Communication
for Business
and the Professions

Communication for Business and the Professions

Sixth Edition

Patricia Hayes Andrews
Indiana University at Bloomington

John E. Baird, Jr.
Baird Consulting Corporation

Madison Dubuque, IA Guilford, CT Chicago Toronto London
Caracas Mexico City Buenos Aires Madrid Bogota Sydney

Book Team

Editor *Stan Stoga*
Developmental Editor *Steve Lehman*
Production Editor *Jayne Klein*
Art Editor *Tina Flanagan*
Photo Editor *Carol Judge*
Visuals/Design Developmental Specialist *Janice M. Roerig-Blong*
Production Manager *Beth Kundert*
Visuals/Design Freelance Specialist *Mary L. Christianson*
Marketing Manager *Pamela S. Cooper*

Brown & Benchmark
PUBLISHERS

A Division of Wm. C. Brown Communications, Inc.

Executive Vice President/General Manager *Thomas E. Doran*
Vice President/Editor in Chief *Edgar J. Laube*
Vice President/Marketing and Sales Systems *Eric Ziegler*
Vice President/Production *Vickie Putman*
National Sales Manager *Bob McLaughlin*

 Wm. C. Brown Communications, Inc.

President and Chief Executive Officer *G. Franklin Lewis*
Senior Vice President, Operations *James H. Higby*
Corporate Senior Vice President and President of Manufacturing *Roger Meyer*
Corporate Senior Vice President and Chief Financial Officer *Robert Chesterman*

The credits section for this book begins on page 483 and is considered an extension of the copyright page.

Cover design by *Anna Manhart*

Cover photo: Inset © Mike Malyszko/FPG International; Large © Telegraph Colour Library/ FPG International

Partial interior design by *Fulton Design*

Copyedited by *Marilyn Taylor*

To our parents:
Arthur L. Hayes and Helen D. Hayes;
John E. Baird and Eleanor B. Baird.

Contents

Preface

ithout question, communication is important to an organization. Thousands of books, articles, and speeches have arrived at the same conclusion: Without communication, organizations could not exist. At present, however, a trend that is sweeping American business and industry is changing the role of communication in organizations. "Participative management" in its various forms is increasingly replacing other styles of management as the preferred method of decision making and governance in organizations. For example:

"Self-managed work teams" in many businesses allow employees to set their own work methods, select new employees and discipline current ones, monitor quality and productivity, and perform other functions traditionally assigned to "supervision" or "management."

"Shared governance" systems in hospitals have provided nurses with opportunities to establish their own work schedules and systems of rotation between units and shifts, to set and monitor standards of patient care, to develop methods for improved staff education, and so on.

Employee advisory groups have provided top-level company executives with important feedback concerning pending decisions and actions and with important advice about the perceptions and problems of employees.

Problem-solving groups composed of nonsupervisory staff have identified and solved work-related problems in organizations of all types, resulting in improved efficiency and millions of dollars in savings.

As this trend continues, managers and supervisors increasingly will have to play the role of "facilitators" rather than "order-givers," and nonsupervisory employees will have to contribute their minds (as well as their hands) to the achievement of organizational goals.

Such fundamental changes in the way organizations are managed ultimately will place the burden of communication effectiveness on all levels of the organization, not just on members of management. For example, an employee in a typical company can expect to

Participate in one or more group problem-solving projects.

Be asked to contribute his or her ideas for improving work.

Deliver to management all or part of a presentation outlining ideas or proposals.

Work informally with peers and superiors in making decisions previously reserved for management alone.

All of these activities require communication skills and sound judgment by organization members at all levels. Knowing this, forward-thinking organizations now are training current staff in communication skills and recruiting people who are skilled communicators and whose values and principles are consistent with those of the organization. Now more than ever, getting and keeping a job requires excellent communication skills.

The structures and functions of communication in organizations are virtually countless. The situations in which you encounter other members of the organization, the topics you discuss, and the effects you seek are of infinite variety and number. Obviously, it would be impossible for us to provide you with a text that offers advice for communicating well in every situation that you might encounter. Instead, we have selected some of the more general types of situations you will face and then described communication strategies and skills that are widely applicable to different specific situations within those general categories. Thus, after considering in more theoretical terms the nature of organizations and organizational communication, we examine one-to-one situations such as interviews or informal conversations, group situations such as staff or employee group meetings, and one-to-group situations such as formal presentations to either small or large audiences. Remember as you read that our purpose in each of these sections is, first, to analyze the demands placed upon people in each situation and, second, to present strategies and techniques by which you might meet those demands to communicate with maximum effectiveness.

Like the previous five editions, this sixth edition emphasizes skills acquisition in the context of organizational communication theory and research. In this edition, we have expanded or added several subjects. Specifically, new material has been added in each of these areas:

1. Technology and its impact on organizational communication
2. Organization theory
3. Managing diversity
4. Reengineering
5. Globalization
6. Quality
7. External communication channels
8. Empowerment
9. Surveillance as an ethical issue involving employee rights to privacy
10. Collaborative conflict management

We have continued our practice of including many real-world illustrations based on the testimony and experience of successful managers whom we have known. As in earlier editions, we emphasize business and industry *and* the professions. We do this with the belief that those of you who read this text are preparing for diversified careers in education, law, agriculture, and the health sciences, as well as in business and other professions. To that end, we have again concluded the book with an appendix on careers in communication, suggesting positions and career options available to those with communication training and skills.

As in the previous edition, we devote much of the first section to the importance of effective communication practices in developing a productive and satisfying organizational climate. We use numerous examples from contemporary business literature and from our consulting experience. We also establish the relationship between theory and practice. The second chapter, for instance, discusses contemporary management theories, linking them to communication practices. Management is presented separately from small group leadership and is clearly tied to actual behavior and communication skills.

The sixth edition's major changes appear in chapters 1, 2, 3, 4, 9, and 11. The first chapter articulates the nature of organizational communication in an increasingly global and technologically sophisticated world. Chapter 2 presents a major new section on issues facing contemporary managers, focusing on empowerment, globalization, quality, reengineering, and managing diversity. The third chapter reorganizes the traditional material on formal communication channels and adds a unit on external channels. In the fourth chapter, the employee rights section is enhanced by further examining the right to privacy and emphasizing ethical issues presented by electronic technology and the potential for surveillance—of both individuals and entire organizations. Chapter 7 presents new resumes for students to examine as potential models and critical exercises. In chapter 9, we have added a major section on using technology to support groups with a special focus on group support systems. Chapter 10 now includes the material on approaches to the study of leadership but presented in the specific context of small group leadership rather than within the more general perspective of management (as in earlier editions). Chapter 11 minimizes the material on mediation and emphasizes instead broader notions of conflict management by acknowledging diverse conflict styles, introducing a collaborative model of conflict management, and discussing technology as a potential conflict management tool. Finally, the public speaking chapters provide a number of fresh examples, with chapter 13 presenting a detailed model speech outline.

As in the past, our book is peppered with Business Briefs—some depicting contemporary illustrations of theories, research, or principles we are discussing and others presenting overviews or summaries. Each attempts to highlight or illustrate important concepts elaborated in the text. *Over fifty percent* of the briefs *are new* to this edition.

Many people have contributed to our personal communication effectiveness. We think it appropriate to acknowledge their contribution to our still-developing skills. Professors J. Jeffrey Auer, James R. Andrews, Raymond G. Smith, Richard L. Johannesen, Robert G. Gunderson, Paul Batty, and Dennis S. Gouran and colleague Herbert G. Melnick taught us by word and example the techniques of effective communication.

Our friends and colleagues at Indiana University and Melnick, Baird, Williams and Fisher, Inc., have shown us the pleasures and successes that good communication can bring. We would also like to thank the reviewers of this edition for their suggestions and comments. They are Claudine SchWeber, University of Maryland University College; Brant Short, Idaho State University; and Robin Vagenas, University of Delaware.

Finally, we are indebted to our parents, whose encouragement, support, and love have been sustaining forces in our lives. To them, we again dedicate this book.

Patricia Hayes Andrews
John E. Baird, Jr.

Communication in Organizations

PART

1

*The unquestioned
authority of managers
in the corporation has
been replaced by . . . the
need for managers to
persuade rather than to
order, and by the need to
acknowledge the
expertise of those below.*

—ROSABETH MOSS KANTER
THE CHANGEMASTERS

CHAPTER 1

An Introduction to Communication in Organizations

hink for a moment about success. What does success mean to you? What do you want for yourself, on both a short-term and a long-term basis? Short term, your goals may be relatively specific: obtaining an entry-level job with some organization, being promoted to some higher level position, getting a raise, achieving a particular grade in a certain class, or graduating at a certain time. Long term, your goals may be less well defined, but definite nevertheless: financial security, happiness, status, love, the chance to make a lasting contribution, and so on. Whatever your goals—whatever success means to you, both short term and long term—a few important facts hold true:

1. Much of your professional success will be achieved through your participation in some organization or group of organizations.
2. Your professional success will be determined to a significant extent by your skills as a communicator.

Let us examine each of these facts one at a time. First, the success you achieve will probably come through some organization. The reason for this is simple: our society is composed almost entirely of organizational entities. Indeed, whenever human beings gather together for the purpose of accomplishing some goal, organizations are born. Some are informal and loosely structured; most are characterized by deliberate structuring and formal divisions of power, labor, and authority. Whatever their nature and scope, however, we seldom escape their influence. We are born in organizations, educated by organizations, work for organizations, and spend much of our leisure time in organized activities.

Second, your ability to succeed will be determined largely by your skills as a communicator. This is true in a number of respects. Your ability to enter an organization in the first place depends heavily upon your communication skills. Hafer and Hoth surveyed 37 companies representing a broad range of industries, from manufacturing to public service.[1] They asked employment officers in those companies to rate a list of job applicants' characteristics according to how important those characteristics are in their selection decisions. These characteristics are listed, in order, in Business Brief 1.1.

While oral communication is listed first, it is important to note that many of the other characteristics are also types of communication skills: appearance is an element of nonverbal communication, for example, just as enthusiasm, assertiveness, loyalty, maturity, leadership, and initiative are typically shown most clearly through communication behavior. And as we shall see very clearly in a later chapter, the employment process itself is an exercise in oral and written communication. Perform well in that process, and you have made the first step toward success.

Once you have joined an organization, your ability to move up, to obtain additional responsibilities, and attain higher status, will be determined by two important elements: your technical skills and your communication skills. You perform your job well by skillfully completing your assignments. As others learn of your accomplishments, however, you gain prominence and begin to move up within the organization. Written memoranda, for example, are important "advertisements" of your identity, your achievements, and your skills as a communicator. Meetings, everyone's favorite target for criticism, also provide opportunities for you to demonstrate your knowledge and communication skills. Presentations of project proposals and progress reports give you a chance to create a positive impression in the minds of the people in power in the organization. Certainly, doing your job well is important. But communicating effectively is equally important (see Business Brief 1.2).

When one reaches the top of an organization, communication activities occupy virtually all of one's time. Several years ago, the administrator of a large hospital kept a detailed record of his activities during ten consecutive work days. Of his 5,186 minutes, approximately 70 percent was spent in oral communication, about 17 percent in writing, and less than 13 percent in activities involving no form of communication.[2] To get to the top requires communication skills; to perform effectively once you get there requires even greater skill.

Clearly, communication skills are crucial for upward mobility in any organization, regardless of specific job or profession. But there are also a substantial number of positions (apart from management) that place a particular emphasis on communication. These positions include personnel interviewer, employee relations representative, training coordinator, speech writer, customer relations representative, fundraiser, consultant, sales representative, and investment account executive. We discuss the specific knowledge and skills needed for effective performance in these and other careers in the "Careers in Communication" appendix at the end of this book.

Of course, as we move toward the year 2000, organizations are changing, sometimes at an unprecedented pace. Some changes have been brought about by advances

The higher you move in an organization, the more important communication becomes to your overall job performance. Indeed, some believe that communication style becomes more important than technical skill.

Andrew Sherwood, president and CEO of Goodrich & Sherwood Company, the human resources firm, says that "meeting goals and objectives are quantitative measures of 'what' you do on the job—'what' you're being paid for. When you begin your career, and until about age 35, 'what' criteria are generally used to judge work performance. After age 35, however, when most people move into middle management or beyond, performance criteria begin to shift and style becomes more important."

After this point in your career, "how" you do your job becomes most important. The "how" criteria include such things as "how you relate to your superiors, how you interact with your peers, how you handle and motivate people, and how you communicate," Sherwood explains. "The higher you rise in your company, the more visibility you have, the more you become a public figure—the more important 'how' you do your job becomes," he says.

Sherwood's conclusions are based on interviews with over one hundred company executives. When he asked them to rank performance criteria, middle managers said good performance is composed equally of "how" and "what" factors; vice-presidents felt performance is 70 percent "how" and 30 percent "what," and corporate presidents said the value of "how" to "what" is 90/10.

From "As You Climb the Ladder, Style Counts," *Management Review* 76 (May 1987): 9.

in modern technology, others by developments in the economy, and still others by the increasingly global environment. The world marketplace has many participants, of which the United States is only one. Over 100,000 American companies are doing business abroad; about one-sixth of our nation's jobs come from international business. American-made products are increasingly rare. At the same time, jobs are changing. Cetron, Rocha, and Luchins predict, for instance, that five of the ten fastest growing careers between now and 2001 will be computer-related.[3] The typical large business will be information-based, composed of specialists who guide themselves based on information from colleagues, customers, and top managers. Even now, one out of every two Americans works in some aspect of information processing. The new technologies offer change as well as opportunity.

Recognizing these changes, the purpose of this book is to help you develop the communication skills you will need to be successful in whatever career and organization you choose. We begin, then, by defining and examining organizations and organizational communication.

Definitions

Communication theorists have defined *organization* in various ways:

"a stable system of individuals who work together to achieve, through a hierarchy of ranks and divisions of labor, common goals"[4]

"an information and decision system"[5]

"the complex pattern of communication and other relations between human beings"[6]

"social relationships . . . interlocked behavior centered on specialized task and maintenance activities"[7]

In these definitions are common threads: goal-directed behavior, coordinated actions, information sharing, decision making, and human relationships. These elements in turn emphasize the importance of communication in organizations. Communication is a process involving the transmission and reception of symbols having meaning in the minds of the participants. Communication is not merely an important activity in organizations; rather, it is the lifeblood that allows organizations to exist. No human relationship could be maintained, no organizational objective achieved, no activities coordinated, and no decisions reached without communication. Perhaps Bavelas and Barrett expressed it best in their classic article on organizational communication when they noted:

> It is entirely possible to view an organization as an elaborate system for gathering, evaluating, recombining, and disseminating information. It is not surprising in these terms that the effectiveness of an organization with respect to the achievement of its goals should be so closely related to its effectiveness in handling information. . . . Communication is not a secondary or derived aspect of organization—a "helper" of the other presumably more basic functions. It is rather the essence of organized activity and is the basic process out of which all other functions derive.[8]

Not surprisingly, when Peters and Waterman had concluded their "search for excellence" they said: "What does it add up to? Lots of communication. All of Hewlett-Packard's golden rules have to do with communicating more. . . . The name of the successful game is rich, informal communication. The astonishing by-product is the ability to have your cake and eat it, too; that is, rich, informal communication leads to more action, more experiments, more learning, and simultaneously to the ability to stay better in touch and on top of things."[9] In short, the effectiveness of communication in an organization usually determines how successful that organization will be.

The Communication Process

To acknowledge the importance of communication is crucial. Equally critical, however, is to understand it as an interesting and complex process. Early models of communication failed to do this. They conceptualized communication as *linear*, largely a one-way process involving the flow of information from a source to a receiver. These models

also focused on channels, so that communication was viewed as a conduit through which individuals attempted to accomplish their goals. Barriers to effective communication were viewed as noise, or anything that interfered with or distorted the message's movement through the channel. Noise might involve anything from crackling telephone wires to garbage on a computer screen to the receiver's attitudes—any one of which might affect message reception and interpretation.

More contemporary models of communication are *transactional,* emphasizing communication as a two-way, reciprocal process of mutual message exchange. Gerald Miller articulates the nature of this process:

> Process implies that particular instances of . . . communication should not be thought of as discrete events with identifiable beginnings and ends, but rather as parts of a dynamic, on-going whole which has no clearly defined temporal boundaries. In particular, process stresses the *transactional* nature of . . . communication, rather than conceptualizing it as a unidirectional, linear act.[10]

The transactional view is also described by communication scholars Wenburg and Wilmot:

> All persons are engaged in sending (encoding) and receiving (decoding) messages simultaneously. Each person is constantly sharing in the encoding and decoding process and each person is affecting the other.[11]

The transactional perspective declines to make a sharp distinction between the roles of source and receiver since one person plays both, and often at the same time. Unlike the linear view, verbal and nonverbal feedback is considered central to the transactional model. How meaning is constructed is another concern. The linear view posits the notion that the meaning of a particular message resides with the sender, whose challenge is to use a message channel effectively. By contrast, the transactional view is more oriented toward the receiver and to the construction of a message's meaning in her or his mind.[12] In short, people grow to share meanings through mutual experiences and by negotiating shared interpretations.

As human beings work together in organizations, they often share information and experiences. Over time, they grow to embrace similar goals and values. When they do, negotiating common interpretations of events, persons, and messages may come easily. Under less harmonious circumstances (involving, for instance, interpersonal conflict), negotiating common interpretations of reality may be more demanding. The transactional model of communication is quite compatible with several contemporary views of organizing and managing (soon to be discussed).

Within the framework of the transactional model, then, *organizational communication* is that process wherein mutually interdependent human beings create and exchange messages and interpret and negotiate meanings, while striving to articulate and realize mutually held visions, purposes, and goals. Organizational communication is influenced by the reality of hierarchies. However, as organizations have become flatter

Figure 1.1
Elements of communication in an organization.

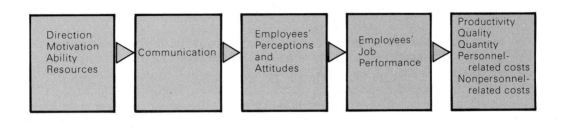

with hierarchical layers reduced, the communication challenges begin to change. Managers exchange some measure of control in return for shared responsibility for outcomes. Now motivation is as much a question for peers who work together in teams as for their formally appointed leaders. Even so, in organizations, the tensions remain—between the desire to cooperate for the good of all and the need to compete so as to promote oneself, between one's professional demands and one's private life, between those formally called "labor" and those formally labeled "management." Each organization is unique, and it is only by studying the organization's communication practices, patterns, and processes, that we will come to understand the organization itself.

The Role of Communication in Organizations

We already have made the claim that communication is vital to the very existence of an organization. To understand the validity of that claim, one must understand the role communication plays in an organization's life. Figure 1.1 illustrates specific elements of that role.

At the far right of the figure are the elements composing an organization's productivity: the quality of the work done in the organization, the quantity of the work completed, the personnel-related costs involved in getting the work done (such as turnover or absenteeism), and the nonpersonnel costs of getting work done (such as wasted materials or scrap). Naturally, organizations want to improve productivity by maximizing the quality and quantity of work completed and minimizing the personnel and nonpersonnel costs involved in work performance.

Just to the left is the primary factor that determines productivity in organizations: the employees' job performance. What employees do in the workplace determines how much work gets done and how well it is done, how costly their own behaviors are, and to a large extent how much is spent on materials and equipment.

At the far left are the four major factors that ultimately shape an employee's performance:

1. The directions the employee receives concerning what to do and how to do it.
2. The employee's motivation to do the job.
3. The ability of the employee to do the job.
4. The resources provided the employee to do the job.

What must occur, then, is the translation of these four factors into employee job performance. The key elements translating motivation, direction, ability, and resources into job performance are in the middle of the figure: perceptions and attitudes. In short, what employees do at work is determined largely by how they perceive the work environment and how they feel about work.

Often, employees misunderstand instructions given them, and errors in their job performance are the predictable result. Just as often, the organization fails to communicate expectations clearly to employees. Those employees in turn perform as they think the organization wants them to, relying on their perceptions (or just plain luck) to guide their efforts. Finally, employees have attitudes toward all elements of their work lives: their jobs, their working conditions, their supervisors, their coworkers, their promotional opportunities, their pay and benefits, and so on. Those attitudes influence their willingness to work effectively and their commitment to the organization's goals and objectives. For example, employees who feel they are not being paid a competitive wage may not work very hard, and employees who actively dislike their immediate supervisors may even do things destructive to the company, such as sabotaging equipment or stealing supplies. Therefore, employees' job performances stem directly from their attitudes and perceptions.

Where do those attitudes and perceptions come from? Communication, in the form of the things employees hear from management, supervisors, and their coworkers; the things employees hear about their organization from outside sources; the written and oral guidelines with which employees are provided; the instructions that employees receive. All this and more compose the communication in which employees participate every day. By shaping the attitudes and perceptions of employees, communication serves to convert external communication from the work environment into internal thoughts and feelings that, in turn, control employees' behaviors.

Again, the lesson should be clear: without communication, there would be no organizations.

The Nature of Organizations: Historical Perspectives

In the preceding section, we dealt with the question of productivity. We asked, "What is it that determines how productive an organization is?" Our answer, of course, was that productivity comes largely from the job performance of employees, which in turn comes from their attitudes and perceptions, which in turn are determined by communication.

For centuries, people have been asking the same question. The answers they developed are important, for the theories people followed in the past have shaped current thinking about organizations and employee performance. For that reason, we will review briefly some historical and current perspectives on organizational functioning.

Historical Perspectives on the Nature of Organizations

Perspective	Primary Focus	Communication Practices
Classical	Organization structure Work efficiency Monetary rewards	Primarily downward Impersonal in nature
Human Relations	Informal group norms Intergroup/interpersonal relations Employee morale	Downward and upward Lateral People-related concerns
Human Resources	Development of human potential Morale and productivity Satisfaction through achievement	Participative decision making Downward and upward Written and oral
Systems	Interaction of organizational parts Social and economic rewards	Internal and external Lateral Importance of feedback
Cultural	Norms, values, roles Behaviors that are rewarded Impact of culture on productivity	Focus on organizational tasks and characteristics Informal and formal
Teamwork	Team-based productivity Task-based rather than function-based organization Individual and group rewards	Lateral and upward Participative problem solving Conflict management

The Classical School

In the late nineteenth and early twentieth centuries, the industrial revolution had taken hold. Factories were in wide use, and the assembly-line technique of production was about to be implemented in the Ford automobile plants. Because so much of the technology of manufacturing was new then and because the techniques for large-scale production were just being developed, management theorists of that age focused largely on work methods as the source of performance improvement. The view that developed at that time is now called the *Classical school* of organization theory, or the school of *Scientific Management*.

One leader of this school of thought was Frederick Taylor.[13] Taylor's approach to organizations was highly structured and mechanistic. His famed time-and-motion studies attempted to break down each minute aspect of a given job and match each worker with the task he could most efficiently perform. Taylor believed in instigating a competitive spirit in organizations by rewarding workers on the basis of their individual output. Praising workers or encouraging creativity never crossed Taylor's mind as being potentially motivating. Rather, he believed that real rewards would invariably be of a monetary nature. Taylor saw no particular clash between the interests of the organization and the welfare of the workers. Rather, he assumed that if individuals could increase their own prosperity while contributing to the organization's efficiency, then everyone would be satisfied. Such a view proved unrealistic. With the growing strength of labor unions in the 1930s, both workers and labor leaders bitterly opposed Taylor's views. They witnessed jobs being eliminated because of Taylor's efficiency-training techniques. This resulted in rises in unemployment. They argued further that those workers who learned to produce with dazzling efficiency were seldom fairly compensated for their extraordinary productivity.

Other writers who contributed to the Classical tradition include Fayol, Gulick and Urwick, and Weber.[14] Taken together, their writings centered almost exclusively on the *structure* of formal organizations. Labor was to be divided according to strict principles of specialization, such as function or process. They believed that the more a task could be divided and hence the simpler the worker's job, the more efficient the organization would become. These classicists stressed the formal organizational hierarchy, the need for clearly structured chains of command, and appropriate discipline and obedience to authority.

Probably the most influential work growing out of the Classical tradition was German sociologist Max Weber's *The Theory of Social and Economic Organizations*. In this work, Weber focuses on bureaucracy, defining it essentially as a social invention that relies on the power to influence through rules, reason, and law.[15] As with other Classical doctrines, bureaucracy is based on the belief that rationality and predictability are desirable goals for both individuals and organizations. Thus, a highly bureaucratic organization typically attempts to maximize these qualities by carefully structuring the organization, by stipulating specific employee rights and duties, and by outlining procedures for dealing with offenders. Classical bureaucracy also encourages impersonal, highly professional interpersonal dealings, based on the belief that, through impersonality, justice

The thinking embodied in the Classical school still can be found in many organizations today. For example, the ways in which some large corporations select new chief executive officers frequently reflect an emphasis on such Classical factors as moving up through the ranks, understanding the company bureaucracy, and demonstrating technical competence.

In recent years, some celebrated instances of chief executive officer removal have occurred. For example, Robert C. Stempel resigned his position as chairman of General Motors Corporation in October 1992, under considerable pressure from his board of directors. Similar situations were seen recently when Tom H. Barrett resigned as chairman and chief executive of Goodyear Tire & Rubber Company and Kenneth H. Olsen resigned the presidency of Digital Equipment Corporation. Both had been long-time company men—Barrett had spent thirty-eight years with Goodyear, and Olsen had founded and spent thirty-five years with Digital—and both had been under intense pressure from their boards of directors. Like General Motors, both Goodyear and Digital had faced significant changes in market demands and competition.

Some management experts claim that the chief executive officers of most big companies are the products of ponderous, deliberate, and often very highly structured management-succession systems. Particularly in old-line industrial organizations, these individuals often joined their companies right out of school and worked their way up through the ranks, assuming greater and greater management responsibility along the way. Like Stempel, they exhibited a high level of competence in the lower-level jobs they held and were well-respected inside their companies, but they were perhaps unable to respond to the complexities and rapidly changing environment business leaders face today.

Leaders groomed in one business environment would thus wind up ill-prepared for another. In short, many executives who have moved up in the Classical tradition risk being the right leaders, but for the wrong times.

From Amanda Bennett, "Many of Today's Top Corporate Officers Are the Right People for the Wrong Time," *Wall Street Journal*, 27 October 1992, pp. B1–B3.

and impartiality can be ensured. Weber reinforces this point by noting that the selection and promotion of workers should be based solely on technical competence.

In organizations managed by people who adopted the Classical philosophy, communication took on certain characteristics. As a rule, communication was almost exclusively downward. Executives issued general orders and plans to their managers, who in turn issued the same orders (perhaps with more specific instructions) to their employees. The content of those communications was almost exclusively work-related; social activities were not generally sponsored by employers, nor were they discussed at work.

Upward communication was virtually nonexistent. Employee suggestions were rarely solicited. Nor were they eagerly accepted (after all, time-and-motion experts had been hired by management to identify the best ways of working; what could employees possibly have to offer?). Employee complaints were rarely expressed, and those employees who did express them were often encouraged to leave. Personal problems simply were not talked about in communications with management. Conflicts were handled through the chain of command and usually were resolved through decisions made by the chief executive officer. In effect, a very rigid, militaristic hierarchy was maintained, with work-related communication flowing downward through the chain of command.

The Human Relations School

The second major school of organization theory, the *Human Relations school,* assigned considerably more significant and varied roles to communication. It represented, in part, a reaction to Classical formalism. It also developed as a logical outgrowth of socioeconomic considerations. Although the research that provided the foundation for the Human Relations movement began in the late 1920s, the major impact of the movement was not actually felt in the world of business and industry until the 1940s and 1950s.

The United States experienced general economic abundance following World War II. Larger numbers of individuals attended college and subsequently entered organizations as professionals. Before this time, individuals either worked their way up through the ranks of organizations to top management positions, or they were brought into the organization because of their relationships (friendship or family) with the organization's executives. But with the post-World War II increase in well educated, relatively independent white-collar workers, organizations were forced to become more cognizant of workers' needs. Hiring trained white-collar personnel proved a costly venture, and organizational executives quickly perceived that keeping these individuals satisfied (and thus maintaining them as members of the organization) was a task to which they should be committed. A concern for employee happiness was, in many ways, a natural child of the times.

The empirical foundation of the Human Relations movement was established in the mid-1920s, when the National Academy of Sciences investigated the relationship between lighting intensity and productivity and found the proposed relationship to be nonexistent; that is, good lighting apparently neither aided nor hindered workers' productivity. The site of the research for this project was the Hawthorne Plant of the Western Electric Company near Chicago, an organization noted for its reasonable wages and considerate treatment of employees. Plant executives were troubled by the puzzling results of the study and decided to invite a team of researchers from the Harvard Graduate School of Business, under the direction of Elton Mayo, to investigate the situation. Mayo and his associates conducted studies over a period of years and found that variations in working conditions were not systematically related to worker productivity or satisfaction. Rather, the critical factor was the workers' perceptions of the special attention they were receiving. Overt observation by the Harvard research team, interviews with top company executives, and monthly checkups by the company doctor convinced the Hawthorne plant employees that something most unusual and undoubtedly important was going on—and that *they* were a significant part of it.

Thus, even under conditions of poor lighting, longer work days, and fewer rest pauses, workers in this study *continued to increase their productivity.*

Mayo's Hawthorne studies also revealed the importance of the informal work group as a source of worker motivation. Specifically, these informal groups established production standards and enforced their norms through pressure for uniformity.[16] Wage incentive plans often failed because they were based on Classical concepts of people as independent, economically motivated beings. In contrast, Human Relations theorists advanced the notion of men and women as *social beings.* Since they were social beings, the roots of their work motivation lay, not within themselves, but within the dynamics of the small work groups to which they belonged and in which they discovered their most meaningful social relationships.

While the Classical view represented an extreme adherence to task-oriented considerations, the Human Relations school overemphasized people-related concerns. Critics of the Human Relations school have maintained that the movement was manipulative and insincere—that it feigned an interest in workers' needs and happiness, while actually manipulating them as a means of increasing organizational productivity. Moreover, in the quest for the happy organizational family, some companies soon discovered that satisfied workers were not necessarily extremely productive on the assembly line—a sobering discovery!

Although some organizations have exploited the findings of the Human Relations school, the movement nevertheless made substantial contributions. Founders of the movement were motivated largely by a genuine concern for workers' happiness. They believed that the most satisfying organization would also be the most rational and efficient one. They emphasized employee satisfaction as a valuable management goal. Equally important, the Human Relations movement provided the groundwork for future theories, many of which are successfully practiced today.

The Nature of Organizations: Contemporary Views

The Human Resources School

Many current theorists now believe that an organization's most important resource is its people. While technology and interpersonal relationships remain important, the *Human Resources school* emphasizes the development and use of human beings in ways that maximize organizational productivity. Championed by such contemporary theorists as McGregor, Likert, Blake and Mouton, and Miles, Human Resources theorists stress participative organizational decision making and effective management-employee relations.[17] The Human Resources model is based on the belief that each individual desires and is capable of contributing to both the organization and society in general. All workers are considered untapped resources of creative suggestions and ideas. Management's job is to discover how to reveal those talents and allow each individual to contribute to the organization in increasingly diversified ways. Managers accepting Human Resources ideas encourage subordinates' participation in significant decision making (particularly that affecting their work directly). In general, workers are prompted to

From Stephen Franklin, "Training, Empowering Employees Pays off for Auto-Parts Producer," *Chicago Tribune,* 20 December 1992, Sec. 7, p. 1.

exercise self-control and self-direction whenever the organizational task permits. The Human Resources approach has dual goals: increased employee satisfaction and morale, and improved organizational decision-making effectiveness—both of which are viewed as integral parts of the *same* process.

Communication according to the Human Resources school is marked by several important characteristics. First is the heavy emphasis on *upward communication*. Employee participation in decision making is actively encouraged through various suggestion systems, departmental meetings, and other communication events, which we will review in the next chapter. In addition, employee ideas are often rewarded through incentive or award systems that provide employees with diamond rings, pen and pencil sets, or a percentage of the money saved by their cost-saving suggestions. Surveys are conducted to assess employee opinions and perceptions. In short, much effort is devoted to involving employees in the communication process and to using their contributions whenever possible.

In organizations managed by Human Resources principles, downward communication is used to keep employees informed of current events and to provide them with instructions and guidelines for behavior. However, just as often, downward messages present matters for employee consideration—plans or decisions about which management wants employee input or involvement. In these cases, downward communication serves to stimulate upward messages. Finally, management must respond to the input provided by employees; thus, downward communication may tell employees what steps management has decided to take in response to employee suggestions, what things management has chosen not to do, or what progress is being made on current projects. Most of these messages are communicated via written channels, although face-to-face meetings between each level of the organization may be used to convey this information as well.

The Systems School

Another school of organization theory, the *Systems school,* grew out of an already established theoretical framework called *general systems theory.* At the time this theory was applied to organizations, it had already influenced several areas of scientific thought, including economics, biology, logic, and sociology. The central principle of general systems theory rests on the idea that the whole is more than the sum of its parts; each part must be considered as it interacts with, changes, and is changed by every other part within the system. The parts, or subsystems, of any given system are assumed to be interdependent, and it is primarily through *communication* that this interdependence is facilitated. In examining the systems approach, it is important to recall that it represents a *perspective* from which organizations can be viewed. It is not geared toward offering management techniques.

The application of systems theory to the study of organizations has produced two important effects. First, it has integrated the concepts stressed by earlier schools. Second, it has made communication central to an understanding of organizations.

By integrating concepts from earlier schools, Systems theory views the organization as a social system in which issues of structure, hierarchy, span of control, and other Classical principles are of equal but no greater importance than the Human Relations concept of participative decision making, morale, and informal group influence. Thus, the two previously distinct domains of task-oriented and people-oriented concerns must be considered interdependently. The *formal* organization, with its administrators and structural constraints, is often most clearly understood by examining it in the context of *informal* work groups with their leaders and relatively free-flowing communication. The Systems view of human beings is also more complex. Workers are believed to be motivated both by social incentives (for example, peer pressure and status symbols) and by economic rewards (such as increases in salary and fringe benefits).

The other main outgrowth of the Systems school is its definition of communication as an essential element of organizations. Indeed, some believe that organizations can best be understood from a communication perspective.[18]

Although a number of organization theorists have discussed the Systems approach to organizations,[19] perhaps the work with the greatest initial impact was Daniel Katz and

Robert Kahn's *The Social Psychology of Organizations*. Katz and Kahn conceive of organizations as open systems; in fact, they believe that "social organizations are flagrantly open systems in that the input of energies and the conversion of output into further energy input consist of transactions between the organization and its environment."[20] Thus, the distinction is drawn between open and closed systems. The former are dynamic, everchanging, and particularly responsive to environmental concerns. The latter are static, predictable, and devoid of environmental interaction. Boundaries defining the closed system are fixed, but those associated with the open one are necessarily flexible and ever permeable. In fact, the precise line or boundary between the organization (open system) and its external constituency (environment) is forever variable. Figure 1.2 represents our model for viewing an organization from an open systems perspective.

This model presents several key components necessary to our understanding of organizations as open systems. To begin with, organizations are always involved in some process of *transformation*. Organizations usually develop in response to the felt needs of the societies, cultures, and environments in which they operate. When we create organizations, we believe that we can fill a void, produce a new or superior product, or create a better, safer society. But no organization can begin without resources: raw materials, buildings, people—in short, energy. The energy the organization draws from its environment is called *input*. Clothing manufacturers require inputs of wool, cotton, machinery, and laborers to produce garments. Colleges must have administrators, buildings, faculty, students, and libraries to contribute to a knowledgeable society. Churches need ministers, laypersons, places of worship, and religious literature to spread the doctrine of their faith. In all of these examples organizational goals are implicit. Whatever the *reasons* for the organization's existence, whatever its goals are construed to be, the organization's *output* should reflect those goals.

When organizations fail to produce output reflecting their goals, we say they lack *accountability*. For an organization to be accountable (to actually do or produce what it claims to be doing or producing), some process of *transformation* must occur within the organizational structure. Automobiles exist because steel, rubber, and plastic have been changed by workers and machinery into a completed automotive product. The automobile represents design and purpose, and it reflects one reason for the existence of Ford or General Motors.

Each of you will likely be transformed by your educational experiences. Your knowledge, interests, values, and career objectives may be altered substantially during this time. In a similar manner, most organizations, from the smallest family business to the greatest international corporation, take input from their environment and transform it into output in accordance with their goals.

Although some organizations are more interactive with their environments than others, *all* organizations must remain relatively open to survive. Organizations cannot exist as static systems, but healthy organizations must remain reasonably *balanced*. The concept of balance, though not actually depicted in the model, involves a combination of the input-transformation-output variables elaborated above. Organizations achieve balance by importing more than they export. The balanced system is capable of generating sufficient environmental input to ensure its survival. Universities, for example,

Figure 1.2
An organization from a systems perspective.

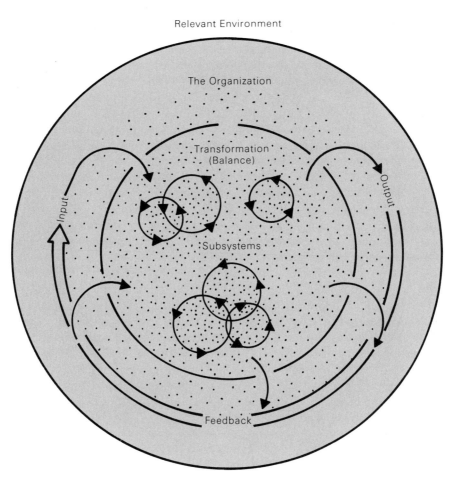

Dotted area: presence of formal and informal communication.

always admit more students than they graduate. Manufacturing companies maintain large reserve supplies of essential raw materials in anticipation of inflationary prices on those goods. And most organizations request more government support than they actually need with the hope that, when cuts are made, they will be able to operate with adequate funds.

Figure 1.2 shows a broken line depicting the boundary between the organization and its *environment*. This demonstrates the fact that in one sense both organization and environment are part of the same continuous process. The actual boundary separating a given organization from its environment is open to interpretation. An organization's environment does not include everything in the world beyond its immediate scope. Rather, the environment is more profitably viewed as those physical and social factors outside the system's boundary that are directly considered in the decision making of individuals in the system.[21] Our primary concern is with the *relevant environment,* which is useful for understanding organizational behavior. No organization can be viewed in isolation, for each is as much a product of its environment as it is a contributor to it.

Within each organization are a number of parts or *subsystems,* each serving definite and often interdependent functions. Our model depicts this interdependence with overlapping subsystems—each affecting and being influenced by the others. Different subsystems within the same organization may be aimed at different, or even conflicting, subgoals. In the long run, however, they ought to move in the same general direction, furthering the purposes of the organization of which they are integral parts.

The final factors depicted in our model are *communication* and *feedback.* Clearly, communication dominates the Systems approach to organizations. Communication is everywhere. It passes up and down formal channels in the organizational hierarchy; it moves quickly within and among small informal work groups; and it passes through organizational boundaries and into the environment, often to be recycled as feedback. Indeed, communication between organizational systems and their environments has become an increasingly important priority for many organizations. Recently, General Motors began a new practice in its Flint, Michigan, manufacturing facility, where the Pontiac Fiero is built. When a car is sold, the dealership sends the name and telephone number of the purchaser to the manufacturing plant. Then, a few weeks later, one of the line workers calls the purchaser to ask how he or she liked the automobile. The information about the car obtained from those telephone calls is passed back to facility management and used to make changes in styling, production, engineering, and marketing and ultimately to improve the car itself. This sort of worker-customer communication is unique and illustrates the "open systems" nature of today's organizations.

The Cultural School

Several recent works have argued that the key to an organization's success is the culture that exists in that organization. Briefly, an organization's culture consists of "a system of shared values (what is important) and beliefs (how things work) that interacts with a company's people, organizational structures, and control systems to produce behavioral norms (the way we do things around here)."[22] Culture is not simply a component of the organization. Rather, as Pacanowsky and O'Donnell-Trujillo note, "a culture is something an organization *is.*"[23]

No profile for an ideal organizational culture exists. In fact, some scholars explicitly say that one organization's culture cannot be compared with another's. However, others believe that certain cultures are healthier, more productive, and more satisfying than others. Peters and Waterman reported, for instance, that the effective organizations they studied (including McDonald's, Hewlett-Packard, and the Dana Corporation) were characterized by certain sets of values and accompanying behaviors. In particular, Peters and Waterman identified eight themes or value sets:

1. *A bias for action.* Rather than discussing problems at length, excellent organizations acted quickly. Although careful in their problem analysis, they refused to become bogged down in an information swamp.
2. *Close to the customer.* Each of these organizations was committed to providing the highest level of service with customer needs considered as paramount. Each was known for innovation, responsiveness, and reliability.
3. *Autonomy and entrepreneurship.* Employees were encouraged to be creative and take risks. Leadership was widely shared. Those who came up with excellent innovations were rewarded with enhanced responsibility and authority.
4. *Hands-on, value-driven.* Organizational leaders made every effort to clearly communicate those values seen as central to the organization's mission and identity. Everyone was committed to the organization's philosophy and values and felt a part of the value-shaping process.
5. *Stick to the knitting.* Excellent companies stayed with the businesses they knew best. They did not diversify beyond what they knew, either in terms of technology or customers.
6. *Productivity through people.* These companies recognized that they could only be successful if each person was valued and encouraged to work to her or his full potential. Artificial barriers between management and workers were discouraged.
7. *Simple form, lean staff.* These organizations were run with simple structures that emphasized decentralization and fewer layers of hierarchy. Self-motivation and self-management were encouraged.
8. *Simultaneous loose-tight properties.* Autonomy and entrepreneurship were encouraged at all levels of the organization. Decision making was often decentralized, but basic values were widely shared and supported throughout the firm.[24]

Thus, in the organizational cultures that Peters and Waterman deemed "excellent," leaders talked openly and freely about their values, and they sought to meet with and involve workers at all levels of the organizational hierarchy. Other scholars have sought to describe the attributes of empowering organizational cultures. We will return to the concept of empowerment in chapter 2.

Deal and Kennedy, in their book *Corporate Cultures,* provide an in-depth analysis of the cultures that typify today's organizations.[25] In their view, there are four basic types of organizational cultures: the "tough-guy, macho culture" where individualistic employees take high risks and get quick feedback about the correctness of their actions; the "work hard/play hard" culture where everyone maintains a high level of low-risk activity; the "bet-your-company" culture where big-stakes decisions are made regularly and feedback comes slowly; and the "process" culture where people focus not on what is done, but on how it is done—in other words, a bureaucracy.

Besides classifying several different types of cultures, Deal and Kennedy identify four key attributes of organizational cultures. First are *values*—the shared views, philosophies, and beliefs of organizational members. An organization's values establish the tone, set the direction and the pace, and suggest appropriate attitudes and courses of action. One can often glean some insight into an organization's values by listening to the way its members communicate among themselves. In large research-oriented universities, for example, professors commonly speak of their teaching *loads* while referring to their research *opportunities*. In this way, they suggest that teaching is a burden and research a pleasure, a view quite consistent with the values of the university as revealed in hiring and promotion practices and other forms of rewards.

Those organizational members who personify and illuminate the organization's values are *heroes,* the second cultural attribute identified by Deal and Kennedy. Often, these heroes occupy the top position in their organizations. Such chief executive officers as Jan Carlzon at SAS, Chichael Harper at ConAgra, Sir John Harvey-Jones at Britain's Imperial Chemical Industries, Yutaka Kume at Nissan, Lee Iacocca at Chrysler, and Ted Turner at Turner Broadcasting articulated and reflected their organization's vision and values. Their actions showed by example the way others should think, behave, and talk. Their language was quoted often, and their way of discussing the world was imitated by others throughout the organization. Thus, they influenced their organization's sense of social reality. An extremely charismatic dean at a large midwestern university, for instance, significantly influenced faculty perceptions of higher-level campus administrators by consistently referring to the administration building and the lowlands surrounding it as the "swamp." In very little time, everyone was talking about the "swamp," which virtually replaced the hall's official name on campus. It took little imagination to recognize and label the sorts of slithering, untrustworthy creatures who inhabit such unsavory places. Much to the dean's delight, the metaphor was a great success! Clearly, it is the hero who defines the allies and the enemies, who writes or sanctions the slogans, and who regularly participates in the third cultural attribute, *rituals and rites.*

Through rituals, organizational members celebrate and reinforce their beliefs, applaud their heroes, and share their visions of the future. In Christian religious organizations, for example, rituals abound, as people marry, celebrate communion, baptize their children, and bury their dead. While these sorts of rituals are shared by many different denominations, each church develops distinctly different traditions regarding how each ritual is enacted. Within the same denomination in a single community, for example, one church celebrates Holy Communion by passing a basket of tiny wafers down the pews. No one kneels, and individual glasses are used for drinking the wine. On the other side of town, however, the congregation comes forward, kneeling together around a large altar. The minister breaks a loaf of bread in half and passes it from person to person, each of whom breaks off small pieces to dip in a communal wine cup. Although these rituals are quite different in method and detail, they celebrate common beliefs, and the recited liturgies are virtually identical. The church's hero, the pastor, leads the congregation through this ritual by taking communion first, as an actual example before them; beginning the recitation of the liturgy; and inviting others to join in.

Although rituals are of obvious importance in religious organizations, they are also evident in other kinds of organizations as members are initiated, promoted, honored, and retired. Whatever the organization's values, members who attend or participate in rituals will be reminded of them and often urged to believe in and live up to them.

The final cultural attribute discussed by Deal and Kennedy is the *communication network*. While rites and rituals represent the ultimate form of formal organizational communication, communication networks are *informal* channels of interaction, typically used for influencing members' perceptions of reality and indoctrinating them to hold the right attitudes and behave in appropriate ways. Networking begins even before the individual formally joins an organization. The job candidate is taken out to lunch by a group of his or her peers who proceed to tell stories about the organization, gossip about its heroes and villains, and enlighten the candidate as to the ways of upward mobility. Later, networking continues over coffee breaks, lunches, dinners, parties, and other social events. One can learn a great deal from these informal interactions, and in such contexts, many feel free to raise questions and make comments that they would never share in more formal settings. Are women really taken seriously here? What about minorities? How ethical are our leaders? Although these kinds of questions may never be posed directly, answers to them can be gleaned by listening to the stories told by those who already belong. At a cocktail party during a job interview visit, a friend was regaled with tales of mismanagement and sexism. At a formal level, everything looked good— official policy statements, pay and other incentives, work environment. She decided to take the job. A year later, after she was passed over twice for promotions (even though she had sold more than any of her male competitors) and sexually harassed by her immediate supervisor, she quit. At least in this case, the informal channels revealed a more accurate picture of the organizational culture than any formal statement of policy.

These four cultural attributes provide a useful perspective for examining organizations. They do not provide a magic formula for success, but they do point to questions that every organization should consider:

What are our values?

How clearly and in what ways have we articulated them?

Are they widely understood and accepted? Are there significant subgroups among us who fail to appreciate them?

If so, how can we reassess and perhaps renegotiate them?

To what extent do those who lead or are honored by the organization truly reflect our values? If not, why not?

Are there others equally worthy of recognition?

Are we satisfied with the nature of our rites and rituals?

Do they remain meaningful to those for whom they are intended? If not, how might we change them without alienating those for whom they are presently meaningful?

Do we recognize the meaning and potential value of our informal communication interactions?

In recent years, dramatic changes in the cultures of several major corporations have been brought about almost entirely through the efforts of the individual in charge of those organizations. For example, Yutaka Kume almost single-handedly changed the culture of Nissan from a lumbering, bureaucracy-ridden organization into a fast-moving, highly successful company by taking such actions as subdividing the organization into three market-oriented groups, putting a complaint desk in every dealership, changing the procedures by which new cars are engineered, rotating managers through assignments in all areas of the company, changing the basis of personnel decisions from seniority to performance, and minimizing organizational rank by banning the practice of putting titles on employees' name badges.

Similarly, Sir John Harvey-Jones changed the culture of Britain's Imperial Chemical Industries in only five years by reorganizing the top management team and the divisions of the company, developing and communicating a new vision and strategy for the company, and becoming personally visible throughout the organization.

In both instances, actions taken by the chief executive officer transformed the organization by creating new sets of values and priorities and discarding old, outmoded assumptions and practices.

From John P. Kotter and James L. Heskett, *Corporate Culture and Performance* (New York: Free Press, 1992).

Are the values we formally embrace reinforced or denied by our words and actions in informal contexts?

How can perceived inconsistencies be resolved or managed?

Every organization has a culture. Some are stronger or healthier than others. All are complex and dynamic and, as a result, potentially difficult to change. Organizational culture and organizational communication are surely intertwined. In fact, effectively managing communication is perhaps the key to shaping an organization's culture.

The importance of the Cultural school is the emphasis it places on the value systems, norms, and behaviors composing an organization. People behave in certain ways because they believe they are expected to behave in those ways and because they believe the organization will reward them for conforming to those expectations. To understand why an organization is successful or unsuccessful, the Cultural school holds, you first must understand the values and norms that make up those expectations. By analyzing the communication behaviors that occur within an organization, you can identify its values, heroes, rites, and rituals and, in so doing, determine what sort of culture it contains.[26]

Teamwork: An increasingly common concept in the contemporary organization.

The Teamwork School

Increasingly, theorists have been adopting the position that productivity in an organization is the result of communication in all directions: upward, downward, and lateral. Such communication fosters the development of work teams. The "teamwork" and "team work" (that is, the sense of team identity and the tasks performed by this work team) achieved by these groups determines how successful the organization is. A news release by the *Behavioral Sciences Newsletter* states:

> If we had to pick one theme that dominates all the various approaches to productivity through human resources, we would say it is the idea of "the team." Whether we are talking about sociotechnical systems, quality circles, self-managing groups, or task forces, the common thread is that such efforts work precisely because, by integrating the activities and skills of individuals, they create a force that makes the most of those individuals, yet is somehow greater than the sum of the parts.[27]

In his widely acclaimed book *Theory Z,* William Ouchi describes the predominance of work teams throughout Japanese industry and argues that this approach to productivity is one of the reasons the Japanese have been so successful over the past several decades. He notes that the "Type Z company is characterized by many cohesive and semi-autonomous work groups even though a Z company seldom undertakes any explicit attempts at teambuilding."[28]

Edward E. Lawler, in his book *High-Involvement Management,* takes the perspective that entire organizations should act as teams, with every level participating to some degree in decision making and problem solving. "No more fundamental change could occur than that involved in moving power, knowledge, information, and rewards to lower levels," he claims.[29] "It changes the very nature of what work is and means to everyone who works in an organization. Because it profoundly affects the jobs of everyone, it can impact on the effectiveness of all work organizations."

Lawler points out, however, that teams are not appropriate in every organizational context. Most agree that teamwork is most effective when a task entails a high level of interdependency among three or more people.[30] For instance, complex manufacturing processes common in the auto, chemical, paper, and high-technology industries can benefit from teams, as can complicated service tasks in insurance, banking, and telecommunications. In most cases, simple assembly-line activities are less amenable to teamwork. As Lawler points out, the more complex the task, the better suited it is for teams. Presumably, when the right kind of task is matched with the team approach, the result will be greater problem-solving speed and effectiveness. Dumaine contrasts this with the traditional approach to problem solving in a hierarchical organization: "A person with a problem in one function might have to shoot it up two or three layers by memo to a vice-president who tosses it laterally to a vice-president of another function who then kicks it down to the person in his area who knows the answer. Then it's back up and down the ladder again."[31] The rewards of teamwork come in the form of enhanced responsibility. Nevertheless, with fewer middle management positions, opportunities for advancement are diminished. And managers must recognize that organizing teams is a long, difficult process. Everyone involved must learn to think differently about themselves and how they approach their work and one another. Advocates of teamwork, however, are convinced that the results are worth the time and effort.

Many American organizations already have instituted various team approaches to managing and communicating. For example, as a part of its successful campaign to improve quality, Ford Motor Company launched a major effort in 1979 to change its culture to being more participative and employee-oriented. As a part of that change, in 1985 it announced a new set of company values that would be important to organizational and individual success:

Producing high-quality products at a cost the customer would consider a good value

Participative management and employee involvement

Continuous improvements in all aspects of the business

Teamwork[32]

Many other companies have also become more participative. Nearly all of Motorola's fifty-seven thousand U.S. employees are involved in some stage of its "Participative Management Program."[33] Honeywell, Xerox, General Motors, and Westinghouse, among

Epson, the world's leading maker of printers for personal computers, has instituted a new and bizarre-sounding method of developing new products. It's called "scrum and scramble." This method, also known to company insiders as the "rugby-team" approach to product development, is vastly different from the traditional "relay-team" approach.

Using the traditional approach, one group of specialists "passes the baton" to the next group: concept development gives their ideas to people in feasibility testing, who turn their results over to product design, who give their plans to production design and tooling, who pass their work to pilot production, who finally turn their methods over to full production. By contrast, under the "scrum-and-scramble" approach, a hand-picked, multidisciplinary team, with its members working from start to finish of the development process, "goes the distance as a unit, passing the ball back and forth," according to Professor Hirotaka Takeuchi of Japan's Hitotsubashi University. The team usually has a high degree of autonomy and often includes representatives of key suppliers.

From Christopher Lorenz, "For Epson, 'Rugby Team' Angle Computes." *San Francisco Examiner,* 12 July 1987, p. D-3.

others, have publicly committed themselves to using a more participative approach to organizing and managing people. Hundreds of companies are using quality circles or some other form of group problem solving to involve employees in identifying and resolving work-related problems. Clearly, as Lawler claims, "participative management is an idea whose time has come."[34]

The Teamwork school thus contains elements of the Human Resources school, the Human Relations school, and the Systems school; yet it also has characteristics of its own. Communication in this sort of organization moves in all directions, including laterally in informal meetings between peers. Spontaneous problem solving is encouraged, and conflict is resolved at the lowest level possible. Opportunities are created for employees in different departments to meet and talk with one another, and formal task teams are created whenever appropriate. Above all, communication cuts across formal organizational boundaries, occurring between people directly involved in getting the work done.

One key to teambuilding is having all group members share the same official status. Thus, in many teams no one is appointed leader. Each person is expected to contribute to the team's effort in diverse ways. Kormanski and Mozenter provide an excellent profile of the characteristics of effective team members:

Are understanding and committed to group goals

Are friendly, concerned, and interested in others

Acknowledge and confront conflict openly

Listen to others with understanding

Include others in the decision-making process

Recognize and respect individual differences

Contribute ideas and solutions

Value the ideas and contributions of others

Recognize and reward team efforts

Encourage and appreciate comments about team performance[35]

As team-oriented participative management becomes more prominent in American business and industry, skills in providing informal leadership and working with others to solve problems will take on ever greater importance.

Summary

At the beginning of this chapter, we made two assertions: first, much of your professional success will come through participation in some organization (or groups of organizations), and second, your professional success will be determined to a significant extent by your skills as a communicator. Learning to function effectively in an organizational setting requires considerable understanding of organizations, how they are structured, and the underlying principles that have influenced their traditions and contributed to their culture. Developing communication skills that will contribute to your professional success is equally important. Many employees understand their organizations rather well. They accurately perceive the management philosophies and practices that affect their daily lives. But because of their own lack of experience with or knowledge of effective communication practices, they cannot influence others in the organization. Nor can they do much to enhance their own upward mobility.

The inability to communicate effectively in organizations can result in feelings of powerlessness, anonymity, and the experience of being passed over when important committee assignments are made or promotion opportunities arise. It is simply not enough to know your stuff. You must also be able to communicate with others about your knowledge, ideas, and suggestions for change. To be able to inform others, to ask good questions, to listen carefully, and to persuade others—these are the basic elements of effective communication.

In this book, we take the view that the principles of effective communication are fairly consistent across diverse situations. Even so, each situation requires some skills that are situation-specific. Speaking to several hundred people is very different from speaking to a board of ten members. Trying to persuade a customer to buy a television is different from trying to persuade your boss to give you a raise. Conducting a disciplinary interview is strikingly different from conducting an employment interview. Recognizing and adapting to these differences is a critical part of learning to communicate effectively. Later in the book, we will discuss communication in diverse settings. But in the next few chapters, we will continue to establish the foundational knowledge upon which specific skills are built by exploring management and leadership, communication channels and networks, the development of human relationships, and, of course, ethics.

Questions for Discussion

1. Why is communication so important to success in an organization?
2. Since everyone already knows how to talk to one another, why would formal training in communication skills be helpful for organizational success?
3. How is communication a "process" in an organization?
4. How might communication serve to translate workers' abilities into job performance?
5. How would each organizational theory view money as a motivator of employee performance?

Exercises

1. Think of an organization for which you have worked or with which you are very familiar. Which organizational theory seems to prevail in this organization? Cite specific examples to support your views.
2. From the business section of a newspaper, clip articles that refer to any organizational practices that illustrate principles of one of the organizational schools of thought.

Management Theory and Practice

he significance of effective leadership for successful organizational functioning was clearly articulated by Hersey and Blanchard when they wrote, "The successful organization has one major attribute that sets it apart from unsuccessful organizations: dynamic and effective leadership."[1] Yet the concept of leadership is not always easy to define. What are the qualities of an effective leader or manager? Is it possible, for instance, to sketch the profile of an ideal manager? If so, what role would communication play? What kinds of communication behaviors should an effective manager be able to exhibit? To what extent should those behaviors vary as the manager is confronted with different leadership problems or organizational situations?

In this chapter, we want to respond to these questions by examining several contemporary management theories, considering diverse issues confronted by contemporary managers and, based on theory, research, and our experience, present some basic principles of management. Before we turn our attention to these tasks, however, we need to take a moment to consider the centrality of communication to effective management.

One way of exploring the kinds of skills needed for effective management is to begin by looking at what the typical manager does with his or her time. Several studies conducted during the past two decades have revealed that managers are almost constantly communicating. Mintzberg's extensive research with dozens of executives, involving direct observations and detailed log-keeping, found that verbal interaction accounted for 78 percent of these managers' time. Moreover, Mintzberg's investigation excluded desk work, defining verbal interaction as scheduled and impromptu meetings, phone calls, and tours![2] Based on this and similar studies, we would have to conclude that any activity that consumes so much of anyone's professional time is bound to be important. Managers who suffer from poor communication skills are likely to feel frustrated most of the time. And they are even more likely to be surrounded by a number of unhappy and unproductive subordinates.

Management Skill Clusters

As we acknowledge the significance of good communication skills for effective management, it is equally crucial to recognize the importance of other management competencies. Communication skills do not exist alone. Typically, they are interdependent with other skill clusters. In general, the good manager needs three sets of skills or skill clusters to flourish: *technical expertise, conceptual ability,* and *human relations, or communication, skills.* Let us consider each briefly.

Managers with *technical expertise* know their own jobs and are capable of understanding and guiding the job performance of their subordinates. Indeed, most people in management positions were promoted in the past because of their performance on the technical elements of their jobs. But two common problems arise. Some managers remain convinced that their subordinates cannot do their jobs as well as the managers themselves. As a result, these managers either delegate too little (in effect, doing subordinates' jobs for them), or they watch their subordinates too closely, insisting that things be done "the way I used to do it." Other managers simply fail to keep up with or lose interest in their original area of technical expertise. By so doing, they become unable to evaluate their subordinates' performance effectively or to provide assistance and guidance when needed.

The second skill cluster is *conceptual ability*. This cluster is broadly defined to include the manager's ability to think creatively, to see interrelationships, and to understand the organization as a complex social system. This concept takes on different meanings as one moves up the hierarchy. Lower-level managers must understand the way their jobs relate to others in the immediate environment and comprehend the ways in which their departments are interdependent. A vice-president in that same organization, however, needs to understand how the organization as a whole might influence or be influenced by its relevant environment. The vice-president also needs a sense of vision concerning the organization's mission and future goals.

Third, the excellent manager needs good *human relations, or communication, skills*. This is the broadest of the skill clusters because it includes the ability to motivate employees, interaction skills, and the ability to function effectively in dyadic, small group, and public communication settings. Regardless of his or her management rank, every supervisor or manager needs to know how to listen to others' ideas, how to conduct meetings, how to motivate subordinates to perform to the best of their ability, and how to speak clearly.

Figure 2.1
Needed management skills over time.

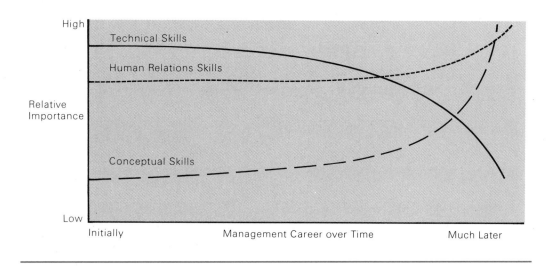

To what extent is each of these skill clusters important to success as a manager? Although there is no absolute answer to that question, in most organizational settings one can rely on these generalizations:

1. At the beginning of a management career, the need for technical expertise will be great. Over time, however, that need will diminish.
2. The need for conceptual ability will increase over the span of a management career. A first-line supervisor can get by with less; a member of the executive board will need a great deal more.
3. Human relations skills are crucial, regardless of where a person is in her or his life as a manager. They are important from the very beginning, and that importance grows over time.

Figure 2.1 depicts the relative importance of the three skill clusters during a manager's career. Although all three skill clusters are crucial when viewed from the total perspective of a management career, *human relations, or communication, skills are more consistently and enduringly related to success as a manager than either technical skill or conceptual ability.*

Whether or not managers view communication skills as being crucial to their effectiveness will depend, in part, upon their notion of what good management is all about. In many cases, managers' views may be guided by some theoretical approach

Theory X versus Theory Y

	Assumptions about People	Implications for Communication
Theory X	People are lazy and try to avoid work.	People need orders and careful monitoring.
	People cannot think for themselves.	People must be told what to do and how to do it. Upward communication is not necessary.
	People are interested only in money.	Pay must be stressed as the available reward.
Theory Y	Work can be as natural as play.	People should be allowed autonomy.
	People can be self-directed.	Give general goals, but let people formulate methods.
	People can think for themselves.	Use participative decision making.
	People want nonmonetary rewards.	Use positive feedback to motivate; help people feel a sense of accomplishment.

that suggests certain tenets of human nature and behavior upon which managers should base their approach to motivating subordinates. In the next section, we will briefly consider several of these contemporary management theories.

The Manager as Leader

McGregor

Theories of organization and philosophies of management are often closely associated. Classical organization theory provided the impetus for Douglas McGregor's first theory of managing human behavior.[3] McGregor labeled this approach "Theory X." In the spirit of scientific management, its central principle is one of direction and control through the exercise of authority. The Theory X manager makes most decisions alone, issues many orders and commands that flow downward through appropriate formal channels, displays little interest in acquiring suggestions and information from those near the bottom of the organizational hierarchy, and generally treats workers as economic beings who are most readily motivated through wage incentive plans and other monetary management methods.

Unfortunately, as McGregor points out, supervisors who manage their workers in accordance with the principles of Theory X often create climates of distrust, fear, and misunderstanding. Because so little information flows upward through the hierarchy (and the information actually reaching the top is usually filtered and considerably distorted), decision making is based on only partial and often inaccurate data.

As an alternative to this authoritarian approach to management, McGregor advocates a second management philosophy, "Theory Y."[4] Based in part on the Human Relations movement and the findings of the Hawthorne studies, Theory Y emphasizes the social nature of workers. It contends that human beings can be meaningfully motivated to work productively only when organizations fulfill their higher-level needs for belonging, esteem, and self-actualization.[5]

Theory Y further argues that workers prefer self-control and self-direction over being directed and controlled by executive commands. Managers practicing the principles of Theory Y encourage the flow of messages up, down, and across the organization. They are sensitive to employee feedback and facilitate frequent, honest interaction in an atmosphere of confidence and trust.

According to McGregor, Theory Y management results in improved communication accuracy and decision-making quality. The central principle of Theory Y is the integration of individual and organizational goals. The theory maintains that through a cooperative effort, both parties have the greatest potential for fulfillment.

A number of criticisms have been leveled against McGregor's theories, the strongest of which focuses on the apparent polarization of Theory X and Theory Y.[6] Critics maintain that this polarization oversimplifies a complex situation by implying that there are only two managerial extremes and no middle ground—or, for that matter, any possible combination of the two extremes. In his later writings, McGregor attempts to clarify his position by arguing that any leader can blend the two theories, depending upon the situation and personnel involved.[7]

Likert

A similar approach to management theory that provides a wider range of managerial alternatives is the systems approach of Likert and his colleagues.[8] Likert's research suggests that most management styles can be classified as belonging to one of four possible systems. System 1 parallels McGregor's Theory X. It focuses on centralized decision making, conflicting organizational and individual goals, a preponderance of downward communication (to the exclusion of adequate upward communication), and a general atmosphere of distrust.

Next on the continuum are Systems 2 and 3. System 2 involves greater interaction between managers and subordinates, but the confidence demonstrated by superiors is often condescending. Decision making is somewhat more diffuse, but significant decisions continue to be made at the top of the organization. System 3 moves in the direction of integration and is characterized by increased interaction throughout the organization, with communication occurring within an atmosphere of general trust and confidence.

Specific decisions are made by more members of the organizational family, although policymaking continues to be carried out at the top.

The final Likert system approximates McGregor's Theory Y. System 4 focuses on complete manager and subordinate trust and confidence; the unrestricted flow of messages up, down, and across the organization; and shared participation in decision making, goal setting, and evaluation. The central concept of Likert's fourth system is "participative decision making." According to this notion, organizations should permit employees to participate in making decisions that directly affect them, particularly if they must execute them.

Likert's research in the early 1960s found that System 4 organizations had the highest level of productivity and System 1 the lowest. He also noted that managers' personal preferences leaned toward the System 4 approach and that the most successful managers worked to develop a "supportive" climate within their organizations. Subordinates usually perceived these supportive (System 4, Theory Y) managers as friendly and helpful, genuinely interested in the well-being of each employee, and trusting in the ability and integrity of all workers. Unfortunately, Likert also found that most managers worked in organizations that adhered to Classical notions and thus followed the System 1 approach.[9]

As we noted in the previous chapter, many U.S. companies today are moving toward the more participative, System 4 approach Likert advocated. A study by the U.S. Department of Labor, for example, noted that nearly half of some five hundred U.S. businesses or business units of major corporations that had been surveyed had instituted some form of employee involvement program.[10] Xerox, Dayton Power and Light, Preston Trucking Company, and A & P stores were but a few examples cited in the study.

Probably the most serious criticism of Likert's theory focuses on his basic notion that organizations employ consistent systems of management throughout; that is, a given

Blake and Mouton's Managerial Styles

Style	Concern for Production	Concern for People
Impoverished	Low	Low
Task-Oriented	High	Low
People-Oriented	Low	High
Middle-of-the-Road	Moderate	Moderate
Team-Oriented	High	High

organization can be categorized at *all* levels as, for example, System 2. It is quite possible, and often probable, that different departments or units of an organization will be managed differently or that there will be differences between organizational levels (so that, for example, top-level staff are managed by means of System 4, while the rank and file are managed by some other approach, possibly System 1).

Blake and Mouton

A third approach to the study of management is based on the findings of small group research on leadership. Two types of leadership behavior predominate in this research: that which concerns itself with the *task* before the group or organization, and that which focuses on the *socioemotional* maintenance of the group itself.[11]

Basing their approach on these two basic leadership dimensions, concern for employees and concern for production, Blake and Mouton have developed a leadership grid for the scrutiny of managerial behavior.[12] According to their theory, there are five possible managerial styles. The first, the *impoverished style,* is illustrated by the manager who cares neither for people nor for productivity. He or she provides no guidance for employees, avoids involvement in any conflict, delegates decision-making responsibilities to others, and prefers to leave others alone and to be left alone. Actually, this person is a manager in name only and a leader in no sense of the word.

Another style Blake and Mouton identify is the *task-oriented style.* As the name implies, this kind of manager demonstrates a low concern for people and a high concern for production and is a direct parallel to McGregor's Theory X and Likert's System 1 managers. Thus, the task-oriented manager issues commands, cares little for employee feedback, and bases his or her reward system on concepts of lower-level need satisfaction.

A third style represents the opposite of the managerial approach just described. It is totally *people-oriented.* These managers are entirely interested in interpersonal relationships, to the exclusion of any concern for organizational productivity. They smooth over conflict, reward extravagantly, and promote good fellowship and harmony—at the expense of the organization.

The fourth style is the *middle-of-the-road* approach, emphasizing moderate concern for both people and production. Managers espousing this philosophy probably fall somewhere near Likert's System 3. They generally support participation in decision making and encourage teamwork and employer-employee interaction, but they are not totally committed to the concept of integration.

Finally, Blake and Mouton point to the fifth style, the *team manager*. This person has high concern for both people and production; thus, he or she parallels the Theory Y, System 4 managers already discussed. The team manager strives to maintain the group while accomplishing the organizational task. He or she confronts and resolves conflict, encourages consensus in decision making, and seeks candid and spontaneous employee feedback in an atmosphere of trust and mutual respect.

Probably the greatest advantage of Blake and Mouton's approach to management is the fact that their grid may be applied to each manager within the organization. Thus, it allows for individual analysis and assumes that different philosophies of management are often operative within the same organizational setting. As with McGregor and Likert, however, each manager is classified with regard to his or her basic approach, allowing little room for the adoption of different managerial styles with varying tasks and personnel.

Hersey and Blanchard

Like Blake and Mouton, Hersey and Blanchard focus on two elements of leadership: managing work and managing people. However, unlike other management theorists, Hersey and Blanchard do not make static assumptions about both managers and workers. In their examination of leadership styles and employee needs, they acknowledge the inevitability of some change, as well as the potential for growth. Their theory of leadership affirms the need for a dynamic leadership approach in which the manager's effectiveness is determined by his or her ability to assess accurately the needs and abilities of employees and adjust his or her leadership strategy accordingly.[13]

According to Hersey and Blanchard, an effective manager should begin by assessing a subordinate's maturity, which they define as the "willingness and ability of a person to take responsibility for directing his or her own behavior."[14] Actually, there are two dimensions to maturity in any work environment: (1) *psychological maturity*—the willingness or motivation to do something, the belief that responsibility is important, and the confidence to complete tasks without extensive encouragement, and (2) *job maturity*—the ability or competence to do something, the knowledge, experience, and skill needed to carry out work without the direction of others.[15]

Hersey and Blanchard recognize that a number of important situational factors exist in any organizational environment. They remain convinced, however, that the behavior of the manager in relation to individual employees in the work group is the most crucial. Consequently, these researchers describe four leadership behavior categories, any

Hersey and Blanchard's Management Styles

High task/low relationship: One-way communication in which leader defines roles, tells people how and when to accomplish tasks. Most appropriate when employees are low in job maturity and psychological maturity.

High task/high relationship: Two-way communication and joint problem solving are encouraged. Most appropriate when employees are low in job maturity but high in psychological maturity.

Low task/high relationship: Shared decision making, with manager acting mainly as a facilitator. Most appropriate when employees are high in job maturity but low in psychological maturity.

Low task/low relationship: Employees left on their own, with minimal supervision. Most appropriate when employees are high in both job and psychological maturity.

one of which might be appropriate, depending upon the maturity level of the employees concerned. These are presented in Business Brief 2.5.

Hersey and Blanchard's situational approach to management has been labeled the "Life Cycle Theory of Leadership" in that it examines leader-subordinate interactions over an extended period of time and assumes that changes, adjustments, and growth will occur. If a manager is dealing with an individual or group of employees whose psychological and job maturity are low, he or she would begin by emphasizing task-oriented leadership. As the employees' maturity level increases, the manager would decrease task behavior and increase relationship behavior until a moderate level of maturity is attained. Ultimately, with increases in maturity, the manager begins to decrease both task and relationship behavior. At this point, employees possess both job and psychological maturity and are capable of providing their own reinforcement. Hersey and Blanchard believe that when high levels of maturity are reached, employees accept the reduction in close supervision and attention as an indication of the manager's confidence and trust.[16]

Perhaps the greatest contribution of Hersey and Blanchard's approach is its recognition of employee differences and changes in maturation over time. While managers hope for highly mature employees, most work with at least some individuals who are less talented and motivated. Hersey and Blanchard's theory accepts the fact that some workers may never reach high levels of maturity. In those instances, these writers contend that the manager's task is to provide highly task-oriented leadership.

Although their theory has provided interesting and useful insights into leadership, Hersey and Blanchard have yet to address some important questions. Among them are: How do we train managers who can accurately identify the maturity level of employees? Should we be satisfied with allowing workers to remain at low maturity levels throughout their productive lives? If not, what strategies can encourage their growth and maturation? Do employees ever really mature beyond the need for managers who demonstrate a real concern for relationships? Is this a desirable goal?

Herzberg

An alternative approach to the study of management is offered by Herzberg, whose research led to the development of his motivation-hygiene or two-factor theory of organizational behavior.[17] Herzberg's theory is an attempt to organize findings from an interviewing study conducted with 203 accountants and engineers. The researchers asked the interviewees to recall a time when they felt particularly good about their jobs. Subsequent probing sought to determine the reasons for the good feelings and their impact on both job performance and overall sense of well-being. After a positive sequence of events was completed, the interview was repeated with the workers being asked to focus on a time when they had negative feelings about their jobs. Again, probing questions were used to get at the reasons for those negative feelings.

Herzberg concluded from this study of "critical incidents" in workers' work lives that five factors stood out as the primary determinants of job satisfaction: *responsibility, advancement, work itself, achievement,* and *recognition.* He believed that the first three were of greatest importance and was struck by the fact that these five factors appeared very infrequently when people were describing events that made them feel negatively about their jobs. Therefore, when one of these factors was present, Herzberg concluded, workers were satisfied. However, when these factors were absent, workers were not necessarily dissatisfied. Instead, they had neutral feelings. Herzberg named these five factors "motivators," since when they were present, they seemed to motivate employees to perform well.

An entirely different set of factors was found to determine job dissatisfaction. The major dissatisfiers emerged from the interviews as being *company administration and policy, supervision, salary, interpersonal relations,* and *working conditions.* Herzberg concluded that these factors produce job dissatisfaction when they are not present or are poorly handled, but that they seemed to have no role in making people feel good about themselves and their work. He named these dissatisfiers "hygiene factors."

According to Herzberg, motivator and hygiene factors are each presumed to reflect different systems of human needs. Hygiene factors supposedly are derived from lower-order biological needs (hunger and thirst, for example) plus all of the learned ones associated with those primary drives (such as the desire for money to buy food). Motivators, on the other hand, spring from peoples' unique ability to achieve and grow. People need challenge and a sense of achievement to feel fulfilled, and this is reflected in the motivators.

The implications of Herzberg's theory are important. A company that emphasizes pay to motivate performance, for example, may be wasting its time and resources; at best, pay can only avoid dissatisfaction, while true motivation must come from the nature of the work itself. While hygiene factors are important, and failure to satisfy hygiene needs can generate much organizational distress, Herzberg believed that companies are wrong when they assume that preventing dissatisfaction will automatically generate positive feelings and produce increased motivation and productivity. At best, emphasis on hygiene factors can only relieve dissatisfaction temporarily, and demands for better pay and benefits eventually will resurface.

Therefore, Herzberg felt that it is especially important for organizations to recognize and respond to their employees' needs for personal growth. In addition, he stressed that the way to satisfy the motivator needs at work is by "job enrichment," a process by which jobs are made more meaningful. Some of his job enrichment principles are:

1. Increasing the accountability of people for their own work.
2. Granting additional authority to employees.
3. Introducing new and more difficult tasks as employees develop greater skills.
4. Involving employees in identifying and solving work-related problems.

In recent years, there has been some criticism of Herzberg's methodology and reliance on "critical incident" reports.[18] Indeed, there is ample evidence that pay can serve both as a dissatisfier and as a motivator (in fact, most companies now use some form of pay-for-performance system). Nevertheless, much of the emphasis seen today on empowering employees and involving work teams in identifying and solving production problems is a direct reflection of Herzberg's theories concerning the intrinsically motivating characteristics of work.

The Japanese Approach to Management

During the 1970s and 1980s, American managers invested much time and money studying Japanese approaches to management because of the fine quality of Japanese products and the general productivity of their organizations. While the American and Japanese cultures differ significantly in many ways, it is still possible to examine Japanese management and discover several relevant principles.

Extensive studies of Japanese organizations have demonstrated that Japanese managers stress the following:[19]

1. *Bottom-up initiative.* Japanese managers believe that change and initiative within an organization *should* come from those closest to the problem. So they elicit change from below. Top-level Japanese managers see their task as creating an atmosphere in which subordinates are motivated to seek better solutions.

2. *Top management as facilitator.* Japanese managers do not view themselves as having all the answers. When a subordinate brings in a proposal, the manager neither accepts nor rejects it. Rather, he tactfully, politely asks questions, makes suggestions, and provides encouragement.

3. *Middle management as impetus for and shaper of solutions.* In the Japanese system, junior (middle) managers are initiators who perceive problems and formulate tentative solutions in coordination with others; they are not functional specialists who carry out their boss's directives. Because so much emphasis is placed on coordination and integration, solutions to problems evolve more slowly, but they are known and understood by all those who have been a part of the solution generation process. Horizontal communication is stressed as essential to the coordination of problem-solving efforts.

4. *Consensus as a way of making decisions.* The Japanese are less inclined to think in terms of absolutes, that is, the solution (which is right) versus the alternatives (which are wrong). Rather, they recognize a range of alternatives, several of which might work and all of which possess advantages and disadvantages.[20] When a group makes a decision, all members become committed to the chosen solution. From a Japanese perspective, that commitment, and the ensuing dedication toward working to make the solution successful, is probably more important than the objective quality of the decision. The Japanese have an interesting concept of consensus. Those who consent to a decision are not necessarily endorsing it. Rather, consent means that each person is satisfied that his or her point of view has been fairly heard, and although he or she may not wholly agree that the decision is the best one, he or she is willing to go along with it and even support it.[21]

5. *Concern for employees' personal well-being.* Japanese managers have a kind of paternalistic attitude toward their employees. Traditionally, Japanese organizations have offered their workers housing, extensive recreational facilities, and lifetime employment. The Japanese believe that it is impossible to divorce a worker's personal and professional lives. Good managers express concern for workers as persons with homes and families as well as for the quality of the products the workers produce. Managers typically work alongside their subordinates, counsel them regarding their personal lives, and encourage much peer interaction.

It is interesting that principles that are considered by many to be advantages of the Japanese system can also be viewed as problems, at least from an American perspective. There is a fine line between encouraging consensus and forcing it. When groups place too much emphasis on being agreeable and conforming to organizational expectations, poor-quality decision making is a likely outcome. Moreover, the Japanese notion of taking care of employees can extend into an extreme form of paternalism with which few well-educated Americans would be comfortable. It is appropriate to protect children or others who cannot think for or look after themselves. But professionals hardly fall into these categories. Most Americans would prefer an organizational system that makes it possible for them to function as mature, intelligent human beings, responsible for their own security and well-being.

Finally, some authors have suggested that Japanese-style management as adapted to American organizations is little more than a tool for even greater management control.[22] Employees who have a life commitment to a particular organization, for instance, become vulnerable. Since they do not perceive viable options, they are more likely to tolerate existing work conditions, even if they find them unpleasant. Employees are also encouraged to become generalists rather than specialists. Thus, their expertise in a particular area is rarely sufficiently developed so that the organization actually grows to depend on them as irreplaceable employees. Instead, substitutes are readily found. Moreover, should employees who have worked in this kind of organizational environment decide to abandon their commitment to this organization after a few years of working as generalists, they would be poorly equipped to move into other American organizations since they would be competing with specialists.

The body of research on Japanese organizations continues to grow. Recent research suggests that one cannot generalize across Japanese workers—that males and females, young and old, differ in their decision-making style and management preference. One study reported that Japanese workers were more passive than commonly thought, preferring to be persuaded of the value of a decision by their supervisor over making the decision themselves.[23] However, a different study found that Japanese managers place a far greater emphasis on corporate participation and cooperation than their American counterparts.[24] Thus, a consistent and coherent view of Japanese organizations does not yet exist.

As with the other approaches to management we have examined, the Japanese approach is interesting. In reminding us of the value of the individual, the need for participative decision making, and the potential of facilitative management, it has been extremely useful. It is not a panacea, however. Because of extreme differences between the Japanese and the American cultures, some Japanese management practices are simply poorly suited to American organizations.

Self-Management

As we noted in the previous chapter, the Teamwork school of organizational theory now is beginning to emphasize informal leadership in place of formal management. In an article titled "Who Needs a Boss?" *Fortune* describes self-managed "superteams" that typically consist of between three and thirty workers, "sometimes blue collar, sometimes white collar, sometimes both."[25] For example, teams in a General Mills cereal plant in Lodi, California, schedule, operate, and maintain machinery so effectively that no managers are present on the night shift. Similarly, after organizing its home office operations into teams, Aetna Life & Casualty reduced the ratio of middle managers to workers from one to seven down to one to thirty (and at the same time improved customer service).

Responsibilities often undertaken by self-managing teams include such traditional management functions as preparing an annual budget, timekeeping, recording quality control statistics, monitoring inventory, assigning jobs within groups, training other team members, adjusting production schedules, modifying production processes, setting team goals, resolving internal conflicts, and evaluating team performance.[26]

Leadership within self-managed teams usually emerges informally. Once company management has trained team members in basic problem-solving and group-dynamic skills and defined for them their scope of responsibility and authority, they allow the team to develop their own procedures and relationships. Team members most skilled in group communication techniques are most likely to emerge as the informal leaders.

Self-managed teams have proven extremely effective in many organizations. During their weekly meeting, a team of Federal Express clerks identified (and eventually resolved) a billing problem that had been costing the company $2.1 million a year. In 3M, cross-functional teams tripled the number of new products produced by one division. Teams of blue-collar workers at Johnsonville Foods of Sheboygan, Wisconsin, helped increase production by more than 50 percent over four years.

Despite such successes, the spread of self-managed teams has been relatively slow for several reasons. First, it requires a great deal of mutual trust between top management and employees—trust that may take years to build (and only a moment to undo). Second, middle managers often feel highly threatened by the concept because they believe it will reduce their power and influence. Thus, they may openly or covertly oppose the process. In addition, implementation of self-managing teams often takes a long time (eighteen months to two years is common), and training employees in self-management skills can be time-consuming and expensive. Nevertheless, the benefits of self-management have been dramatic enough to convince many organizations to commit to this new management style.

Management Theory in Perspective

Our discussion of approaches to management is not intended to be exhaustive but only indicative of some of the existing significant theories. The concepts of management and leadership are often used interchangeably. Yet, the notion of leadership extends far beyond that of management. Managers are, by definition, appointed leaders—that is, selected by the organization to serve in positions of coordination, integration, and decision making. Many organizations meet their goals without effective management; they *cannot meet their goals without effective leadership.*

We have all had experiences with ineffective managers. They can be found in schools, churches, hospitals, small private firms, and large corporations. In the clever film *Nine to Five,* we are delighted to observe the authoritarian, abusive boss who is bound, gagged, and kept captive in his own home for six weeks while three female employees, including his own secretary, try to prove him a crook. While he is "tied up," these three women also take the liberty to initiate several changes in the office. They have the place redecorated, institute flexible work hours, start a day-care center and an alcoholism rehabilitation program, begin to hire the handicapped, and remove the time clock. When, at last, the boss returns, he is at first horrified and later stunned to discover that productivity is up by 20 percent!

The movie is a comedy, but the point it makes is provocative. These three women, who had never been allowed to make decisions before, demonstrated their ability to take risks, make tough decisions, and deal with their fellow employees in compassionate and creative ways. The effectiveness of their leadership could not be questioned.

It is possible for nearly any employee to provide leadership. We concur with Tanenbaum, Weschler, and Massarik, who define leadership as "interpersonal influence, exercised in a situation and directed, through the communication process, toward the attainment of specialized goal or goals."[27] Our concept of leadership, then, is functional. It permits and encourages the spread of decision making and problem solving throughout the organization as a whole.

Issues Facing Contemporary Managers

Empowerment

To what extent should power be shared? How is sharing power and effective leadership related? In an attempt to answer these questions, Bennis sought to identify the defining characteristics of excellent leaders by interviewing ninety individuals who had been nominated by their peers as the most influential leaders in all walks of life. Bennis found that these individuals all shared one significant characteristic: they made others feel powerful.[28] Together with others, these leaders were able to accomplish exceptional organizational goals. Bennis concluded that empowering others consistently produced several important benefits. First, those who felt empowered reported feeling important and valued by their fellow workers. They also developed a conviction that learning and competence really matter and sought to behave in ways consistent with those convictions. They perceived themselves as part of a team or as embedded within a community. Finally, they came to view their work as more engaging and challenging than ever before.

Bennis's research suggests many positive outcomes associated with empowering workers. You may be wondering, however, *how* managers might approach empowerment in terms of their attitudes, behaviors, and communication practices. Several researchers have pursued these issues, attempting to describe the culture, practices, and behaviors that might typify an empowering organization and its leaders. Conger, for instance, describes several specific managerial techniques and strategies:

Involve subordinates in the assignment of work. Normally, it is the manager who makes work assignments. Thus, when subordinates are permitted to make decisions about which tasks they choose to tackle, they are sharing some of the manager's authority.

Provide a positive, collaborative work environment. Whenever individuals are able to set aside formal role relationships and focus on common problems while seeking mutually acceptable solutions, they move in the direction of empowerment.

Reward and encourage others in visible and personal ways. For most individuals, the value of a reward is increased when it is awarded in public and when it is very personal (in the context of professional good taste). Acknowledging the excellent performance of someone during a public speech or reading aloud a letter praising someone's fine work during a staff meeting might serve as such visible recognition.

Express confidence. The manager who shares a difficult task with others, who actually involves others in demanding, challenging problem solving, communicates the message that she is confident that others are up to the challenge. While sentiments of confidence can be expressed verbally, taking actions that demonstrate confidence and trust may communicate an even more powerful message.

Foster initiative and responsibility. One especially effective manager encouraged his subordinates to identify problems within the organization and come to him with ideas for how to solve them. He consistently expressed tremendous enthusiasm whenever a subordinate identified a legitimate problem and offered a sound, promising, or innovative solution. This manager prodded subordinates into being problem detectors and problem solvers—thus, encouraging energetic, intelligent, and responsible employee behavior.

Build on success. The wisest managers are those who applaud and celebrate others' accomplishments. Rather than being threatened by those beneath them, these managers point to others' successes with genuine enthusiasm, reward them generously, and challenge them to excel even more.[29]

Another approach to describing empowering organizational cultures has grown from Pacanowsky's long-term study of W. L. Gore & Associates. Pacanowsky offers several "operating rules of the empowering organization" and suggests that they might serve as a model for other organizations. His rules include:

Distribute power and opportunity widely. This focuses on letting people own the problems they are interested in, decentralizing the process by which important decisions are made, and emphasizing the power to accomplish (rather than the power to dominate).

Maintain a full, open, and decentralized communication system. Information in this sort of organization flows freely, with fewer distortions and less attention to impression management. Mistakes are tolerated as people learn, grow, take risks, and keep on working.

Use integrative problem solving. This approach distributes problem-solving responsibilities among functional work units. Power, information, and opportunity are genuinely and widely distributed. Task forces are used abundantly. With new configurations of people coming together to solve problems, innovation and creativity are encouraged in a climate that fosters visibility for many and nurtures a "we" attitude among everyone.

Practice challenge in an environment of trust. Individuals will be better problem solvers when they participate in debate and lively conversations about the relative strengths and weaknesses of competing courses of action. Ideas are to be challenged and concerns expressed—but criticism and challenge must be offered in a spirit of support rather than in a spirit of one-upmanship. Ultimately, after issues have been thoroughly discussed, people must be given the chance to act according to their best information and judgment.

Reward and recognize people so as to encourage a high-performance ethic and responsibility. The best rewards grow from giving others increased power and opportunity, rather than from instituting "employee of the month" awards. Thus, the emphasis is upon internal rather than external incentives. As individuals are given greater responsibilities, their credibility is also enhanced.

Become wise by living through, and learning from, organizational ambiguity, inconsistency, contradiction, and paradox. Most organizations exist in complex, ambiguous environments where information is equivocal and decision making is shrouded in uncertainty. Organizational values are often characterized by inconsistencies. People are encouraged to excel as individuals, while, simultaneously, cooperative teamwork is praised and rewarded. Learning to live with these apparently conflicting realities is critical to empowerment and growth.[30]

Finally, some scholars have offered a more theoretical approach to defining empowerment. Based on the notion of empowerment as a process of creating intrinsic task motivation by providing an environment and tasks that increase feelings of self-efficacy and energy, Thomas and Velthouse have developed a conceptual model that specifies four dimensions of empowerment: impact, choice, competence, and meaningfulness.[31] *Impact* is related to whether accomplishing a particular task or job will make a difference in the scheme of things. In theory, the greater the impact employees believe they have, the more internally motivated they will be.[32] The second dimension, *choice,* means the degree to which personal behavior is self-determined. According to this model, the more individuals are given the opportunity to select tasks, to decide how they should be accomplished, and to elect to take responsibility for their outcome, the more empowered they should feel. The third dimension is *competence.* For empowerment to be possible, those to whom tasks are assigned must possess the necessary skills, knowledge, experience, and other qualifications to enable them to move forward with confidence and competence. Finally, *meaningfulness* is crucial. This dimension points to the value of a task or job in relation to the individual's own beliefs, ideals, and standards. The more closely a task is consistent with someone's value system, the more conviction he or she brings to its accomplishment. Without perceived meaningfulness, a sense of empowerment is unlikely.[33]

Taken together, the empowerment model and practical guidelines provide a broad vision of what empowerment might actually mean on a day-to-day basis. Even so, several questions remain. Can an empowering organizational profile ever be identified, or must each manager define empowerment in terms of her or his specific organization? Is empowerment possible in all kinds of organizations? Does empowerment grow from the

From Michael E. Pacanowsky, "Communication in the Empowering Organization," in *Communication Yearbook 11,* ed. J. Anderson (Beverly Hills: Sage, 1987), p. 378.

relationship between the manager and the employee, or is it rooted in the employee's own intrinsic need for self-efficacy? To what extent are there individual differences; that is, does every employee want to be empowered?

Globalization

As technology and transportation continue to shrink our world, members of organizations increasingly will be confronted with the challenges inherent in dealing with people from other cultures. While barriers of language and custom pose many difficulties for communicators, even more fundamental are differences in values and ethics. In parts of Africa, for example, a celebration at the conclusion of a business deal (a party for which you might be asked to pay) would be considered a sign of friendship and lasting business relationships, not a payoff by you in exchange for cooperation from your customers. Similarly, in many parts of the world, custom, law, and religion all support the denial of women's personal and professional rights of equality, much to the frustration of American female business executives. Yet each of these practices is part of some culture's ethical standards and value systems.

Hodgson argues that the key steps to overcoming the hurdles posed by cultural differences are these:

1. Become sensitive to the customs, values, and practices of other peoples—the things they view as moral, traditional, practical, and effective.
2. Do not judge customs different from your own as being immoral, corrupt, or inappropriate; assume they are legitimate until proven otherwise.
3. Find legitimate ways to operate from others' ethical and commercial points of view; do not demand that they operate by your customs or ground rules.
4. Conduct relationships and negotiations as openly and aboveboard as possible.
5. Avoid rationalizing borderline actions, and refuse to do business when suggested actions violate or seriously compromise laws or fundamental organizational values.[34]

A survey of globalization practices by major U.S. companies conducted by Runzheimer International revealed that:

1. The companies have an office or operation in an average of twenty different countries.
2. The companies employ an average of 6,331 employees in countries outside their home location.
3. Fifty-seven percent of the companies provided no formal training to brief their employees on the countries to which they were assigned; 30 percent did provide such training.
4. Sixty-seven percent of the companies that did provide formal training included training for nonemployee family members.

Survey results presented in "HR from a Global Perspective," *Personnel Journal* 72 (October 1993): 87.

Consider, for example, bribery. Most governments and organizations have statutes against most forms of private payoff. Yet in some African countries, ancient traditions take precedence over laws or company policies. Payoffs have become the norm and are rooted in such traditional practices as the Nigerian "dash" (private pay for private service), which are an expected part of business transactions.

Some companies have sought to promote globalization through the development of strong organizational cultures designed to facilitate adaptation to different environments. Asea Brown Boveri, Inc., an electrical-engineering giant, has 213,000 employees worldwide and lives by the motto "think globally, act locally." The company is tightly focused on making money, and it is managed in a hands-on, action-oriented style. Yet members of management are strongly encouraged to be sensitive and adjust to the cultures of the countries in which they work.[35] Indeed, one culture difficult for the senior management team (most of whom are Europeans) to understand is that of the United States: most seem puzzled when told, for example, that they cannot ask a person's age or marital status during an employment interview. Nevertheless, these executives work to adapt to this "strange" set of cultural practices.

Another instance of cultures being merged occurred in 1993, when London-based British Airways formed an alliance with Virginia-based USAir. To begin blending the two organization's corporate and national cultures, the companies initiated an exchange program in which management personnel from one company "shadowed" their counterparts at the other to learn how they did business, made decisions, and managed employees. For example, an individual from British Airways worked side-by-side in Washington, D.C., with USAir's director of employee relations, learning how the company makes key personnel decisions. In turn, the USAir executive then went to London to spend several weeks at British Airway's headquarters, observing its personnel management processes.

The two airlines also initiated a series of training programs to help employees recognize and deal with cultural differences. In addition, they formed working committees within major departments (comprised of representatives from both organizations) to work out programs and procedures by which both companies could work as partners. Through these sorts of efforts, the organizations helped their people to develop greater sensitivity to and appreciation of their cultural differences.

While sensitivity to cultural norms and an avoidance of being judgmental about unfamiliar practices are important, more specific advice concerning communication behaviors also can be provided. DeVries suggests that when corresponding with people outside the United States, we ought to make sure that the words and phrases we use do not confuse, frustrate, or offend others. For example, we should try to avoid the use of slang (such as *two-bit, blackball* or *off-the-wall*), jargon and buzzwords ("ballpark figure" or "across the board"), and cliches ("back to the drawing board" or "dog-eat-dog") that might be difficult to interpret.[36] Similarly, Huber recommends that we speak slowly and enunciate well when addressing those for whom English is not their first language, avoid idioms and sarcasm, be careful in our use of humor (which often does not translate well), and realize that people from other cultures may be reluctant to ask questions or provide feedback.[37]

As the "global village" continues to shrink and more companies establish a presence in countries other than their home base, the ability to interact with and adapt to other cultures will take on increasing importance. Many companies are attempting to help their employees develop skills in cross-cultural communication, but the most successful people are likely to be those who, on their own, prepare for increasing globalization.

Quality

At a conference in Tokyo in 1990, Joseph M. Juran, a renowned American quality consultant, made a startling prediction. Speaking to a group of Japanese executives who for years have used his total quality control methods to defeat their American competitors, Juran declared that America is about to bounce back. In his view, "made in America" again would become the symbol of world-class quality.[38]

Juran's speech was merely one example of American businesses' new focus on quality. Business schools are revamping their curricula to focus on the "quality imperative," many companies are establishing executive positions to oversee quality improvement, and the national Malcolm Baldrige Award has been established to formally recognize companies that have achieved high quality in their products or services. Moreover, Juran's primary competitor in Japan, Dr. W. Edwards Deming, has been elevated to near-guru status by U.S. business executives eager to learn his approaches to quality management.

This new focus on quality is driven largely by economic necessity: American executives have discovered that people no longer will buy products or services of inferior quality, and products made in other countries (such as automobiles, consumer electronics, and office technology) often are of quality vastly superior to products made in the United States. Thus, many organizations have launched companywide programs designed to achieve dramatic improvements in product quality and, ultimately, customer satisfaction.

Several types of communication have become central to the quality-improvement drive. *Communication with customers* has taken on primary importance: through formal and informal customer surveys, improved customer relations training for employees, face-to-face meetings between customers and workers, and other innovative approaches, companies have attempted to assess and respond to customer needs more effectively. *Communication with suppliers* similarly has become more prominent, since high-quality products cannot be made with poor-quality supplies or materials. Many organizations have invited suppliers to tour their facilities and meet with their employees, all in an effort to improve coordination and quality. And some companies (such as Ford Motor Company) have established formal quality standards that suppliers must meet if they want to continue to sell their products to the organization.

Various forms of internal communication also have taken on increased importance in the quality-improvement effort. Most "total quality management" (TQM) or "continuous quality improvement" (CQI) efforts make heavy use of employee teams or problem-solving task forces. However, a team approach requires many other changes in organizational communication practices, including shifting management style from authoritarian to participative, developing channels for communicating employees' ideas and suggestions upward, and training employees and members of management in group problem-solving skills.[39] In addition, pay systems often must be restructured to reward team rather than individual achievements, new methods of collecting quality-related data must be developed and instituted, and new methods for communicating changes in customer satisfaction and product or service quality improvements must be devised.[40]

Communication downward about the mission and objectives of the organization also becomes even more important during a TQM effort. All members of management and all employees must be helped to understand clearly the nature of their business, the mission and values by which that business is conducted, the expectations and demands of the customers the business serves, and the ways in which TQM helps to improve customer satisfaction and the ultimate success of the organization. A quality-improvement program initiated without this fundamental education is likely to be viewed as merely this year's fad and to fail over the long term.[41]

Two final communication-related principles are also key to the success of a quality-improvement effort. First, the effort must be undertaken for the right reasons, and those reasons must be communicated clearly to and supported by all involved. Research reported in 1992 by the University of Southern California's Center for Effective Organizations suggests that some of the most common motivations include improving morale, motivating the work force, improving job skills, managing change, instilling ethics, strengthening management skill, and reducing costs. But the most frequently reported motive by a large margin was the desire to improve quality and productivity. This last motive is appropriate; the others are likely to cause management and employees to view a quality-improvement effort as a sham, since the effort is in fact intended to accomplish something else. Again, the desire and need for improved quality and productivity must clearly be communicated.[42]

Second, the TQM effort must have support from the very top of the organization—the chief executive officer. Caudron argues that "without a doubt, the most important

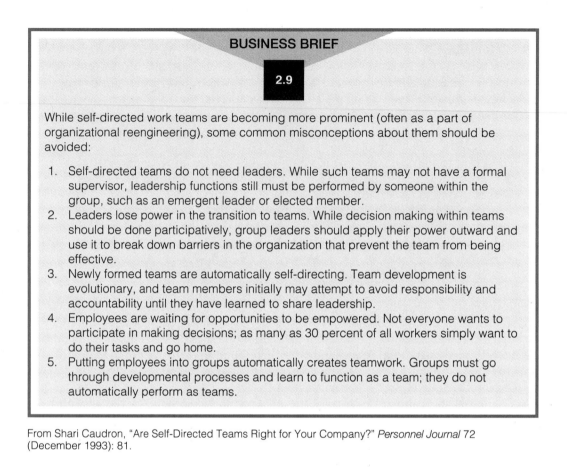

BUSINESS BRIEF

2.9

While self-directed work teams are becoming more prominent (often as a part of organizational reengineering), some common misconceptions about them should be avoided:

1. Self-directed teams do not need leaders. While such teams may not have a formal supervisor, leadership functions still must be performed by someone within the group, such as an emergent leader or elected member.
2. Leaders lose power in the transition to teams. While decision making within teams should be done participatively, group leaders should apply their power outward and use it to break down barriers in the organization that prevent the team from being effective.
3. Newly formed teams are automatically self-directing. Team development is evolutionary, and team members initially may attempt to avoid responsibility and accountability until they have learned to share leadership.
4. Employees are waiting for opportunities to be empowered. Not everyone wants to participate in making decisions; as many as 30 percent of all workers simply want to do their tasks and go home.
5. Putting employees into groups automatically creates teamwork. Groups must go through developmental processes and learn to function as a team; they do not automatically perform as teams.

From Shari Caudron, "Are Self-Directed Teams Right for Your Company?" *Personnel Journal* 72 (December 1993): 81.

contributor to the successful implementation of any quality-improvement effort is top-down leadership."[43] For example, when the Atlanta-based Ritz-Carlton Hotel Company initiated TQM, the process achieved little until Horst Schulze, president and CEO of the company, demanded that quality improve. He and other senior leaders adapted the practice of staying a week at each new facility when it opened, modeling for new employees the correct ways to interact with guests. Indeed, Schulze's direct involvement was one of the many reasons the company received the Baldrige Award for quality in 1992.

It seems likely, then, that the growing concern for quality among American businesses will increase the emphasis placed on teamwork and group problem solving and on effective communication between organizations and their customers and suppliers.

Reengineering

Related to the quality imperative is the effort underway in many organizations to reengineer the ways in which work is done. Many organizations have developed layer upon layer of management, creating bureaucracies that significantly slow work

Harlow Jones has worked as an industrial mechanic at the USG Interiors, Inc. ceiling tile plant in Walworth, Wisconsin, for nearly thirty years. But nothing prepared him for the task he performed as a part of the company's efforts to empower employees.

A fellow maintenance worker had been fired for failing to padlock the starter switch on a machine that was jammed and in need of repair—a clear violation of company safety policies. Jones's name, along with those of two other employees, was picked out of a hat to form a three-employee panel that heard the fired worker's appeal of management's decision. It was the first time that Jones had a voice in whether an employee was to be fired, and his panel's decision was to be final.

The committee unanimously upheld management's decision.

Employee review committees are but one element of the company's new team-oriented approach. Time clocks have been eliminated, problem-solving teams of employees have been formed, and a gain-sharing incentive pay system has been implemented for employees to share in company profits. A random sampling of employee opinion about these changes drew mostly positive responses, although one employee reacted angrily to peer involvement in hiring and firing: "That's management's job," he said.

From Merrill Goozner, "Workers Get Bigger Role as USG Revamps," *Chicago Tribune,* 27 May 1991, Sec. 4, pp. 1–2.

processes and decision making and hamper organizational achievement. In an effort to regain the efficiencies they enjoyed as smaller firms, many companies are attempting to recreate themselves.

Briefly, reengineering involves radically changing and reinventing the way work is done in an organization. According to the cover story in a recent issue of *Business Week,* this typically involves seven key elements:

1. *Organizing around processes, not tasks.* Just as some automobile manufacturers have abandoned traditional production-line approaches in favor of having work teams build entire cars from the ground up, so too are many companies attempting to change how they organize themselves and their work. Rather than creating a structure around functions or departments, some companies are attempting to build themselves around three to five core processes with specific performance goals.

2. *Flattening the hierarchy.* Organizations that are reengineering are attempting to "de-layer" themselves by eliminating entire categories of middle-level managers, doing away with work that does not add value to the company's key products or services, and cutting the activities within each core process to a minimum.

3. *Using teams to manage everything.* Work teams are being made the building blocks of the organization. Indeed, more and more employee teams are being taught to manage themselves, without supervision, and to achieve clear goals and objectives for which they are held directly accountable.

4. *Letting customers drive performance.* In some companies, customer satisfaction has replaced profitability or stock appreciation as the primary driver and measure of performance. These organizations realize that profits and higher stock prices come only as a result of satisfying customers.
5. *Rewarding team performance.* Most organizations use performance evaluation and pay systems that reward individual achievement, not teamwork. Since the management principle "what gets rewarded gets done" can either support or hamper team performance, many companies are developing some form of team-based awards (augmenting or, in some cases, entirely replacing individual pay increases).
6. *Maximizing supplier and customer contact.* As is often the case in TQM programs, reengineering frequently seeks to bring employees into direct, regular contact with suppliers and customers. Indeed, some organizations have added supplier or customer representatives as full working members of employee problem-solving teams as a means of facilitating organization-environment communication.
7. *Informing and training all employees.* Management of companies that are reengineering must communicate information fully and frequently, not just on a "need to know" basis. Financial data traditionally withheld from employees must be communicated so everyone can monitor and feel a part of the organization's progress.[44]

To create a "horizontal corporation," McKinsey and Company recommend, senior management must identify clearly their strategic objectives, analyze key competitive advantages to fulfill those objectives, define core processes and focus on what is essential to achieve the goals, reorganize around those processes rather than by traditional function, eliminate all activities that do not contribute to achievement of the key objectives, cut function and staff departments to a minimum, appoint a manager or team as the "owner" of each core process, create multidisciplinary teams to run each process, set specific performance objectives for each process, empower employees with authority and information to achieve goals, and revamp training, appraisal, pay, and budgeting systems to support the new structure and link it to customer satisfaction.[45]

Like TQM, reengineering will place increasing emphasis on the communication and problem-solving skills of organizational members.

Managing Diversity

During a period of rapid growth in the late 1980s, GE Silicones in Waterford, New York, hired several chemical engineers and other professionals in several key initiatives, including formation of a total quality management department, expansion of its research and development function, and reorganization of its manufacturing operation. Nearly 30 percent of the new hires were women or minorities, some of whom objected to several of the company's current practices, including:

The presence of pinup-style calendars in work areas

The lack of women's rest rooms in the plant

Managers' condescending attitudes toward women

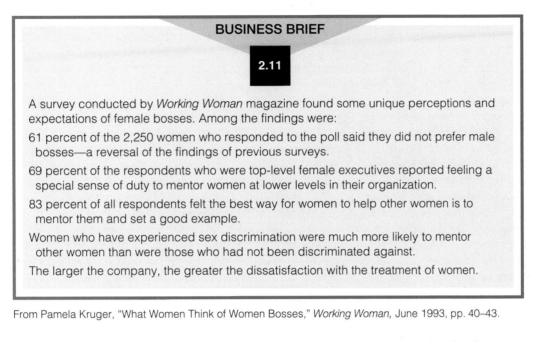

From Pamela Kruger, "What Women Think of Women Bosses," *Working Woman,* June 1993, pp. 40–43.

Managers' reluctance to give women work assignments that were considered to be difficult and therefore more suitable for men

Lack of advancement opportunities for minorities and of minority representation in management ranks

Company management quickly realized they were not in tune with today's diverse work force and took steps to manage the diversity of their employees more effectively. Initially, they formed a steering committee of volunteering employees to oversee the development of programs to improve the management of a culturally diverse employee population. Using that committee's recommendations, they then embarked on two major efforts: teamwork and diversity training.

The teamwork initiative consisted of forming teams of volunteers representing a cross-section of the organization to investigate a variety of cultural diversity issues raised by employees. These issues included family leave, flexible hours, working couples, minority recruitment, personal and professional development of employees, and mentoring. The teams worked to find ways to manage those issues and ultimately produced new company policies on family leave, child care services, job sharing and flextime, mentoring, and relocation.

The diversity training initiative began with top management, who attended a three-day workshop on attitudes and stereotypes that impair communication with a diverse work force. Through role-playing, group exercises, and written inventories, workshop participants were helped to understand themselves and their assumptions and biases more thoroughly and to develop skills for overcoming those stereotypes to communicate effectively with others.

Ultimately, diversity training was provided to all levels of the organization. The training program included a videotaped instructional presentation, question-and-answer sessions, reviews of organizational policies, and, occasionally, role-playing.[46]

The experience of GE Silicones typifies those of many organizations. Starting with a realization that the composition of today's work force has changed dramatically (so that white males, in fact, are now a minority of the employee population), companies have worked to involve employees in developing ways to manage more effectively. Rather than focusing entirely on past practices and written procedures, these organizations have sought to identify the needs of their employees and then adapt their practices accordingly.

The Prudential Insurance Company, for example, surveyed its African-American workers in 1988 to determine why so many were leaving the company and discovered that these individuals felt management was insensitive to diversity issues—a feeling shared by the company's female, Asian, and other minority employees, the firm later discovered. In response, the company initiated an organizationwide diversity training program, instituted a policy of holding all managers accountable for improving diversity, formed diversity councils to monitor the effectiveness of diversity efforts, and required all senior-level managers to submit plans telling how they would address bottom-line diversity issues.[47]

Similarly, Hewlett-Packard found in 1988 that its minority employees had more negative attitudes than the rest of the employees toward company pay and promotional practices. As a result, it too instituted new training, communication, accountability, and developmental programs.[48]

While increased emphasis on effectively managing work force diversity generally has produced positive results, not every experience has been a good one. For example, in 1988, Lucky Stores Inc., a California-based grocery store chain, conducted workshops to increase sensitivity among its store managers. During those workshops, the participants were asked to mention stereotypes they had heard about women and minority-group members. Though the intent of the exercise was to expose potential prejudice and deal with it, to the company's horror, notes from this session later turned up as evidence in a sex-discrimination lawsuit arguing that female employees were not being promoted equitably. The company lost the suit in part because the court decided that some of the stereotypes mentioned during the workshop amounted to management bias.[49]

Ultimately, the key to managing diversity effectively is valuing rather than suppressing differences and developing skills in listening and adapting to others.[50] Realizing, for example, that some cultures (such as Asian, Hispanic, Native American, or African-American) place great value on body language and other nonverbal cues, while others (such as Northern European, Swiss, or Anglo-American male) focus more on verbal behavior can help one to adapt his or her behavior more effectively to others.[51] As the work force becomes increasingly diverse, such communication skills will take on added importance.

Practical Guidelines for Effective Management

Perhaps after having read the first sections of this chapter, you are convinced that the definition of a good manager varies so significantly with the situation that it is

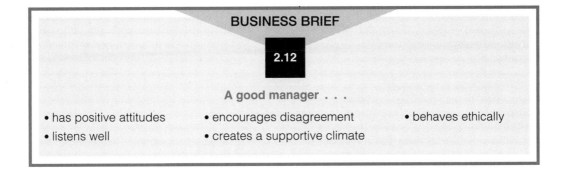

simply impossible to construct the profile of an "ideal" manager. You are probably correct. Almost any complex human skill will be influenced by the situation in which it is being demonstrated or studied. This is particularly true of skills that are based on communication and are performed in complex social structures such as organizations. But even as we recognize the need for flexibility in viewing both management and leadership, we must also acknowledge that in most organizational settings, the majority of excellent managers seem to possess some common attributes. In this final section, we would like to explore these attributes, offering them as guidelines for effective management practice.

Having Sound Attitudes

The good manager regularly examines his or her attitudes toward fellow workers.

Any manager can memorize communication rules; most can learn effective communication strategies and tactics. But that is no guarantee that they will become excellent managers, particularly when measured over the long run. For instance, anyone can learn the rule, "Your employees will feel more valued if they believe you are listening to them." What you derive from this rule and are able to do with it, however, will largely depend upon your underlying attitude toward those employees. Many managers are most interested in what they believe to be the positive relationship between employees feeling valued and their subsequent productivity. They do not see improved morale as an end in itself. Nor do they value their employees' ideas. Thus, they pretend to listen, with the goal of using this communication technique as a method for improving productivity.

As a general rule, those managers who most successfully use such communication techniques as supportive listening, participative decision making, and openness are those who genuinely believe that their subordinates have ideas worth hearing, that their decisions will be improved by sharing the decision-making process with others, and that every employee is an individual worthy of respect and capable of growth. When, in contrast, communication techniques are used to manipulate or control others, they tend to be far less effective. That's why it is so important to examine one's communication skills and techniques in light of one's attitudes toward others. Several of the excellent companies praised by Peters and Waterman intentionally use language designed to upgrade the status of the individual. In McDonald's, employees are called "crew members"; in Wal-Mart, they are called "associates."[52] In distinguished universities, even the youngest assistant professor is referred to as a "colleague." Such language reflects an underlying attitude of respect.

Listening Well

The good manager is a good listener.

Most managers take their listening skills for granted. They generally assume that they are good listeners. After all, they reason, all you have to do to listen is sit quietly and nod your head affirmatively from time to time. They assume further that it is much easier to listen than it is to talk. Nothing could be less true. Listening is difficult. It takes time and energy and a real desire to hear what the other person is trying to say, whether or not that person is a skilled communicator and whether or not we like what we are hearing.

In chapter 5, we will discuss listening in greater detail. Here, let us simply point out that listening is considered by many supervisees to be the most valuable trait that a supervisor can possess. Even if subordinates don't get what they want, even if the decision doesn't go their way, they can accept it if they feel that they have been heard and understood and that their ideas have been given serious consideration. Drake lists "staying in touch with people" as one of the eight traits that distinguish today's successful corporate leaders: "By listening to them with an open mind, the CEO may garner valuable 'second opinions' to weigh against the filtered information that flows to the top of most large organizations."[53]

Encouraging Dissent

The good manager encourages others to express views that differ from his or her own.

We all like to learn that others agree with us and think our ideas are great. We are usually less eager to discover that others think our notions are poorly conceived, badly timed, or wrong in other regards. It takes courage to accept criticism when it is offered. It takes even greater strength to actively encourage criticism. Yet, years of research on decision making have convincingly demonstrated that ideas are usually better, decisions more rational, and plans more likely to succeed if they have stood the test of critical examination. Since most managers are not capable of viewing their own ideas with a completely dispassionate critical view, they need the feedback of others to keep them from making serious blunders. Wheeless, Wheeless, and Howard provide these guidelines for managers wishing to enhance their subordinates' job satisfaction: "the supervisor should be flexible in dealing with others' opinions, tolerant to differences of opinions, open-minded, encouraging of input, willing to try new ideas, willing to listen, etc."[54]

All of the guidelines we have discussed so far are interrelated. No manager can really be a good listener if he or she does not believe that others' ideas are worthy of consideration. Neither can dissent be encouraged if the dissenting views are not viewed as potentially valuable.

Creating a Supportive Climate

The good manager creates a supportive organizational climate.

Being a supportive manager does not imply that one cannot offer candid feedback on employee performance, some of which may be negative. It does suggest, however, that as a supportive supervisor, you might be willing to work with the employee to set realistic improvement goals and to assist in training, counseling, and problem solving. Being supportive often means standing by subordinates, even when they make mistakes. It also means actively affirming employees as human beings, even when it is necessary to suggest changes in their work behavior.

Robert Levering reports that, in becoming "a great place to work," Preston Trucking had to develop a more supportive climate.[55] Before the change effort began, supervisors often referred to workers as "scum, garbage, or idiots." Consultants assisting the change effort prescribed a simple approach to becoming more supportive: Preston's managers should find and praise four acts that an employee does correctly for every one action they criticize. This action alone set the stage for development of a new, more participative management style that ultimately brought about significantly improved productivity and morale.

To translate supportive management into specific terms, it is useful to think about the kinds of attitudes a supportive manager might convey as he or she interacts with subordinates. Specifically, the supportive manager is likely to be:

1. *Descriptive* rather than evaluative—nonjudgmental; slow to question others' standards and values; willing to seek additional information.
2. *Problem-oriented*—interested in defining mutual problems and cooperatively seeking solutions rather than in identifying individuals who can be blamed.
3. *Spontaneous*—straightforward, honest, and tactfully direct; unwilling to deal with others in manipulative ways.
4. *Respectful*—interacting as an equal; demonstrating and seeking mutual trust and respect; encouraging participative planning while deemphasizing status, power, and formal role relationships.
5. *Empathic*—attempting to see issues and problems from others' perspectives; identifying with others' needs, interests, and values.
6. *Provisional*—willing to admit that one could be wrong; open to new ways of doing things; tentative in one's views.[56]

Again, we are reminded of the importance of having the right attitudes toward fellow workers. These supportive behaviors are very difficult to exhibit if one's attitude toward others is one of suspicion, distrust, or lack of respect. There is also room here for the self-fulfilling prophecy: treat workers as equals, as if their views are worthy of consideration, and they are likely to exert great effort to show themselves deserving of such faith and responsibility.

Being Ethical

The good manager is ethical.

In chapter 4, we address the issue of ethics in detail. Here, we simply identify ethical behavior as essential for effective management. Ethical managers know and understand the rules. They go beyond that, however, to find out what the rules mean and what they are intended to accomplish. Then they proceed to work within the spirit of the rule rather than simply obeying it in a superficial, procedural sense. Every smart executive knows, for example, what affirmative action policies are intended to accomplish. But he or she also knows how easy it is to just put through the paperwork and do what the rules require while still hiring as if there were no rules. The ethical manager uses affirmative action procedures as a technique for giving every applicant an equitable opportunity for employment.

Ethical managers, then, are fair. They are fair in hiring, fair in promotion, and just in dealing with grievances or disciplinary actions. They have high standards for themselves, as well as for others. They are honest. They are committed to the good of the organization, their employees, and society as a whole rather than simply to the advancement of their own careers. They are interested in fair pricing, fair wages, honest advertising, and giving credit to those responsible for excellent ideas and innovations. They are as interested in the high morale of their employees as they are in the company's profits. We all value the opportunity to work for managers such as these. In the long run, these men and women generally see increased productivity in their organizations.

Summary

Every manager must decide what style or approach to management he or she prefers. Often that style will vary, and appropriately so, with the demands of the situation. Yet, for most of us, the choice of a management style reflects our underlying beliefs about our fellow workers and their abilities, interests, and needs. Some managers take the view that people prefer strong leaders who take decisive actions. Others feel compelled to consult with representatives of every group who will be affected by the decision about to be made. Some view employees as highly motivated. Others think of them as fundamentally lazy. These kinds of beliefs are translated into communication behaviors. Some managers give more orders than others. Some ask more questions. Some are better listeners. Some do most of the talking.

It is our view that in almost any organization, the preferable management style is one that encourages others to participate, respects the views of subordinates, values listening as much as talking, and encourages others to exert leadership appropriately. Every organization needs employees who are capable of influencing others, completing tasks without close supervision, suggesting constructive changes, and thinking in independent and creative ways. These forms of leadership behavior should be widely distributed across the organization rather than concentrated at the very top. Thus, the most effective managers often share leadership roles with others while remaining role models themselves. They demonstrate high expectations and goodwill toward their fellow employees, a willingness to listen and tolerate dissent, and high personal and professional integrity.

Questions for Discussion

1. What is leadership?
2. Compare and contrast Theory X and Theory Y.
3. Which approach to management do you prefer? Why?
4. React to Japanese management practices. Do you think they would work in most American organizations? Why or why not?
5. How would you describe an "empowering" organizational culture? Have you ever been a part of such an organization? Briefly, describe your experience.
6. If you were asked to construct a profile of an effective manager, what characteristics would you include? Why?

Exercises

1. Choose an individual who currently serves in a leadership position and arrange to interview this person. Ask her or him to describe their philosophy of or approach to leadership/management. How does he or she make decisions or solve problems? After the interview, write a brief essay in which you describe the theory (ies) of management that best characterizes the leader you interviewed.
2. Find an organization that is culturally diverse. Talk to a member of that organization regarding how that diversity is managed. Share your findings with the class.
3. Talk to at least three people who have held several jobs. Ask them to describe organizational situations in which thay have felt especially empowered—or, by contrast, not at all empowered. What factors contributed to each?
4. Adam Smith, author of *Wealth of Nations,* is generally credited with the development of the principles that are the basis for current industrial production techniques, such as specialization and division of labor. Unfortunately, he also developed something else—a philosophy of management. His workers (in the mid-1700s) were young boys whose natural instincts were not to spend eighteen hours a day in a factory making pins out of wire. Consequently, he had to manage them rather carefully.
   a. Which of the management theories we have examined seems similar to Smith's approach? Why?
   b. Specifically describe the characteristics of the theory you chose that seem most applicable to children rather than adults.

Communication Functions, Channels, and Networks

As we have seen, communication, both oral and written, is a predominant form of organizational behavior. People in today's organizations spend a great deal of time communicating; the higher they go in the organizational hierarchy, the more time communication consumes. However, as Peter Drucker points out, all is not well: "We have more attempts at communications today . . . yet communications has proven as elusive as the unicorn. The noise level has gone up so fast that no one can really listen anymore to all that babble about communications. But there is clearly less and less communicating. The communications gap within institutions and between groups in society has been widening steadily—to the point where it threatens to become an unbridgeable gulf of total misunderstanding."[1] In short, while people in organizations today spend a lot of time engaged in communication-related activity, they are not very successful in communicating.

During the past twelve years, the authors have consulted with over five hundred different organizations. Our experiences consistently have borne out Professor Drucker's observation: communication is not done very well in most organizations, despite the flurry of communication activity. Generally, we have found five basic causes of communication failure:

1. *Communication in most organizations is activity-oriented, not results-oriented.* When consulting with hospitals, for example, it is our practice to ask the hospital administrator to show us the hospital's employee handbook. Then we ask him or her, "Do you feel this is a good employee handbook?" Typically, his or her answer will be yes, followed by such reasons as: It has won national awards for design and layout; it costs us a lot of money to produce; my picture is on the inside cover; consultants helped us to develop it; and so on. When we then ask, "But does it do what it is supposed to do?" we typically receive a puzzled look and a long silence in response. Communication is a tool designed to produce some effect upon its receiver. Too many organizations, however, view communication as something that "ought to be done," losing sight of the impact their communications should have.

2. *Communication often is one-way.* Management frequently assumes that, as long as they are sending messages regularly to the rest of the organization, they are communicating. They therefore engage exclusively in downward communication, receiving little or no feedback from lower levels of the organization. As a result, they often do not know if their downward messages were received, understood, believed, or approved of by employees, and they cannot adjust future messages to employees' needs or characteristics. To be effective, communication in organizations must flow not only downward but upward and laterally.

3. *The impact of communication is not measured.* This problem is related to the preceding one. In many organizations, management receives informal feedback. However, no systematic attempt is made to measure the impact of communication in terms of the objectives or results the communication was supposed to achieve. If, for example, the employee handbook is designed to inform employees about

company benefit programs, actual measures should be taken to determine how much information employees get and retain about benefit plans by reading that handbook. In effect, management must clearly define the results they want their communication systems to achieve and then regularly measure the extent to which those results have been produced.

4. *Communication is not responsive to employee needs.* When defining the objectives of their communication systems, management should first ask employees what information they want or need. Then they can tailor downward messages to meet those needs. Rarely, for example, do companies ask new employees what information they would like to receive in their orientation meetings; rather, they assume that the information they are providing is exactly what the employees need. When we interview incoming employees about their concerns and desires, we find an entire body of information is needed that company orientation programs do not provide.

5. *The people who implement communication systems lack the necessary communication skills.* Department meetings cannot be effective if the department heads conducting them lack meeting leadership skills. Employment interviews do not select the best available candidates if the interviewers are unskilled. Communication systems and opportunities are not enough; the people who use those systems must have skills as communicators.

As the preceding discussion indicates, communication in organizations has two basic elements: *communication systems* (the meetings, publications, conversations, and so on in which messages are transmitted) and the *communication skills* of the people participating in those communication systems. In this chapter, we will focus on the systems through which people in organizations communicate. In later chapters, we will discuss the skills you need to communicate effectively.

Settings for Communication Activities

Communication in organizations takes two basic forms: written and oral. Written messages come in a wide variety of forms: booklets, manuals, newsletters, reports, letters, memoranda, posters, and so on. Oral communication settings include the *dyad* (or interpersonal setting), the *small group,* and the *public communication* setting, all three of which we will discuss in this book. The executive spends approximately 75 percent of his or her time communicating—occasionally with large groups, but more often in interpersonal and small group contexts.[2] Probably the most extensive inventories of organizational communication behaviors were conducted by Clark. He surveyed one hundred business executives, asking them to rate the importance of twenty-one types of communication behaviors typically found in business. Importance was defined as the extent to which the behavior was used in the organization and the significance of the behavior in contributing to the accomplishment of the organization's goals. According to these executives, the types of communication most often used and most influential in promoting organizational success were, in order, interpersonal communication, group communication, and public speaking.[3] In general, studies have revealed that for employees from all levels of the organizational hierarchy, both interpersonal and small group communication activities occupy the majority of their significant communicating time.[4]

Communication Functions

Within each organizational setting, communication performs a variety of functions. One central function within all organizational systems is _information exchange_. In a broad sense, any organization that does not exchange information with its environment will die. The organization both effects change in its environment and responds to change in order to survive. Such changes would not be possible without the possession of considerable information on which to base intelligent behavior. Thus, the exchange of information serves the basic function of organizational maintenance.

As members of organizations, we must possess adequate information to function productively every day. We must also exchange sufficient information so that our goals are somehow integrated and coordinated with those of others in the organization. Obviously, the separate rules and tasks of any organization do not exist in a vacuum. Rather, we must accomplish each task in coordination with other individuals, groups, and departments. In one of the early texts on organizational communication, Haney presents a tragic case involving the mismanagement of information exchanged in a hospital.[5] In this case, a deceased patient who was not immediately removed from his room was visited by his wife, who, upon finding her husband dead, collapsed and died of a heart attack herself. This tragedy occurred because rotating nurses in charge of the situation did not exchange clear messages and failed to notify appropriate authorities the minute they knew their patient had died. Although most instances of mismanagement of information exchange do not have such tragic outcomes, the smooth, timely, and undistorted flow of information remains an important goal of all organizations.

Persuasion is a second major function of communication within organizations. Information exchange and persuasion are not distinct. When a supervisor tells us how to replace the paper in the copying machine, how to fill out grant request forms, or how to deal with a disciplinary problem, on the surface he or she is informing us about how to perform our jobs. But such information clearly does more than inform. It also persuades that the procedure in question is not only acceptable but often preferred or even _required_.

From the time we enter an organization, we are bombarded with ideas, information, and attitudes whose purpose is to effect some change in us. Whenever we join an organization, we immediately encounter some of the more common forms of persuasion. We may be told succinctly and directly how to function in our daily jobs and how those jobs fit into the overall organizational plan. At a more subtle level, our initiation may involve a strategic indoctrination aimed at encouraging us to conform to the values, standards, and needs of the organization. Schein refers to this latter process as "organizational socialization."[6] Although some socialization is probably inevitable and in some

sense beneficial, Schein maintains that what organizations really need are creative people who accept *crucial* organizational values but are richly diversified in other significant respects. Most healthy companies are filled with professionals who are united in their dedication to the organization's goals of high-quality products, employee satisfaction, and productivity. Even so, their ideas about what precisely constitutes quality, how to keep workers happy, and how to achieve maximum productivity are probably quite different. Although organizations can command a great deal of conformity, only through a process of mutual organizational and individual influence is innovation and growth likely to occur in the long run.[7]

The Cultural school of thought rests heavily on the ability of organizations to convince their members to behave in certain ways. As Deal and Kennedy describe in *Corporate Cultures,* organizations establish and maintain their cultural identities by instilling their value systems into all members of the organization.[8] The Pepsi-Cola Company adopted a new culture several years ago, changing from an organization content with being second to Coca-Cola to one that was determined to become number one. This new culture developed when the company persuaded employees to adopt a competitive attitude toward other companies and even toward one another.

A third major communication function is *evaluation.* When we evaluate, we process, interpret, and judge. Each of us is evaluated before entering the organization through applications and employment interviews, and the notion of evaluation is really inherent in the organization's hierarchy. Supervisors evaluate their subordinates just as higher executives judge lower-level supervisors. Worker evaluation sheets, memos, organizational progress reports, interviews, and personal and small group conferences are a few examples of common organizational evaluation procedures.

A fourth function of communication is to *solicit feedback.* From a historical perspective, several factors have impeded feedback in organizations. As Anthony suggests, some employees simply are not interested in communicating to management or participating in decision making; others are afraid to communicate (fearing reprisals from management or ostracism by their peers); still others are unaware that management expects them to communicate; and some simply believe that management has no interest in their thoughts and concerns and will not respond to them.[9]

As we have seen in earlier chapters, important changes have begun as top management in many organizations has recognized the need to solicit feedback from employees. Ewing describes these changes as they have taken place in General Motors:

> . . . at a Lordstown, Ohio plant of GM in 1972, a young worker told U.S. Senator Charles Percy: "Every time I pass through those plant gates to go to work, I leave America and my rights as a free man. I spend nine hours in there, in prison, and then come out into my country again." Today, perhaps several hundred corporations are seriously experimenting with different ways to encourage an "open society" at all levels. . . . At their operations in Tarrytown, New York, and Warren, Ohio, as well as at other enormous GM plants, management now encourages employees to speak out, to participate in decision making, to plan, to do some of their own managing.[10]

Through a variety of methods, many of which we will describe in the next section, organizations now solicit communication from their employees.

Taken together, the communication functions we have outlined influence the effectiveness and efficiency of the organization. The amount, clarity, and appropriateness of information exchanged, the ability of the organization to socialize and influence its members, the impact of evaluations, and the success of attempts to solicit feedback all determine the characteristics, and ultimately the success, of a particular organization. In the next section, we will review some of the channels that organizations use to achieve these functions.

Formal Communication Channels

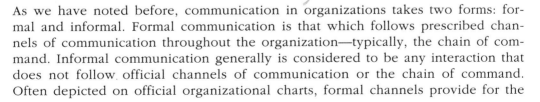

As we have noted before, communication in organizations takes two forms: formal and informal. Formal communication is that which follows prescribed channels of communication throughout the organization—typically, the chain of command. Informal communication generally is considered to be any interaction that does not follow official channels of communication or the chain of command. Often depicted on official organizational charts, formal channels provide for the structured flow of upward, downward, and, occasionally, horizontal communication. Hierarchy, chain-of-command, specialization, and other classical principles are incorporated into this structuring of communication behavior.

Downward Communication

Messages flowing from upper organizational levels to lower ones constitute *downward communication*. Through downward communication, organizations direct the activities of employees, instruct them in proper behaviors and work methods, persuade them to adopt certain attitudes and ideas, evaluate their performance on the job, solicit upward communication, and provide entertainment—the functions of communication we described earlier.

In modern organizations, downward communication takes a variety of specific forms. In describing some methods used by companies to communicate their benefits plans to employees, for example, Hourihan discusses three "generations" of benefits communication: the printed materials provided by insurance companies themselves (which are written from the insurer's viewpoint using highly technical language), written communications from the employer (such as an annual computerized benefits statement for each employee), and a large meeting presentation using dual-projector slide shows and professional speakers, with a social event afterwards (cocktails and dinner) in which the questions about benefit programs can be discussed and answered.[11] Through this description, he also illustrates a current change in emphasis in downward communication, with companies moving from a traditional reliance on written messages to greater face-to-face interaction.

Types of Downward Communication

Communication from higher to lower levels of an organization occurs through a variety of written, face-to-face, and electronic channels.

Written forms of downward communication often include:

Employee handbooks, which are given to employees when they first join an organization and summarize the mission, values, policies, and pay and benefits practices of the organization.

Job descriptions and work procedures and protocols, which typically are given to supervisors and managers to help them govern employees' day-to-day behaviors.

Newsletters and publications, which carry information ranging from social activities to important organizational decisions and events.

Bulletin boards, on which are posted important notices (particularly those required by various governmental agencies), but which frequently are ignored by passersby. Some companies use electronic bulletin boards that provide constantly changing messages and thus attract more interest.

Letters and memoranda, which may be sent to employees' homes, distributed in paycheck envelopes, or handed out by supervisors and managers to facilitate conversation with staff.

From "What Employees Want to Know," *Communication Briefings* (December 1993): 3.

Written downward messages offer the advantages of being relatively permanent, easily distributed, and time-efficient for the receivers, who can read them whenever it is most convenient. In addition, these messages can serve as legal documentation of a company's philosophies and practices, thereby helping to defend the company (or convict it, if the messages are inappropriate) in court proceedings. However, written messages do not allow discussion between sender and receiver, thereby hindering clarification or debate of unclear or controversial information.

Face-to-face interaction also provides opportunities for downward communication:

Employment interviews often are one of the first instances of downward communication employees encounter and are useful for transmitting information about an organization.

Performance evaluations tell employees how effectively they have performed over the last six months or year (in the view of their supervisor) and offer suggestions for improving performance in the future.

Corrective interviews let employees know when they have violated a company rule or policy and provide them with guidance for improving behavior or job performance.

Disciplinary interviews often are used after corrective interviews have failed to improve behavior and mete out some form of punishment in addition to advice for behavioral improvement.

Department or unit meetings involve groups of employees and their supervision or management. As channels for downward communication, such meetings often discuss what one author calls the "4 P's": progress (how we are doing), people (who are changing jobs), policy (what is unclear or changing), and points (anything that arises during the meeting).[12]

Mass meetings often are used by top-level executives to communicate important information to large groups of employees. Often taking the form of town hall meetings, these forums are used to make important announcements, explain significant events, initiate companywide programs or processes, or keep employees up-to-date on the organization's progress.

Educational and orientation programs can be used to indoctrinate and educate new employees about companywide practices, benefits, pay procedures, and so on or to teach employees new information and skills related to their jobs.

Recently, a variety of electronic media has been developed to facilitate downward communication:

Video presentations often are used during department or unit meetings to show a top-level executive presenting important information. In large organizations where personal visits by senior executives are impractical, this can be an effective means of increasing contact between management and staff. Some companies also place video monitors in high-traffic areas (such as near cafeteria entrances or in break rooms) and replay the message constantly so it can be viewed by passersby.

Electronic mail (E-mail) is a computer-based system whereby messages are sent from one personal computer user to another. Messages are retained in the receiver's electronic "mailbox" until she or he decides to read them. Most E-mail systems allow the receiver to scan a summary of the names of message senders and topics and then to read the messages that seem to have the highest priority.

Voice messaging (V-mail) is a telephone-based system whereby callers leave brief recorded messages for the receiver. Such systems can range from relatively simple telephone answering machines to extremely sophisticated organizationwide networks. Again, the receiver can decide when to take his or her recorded messages, although those messages typically must be listened to in the order in which they were received.

Computerized bulletin boards are used in some companies to send brief announcements. For example, some companies post different announcements each day, and anyone who turns on her or his personal computer automatically sees the announcement come up on the monitor.

Telephones have been in use for years, of course, and remain one of the most frequently used channels for downward communication in organizations.

Problems with Downward Communication

In most organizations, a variety of problems commonly afflict downward communication. Frequently, for example, *messages are not received*. Announcements or letters often are not read, meetings are poorly attended, needed corrective interviews are not conducted, and so on. But just as frequently, *information overload* occurs. Too many messages are sent by management so that employees are bombarded with letters, memos, bulletin board announcements, meetings, and the like. As a result, the impact of any one message becomes diluted. *Organizational bypassing* often can occur as well, with top management communicating information directly to lower levels and, in the process, omitting one or more members of middle management who then must obtain the information from their staff. *Distortion or filtering* can also occur as one person passes a message on to another, who in turn communicates that message to a third, and so on. At each link in the communication chain, the message is changed and filtered slightly so that by the time it reaches its final destination, it may bear little resemblance to the original form.

Downward communication can serve as an effective substitute for cash or promotions by providing recognition for employees. *Communication Briefings* suggests formally acknowledging employees' sacrifices, reminding them frequently of how much they are valued by the company, involving them deeply in making decisions, offering them opportunities to learn new skills, giving them new titles or greater visibility, having lunches or coffee breaks involving upper management and employees, and providing inexpensive tangible rewards symbolic of the company's appreciation (such as pens or plaques). Such efforts can be extremely useful in organizations that simply do not have the funds to provide pay increases to all employees.

From "How to Keep Good Workers," *Communication Briefings* (July 1993): 5.

Effective downward communication most often is achieved through a thoughtful and strategic *combination* of oral, written, and electronic messages. Written messages are easily distributed and consistent in form, but do not allow feedback or further discussion. Oral messages allow interaction, but may be transmitted inconsistently (or not at all) from person to person or group to group. Electronic messages often limit interaction as well and may require a certain level of skill and technological sophistication that not all organizations or employees possess. Thus, the most effective downward communication process might be written or electronically communicated announcements, followed by individual or group discussions that are then summarized in writing for permanence. For particularly important messages, this approach to combining written, face-to-face, and electronic media is usually most effective.

Upward Communication

Communication sent from lower to higher levels of an organization constitutes *upward communication*. Like downward communication, messages flowing upward are vital to an organization's success. Employees' ideas, concerns, reactions, and recommendations are extremely valuable resources that are tapped only when upward communication works effectively.

Types of Upward Communication

Like downward communication, upward messages can be sent in writing, orally, or via electronic media. Some commonly used written channels include:

Employee opinion surveys, which ask employees to report anonymously their perceptions, attitudes, and values so that management can determine what actions, if any, are needed to improve employees' feelings toward the organization.

"Write to know" or "gripevine" systems, which typically allow employees to write messages, often anonymously, to management and to see their answers published in an employee newsletter or posted on a bulletin board designated for that purpose.

Suggestion boxes or suggestion systems, which are often effective in obtaining employee input, although their effectiveness tends to wane over time. Typically, these systems provide some recognition and reward to employees whose suggestions save money or improve operations in the organization.

Letters and memoranda, which are frequent channels for upward as well as downward communication.

Upward communication also occurs frequently via face-to-face interaction:

Open door policies tell employees that they are welcome to enter any manager's office with a question or concern whenever they wish. However, managers' doors too often literally are not open, and employees too often are afraid to walk through those doors even when they are open. Thus, a more effective policy is the "open floor" approach, whereby managers leave their offices and "manage by walking around," having informal conversations with employees in their workplaces.[13]

Employee counseling provides an avenue for addressing employees' personal problems, as well as their work-related concerns. Many companies provide employee assistance programs through which employees can see trained counselors to obtain help with marital and financial problems, substance abuse issues, emotional and psychological difficulties, and so on.

Formal grievance procedures give employees some recourse when they have a complaint or feel they have been treated unfairly. In unionized companies, shop stewards or union business agents assist employees with their grievances, which typically are presented to successive levels of management until a solution is reached or taken to outside arbitration if a solution cannot be agreed upon. Nonunion companies occasionally have trained ombudspersons to assist grievants and may use employee committees to hear and resolve grievances.

Department or unit meetings should serve as effective channels for upward and downward communication, with announcements being made and employee input sought by the manager conducting the meeting.

Individual interviews similarly should promote both upward and downward communication. During corrective or disciplinary interviews, the employee's reactions should be solicited and heard, and his or her ideas for behavioral improvement should be sought and integrated into a plan of action. During performance evaluations, the employee's perceptions of her or his own performance should be elicited, as should ideas for improving performance in the future. Indeed, every face-to-face interaction offers an important opportunity for upward communication.

Advisory committees are formal bodies of employees who provide management with information about employee concerns, perceptions, and reactions. For example, Purdue

While performance evaluations traditionally have been used as a tool for downward communication, some companies are instituting upward appraisal systems as well. In 1992, AT&T developed a 40-question survey asking subordinates to evaluate the effectiveness with which their supervisors show respect, emphasize helping customers, promote teamwork and innovation, and maintain high standards. MassMutual Insurance instituted a similar system of written surveys in 1987, asking employees to evaluate the effectiveness of their supervisors and managers.

Employees at AMOCO Corporation requested opportunities for upward appraisals, and a 135-question feedback instrument was developed as a part of the week-long mandatory training session for middle-level managers. And when Deloitte & Touch, the professional services firm, realized that its service is its employees, it instituted a process whereby those employees could express, anonymously and in writing, their satisfaction with their management.

Each of these systems is based on the realization that a manager's "customers" are the people who work for him or her (and thereby are the recipients of that manager's communication skills) and that an assessment of "customer satisfaction" is an important element of improving managerial performance.

From Catherine Romano, "Fear of Feedback," *Management Review* 82 (December 1993): 38–41.

University uses its Clerical and Service Staff Advisory Council to obtain advice from employees and hear their concerns, and Cedars-Sinai Medical Center in Los Angeles makes similar use of its Employee-Management Advisory Committee.

Task forces and problem-solving groups often are formed to empower employees to identify, analyze, and resolve work-related problems. Quality circles and other participative problem-solving groups typically are used within individual departments, while task forces frequently involve people from a variety of areas throughout an organization. Both types of groups can be extremely valuable in improving the operation of an organization.

Formal presentations often involve someone at a lower organizational level speaking to a group of higher-level executives or managers. These speeches may be progress reports, proposal presentations, project summaries, or simply regular updates. But, in every case, they represent important opportunities for the speaker to perform in front of an influential decision-making group and may determine the progress of the speaker's career.

Electronic media also may be used to communicate messages upward:

Telephone hot lines may be used to encourage employees to express their feelings or report problems anonymously. For example, at one division of General Electric, more

From "Suggestion Systems: An Answer to Personnel Problems", *Personnel Journal* 59 (July 1980): 552–53.

than 100,000 calls were processed during a single year, with topics ranging from questions about rumored salary increases to complaints about sexual harassment.[14]

Electronic mail and *voice messaging* often are used for upward as well as downward communication. Indeed, since many executives spend most of their time in meetings, these systems often are the only way in which these people can be reached by others in the organization.

Problems with Upward Communication

Upward communication has its share of problems in organizations. First, *upward communication is subject to substantial distortion*. Specifically, as subordinates we are especially reluctant to communicate negative information to our superiors. Instead, we make every attempt to send messages aimed to please management and not without good reason. Tompkins has noted that negative ("bad news") feedback is discouraged by superiors, who tend to reward *positive* feedback rather than *accurate* feedback.[15] As a result, in most organizations, monthly reports present a positively exaggerated account of performance and productivity. Attempts to improve the climate of the organization as well as the utilization of human resources have led to the encouragement of open, honest communication in all directions. Studies have demonstrated that when fear of punishment is reduced and trust runs high between employees and management, the accuracy of upward communication is greatly facilitated.[16] Accurate upward communication is also more likely to occur when the supervisor is perceived as friendly, approachable, and considerate.[17]

Second, *some members of the organization actively discourage upward communication*. Weak supervisors, for example, will perform the organizational ritual called "CYA" (cover your posterior) by attempting to block communication between their employees and other members of management. They discourage employees from participating in opinion surveys, fail to conduct departmental meetings, falsify their monthly reports, and sharply criticize employees who "go around them" by talking to management or "hang out our dirty laundry" by taking problems to the personnel department. Naturally, it is imperative that top management discover and deal with these situations as quickly as possible.

Third, *upward communication can be intimidating* to some employees. Many find it difficult to talk to their superiors, choosing instead to smile and answer "everything's fine" when asked how things are going. Entering a manager's office via the "open door" policy is virtually impossible for them, and writing a letter to the editor of the newsletter is too challenging. In many organizations, there is a "silent majority" of employees who simply are nervous about talking to the people over them.

Upward communication also can be intimidating to management. As Zaremba notes, "People, no matter who they are and how confident they might appear to be, are reluctant to solicit rejection." Since upward channels allow criticism or negative feedback from employees, he concludes, "a simple reason upward communication networks are not used effectively is because few people want to invite such criticism."[18]

Last, *employees simply may not know that management wants them to communicate upward.* While employees may want to contribute their ideas, express their thoughts, or voice their concerns to management, they often believe (with some justification) that reprisals might be taken against them if they complain or that management simply is not interested in their input. For that reason, as Jablin points out, most organizations must provide systems designed specifically to promote upward communication.[19]

Horizontal Communication

The final formal communication channel involves exchanges of messages among individuals on the same organizational level, or *horizontal communication*. Traditional organizations discouraged horizontal exchanges between individuals in different divisions because messages were supposed to be passed vertically throughout the organizational hierarchy. The assumption was that by following vertical flows, each message would touch all appropriate points of authority. Rank-and-file workers were neither expected nor trusted to work out their own problems without the assistance of their superiors. Even so, you may recall that Classicist Fayol advocated direct horizontal communication whenever the situation demanded immediate action. Fayol pointed out that there are many organizational operations where there is little chance of success without rapid execution.[20] When a power failure occurs, when someone is injured, or when costly machinery malfunctions, decisive action by employees immediately involved with the problem may be the only sensible course of action.

Types of Horizontal Communication

Progressive organizations have implemented a variety of programs designed to improve horizontal communication and teamwork. Most of the written, face-to-face, and electronic channels listed above frequently are used for lateral communication as well, but some other channels may also be utilized:

Several methods can be used to build a sense of teamwork among organizational members. In its simplest form, team building is the guided discussion of several questions, through which the team members examine themselves and decide how their teamwork might be improved. Questions commonly considered in team building meetings include:

What would we be like if we were an ideal team?

What are we like now as compared to that ideal?

How do we need to change?

How can we change?

How, specifically, will we change?

What things can each of us do to help other team members more?

What things can each of us do to support and encourage other team members to adhere to the commitments we have made?

The decisions made by the group are written down and distributed to each member, as well as to any person to whom the team reports. When done well, the team building meeting (or series of team building meetings) will improve the relationships among team members and, in so doing, improve communication and cooperation among them.

Based on William I. Gordon and Roger J. Howe, *Team Dynamics* (Dubuque, Iowa: Kendall/Hunt, 1977), and William G. Dyer, *Team Building: Issues and Alternatives* (Reading, Mass.: Addison-Wesley, 1977).

Team building seminars often are conducted by trained specialists to improve relations among individuals or groups that interact with one another in the workplace. Top-level executives, for example, may by taken on team building retreats lasting several days, while nonsupervisory employees may simply meet in break areas to discuss ways of working together more effectively.

Cross-departmental visitation is a simple but effective method for improving lateral communication. One department manager, for example, may invite the manager of another department to visit her or his work area, talk with employees, and discuss more effective and efficient ways in which the two departments might work together.

Committee meetings occur when representatives from different departments or units meet to hear announcements or discuss problems of mutual concern. Most organizations, for example, conduct department head or management meetings designed to build horizontal communication. Too often, however, these meetings are dominated by the leader and serve only as a channel for downward messages.

Work teams are being used with greater frequency to manage the operation of individual units in an organization. Semiautonomous or autonomous groups of employees often meet to plan their work schedules, assign duties, review their own performance and progress, and even hire or dismiss team members.

The growing importance of horizontal communication is illustrated by a feature article in *Business Week,* which lists seven steps needed to gain "quantum leaps" in performance: 1) organize around process, not task; 2) flatten hierarchy; 3) use teams to manage everything; 4) let customers drive performance; 5) reward team performance; 6) maximize supplier and customer contact; and 7) inform and train all employees.[21] As organizations eliminate unneeded levels of middle management, horizontal communication will continue to take on greater importance.

Problems with Horizontal Communication

Kanter, in her book *The Change Masters: Innovation for Productivity in the American Corporation,* describes the thinking that typifies too many organizations today:

> In the traditional mechanistic bureaucracy, the isolation of departments and levels means that people will see only local manifestations of problems, and they will perhaps appear puzzling or idiosyncratic. Furthermore, the message to the troops is clear: keep the lid on; the messenger with bad news will be shot. Because each segment is expected to do its work without troubling any other segment, communicating primarily in prespecified ways and mostly to transfer good news (results or output), then identification of a problem is a sign of failure likely to get the identifier in trouble.[22]

As Kanter indicates, horizontal communication should serve to solve problems, promote cooperation, and improve the overall effectiveness and efficiency of the organization. Unfortunately, *most organizations do little to encourage horizontal communication.* In fact, highly competitive organizations may even discourage it. The employee who is eager to obtain some reward for his or her work, whether it be a promotion, a pay increase, or a word of praise, may not be willing to share his or her bright ideas or coveted data with peers who are after the same, usually limited, rewards. When managers cling to Classical administrative tenets, they may believe that their workers will, in fact, be more productive in an atmosphere that encourages *competition* and rewards selectively. When this is true, horizontal communication usually decreases or becomes routine.

Even when organizations want colleagues to communicate freely and frequently, such a goal is not readily accomplished because of *specialization.* The highly skilled machinist uses a specialized vocabulary, as does the neurosurgeon, the corporate lawyer, the engineer, the chemist, and the accountant. Yet many large organizations bring all of these specialists together under the same professional roof. While informal social chitchat may be manageable, serious exchanges of task-relevant information are far more difficult. One way of dealing with this problem is to hire employees who have a good general background of education and experience, with their specialization representing only one aspect of their interest and skill. In general, organizations need to hold regular meetings that bring together individuals from different divisions. These people take turns talking about their work, skills, and frustrations in jargon-free language that can be understood by those not familiar with their areas of specialization.

Given the many obstacles of horizontal communication, it is not surprising that McClelland and Wilmot, in their survey of communication practices, found that 60 percent of employees in a variety of organizations feel lateral communication is ineffective.[23]

External Communication

Increasingly, organizations are realizing that effective communication with external audiences is crucial. Certainly, communication to potential customers (in the form of advertising or public relations) long has been an important element of organizational communication. Now, however, companies have come to realize that effective communication with suppliers, customers, consumers, governmental agencies, and the general public all are vital to organizational success.

Types of External Communication

Communication between an organization and its environment can involve many of the same types of written, face-to-face, and electronic channels used for internal organizational communication. For example, some commonly used written channels include:

Newspaper and magazine press releases distributed by an organization to communicate its message to readers and *newspaper and magazine stories* written about an organization that may carry information the organization would just as soon not have communicated (such as an unfavorable review of the organization's products or some internal scandal the organization wished to suppress).

Brochures and publications that describe the products and services of the organization to prospective customers, summarize the financial achievements of the organization for shareholders and the public (in the form of quarterly or annual reports, for example), or recruit new organizational members.

Letters sent to the homes or businesses of potential or current customers or the public at large. Many hospitals, for example, have adopted the practice of sending personalized letters to people throughout the communities they serve, describing new services they offer or dramatic medical cases they have handled. Most junk mail sent to "Occupant" typifies this sort of external communication.

Face-to-face communication also can be used by organizations to communicate with their environment:

Tours of company facilities, conducted for members of the general public or for the media, can be useful in acquainting the public with company operations.

Large group meetings often are conducted for shareholders or for the public at large. For example, when two Massachusetts hospitals—Leonard Morse Hospital in Natick and Framingham Union Hospital in Framingham—merged to form MetroWest Medical Center, the chief executive officer of the new organization, Murray Leipzig, used large town meetings effectively to respond to and defuse community concerns about losing their community hospitals.

Seminars and workshops may be provided by organizations either as the core of their customer services (such as by consulting firms specializing in supervisory and management training) or to augment their services and products (as when technicians from IBM teach customers how to use their newly purchased hardware).

Sales and proposal presentations are used in individual and group settings to convince potential customers to buy the organization's products or services.

Customer or supplier meetings increasingly are being used to improve service, either by having customers communicate their preferences and expectations directly to groups of employees or by having suppliers meet with employees (their customers, in effect) to hear concerns and preferences regarding the supplier's services or products.

Employment interviews are an often-overlooked channel of communication with the environment. For every position filled, there may be several candidates rejected. Yet those candidates' perceptions of the organization are strongly shaped by their interview experiences, making this an important channel of external communication as well.

Electronic media also play a key role in external communication:

Radio and television serve as channels both for advertising and public service announcements by organizations and news about those organizations.

Telephone communication is key for most organizations; many companies provide in-depth training for employees in telephone courtesy and monitor employees' communication performance in telephone conversations with customers.

Electronic mail and voice messaging are important for communication with the environment as well. Some companies use E-mail extensively to get information from or communicate it to their environment, and many use V-mail to record messages for people who were unavailable when the call arrived.

Teleconferencing via satellite is used by many organizations to conduct news conferences or provide information to external audiences. A few organizations use this channel for internal communication as well, although it tends to be too expensive for frequent internal use.

Video communications often are prepared and released to news services, customers, and other organizations in the environment as a means of communicating the organization's message in an interesting, compelling manner.

Communication to external audiences suffers from many of the same problems that afflict upward, downward, and lateral communication within organizations, such as information overload, unreceived messages, and filtering and distortion. Indeed, organizations have far less control over the distribution of messages sent to external audiences than they do over internally communicated messages, making these problems even more likely to occur.

Regardless of the external channel or channels chosen, several principles should be observed to minimize the impact of potential communication breakdowns. Communication consultant Frank Corrado claims that a formal plan for managing issues should be developed by every organization and that communication with external audiences should be carefully coordinated with internal communications.[24] In addition, the impact of external communication should be carefully and continually evaluated to ensure that the desired effects are being achieved. In this manner, then, relationships between organizations and their environment can be more effectively managed.

The Communication System: Informal Dimensions

Within every formal organization there also exists an informal organization. The Hawthorne studies were the first to document this. Within this informal structure, a great deal of communication behavior occurs. Much communication in large organizations is informal, springing up whenever an individual feels a need to communicate with someone with whom he or she is not connected by a formal organization channel.[25] Whereas formal communication consists of messages the organization recognizes as official, informal messages do not follow official lines. According to Tompkins, informal networks often develop through accidents of spatial arrangement, similarity of personalities, or compatibilities of personal skills.[26] For example, employees may end up talking simply because they have adjacent offices, enjoy NCAA basketball, or feel similarly about the present federal government's leadership. Of course, what they share at an informal level will affect their ability to communicate about their jobs. Most employees are involved in several networks at the same time: some grow from political ties, others from technical interests, and still others from social preferences.[27]

As you might expect, informal communication is by far the dominant form of oral interaction in organizations. Indeed, Deal and Kennedy suggest that 90 percent of what goes on in an organization has nothing to do with formal events. Rather, the informal network, the "hidden hierarchy," is in reality how an organization operates.[28] And the operation of informal networks is not necessarily bad. Peters and Waterman noted in *In Search of Excellence* that "the excellent companies are a vast network of informal, open communications. The patterns and intensity cultivate the right people's getting into contact with each other, regularly, and the chaotic/anarchic properties of the system are kept well under control simply because of the regularity of contact and its nature (for example peer versus peer in quasi-competitive situations)."[29]

It is important to note that top-level management also benefits from informal communication. "After closely observing fifteen better-than-average general managers in action, professor John Kotter of the Harvard Business School concluded that his subjects got work done not by giving orders or churning out reports, but mostly by talking to people—asking questions, making requests, maybe prodding a bit. These conversations often consisted of nothing more than a two-minute encounter in the hallway or on the phone."[30]

It is not uncommon to find writers referring to informal message behavior as "grapevine" communication. Information introduced into the grapevine travels quickly because it is not inhibited by structural constraints. Although we tend to discredit publicly information we receive through the grapevine, research has shown that it is amazingly accurate. Scholars have consistently reported 78 to 90

Informal communication in an organization's environment can be extremely important. On September 1, 1993, Snapple Beverage Corporation began an advertising campaign to rebut rumors in the San Francisco Bay-area black community that the company supported the Ku Klux Klan. One rumor suggested that a small letter K printed on Snapple labels stands for the KKK. But the symbol means that Snapple, like Coca-Cola and other famous products, meets kosher dietary standards. Another rumor contended that the illustration on the label of Snapple iced tea portrays ships bringing black slaves to America. But the photo, from the Bettmann Archive, is of a famous drawing of the Boston Tea Party.

In other situations, underground rumors have been devastating to companies. Procter & Gamble battled a rumor for nearly ten years that its 140-year-old logo of a man-in-the-moon face and cluster of thirteen stars was a symbol of the devil. Despite lawsuits and an intense public relations campaign, P&G could not dispel the myth and in 1991 was forced to redesign the logo. McDonald's spent a year and a small fortune trying to dispel the 1978 rumor that it was using red worms in its hamburgers to boost their volume and protein content. Reports at the time said hamburger sales dropped sharply at about 20 percent of McDonald's stores.

In Snapple's case, the company fought back by advertising in local newspapers and on radio stations. Eventually, the rumors were quelled, but sales of Snapple's iced tea and other beverages suffered.

From John Eckhouse, "Snapple Fights Rumors That It Supports KKK," *San Francisco Chronicle,* September 1993, p. B1.

percent accuracy figures in their extensive studies of grapevine communication in organizational settings.[31] When errors do occur, however, they are often of a critical or dramatic nature.

Probably the most negative attribute of the grapevine is that it serves as a network through which *rumors* travel. Unlike much grapevine activity, which consists of verifiable informal communication, rumors are unconfirmed; that is, they are devoid of supporting evidence or cited sources. Rumors develop in part because employees perceive the formal communication system as inadequate. Whenever there are organizational policies that foster secrecy or superiors and subordinates who regard each other suspiciously, rumors are likely to flourish. For some, participation in rumor transmission may serve as an emotional safety valve to relieve frustrations and worries.

In their classic study of rumor transmission, Allport and Postman noted that rumors spread both as a function of their *importance* and their *ambiguity*.[32] If you are up for promotion and you hear through the grapevine that a promotion decision has been made, you are quite likely to discuss this rumor with others, especially your friends. The issue is vital to you and the message is ambiguous. Who was promoted? When did it happen? Why haven't you been officially informed? Myth has it that certain people

Figure 3.1
Typical rumor transmission pattern: the cluster chain.

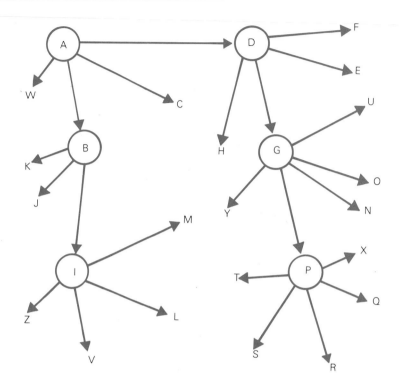

Note: Only circled letters represent active rumor transmitters

function as specialists in rumor transmission, but research does not confirm this notion. Whether or not an individual will pass on a rumor usually depends on the individual's degree of interest in the rumor, perception of others' interest in the rumor, access to others, and personal goals. Relatively few people who receive rumors actually transmit them. Those who do often tell a cluster of others, only a few of whom will send the message further.[33] Figure 3.1 depicts a typical rumor cluster chain. Like other grapevine information, rumors spread quickly. One journalist described rumors this way: "With the rapidity of a burning powder trail, information flows like magic out of the woodwork, past the water fountain, past the managers' doors and the janitor's mop closet. As elusive as a summer zephyr, it filters through steel walls, bulkheads, or construction glass partitions, from office boy to executive."[34]

The grapevine is a part of organizational reality—a natural outgrowth of humans being together. Managers who do not admit to the grapevine's existence usually have trouble. Managers who try to stamp out the grapevine with such policies as "Employees must not discuss their salaries with each other" also have trouble. Policies to that effect simply tend to drive the discussions underground.

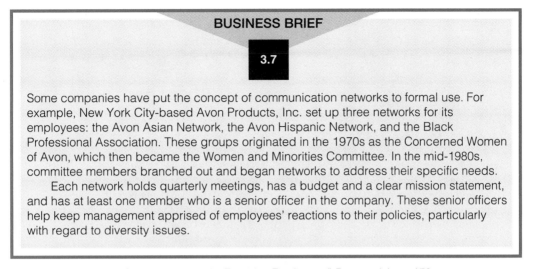

From Charlene Marmer Solomon, "Networks Empower Employees," *Personnel Journal* 70 (October 1991): 51–54.

Davis, who has studied grapevine communication for more than twenty years, believes that management should accept the grapevine as an inevitable fact of organizational life. He points out that "if properly guided, it can help build teamwork, company loyalty, and the kind of motivation that makes people want to do their best. It may weld the group together more effectively than company policy and other formal tools of the organization."[35] It is vital that managers be in touch with informal networks, participate in them, learn from them, and use them carefully to disseminate information.

Esposito and Rosnow suggest that managers do several things to defend against destructive rumors: keep employees informed (so that rumors do not occur to fill an information void), heed rumors (to identify employee concerns), act promptly (before rumors spread and attitudes harden), and enlighten personnel (teaching them about the potential destructiveness of rumors).[36]

Summary

In this chapter, we have demonstrated the importance and diversity of communication within and between organizations. In writing, in face-to-face conversation, and through electronic media, we continually exchange information, convey our ideas and attitudes, render judgments, and assist in making decisions. Your future organizational experiences may take you into a business firm, hospital, school, or industrial organization. You may function as a marketing analyst, accountant, teacher, cook, or executive. Whatever the organization or the specific function you fulfill, your daily activities, productivity, and pleasure will be greatly influenced by the quality of your communication interactions.[37]

What effect do these information systems have on organizations? Economist Peter Drucker makes this prediction:

The typical large business 20 years hence will have fewer than half the levels of management of its counterpart today, and no more than a third the managers. In its structure, and in its management problems and concerns, it will bear little resemblance to the typical manufacturing company, circa 1950, which our textbooks still consider the norm. Instead it is far more likely to resemble organizations that neither the practicing manager nor the management scholar pays much attention to today: the hospital, the university, the symphony orchestra. For like them the typical business will be knowledge-based, an organization composed largely of specialists who direct and discipline their own performance through organized feedback from colleagues, customers, and headquarters. For this reason, it will be what I call an information-based organization.

So far most computer users still use the new technology only to do faster what they have always done before, crunch conventional numbers. But as soon as a company takes the first tentative steps from data to information, its decision processes, management structure, and even the way its work gets done begin to be transformed.

Peter F. Drucker, "The Coming of the New Organization," *Harvard Business Review* (January–February 1988): 45–46.

Each organization anticipates certain patterns of interaction. These patterns reflect the strategic plan of the organization. They also suggest appropriate approaches to information exchange, problem solving, and decision making. Thus, formal channels exist on paper and in practice. They may serve to clarify role relations and prevent message overload, but they often create unnecessary barriers to open communication. Increasingly, the task of the manager has been to find improved formal communication channels while acknowledging the significance, frequency, and potential usefulness of informal channels and networks. The manager's challenge for the future is to successfully integrate the new information technologies.

Questions for Discussion

1. In your opinion, why has the amount of communication in organizations increased but the quality of communication not improved?
2. What might cause an organization to take an "activities" approach to communication rather than a "results" approach?
3. Why might management be more comfortable with one-way communication?
4. In which communication setting does the most important business of an organization typically get done? Why do you think so?

5. What effect does superior-subordinate trust have on communication?
6. What do you see as being the potential benefits of the so-called information age? Potential problems?

Exercises

1. Contributors to the Human Resources model of organizational behavior stress improved decision making. One might argue that decision making is the most important function that communication serves in organizations. Support or defeat this argument, making some reference to other communication functions.

2. Michael Johnston is a top supervisor in a large food manufacturing corporation. He must communicate some bad news to a number of the organization's employees (all of whom are under him in the organizational hierarchy). New, more stringent health regulations will require them to wear special caps to cover their hair, to wash their hands frequently with a special antibacterial soap, and to have two checkups per year with the company physician (instead of the present one).
   a. Given your knowledge of downward communication, how should Johnston approach the communication of this information?
   b. Should he utilize both formal and informal channels and both oral and written modes of communication? Why or why not?
   c. What problems might he encounter, and what strategy might he use for overcoming them?

3. You are administrative assistant to the vice-president for sales in a moderately sized business firm. While your boss is extremely bright and superbly competent in her area of marketing, sales, and public relations, she tends to run a fairly authoritarian operation with minimal desire to let others assist her in decision making. She neither seeks nor is she particularly receptive to feedback from anyone. While many lower-level employees are reluctant to discuss problems with *her,* they often come to *you* to complain about both task-related problems and the fact that they are frustrated with the managerial style of the vice-president. You have known this woman for many years—first as a friend and only recently (six months) as a boss. You have high regard for her as a person, but you are appalled at the lack of congruence between her general humanitarian philosophies and her conservative, rigid style of leadership.
   a. Using your knowledge of communication behavior, how would you approach this situation?
   b. How might your upward mobility aspirations figure into this?
   c. Consider your probable feelings with regard to trust and status.

4. Consider an organization with which you are very familiar. What systems of upward communication does that organization use? What systems of downward communication? What systems of horizontal communication?

5. Consider an organization you know well. List instances within that organization in which you have observed each of the functions communication plays in an organization.

Ethics and Values and the Organization

hroughout your life you will face decisions about what is "right" and "proper" and "fair." You may decide, for example, how to rear your children, what life occupation you want, and how you should use your material possessions. On the job, you will have to consider how to communicate bad news to your superiors, how to promote your product or service (and indeed, yourself), how carefully to report your business expenses to your employer and/or the Internal Revenue Service, or how to use your power responsibly in dealing with subordinates. All of these decisions about what is "right," "proper," or "fair" are *ethical* decisions.

Similarly, the organizations in which you work will struggle with ethical concerns: how employees should be treated, how products or services should be priced, how the environment should be protected, how they should fulfill their social responsibilities, and so on. And as a member of those organizations, you will need to decide how you feel about their ethical decisions and, if you disagree, what you should do about it.

In this chapter, we will examine several different perspectives for making ethical judgments. One or more of these perspectives might guide the actions and underlie the judgments you make as an individual; they also influence the behavior and worldview of every organization with which you are or will be associated. Part of our discussion will focus on both traditional and evolving American value systems and their impact on organizational values and ethical standards. Before turning to these tasks, we might begin by defining ethics in the context of the modern organization.

Perhaps Bowen H. McCoy, managing director of Morgan Stanley & Company, Inc., investment bankers, put it best when he said:

> Ethics involves the art of integration and compromise, not blind obedience and conformity. Ethics calls for tolerance of ambiguity; yet, it is an action-oriented, interpersonal process. [It] signifies a heightened ability to seek truth that stems from core beliefs and to decide consciously on one's action in a business context. Ethics deals with free choice among alternatives. In a practical sense . . . ethics is wrapped up with the integrity and authenticity of the businessman and the business enterprise.[1]

Ethics goes far beyond simple questions of legality or illegality—of bribery, theft, or collusion. Ethics considers what our relationships are and ought to be with our employers, coworkers, subordinates, customers, stockholders, suppliers, distributors, neighbors, and all other members of the communities in which we operate. As Solomon and Hanson note, ethics is "a way of life," not a set of absolute principles divorced from day-to-day life. "It is the awareness that one is an intrinsic part of a social order, in which the interests of others and one's own interests are inevitably intertwined."[2]

Why Be Ethical?

In recent years, an alarming number of "unethical" situations have arisen in American business. For example, Ivan Boesky was found to have engaged in "insider trading," an unethical and potentially illegal practice for investment counselors. Chrysler was found to have disconnected the odometers in "new" cars that had been driven by their executives. Barry Minkow, founder of ZZZZ Best, was accused of money laundering, fraudulent credit card usages, phony business contracts, and connections to organized crime. Directors of savings and loan associations were found to have defrauded depositors, in many cases depriving people of their life savings. In these and many other situations, prominent business organizations or individuals behaved in ways that seem not to have been ethical.

But why should we be concerned about ethics in the first place? Why is it important to behave ethically if unethical behavior might provide us with some advantage in the competitive business world? Although each of us must answer these questions to his or her own satisfaction, recent events suggest the following.

First, unethical behavior can have seriously damaging consequences. These consequences can affect both the person committing the practice and the people that practice touches. In some of the cases noted above, for example, innocent investors lost large amounts of money and some of the perpetrators were sentenced to jail. But beyond that, the people and organizations (and indeed, entire industries) who were involved lost credibility. And once your image is so tarnished that people no longer are willing to believe or put their faith in you and your business, failure is almost certain.

Second, ethical behavior usually has important positive consequences. Honesty in business dealings allows others to trust you and your organization, and makes you far more effective in your dealings with them. Indeed, business in general depends on the acceptance of rules and expectations, mutual trust and fairness. Simply put, ethical behavior is good business.

Third, your behavior serves as a model, both to yourself and to others. If you behave ethically and discover the effectiveness of such behavior, you are more likely to behave ethically in the future. Similarly, the people with whom you work (particularly your subordinates) will be more likely to engage in ethical behaviors. Conversely, if you behave unethically and get away with it (or even gain some short-term profit from it), you become more likely to continue your unethical behaviors and to promote such behavior by others.

Fourth, our own observations indicate that ethical errors end careers more quickly and with more finality than any other mistake in judgment. Lying, stealing, cheating, reneging on contracts, and so on undermine the very foundation upon which the business world is built and thus are not readily forgiven or forgotten. For every newspaper headline discussing major breaches of ethics, there may be hundreds of "minor" situations where an individual is fired (or "asked to resign") for unethical behavior, or where an executive or manager is put in a dead-end career track by a company wishing to avoid a public relations scandal.

Finally, ethical behavior is intrinsically valuable. Knowing that you are honest, that you behave humanely in your dealings with your fellow employees, that you are fair in your evaluations of others, and that you are concerned for the welfare of the whole organization and the society it serves—these are important self-perceptions, ones that carry no price tag.

Ultimately, the need for ethical behavior might best be expressed by the old maxim, "what goes around comes around." When we have unimpeachable integrity in our dealings with other people, we earn their trust and make them more willing to support us and our organization. Conversely, when we lack integrity, we promote mistrust on the part of those with whom we deal and, as managers, create employees who are ashamed of their organization and the products or services they provide. Since they feel their work is not worthy, they cease to care.

Some Ethical Perspectives

We have already stated that ethical concerns are involved in much organizational activity. Every day, employees must decide how to conduct themselves ethically. Consider the following examples: (1) a doctor must choose whether or not to prescribe a drug for a patient suffering from a largely psychosomatic illness; (2) an insurance salesman tries to decide how to convince an elderly couple to purchase his company's homeowner's insurance; (3) a division head must decide how to present financial data reflecting poorly on her own department in the monthly report; (4) a teacher must determine how to handle a severe discipline problem developing in his classroom; (5) a committee member must decide whether or not to voice her objections to a proposal favored by most other committee members, including her boss; and (6) a vice-president must decide which of two equally qualified employees ought to be promoted. While all of these situations have pragmatic dimensions, they all involve issues of right or wrong, good or bad, fair or unfair—dimensions of ethical significance.

Ethics can be viewed from several perspectives, each of which provides a different basis for making judgments. Depending on the specific perspective employed, the answer to any given ethical dilemma will vary.

Hosmer describes three general approaches to ethical decision making in business.[3] *Economic analysis* bases ethical judgments on impersonal market forces. This school of thought holds that managers always should act to maximize revenues and minimize costs and that this strategy itself will ensure that society gains the greatest benefit over the long term. This approach, however, does not take into consideration the well-being of some segments of society (for example, the poor and minorities, who do not or cannot participate in corporate ownership), nor does it exclude the use of questionable practices (bribes, environmental pollution, hazardous working conditions, or unequal treatment) that might improve an organization's bottom line. In effect, it is an impersonal approach that considers people a means to an end and takes no account of the nature of those people themselves.

Legal analysis reduces ethical judgments to a matter of law. Anything that is illegal is unethical. If a given behavior falls within legal limits, no ethical question can be raised. This approach has the advantage of ensuring simple ethical decisions: one has only to investigate the law, the rule, or the regulation covering a particular behavior. Thus, if a specific managerial practice is within the legal limits of an organization, the practice is considered ethical. While some may take great comfort in guiding their decisions and behavior by legal standards, this perspective often leads to oversimplification and superficiality. For example, the law does not prohibit lying except under oath in a court or in some formal contracts. Moreover, the law tends to forbid negative actions but does not encourage positive ones (for example, no law requires someone to go to the aid of a drowning child). Finally, some laws in and of themselves are morally objectionable to some: until the early 1960s, some areas of the United States legally required racial discrimination, and even now laws concerning abortion, homosexuality, or religious observances in schools are repugnant to many.

Philosophical analysis seems more likely than the first two to provide useful guidance in making ethical decisions. However, a wide variety of such philosophical perspectives is available, including the following.

Religious Perspective

Within the framework of every world religion, there are crucial moral and spiritual injunctions that might be used to measure the ethics of a given behavior. Most religions teach that behavior such as lying, committing adultery, slandering, and murdering are wrong. From a Judeo-Christian perspective, for instance, Christians are taught to love their neighbors as themselves, discouraging any remark or behavior of harmful intent directed toward another person. The Taoist religion stresses empathy and insight as roads to truth, deemphasizing reason and logic.

Some writers have attempted to apply these standards to certain facets of organizational behavior. McMillan discusses the concept of "multiple neighbors"—of organizational accountability extending to owners, employees, clients, customers, and the general public.[4] Although some contend that business persons are dishonest and deceitful, others suggest there is a trend toward more positive Christian values. Alderson believes that a good deal of business conduct is controlled by rules of morality, many of which have the force of law. He contends that most business persons keep their word when they make a promise, devote many hours to civic institutions and social concerns, and try to influence others to give their best, not only for the sake of the firm but also for the sake of themselves and their families.[5] The religious perspective thus provides some ethical guidelines, but leaves one with the problem of deciding which set of religious teachings he or she should follow.

Utilitarian Perspective

From a utilitarian perspective, usefulness and expediency are the criteria used to make ethical judgments. Taking this approach, one would conclude that a behavior is ethical if it provides the greatest benefits to the greatest number of people. A utilitarian critic judging the effectiveness of a public speech would be mainly concerned with whether or not the speech actually got the vote, changed the belief, or positively stimulated the audience. Techniques used to achieve the speech's purpose would be judged in terms of practical results. One might evaluate the worth of an advertising campaign, an incentive plan, or a public relations program from the same perspective.

While it is probably safe to say that the utilitarian view has less intrinsic appeal as an ethical perspective, it still has great practical significance. There would be no persuasive appeals, marketing strategies, or incentive plans without some pragmatic goal in mind. Organizations must be concerned with the ultimate effects of their plans, policies, and procedures, and laudable means that fail to promote important organizational goals should be subject to criticism, just as questionable goals themselves should be scrutinized. However, ends do not always justify means, and the rights of the minority must not be sacrificed for the "good" of the majority. Thus, this perspective, too, has its limitations.

Universalist Perspective

While the utilitarian perspective considers the outcomes of an action, the universalist perspective holds that because outcomes are too difficult to predict or control, we should focus on intent. In effect, the morality of an action depends on the intentions of the person making the decision or performing the act. If that person wishes the best for others, his or her actions are ethical even if, due to the person's clumsiness or ineptitude, those actions end up hurting someone. This approach holds that there are certain universal duties people have in dealing with one another (hence the "universalist" perspective), such as telling the truth, not taking another's property, and adhering to agreements, and that if our intent is to uphold those duties, we are behaving ethically.

Under this approach, people are seen as ends rather than means. They are worthy of dignity and respect, not tools to be used by us for our own purposes. Perhaps that is the greatest lesson the universalist approach teaches. On the other hand, it is difficult to determine what "intent" is (even our own motives for performing various actions may be unclear to us), and in business, people at times *do* serve as a means to an end: for example, customers are a means of making money and earning a living, and employees are a means of getting work done.

Humanist Perspective

Some writers attempt to make ethical judgments philosophically by isolating certain unique characteristics of human nature that should be enhanced. They then look at a particular technique, rule, policy, strategy, or behavior and attempt to determine the extent to which it either furthers or hampers these uniquely human attributes. Aristotle believed, for example, that truly human acts were performed by rational persons, individuals who recognized what they were doing and chose freely to do it.[6] In the case of a persuasive speaker, for example, his or her persuasive appeals and strategy should be judged in terms of their tendencies to enhance or reduce the listeners' rationality and their decision-making ability.

Contemporary writers have identified such uniquely human attributes as the individual's symbol-using capacity; the need for mutual understanding; the motivation to serve both self and others; and the necessity for rational, reflective thought. Burke talks of the human need to transcend individual differences and to communicate cooperatively.[7] In her book *The Worth Ethic,* Kate Ludeman argues that "the Worth Ethic is a belief in your indelible self-worth and the fundamental and potential worth of others. . . . Worth Ethic managers commit themselves to help employees develop and use their skills and talents."[8]

One might infer from these statements that the ethical organization would encourage its members to communicate fully, freely, and cooperatively. Thus, organizational incentives aimed at encouraging cooperative deliberation should be encouraged, whereas competitively oriented programs should be deemphasized.

Political/Cultural Perspective

Political systems and specific cultures provide another perspective from which to view ethical behavior. Within any given cultural or political context, there exist certain values or processes that seem basic to the well-being and growth of society. Values govern the way we behave as well as the kinds of goals we seek throughout our lives. Rokeach defines a value as "a type of belief, centrally located within one's total belief system, about how one ought or ought not to behave, or about some end-state of existence worth or not worth attaining."[9] Thus, values provide standards for judging our own and others' behavior.

Of course, cultural perspectives are widely diversified. Haiman believes that the development of the human capacity to reason is a goal to which our American society is inherently committed and labels as unethical any behavior or technique that attempts to circumvent or demean the individual's ability to reason.[10] Wallace further asserts that the essential values of democracy are belief in the dignity and worth of the individual, faith in equality of opportunity, belief in freedom, and belief in each person's ability to understand the nature of democracy.[11] Finally, John Gunther wrote in *Inside USA,* "Ours is the only country deliberately founded on a good idea."[12] This idea combines a commitment to each person's inalienable rights with the belief in an ultimate moral law.

Dialogic Perspective

An interesting viewpoint for making ethical judgments has emerged from scholarship on the nature of ethical human communication as dialogue rather than monologue.[13] According to this perspective, the attitudes that individuals in any communication transaction have toward one another are an index of the ethical level of that communication. Some attitudes are believed to be more fully human, facilitative of self-actualization, and humane than other attitudes. According to Johannesen, for example, when people communicate from a dialogic perspective, their attitudes are characterized by honesty, trust, concern for others, open-mindedness, empathy, humility, sincerity, and directness. They are nonmanipulative, encourage free expression in others, and accept others as persons of intrinsic worth, regardless of differences of opinion or belief. Communication as monologue, on the other hand, is characterized by such qualities as deception, superiority, exploitation, domination, insincerity, distrust, and so forth. Freedom of expression is stifled, and others are viewed as objects to be manipulated.[14]

In using this perspective, you would observe any behavior, advertisement, speech, managerial practice, or organizational policy and determine the degree to which it reveals an ethical dialogic attitude or an unethical monologic attitude toward its intended audience. For the dialogic critic, any communication act or attitude that promotes deception, exploitation, or domination is unethical, regardless of the situation.

Situational Perspective

Some writers are less universal in their approach to ethics, believing it impossible to set definite ethical guidelines apart from the specific situation. They believe ethical criteria vary as factors in the communication situation vary, as the needs of the listeners vary, and even as role relationships change. According to this view, receiver expectations and knowledge levels are especially critical determinants. For example, we often expect hyperbole in political speeches and filter our responses accordingly. We do not, on the other hand, anticipate exaggerations from a college professor giving a lecture or from a doctor explaining the nature of an illness.[15] Thus, in the political context, hyperbole might be acceptable; but in the educational or medical setting, it would be taken literally and therefore should be considered unethical.

Another kind of situation where normally unethical behavior might be considered acceptable, and even desirable, is a situation involving crisis. From the situational perspective, the leader who uses emotional appeals in order to get people to act quickly when their lives are endangered would not be downgraded for bypassing human rational processes. The situational critic is quite likely to scrutinize carefully the end or goal in judging the means. The same means would be judged differently given different situations.

In his controversial book *Humbuggery and Manipulation: The Art of Leadership,* F. G. Bailey argues that political leadership is a special situation requiring special ethical judgments. He claims that leaders are "inescapably polluted by what they do, and, since leadership is by its very nature defiling, it follows that moral judgments are as appropriate in this regard as they are about foul weather." He continues by asserting that "no leader can survive as a leader without deceiving others (followers no less than opponents) and without deliberately doing to others what he would prefer not to have done to himself." Bailey concludes that "leaders everywhere must set themselves above the morality of their own society."[16] Unfortunately, it is all too easy to list political leaders, past and present, who have followed this school of thought.

Clearly, there are a variety of approaches to making ethical judgments, and each approach has its advantages and limitations. Perhaps the best thing to do in any given situation is to ask oneself a series of questions designed to test an action in terms of almost all of these approaches. The questions might include the following:

Would I want this action to be broadcast on the six o'clock news?

Would I want my boss and top management to know I did this?

Would I want my parents to know I did this?

Would I want my spouse or family to know I did this?

Would I want my customers to know I did this?

Would I want my subordinates to know I did this?

Would I want this action to be announced to my church congregation, with me present, during next Sunday's service?

Would I do this if a police officer were standing or sitting next to me?

Is doing this "good business"?

Ethical Perspectives

Perspective	Ethical Guidelines
Economic analysis	Striving to maximize revenues and minimize costs automatically leads to long-term ethical behaviors.
Legal analysis	Stay within the boundaries of the law.
Philosophical analysis	Adhere to principles embodied by one or more philosophical perspectives, such as:
Religious	Follow moral and spiritual injunctions taught by a particular religion; love your neighbor as you do yourself.
Utilitarian	Do what achieves the greatest good for the greatest number.
Universalist	Have the best of intentions; do what maintains the dignity and worth of others.
Humanistic	Enhance the unique human characteristics: reasoning, reflective thought, motivation to serve self and others.
Political/Cultural	Follow society's values and norms.
Dialogic	Promote and show trust, concern for others, open-mindedness, empathy, humility, sincerity, and directness.
Situational	Take into account receiver expectations and knowledge levels when making judgments.

Will doing this promote trust in me by others?

Will I be able to sleep at night knowing I've done this?

Would I want others to do this to me?

Even these questions provide an incomplete guide. For example, a professional football player who also happens to be homosexual might well answer no to most of these questions, not because he feels his lifestyle is unethical but because he fears the reactions of teammates, coaches, other players, his family, the public, and so on—people who have a different set of ethics. Nevertheless, if as you contemplate some action you find the answer to many of these questions to be no, you should consider carefully whether this action is truly ethical.

Values in Transition and Organizational Leadership

At the base of any ethical perspective is a value system that serves as a guide for judging one's own and others' behavior and that resists change. Our own values come from a variety of sources: family, peers, institutions (church, school), previous experience (traumas, successes, disappointments), the media (television, radio, books, newspapers and magazines), professional roles and models (job expectations, organizational leaders, heroes), company policies, and our own personal codes of ethics (developed through experience with ethical conflicts and pressures). But the value systems to which we are exposed can change, and these changes in turn produce changes in human behavior, including communication.

Certainly not everyone embraces new values at the same rate; yet, there is some evidence to suggest that within our society values are in a state of transition. Trist believes that values in most postindustrial societies are changing in the following ways: from achievement to *self-actualization,* from self-control to *self-expression,* from independence to *interdependence,* from endurance of distress to *capacity for joy.*[17] The implications of these kinds of value changes for human interaction within organizations, as well as for society in general, are far-reaching.

As organizational employees, when we desire *self-actualization* as a form of achievement, we become concerned with more than simply completing a given task. The interest now is in relating that finished task to our individual growth needs. Organizations in tune with this new value emphasis demonstrate great concern for fulfilling us as individuals as well as advancing organizational goals, recognizing that the two are reciprocally stimulating.

The traditional value of self-control emphasizes a kind of stoic philosophy in which individuals do as they are ordered, obey the rules, and suffer with controlled silence any indignities that may occur. Certainly in the past, men and women have quietly questioned the system without really making themselves heard because of the fear of losing their jobs. Moreover, they were conditioned to the idea that deference toward the views of higher ranking organizational officials was a virtue. The more contemporary emphasis, on the other hand, is upon *expressing oneself* and contributing one's views, both personally and professionally. Managers spend more time listening and less time giving orders, put more effort into responding to employees at a personal level, and recognize the potential worth of all individual contributions to the decision-making process.

The notion of *interdependence* is a particularly critical organizational value. In many ways individuals retain their independence, but there is increased sensitivity to the fact that all persons need others and their compassion and understanding in order to be deeply fulfilled throughout their lives. It is within social and organizational contexts, for example, that we most often satisfy our needs for love, belonging, esteem, and self-actualization. While each person may be reasonably independent in terms of meeting his or her basic physiological and security needs, other kinds of goals can be achieved only through interpersonal interaction and reciprocal trust.

Finally, individuals are growing to expect a great deal from their lives as well as from their multiple organizational affiliations. The *capacity for joyful living* is a major goal of most contemporary lives. Work, then, should be satisfying, stimulating, and fulfilling. In and of itself, work is neither good nor bad; rather, it is the personal reaction of the worker that determines its worth. Obviously, not all jobs are ultimately satisfying for the individuals who perform them. Clearly there are jobs to be carried out in organizational contexts that are far from glamorous and, in some instances, are barely tolerable.

Even so, the fact that our society is deeply concerned about personal enrichment as well as organizational productivity represents a major advancement in allowing human beings to live fully and joyfully.

In their book *In Search of Excellence,* Thomas J. Peters and Robert H. Waterman report that "every excellent company we studied is clear on what it stands for, and takes the process of value shaping seriously. In fact, we wonder whether it is possible to be an excellent company without clarity of values and without having the right sorts of values."[18] Increasing numbers of managers, scholars, and writers are stressing the importance of organizational values and cultures in building a strong, creative, and productive work force. Based on their survey of nearly fifteen hundred managers and executives, Schmidt and Posner point out that a growing number of executives are discovering that one of their key responsibilities is the management of meaning—"that they give powerful direction through the heroes they applaud, the mission statements they issue, and the organizational accomplishments they celebrate."[19] For example, the general manager of a major fast-food chain recently modified his company's mission statement to emphasize product and service quality rather than financial return to investors as a way of clarifying the values he wants his colleagues to espouse.

In spite of the positive emphasis we have discussed thus far, many believe that as a *nation* we are faced with a moral crisis. A *Time* magazine cover asks, "What Ever Happened to Ethics?" and continues, "Assaulted by sleaze, scandals, and hypocrisy, America searches for its moral bearings." Although many of the unethical incidents discussed in this issue focus on government employees and leaders, the problem is clearly not confined to the public sector. As Harvard sociologist David Riesman has put it, "What we have now is a transaction mentality. No longer do we have an endowment mentality that asks what we can contribute to an organization."[20]

In some instances, self-serving attitudes on the part of individual employees manifest themselves in white-collar crime. It is estimated that common street crime costs our country about $4 billion a year. But white-collar law-breaking drains at least $40 billion from corporations, governments, and other organizations, not to mention the price paid by millions of consumers and taxpayers. Sometimes business crime occurs on a relatively small (if insidious) scale, as in the case of the two New Jersey tow-truck operators who were convicted of pouring oil on a freeway ramp to cause accidents and boost their business! In other instances, the crime is significantly more far-reaching. Marvin Warner, a financier and former ambassador to Switzerland, was sentenced to prison for his role in the collapse of Cincinnati's Home State Savings Bank, which forced the temporary closing of seventy other thrift institutions in Ohio and cost the state an estimated $226 million.[21] More recently, Phoenix financier Charles H. Keating, Jr., was condemned by a federal judge for "looting" the Lincoln Savings and Loan Association, "dipping into Lincoln's coffers and taking money" to which he was not entitled.[22]

In many instances, white-collar crimes not only cost a great deal of money but also threaten lives. Several U.S. airlines have been accused of endangering passengers by cutting back on maintenance. Some construction firms used asbestos in their building materials long after they knew it was unsafe. A. H. Robins Company made and sold the Dalkon Shield, a dangerous intrauterine contraceptive device. NASA launched the *Challenger,* even though several engineers at Morton Thiokol, the rocketmaker, spent most of the night before the launch pleading futilely for a precautionary delay.

If moral disarray exists, who is to blame? In a poll for *Time* conducted by Y. C. Shulman, more than 90 percent of the respondents agreed that morals have fallen because parents fail to take responsibility for their children or to provide decent moral standards and examples; 76 percent saw lack of ethics in business people as contributing to tumbling moral standards; and 74 percent decried failure by political leaders to set a good example.[23] Moral leadership, according to Sissela Bok, professor of philosophy at Brandeis University, should come from people in public office. She echoes Aristotle's view that people in government exercise a teaching function. And in any organization, most believe that ethics should start at the top. But it is clearly reciprocal. Leaders are invariably creatures of the people, embodying our most visible warts.

It is likely true, as Ezra Bowen has written, that Americans need to reexamine the values that society "so seductively parades before them: a top job, political power, sexual allure, a penthouse or lakefront spread, a killing on the market." The real challenge, according to Bowen, becomes "a redefinition of wants so that they serve society as well as self."[24]

What, then, are the most important values an organization can stress? Surveys reveal that managers at all levels seem to place the highest value on *integrity* and *competence* in their superiors, peers, and subordinates.[25] Moreover, American managers thrive in companies that stand for values they can embrace in their personal lives. Excellent companies have clear values that make sense to their employees—and they reinforce these values through everything they do. In his American Management Association *Memos for Management: Leadership,* James L. Hayes points out that ethics are just as much a part of everyday business practices as they are embedded in broad corporate philosophy. Hayes reports that managers lack credibility on the big issues if they have demonstrated a lack of moral fiber when it comes to handling the smaller, everyday ethical issues. He goes on to define "moral fiber" as "respect for the customers and employees and sensitivity to the concerns of society in general."[26]

Similarly, in *Thriving on Chaos,* Tom Peters argues that "without doubt, honesty has always been the best policy. The best firms on this score have long had the best track records overall—Johnson & Johnson, IBM, S. C. Johnson (Johnson Wax), Hewlett-Packard, Merck, Digital Equipment."[27] Thus, managers should "demand total integrity" from themselves and their people: "if a promise (even a minor one) is not kept, if ethics are compromised, and if management behaves inconsistently, then the strategies necessary to survival today simply can't be executed."

Presumably, every individual prefers to work for an organization he or she believes to be guided by ethical principles. In the Schmidt and Posner survey, 80 percent of the respondents agreed that the organizations for which they worked were guided by highly ethical standards. The strongest vote of confidence came from top management, however, while younger respondents and those of lower rank provided answers that implied more cynical views. All respondents, regardless of rank or experience, agreed that their bosses had the greatest influence on their own professional ethical conduct. And those bosses generally prefer ethical behaviors themselves: Schmidt and Posner concluded their report by noting that the profit motive and ambition, for example, do not receive the highest rating on most managers' lists of most admired qualities. In fact, both rank "well below responsibility, honesty, and imagination."[28]

Organizations and Critical Ethical Issues

Organizations face a wide variety of ethical issues today. While it is impossible to examine every such issue, a brief review of some key issues is useful.

Advertising

A key element of most organizations' public relations and sales efforts is advertising. Each year, over $100 billion is spent by companies to convey information about their products or services. Yet critical reactions to advertising seem to be growing almost more rapidly than the industry itself. As one Harvard professor of business administration has put it, "Wherever we turn, advertising will be forcibly thrust on us in an intrusive orgy of abrasive sound and sight, all to induce us to do something we might not ordinarily do, or to induce us to do it differently."[29] What are the major criticisms of advertising? Probably the most frequent complaint centers on the issue of *truth and distortion*. Studies have demonstrated that distortion and deception in advertising are quite disturbing to consumers, particularly to those in the higher-income brackets.[30] Consumers are demanding more fact and less fluff or "puffery," as one critic so aptly put it.[31]

Another basic concern among critics of advertising is the *omnipresence of advertising* in our lives. In less than a generation following World War I, advertising "swept across the land as a powerful revolutionary force."[32] Today, advertisements jump at us from billboards, scream at us from neon signs, and overwhelm us from our television sets to the tune of four to six in a row between program segments. This deluge of advertising messages in turn places increasing emphasis on message content, creativity, and uniqueness. As an article in the *Journal of Advertising Research* points out, "With the average consumer exposed to about 1,000 advertising messages every day, it takes a powerful message to rise above the surrounding 'noise level.' "[33]

Clearly, not every product innovation actually represents an improvement—or, more important, fills a consumer need. Many critics are concerned with industries' attempts to *create consumer needs* and *artificially stimulate consumption*. Often these attempts are not particularly successful (for example, few people apparently needed a "new" Coca-Cola). Even so, it seems that the appropriate role of advertising is *not* to shape consumer preferences to suit the needs of the competitive production system, but to assist consumers in translating their preferences rationally into a demand that producers would then satisfy.[34]

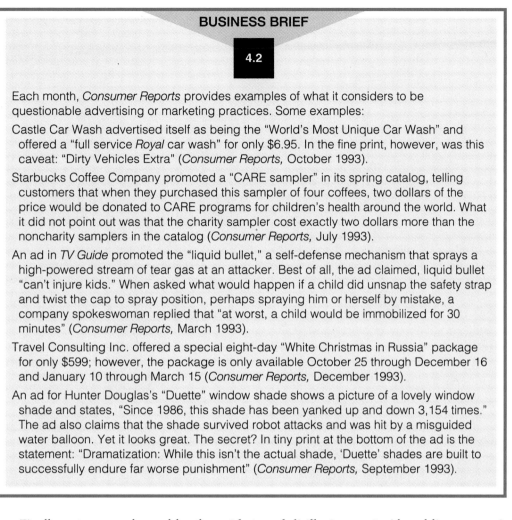

BUSINESS BRIEF

4.2

Each month, *Consumer Reports* provides examples of what it considers to be questionable advertising or marketing practices. Some examples:

Castle Car Wash advertised itself as being the "World's Most Unique Car Wash" and offered a "full service *Royal* car wash" for only $6.95. In the fine print, however, was this caveat: "Dirty Vehicles Extra" (*Consumer Reports,* October 1993).

Starbucks Coffee Company promoted a "CARE sampler" in its spring catalog, telling customers that when they purchased this sampler of four coffees, two dollars of the price would be donated to CARE programs for children's health around the world. What it did not point out was that the charity sampler cost exactly two dollars more than the noncharity samplers in the catalog (*Consumer Reports,* July 1993).

An ad in *TV Guide* promoted the "liquid bullet," a self-defense mechanism that sprays a high-powered stream of tear gas at an attacker. Best of all, the ad claimed, liquid bullet "can't injure kids." When asked what would happen if a child did unsnap the safety strap and twist the cap to spray position, perhaps spraying him or herself by mistake, a company spokeswoman replied that "at worst, a child would be immobilized for 30 minutes" (*Consumer Reports,* March 1993).

Travel Consulting Inc. offered a special eight-day "White Christmas in Russia" package for only $599; however, the package is only available October 25 through December 16 and January 10 through March 15 (*Consumer Reports,* December 1993).

An ad for Hunter Douglas's "Duette" window shade shows a picture of a lovely window shade and states, "Since 1986, this shade has been yanked up and down 3,154 times." The ad also claims that the shade survived robot attacks and was hit by a misguided water balloon. Yet it looks great. The secret? In tiny print at the bottom of the ad is the statement: "Dramatization: While this isn't the actual shade, 'Duette' shades are built to successfully endure far worse punishment" (*Consumer Reports,* September 1993).

Finally, many are alarmed by the *widespread disillusionment* with public communication, especially political communication and advertising. Some have even contended that unethical practices in advertising could be self-destructive.[35] Some evidence suggests that fewer and fewer people believe the advertising they read and hear.[36]

Although some have taken a dim view of contemporary advertising, other writers are more supportive. Kottman argues that most factual statements in contemporary advertising are *true*. He contends that only the *image* of advertising is tainted with untruthfulness.[37] This image has developed because of the relatively few advertisements that contain false statements and because people often fail to make a distinction between factual statements and value judgments. Advertisements fall largely within the realm of the latter and, as such, represent expressions of opinion or estimates of certain aspects of reality. A more fruitful way of viewing advertisements might be in terms of "acceptable" or "unacceptable" rather than "true" or "false."

Levitt offers a provocative defense of contemporary advertising. He compares advertising with poetry, arguing that embellishment and distortion are among advertising's socially acceptable aims:

> Consider poetry. Like advertising, poetry's purpose is to influence an audience; to affect its perceptions and sensibilities; perhaps even to change its mind. Like rhetoric, poetry's intent is to convince and seduce. In the service of that intent, it employs without guilt or fear of criticism all the arcane tools of distortion that the literary mind can devise.[38]

Levitt goes on to point out that consumers do not *want* factual descriptions based on literal reality. Instead, they desire the promise of love, charm, and elegance. As Charles Revson of Revlon, Inc., once put it, "In the factory we make cosmetics; in the store we sell hope." As a society, then, we demand symbol as well as substance, promise as well as experience, and imagery as well as reality.

In a sense, all of these defenses lead to the conclusion that advertising should be judged by a special set of ethical standards. Advertisers recognize certain "truths" about their audience. Among them are that people expect exaggeration whenever they view advertising, that they hope to be promised effects beyond realistic expectations, and that they largely understand the rules of the game. Galbraith once pointed out that "the merest child watching television dismisses the health and status-giving claims of a breakfast cereal as 'a commercial.' "[39]

The ethical complexities of advertising have attracted the attention of regulatory agencies over the years. As early as 1962, the American Association of Advertising Agencies prohibited its members from knowingly producing advertising that contained: (1) false or misleading statements or exaggerations, visual or verbal; (2) testimonials that do not reflect the real choice of a competent witness; (3) misleading price claims; (4) comparisons that unfairly disparage a competitive product or service; (5) claims insufficiently supported or that distort true meaning or practicable application of statements made by professional or scientific authority; (6) statements, suggestions, or pictures offensive to public decency. These kinds of guidelines, of course, must remain flexible, and many of their major terms—such as *misleading, competent, unfairly, true meaning,* and *offensive*—are open to interpretation.

The Federal Trade Commission (FTC) has also taken an active role in ensuring that facts are available to support claims made in advertising.[40] In 1972, for instance, in a case involving Unburn sunburn lotion, the commission took the position that not only must evidence be presented to support the advertiser's claims, but the substantiation should provide a "reasonable basis" for believing the claims are true.[41] In other words, the quality of evidence is important.

These guidelines had important implications in a series of three cases involving the major analgesics manufacturers. Specifically, American Home Products (maker of Anacin and Arthritis Pain Formula), Bristol-Myers (manufacturer of Bufferin), and Sterling Drug (maker of Bayer Aspirin) were all making claims concerning their products' superior efficacy and/or freedom from side effects. Based on extensive investigation of these claims and supporting evidence, an FTC administrative law judge issued an order requiring

American Home Products to disclose that its pain reliever was aspirin and to cease making claims that stated or implied that its pain reliever was an "unusual ingredient."[42] The FTC continues to actively investigate advertising claims in a variety of other industries, including automobiles, dentifrices, tires, hearing aids, and antiperspirants.

Advertising is likely to continue to be a controversial ethical issue for many years. Assessing the ethics of any one advertisement will largely depend on the perspective one takes. Economic and legal analyses would suggest that virtually all advertising is ethical, for it promotes the bottom line of business and violates no laws. Universalists might argue, however, that advertising treats people as means to an end and does not provide dignity or respect. People taking the dialogic perspective would criticize the inherent manipulativeness of many advertisements. Given the pervasiveness and impact of advertising today, it is important that we monitor the ethical implications of advertising practices, regardless of the perspective we take.

Service Versus Profit

Most business theorists argue that good service means better profits—that maximizing the services provided to customers ultimately improves an organization's bottom line. In health care, however, that principle does not necessarily hold true.

In the mid-1980s, the federal government became increasingly concerned about rapidly rising health care costs. As a result, in 1983, Congress enacted the Medicare prospective payment system, which established fixed amounts that would be paid to hospitals for each of 468 different types of treatments (Medicare would pay a certain amount for appendectomies, a certain amount for tonsillectomies, and so on). Prior to that time, Medicare and Medicaid had paid hospital charges regardless of the amount. Under the new plan (which uses changes based on diagnosis-related groups), hospitals whose actual costs fell below the fixed levels could keep the difference, while hospitals whose costs were above the established levels suffered losses. Since 40 percent of all hospital patients on the average are covered by Medicare, this represented a significant change in health care funding. Soon after, other private insurers implemented similar plans of their own.

Hospitals responded to these financial pressures in several ways, most of which involved attempting to reduce the costs of providing care.[43] Reducing patients' length of stay was a key element of cost reduction: for example, by reducing from five days to three the amount of time an appendectomy patient spent in the hospital, hospital administrators could reduce the cost of delivering care to that person. "Get 'em out quicker and sicker" became the motto for many hospitals.

Many health care organizations also began marketing their services more aggressively, with ethical implications. One such situation involved a Chicago-based hospice (hospice programs are designed to provide care at home for terminally ill patients believed to have six months or less to live). In two memos sent to employees, hospice management offered to pay cash bonuses to nurses who recruited patients and directed them to immediately hospitalize all patients admitted during the weekend as well as all patients who were at home when they first signed up (despite federal guidelines requiring that no more than 20 percent of hospice care is to be in a hospital). One memo from an administrator stated that "the low census in both inpatient units cannot continue to occur. Quite frankly, it is strangling us financially."[44] More than a dozen employees quit their jobs in the organization, saying they were disturbed by what they viewed as unethical practices.

Finally, many health care organizations have begun to take other steps to reduce costs and improve their financial strength: reducing the number of staff (including the number of people who provide care directly to patients), reducing or eliminating services and treatments that have proven unprofitable, conducting fewer routine tests, and attempting to control equipment and supply costs. Still, over one hundred hospitals have been forced to close each year, and continued financial pressures are expected.[45]

Health care administrators and managers thus face a variety of ethical choices: What level of care is good enough? Should services offered be based on community needs, financial realities, or some compromise of the two? How far should a health care organization go in trying to increase its business volume? How much work can reasonably be demanded of hospital employees? Ultimately, the answers to ethical issues like these will determine the quality and type of health care we receive in the future.

Social Responsibility

In response to the question "Do corporations have social responsibilities over and above their obligations to their stockholders?" most would answer "Of course!" But the scope of that responsibility remains an area of some controversy.

One interesting example is provided by Control Data Corporation and its founder, chairman and chief executive officer William C. Norris. During 1967, when riots erupted in a depressed area of Minneapolis not far from Control Data's headquarters, Norris responded in a manner that should serve as a model of social responsibility. "You can't do business with the town on fire," he said. "So you stop and think why this has happened. It happened because of inequities. The people felt so damn frustrated that this was their way of expressing themselves."[46] Thus, in 1968, Norris and Control Data opened a new plant in the riot-torn area of Minneapolis and provided their new employees with a child-care center and intensive job training (including basic courses in computer skills). In 1970, they opened a second plant in St. Paul. The company went on to launch programs to revitalize urban and rural areas, create jobs through small business development, provide training to prison populations, and meet other social needs.

More recently, a major shoemaker was accused of shirking its social responsibilities. Operation PUSH, a Chicago-based civil rights group founded by, among others, Reverend Jesse Jackson, demanded that the Nike shoe company change the composition of its management and board of directors. Their reasoning: since African-Americans compose a significant portion of Nike's athletic footwear market, African-Americans should hold prominent positions in the company as well. When Nike refused Operation PUSH's demands for detailed financial information about the company and changes in the organization's structure (and indeed, countered with similar demands for detailed information about Operation PUSH), leaders of Operation PUSH declared economic war and attempted to organize a boycott of Nike products.[47] That boycott generally has proven unsuccessful.

Again, questions arise: Do corporations have an ethical responsibility to support their communities and assist in the resolution of social problems? Does any group have the ethical right to declare itself the spokesperson for some segment of society and make demands on manufacturers who sell their products to that segment? Relations between organizational systems and their environment will continue to raise ethical questions in the future.

Employee Rights

The treatment of employees by their superiors involves a myriad of ethical issues. Most theorists imply that employees have certain basic rights and that the ethics of management's treatment of employees can be judged, at least in part, by the extent to which those rights are upheld. We will consider just a few of those rights here.

The Right to Fair and Equitable Treatment

In recent years, government regulations, often in the form of affirmative action policies, have required equitable procedures in screening, hiring, promoting, and terminating employees.[48] Discrimination on the basis of race, religion, national origin, or sex is strictly forbidden, according to the law.[49]

Discrimination on the basis of age is becoming a particular concern. The Bureau of National Affairs reports that "age discrimination actions challenging employer decisions represent the hottest area of employment discrimination litigation today." In its view, the aging of the American work force, combined with increased employee awareness of their rights under the Age Discrimination in Employment Act of 1967, should lead employers "to expect to be sued whenever they make an employment decision—especially a termination decision—that is perceived to be adverse to the interests of an older worker."[50]

Another issue of concern is sexual harassment. As more women have entered the work force, problems with sexual harassment have grown. Cornell University conducted one of the first studies of sexual harassment and reported that 92 percent of 155 respondents viewed sexual harassment as a serious problem and 70 percent had personally experienced some form of harassment.[51] However, the question of what exactly constitutes harassment has remained complex. In its most obvious form, sexual harassment occurs when a person's supervisor requests sexual favors under the threat of denying promotion, pay increase, or even termination. But this is a narrow definition, describing only the most stereotypic cases.

In 1980, the U.S. Equal Employment Opportunity Commission (EEOC) issued guidelines stating that sexual harassment is a violation of Title VII of the 1964 Civil Rights Act. It defined harassment as occurring when

1. Submission to the sexual conduct is made either implicitly or explicitly a term or condition of employment.
2. Employment decisions affecting the recipient are made on the basis of the recipient's acceptance or rejection of the sexual conduct.
3. The conduct has the purpose or effect of reasonably interfering with an individual's work performance or creating an intimidating, hostile, or offensive working environment.[52]

Women: entering the work force in record numbers with the hope of encountering an equitable work environment.

Clearly, according to this broad definition, much sexual harassment is fairly subtle. It could be viewed as including leering, staring, or verbal harassment, such as sexual joking or referring to women as "girls," or even making sexist comments such as "women are just too emotional to take the pressure."

Apart from legal definitions of harassment, some researchers have concerned themselves with the ways that women themselves define harassment. One study, for instance, found that while close to 80 percent of women considered sexual propositions, touching, grabbing, and brushing as harassment, only 50 percent thought that sexual remarks and suggestive gestures were sexually harassing. Although most believed that staring and flirting were perhaps the most frequent form of female-directed attention, most did not view such behaviors as harassment.[53] It is also important to note here that even though the majority of cases of sexual harassment involve *women* as victims, the EEOC guidelines apply equally to *men*. In fact, a different UN survey conducted in 1975 found that 50 percent of females and 31 percent of males had experienced some form of sexual harassment.[54] The *Wall Street Journal* notes that sexual harassment can involve gay workers harassing others, women harassing men, subordinates harassing managers, and outside vendors harassing customers.[55]

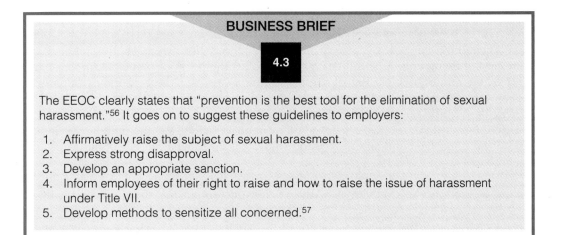

The financial and human costs of sexual harassment can be immense. The financial costs include fines and other legal settlements, which can be substantial. Moreover, if the employer is a contractor with the federal government, it may lose its federal contracts. The human costs of sexual harassment are equally great. Victims suffer embarrassment, intimidation, helplessness, and anger.[58] In many cases, the victims live with these feelings rather than confront the offender, for fear of retaliation. Several studies report that some victims eventually suffer from serious psychological problems requiring medical attention because of the harassment.[59] More frequently, however, these emotional problems lead to increased absenteeism, reduced efficiency, and even resignations.[60] Thus, even in small businesses (with fewer than fifteen employees) where EEOC guidelines are not binding, employers should still be concerned about lowered morale and productivity. In most instances of harassment, both the victim and the perpetrator ultimately suffer.

Many companies have taken steps to avoid incidences of sexual harassment. One study revealed that over 27 percent of *Fortune* 500 respondents said they hold EEOC or affirmative action training programs and seminars for employees; 20 percent provide continuing education through company magazines or journals, films, and training sessions of various kinds. Slightly more than 9 percent said they included sexual harassment topics as part of supervisory training.[61] Some companies have made major advances in addressing the problem. DuPont, for example, invested $500,000 to develop a program designed to teach employees how to avert sexual harassment, rape, and other safety risks.[62]

The Right to Privacy

Most would agree that employee offices or lockers, files, telephone conversations, personnel data, outside activities, and so on should not be invaded by their employers—that people have a right to privacy at work. Yet the limits of employee privacy are being pushed back almost daily. For example, as chapter 7 will describe in some detail, employees now are being tested in a variety of ways by their employers: for drugs and alcohol usage, for AIDS, for honesty (using polygraphs), and for job skills.[63] Employees subjected to such tests often object that "what I do on my own time is my own business" (including, supposedly, taking drugs). Yet three Northwest Airlines pilots were convicted of flying under the influence of alcohol as the result of participating in a party on their own time the night before the flight. Employees at a meat-packing company in Monmouth, Illinois, objected to random drug and alcohol testing conducted by their employer, despite the fact that their jobs required them to use extremely sharp knives to butcher hogs and the testing was designed to improve safety. As one company foreman said to this consultant and author: "We try to protect those who are too dumb to protect themselves."

Electronic monitoring of employee performance also has increased. An estimated 10 million workers in the United States have their work output measured electronically or their phone conversations listened to in the workday. Employees who often are monitored include telephone operators; airline, auto rental, and hotel reservation clerks; telemarketing sales and order clerks; insurance claims processors; and newspaper classified ad and circulation workers. "Not only are their keystrokes, customer contacts and unproductive time measured by computers, but their conversations also are often secretly monitored by supervisors checking on employees' efficiency and effectiveness."[64] Critics raise concerns that such monitoring increases work stress (bringing about "electronic sweatshops") and may lead to a loss of freedom. However, Alan Westin, professor of public law and government at Columbia, disagrees: "The premise that a conversation between an employee and a customer on the employer's premises in the name of the employer's business is somehow a private chat is 180 degrees wrong. Monitoring in principle is essential to assuring the quality of customer service work."[65] Nevertheless, legislation to limit employer monitoring of employees is pending.

Another area of growing controversy concerning employees' rights to privacy involves the use of electronic and voice mail. In 1993, for example, *Macworld* magazine published a survey showing widespread eavesdropping by employers. Based on responses from 301 businesses employing over 1 million workers, *Macworld* estimated that as many as 20 million Americans may be subject to electronic monitoring on the job.

The *Macworld* survey found that more than 21 percent of the respondents have searched employees' computer files, electronic mail, voice mail, or other networking communications. Of those who admitted to snooping, 74 percent had searched computer work files, 42 percent had searched electronic mail, and 15 percent had searched voice mail.

Why had these searches been conducted? To monitor work flow, investigate thefts, or prevent industrial espionage, some said. But whatever the purpose, there are no legal limits placed on employers spying on their employees in the workplace. They are free to view employees on closed-circuit television, tap their telephones, search their E-mail and network communications, and rummage through their computer files with or without employee knowledge or consent, twenty-four hours a day.[66]

In response to concerns about surveillance of employees, AT&T adjusted its practices of monitoring telephone operators to check their service to customers. Initially, the emphasis of the effort was on discipline. First-level supervisors monitored operators to check their conformity to standards of courtesy, customer relations specialists randomly surveyed customer opinions of operators' effectiveness, and the information collected was used to evaluate (and sometimes fire) individual operators.

Now, as a part of AT&T's move toward self-management, operators monitor each other at thirteen AT&T operator services offices. Operators learn what they are doing well and what they need to improve, but they learn from one another, not a supervisor. The operator teams decide among themselves how best to monitor one another's performance, and they evaluate each other on the basis of "customer attributes"—eight behaviors customers have said are important—rather than on what management thinks customers want. The focus of monitoring thus has shifted from being evaluative to attempting to develop improved skills among operators.

From Jennifer J. Laabs, "Surveillance: Tool or Trap?" *Personnel Journal* 71 (June 1992): 101.

The Right to a Safe and Healthful Work Environment

The Occupational Safety and Health Administration (OSHA) was established to ensure that employers provide safe working conditions for their people. Yet abuses occur. Scientists from Argonne's Center for Human Radiobiology, for example, found nine breast-cancer deaths in a group of 463 women who had worked in a Luminous Processes plant in Ottawa, Illinois, painting clock and watch dials with radium. These women reported that safety precautions were almost nonexistent and that workers were constantly contaminated with the radioactive material. In fact, they stated that company officials told them that radium was safe to handle. Women at the plant sometimes painted their fingernails with radium paint; others took pots of radium paint home to paint light switches that would glow in the dark. Workers routinely contaminated their hair, arms, legs, and feet with the radioactive material accidentally while they worked, and they wiped paint-covered hands on the front of their work smocks.[67] The plant closed in 1978.

While the need to protect workers in the workplace would seem incontrovertible, many important issues remain. For example, many major U.S. corporations (including American Cyanamid, Olin, General Motors, Gulf Oil, Dow Chemical, Du Pont, Union Carbide, and Monsanto) have policies concerning fetal protection that prohibit women from working in areas that might endanger pregnancies. "I can't go anywhere," said Patricia Briner, who fills batteries with acid for Milwaukee-based Johnson Controls, Inc.

"The good jobs are in departments where lead is used—and women aren't allowed to work in them. The company says it's too dangerous. That includes women who aren't pregnant and who don't ever intend to become pregnant."[68] A spokesman for the company said that, according to company research, lead exposure "has a minor impact on men, but an overwhelming evidence indicates risk to fetuses. It would be unconscionable to expose women to it. We're trying to do the right thing."[69] The Supreme Court in 1991 determined that Title VII of the U.S. Civil Rights Act, which prohibits discrimination in job assignments, took precedence in this instance over OSHA regulations, which require companies to take steps to protect third parties (such as fetuses) from workplace dangers, and ruled that Johnson Controls's policy discriminated against women.

The Right to Conscientious Objection

Despite organizational rules prohibiting insubordination, most would agree that employees should have the right to refuse orders that violate their principles (such as falsifying figures in a financial statement, giving or accepting bribes, or lying to government agencies). Yet controversy still surrounds the actions one should take when one sees an organization engaging in unethical practices. In such situations, should an employee blow the whistle on his or her employer?

The prototypical case of a whistle-blower involved Dan Gellert, a pilot for Eastern Airlines. He became concerned about the safety of the Lockheed 1011 airplane. In flight simulation, the automatic pilot would disengage without warning about ninety seconds before landing (or about two thousand feet above the ground). He reported his concerns to company management, who said, "We'll look into it." On December 29, 1972, an Eastern Airlines L-1011 crashed, killing 103 people. Gellert took his report to the top of the company, who ignored him. Then he sent his report to the National Transportation Safety Board. While his actions did prompt some needed adjustments in the automatic pilot (done quietly by the company), he was demoted and then grounded by the company. He went through grievance procedures for seven months and then sued. Ultimately, he won more than he had sued for ($1.6 million).

The movie *Silkwood* was based upon Karen Silkwood's fight against Kerr-McGee to improve safety for nuclear plant workers—a fight in which she blew the whistle on the company. Other similar situations have developed since. For example, in 1989, an employee of Pacific Gas & Electric claimed he was fired for raising safety concerns about the construction of the Diablo Canyon nuclear plant. In his suit, he alleged that he was fired because he brought to management's attention discrepancies between the "as built" drawings for the plant and actual conditions at the facility. These differences, he felt, affected the safety of the plant, which is located near the San Andreas fault.[70]

Government agencies gradually have developed guidelines for protecting whistle-blowers. For example, in November 1988, the Occupational Safety and Health Administration issued final rules outlining procedures the agency will use to investigate cases in which employees in the trucking industry allege that they were fired or otherwise subjected to retaliation by their employers for voicing complaints about health or safety conditions. In 1990, Wisconsin enacted new employment laws under which employers would be liable for retaliating when they believe that an employee has filed a complaint, even if the employee has not actually filed. New Jersey already had enacted a Whistleblower Act in 1986.

Whistle-blowing is controversial because it puts into conflict two employee obligations: loyalty to the employer and responsibility to society.[71] Some argue that employees should exhaust every possible avenue within the company before they make their concerns public. Yet many companies provide no such avenues for employees in the first place. Because there is no one to whom an employee can "conscientiously object," he or she may be forced to go outside to a government agency or the media. And because they are eager to protect their public image, some companies try very hard to discourage this sort of public airing of their dirty laundry.

Certainly, employees have many rights beyond those discussed above: the right to (qualified) free speech (to complain, for example, but not to defame the company in public), the right to due process, the right to participate in outside activities, and so on. Each of these rights leads to important moral and ethical judgments.

Surveillance

Just as employees' rights to privacy can be jeopardized by new electronic technology, so too can technology threaten the rights of citizens who may not be organizational members or of entire organizations themselves. Consider some recent examples:

In June 1993, executives of Procter & Gamble in Cincinnati complained to police that company information was being illegally leaked to the press. To identify the source of the leak, Cincinnati Bell Telephone Company, acting in response to a subpoena from a grand jury, searched the phone records of every one of its 655,000 customers in the 513 and 606 area codes. Procter & Gamble executives later admitted that this might have been an error in judgment.

Lotus Development, a software manufacturer, and Equifax, a company that compiles financial information about individuals, developed a plan to sell a data base that would have allowed anyone with a personal computer to purchase a list of names, buying habits, and income levels of selected households. Small businesses, such as pharmacies, pizza parlors, and dry cleaners, would have been able to get all such information on potential local customers. Public uproar forced the companies to scrap their plan.

The Employer's Information Service, based in Gretna, Louisiana, is creating a massive data bank on workers who have reported on-the-job injuries. For a fee, employers can request a report on prospective employees, including a history of prior job injuries and a record of worker's compensation claims and lawsuits. To keep from being added to other data banks, workers in Idaho are suing that state's industrial commission to prevent it from releasing such records.[72]

Increasingly, organizations are developing or acquiring technology to spy on their employees, the public, or other organizations. But the biggest threat to privacy is not video surveillance cameras, listening devices, or telephone answering machines—it is the computer.

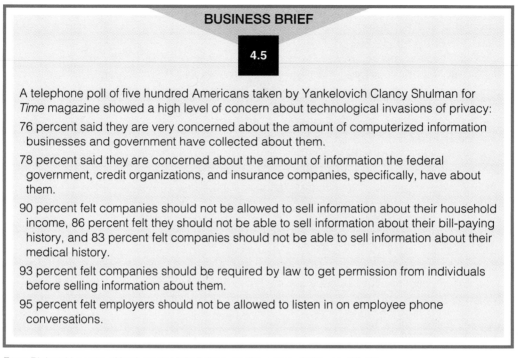

From Richard Lacayo, "Nowhere to Hide," *Time,* 11 November 1991, pp. 34–40.

To obtain a credit card, mortgage, driver's license, or admission to a hospital, people typically must complete forms that ask for a variety of information about their financial, medical, and family histories, their buying habits, and so on. In turn, these data are often sold to other organizations (as when a state government sells lists of driver's license holders to advertisers) that use the information for their own purposes. Such information routinely is made available to government agencies, mortgage lenders, retailers, small businesses, marketers, and insurers. Credit reports, for example, are used by banks to determine whether they will give someone a mortgage, and medical records are used by insurance companies (and sometimes potential employers) to determine whether someone will be covered (or hired). And marketers use information about income and buying habits to target recipients of their mail-order and telephone solicitations.

Three huge organizations—TRW, Equifax, and Trans Union—dominate the consumer-data industry. Every month, these companies purchase computer records, usually from banks and retailers, that detail the financial activities of almost every adult in the United States. While these organizations have argued that their data bases do not disclose truly confidential details, Equifax used credit card use patterns and census data to develop projections of each card user's estimated annual income—information it then sold to its customers. Only when this practice proved too controversial did Equifax discontinue selling this information, in the summer of 1993.

Other forms of technology are also becoming more sophisticated. A number of catalog retailers and financial companies now make use of an updated version of "caller ID," which in its simplest form displays the telephone number from which an incoming call has been placed. The more sophisticated version displays the caller's name, telephone number, and credit history almost as quickly as the call is answered.

Certainly, concern is rising about the use of technology to invade the public's privacy. Yet privacy cannot be taken as having inherent value. For example, with U.S. banks being used as conduits for drug money, law enforcement officials have pressed banks to report any suspicious movement of cash. Although such reports may conflict with traditional concepts of bank-client confidentiality, most banks have been willing to comply. In addition, some business groups argue that controlling their sale of data about their customers violates their property rights; the information is theirs, they claim, and they should have the right to sell it to whomever they choose.

Ultimately, some of these issues may be resolved via legislation. For example, Congress soon is expected to review the appropriateness of the automated dialing machines, used by telemarketers to call every number in a telephone exchange, one after another, to make a recorded sales pitch. Some also have proposed that the 1974 Federal Privacy Act, which defends citizens from government misuse of data, should be extended to cover private industry as well and should be enforced more stringently. But important questions remain. Do the rights of organizations take precedence over the rights of individuals? To what extent should government be involved in regulating the actions of private organizations? And when does an organization's use of personal data about individuals become unethical?

Building Organizational Ethics

As organizations have come to realize the importance of ethical behavior, they have attempted to develop a sense of organizational ethics in a variety of ways. Each of these involves communication.

Corporate Mission Statements

Increasingly, organizations are seeking to establish a system of ethics by developing a statement of mission that tells employees what the organization is about and where it is going, builds a set of values with which everyone can identify, and supports cohesiveness and productivity. According to Jerome Want, a mission statement should separate a company from its competition and provide it with a sense of identity, legitimacy, and direction.[73] Its primary components are the following:

Purpose of the organization. The mission statement should clearly outline the reasons for the organization's existence, the primary businesses in which it engages, and the products and services it provides (and the manner in which they should be provided).

Principal business aims, such as market share, profitability, or size; strategies for achieving growth or optimizing productivity; and impact on the competition.

Corporate identity, or how the company wants to be perceived by its customers, competitors, the business community in general, and its employees.

Policies concerning the philosophy and style of leadership managers should use, the relationships among senior management, owners, shareholders and the board of directors, and the overall decision-making structure of the organization.

Values, or a clear set of business standards against which the company and its members' actions should be judged. Typically, statements of values allow the company to be judged from several different perspectives: those of customers, competitors, employees, regulatory agencies, and the general public. As Weiss notes, these values should be simple and easy to articulate, apply to internal as well as external operations, and be communicated early and often even during the recruitment and selection process.[74]

Codes of Ethics

Many companies have attempted to ensure ethical behavior by their members by establishing a code of ethics. Indeed, Davis reports that more than two hundred of the *Fortune* 500 now have their own codes of ethics.[75] While these codes vary somewhat, they have some common characteristics:

They speak to activities that often cannot be closely supervised by company management (such as honesty with customers or mutual respect among employees). Thus, motivators such as fear or coercion cannot be applied to these activities, making the individual employee's ethics all the more important.

They ask more than might otherwise be expected (such as avoiding criticisms of competitors during sales calls or taking pains to help customers).

They contribute to the long-term success of the organization only to the extent that they are upheld by members of the organization. That is, they depend on voluntary cooperation by management and employees alike to ensure ethical behavior.

Simply announcing a code of conduct to all staff, posting the code on bulletin boards throughout the company, or having new employees sign a copy of the code as a part of their orientation will not ensure cooperation. Individual managers must serve as role models of the code, and organizational rewards and punishments must be applied to encourage following the code's provisions.

Corporate Mottos

Corporate mottos are a little-used means of communicating an organization's guiding principles, sentiments, or philosophies. Research conducted by Hershey found that most *Fortune* 100 companies have never thought of a motto as a vehicle for transmitting corporate values to employees, but many use slogans to exhort workers or impress customers.[76] The mottos Hershey found included "*semper fidelis*" or "always faithful" (the U.S. Marine Corps); "We always get our man" (Royal Canadian Mounted

Presented below is the mission statement developed by a small Chicago-based company:

Mission Statement

Our mission is to manufacture wire, cable, and related products which enhance the day-to-day lives of the people who work and live in the buildings, use the computers and appliances, and enjoy the parks and golf courses of which our products become an integral part. We will achieve success by working together to make XXXXX a profitable, quality company:

Committed to Manufacturing Quality Products

Our first commitment is to provide our customers with quality products which are innovative and technologically responsive to their needs, at competitive prices.

Committed to Providing Quality Service

We likewise are committed to providing our customers with service which is responsive, flexible, dependable and tailored to their unique problems and demands.

Committed to Pursuing Quality Work Life

We commit to establishing and maintaining the kind of environment in which our employees want to work—one which encourages each person to achieve his or her highest potential, provides equal opportunities to all, and gives all employees a chance to make a meaningful contribution to the fulfillment of our mission and to be recognized for their accomplishments. A safe work environment also is critical, and every employee must be committed to their own safety and that of their fellow workers.

Committed to Developing Quality Relationships

We commit to establishing and maintaining high quality relationships among all XXXXX personnel. This means that everyone strives to understand and follow the Company's objectives and policies, communicates with one another, acts in a professional manner, and tries at all times to treat one another with respect, dignity and cooperation. It also means that every XXXXX employee has the opportunity to speak with any other person in the Company, so that all managers maintain an "open door" policy for all employees.

Committed to Contributing to Quality Community Service

We are committed to serving the communities from which our people come. We strive to improve quality of life in those communities through our support of community organizations and projects, through encouraging service to the community by employees, and by promoting participation in community services.

Reaching Quality in Individual Performance

We pledge to make our time at work "quality time," to working with a sense of urgency, dependability, accuracy, and consistency, and to making each working minute count toward the achievement of our mission.

Police); "Neither snow, nor rain, nor heat, nor gloom of night stays these couriers from the swift completion of their appointed rounds" (U.S. Postal Service); "The difficult we do immediately; the impossible takes a little longer" (U.S. Army Corps of Engineers); and "To keep it, you have to give it away" (Alcoholics Anonymous). A Cleveland-based health organization took the saying "Sometimes you eat the bear, and sometimes the bear eats you" and made it into its motto of the year: "Eat More Bear." Hershey claims that the ideal corporate motto would convey and promote a core philosophy of an organization, have an emotional appeal, and be somewhat of a mystery to the general public (thus reinforcing cohesiveness among organizational members). He found no corporate motto that meets all these criteria.

Work Rules

Most companies try to ensure ethical behavior by developing and enforcing work rules. Typically, rules prohibit such actions as gambling, assaulting others, destroying property, theft, or trying to sell things to other employees at work. Yet these rules also tend to be somewhat loosely enforced: office pools gamble on the outcome of football games or buy state lottery tickets, employees conduct Tupperware parties, and so on.

The way in which a company develops and enforces its rules may reveal more about its ethics than the rules themselves. Steelcase, the nation's largest manufacturer of office furnishings, developed a form of participative management to enforce adherence to its values and policies. As a first step, a committee representing a cross-section of the entire company classified rules violations into three categories: Class I offenses (failing to punch in, gambling, unauthorized use of company telephones), which call for penalties of one to sixty points; Class II offenses (careless workmanship, destruction of company property, theft up to ten dollars), which call for assessments of sixty to 120 points; Class III offenses (under the influence of alcohol or drugs, assaulting a supervisor, drinking on company time), which call for eighty to 110 points. Employees accumulating 160 points are dismissed. Whenever an employee reaches eighty points, an Employee Performance Improvement Committee (comprising the plant manager, area superintendent, employee's foreman, employee relations representative, and a professional from the company's counseling center) meets with the employee to encourage performance improvement. If the employee goes on to reach one hundred points, the committee meets again. And even those employees who reach 160 points may not be through with the company: many are rehired; and of those given a second chance, 80 percent succeed.[77]

Management Behaviors

The real key to developing organizational ethics seems to be the behaviors of individual supervisors and managers. Dolecheck advises four approaches a manager or supervisor should take to improving ethics.[78] First, a manager should *emphasize and discuss ethics continually*. A code of ethics becomes real only when a manager talks about it by encouraging subordinates to raise ethics-related issues, doubts, or concerns, by referring to it when answering questions or making decisions concerning quality, safety, work methods, and so on, and by keeping others' attention focused on it. Second, it is important that the manager *develop realistic goals.* People faced with goals they cannot achieve are tempted to cut corners, sacrificing ethics for achievement. Third, by *identifying areas that are vulnerable to unethical practices,* a manager might avoid ethical problems by discussing with employees the sorts of temptations that might arise. Finally, *encouraging reporting of unethical activities* lets everyone know that he or she has a role in enforcing ethical standards and indicates the manager's serious intent in ensuring ethical behavior.

As members of organizations, we must promote ethical behaviors by serving as role models. As Weiss notes, "values cannot be taught, they must be lived." People emulate what they see, not what they are told. If they see unethical behaviors or tolerance for improper practices, they will cease to believe any written codes of ethics. Richard Zimmerman, chairman and CEO of Hershey Foods Corporation, refers to his company's value system as an "anchor" for the organization and asserts that "each manager must have a grip on those clearly defined values and be able to demonstrate them through their own behavior to employee groups." President and Chief Operating Officer Kenneth Wolfe agrees: "There is no grey area on ethics at Hershey. Here, you will never bend the ethical standards of doing business."[79]

Some Difficulties with Making Ethical Judgments

It is clear that ethical judgments will take on increasing importance in the future. The U.S. Department of Labor, in its research bulletin *The Changing Role of First-Line Supervisors and Middle Managers,* concluded that "many middle managers and first-line supervisors find the managing job more difficult, because they must learn to manage by principle rather than by policy. Many of the new work systems are built on the premise that each situation must be evaluated on its own merits and that actions are taken based on doing 'what's right' for the business and the people involved."[80]

But making ethical judgments often means being concerned with the motives, intentions, and even the sincerity of individuals and organizations, and there are several difficulties in making these kinds of judgments. Regardless of the act committed, it is extremely *difficult to evaluate* with certainty *another's motives.* Behavior or language may seem incriminating and may have actually functioned destructively. To measure the effect of the act is not the same, however, as judging the intentions of the actor. Former President Richard M. Nixon was quick to take advantage of this fact in admitting that though his actions in the Watergate affair had been unfortunate, his motives remained pure.

The difficulty of determining intentions is compounded when one faces *the task of establishing truth.* Philosophers from the time of Plato have debated the nature of truth and the problems associated with establishing its essence. Before one can evaluate whether or not an individual or an organization is on the side of good, it is imperative that one have a reasonably clear conception of the difference between good and bad, right and wrong, true and false. To continue the previous example, consider the number of American citizens who, after bombardment by newspapers, television, and scores of books, still are uncertain of the true version of the Watergate cover-up. Although this is a fairly complicated example, most of the issues about which we daily make important ethical judgments are neither simple nor obvious.

In discussing the situational perspective above, we hinted at another difficulty with making ethical judgments, *the problem of establishing universal ethical standards*. If ethics do vary with the culture, the time, the receivers, and the communicators, then it may be that even the establishment of flexible criteria is virtually impossible. If, on the other hand, one engages in the quest for absolutes, he or she runs the risk of rigidity and dogmatism. While the best solution is probably to seek a kind of middle ground using flexible guidelines, the most appropriate spot to rest on the flexibility ↔ rigidity continuum is a serious question and a matter of great significance.

Finally, while few would argue the importance of struggling with ethical issues, it is crucial to recognize that *ethics represent only one relevant dimension for judging any work or act*. We are all familiar with the public speaker who, while uninspiring, poorly prepared, and inept at delivery, is nonetheless clearly *sincere*. Many fine organizations owned and managed by men and women of honor and integrity go under every year because of inefficient and ineffective management. Many tasteful, creative advertisements and other public relations efforts fail to capture the public imagination and vanish. The point we are trying to make is that ethics are important, and they tend to be ignored rather than overemphasized. It is still critical to remember that they must continually be viewed along with the practical considerations so vital to the lives of organizations and individuals.

Summary

Ethical decisions and value orientations are deeply embedded in organizational structures, reflecting the society and culture in which they exist. We must evaluate both organizational and communication ethics from various philosophical perspectives, including religious, political, utilitarian, universalist, dialogic, and situational. However, evaluation from any ethical perspective is made more difficult by such complexities as judging the motives of others, determining the nature of truth, establishing absolute guidelines, and attempting to combine ethical concerns with other more pragmatic issues, including practical effectiveness. Despite these difficulties, the contemporary thrust of organizational leadership and behavior embraces a compelling appeal for a sense of ethics within the context of social responsibility.

Questions for Discussion

1. Compare and contrast the religious and universalist ethical perspectives. In what ways might they be interrelated?
2. From a political/cultural perspective, discuss ethics in contemporary American society. How does this perspective influence organizations within this society?

3. Discuss the assertion that the end justifies the means. Are there any particular kinds of situations in which this position might be defensible? Elaborate with at least one example.

4. Those who espouse a legal perspective refer to specific books, sets of rules, or bodies of law to find the answers to ethical questions. Do you do this? If so, in what kinds of situations? Do you feel that legalism is an intelligent approach to ethics?

5. It is not uncommon for individuals to vary their ethical perspectives, depending on the precise nature of the situation in which they find themselves. Can you justify this point of view?

6. What is your view of contemporary advertising in terms of ethics? Are deception, the creation of artificial consumer needs, and other issues discussed in this chapter of significance from your ethical view? Elaborate.

7. To what extent do consumers expect and accept deception in advertising; that is, are they buying illusions of hope, images of beauty, and so forth when they buy soap and makeup? What does this say about American society?

8. What should an employee do when he or she feels his or her immediate supervisor is doing something unethical? Outline a series of actions that an employee might take.

9. How would you define ethics from the vantage point of your present organizational affiliation?

Exercises

1. Choose any prominent persons (such as an educator, religious leader, politician, lawyer, or executive) and discuss her or his behavior from an ethical perspective. What is the apparent value system of this individual? On what is it based? From your own view, is this person's behavior ethical? Be specific.

2. Select any three advertisements. Consider their bases of appeal, operating assumptions, and general taste. To what extent is each a reasonably accurate representation of reality? How would you rate each in terms of *your* ethical perspective?

3. Choose an executive with a moderate to large organization. Arrange for an interview. During the interview, discuss his or her philosophies of management, relating them to his or her own values and those of the organization. Try to fit this individual's perspective into the value changes suggested by Trist.

4. Contact several major organizations that have branches near your community. Ask them whether or not they have written procedures for dealing with discrimination and/or sexual harassment. If they do, obtain copies. Do they seem adequate? If not, how could they be improved?

5. You are the manager of a newly established realty company in a medium-sized town in the Midwest. While the organization has nationwide branches, your office is new, and you are relatively free to run it as you prefer—so long as you operate in the black. Your fifteen years of experience in the real estate business has taught you that it is a competitive, exciting, and in some senses treacherous business. Yet one of its major purposes is to serve the public.

a. What values would influence you most in building your organization? Why? (Refer to Trist's scheme and try to determine where you might fit.)
b. How would these values be reflected in your hiring and handling of employees, especially fellow real estate agents?
c. How would your values relate to your handling of the public?
d. What is the ethical basis for your particular values? Elaborate.

6. Imagine yourself as a fairly new employee in a rapidly growing firm. You have high hopes for rapid promotion, but your boss is a person who presents certain problems. His ideas of how to manage are very command-oriented, whereas yours are much more democratic. His political views are conservative (far to the right of George Bush); yours are just left of Ted Kennedy. He loves sports; you loathe sports. Unfortunately, he often asks for your views on all of the above and on other painful issues as well. What do you do? Do you articulate your true opinions? Do you pretend to agree? Do you downplay your views or simply attempt to change the subject? Is it possible to distort your position in some areas but not in others? *What is the relationship here between the ethical and the political thing to do?* What ethical perspective would you use to resolve this dilemma? Why?

Dyadic Communication

PART

2

Whether I'm selling or buying, whether I'm hiring or being hired, whether I'm negotiating a contract or responding to someone else's demands, I want to know where the other person is coming from. I want to know the other person's real self.

—MARK H. McCORMACK

WHAT THEY DON'T TEACH YOU AT HARVARD BUSINESS SCHOOL

Fundamentals of Communication

Establishing Human Relationships

As organizations become more technologically sophisticated, one might expect human relationships to take on decreasing importance. Quite the contrary, argues John Naisbitt in his best-seller, *Megatrends: Ten New Directions Transforming Our Lives*. He contends that people have a need to be together. Even when most work is done by computer and people have the choice of working in their own homes, he says, "very few people will be willing to stay home all of the time and tap out messages to the office. People want to go to the office. People want to be with people, and the more technology we pump into the society, the more people will want to be with people."[1] To be successful in tomorrow's organization, you will need to establish and maintain good relationships with others.

In many respects, then, this chapter will serve as a basis for all the chapters that follow. We will consider human relationships and the communication behaviors that compose them. After examining the components of relationships, we will discuss the specific communication elements that bring those relationships about: receiving and sending. Then we will offer some communication strategies whereby relationships in all settings—dyadic, group, and organizational—might be improved.

The Nature of Human Relationships

Several theorists have tried to identify the dimensions that make up our relationships. Timothy Leary and his associates concluded from their studies of therapists and patients that relationships have two dimensions: dominance (that is, the extent to which each person makes decisions the other follows) and affection (the extent to which each person likes the other).[2] Later research by Schutz suggested three dimensions: control (or dominance), affection, and inclusion (or the extent to which people identify and interact with each other).[3] Bales observed relationships in groups and found them to consist of positiveness-negativeness (or attraction), power (or dominance), and movement toward the group goal (a group task-related dimension).[4]

If you think about your relationship with someone at work, you probably will see the validity of these dimensions. You have feelings toward that person, just as he or she has feelings (likes and dislikes) toward you. One of you probably has higher status and/or greater influence over the relationship than the other. Certainly, you interact and identify with each other to some degree. Thus, research and our own experiences point to three relationship dimensions: *attraction,* an index of liking or affection; *dominance,* a measure of power or control; and *involvement,* an index of identification with the other person, of unity, and of active inclusiveness. To these should be added a fourth dimension, *situation,* which considers the physical, social, and task environment of the encounter, for all three have some impact upon relationship development.

Attraction

The first dimension considers the degree to which the participants feel positively or negatively about one another. Many factors influence the extent to which we are attracted to someone else. The first of these is *physical proximity*—the sheer accident of physical location determines to a large degree those to whom we will be attracted. Employees working in the same department, for example, see one another relatively often, and relationships between them are likely to form as a result. But we need to emphasize that while contact produces feelings about others, those feelings are not necessarily positive. That is, to dislike someone intensely, we would need to see them frequently as well. Thus, physical proximity simply causes us to come into contact with others, giving us an opportunity to form opinions about them and develop attraction toward (or repulsion from) them.

Although society tells us that we should not judge a book by its cover or judge people by their appearance, research indicates that we do exactly that. Indeed, *physical attractiveness* seems to be the second major determinant of our attraction to someone else. People who find one another physically attractive, regardless of sex, are more likely to talk with one another and form friendships. Conversely, people who are extremely unattractive have fewer social contacts and, as a result, fewer friendships.

Third, attraction is influenced by *interpersonal similarity*.[5] A substantial body of research demonstrates that we prefer the company of people who are like ourselves. Similarity in attitudes, values, socioeconomic status, and background determines to some extent the degree to which people are mutually attracted.[6] In organizations, this tendency has been shown to be related to satisfaction with supervisors—employees who were similar in important respects to their immediate supervisors were more satisfied with supervision than were employees who were significantly different from their supervisors.[7] In employment interviews, the interviewers gave more positive evaluations to applicants who were similar biographically to themselves.[8] Clearly, we are more attracted to people like ourselves.

Two final determinants of attraction are *status* and *personal rewards*. People holding status higher than our own are more attractive to us, while people of lesser status tend to be less attractive. People who provide us (or potentially can provide us) with personal rewards are more attractive, while those who will not or cannot reward us are less attractive. Not surprisingly, we are more attracted to people who evaluate us positively or give us praise and less attracted to people who criticize us.[9]

Dominance

The ability of one person to exert some control or influence over another seems to be a product of three things: the characteristics of the person trying to exert influence, the characteristics of the person receiving the influence attempts, and the influence strategies employed by the person trying to dominate.[10] A person is more influential if he or she wants to exert influence in the first place, if he or she is perceived as an expert in the topic area under discussion, if he or she is skillful in exerting influence, and if he or she has higher status than the people being influenced. On the other hand, the recipient of the influence attempt is more likely to be influenced if he or she wants to obtain rewards or avoid punishments controlled by the source, if he or she likes the source, or if he or she can be convinced that the source's recommendation is the right thing to do. All of these characteristics of sources and recipients come into play in the organizational setting.

Involvement

A third dimension considers the degree to which we are involved with someone else, or the breadth and depth of our relationship with him or her. Some relationships are rich and intense; others are quite superficial. Social psychologists Altman and Taylor suggest that relationships develop in increments, moving from superficial to more intimate levels.

> As two individuals learn more about each other, largely through observing each other's behavior and through self-disclosure, their relationship grows in importance. The number of topics discussed (breadth) and the depth of information shared suggest whether the relationship can be defined as casual or intimate. With casual relationships breadth is often high, but depth is low. The most intimate relationships have high breadth and depth. As individuals disclose information that is central to the relationship, depth increases.[11]

Altman and Taylor's model, referred to as social penetration theory, is useful in understanding the dimensions of involvement and the communication elements that contribute to intimate relationships. Many individuals function effectively in professional settings by maintaining mostly casual relationships. But when greater intimacy is desired, increasing both depth and breadth of interaction can be helpful.[12]

Situation

The fourth human relationship dimension existing between people is the situation, which considers environments in which communication occurs. Three aspects of the situation seem particularly influential in interpersonal relationships. First, the *physical environment* influences interaction among the individuals.[13] Such things as office furniture arrangement can influence the dominance dimension of interpersonal relationships, while the attractiveness of the surroundings may influence interpersonal attraction. Second, the *social environment* affects interaction.[14] The number of persons present, the role behaviors expected of the interactants, and the social hierarchy have some impact upon relationships. Finally, the *tasks and purposes present* in the encounter affect relationship development. This aspect of the situation takes into account both the observable goals of the individuals and the motivations underlying their behaviors.

From the preceding description of situation, it would seem that all relationships are situationally determined. However, the distinction must be made between long- and short-term situations. In the long term, the president of an organization is higher in dominance than the manager of employee relations. When discussing actions that should be taken during an employee strike, however, the manager is dominant by virtue of his or her expertise. Employees presenting their quality circle's recommendations to top management are dominant during that particular meeting, although their long-term status is much lower than that of the people to whom they are speaking. Finally, while everyone attending a meeting may hold the same job in the organization, the person who, by luck or design, is seated at the head of the long conference table probably will exert the most dominance during that meeting. Thus, while the organization itself might be considered a situation that influences attraction, dominance, and involvement, our intent here is to call attention to short-term influences that affect relationships in organizations.

Interactions

Last, it is important to realize that the four dimensions do not operate independently. They interact so that changes in one of them often produce changes in others. For example, attraction and dominance interact to make high-status individuals more attractive than low-status individuals.[15] And this interaction makes people of low status desire to communicate more with individuals having high status than vice versa. Attraction and involvement also are related. Mutually attracted people are more likely to share personal (involving) information about themselves, and this sharing, in turn, seems to increase attraction.[16] We already have seen that situations produce changes in both attraction and dominance and that physical and social surroundings influence people's tendencies to become involved with one another.[17] Thus, human relationships represent a complex network of mutually influential dimensions.[18]

To help you to establish and manage relationships effectively, we will consider in the next section the specific communication skills that compose relationships in organizations.

Perception

Haney defines perception as "the process of making sense out of experience."[19] That is, we encounter environments, experience them through our senses, and then try to sort out experiences so that they become meaningful to us. While all of our experiences necessarily involve perception, the most important ones are those that demand perception of people. Therefore, the process of person perception will occupy most of our attention in this section.

Stages of Perception

Although complex, the perception process seems to involve three successive stages: *selecting, sorting,* and *interpreting.* The first, selecting, involves both involuntary and voluntary choices. The world presents an infinite array of message stimuli, so that to attend to all of them is utterly impossible. We must make some choices concerning which stimuli we will attend to and which we will ignore. Actually, to some degree, these choices are made for us. Our *physical location* is one factor determining our perceptions. By making certain stimuli available to us, our location limits the experiences we can have and hence the things that we can perceive. But even within our location, we are further limited as our *physiological capacities* make some stimuli imperceptible to us. For example, we cannot hear sounds below twenty or above twenty-thousand cycles per second, even though many sounds fall outside that relatively narrow range. We cannot hear a dog trainer's whistle to which a dog will respond immediately. Our eyes are able to see only about one-seventieth of the light spectrum. Of the things that our eyes can see, our brain can assimilate only about one-ten-thousandth. Before we ever begin deliberate selection of available stimuli, then, a great deal of selection already has occurred.

When we finally enter the realm of things our location and senses allow us to receive, another set of factors enters into the perceptual selection process. Particularly important is *psychological comfort*. Just as we seek to be comfortable physically, so too we select information that makes us psychologically comfortable. To a lesser degree, we avoid information that creates psychological discomfort. We tend to seek information that reinforces views we hold and to avoid information that fails to do so. The reason for this behavior seems to lie in our need for self-esteem, or the need to think well of ourselves. Agreeable information implicitly tells us that we are right or that our ideas are good ones. Disagreeable information tells us that somehow our ideas or beliefs are defective and that we are in need of change. Clearly, reinforcing information makes us comfortable about ourselves; conflicting information may make us uncomfortable.

A second factor is *interest*. We tend to select those things that are interesting to us and ignore things that are not. Perhaps *importance* might be a better term, for the reason something is interesting to us in the first place is that it holds some importance for us. For example, if you are at a party where groups of people are standing around talking, try saying softly the name of one of the people in an adjacent group. Even though that person probably has not heard anything you said before that point, he almost certainly will hear his name. The reason is simple: a person's name is the single most interesting (important) word in the world to that person. Or suppose you were considering buying a car and had almost settled on a certain Buick. Suddenly it seems as though everyone is driving that kind of car. Actually, those cars were there all the time; you just did not perceive them because they had not been important to you until now. Probably you have had similar experiences, all of which illustrate the point that we perceive things that are particularly important or interesting to us.

Perception occurs according to a third factor, *past experience*. To a large degree, we perceive what we expect to perceive. Consider the triangles presented in figure 5.1. Quickly read each of them aloud. Usually, these figures are read as "Dumb as an ox," "Bird in the hand," "Busy as a beaver," and "Paris in the spring." If you saw them that way, look again—you missed something. Unfortunately, this phenomenon of seeing what we expect to see also occurs when we observe people. If we expect them to be obnoxious, they often become that way, regardless of what they actually do. In essence, our prophecies become self-fulfilling.

In addition to molding our expectations, past experience influences perception by creating habitual ways of seeing the world. Figure 5.2 presents another example. There you will find a square consisting of three rows having three dots each. Your task is to connect all nine dots using only four lines and never lifting your pencil from the page. Simple, right? Try it a few times. Unless you have seen this before, you probably will have some difficulty figuring it out. Blame it on past experience. We are used to seeing the world in certain ways, and in this instance, we tend to perceive the figure as a square. Thus, we operate within the limits of the square, trying to find some way to draw four lines. As long as you let perceptual habit confine you to the square, you will be unable to solve the problem. You have to go beyond the square to solve it successfully. This principle also applies to people. If you let past habits of perception limit your observations of the people you meet, you probably will not perceive new people accurately.

Figure 5.1
An exercise in perception.

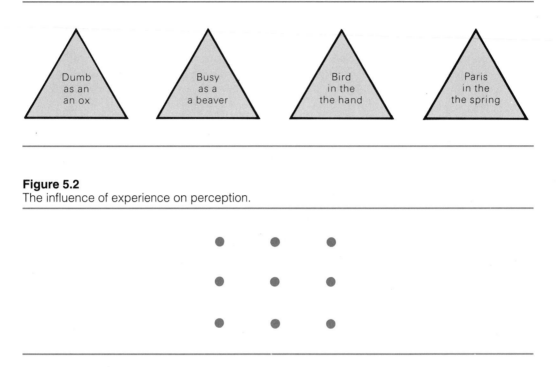

Figure 5.2
The influence of experience on perception.

A final set of variables influencing our selection choices consists of the *characteristics of the stimuli* we encounter. First, we tend to select, often involuntarily, stimuli that are very *intense*. Loud noises, bright lights, and strong smells all attract our attention. To be certain of getting someone's attention, you need only *scream*. But if you continue screaming, the effect wears off. Hence, you need to use another stimulus characteristic, *change*. Our attention is attracted if a stationary object suddenly moves, a moving object stops, or a loud noise becomes soft. While intense stimuli initially gain our attention, variations in the stimuli are needed to maintain attention. *Novel* stimuli also get attention. In communicating, novel behaviors include humor, unbelievable (but true) statements, profanity, and sometimes silence. Finally, *repetition* adds emphasis and, in so doing, draws attention. As we shall see later, each of these stimulus characteristics can be used when transmitting messages to ensure that the receivers are listening. For now, simply be aware that you heed, often unintentionally, stimuli that have the preceding characteristics.

After we have completed the selection stage of perception, determining to which stimuli we will and will not attend, we move to the second stage, *sorting*. We do not perceive things to be random, unrelated occurrences. Rather, we tend to organize our perceptions into coherent patterns. Generally, this process of organization moves through two phases. First, we give things structure. Several laws seem to govern this.

Figure 5.3
Physical proximity and closure.

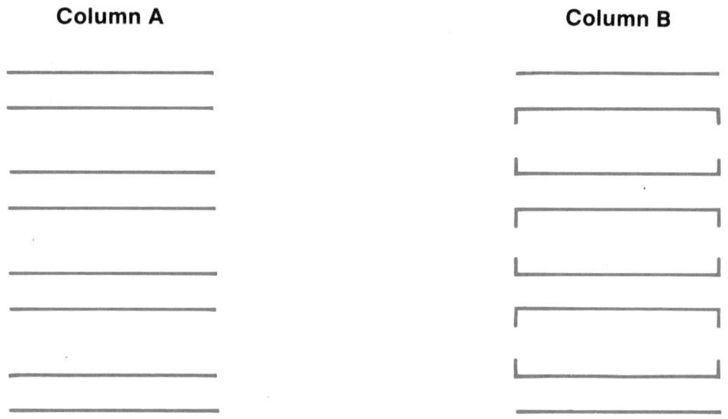

For example, we tend to group together things that are located in close proximity. In figure 5.3, Column A presents eight lines. Although no special relationship exists between any of them, we tend to group them into four pairs simply because of their physical location. Column B adds a second law, closure. We tend to fill in incomplete figures, perceiving the entire figure as though the complete object were there. Thus in Column B, we group the lines differently, tending to see three rectangles with single brackets at the top and bottom of the column. In addition, resemblance affects structure: we group together things that look alike. Finally, we structure our world according to "common fate," relating things that seem to be acting in the same way or moving in a common direction.

When we have selected and sorted stimuli into some coherent pattern, we move to the third stage of perception, *interpretation*. Here, we finally make sense of the things we have experienced. Again, several principles seem to govern the interpretations we form. We interpret people and things in terms of their *context*. For instance, our perceptions of people may change from one context to the next. Someone drinking at a party usually is judged a "social drinker." The same person performing that same behavior in a different context, such as a back alley or a gutter, would be judged a "derelict" or "wino." Yet, only the context has changed.

When encountering people, we also tend to interpret them in terms of our perception of their *intent*. Unless the behaviors we observe are clearly unintentional, we typically assume that they are done deliberately and for a specific purpose. We seek to determine what that purpose or intent is. Usually, that determination is based upon our self-perceptions, as we ask ourselves, "Now what would I be after if I were doing that?" To a large degree, then, these judgments of intent are based on our perceptions of our own behavior, since we operate on the assumption that other people are like ourselves.

Related to the second principle is a third, *projection*. Essentially, we tend to project onto other people our own characteristics. Classical projection involves two processes: attributing our undesirable characteristics to people we dislike and refusing to acknowledge that we possess those characteristics in the first place. On the other hand, attributive projection occurs when we attribute our own favorable characteristics to people we like. Rationalized projection occurs when we attribute thoughts, intentions, or characteristics to other people without knowing why we do so. An incompetent worker would find it discomforting to confront his own incompetence, so instead he attributes his failures to his supervisor, claiming perhaps that "she's always out to get me." While the supervisor may, in fact, have no such motivation, this sort of projection is a handy device with which to rationalize away things that would trouble the worker if he confronted them directly.

Another determinant of interpretation is the *label* we attach to the thing we are perceiving. People really are ambiguous objects. We can see that they are people, but not much more. Any information we can obtain about them helps us to determine what they are about. One such bit of information is the labels other people provide. Before meeting someone, we might be told that "He's a creep" or "She's a genius." When interpreting this person's behavior, these labels may serve as a sort of filter through which our judgments would pass. Thus, we would have developed a kind of individualized stereotype whereby we judged the person in terms of the label attached to him or her, rather than on the basis of the behaviors we actually observed. Clearly, these sorts of judgments are highly unreliable. We would be well advised to rely on our own observations, ignoring as much as possible the labels with which other people provide us.

The final source of interpretation is *familiarity*—the one saving grace in the perceptual process. While context, intent, projection, and labels all tend to lead us astray because they all are based upon something other than the object being perceived, familiarity considers the extent to which we have developed an acquaintance with the object. As a rule, the more familiar we are with something, the more accurately we are able to perceive it. Certainly, this is true with people. The better we know them, the more accurately we come to interpret their behaviors. Despite initial misjudgments, then, we still may be able to develop an accurate view of a person simply by making repeated observations or by increasing our familiarity with him or her.

To this point, we have explored the process through which we proceed when perceiving anything we encounter in the environment. When we must deal specifically with people, however, as we do in organizations, additional factors become important. In the next section, we shall examine several unique elements composing our perceptions of people.

Person Perception

In this section, we will discuss two aspects of our perceptions of other people: the *kinds of information* we use to make judgments about them and the *process by which* our *perceptual judgments form*. An understanding of each aspect is crucial to the development of our abilities to perceive other people accurately.

Perception of Culture and Person

As American corporations hire increasing numbers of immigrants, cross-cultural misunderstandings will occur with greater frequency. For example:

In the United States, calling attention to oneself (particularly to professional achievements) is considered a sign of self-respect. For many Asians, however, calling inordinate attention to oneself may be rude and unprofessional. In an employment interview, this cultural clash could result in a Vietnamese applicant being viewed as "lacking self-esteem."

While direct eye contact is valued in the United States, other cultures avoid eye contact as a sign of respect or deference. An applicant from such a culture probably would be viewed as "unassertive" or "untrustworthy."

Rather than risk losing face or ridicule for misusing an English word, some foreign-speaking workers will simply remain silent. Their American managers often assume they simply have no suggestions or ideas to contribute.

In parts of Asia, the Hispanic countries, and much of Europe, to initiate even the simplest task without being told specifically to do so is considered a defiance of authority. From the American viewpoint, this "lack of initiative" may be interpreted as laziness or a lack of self-confidence.

As the American workplace becomes increasingly multicultural, we must improve our skills in perceiving people. Rather than interpret others' behaviors in terms of our own cultural norms, we must communicate more carefully and thoroughly to ensure that we understand what others do.

From Sondra Thiederman, "Communication: Overcoming Cultural and Language Barriers," *Personnel Journal* 67 (December 1988): 34–40.

The judgments we make about people are derived from some rather specific bits of information. One obvious source of information about people we meet is their *verbal behavior*—the words they speak. However, encounters occur where no words are exchanged or where the words are used to deceive. While we tend to rely heavily upon verbal behavior for information about the person speaking, this source of information can prove unreliable. We therefore look to the person's *nonverbal behavior* as well. The cues that accompany the words the individual speaks (or that operate in the place of words) provide us with a great deal of information about that person. Nonverbal cues may be divided into "static" and "dynamic" characteristics. Static cues include facial features, physique, vocal qualities, clothing, or other elements of the person (such as jewelry, makeup, or hair style) that change slowly. Dynamic cues are bodily orientation (direction in which the person is facing),

Figure 5.4
The process of making perceptual judgments.

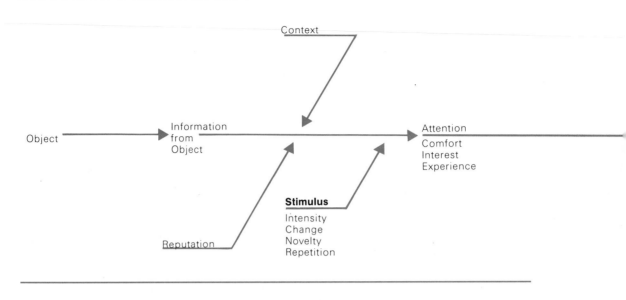

physical location, posture, gestures, facial expressions, eye contact and direction of gaze, tone of voice, and rate or fluency of speech. These cues help us to form more accurate judgments about people we encounter.

The *context* in which we meet people similarly influences our perceptions of them. Research suggests, for example, that when we meet someone in a pleasant, attractive room, we will react more favorably to that individual than if we were to meet that person in a disagreeable setting.[20] The impact of our surroundings seems to generalize to the people we confront in that context so that our perceptions of those people are influenced.

The *reputation* of the people we meet also has an impact on perception. As we already have seen, we use labels to interpret things that otherwise would be ambiguous. So it is with people. When we form judgments of people whom we have encountered recently, we rely rather heavily—too heavily perhaps—on the labels supplied by people whose opinions we respect. Certainly, other people's observations may be useful to us. However, our own observations should take precedence when we judge others.

Having seen the sorts of judgments we make about others and the pieces of information we use to make them, we turn finally to the process by which perceptual judgments occur. Figure 5.4 is a graphic representation of this process.

At the beginning of the process lies the object or person to be perceived. Available to us is some, but by no means all, information about that individual: information provided by actions of the person, information about the person provided by other people, and information from the context that influences our perceptions of the person. This information consists of a myriad of cues that vary in intensity, change, novelty, and repetitiveness. Consequently, some of these cues attract our attention while others do not.

Figure 5.4
(continued)

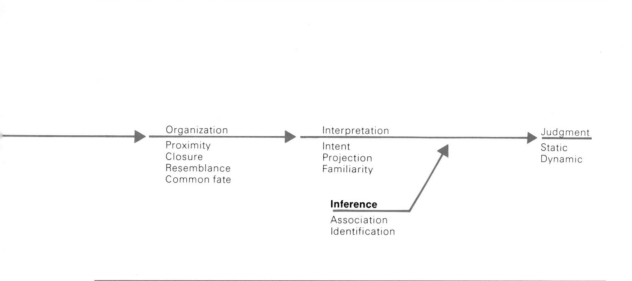

Our attention also is directed by psychological factors: comfort, interest, and experience. Parents often overlook faults in their children that are all too obvious to others; supervisors looking for laziness in workers usually are able to perceive it; and psychiatrists experienced in diagnosing psychological disorders are able to perceive and interpret behavioral cues unobservable to most of us. The attended cues, then, are placed into some coherent pattern according to the organizational rules of proximity, closure, resemblance, and common fate. Subsequent interpretation of this pattern is carried out according to perceived intent, projection, and familiarity. But before the final judgment is rendered, one last element enters the perceptual process: inferences.

Within each of us rests a set of presumptions or rules by which we classify and respond to other people. These rules seem to be of two sorts: *association rules,* which hold that particular characteristics are associated ("People who lack ambition are unlikely to succeed" or "Intelligent people are influential"); and *identification rules,* which provide keys for identifying people who have a particular characteristic ("People who refuse to lend money are stingy" or "People who call other people obscene names in public are impolite and insensitive").

Basically, there are four different approaches to or sources of rules.[21] First, *induction* provides us with rules that are based on our own experiences. We may, for example, interact with several people who have an Ivy League education and find them to be quite arrogant. Based on these unpleasant encounters, we may infer that all people with Ivy League degrees are aloof and arrogant. From that point on, we will expect to encounter an arrogant attitude whenever we are introduced to someone with a degree from Harvard or Yale. On the other hand, *construction* occurs when we invent our own rules. For example, people who have decided that "women are too emotional to be good managers" have likely constructed this rule without any direct experience or information to support it. Indeed, most instances of prejudice or stereotyping involve self-constructed rules.

The third source of rules is through *analogy*. When we draw an analogy, we reason that when one person acts in a particular way, everyone else who is like that person will act in the same way. If an elderly woman hires a young teenager to mow her lawn and the boy proves to be irresponsible, she may conclude that all teenagers are irresponsible. Finally, other people may supply rules to us, so that we obtain them through *authority*. Parents, friends, colleagues, and others with whom we identify may tell us that "People who _____ are _____ ." The blanks can be completed in endless ways. For example, "People who use drugs are no good," "People who come to work late are lazy," "People who hang around bars are asking for trouble," and so on. Of course, we may accept or reject these rules. One powerful authority, incidentally, is television. We know that people obtain information about what types of people do what types of things from the television shows they watch and that, ultimately, they begin to react to others in ways they have observed on television.

We use these approaches to rules to form impressions of others and to make inferences about their attitudes, aptitudes, and likely actions. In these ways, we use our own inferential processes to make judgments about all kinds of people in all kinds of contexts.

In view of the complexity of the process of person perception, you might expect perceptual problems to be common in everyday work settings. And you would be right. Perceptual disagreements have repeatedly been shown to affect the climate of organizations adversely. Several studies have demonstrated that a lack of congruity in role perceptions between two people is associated with higher interpersonal tension and lower evaluations by each of the other person's job performance.[22] Moreover, this tension is often related to decreases in interpersonal attraction.

Numerous investigators have reported that pairs agreeing on appropriate role behaviors tend to be more mutually attracted than pairs holding incongruent role expectations, and some have noted that violations of interpersonal role expectations produce strain and stress.[23]

This lack of congruence also seems to have an impact on job satisfaction. Investigators have found that perceptual ambiguity between superiors and subordinates concerning the latters' role responsibilities is associated with subordinates' dissatisfaction, anxiety, and lack of job interest. These harmful effects of perceptual breakdowns demand that care be taken to ensure accurate perceptions between organizational members.

How can we improve the accuracy with which we perceive people we encounter? Although there is no simple method, we can suggest four techniques that may prove helpful.

First is the method termed *consensual validation,* which involves seeking the agreement or consensus of other people concerning the nature of "reality." In essence, you simply ask others what they think. There are some dangers here, such as the chance of asking people whose perceptions are as strange as our own or making ourselves vulnerable to manipulation by those whom we consult. But for the most part, consensual validation is a useful means of determining whether or not we perceive others accurately.

Second, we can use *repetitive validation,* observing the person several times, to determine whether our first impressions were correct. This method may not solve the problems posed by stable stereotypes and prejudices, but it may aid us in the selection and organization stages of perception.

Third, *multisensory validation* involves the use of other senses to confirm what one sense has received. A desert mirage seems real only as long as we look at it. When we try to touch it, it disappears. Or people may present themselves in a certain way, causing us to derive a perceptual conclusion about them; but if we listen to them, we may discover that they are not the way they look at all. Thus, we ought not rely on just one sense when perceiving others.

Last, with *comparative validation,* we get some indication of perceptual validity by comparing this new perception with experiences of the past. Using this technique, we might ask ourselves, "Does the behavior I am now seeing fit with the behaviors I have seen from this person in the past?" The answer to that question has important implications for our judgments of this person. If the behavior is consistent, perhaps we are in a position to make a judgment about his or her traits; if the behavior is inconsistent, we may need to find out why.

Although any of these four methods may prove useful in increasing perceptual accuracy, our main point is this: Rather than accepting the things we perceive at face value (instead of forming judgments immediately on the basis of what we perceive at the moment), we need to check our perceptions before we judge and act. If we take care in forming perceptions, or if we resolve that we are going to suspend judgment until we have made all the observations we can, we will have done much to improve our perceptions of the people we encounter.

Listening

In organizations, *listening is crucial for several reasons.* First, it provides us with information. To do an effective job at work, there are things we must know: what our job is, how it interacts with other jobs, what our superiors expect of us, and what is going on throughout the company. In business, this sort of information is rarely published. Usually, it is given to us orally, either in formal meetings or informal conversations or interviews. If we listen well, we will assimilate the information we need to succeed. If we do not, we probably will find ourselves in trouble. In addition, listening allows us to think critically. By comparing and analyzing what we hear, we can arrive at conclusions that are more likely to be correct. From these two benefits comes another: good listening makes us better senders. If we correctly interpret what people say to us, we are more likely to respond to them in appropriate ways. To a significant extent, then, our success in organizations depends upon our ability to listen well to the things others say to us.

Unfortunately, there are several barriers to listening that affect all of us. A recent study of perceived listening needs of managers of training in over one hundred *Fortune* 500 industrial organizations revealed that poor listening was one of the most important problems they faced, leading to ineffective performance and low productivity.[24] These training managers pointed out that listening was particularly problematic during meetings, performance appraisals, and in any context involving superior-subordinate communication. Campbell has discovered several sources of systematic error that seem to inhibit listeners' understanding. These include:

1. *Length of the message.* Listeners tend to shorten, simplify, and eliminate detail from the messages they receive, thus losing information and accuracy. The longer the message, the greater the loss.

2. *Middle of the message.* Dispute continues among communication scholars over whether listeners best remember the first or the last things they hear. But everyone agrees on one thing: listeners tend to forget the middle of the message.

3. *Rounding off the message.* Listeners tend to tailor messages to suit their own needs or beliefs, thus distorting the messages' actual content. For instance, an eager employee proposes some bright idea to his boss, who responds with, "That's an interesting idea. Let me give it some thought." Because of his need to feel that the boss responded with affirmation and enthusiasm, the employee may round off her message and "hear" that the boss has endorsed the idea.

4. *Expectations.* In some situations, we are confident we know what the source is going to say. As a result, no matter what that person says, we hear what we expect. For instance, one of your authors came home in the middle of the afternoon one day to find her husband sitting in the family room. As she walked past him (with her arms full of groceries), she "heard" him say what he often says, "I came home early because I just get sick of that office." When she only responded with, "Yeah, I know," he said, "Are you listening to me? I said I came home early because I got really sick in the office." While arguably this example could illustrate the middle-aged hearing loss of one of your authors, her expectations also played a key role. Needless to say, once she had heard the real message, she responded with much greater concern.

5. *False agreement.* When confronted with a source we respect or admire, we often modify her message so that it more closely coincides with our own attitudes and beliefs. Knowing that someone with high credibility possesses views that differ significantly from our own can produce tension. One way of avoiding this tension is to simply "hear" a higher level of agreement than actually exists.

6. *Dichotomous listening.* We have a tendency to polarize the world, to create dichotomies in which things are either one way or the other—right or wrong, good or bad, beautiful or ugly. Most speakers express ideas falling somewhere between these extremes; but we are inclined to assign those ideas to one category or the other.[25]

As Campbell's list suggests, listening problems present themselves in varied forms. Other factors can lead to what Goffman calls "alienation" in communicative interactions. Each interferes with listening accuracy:

1. *External preoccupation.* Whenever we give our attention to something or someone other than the person speaking to us, we are allowing external preoccupation to become a problem. Preoccupations can take many forms—suddenly becoming aware of how long someone is talking (and perhaps glancing at our watches), thinking about a dreaded meeting we have to attend later in the day, or becoming aware of how cold

In the summer of 1992, a high-tech marvel arrived on the shelves of AT&T stores: the video phone. For $1,499, the buyer could purchase what looked like a telephone with a little flip-top television attached. It could be plugged into a regular telephone jack and dialed like a regular phone. If the person at the other end had the same device, the caller could see a flickering, color image of that person during the call.

Of course, that person could see the caller, too. And that was what transformed the common experience of a telephone call into something considerably more complex. The person who works at home, for example, and often dresses casually (to put it kindly) when calling important contacts now may have to consider what he or she wears. In addition, because the video phone would provide a kind of window into one's home that could be opened, in effect, at any time by any caller, it could break down barriers between public areas and places previously considered private.

Even those who are not concerned about their appearance or surroundings would need to learn to use the video phone effectively. For example, sudden movements, such as rearing one's head back to laugh, can look uncoordinated or awkward when transmitted over video phones, and facial expressions often look strange or unnatural when seen via the video phone's somewhat jerky, almost slow-motion picture.

Some businesses were among the first to obtain the video phone. For example, hospitals installed video phones in their birthing centers to let new mothers show their babies to grandparents and relatives. AT&T officials predict that in ten years, the video phone will be as common as today's cordless phone.

From Matthew Nickerson, "Looks Count for a Lot on Video Telephone," *Chicago Tribune*, 26 December 1992, pp. 1, 16.

it is in the room. These sorts of thoughts—which are external to our interaction of the moment—diminish our ability to truly attend to what the other person is saying to us.

2. *Self-consciousness.* Occasionally, we become overly focused on ourselves—perhaps preoccupied with our appearance, grammar, or how we are coming across. For instance, in a job interview, we may become so preoccupied with the sort of impression we are making that we have to ask the interviewer to repeat a question. We simply did not hear it.

3. *Interaction-consciousness.* At times, we may become too preoccupied with the progress of the interaction, neglecting the messages and concentrating only on keeping talk going. Hosts and hostesses suffer from this type of alienation. They don't care what people say, as long as they say something.

4. *Other-consciousness.* Another source of distraction may be the speaker him or herself. We can become so involved with the speaker emotionally that we are unable to deal objectively with what he or she is saying. Or the speaker's physical appearance may be distracting. In either case, we become too preoccupied with the speaker to really listen to what he or she is saying.[26]

Given the list of things that can go wrong in listening, it is hardly surprising to discover that listening errors are both common and expensive. Chicago consultant Bridget Maile, head of Innovative Management Technologies, contends the average listening mistake costs a company about fifteen dollars in lost time, materials, and deadlines.[27] All told, the listening errors made each day by each employee probably cost organizations millions of dollars in lost efficiency or wasted effort.

There are several techniques you may find useful in improving listening. One is called the HEAR formula. HEAR is an acronym formed by the first letter of the four words you should remember when trying to listen to someone: *helpful, empathic, attentive,* and *responsive.*

To be *helpful* when listening to someone, you should make it easy for her to talk with you. One way to do this is to minimize the waiting time and maximize the meeting time for that person. In other words, when someone comes to talk with you, you should not keep that person waiting, cooling her heels, while you do something else because this communicates to her that you have more important things to do and that listening to her is not among your priorities.

Similarly, while meeting with another person, you should try to convey the impression that you have all the time in the world—that nothing could be more important than that meeting with that person. This means avoiding glances at your watch or the clock on the wall, not fidgeting, and not giving the impression that you need to get this meeting over as quickly as possible. Even if you are pressed for time, you must always try to convey to the other person the feeling that the time you do have is all his.

Helpfulness also is improved by making the environment as attractive and informal as possible because attractive and informal settings encourage interaction. Similarly, you should eliminate potential distractions (take the phone off the hook or move to a private location), and when the meeting is over, you should thank the person for talking with you and invite him to meet with you again some time soon. All of these things help people to talk with you—an important element of being an effective listener.

To be *empathic,* you need to show the other person that you truly understand how she feels and that you care about those feelings. This is very different from sympathy, in which you simply feel sorry for the other person. Most people want empathy; they may resent sympathy. To improve the empathy dimension, you first should ask about the person's well-being; show you care about her as a person, regardless of the topic under question. Then, when she is talking to you, you should occasionally use some of the "active listening" techniques we discuss in the next chapter, such as paraphrasing the things she has just said or reflecting back to the person the feelings she seems to be experiencing.

Attentiveness means demonstrating to the other person that you are indeed listening to his or her point of view. To improve the attention you show, first suspend your reactions; do not react until you have heard everything the other person has to say. To the greatest extent possible, withhold judgment and emotions; when you react, do so as logically and calmly as possible. When you disagree, show you understand the other's points before you begin to present your own. Paraphrase or summarize the person's ideas and let him or her know that you did, indeed, understand what was being said. Then present your ideas. Finally, you might periodically summarize the points the other

Effective Listening: The HEAR Formula

To Be Helpful:	Minimize waiting time
	Act unhurried
	Make environment attractive
	Eliminate potential distractions
	Invite future interactions
To Be Empathic:	Show the other's feelings are understood
	Show the other person is cared about
	Use active listening techniques
To Be Attentive:	Suspend your reactions
	Show understanding before disagreeing
	Paraphrase and summarize
To Be Responsive:	Maintain eye contact
	Use nonverbal reinforcement
	Ask questions
	Let other person talk

person has just covered ("Let me see. You said that Bill first went to . . . and that he then. . . . Is that right?"). You should always avoid distractions or directing your attention somewhere else when someone is talking to you.

Finally, you should listen *responsively,* showing that you not only are paying attention, but that you are actively interested in the person and the topic. Maintain eye contact by looking at people most of the time they are talking to you. Use nonverbal reinforcement (such as nodding your head occasionally and sitting up straight, leaning slightly toward the speaker) to show responsiveness, or use vocal prompts such as "uh-huh," "um-hmm," "OK," and so on. When appropriate, ask questions to display your interest and to get useful information. Avoid giving advice unless you are explicitly asked to do so. And above all, let the other person do the talking.

You also can improve your listening efforts by using some of the techniques of *active listening.*[28] Essentially, active listening is using "sending" communication behaviors to help the other person communicate more clearly with you. We will examine some of these techniques in chapter 6.

Sending Messages

We must again emphasize the importance of skill in sending messages to other people. Just as listening and perceptual skills are vital to the establishment of desirable relationships in organizations, so too is skill in the use of verbal and nonverbal symbols. For example, Sullivan reported the results of research comparing successful company presidents with average college graduates.[29] The findings showed that presidents excelled in several areas, including (in order): verbal skills, mathematical reasoning, logical thinking, personality (presidents were more dynamic and assertive, with more positive attitudes toward other people), energy and drive, ascendance (presidents had more leadership confidence and assertiveness), personal relations (presidents had greater ability to get along with others and, perhaps surprisingly, were kinder, more sympathetic, understanding, tolerant, and warm-hearted), and values (most presidents placed high value on gaining power and responsibility and on attaining the financial rewards that go with those objectives). The importance of verbal skill is therefore obvious; what is less obvious is that each of these other qualities manifests itself in various communication behaviors. As we have said repeatedly, your ability to succeed is directly tied to your ability to communicate.

The Effects of Words

When speaking to others, we use words that have an impact on two parties: those to whom we speak and ourselves. For years, a group of scholars called *general semanticists* have studied the impact of words on their users and their recipients, and they have identified some common problems that stem from the ways in which we use our language.[30]

Allness is one such problem, often caused by the word *is*. When we attach a label to someone, as when a foreman complains about a worker that "he is lazy," or a worker says of a foreman, "He's a slave driver," we implicitly state that the label is all that the person is. A lazy worker is lazy, and nothing more. A slave driver is nothing except that. Thus, we overlook the person's other, perhaps more desirable, characteristics. We forget that his behavior may have resulted simply from having a bad day, and, indeed, we lose sight of the person's humanity.

Categorizing is another danger of language. To some degree, we have to attach labels to people: he is a foreman; she is an executive. But these labels sometimes cause us to ignore differences between people whom the label fits. In truth, every individual is different, so to treat the members of a certain category the same way is to deal with them impersonally and inappropriately.

Time-fixing is the tendency for words to ignore the fact that people change through time. When we label someone "lazy," we tend to see the person that way over time. But people change continuously, so to assume that a person is lazy now because he or she was lazy yesterday or last week is often inaccurate.

Polarization occurs when words cause us to think in dichotomous or polarized terms. The person who polarizes thinks in either-or terms, refusing to acknowledge shades of gray. Since in reality most things and people fall somewhere between the extremes, this tendency for language to cause us to see things as opposites produces a perceptual distortion of the actual situation.

All of these pitfalls are potential problems because they cause us to lose sight of the reality with which we are dealing and to focus instead on the "word maps" that inadequately represent that reality. As a result, we and our listeners begin to deal with people as objects, stereotypes, labels, or other dehumanized elements of our environment. Such thinking can only harm relationships in organizations.

Improving the Use of Language

Today, many organizations are recognizing and responding to the problematic aspects of language. "In big organizations with massive, complex operations, there's a tendency to think in terms of labels," remarked A. W. Clausen, who headed Bank of America during the 1970s. "Those people over there are tellers, those are managers, these are officers. These are grade 20s, grade 15s, grade 30s, and so on. The names are forgotten along with sensitivities, anxieties, frustrations. The tendency is to dehumanize."[31] Such dehumanization can be avoided only if we use words carefully.

But what can we do to overcome the problems language poses? Semanticists have developed several devices designed to help us use words better. The mental use of *etcetera,* for example, helps us to overcome the problem of allness. Whenever we attach a label, we should use *etcetera.* Thus, "he or she is an executive, etcetera" reminds us that the label does not say all there is to say about the individual. "Indexing" helps us deal with the problem of categorizing by asking us to attach mentally an index number to each member of the category of which we speak: student 1, student 2, and so on. In this way, we remind ourselves that each member is an individual. "Dating" or mentally attaching a date to every observation we make (for example, "He is lazy, May 13, 1993") reminds us that people change constantly and that we must constantly reassess the conclusions we have drawn.

On a more specific level, Hegarty suggests some verbal habits to avoid if words are to be used to your greatest advantage.[32] There are, he claims, some verbal behaviors that either annoy other people or cause them to draw unfavorable conclusions about the speaker. Among them are the following:

1. Repeated use of the same conversational closing, such as "take care" or "take it easy." These are both impersonal and indicative of a lack of creativity and thoughtfulness.
2. Repeated use of the same designation (referring to everyone as "you guys"), the same modifier (calling everything "cool" or "tremendous"), the same expression ("wow" or "good grief" or "no kidding"), the same cliché ("a stitch in time" or "strike while the iron is hot"), or conversational fillers such as "you know" and "like." These become annoying and show sloppy mental habits.
3. Mistakes in usage, such as the double negative ("They can't hardly expect us to do that!"; "Irregardless"; "He never did nothing"); misuse of *do* and *did, don't* and *doesn't* ("He don't have any right to do that," "She admitted she done it"); misuse of *knew, know,* and *known* ("He knowed we couldn't do it"); misuse of *gone* and *went* ("I wish I had went"); misuse of personal pronouns ("They fired him and I," "They did it to her and myself"); misuse of *was* and *were* ("They was going"); use of "dem" and "dose" ("I don't like dose guys").

Mistakes in grammar and pronunciation call undesired attention to you. It makes no difference whether you grew up in the hills of West Virginia or on the streets of Chicago's South Side; improper use of the language will hurt your credibility in an organization and probably limit your ability to rise in the hierarchy. Be sure your English is good.

The final recommendation we can offer in the effective use of language concerns courtesy. Too often, people in organizations are under pressure and, as a result, begin treating one another discourteously. Barton discusses the use of "put downs and vulgarity" in business, claiming that "managers who use vulgarity often feel it adds an extra bit of shock and sophistication to their interchanges with employees. In most cases, however, it alienates employees and places them on the defensive. Using put downs, snappy replies, and vulgarity destroys the speaker's credibility."[33] The person who can remain courteous even in a crisis impresses everyone else with his or her coolness under fire and professionalism in dealing with others. Such basics as saying "please" when making a request (rather than ordering someone to "Get me the Watsis file") or saying "thank you" when a request is fulfilled (instead of taking the Watsis file without even looking up) help enormously in gaining and maintaining the respect and cooperation of others.

With all of these recommendations in mind, then, we move to the nonverbal elements of communication in human relationships.

Nonverbal Symbols

Verbal symbols are of undeniable importance, forming the basic unit of our communications with others. But of at least equal importance are the myriad of unspoken, nonverbal cues that accompany spoken messages. Indeed, Birdwhistell argues that these cues are even more important than words.[34]

Roles of Nonverbal Cues

To understand nonverbal cues as they operate in human communication, we need to consider the roles they play or the things they do when people interact. These roles become most apparent when we consider nonverbal cues as they relate to verbal messages. To see nonverbal messages in action, consider this hypothetical situation. You walk into the company president's luxurious office to ask him to give you a raise. During the encounter, the nonverbal cues you receive perform the following roles:

1. *Repeating.* "Sit down," the president says, pointing to a chair in front of his huge desk. His nonverbal cue, a hand gesture, serves to repeat the message he has spoken. "Would you care for a cigarette?" he asks, holding a box out toward you. Again, his gesture repeats his words.
2. *Contradicting.* "You know," he begins as you light your cigarette, "I'm a simple man. I've always been satisfied with little things." His office with its wood paneling, leather-upholstered furniture, deep-pile carpet, and teak desk contradicts his words. "Now, I've always been happy to talk to people who are eager to improve their lot

in life." He kept you waiting nearly an hour in his outer office and now speaks to you with a scowl on his face. His nonverbal cues thus suggest that he is anything but happy to see you.

3. *Substituting.* "And I wish the company had enough money to give everyone who deserves it a raise. But. . . ." His voice trails off, and he shrugs and shakes his head. These gestures substitute for words. He does not have to say, "No, and there's nothing I can do about it." His nonverbal gestures have said it for him.

4. *Elaborating.* Suddenly, the president bursts into tears. Between sobs, he manages to stammer, "I hate having to do this. You can't know how bad I feel about not being able to give you a raise. Sometimes this job is hell!" His words express his feelings, but his actions elaborate on them, showing us just how much he means what he says.

5. *Accenting.* Slowly, the president rises from his chair, struggling to regain his composure. "Darn it!" he explodes, pounding his fist on the desk. "Darn it, I'm going to give you that raise, even though we can't afford it. It won't be as much as you asked for—three cents a week, in fact—but we need to do something for employees as faithful as you." His fist pounding serves to accent his "darn its," and his rising out of his seat likewise accents both his dominance and his beneficence.

6. *Regulating.* "I'm glad you came in here," he concludes, extending a clammy hand. "We need to talk like this more often." He then sits down, turns away, and begins reading the *Wall Street Journal*. The role of these last behaviors is to regulate or control the interaction. In essence, he is saying, "Our conversation is now over. No further communication is desired. Please leave."

Thus, the roles of nonverbal cues are determined largely by their relationships to spoken messages. Nonverbal behaviors may produce or change meaning by repeating the verbal message, contradicting it, substituting for it, elaborating on it, accenting parts of it, or regulating it. Each of these functions is important, as our example demonstrates, and each of them shows the crucial nature of nonverbal communication in our everyday interactions.

Impact of Nonverbal Cues

Although nonverbal cues can be divided into any number of categories, researchers typically have placed them into six. We will consider each category individually, noting how the behaviors and cues in each seem to influence human communication.

Environment

The physical setting in which communication occurs constitutes the environmental element of nonverbal communication. As you might suspect, the work environment is important, particularly from the viewpoint of those within that environment. A study by the Buffalo Organization for Social and Technical Innovation showed that satisfaction with work space created an extra sixteen hundred dollars of productivity annually in a white-collar worker.[35]

From Jose Martinez, "Can You Be Categorized as Visionary or Stabilizer?" *Chicago Tribune,* 15 March 1992, Sec. 7, p. 7.

According to Steele, the dimensions and functions that immediate physical settings have for people include the following:[36]

1. *Security and shelter:* protection from harmful or unwanted things, such as a roof keeping out the rain or thick walls keeping out sounds. Such protection can include both physical and psychological security; privacy, for example, may be provided or prevented by the physical surroundings.

2. *Social contact:* arrangements that permit or promote social interaction, such as the water cooler around which people accidentally come into face-to-face contact; takes into account the arrangement of facilities, locations of people in relation to one another, and amount of mobility allowed by the setting. Some locations are high-contact (such as desks near doorways), while others are low-contact (desks in a back corner of a room). The presence or absence of central gathering places (such as break areas or coffee machines) also is influential in promoting or discouraging communication.

3. *Symbolic identification:* the messages sent by settings that tell someone what a person, group, or organization is like or what his, her, or their position in the organization is. Companies will select arrangements, furniture, and so on to project a certain image or corporate culture both to their employees and visitors. For example, at Systek Corporation in Oak Brook, Illinois, Rick Wargo, director of

national sales, selected teak furniture for all of his sales staff. The reason for his choice was that "Systek is a people-oriented company and the wood has a warmth much greater than steel."[37]

The physical arrangement has clear implications for the dominance dimension of organizational relationships. The relative status of individuals, groups, and entire departments is communicated by the arrangement of the physical environment.

In large buildings, individual floors often express the dominance implicit in the hierarchy. The corner offices on upper floors are occupied by senior executives or department heads. Middle offices are occupied by executives of lesser status. The most powerful executive has the largest office with the most windows and best view. Middle management personnel have one-window offices. Employees on the lowest rungs—clerks, secretaries, typists—work together in a large, open room.

Similarly, accessibility is inversely related to status. Presidents often have two or three secretaries and two or three waiting rooms one must go through to get to them. Lower-level managers have one secretary and no waiting room. Even in the open areas, there are status differences. Recently we observed one large room housing a personnel manager, the personnel assistant manager, and several secretaries. As figure 5.5 shows, the manager had a corner cubicle, the assistant manager had a corner desk with two screens one had to go around to see him, the secretaries had desks in the center of the room, and the low-status clerk-typists had desks in the front of the room nearest the door. Thus, the more important you are, the more difficult it is to see and communicate with you.

This odd characteristic of organizations, incidentally, is one communication-related problem with severe implications. The people who must be involved in organizational communication are the executives. The more important an executive is, the more crucial it is that he or she be in the communication network. Yet organizational arrangements work to produce the opposite effect. Important executives are inaccessible, while clerk-typists are a part of virtually everything. It is small wonder, then, that studies of organizations repeatedly have found executives to know far less about organizational matters than do lower-level secretaries and clerks.[38]

Furniture arrangement is another important element of the environment. Michael Korda, a publishing house executive, describes how placement of a desk and chairs in an office can influence the dominance the occupants exert over their visitors.[39] Figure 5.6 illustrates three office arrangements, each exerting a different level of dominance. In the first arrangement, power is minimized. The visitor sits next to the desk, making him or her virtually equal to the occupant and forcing the occupant to assume a relatively uncomfortable position to talk to him or her. In the second arrangement, the occupant is more powerful. He sits regally behind his desk, which is interposed between him and his visitor. But the third arrangement is most dominant of all. The visitor sits with his or her back to the wall, occupying minimal space, while the occupant has the remainder of the office in which to move about. This, coupled with the interposed desk, makes the situation the most domineering.

Finally, things within the environment can communicate information about the individual occupant. One study found, for example, that the presence of aesthetic objects (such as paintings, a color calendar, and a potted fern) in a faculty member's office

Figure 5.5
Accessibility as related to status.

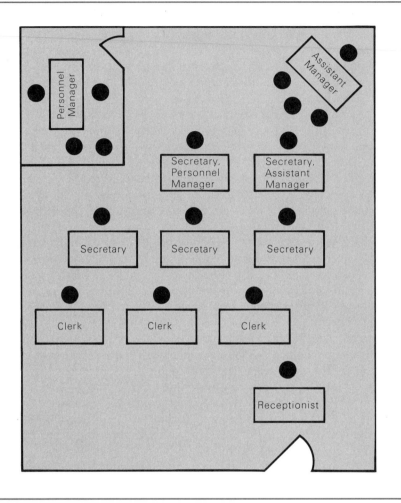

significantly increased perceptions of his or her authoritativeness and trustworthiness. The same study also discovered that the presence of profession-related objects (including award plaques and a professional-looking library) in a faculty member's office produced a similar effect.[40]

While environments influence perceptions of status, professional competence, and so on, it is worth noting that people may arrange their environments differently because of their status. One study found that high-status occupants tended to "place their desks between themselves and the door rather than against a side or back wall."[41] Low-status occupants were more likely to place their desks touching a wall, thus demonstrating that, while environments affect their occupants, occupants also shape the environment.

Figure 5.6
Furniture arrangement as part of environment.

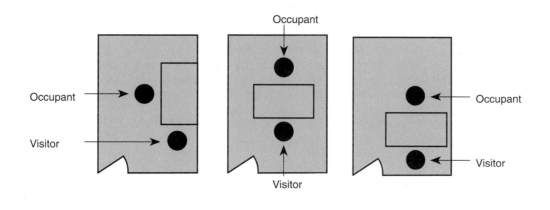

4. *Task instrumentality:* the appropriateness of facilities for carrying out tasks. This function considers specific settings and tasks, such as the soundproof room needed for taping records, the locations of groups that work together, the presence of equipment, and sensory conditions. While physical environments affect interaction, perceptions of status, and the like, it is important to remember that they are constructed to get work done. Offices are arranged in ways that theoretically will enhance productivity; production lines are similarly set up to promote work. Industrial engineers and architects have traditionally concerned themselves only with the task instrumentality of the environments they design. Only recently have they begun to focus on the impact of environments on the relationships among the people working within them.
5. *Pleasure:* the gratification the place gives to those who use it, such as the views employees enjoy from the sixtieth floor of the Sears Tower in Chicago. This factor includes the absence of unpleasant stimuli (noise, smells, temperature) and the presence of pleasant stimuli (music, colors, and other visual stimuli). However, it is important to remember that pleasure is an individual thing; conflicts over what stimuli are pleasurable sometimes occur among organizational members.

In each of these important respects, then, the physical environment shapes the interrelationships of the people who work within it.

Proxemics

Proxemics is the placement of individuals relative to other individuals—their physical closeness—as well as the way they communicate through interpersonal space and distance. In general, people tend to sit close together when they are involved in a group working on a common problem. But if the same group is given individual tasks to work on for a few minutes, they will tend to move farther apart. Overall, groups perform better, more persuasively, and more cooperatively at close, face-to-face distances (eighteen

One high-tech manufacturing firm thought it would improve employee morale by playing music over the building's loudspeakers while people worked. When management asked employees whether they wanted music, the response was overwhelmingly affirmative. However, as soon as the music began, so did the conflict. Some employees wanted a rock station; many others wanted country and western; still others wanted salsa, reggae, jazz, or soul. One employee wanted classical. Cliques of music lovers formed, and conflict between them was common. Finally, management had to stop the music altogether. While some organizations are able to overcome problems such as these (the Chicago Cubs, for example, allows its employees to play their own radios in the locker room, with the result that player interviews must be conducted through a background din of five different radios, each blaring a different kind of music), conflicts over what is "pleasurable" are not uncommon.

inches versus thirty-six inches). But if the group describes itself as "crowded," these positive characteristics begin to disappear.[42]

Gender differences have been found in reactions to group density. American women tend to sit closer together in groups than do men. All-male groups sit farthest apart, mixed-sex groups at an intermediate distance, and all-female groups closest together. It has been argued that women in groups are more likely to develop warm, close, affiliative relationships than are men. In general, males have been found to prefer meeting in large rooms and to give each other higher ratings in that setting, while women prefer smaller meeting rooms. Several studies have concluded that dense environments have a more adverse effect on males than on females.[43]

The seating arrangement of a group of people is particularly important in proxemics. A great deal of evidence suggests that seating has a significant impact on patterns of communication. Research indicates that people seated directly across a table from one another communicate most often and that people seated at the end of the table communicate more with the entire group than do people seated in any other position. These effects on interaction in turn have an effect on group leadership; people seated at the ends almost always emerge as group leaders by virtue of their easy access to all the other members.[44] Our physical proximity to other group members, then, influences our ability to influence them.

Proxemics in groups has an impact on the involvement dimension of human relationships by encouraging or discouraging interaction among the people present. Again, some organizations are taking this into account. Peters and Waterman report that

The president of a company on our list recounted what he allowed was an important recent activity: "I got rid of the little four-person round tables in the company dining room, replaced them with army mess tables—long, rectangular ones. It's important. At a little round table, four people who already know each other will sit down and eat lunch with each other day in and day out. With long mess tables, strangers come in contact. Some scientist gets talking to some marketer or some manufacturer from some other division. It's a probability game. Every little bit enhances the odds of important idea exchange."[45]

Artifacts

The things with which we decorate our bodies also are important in communication. In most organizations and in society as a whole, clothing seems to be a strong indicator of status. The implications of this clothing-status relationship become apparent when we consider a study conducted by Lefkowitz, Blake, and Mouton, who observed the conformity behavior of pedestrians in a large city.[46] An accomplice wandered about the city violating the "Don't Walk" sign at street corners while the experimenters watched the behavior of other pedestrians to determine whether they followed his example. This was done on two consecutive days. On the first day, the accomplice wore a high-status outfit—a suit—and carried an attaché case. On the second day, he was dressed in a low-status janitor's outfit. The results were startling. When the accomplice was well dressed, several people followed him across the street; but when he was poorly dressed, no one followed him. The researchers concluded that status, as shown by one's clothing, has an impact upon one's ability to influence other people.

A variety of works have been published dealing with the impact of clothing upon success in the organization. *Dress for Success* probably is the most widely read, although many others also are on the market.[47] Our own observations, however, indicate that the rules suggested by *Dress for Success* and other such works do not hold in today's organization. Rather, a variety of factors determine which "uniform" is most appropriate in a particular company. Many organizations have a dress code for their employees, and many require (and often provide) uniforms.

Still other differences are found in different industries: financial institutions (for example, banks and insurance companies) seem to value conservative, dressy outfits (such as blue three-piece suits for men and conservatively colored suits for women). Newer high-tech companies (such as Apple Computer) encourage employees to dress more casually, and a three-piece suit worn in their manufacturing plants would be regarded as strange. Interestingly, however, the father of high-tech, IBM, traditionally has had an unspoken rule that everyone wears blue suits and white shirts or blouses, and only recently has that norm been relaxed to allow colored shirts and less conservative suits. Small manufacturing concerns almost always are shirtsleeves organizations; supervisors and managers wear slacks and open-collared shirts rather than blue jeans and T-shirts, but rarely do people wear suits.

There also are regional differences in clothing preferences: companies in or near large cities in the East and Midwest encourage more conservative, dressier appearances; companies in smaller communities tend more to emphasize sport coats or shirt sleeves; companies in the West and South are also less formal, varying from sport coats to very casual dress, depending on the industry. Note, however, that we are speaking here in terms of men's clothing. Norms for women's clothing still have not become clear enough for us to draw any firm conclusions.

In any event, what is important is that every organization has its norms for appearance. By adhering to those norms, and perhaps developing an appearance just slightly "better" than that expected by the organization, you can enhance your own credibility to some degree. However, by violating the norms and dressing to either extreme (too casual or too dressy), you may harm your image in the organization and even be subject to disciplinary action. It is also important to dress in a way that makes you feel good about yourself. Research has shown that those who feel inappropriately dressed often exhibit hostility, withdrawal, or aggression. However, those who feel positively about the way they are dressed tend to be more outgoing, friendly, happy, and relaxed, and they report feeling more confident.[48]

Kinesics

The category of kinesics includes general body movements—postures, gestures, facial expressions, and eye behavior. Each of these has been found influential in communication. In studies of body posture, Mehrabian found a close relationship between posture and liking for the other person.[49] For example, when confronting someone they intensely dislike, women tend to look away from the other person as much as possible. If they like the other person, they vary their direction of face, sometimes looking squarely at that person and sometimes looking away. When dealing with a total stranger, they tend to look directly at that person. No consistent results were obtained for males. For both sexes, however, leaning forward seemed to indicate liking for the other, while leaning backward seemed to convey negative feelings. Experts on nonverbal communication agree that our posture communicates much about our moods and emotions. We judge whether others are happy, sad, confident, or determined based on the way they carry themselves. In general, wider, more open body postures result in more perceived credibility and persuasive power, whereas narrower postures (legs and arms held close together) reduce status.

While the effects of gestures upon others remain somewhat a mystery, we do know something about the factors underlying a person's gestural behavior. Mehrabian and Williams observed that people trying to be persuasive show more gestures and head nods and fewer postural shifts than others.[50] O'Connor and Baird found that emergent group leaders tend to show more positive head nods and gesticulations of the shoulders and arms than do nonleaders.[51] When gestures are tied to the rhythm of our speech, they appear to help listeners follow our remarks. People who are relaxed as they communicate tend to use more gestures and to use gestures that are more natural and conversational. Highly nervous speakers may use no gestures at all, too many repetitive gestures, or touch themselves (for example, by playing with hair or jewelry)—all of which are perceived as signs of nervousness or discomfort.[52]

We may also use kinesic communication to control or regulate interpersonal communication. One example is turn-taking. We may signal the end of our turn by stopping or by relaxing our hand movements. We may shift our heads or eye position, or change our posture. Most important, we can signal our desire to talk by leaning forward and/or using gestures prior to speaking. In group settings, dominant persons are often seen leaning forward and using gestures to maintain the floor, preventing interruptions from other group members. Some scholars believe that it is largely kinesic behavior that determines who talks when and for how long. Listeners' kinesic movements are also important to observe since they provide clues as to who really is being listened to and whose opinions are valued. Listeners typically turn their bodies toward someone they want to hear. By not turning toward someone who is speaking, they communicate the opposite attitude.[53]

Facial expressions and eye contact are other areas of kinesics that seem important in communication. Rosenfeld noted that people seeking approval seem to smile more frequently, and Mehrabian and Williams observed that people trying to persuade others also showed an increase in facial activity.[54] Several studies have shown that, unlike other aspects of nonverbal communication, basic facial expressions are rather universal, carrying the same fundamental meaning throughout the world.[55] Because we all feel that we are pretty good at reading others' facial expressions, we sometimes believe that we can accurately assess others' reactions to what we or others are saying. But often we are inaccurate because most people mask or conceal their facial expressions with "public faces." Studies of eye contact in human communication have identified the situations in which we seek or avoid eye contact with others. Generally, we will seek eye contact with others when we want to communicate with them, when we are physically distant from them, when we like them, when we are extremely hostile toward them (as when two bitter enemies try to stare each other down), or when we desire feedback from them. Conversely, we avoid contact with others when we wish to avoid communication, are situated physically close to them, dislike them, are trying to deceive them, or are uninterested in what they have to say. Given the positiveness of eye contact, we should find that it improves communication—and indeed it does. Some investigators have found that messages accompanied by eye contact were more favorably interpreted by observers than were messages sent without eye contact.[56] Indeed, aversion of eye contact in a group setting is sometimes perceived by others as an indication of disinterest, apathy, rudeness, shyness, nervousness, or even dishonesty or deceit! Eye contact also seems indicative of status—Mehrabian noted that high-status individuals usually receive more eye contact from other group members than do individuals of low status.[57]

Touch

The fifth aspect of nonverbal behavior, touching, is perhaps the most primitive. Even in the womb, the child can be stimulated by touch.[58] As a form of communication, touching is very important. Montagu argues that a person's social and psychological development is hampered if that person receives too little touching from others early in life.[59] Although touching can serve many different functions, including sexual expression, from an organizational perspective, two are especially important: *expressing supportiveness* and *communicating power or dominance*.

Touching in a supportive way can take many forms—putting our arms around other people, patting them on the arm or hand, holding their hands in our own. Generally, we do not touch people we dislike (unless we are fighting with them), so the act of touching someone communicates a general message of liking and support. Through touching we can communicate consolation, empathy, liking, and varying degrees of commitment. In organizational settings, a common form of touching is the handshake.

From J. T. Auer, *The Joy of Selling* (Toronto: Stoddard Publishing, 1992), pp. 45–51.

Used for meeting others, greeting others, and saying goodbye, the handshake, while expected as a professional gesture for both men and women, is a fairly minor social affair. In general, in casual encounters, we keep touching at a minimum. As relationships develop, the nature and frequency of touching change dramatically.

Some management theorists have warned about appropriate uses of touching. Blanchard and Johnson, in their popular book, *The One Minute Manager,* point out that managers should only touch others when they are communicating something positive, such as encouragement, reassurance, or support. They view negative touching, associated with criticizing, admonishing, or disciplining as quite inappropriate.[60]

One of the reasons that Blanchard and Johnson offer this advice to managers is because of the power/dominance function of touching. That is, it is the high-status person who has the power to touch. It is the police officer who touches the accused, the teacher who touches the student, the doctor who touches the patient, and the manager who touches the employee. As Nancy Henley points out in *Body Politics,* it would be a breach of etiquette for the lower-status person to touch the person of higher status.[61] Henley further argues that in addition to indicating relative status, touching also demonstrates the assertion of male power and dominance over women.

Whether or not Henley's assertion is true, much research has examined gender differences in touching. Mothers have been found to touch children of both sexes and of all ages a great deal more than fathers do.[62] Women touch their fathers more than men do. Female babies are touched more than male babies. And women reportedly have a greater desire to be held than do men.[63] In general, more touching reportedly occurs among opposite-sex friends than among same-sex friends. However, since our culture tends to frown on same-sex touching, many people may not feel comfortable acknowledging the extent to which they touch those of the same sex.

Whatever gender differences exist, cross-cultural differences are more apparent. In one study, for example, students from the United States reported being touched twice as much as did students from Japan.[64] In Japan, there is a strong taboo against strangers touching, and the Japanese are especially careful to maintain adequate distance. Another obvious cross-cultural difference is in the Middle East, where same-sex touching in public is extremely common. Men will walk with their arms on each other's shoulders, a practice that would not be comfortably received in the United States, except in specific situations, such as locker-room celebrations.

These cross-cultural nonverbal differences can cause real problems when people from different countries and cultures attempt to interact effectively. The Japanese, for instance, may be perceived as distant or aloof, while southern Europeans may be viewed as pushy or aggressive. An awareness of and sensitivity to cultural differences in touching behavior are crucial as people from different cultural backgrounds try to work together in organizations.

Vocalics

Aspects of the voice—pitch, volume, quality, and rate—that accompany spoken words make up the final category of nonverbal cues, vocalics. Apparently, people make several sorts of judgments about others on the basis of vocal cues. As Addington discovered, we judge personality characteristics on the basis of voice. Among the responses he found to various types of voices were:

1. *Breathy voices.* Males having this characteristic were rated young and artistic. Females were rated pretty, petite, effervescent, and high-strung.
2. *Nasal voices.* Males and females both were given a wide variety of negative characteristics.
3. *Throaty voices.* Males were rated older, realistic, mature, sophisticated, and well-adjusted. Females were termed masculine, unintelligent, lazy, ugly, sickly, careless, naive, neurotic, and assigned a variety of other undesirable characteristics.
4. *Flat voices.* Males were rated masculine, sluggish, cold, and withdrawn. Females received identical characterizations.[65]

Another judgment that is based on vocal cues is speaker recognition. On the basis of vocal cues alone, we can accurately recognize the identity of the person to whom we are listening (provided, of course, we already are acquainted with that person and his or her voice).[66] On the basis of voice we also may be able to recognize personal characteristics of the speaker, such as age, sex, or race.[67] Vocal cues give us hints about the emotional state of the speaker—whether he or she is happy, sad, angry, or pleased.[68]

Perhaps the most important function of vocalics is modifying our verbal messages. For instance, researchers have identified at least two dozen ways of saying yes.[69] There are definite yeses and wishy-washy yeses, happy and sad ones, seductive, confused, and assured ones. When we interact with others, they will believe our vocal meaning whenever our verbal and vocal messages are at odds.

Our intent in this section on nonverbal cues has been primarily descriptive. We have sought to sensitize you to the nonverbal cues encountered when communicating with others in almost any setting. By putting this knowledge into practice, you should be able to communicate more effectively in your daily encounters with other people.[70]

Using Communication Skills to Improve Relationships

To this point, we have reviewed the nature of human relationships and the verbal and nonverbal communication elements that allow those relationships to exist. In this final section, we turn to some broader strategies for improving relationships in the organizational setting.

As we saw earlier, relationships consist of three basic dimensions: attraction, dominance, and involvement. These three vary according to the situations in which the inter-actants find themselves, and these dimensions influence one another. Nevertheless, we will consider each of them again briefly, noting some ways in which each might be strengthened in the organizational setting.

Attraction

It would be foolish for us to try to present "ten ways to make people like you." There simply is no sure-fire formula for making oneself attractive to everyone, despite the many paperback books that claim there is. We can, however, point to some behaviors that, in the view of several authors, drive people away and thus impair the attraction dimension of relationships. Obviously, our recommendation will be to avoid these behaviors.

Hegarty claims that certain verbal behaviors prevent the development of good relationships in organizations.[71] One such behavior is complaining. While occasional complaining may bring people together for periodic gripe sessions, constant complaining becomes irritating to everyone—particularly one's superiors in the organization. An occasional complaint among friends may promote group cohesiveness; continual complaining, Hegarty argues, brings about social isolation. Avoidance of complaining and maintenance of a generally positive attitude will enhance your success on the attraction dimension.

Yet another method to improve the attraction element of organizational relationships is "showing the right attitude." This consists of such specific behaviors as speaking as if you like your work; taking a cooperative ("What can we do to solve this problem?") rather than authoritative ("What are you going to do to solve this problem?") approach to problem solving; taking the attitude that your subordinates work with you, not for you; attacking issues and problems rather than personalities;

treating others as equals; and using many of the listening techniques we discussed earlier in this chapter. All of these things demonstrate your liking for others and increase the likelihood they will regard you positively in return.

Dominance

In an organization, the dominance dimension is determined both by organizational rank and by situational variables dictating who is in control for the moment. There are several methods for influencing others' behaviors. First is *simple force*—threats or physical actions—to gain compliance. Since this method tends to produce resistance, hostility, or resentment and is unjustifiable from most ethical perspectives, it is the least desirable influence method.

We can also *control rewards and punishments*. We know that people want to satisfy their needs. Thus, we can suggest to them that by doing what we recommend, they can satisfy needs presently unsatisfied, satisfy needs that now are only minimally satisfied, or continue satisfaction of needs now threatened. Conservationists employ the threatened-needs strategy, telling us: "Sure, everything is fine now. But watch out for the future. Unless we conserve fuel, land resources, and clean air, we will be in serious trouble soon." In other words, needs are satisfied now; but unless we make some change, the satisfaction will stop in the near future.

Still another influence strategy involves *obligation*. In our society, there exists a norm of "reciprocity," which tells us that we ought to respond in kind to behaviors we receive. If someone rewards us, perhaps by doing us a favor, then we feel obligated to reward him or her in return. As communicators, we may use an obligation strategy by reminding others of benefits they have accrued or rewards they have experienced and by suggesting that they now have a chance to show their appreciation by, for example, making a financial pledge or voting for a particular issue.

Controlling the environment is yet another influence strategy. Instances of this sort of influence are rather common. Confronted by several rowdy students, a teacher may put them all in the front row of the classroom so that they may more easily be intimidated or scatter them throughout the classroom so that they are removed from one another's influence. Similarly, upon perceiving a group of troublemakers, the foreman of a production line may place them on different shifts or scatter them throughout the assembly line.

Some individuals point to the positions they hold as a strategy for getting others to comply. Thus, *legitimate power* lets an individual exert influence simply because the recipient believes he or she has the right to do so.[72] The father who answers his child's "Why?" with "Because I told you to" exerts power of this sort. He has only to tell his child what to do. His position as parent gives him the authority to exert influence without question. Similarly, an organization's hierarchy confers legitimate power to people of high status. They command and their positional power causes their subordinates to obey.

We can also exert influence through *reason*. If we can convince someone that our point of view is correct, then he or she will willingly accept our influence. In our view, this influence strategy is most desirable, producing compliance for the best possible reason—because it is believed to be right.

As we repeatedly have indicated throughout this text, managerial effectiveness in today's rapidly changing environment depends on influence, the ability to get things done through people over whom one has no formal control. Jane Carroll Jackson, vice-president of the Forum Corporation, outlined the results and implications of research by her company on influence as a process and as a management tool.[73] Based on data obtained from four thousand individuals, Jackson defined a three-part model of effective influence behavior.

Part one is *building influence*. This involves a core practice of being supportive and helpful to others. In effect, you first must develop good personal relationships with other people (relationships with high degrees of attraction and involvement), and then you can exert influence without giving orders or relying on your positional authority. Part two is termed *using influence*. Jackson claims that sharing power is the core practice that allows for trying new ideas and working through alternatives. While the manager remains the dominant person in the situation, he or she asks for input from the subordinate individual and involves him or her in making the decision. *Sustaining influence* is the third part. In this element, trust forms a basis for gaining consensus and demonstrating openness. Even when the decision has been made, the dominant individual remains open to suggestions and criticisms, and subordinates feel enough trust in their superior to speak their minds without fear of reprisal.

Not long ago, it was enough for an executive to "dress for success"—to wear power ties, navy suits, and other clothing conveying and contributing to the success the executive sought. Now, however, there is a growing recognition that the ingredients for success go beyond clothing and include such nonverbal communication factors as animated gestures, well-timed smiles, and careful use of vocal pitch.

Some executives now are obtaining training in theatrics in an effort to enhance their corporate presence with a polish worthy of the stage. Dave Schopp, owner of a Chicago-based printing company, hired an acting coach to strengthen his "lifeless business presentations" after more traditional measures had failed. "I've been to Dale Carnegie and have used corporate facilitators, but I still was looking at blank stares when I addressed an audience," Schopp says. "Facial expressions and mannerisms are so important when you need people to listen."

The Player's Workshop of Second City, a school for improvisation with ties to the famed Chicago comedy troupe, conducts workshops in which participants are taught "basic skills to heighten awareness that will bring them control in a variety of situations, business or otherwise," according to Josephone Racidi Forsbeg, founder of the school. During weekly three-hour sessions, students are taught to act out different roles in spontaneous situations. Often, sessions are videotaped and played back for critique by class participants.

John Ransford Watts, Dean of the School of Theatre at De Paul University, reports seeing a rise in the number of business executives and other professionals seeking the help of drama, voice, and acting coaches to improve their communication skills. "There's an enormous number of people in high levels that have skills and knowledge that sit between their ears but they don't know how to transmit that knowledge in a personal way," he observes. "To seek coaching is a good idea, and many executives are coming to this realization."

From Mary Maguire, "Prime-time Executives: Theatrical Training Lifts Careers," *Chicago Tribune,* 19 October 1992, Sec. 4, p. 1.

Involvement

Obviously, frequent interaction with someone else is likely to produce an increasingly involved relationship. As Josefowitz notes, however, in many organizations there are people who are unreachable, stubborn, and impossible to convince and with whom it is difficult to maintain a conversation.[74] These people "switch to automatic and become immune to input from the outside"; they are "unwilling or unable to see the possibility of another way of looking at an issue." They demonstrate their unreachability through lack of eye contact, fidgeting or rigid body posture, apparent interest in other activities or frequent interruptions, yawning, looking at their watches repeatedly, giving "yes, but . . ." responses, or not responding to the topic under discussion.

Josefowitz suggests several strategies for getting through to the unreachable person. First is the direct approach, in which one confronts nonresponsiveness directly, saying such things as "it upsets me when you don't pay attention to me" or "I don't feel you hear me, and I don't know what else to do." Usually, this will alert the person to his or her own behavior (and to the speaker's awareness of that behavior), and it will cause the unreachable person to let his or her defenses down, at least for the moment.

Next is the preventive approach, which can be taken at the beginning of a conversation. The speaker might say, "I know you have had trouble listening to me in the past, but would you please try to hear a different point of view?" Again, the person's behavioral pattern may be broken.

The therapeutic approach, the third alternative, encourages the person to examine both his or her own behavior and the reactions it produces. The speaker might say, "You seem to have difficulty focusing on the discussion and often retreat behind a wall. This really frustrates me because I feel I can't reach you. What can we do to solve this problem?"

During conversations, another method for increasing involvement is *leveling* with the other person—to communicate with him or her openly, candidly, and honestly. As Stagnaro reports, some organizations have adopted leveling as a corporate practice.[75] The ROLM Corporation has adopted communication norms designed to promote leveling. One is the use of tactful phrasing, such as "you might consider this," "this might be helpful," or "we have a problem," to show employees the manager is on their side and that he or she is willing to listen to their viewpoint. Another is the use of the "I perceive" technique, in which managers report to employees how they are coming across to them: "This is how I see you," stated honestly and specifically. Such statements provide employees with important feedback on how others in the organization see them. Note, however, that leveling can have unpleasant results. Occasionally, people are unable to take criticism constructively, and conflict or hurt feelings can result. Before adopting leveling as a general practice, then, an organization and an individual must consider the risks involved.

Rossiter and Pearce discuss at length the concept of "honest" communication, in which one person reveals his or her true and innermost feelings to another.[76] Culbert terms this strategy "self-disclosure," which he defines as "an individual's explicitly communicating to one or more others some personal information that he believes these others would be unlikely to acquire unless he himself discloses it"[77]—that is, the disclosure of personal information, or of hidden secrets, to someone else. The principle of self-disclosure has been illustrated by Joseph Luft, who developed the well-known "Johari Window."[78] This window suggests that people possess four types of information about themselves: things unknown to both themselves and others; things known to them but hidden from others; things known to both themselves and others; and things known to others to which they themselves are blind. These "unknown," "hidden," "open," and "blind" areas are illustrated in figure 5.7. Self-disclosure serves to expand the open area by making known both to the self and to others information now hidden or blind. Thus, the areas on the left of figure 5.7 represent the nondisclosing individual, while the areas on the right represent the individual after self-disclosure.

Figure 5.7
Degrees of self-disclosure.

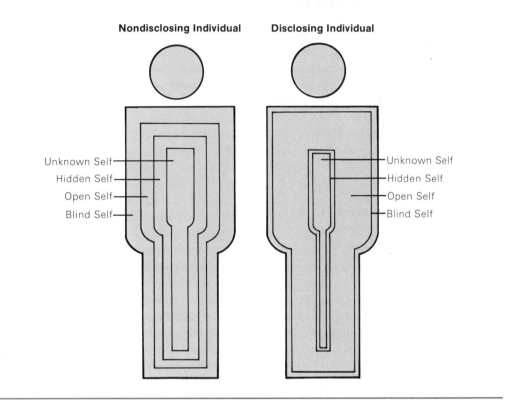

Two important characteristics of self-disclosure deserve consideration. First, it is risky. Since the information is personal, we make ourselves vulnerable to several undesirable consequences by presenting it to others. We risk rejection—a devastating experience. When we are presenting a front or playing some social role, we can always rationalize away rejections when they occur. After all, it was not we they rejected, just our front. But if we present our true selves and are rejected, there is no place to which to retreat—our very essence has been deemed unacceptable. Fortunately, this sort of rejection occurs infrequently. People are usually accepting and understanding when we open ourselves up to them. Nevertheless, the risk of rejection is a real problem that we must consider when deciding whether or not to disclose our true feelings to someone else.

A second source of risk is the possibility that the information we disclose might be used against us. Chester Burger, a management consultant in New York, tells of a corporate vice-president who disclosed his job anxieties to a colleague at lunch one day.[79]

In so doing, he destroyed his image of invulnerability and self-confidence and encouraged the other man to try to take his job—as he soon did. This negative experience reinforces an important point: self-disclosure must be based on trust to minimize the risk of having information you reveal used against you.

Another risky aspect of self-disclosure is that it may force us to confront our own weaknesses, thus discovering things about ourselves we may not like very much. Discovering that we are inadequate in some way is painful. Finding that we are not all we could have become is disappointing. Thus, self-disclosure poses the danger of revealing characteristics we might rather ignore.

If self-disclosure is so risky, why should we try it? The answer is the second characteristic of self-disclosure: it produces better, more involved, more satisfying relationships. Studies repeatedly have shown that we need relationships based upon self-disclosure if we are to be happy and fulfilled.[80] Despite its risks, then, self-disclosure is an important means for establishing more involved, personal relationships with others.

Having seen the benefits of self-disclosure, our next concern is how it might be accomplished. In general, there are five rules to observe when we express our personal feelings to other people:

1. *Self-disclosure should be as immediate as possible.* We should report our feelings as they occur rather than waiting until some later time to discuss them.
2. *Self-disclosure should be voluntary and natural.* We should not reveal personal information because we feel compelled to do so. Rather, revelation should naturally grow out of a relationship that has developed some degree of trust and supportiveness.
3. *Self-disclosure should be self-descriptive.* Good self-disclosure is purely descriptive, noting one's emotions and how they relate to the other person's behaviors. For example, we might describe our feelings by saying, "When you yell at me, I feel angry and resentful."
4. *Self-disclosure should strive to improve the relationship.* Although it is sometimes difficult to anticipate precisely the effects our self-disclosure will produce, we nevertheless should try to determine before disclosing what the effect will be upon our relationship with the other person. If the relationship is likely to be harmed in the long run, perhaps because our true feelings might make the other person defensive or hurt, then we probably should not disclose. If, on the other hand, we think disclosure will help the relationship, then it probably is appropriate. It is crucial here to make a distinction between immediate and long-range effects. It may be painful for the other person to discover that he or she has made us feel hurt or angry, but if through our self-disclosure, he or she can grow to understand how that feeling resulted, perhaps a better relationship can evolve.
5. *Self-disclosure should be as specific as possible.* When reporting our feelings to someone else, we should try to avoid generalizations and speak as specifically as we can about how we feel and why. What incidents have made us feel upset? Are there patterns we can perceive? Why do we react as we do?

While self-disclosure is one useful method of increasing involvement, we still face the problem of encouraging disclosure by the other person. To do so, we must find some means of minimizing the risk that disclosure poses to him or her. One useful method of accomplishing this is through *supportiveness*. That is, our responses should create a climate of support and trust so that the other person feels secure enough to self-disclose to us.

Summary

Our purpose in this chapter has been to consider a fundamental element of the organization's social system: human relationships. In examining the nature of human relationships, we concluded that they consist of four basic dimensions: attraction, dominance, involvement, and the situations in which persons interact. We can develop communication practices that allow us to deal effectively with each of these dimensions. Fundamental to our effective communication skills is learning to listen to others so that we both learn from them and are *perceived* as good listeners. But we must also understand the nature of language and perception and be able to speak clearly, articulately, and influentially. The way we speak is important, as is our ability to use every nonverbal communication element to our advantage, including our attire, our office decorations, our eye contact, and our posture. The basics of effective communication are important in every organizational setting—from the interview to the public presentation.

Questions for Discussion

1. If, as many futurists project, more people will begin to work at home using computers, what effect will it have on organizational relationships?
2. What aspects of an organization with which you are very familiar serve to shape the dominance dimension? Be specific.
3. What are some important factors influencing perception in organizational settings?
4. What are some ways in which we can be helpful as listeners? How can we be attentive? Empathic? Responsive?
5. How do the principles of the general semanticists relate to the attraction dimension? The involvement dimension?
6. Choose an organization with which you are familiar. How does its physical environment communicate what that organization is like? How does the environment promote or inhibit the personal growth of its occupants?
7. What dress code seems to apply to people working in any organization with which you are familiar?
8. What are some possible dangers of open, honest communication?

Exercises

1. Select an organization with which you are very familiar. Describe how the attraction factor is shaped within that organization; that is, how do proximity, attractiveness, and so on play a role in interpersonal attraction there?
2. Think of the most obnoxious, unpleasant person you know. Then list all of the verbal habits that person has that you find offensive. How should these habits be overcome?
3. Choose an organization you know well. How does that organization's physical environment show status differences? How does it control who talks to whom?
4. Think of someone who has some control over your life. Then think of one example of each kind of influence (force, rewards, punishments, and so on) that person uses.
5. Suggest principles related to the dominance dimension of human relationships that you might use to be a better supervisor. How would you use them, generally, if you were supervising the work of ten engineers?

Principles of Interviewing

hile dyadic encounters are frequent in all human interactions, both personal and professional, in organizational settings no form of dyadic communication is more significant or frequent than the interview. It is in the employment interview that we often are initially accepted or rejected by the organization. Subsequent interviews will inform us of our progress, promise, and problems in our daily work activities. In the context of the interview, we will likewise complain and be counseled, provide and receive information, and be praised and disciplined. We will participate in problem solving and persuasion; and often before we retire from or leave the organization, we will reflect on our accomplishments, disappointments, defeats, and triumphs in final exit interviews. Clearly, interviewing pervades all organizational activity—serving a multiplicity of functions, operating at numerous levels within the organizational hierarchy, and continuing throughout the lives of each organization employee.

Interviewing, like all interpersonal communication, normally involves face-to-face interaction (although telephone interviews do occur on occasion) between two parties (interviewer and interviewee) who take turns acting as sender and receiver. However, some other characteristics make interviewing a unique form of dyadic communication. First, interviews are *purposive,* conducted to achieve some specific objective. Informal interactions may have underlying purposes as well, but in an interview, the purpose is more clearly stated and understood by the participants. Second, interviews are more *structured* than informal conversations: The interviewer usually has some preestablished agenda that is followed during the conversation. Implied in this characteristic is a third: Interviews are more carefully *prepared* than are informal conversations. Typically, the interviewer prepares carefully for the interview before it is conducted. Often, the interviewee prepares just as carefully (as before an employment interview). Finally, the *sequence* of the interview is more predictable: The interviewer selects topic areas and asks questions, for the most part, while the interviewee provides responses and answers. In summary, then, interviews are prepared, structured interactions between two or more parties in which questions and answers are used to achieve relatively specific and mutually understood purposes.

Knowledge of interviewing is important, both for short-term and long-term reasons. In the short term, it is likely you will experience these interviews as an interviewee. To participate effectively, you need some knowledge of how interviews function and what the interviewer has (or should have) in mind. In the long term, you may achieve supervisory or management status in an organization. As a supervisor or manager, your success may be determined to a significant extent by your competence in conducting various types of interviews. Your immediate and long-term professional success, therefore, rests to some degree on your understanding of and skill in various forms of interviews.

In this chapter, we will examine the unique nature of interviews as communicative events. Taking the perspective of the interviewer, we will consider the nature of interviews in general and some specific purposes for which interviews are used in organizational settings. Then we will examine some types of interview questions and suggest sequences by which those questions might be organized. Applying our understanding of communication principles, we will discuss the interviewer's role as a listener and respondent.

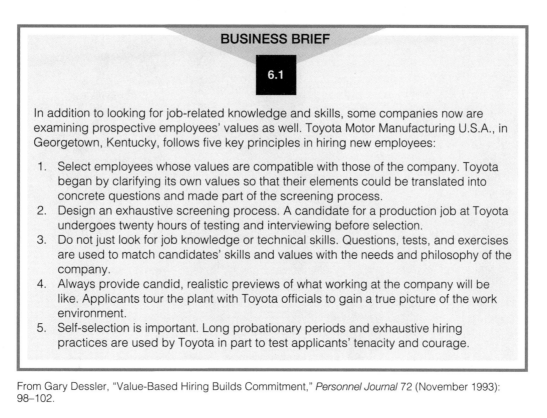

From Gary Dessler, "Value-Based Hiring Builds Commitment," *Personnel Journal* 72 (November 1993): 98–102.

Types of Interviews in Organizations

Employment Interviews

The employment interview will be discussed in the next chapter. It is worth mentioning here that modern advice on job interviews differs significantly from the traditional emphasis on the organization as the sole decision maker, possessing the power to accept or reject each applicant. The contemporary view is that each of us should see ourselves as untapped creative resources, as persons with skills that allow us to contribute substantially to the organization. With this approach, the interview becomes an opportunity for prospective employer and employee to exchange meaningful information and to decide about their mutual compatibility.

Disciplinary Interviews

When an employee violates a policy or breaks a rule, the employer usually initiates a disciplinary interview with that employee. Generally, these interviews attempt to show the employee what he or she did wrong, remind him or her of the rules involved, inform him or her of the disciplinary actions, if any, to be taken, and lay out clear expectations for performance improvements in the future. Such interviews, as we shall see in the next chapter, are highly controlled by the interviewer and often uncomfortable for the interviewee.

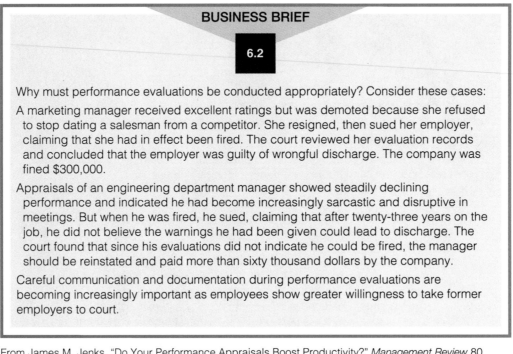

From James M. Jenks, "Do Your Performance Appraisals Boost Productivity?" *Management Review* 80 (June 1991): 46.

Appraisal Interviews

Appraisal interviews also will be discussed in the next chapter. Their function is to review the performance objectives established for the employee in the previous appraisal interview, to review the employee's performance in relation to those objectives, to establish new or revised objectives for the upcoming months or year, and to lay out specific strategies for performance improvement. The appraisal interview may also provide an overall rating of the employee's performance and determine how much pay increase, if any, the employee will receive.

Grievance Interviews

While the disciplinary interview represents the extreme in employer initiation and control, the *grievance interview* is initiated and largely controlled by the employee. The range of employee discontent is wide and may focus on such matters as poor working conditions, incompetent fellow employees, unfair treatment, and inadequate salaries. Managers who believe in the value of employee contributions must recognize that some of these contributions will invariably originate in the form of complaints. They should encourage, and even reward, employees for *accurate* upward communication whether it involves praise or criticism of the organization and its management. The manager who listens to employee grievances and acts in response to legitimate complaints builds the foundation for a productive, harmonious organization.

Counseling Interviews

While most interviews conducted within organizations focus on task-related matters, the *counseling interview* is usually directed toward personal considerations. Organizations are increasingly recognizing the impossibility of disassociating an employee's personal and professional life. Personal problems can, and often do, create and intensify problems at work. A survey in England that focused on executives identified major stress sources, such as the inability to cope with sudden and often unanticipated change, failure to accept thwarted ambitions, and promotions to jobs beyond their capacity.[1] Other increasingly common problems for all kinds of employees are marital discord, alcoholism, fear of retirement, and drug abuse.[2] Alcoholism, for example, affects at least 4 million men and women in the United States work force each year.[3] While counseling interviews are seldom appropriate for rehabilitating employees suffering from such problems, they are often legitimately used to obtain valuable preliminary information and to encourage workers to obtain professional assistance.

Exit Interviews

Most interviews occur periodically throughout the working lives of the organization's employees, but the *exit interview* occurs at the end of those productive years or at a time of change in the employee's organizational affiliation. While there is some evidence to indicate that a moderately high attrition rate can be an asset, most organizations consider high employee turnover to be a problem.[4] Finding good employees is never easy, and the expense of training new ones increases every year. Thus, many organizations conduct exit interviews to learn why employees leave their jobs.

A terminating employee often approaches an exit interview with considerable suspicion, especially if he or she has never been interviewed by a company representative since accepting the job! The employee may worry that the disclosure of negative information might result in lowered recommendations, or the employee may simply prefer leaving the organization on a positive note. It is critical for the interviewer to allay potential suspicions. A candid statement of the purpose of the interview and assurance of sincerity and trustworthiness on the part of the organization are mandatory. Exiting employees must be assured that honest responses will affect neither their futures in other organizations nor the relationships they are leaving behind. Similarly, when employees decide to leave an organization, they ought to approach the exit interview with maturity and sincerity—recognizing that it is partly their responsibility to contribute both positive and negative insights that might make the job a more rewarding one for future employees.

Some interviews involve information exchange, mutual persuasion, and problem solving.

Information-Giving and -Seeking Interviews

Interviews that provide information most often occur during periods of orientation and training in organizations. In the context of *information-giving interviews,* employees are trained, instructed, and coached in particular behaviors. Orientation interviews assist new employees in adjusting to an unfamiliar work environment. Early interviews in organizations provide a structured opportunity for managers to explain job requirements, explicate procedures, and answer questions. Upon accepting a position on the faculty of a major university, the novice teacher-scholar is involved in a number of orientation interviews in which he or she is informed of salary matters and insurance and retirement benefits and generally introduced to the procedures, practices, and expectations of the department in particular and the university in general.

The opposite end of the information exchange continuum is represented by the *information-seeking interview.* Unlike other types of interviews already discussed, those who seek information in interviews are often representing the organization. As we mentioned in chapter 1, the organizational system, if it is to survive, must exchange information and energy with its relevant environment. An organization may seek to discover, for example, the effectiveness of its public relations efforts or the receptivity of its

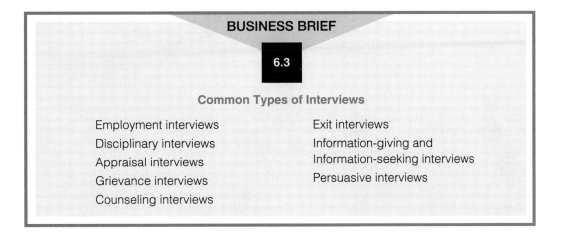

environment to some proposed product modification. It may conduct extensive polls, surveys, and interviews to examine the attitudes of the population or market in question.

Other kinds of interviews fall under the general purpose of seeking information. They involve judicial settings in which a lawyer interviews a client in an attempt to obtain a clear account of the client's view of the case; medical settings where doctors or nurses seek patients' medical histories and descriptions of current disorders; business or government settings in which an executive calls in a staff assistant to be briefed on a particular subject about which the assistant is especially knowledgeable; and journalistic research settings where press conferences and private interviews provide the context for interviewers to elicit facts and opinions from a person of special interest or expertise, often a celebrity.

Persuasive Interviews

While all members of organizations are involved with persuasive exchanges, many employees function primarily in the specific context of *persuasive interviews*. The most common example of this type of interview is the sales transaction in which a salesperson attempts to sell a specific product to a prospective customer. We will return to persuasive interviews in the next chapter.

Conducting Effective Interviews

Although interviewing is a common organizational activity, it is not necessarily an easy one. Perhaps Stewart and Cash put it best in their introductory chapter on interviewing:

> If you . . . tend to believe that interviewing comes naturally—like swimming to a dog— think of your recent experiences: the inept company recruiter who kept answering her own questions; the car sales representative who was determined to sell you a large sedan when you wanted a small economy car; the counselor who told you all of his problems instead of listening to your problems; the public opinion interviewer who asked biased questions; the encyclopedia sales representative with a canned pitch.[5]

To avoid the kinds of problems mentioned by Stewart and Cash, we will consider specific strategies for employment, appraisal, disciplinary, and persuasive interviews in the next chapter. In this section, we will examine some interviewing techniques that apply to all interviewing situations and that you should use regardless of your purpose in the interaction. More precisely, we will discuss the preliminary planning that interviews require, some strategies and questions for interviewing, using probes, coping with inadequate responses, acting as listener and respondent, and closing the interview. Each of these phases is critical to success in conducting any sort of organizational interview.

Preliminary Planning

While there is no certain way to create a climate for ideal interviews, careful preliminary planning can assist you in establishing a potentially constructive interviewing setting. Hopefully, as an organizational member functioning as an interviewer, you will receive some training in the interviewing process. For instance, Carlson's long-range studies with the Life Insurance Agency Management Association resulted in a promising *Agent Selection Kit*.[6] In a three-day workshop, interviewers were taught to use this kit and, through it, to develop flexible knowledge, attitudes, and skills that led to improved interviewing. One of the advantages of this kind of training is that the interviewer learns methods for structuring interviews. Too many untrained interviewers approach each interview without a specific strategy. This is not to imply that you should employ totally canned procedures without sensitivity to the demands of the situation and the needs of each particular interviewee. It only suggests that interviews that are systematic, structured, and guided are more valid than those that are unguided, unstructured, and without design or system.

Most interviews are conducted on the premises of the organization. Many are carried out in the interviewer's own office. When this is the case, the interviewer is responsible for creating the best possible environment in which the interview can occur. First, each interview should be conducted under circumstances that promote comfort and privacy. *Comfort* involves such physical considerations as room temperature and seating comfort, as well as matters related to psychological comfort. The physical distance between you and the interviewee (proxemics) is important, as is the arrangement of the furniture in the room. In the American culture, physical distances of two to five feet seem to be the most psychologically comfortable for conversation. Other potential barriers to communication include chair arrangement, the presence or absence of a desk, notetaking, and tape recording. If you plan to take notes or record the conversation, mention the fact directly and indicate the reasons for the practice. In each instance, you should give careful consideration to the kind of climate you wish to create and attempt to use space, distance, and other verbal and nonverbal factors to enhance the interview setting. Different interviewees will respond differently to the same environmental stimuli. One study revealed that interviewees who expressed high anxiety during an interview perceived the credibility of the interviewer to be higher when there was no desk between them.[7] Low-anxiety interviewees, on the other hand, made exactly the opposite credibility judgments. Similarly, though many interviewees will be relatively oblivious to notetaking, the practice may so inflate the nervousness of some that the wisest route is to stop taking notes.

The interviewee's psychological comfort will also be enhanced if you do all you can to ensure that the interview remains a *private exchange*. Although privacy is absolutely mandatory in the context of counseling and disciplinary interviews, nearly all interviews benefit from a private communication environment. Your secretary should not dash in with urgent messages or put calls through to you. If you must interrupt the interview to deal with some critical issue, apologize to the interviewee.

Depending upon the kind of interview you are conducting, you will probably need to plan the general approach you want to take, the kinds of questions you want to ask, and the kind of information you need to share. If you are conducting an employment interview, you should plan a core of basic questions, read the applicant's resume in advance, and bring information about the job's critical requirements. With a disciplinary interview, you must decide how to describe your perception of the problem and how and when to encourage the interviewee to respond. In the context of a work appraisal interview, you should study your written comments, prepare to make positive comments as well as suggestions for future improvements, and decide how to encourage the interviewee to join you in setting future goals. The kind of planning you do will depend upon the purpose of your interview.

Opening the Interview

The *opening* of the interview sets the tone for the remainder of the communication encounter. Although individual interviewers vary in their interpersonal styles, a generally desirable opening approach is one of warmth (seasoned with professional restraint), interest, and genuine personal concern for the interviewee. This may include a handshake, a smile, and a word of thanks for the interviewee's presence at the interview. The goal is to establish rapport by creating a climate of trust and goodwill. One traditional approach to putting the interviewee at ease is to engage in initial small talk. Some brief exchanges concerning sports, weather, families, and so forth may enhance rapport. But excessive small talk may backfire and cause the interviewee to be anxious and eager to settle down to the serious business of participating in the interview.

Soon after the initial greeting, you should make some *orientation statement*. In some types of interviews, both parties know essentially why they are there. Even so, it is often helpful to state your perception of the purpose of the interview. In many interviews, the interviewees are tense, uncertain, and perhaps overly aware of the status and power of the interviewer. This is especially so in appraisal, employment, disciplinary, and grievance contexts. To assist in overcoming this problem, you might make some early statement expressing your view that the purpose of this interview is for *both* you and the interviewee to exchange information so that both of you might make a wise decision concerning employment, performance, and other factors. This kind of orienting remark not only clarifies the purpose of the interview but may serve to relax the interviewee.

At this point, you may wish to *preview* the kinds of topics you hope to discuss. While a preview is not necessary for selection interviews, previewing can provide some sense of direction for the interviewee, increase interpersonal trust, and improve the overall efficiency of the interviewing process. Once again, it is extremely important to be sensitive to the needs of the person being interviewed. An extended orientation phase is especially helpful with highly anxious interviewees. Richetto and Zima point out that a desirable approach to obviously nervous applicants is to outline clearly the general flow of the interview, the basic topics to be covered, the rationale for covering them, and the ultimate usage of the collected data.[8]

Basic Interviewing Strategies

Each interview must have a goal, and the interviewer usually formulates an overall design that will theoretically lead to that goal. Many interviewees will have their own strategies and goals, some of which will complement and others of which will conflict with your goals as an interviewer. In an employment interview, each of you may have as a mutual goal the discovery of whether or not you should become professionally associated. To achieve that goal, however, both of you may hope to spend a maximum amount of time during the interview gaining information from the other. Clearly, these goals are not compatible, given the time constraints that are usually present. Thus, both interviewer and interviewee must be prepared to adjust to the unanticipated demands of the communication situation.

From your perspective as an interviewer, there are two basic strategies you can adopt. The first is *directive*. Using a directive strategy, you establish the purpose of the interview and strive to control the pacing of the interview and the subjects covered during it.[9] This approach is highly structured. It is particularly applicable when you believe you know the desired interview goal and the precise steps for getting there. One directive approach is to work from a patterned questionnaire. More often, though, the directive strategy will take the form of probing specific topics in a particular sequence with considerable flexibility in follow-up questions and overall structure. The directive strategy is especially efficient for acquiring large quantities of information.

As we mentioned earlier, highly structured interviews tend to have high validity. Nevertheless, the directive strategy has some potential weaknesses. Let us say that you are interviewing several applicants for the position of your administrative assistant or that you are seeing a dozen employees over a two-day period to conduct work appraisal interviews. Let us assume further that you decide for purposes of simplicity and consistency to use a directive strategy. In this case, you may become so dependent upon the planned, frequently used format that you cease to be sensitive to the unique characteristics, demands, and needs of each interview and interviewee. Particularly important aspects of an employee's performance may be left unexplored simply because they do not fit logically into the planned sequence of questions. Using a structured, familiar interview format is somewhat akin to playing the same role in a play over and over again: You must labor to make each appearance *seem* fresh, original, and interesting. No interviewee should leave the interview feeling that he or she has just been exposed to the organization's assembly line!

The second basic interviewing strategy is *nondirective*. When you choose a nondirective strategy, you allow the interviewee to control the purpose, topics to be covered, and pacing of the interview.[10] Nondirective interviewing was developed by therapist Carl Rogers and is most commonly used in counseling situations. The nondirective strategy is seldom employed in its pure form in organizational interviews. However, if you do not possess adequate information regarding an interviewee or his or her problems, the nondirective strategy *may* be used. Even though this approach allows the interviewee to explore whatever areas he or she wishes with only minimal structural constraints, it is not without some interviewer control. Your role is one of empathic, nonjudgmental listening, while permitting the interviewee to structure his or her own thinking with flexible and subtle guidance.

The obvious advantages of the nondirective approach are flexibility and the opportunity to explore interesting subjects in depth. By using this method, interviewer and interviewee can begin to establish an ongoing relationship. Moreover, with this approach, the interviewee has every opportunity for self-expression. Nondirective interviews are not without their disadvantages, however. They are less efficient than directive interviews and can be very time-consuming. Because the interviewees choose most of the content to be pursued, each interview is likely to cover entirely different ground. Thus, as an interviewer, you cannot really compare interviewee responses across several interviews. Nondirective interviews require considerable interviewer sensitivity and excellent listening skills.

While the typical approach to most interviews remains the directive strategy, many interviewers plan several major questions, allowing a great deal of flexibility in the ways in which these questions are pursued by interviewees and providing considerable time for interviewee questions, comments, and insights. This combined approach is practical and allows the interview to be a shared communicative experience.

Questions

A key communication tool used by interviewers is the question. Whatever your overall design, you will ask many questions as a primary means of collecting the data you need to plan and make decisions. You may choose to use one of two basic types of questions: *open* or *closed*. *Open questions* are broad in nature and basically unstructured. Often they indicate only the topic to be considered and allow the interviewee considerable freedom in determining the amount and kind of information he or she will provide. Open questions let the interviewee know that you are interested in his or her perspectives, attitudes, and value system.

Some questions are extremely open ended, with virtually no restrictions, such as: (1) Tell me about yourself. (2) What do you know about General Motors? (3) How do you think this organization can be improved? Other questions are more moderately open: (1) Why did you major in marketing? (2) What can be done to improve this organization's productivity? (3) What do you know about General Motors' new design plants?

Open questions allow the interviewee to talk with relative freedom. Because there are so many different ways to respond to them, they are not very threatening and tend to reduce interviewee anxiety. Often the interviewee will volunteer information for which the interviewer would not have thought to ask. Open questions give the interviewer insights into the interviewee's prejudices, values, and commitments. Of course, open questions are not without their disadvantages. They take a good deal of time, collect much irrelevant information, often require several follow-up questions, demand excellent listening skills on the part of the interviewer, and can be difficult to evaluate following the interview.

On the opposite end are *closed questions*. These are structured, restricted, and often include several possible answers from which to choose. Thus, potential responses are limited. On occasion, a closed question will probe for a brief bit of specific information, such as: (1) When did you first notice that you were drinking excessively? (2) How many years did you consult? (3) What starting salary would you anticipate with this job? Others are even more closed, requiring the interviewee to select the appropriate response from among those you provide, such as: (1) What brand of toothpaste do you presently use: _____ Crest, _____ Colgate, _____ Aim, _____ Aquafresh, or _____ Gleem? (2) Where would you prefer being located with our company:_____ New Orleans, _____ New York, _____ San Francisco, or _____ Chicago?

The most extreme form of the closed question is the *yes/no bipolar question*. Usually the interviewee is allowed to respond only with yes or no, or possibly "don't know." For example: (1) Do you smoke? (2) Do you agree with this church's stand on women in the clergy? (3) Are you familiar with our new drug abuse program? Inexperienced, unskilled interviewers have a tendency to rely heavily on this type of questioning in spite of the fact that it requires maximum questioning effort and generates only small amounts of information per question. Occasionally a yes/no question is appropriate, but long series of such questions should be avoided.

In general, closed questions save time, increase the probability of obtaining relevant responses, are more efficient, and are relatively easy to tabulate following the interview. By using closed questions, the interviewer maintains substantial control over the flow of the interview. On the other hand, closed questions generate limited information and often cause interviewees to respond less accurately (since their views may not fit precisely into any one of the offered alternatives). They decrease interviewee talking time and increase the number of questions the interviewer must generate. Finally, they fail to explore the reasons behind attitudes and opinions and stifle the offering of valuable, but unanticipated, information.

Probing: A Special Kind of Questioning

Sometimes an interviewee will respond only partially to a question, answer it inadequately, or make a provocative point that causes you to desire additional information. When this occurs, you may attempt to stimulate discussion by *probing* for further information. Probes, according to Richetto and Zima, "allow the interviewer to follow up on partial or superficial responses by directing the thinking of the interviewee to further aspects of the topic at hand."[11] Thus, probes may request exploration, elaboration, or justification. Some examples are (1) What do you mean by that? (2) Why did you feel that way? (3) Could you give me an example? Recent research by Tengler and Jablin suggests that probes are frequently used and needed by employment interviewers to obtain substantive responses to open questions.[12]

There are several kinds of *specialized probes*. Two commonly used in employment interviews are *hypothetical* and *reactive probes*. The *hypothetical probe* places the interviewee in a situation, not unlike one he or she might encounter on the job, and asks how he or she would handle the situation. You might say, "Suppose you had been working here for a few months and one day you heard a rumor that drastic layoffs were impending. How do you think you'd react to that?" Hypothetical probes can be useful for determining basic attitudes or approaches to problem solving, but they also encourage a certain amount of second guessing, where the interviewee gives the ideal response (that is, the one she or he thinks you want to hear) rather than an honest response.

You may also choose to use *reactive probes* in which you make a statement simply to get the reaction of the interviewee. Perhaps you ask the interviewee to agree or disagree with a stated position or issue. For example, a high school principal used a reactive probe in interviewing a young woman for a teaching position when he asked the following question: "There are many teachers who believe that most major disciplinary problems should be brought to the attention of the principal, while others prefer to handle these matters without administrative assistance, except in the most severe instances. How do you feel about dealing with discipline?"

In a sense, hypothetical and reactive probes are similar in that they provide a frame of reference and set the stage for the interviewee's response. But the reactive probe focuses on real rather than hypothetical cases. By using such probes, you can gain some insights into applicants' views on pertinent real-life issues without in any way challenging their ideas.

Another method for obtaining follow-up information is the use of *restatement* (sometimes referred to as the "mirror" technique). With this technique, you do not directly request that the interviewee provide additional information. Rather, you restate part or all of the person's comments in such a way that it encourages him or her to continue. In this manner, you can communicate genuine interest, indicating that you are "with" the other person. Restatement does not demand additional information; it simply provides the opportunity for elaboration and deeper examination. Compare the following interviewer responses, one using a probe and the other restatement:

Interviewee: I left my job at the small accounting firm because I found it unchallenging. It was *dull*.

Interviewer (using a probe): How was it dull and unchallenging?

Interviewer (using restatement): You felt it was dull and unchallenging?

Restatement is a technique particularly useful for allowing people to clarify their ideas and listen to their own language without in any way commenting on or evaluating them. The effective use of restatement requires careful listening and personal sensitivity. It should be used only occasionally and with care.

Question Bias

Still another method by which types of questions can be distinguished is based upon the extent to which the question reveals the attitudes of the questioner or suggests the sort of answer that the respondent is supposed to give. For example, "How do you feel about labor unions?" suggests little about the thinking of the questioner. "You don't like labor unions, do you?" suggests quite a bit more. "You wouldn't join one of those pinko-commie anti-American labor unions, would you?" clearly indicates the feelings of the questioner. When biased questions are used accidentally, they place the interviewee in a difficult position; when used carefully, however, they can reveal much about the respondent.

As with other types of questions, unbiased and biased inquiries range along a continuum from very biased to completely neutral. Most of the examples we have offered in this section have been unbiased. For example, "How well do you feel you performed this past year?" says nothing about the feelings of the interviewer and leaves interviewees free to answer as they please without fear of being trapped by the question. Somewhat more biased or leading is the question, "You like working with machinery, don't you?" And, at the most biased end of the scale is, "Are you going to improve your output next month, or should I start a search for your replacement?" Because these three questions vary in their revelations of the interviewer's feelings, they exert different degrees of pressure upon the interviewee to respond in a particular fashion.

In deciding whether to use biased, moderately biased, or completely neutral questions during the interview, you first must take into account your purpose. If you are seeking the interviewee's true feelings or attitudes, you probably should avoid biased questions. If, however, you are trying to persuade the interviewee, biased questions may be useful. Research on attitude change suggests that if we can encourage an individual to state a certain opinion, he or she is likely to adopt that opinion as his or her own. Thus, if the interviewee initially had no intention of changing the behaviors for which you were disciplining him, you might persuade him through a sequence of questions, such as:

"You understand that we have to have people here at work in order to maintain our responsiveness to customers, don't you?"

"You know that absenteeism hurts our ability to get the product to customers when they need it, don't you?"

"You realize that when someone is late for work, we have to move everyone around to cover for him?"

"You know that just as we promise to provide you with pay and benefits, so you promise to come to work regularly and on time?"

"So what are you going to do to improve your attendance record?"

The yes answers produced by the first four questions probably will lead to a constructive plan of action in response to the fifth, while at the same time leading the interviewee to an understanding of the necessity of good attendance. Thus, biased questions produce the same effect that a lecture or series of commands would achieve, but in a more palatable manner.

Finally, biased questions also can serve to test an interviewee. We can use them to determine how independent workers are or how likely workers are to provide socially acceptable responses. For example, if we asked, "Are you biased against moving women into managerial positions?" most male executives would respond, "No." However, if we asked, "Do you think that women are often too emotional to take the daily stresses of management positions?" a "closet sexist" would be much more likely to reveal his true feelings. However, we must use biased questions with care. At times, their use is deceptive and unethical. Their implications may make the interviewee suspicious, angry, or skeptical of our own opinions or judgment. For the most part, then, we are much safer in using neutral questions and relying on the openness created by other interviewing skills to elicit honest answers from the interviewee.

Coping with Inadequate Responses

Unfortunately, not all questions asked in interviews elicit the kinds of responses sought. Interviewee answers may be inadequate in many ways and for many reasons. Sometimes the interviewer's question is not clearly understood because of content, language, or structure. On occasion, interviewees may not know how to respond appropriately because of inadequate knowledge or a misunderstanding of the interviewer's expectations (that is, they are uncertain how much detail and elaboration is expected). Finally, the interviewee may be naturally reticent or may feel that the interviewer is asking for irrelevant or overly personal information.

Whatever the reason, as an interviewer you will encounter many inadequate responses from interviewees. Each will challenge your wits and require you to respond creatively to the interpersonal communication difficulties posed by such interviews. Some responses, for example, are *oververbalized*. They are often the product of compulsive talkers who go on and on, seemingly indefinitely. As we have pointed out, the use of open questions encourages more elaborated responses. When you perceive that you are dealing with a compulsive talker, you would do well to alter your strategy to a more directive one, using closed questions to limit the response range.

Other responses are simply *irrelevant*. They do not deal with the question posed and are frequently offered by interviewees who do not understand the question, do not have the information to respond appropriately, or are poor listeners. When irrelevant responses are offered, it is usually best to restate the question (perhaps at a later time in the interview). One decision you must make is how to pose a clearer question—possibly by stating it as a closed question with distinct alternatives—or by emphasizing key words. For example:

Interviewer: "What is your attitude toward the new payment schedule?"

Interviewee: "A lot of people in my department don't like it. They say it's unfair."

Interviewer: "What is *your* attitude toward the schedule?"

Interviewers quite often encounter *partial* responses or even *nonresponses*. Both are inadequate because they provide little or no information. Interviewees who consistently respond "yes," "no," "I don't know," or "I don't think so," or who only partially and superficially answer questions provide a great challenge for interviewers. If the interviewee's response is incomplete or hesitant, you might nudge him or her by saying: "I see." "And then?" "Yes?" or "What happened next?" Superficial responses might be followed by: "Why do you think you felt that way?" "Tell me more about your reasons for doing that," or "How did you react when that happened?" Vague answers could be greeted with: "What do you mean when you use the word *liberal?*" "How are you using the term *participation?*" or "I'm not sure I understand."

In general, a useful strategy with any reticent interviewee is to phrase all questions in an open manner so that it becomes impossible to answer them sensibly with one-word responses. Nontalkers often lack confidence or are highly anxious about the interview. Thus, the best initial approach is one of extended rapport-building and orientation. It is also imperative that the first question or two be easy ones. If highly anxious persons are asked a difficult question initially, they may never be able to relax and communicate fully and effectively.

Question Sequences

Another important element of effective interviewing is the order in which questions are asked. While a virtually infinite number of sequences could be identified, we shall consider five types, distinguishable by their use of open and closed questions.

The first type of sequence, the *funnel,* begins with open questions and builds upon them with questions of increasing specificity. The funnel sequence is particularly appropriate when interviewees are quite familiar with the topic and feel free to discuss it or when they are emotionally charged and need a chance to express feelings. We might begin by asking a general question about the interviewee's attitudes toward work and then become increasingly specific by focusing on particular aspects of the interviewee's position. If, for example, the interviewee formerly was an effective worker but recently has let her performance slip, we might begin the interview with general questions about the interviewee's morale and overall job satisfaction. Then we would move to her performance over the past several years and become even more specific, considering her most recent performance level. Finally, we could deal with precise elements of her job, such as attendance or amount of work produced, and try to determine those factors that may have caused these elements to go downhill. Of the question sequences used in all types of interviews, the funnel sequence (illustrated in figure 6.1) is one of the most common.

The second sequence, the *inverted funnel,* is the reverse of the preceding. As demonstrated in figure 6.1, the interviewer begins with specific, closed questions and gradually moves to more general, open questions. This approach may be useful if the interviewee is reluctant to talk at all. While open questions might get no response, specific questions (such as, "Did it take you long to find this place?" or "How long have you been working here?") may be an effective way to motivate the interviewee to respond freely. Once he or she is talking, the interviewee may be encouraged to deal with more open questions, demanding greater depth of response. One recent study of employment interviewing suggested that most interviewers use the inverted funnel sequence.[13]

The third and fourth sequences involve combinations of the first two. The *diamond sequence* begins with closed questions, moves to open ones, and then narrows again to specific, closed inquiries. When counseling an employee who seems to have a drug or alcohol problem, we might begin with specific questions about situations similar to his, then move to more open questions about his own life and work performance, and then

Figure 6.1
A comparison of two basic questioning sequences.

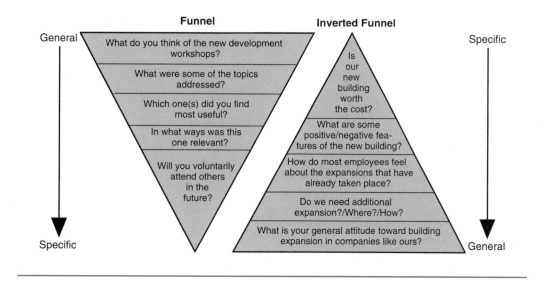

center again upon his own problems and concerns. We begin with a relatively easy topic of discussion (someone else's problems), move to something a little more personal but still not too difficult to discuss (his life in general), and then arrive at the most difficult and the most specific portion of the interview—his own problems and what to do about them. This questioning sequence is often useful in dealing with potentially painful topics or difficult problems.

The *hourglass sequence* begins with open questions, moves to closed questions, and then becomes open once again. When conducting a performance review with a supervisor who has been steadily criticized by her own workers, for example, we might begin with a discussion of people and how motivated they are in very general terms, then move to specific questions about her situation, and encourage her to develop her own supervisory action plan by asking increasingly open-ended questions toward the end of the interview. Such a sequence of questions might include:

"What do you think makes people want to work?"

"How do you think they get these things from work?"

"Does the supervisor play a role in providing these things?"

"Does this apply to your staff as well?"

"Do you provide the things they want or need?"

"What are some things you might do more of as a supervisor?"

"What will you try to accomplish during the next year?"

This sequence is much shorter than the entire interview would be, but it illustrates the open-to-closed-to-open procedure found in the hourglass sequence. This sequence is especially useful if you want to begin by establishing some general principles, then move to a specific application (closer to home), and finally go on to examine some action strategies for the future.

Finally, the *tunnel sequence* uses questions that are all of the same degree of openness. Interviews conducted in shopping centers by market researchers who stop shoppers at random and ask them a series of questions typically follow this pattern. Very specific, factual questions are asked in a rapid sequence to gain maximum information in a minimum amount of time. In contrast, some psychotherapists use exclusively open questions in their counseling interviews with patients. Their goal is to cause the patient to talk and so arrive at a solution to his or her own problem.

Your selection of a question sequence, then, is based largely on your purpose in the interview and your knowledge of the interviewee's state of mind. A reluctant respondent may require use of an inverted funnel. A disagreeable interviewee may be persuaded through a diamond sequence. An uninformed or uneducated interviewee may be taught to apply general principles to his or her own situation through an hourglass sequence. Interviewers must carefully assess their purpose and the nature of the interviewee and then carefully plan their overall questioning strategy.

The Interviewer as Listener and Respondent

We have already discussed listening in an earlier chapter, but the significance of good listening for effective interviewing cannot be overemphasized.[14] The good interviewer/listener is able both to gain a better understanding of the interviewee and to devise better questions that obtain the best possible information.

To listen effectively, there are several basic techniques you might use:

1. *Face the interviewee.* You cannot listen to and observe someone unless you are looking at him or her.
2. *Maintain eye contact.* While you do not want to stare down the interviewee, you want to establish frequent eye contact, both to show your own attentiveness and to open the channels of communication.
3. *Hang on every word.* That is, avoid allowing yourself to be distracted by anything else in the environment, by the person's appearance, or by the things you intend to say next. Too often, we pick up a word or two and immediately begin to rehearse silently the answer we are going to give, missing important information in the process.
4. *Avoid common barriers to listening.* Many such barriers exist.
   a. *Wasting thought power.* We listen and absorb ideas at a rate much faster than people talk. On the average, most of us can talk at a rate of 125 words per minute, while we can think at 400 to 500 words per minute. Unfortunately, this difference in thought and word speed is responsible for many mental tangents; that is, instead of concentrating on what the interviewee is saying, our minds wander off onto other things. We need to use thought speed constructively, analyzing and summarizing what the interviewee has just said, anticipating the next point, and so on.

b. *Listening only for specific facts or details.* Too often we concentrate only on details or facts and lose sight of the overall message and feelings of the other person. Effective listening occurs only when the big picture is kept in mind; you have to maintain a focus on the overall structure and purpose of the conversation.

c. *"Throw-in-the-towel" listening.* When the going gets tough or when it becomes clear that the other person simply is not totally supportive of what we are saying, some of us simply give up and mentally check out. Instead, we should listen even more intently, trying to discover from the other person's words things we can use to further the conversation.

d. *Focusing on the interviewee's personal characteristics.* Often we are distracted by the speaker's mannerisms, appearance, delivery, and so on. When this occurs, we are not listening to the message, but are concentrating on the messenger. We must focus on the message content, not the peculiar appearance or behavior of the interviewee.

e. *Faking attention.* Many interviewers become skilled at pretending to pay attention. They mutter "uh-huh" while the interviewee speaks, they sit with glazed eyes and fixed smiles during conversations, and they generally ignore everything going on around them. In effect, they just go through the motions of the interview and do not really communicate.

f. *Tolerating or creating distractions.* Poor listeners are easily distracted by other things, or they may even create distractions themselves. For example, the sales representative who attempts to listen while flipping through product information sheets provides a distraction for the customer and, in so doing, probably discourages further communication.

Perhaps the best way to improve your listening is to practice active listening methods.[15] Active listening consists of responding, verbally and nonverbally, to the person who is talking to you. These responses should encourage the other person to tell you more, show that you understand the person's words, and indicate that you empathize with her or his feelings. When you listen actively, you may respond to the content of the interviewee's words, your perception of her or his feelings, or important nonverbal cues. Some active listening techniques follow.

Active Listening Methods

As an interviewer, when you respond to something the interviewee has said (that is, to the message content), one goal you may have is to *demonstrate your attention and understanding.* You might do this by *paraphrasing,* where you state in your own words what you think the interviewee just said; by *prodding,* where you give short vocal and nonverbal cues that signal you are listening and encourage the interviewee to continue talking; or by *accepting,* where you state your approval or acceptance of the interviewee's expressed views.

Another way of responding to the interviewee's remarks is to *request further input.* You might do this by *encouraging,* that is, requesting that the interviewee give you more information about what happened, what caused a particular problem ("Could you give me a little more background on what happened right before George became department head?"); by *delegating,* where you place responsibility for solutions or ideas back on the interviewee, thus involving him or her in the solution ("What ideas do you have that I might pass along?" or "How do you think we might solve that problem?"); by *reconstructing,* where you ask the person to recall or imagine the events that led to the topic you are discussing ("How was that decision originally made?"); or by *reversing,* where you ask for an opposite point of view ("You've discussed a number of problems with the new word processing software. Have you found any advantages to it?").

Yet another goal you may have as you listen actively to an interviewee's verbal messages is to *cause him or her to think critically.* You might, for instance, try *testing,* where you ask the interviewee to consider the possible results of a problem, solution, or proposed course of action ("How do you think our regular customers would react if we switched to a cheaper vendor?"); or you might try *confronting,* where you challenge the validity of what has been said ("You say that we are charging too much for those microcomputers, but sales have never been better!"). These techniques, of course, will be effective only if they are used with sensitivity and tact.

A final goal you may have in responding to interviewee ideas and suggestions is to *demonstrate interest and offer help or guidance.* You might do this by *offering,* where you suggest possible alternatives or solutions to a problem; or by *elaborating,* where you build on to what the interviewee has just said, communicating understanding, involvement, and approval ("You're right about the importance of the company getting involved with community service projects. I like the ones you've mentioned, especially the blood drive. We might also consider working with the group that's trying to solve the PCB problem.").

Perhaps more difficult than responding to the interviewee's expressed view is responding to your perceptions of his or her feelings. To do this, you observe reactions that seem to indicate that emotions are present and then tell the interviewee what you have noticed and what you tentatively interpret your observations to mean.

As a general rule, you should respond only to fairly obvious feelings. Your goal is not to "psych out" the interviewee, but to *grow to understand that person's emotions and build a better relationship* with him or her. By being responsive to another's feelings, you not only *show concern* for the individual but *promote rational discussion* by minimizing emotional problems that can get in the way. Therefore, when strong emotions seem evident, you might ask such questions as: "I get the feeling you are really upset about something. Would you like to talk about it?", "You seem really sad today. Is anything wrong?", or "You sound pretty depressed. What has got you down?" By taking the time to encourage the interviewee to share his or her feelings, you show your concern and begin to build a better understanding, which should lead, ultimately, to improved communication.

Finally, as an active listener/interviewer, you may need to respond to the interviewee's nonverbal cues. In some instances, these cues will reinforce the verbal message. On other occasions, they will contradict what is being said. Often, the nonverbal cues will give you insight into the interviewee's true feelings. In chapter 5, we discussed nonverbal behavior in considerable detail, but a few examples of the kinds of nonverbal cues that you might see in interviews may be useful here. For instance, a frown in response to a comment you make may indicate confusion or disagreement; folded arms and sitting back after a comment may suggest anger or withdrawal; rapid hand movements or shifting on the chair may indicate anxiety or nervousness; a smirk on the face may denote an attitude of superiority or disgust; and a variety of other facial expressions may reveal confusion, anger, distrust, or resistance.

Whenever you observe an interviewee's nonverbal behavior that seems unclear, or appears to contradict what is being said, you might ask about it, with such questions as: "I know you said yes, but you look kind of puzzled. Are there some questions you still have on your mind?" or "When I look at you sitting there, kind of slouched down in your chair, I sense that you're not really terribly enthusiastic about taking on this project. Could we talk about it some more?"

When you make observations about an interviewee's nonverbal cues, make your evaluations as tentative as possible. Nonverbal cues can be ambiguous. They may reveal underlying feelings that the interviewee is unaware of or not yet ready to acknowledge or discuss. But if you can approach the subject tactfully and patiently, you may be able to help the interviewee become aware of how she is coming across to others and help clarify her own reactions. But let the interviewee do the interpretation.

Taken together, the ability to ask good questions and the skill and willingness to listen actively will do much to help you become an effective interviewer in a wide variety of interviewing contexts.

Closing the Interview

Perhaps the interviews you conduct will be subject to some external time constraints so that there are only twenty or thirty minutes available. Usually you will be in a more flexible situation that allows you to decide when prolonging the interview would not be profitable. One interviewing researcher points out that in every communication encounter, there are "crucial junctures—those moments in an interview when the next response . . . will determine whether its continuance will be productive or not, whether vital data will be elicited or if tangential information will be forthcoming."[16] Your ability to recognize critical junctures will improve with experience. What is important to remember is that you should terminate an interview whenever you feel that your mutual goals have been accomplished.

The end of the interview is as important as the beginning, and failure to attend to it may result in undermining earlier accomplishments. To thank an interviewee for his or her participation in an interview and to mumble something about "being in touch" is not an adequate conclusion. In general, the tone of the closing should be similar to that of the rest of the interview—appreciative of the interviewee's participation and interest in him or her as a person. You should encourage each interviewee to ask questions and devote the remainder of the interview to exploring the procedure to be used next. In other words, there must be some orientation toward the next step. If the interview has been a selection situation, you should tell applicants what will happen next: who will contact them and when the contact will be made. Or you may make the decision to hire or not to hire right then and inform each applicant accordingly. At the end of an appraisal interview, you and the interviewee should agree on what the interviewee will strive to accomplish during the next few months and discuss how you will keep track of his or her achievements. To close a counseling interview, you might discuss when your next appointment will be. To close a sales interview, you should ask for the sale. In each case, the closing should reflect the purpose of the meeting and should emphasize the things you want to happen as a result of the discussion. And above all, this closing should be prepared every bit as carefully as the rest of the interview. You should not simply assume that the momentum of the interview will carry you automatically into an effective closing.

The Ethics of Interviewing

In a sense, conducting an interview is no different from engaging in other forms of organizational communicative interaction in that ethical behavior is important. But being an interviewer places a special emphasis on the need for ethics. Almost by definition, interviewers are individuals with authority. In most cases, the interviewer has the ability to make some decision affecting the fate or well-being of the interviewee. In employment interviews, the interviewer can eliminate the applicant from further consideration. In disciplinary interviews, the interviewer can choose the terms of the punishment or the nature of the contract employees must fulfill if they wish to remain with the company.

In any interview, the interviewer officially represents the organization, and his or her conduct reflects on the standards, values, and ethics of the organization. The interviewer who asks offensive or illegal questions, who speaks rudely or condescendingly to a fellow employee, or who refuses to listen to the interviewee's explanations or ideas not only reveals him or herself as insensitive or unethical; he or she also suggests that the company condones such behavior. One of our former students was interviewed by a personnel manager who represented a major U.S. manufacturing company. This woman was initially quite pleased when she received the opportunity to interview with this company. During the interview, however, the interviewer asked her several personal (and illegal) questions, focusing in particular on her fiancé's attitude toward the prospect of her traveling all over the country. Not only did this woman leave the interview with a feeling of disgust, she decided that she wanted no further dealings with this organization. Even when she received a letter inviting her to visit the company for a second interview, she declined.

Illegal interviewing practices are always unethical. But unethical interviewing occurs whenever interviewers treat interviewees with disrespect, use their authority to make employees feel powerless or threatened, or refuse to listen or even to give an interviewee the chance to speak. By contrast, the ethical interviewer

shows concern for the interviewee and his or her feelings.

is interested in finding out what the interviewee thinks.

genuinely listens.

demonstrates respect for the interviewee by the way he or she communicates.

plans the interview time so that information exchange can, in fact, occur.

is familiar with the law and other organizational rules to be sure that he or she is operating within a legal framework.

is knowledgeable concerning the organization's code of ethics, either formal or informal.

is sensitive to power and authority differences in the interview setting and seeks to minimize their potentially negative effects.

Behaving ethically as an interviewer is a matter of knowledge, common sense, good will, and hard work.

Summary

In this chapter, we have acquainted you with the types and functions of interviews in organizations. We have pointed out the pervasiveness of interviewing activities, as well as the critical communication functions served by interviews, such as information giving and seeking, persuading, and problem solving. In the interviewing context, we hire people, evaluate them, counsel them, discipline them, sell things to them, solve problems with them, gain information from them, and, occasionally, fire them. Certainly, we also find ourselves on the receiving end of these interview functions. Our ability to function effectively in each of these contexts will contribute to our success in organizational life.

More than any other single factor, the key to successful interviewing is preparation. As we saw in this chapter, we first must analyze our own purposes, and we must consider the attitudes, knowledge, behaviors, and characteristics of our interviewee. Then we must carefully plan the opening of the interview, the types of questions we will ask and the order in which we will ask them, and the way in which we will close the encounter. Moreover, we must take care to listen and react to the interviewee, so that modifications in our interview game plan can be made when needed. Above all, we must resolve to treat the interview as a problem-solving situation, one in which both we and the interviewee have our own needs and in which we work together to develop action plans whereby each of our needs can be met. By taking this sort of approach, we significantly enhance our chances for success as an interviewer.

Questions for Discussion

1. How would you distinguish an interview from other kinds of dyadic encounters?
2. What are some of the types of interviews commonly encountered within organizations? What are some of the characteristics and potential problems associated with each?
3. From the interviewer's perspective, describe the planning necessary for conducting effective interviews.

4. Compare and contrast the following, giving examples of each:
   a. *directive* versus *nondirective* strategy
   b. *open* versus *closed* questions
   c. *probing* versus *restatement*
   d. *hypothetical* versus *reactive* probes
5. Discuss the concept of question bias. How can biased questions be used effectively? Are they ever unethical? How?
6. Compare and contrast the following questioning sequences: funnel, inverted funnel, diamond, hourglass, and tunnel.
7. Discuss the interviewer's role as listener and respondent.

Exercises

1. You have just been hired as a middle-level manager in a small industrial firm. Among the many decisions you must make as you approach the supervisors who will report to you is how you will use interviewing to stay in touch with these employees. Will you conduct appraisal interviews? Exit interviews? Counseling? Take a few moments to consider these questions and then write a brief essay in which you describe your approach to and rationale for interviewing.
2. Assume that you are a personnel director for a growing industrial firm. Part of your job involves interviewing prospective employees for supervisory positions in the organization. Assume further that you have limited interviewing time so that the questions you ask must be carefully chosen. What are five questions you would ask every interviewee and why?
3. Discuss the *kind* and *quality* of each of the following questions that might conceivably be used in a selection interview.
   a. "What is one of the greatest problems you've faced in your life—and how did you try to handle it?"
   b. "How do you feel about our company's stand on false advertising?"
   c. "Do you like to work with people?"
   d. "Do you hope to advance within our company?"
   e. "How do you react to working under a great deal of pressure?"
4. You are in a managerial position in a small advertising firm. In recent weeks, you have lost three of your best writers and designers, in each case to firms no more reputable than your own. You are greatly concerned about this problem since you know that salaries, fringe benefits, and working conditions in your firm are competitive with those in other firms. You are considering conducting exit interviews with these employees.
   a. What approach might you take with these individuals to overcome problems often associated with exit interviews?
   b. Might you consider simply mailing them a questionnaire instead? Why or why not?

c. What specific kind of information do you hope to discover—that is, what reasons might employees have for leaving an organization that are totally unrelated to the organization's reputation and economic benefits?

5. You are a woman being interviewed for a sales position with a company for which you have aspired to work for several years. The organization is firmly established, produces excellent products, pays well, and the potential for upward mobility is great. You want the job very much. The interviewer has asked you several questions you anticipated, but now he says, "I notice you are wearing an engagement ring. How will your marriage and the possible birth of children affect your career?"

    a. How do you feel about this kind of question generally?

    b. Given the fact you want the job, how do you think you would respond?

    c. Would this question alter your attitude toward this organization? If so, how?

Interviewing Applications

In the preceding chapter, we began our study of interviews—a purposive form of dyadic communication between members of organizations. In this chapter, we will apply those general principles to some specific situations that are of particular importance in any organization. First, we will examine the employment interview from the perspective of both the interviewer and the applicant. Second, we will consider the appraisal interview, used to evaluate past levels of performance and to outline future expectations. Third, we will study the disciplinary interview, used when an employee fails to live up to performance expectations or for some reason violates the organization's standards of conduct. Finally, we will discuss the persuasive interview in which the interviewer (often a salesperson) seeks to influence the attitudes and behaviors of the interviewee (who often is a customer or potential customer). For each situation, we will apply the principles discussed in the previous chapter to the objectives present in the interview setting.

Employment Interviews

Of the many functions an interview can serve, none is more important than the employment interview. For the supervisor or manager, this interview determines the quality of his or her people, and this in turn determines how successful he or she will be as a manager. After all, the definition of supervision or management is "getting work done through others." If those others are inept, the work will not be done well, and the supervisor or manager, along with his or her employees, will fail.

For the interviewee seeking employment, the interview is equally important. Failure to make a good impression during an interview may mean failure to get a position for which the interviewee is well qualified. In addition, failure to ask the right questions during the interview may mean accepting a job for which the interviewee is unqualified or unsuited—almost a guarantee of failure. For someone just beginning a career, selecting the right job is of particular importance. Raelin claims that "the characteristics of a person's first job are important in explaining their later employment success."[1] His research suggests that jobs that provide challenge, opportunities for growth, and independence improve one's attitudes toward and aptitudes in work, thus enhancing chances for success in the future. Therefore, first-time job seekers should choose very carefully what positions they accept: their future could depend on making the right choice.

In the following section, we will examine the employment interview from two perspectives: that of the interviewer looking for qualified candidates and that of the interviewee seeking a position. It is important that you understand both roles. If, for example, you are seeking a position, you should know both your own role and that of the "opposition." After all, if you can anticipate their preferences, needs, and interview strategies, you can present yourself more effectively during the interview. On the other hand, as an interviewer, you must also understand the interviewee's role, because part of your job is to help the interviewees present themselves as well and as accurately as possible. You should never make the mistake of eliminating a qualified applicant on the basis of a poorly conducted interview, just as you should never hire an unqualified candidate who happens to be particularly skilled in being interviewed. Only when both parties are skilled in their own roles and have an understanding of the other's role can the employment interview be maximally effective.

The Role of the Interviewer

As the person seeking a new employee, the interviewer must be involved in a number of processes. These include defining the job, recruiting, prescreening applicants, and interviewing. We will consider each in turn.

Job Requirements

You first must determine the nature of the position to be filled and the corresponding qualifications that a potential applicant must possess. This information should be the basis for recruiting and selecting people for the available position. Among the qualifications you should consider are education, experience, knowledge and skills, physical demands of the job, integrity or trustworthiness, contact with other people, and any other special requirements (such as odd working hours or unusual working conditions).

By identifying these requirements, you achieve a number of things. First and foremost, you identify the *bona fide occupational qualifications* (BFOQ) that, under the law, must serve as the basis for your selection decisions. The Equal Employment Opportunity Commission (EEOC) states that such personal factors as age, sex, race, religion, ethnic origin, and veteran's status cannot be involved in hiring decisions unless a BFOQ necessitates incorporation of that factor. For example, if the job is "men's room attendant" in a hotel, sex becomes a BFOQ, and you are allowed to exclude women from consideration. In most instances, however, you must give equal consideration to all applicants without regard to their demographic characteristics, and you must base your hiring decisions in every instance on the requirements of the position itself.

Identifying job requirements also indicates the sorts of applicants you need, the places in which you should recruit for applicants, the information you should look for when reviewing resumes or application forms, and the information you should seek during the selection interview.

Recruiting

When looking for potential applicants, you should consider a number of sources. First, look at *sources in your own organization*. In almost every organization, it should be a policy to promote from within whenever possible. This policy shows employees that they have a chance to grow within the organization and that the quality of their performance will be rewarded by upward movement.

When additional candidates are desired, *employee referrals should be solicited*. Often, employees know people who might be qualified, and they know the organization well enough to have an idea of the type of candidate who would fit the organization.

Advertising in newspapers, radio, and occasionally television is another common re-cruiting technique. *Professional journals, trade association newsletters,* and *other written media* sent to specific types of employees are also commonly used. These sources must be used carefully, for the law prohibits advertisements that may discriminate on the basis of age, sex, veteran's status, or some other characteristic not related to the job.

Public and private employment agencies can provide job applicants. Headhunters have become the most common source for recruiting executive-level applicants, and many recruitment firms handle lower-level positions as well. Most trade schools, busi-ness schools, junior or community colleges, high schools, and colleges and universities have placement offices and counselors who refer students or graduates. Some schools have internship or work-study programs that are excellent sources for part-time employ-ees and, ultimately, experienced help.

Former employees who left the organization on good terms may refer potential appli-cants, or they may even fill in as temporary help. In some cases, changed family situa-tions (for example, a child now old enough to be cared for by someone else) may make a former employee available for work again. In virtually no case, however, should some-one who was terminated by the organization for cause (that is, fired) be hired again.

Screening

When the recruiting sources have produced a group of applicants, the next task is to sort out those who clearly are unsuited for the job. Typically, two pieces of information are used to screen out unqualified candidates—a resume and references. A *resume or application form* should be obtained from each applicant and should present basic in-formation about educational and work history, personal references, short- and long-term goals. Figure 7.1 presents a completed sample application form—one used by a major corporation but modified for use here. Review the information that the applicant has provided and assess the implications of this information. The things you should look for include:

1. *Time gaps.* Are there any time periods unaccounted for? Might these gaps be important? Why?
2. *Education.* Imagine this individual is applying for a position in sales. How would you evaluate his or her educational background? How would you verify it?
3. *Incomplete information.* Are there any instances where more information should have been given? Could the omissions be important? Why?
4. *Employment history.* Does this record show success? Stability? What can you infer from the information given?
5. *Salary.* Is consistent progress shown? What can you infer about the applicant, based upon her or his salary history?
6. *References.* Are the right people listed as references? Do important people seem to be missing? What can you infer?
7. *Appearance of the application.* Is it neat and easy to read? Grammatically correct? Professional-looking? As Arthur points out, the care with which application forms or resumes are prepared often provides insight into the care with which the applicant would do his or her work.[2]

Figure 7.1
Application for employment.

APPLICATION FOR EMPLOYMENT

Name [Last Name First] _Hill, Timothy A_   Date _____

Address _1763 E Washington Mundelein, IL 60032_   Soc. Sec. No. _335-40-7125_

What kind of work are you applying for? _Sales_   Telephone _(312) 665-4013_

What special qualifications do you have? _____

What office machines can you operate? _____

Who referred you to us? _Bob Petrovitch_

SPECIAL PURPOSE QUESTIONS

DO NOT ANSWER **ANY** OF THE QUESTIONS IN THIS FRAMED AREA UNLESS THE EMPLOYER HAS **CHECKED A BOX PRECEDING** A QUESTION, THEREBY INDICATING THAT THE INFORMATION IS REQUIRED FOR A BONA FIDE OCCUPATONAL QUALIFICATION, OR DICTATED BY NATIONAL SECURITY LAWS, OR IS NEEDED FOR OTHER LEGALLY PERMISSIBLE REASONS.

☐ HEIGHT_____ FEET_____ INCHES ☐ WEIGHT_____ LBS. ☐ CITIZEN OF U.S._____ YES_____ NO ☐ DATE OF BIRTH * _1/10/1970_

☐ _____

* The Age Discrimination in Employment Act of 1967 prohibits discrimination on the basis of age with respect to individuals who are at least 40 but less than 65 years of age.

MILITARY SERVICE RECORD

Armed Forces Service _____ Yes _____ No _____ From _____ To _____

Branch of Service_____ Duties_____

Rank or rating at time of enlistment _____ Rating at time of discharge_____

Any disability?_____

EDUCATION

SCHOOL	DATE * FROM	DATE * TO	NAME OF SCHOOL	CITY	COURSE	DID YOU GRADUATE
GRAMMAR						
HIGH	1984	1988	Grace M. Davis High School			yes
COLLEGE	1988	1992	Northwestern University		Psychology/music	yes
OTHER						

* The Age Discrimination in Employment Act of 1967 prohibits discrimination on the basis of age with respect to individuals who are at least 40 but less than 65 years of age.

EXPERIENCE

NAME AND ADDRESS OF COMPANY	DATE FROM	DATE TO	LIST YOUR DUTIES	STARTING SALARY	FINAL SALARY	REASON FOR LEAVING
International Harvester	6/1/92	8/3/96	Salesperson	12,500	22,000	Resigned
James & Luth Interior Design	9/1/90	5/25/92	Sales Representative (part-time)	per hour 5.00	per hour 7.00	Graduated from school

BUSINESS REFERENCES

NAME	ADDRESS	OCCUPATION
James Randall	International Harvester, Chicago IL (312) 555-1212	Sales Manager
Robert James	James & Luth, Evanston, IL (312) 764-5380	Owner

This form has been designed to strictly comply with State and Federal fair employment practice laws prohibiting discrimination on the basis of an applicant's sex or minority status. Questions directly or indirectly reflecting such status have been included only where needed to determine a bona fide occupational qualification or for other permissible purposes. Such questions are appropriately noted on the application.

Although the information supplied on the application form in figure 7.1 is fictitious, the sorts of considerations listed should be taken into account anytime you review a resume or job application.

The *references provided by the applicant* provide the second source of information you should use during the screening procedure. Typically, you would contact references only for those applicants whose written materials have kept them in contention. The purpose of such reference checks is to get more in-depth information about the applicant and to verify the accuracy of the information provided on the application form or resume. When properly done, a reference check may provide information about the employee's motivation level, aptitudes, attitudes and personality, relations with others, general and specific knowledge and skills, general intelligence, judgment and common sense, resourcefulness, integrity, energy level, accuracy and speed of work, ability to handle pressure and meet deadlines, job progress, and leadership and responsibility levels. Obviously, this information goes far beyond that provided on the application form, and it allows the supervisor to make a far more accurate judgment concerning the suitability of a candidate.

As a rule, you should *seek several such references.* Work-related references are best, although personal references may be appropriate, particularly for younger applicants who have little work experience. Consider the total information accumulated during your reference checks when you decide whether or not to pursue the candidate further. That is, one slightly unfavorable reference should not outweigh two or three favorable ones. However, a single, strongly unfavorable reference may be a signal that you should investigate the applicant more thoroughly.

Upon completion of the reference checks, you will have concluded the screening portion of the employment process. At this point, you should have eliminated applicants who clearly are unsuited for the position. You are now ready to undertake the interviewing process.

The Interviewing Process

Despite the many refinements that have been developed in recruiting and screening methods, the interview is still considered the most vital part of the selection process. The interview offers the prospective employee and the employer the opportunity to obtain information, form impressions, and make observations that would not be possible otherwise. Normally, the *objectives* of the employment interview are:

1. To allow the interviewer to obtain enough knowledge about the applicant to determine if she or he is suitable for employment in a particular position.
2. To provide sufficient information about the organization and the particular job for the applicant to decide whether to accept or reject the job, if offered.
3. To treat the applicant in a manner that will create and maintain goodwill toward the organization.

Achievement of these objectives requires careful planning, as we shall see in the following sections.

Conducting the Interview

The first step is to *prepare*. You should review again the requirements of the position, the qualifications you want an applicant to possess, and the information about this specific applicant you have obtained via written materials and reference checks. You should also take care to eliminate potential distractions (such as telephone calls or unexpected visitors) and to make the surroundings as comfortable as possible. Having done all these things, you are ready to meet the applicant.

Gaining rapport is an important first step in the interview. As interviewer, you should be courteous, show sincerity, express interest, and give complete attention to the interviewee's remarks. First impressions are particularly important in an employment interview from both perspectives, and your appearance, conduct, and attitude will influence the applicant just as much as his or her appearance and conduct will influence you.

When you proceed to the questioning, your continuing concern should be to *avoid the problems that commonly occur during employment interviews.* These include (1) asking questions that can be answered with a simple yes or no (and thus reveal little about the interviewee's abilities in self-expression); (2) asking a series of run-of-the-mill questions for which the astute applicant has long since prepared ready-made answers; (3) using leading questions that suggest the "proper" answer to the applicant or asking questions already answered by the resume; (4) asking questions not related to the task at hand. In addition, you must take care to *avoid unlawful questions* and to ask only those that conform to EEOC requirements and the nature of the job itself.[3] To ensure that your interviewing practices are consistent with legal requirements, you should become familiar with the American Psychological Association's *Principles for the Validation and Use of Personnel Selection Procedures* and the EEOC's *Uniform Guidelines on Employee Selection.*[4]

Under current regulations, it is *unlawful* to ask an applicant:

If he or she has *ever worked under another name,* unless the applicant previously worked for your organization under another name. However, if the applicant is female, you can usually request that she indicate her maiden name.

For his *birthplace* or the birthplace of his *parents, spouse, or other close relatives.* This could reveal the national origin or race of the applicant.

For her *birthdate or age.* However, you may ask if the applicant is over sixty-five or under eighteen.

For his *religious affiliation, church, or the religious holidays* he observes.

If she is a *naturalized citizen.* This could easily establish race or national origin.

How he acquired the ability to read, write, or speak a foreign language. This could easily determine ethnic background.

To *provide names of relatives other than father, mother, husband, wife, or minor-age dependent children.* This may reveal national origin, race, creed, or ethnic background of the applicant or spouse.

For the *names of all clubs, societies, and lodges to which she belongs*. This could reveal the individual's ethnic background and color. However, the applicant can be asked to indicate membership in organizations that are not based on ethnic origins or religious membership practices.

To include a photograph with the application for employment.

For *his or her marital status*.

To reveal *the number of his dependents*.

To list *her children by name or age*.

For the *color of his eyes or hair*.

If she owns her own home.

If her spouse works.

For *personal references*, which may discriminate against minorities. Work references are acceptable.

In general, it is crucial: (1) that you ask *only* questions that pertain to the job's critical requirements (BFOQs), (2) that you avoid general interest or curiosity questions, and (3) that you ask the same questions of all applicants. Following these simple guidelines will keep you safely within the law.

Within this legal framework, there are certain question areas on which you can, and should, focus your attention. These include:

The applicant's work experience: A person's work experience is important and is a natural and easy place to start the interview. Some key questions might be:

1. One of the things we want to talk about today is your work experience. Would you tell me about your present job?
2. What are some of the things on your job you feel you have done particularly well or in which you have achieved the greatest success? Why do you feel this way?
3. What are some of the things about your job that you found difficult to do? Why do you feel they were difficult for you?
4. How do you feel about the progress you have made with your present organization?
5. What are some of the reasons you have for leaving your present or last job?
6. What are some of the things you particularly liked about your last job?
7. Most jobs have pluses and minuses. What were some of the minuses in your last job?

How the applicant feels about people: The way the applicant feels about people—her or his coworkers and supervisors—has an important part in determining job success. Here are the kinds of questions that will help you explore this important area:

1. What do you feel were your supervisor's greatest strengths?
2. In what areas do you feel your supervisor could have done an even better job?
3. How do you feel about the way you or others in the department were treated by your supervisor?

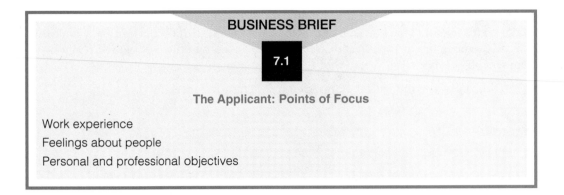

4. How do you feel your supervisor rated your job performance? What evidence do you have to support this conclusion?
5. What kind of people do you like working with? What kind of people do you find most difficult to work with?

The applicant's job objectives: The interviewer needs to know what the applicant's job objectives are in a job or career—what he or she is looking for or wishing to avoid. Here, again, proper questions can be of great help in obtaining such information. For example:

1. What are some of the things in a job that are important to you?
2. What are some of the things you would like to avoid in a job, and why?
3. What is your overall career objective? What are some of the things, outside of your job, that you have done or that you plan to do that will assist you in reaching this objective?
4. What kind of position would you expect to progress to in five years? Ten years?

Besides the kinds of core questions we have just suggested, you will want or need to *use many of the other questioning techniques we discussed in the preceding chapter.* Whenever your initial question does not elicit the kind of information you had hoped to obtain, you probably should follow it up with some kind of probe. Through probes and restatement you can encourage reticent interviewees to go further with their responses so that you obtain a clearer understanding of how they think and feel and what they know.

When you have obtained all the information you need, *be sure that the applicant has a chance to ask questions.* The quality of questions applicants ask may tell you a great deal about their thinking, the extent to which they investigated the organization or position ahead of time, and their familiarity with the field of work. Your purpose is to provide complete, accurate information so applicants can make informed, correct decisions about you and your organization. After all, deceiving applicants to get them to take a job will only result in disillusioned employees once the deception is discovered.

After all of the applicant's questions have been answered, *your final task is to outline the next steps, if any.* If you have reached a decision and have the power to extend an offer at that time, you may choose to do so. Similarly, if you have decided that the employee is not suited to the job, you may also inform him or her of that decision. If you are not in a position to make a decision at that point, tell the applicant what will happen next: when the decision will occur and how it will be communicated. Then follow through.

Preemployment Testing

Many organizations now are conducting various tests of applicants before offering them positions. Greenberg's research revealed four major types of tests commonly conducted:[5]

Drug testing has increased dramatically over the past few years. For example, in 1986, 21 percent of the organizations surveyed conducted drug tests; in 1987, 37 percent were conducting drug tests and 48 percent were doing so in 1988. Most of the respondents said they would not hire an applicant who tested positive for drugs.

Polygraph testing—popularly known as the lie detector—has been severely restricted by federal law. Nevertheless, in states where such testing is permitted, 31 percent of survey respondents indicated they use polygraph tests. Governmental and military units were most likely to conduct polygraph tests of job applicants, followed by banking and financial organizations, health-care providers, and manufacturers.

AIDS testing is perhaps the most controversial. People with AIDS and people who test positive for HIV antibodies are protected by laws preventing discrimination against the handicapped. Moreover, the presence of HIV antibodies does not indicate that a person has AIDS, only that the person has been exposed to AIDS. Nevertheless, some organizations (particularly health-care providers, governmental agencies, and military units) provide AIDS testing, usually on a voluntary basis.

Job skills testing of applicants for non-white-collar positions (such as clerical or secretarial jobs or work on production lines) is increasing.[6] Of the companies surveyed in an American Management Association study, 22.5 percent tested applicants for nonmanagement jobs. Tests of applicants for management positions were far less frequent.

As an interviewer, it is important that you be fully aware of your organization's testing policies and practices and that you tell each applicant of the tests he or she will be required to take. In addition, you should be sure that all applicants for a position take the same tests: selective application of tests has been found to be evidence of discrimination.

Conclusion

Witkin argues that "success on the job is a product of many factors, but failure can be the result of only one."[7] He characterizes the selection process as a "search for the derogatory," in which the interviewer looks for things that may cause the employee to fail and on the basis of those things eliminates contenders from consideration. While this may seem a negative view of employee selection, it is in fact reasonably accurate.

Most important, it emphasizes the need for complete information about each applicant we encounter. The more we are able to learn about an applicant, the better we can determine whether the applicant has a flaw that would prevent effective performance. Working within the requirements of the law, we must do all we can to gain a complete, accurate view of the candidates. By implementing the suggestions outlined above and by reviewing some of the many more detailed works available concerning employment interviewing, you should be able to make maximum use of this important communication tool.[8]

The Role of the Interviewee

Much of the preceding section is also of interest to the job applicant. When seeking a job, you should be aware of the needs and strategies of employers; and you should use that awareness to prepare for your interviews. In this section, we will consider the specific principles that employment interviewees should follow—principles that significantly enhance the likelihood that you will obtain the position of your choice (provided, of course, that you possess the qualifications that the position demands).

Initiating the Quest for Employment

A detailed study of job hunting in the United States revealed that the greater the number of auxiliary avenues used by the job seeker, the greater his or her success in finding a job.[9] The traditional routes include, first, *friends, relatives,* and *former employees.* These individuals can provide the names of people to contact in the organization. You can then address letters of inquiry to specific individuals and not merely to the impersonal "Dear Sir." *Placement agencies* are a second common starting place. College and university placement services are often free and provide students with contacts and interviews. Other placement agencies demand fees and are often affiliated with professional organizations for management, speech communication, accounting, and teaching. General placement agencies find jobs for individuals for a specific fee, often a certain percentage of the first month's or year's salary. In general, these latter services should be approached with caution. A third traditional source of employment potential is *newspaper advertisements.* Responses to ads should include not only the completed application form (if available), but also a resume and a request for an interview. Finally, and less traditional, is the *skills approach* described in the following pages. This can be integrated with some of the other methods, but it does demand that the job seeker engage in considerable preliminary research.

In initiating any employment quest, *make a thorough self-inventory.* Your college major is important, as are work experiences and other kinds of experiences you have had. They are important especially because they indicate something about your values, interests, attitudes, ambitions, and skills. Often we take stock only of our obvious and relatively superficial aspects. We assume, for example, that without a college degree in a specific field, we should never seek employment in that area of specialty. Yet consider the example of the man who, as vice-president for development, saved a small private college from financial disaster. His educational background was in counseling, speech communication, academic affairs, and the ministry. He had never studied development, fundraising, or grant solicitation. His formal knowledge of annual giving programs, capital campaigns, and deferred giving was minimal. Even so, he succeeded in his position because he possessed the *skills* that allowed him to understand people and their needs and interests, to have compassion for them, and to move them persuasively to support causes in which they believed. Thus, his skills were *transferable* from his academic background and professional experiences to the business of fundraising. It is important that you identify and list those skills you possess that might be attractive to a prospective employer.

Researching the Organization

Understanding yourself and your skills can best be accomplished in conjunction with knowledge of the organization. Bolles believes that organizational research should be a major focus of each person's preliminary employment strategy.[10] At the very least, you should learn the location of the organization's plants, branches, and offices; the age of the company; the kinds of services it offers; and its growth and future potential. The list of useful questions, however, could continue: How does the organization rank within its field? Is the organization family-owned? If so, does this influence promotions? How innovative is the organization? What is the existing political situation? Are there imminent proxy fights, upcoming mergers? What kind of image does the organization have in the mind of the public? Does the organization have special hiring policies (such as preferences for employees with previous experience)? What kind of staff turnover does it have? What is the attitude of current employees? Does the organization encourage its employees to further their education? In general, how does communication flow within the organization? Is decision making highly centralized, or is it spread throughout the organization?

Sources of information on organizations are numerous and include the following: Better Business Bureau reports on the organization; chambers of commerce; college libraries; the organization's annual reports; *Dun and Bradstreet's Million Dollar* and *Middle Market* directories; *Fortune's Plant and Product Directory; Standard and Poor's Register of Corporations, Directors, and Executives; Standard and Poor's Industrial Index; Standard and Poor's Listed Stock Reports; MacRae's Blue Book—Corporate Index; Thomas's Register of American Manufacturers; Fitch's Corporation Reports; Business Week; Dun's Review; The Wall Street Journal; Fortune; Who's Hiring Who: Job Directory;* and, finally, anyone affiliated with the organization—college alumni, friends, brokers—who can provide helpful insights.

Presentation of Self in Writing

For many job seekers, the initial contact with the organization is through writing. Dozens of books exist that provide comprehensive guidelines for writing cover letters and resumes.[11] The following discussion focuses on only the *essentials* of both forms of written communication.

To begin with, send each prospective employer an original *cover letter*. The cover letter is important. Sherer's recent investigation suggested that it might have even more impact than the resume in affecting hiring decisions.[12] Whenever possible, address your letter to the specific person who will be actively involved in the recruiting process. The cover letter should be short, and it should describe your areas of interest, special skills, knowledge and experience, and the reason(s) for your selection of this particular organization. The cover letter should not simply reiterate information contained in the resume but creatively amplify it. If, for example, there is a piece of negative information in your resume, such as some low grades in a specific subject, then the cover letter may be used to offer brief explanations or elaborations. In particular, you should describe the abilities you possess and the skills you have that make you particularly well suited for this job. Finally, the cover letter can be used to request additional information about the organization. It should always include the times you are available for interviewing and your phone numbers. In general, cover letters should be neat, clear, checked for spelling, and provide for you a forthright and fresh introduction. Figure 7.2 presents a sample cover letter.

Cover letters are typically accompanied by *resumes* (also referred to as personal fact or data sheets). According to one extensive survey, 98 percent of all organizations prefer to receive both as part of the initial contact.[13] Like the cover letter, resumes should be brief (one to two pages) and should include the following basic information: (1) *personal data*—work and home phone numbers and address; (2) *professional goal or job objective—which recognizes the employer's needs;* for example, "college professor in a four-year liberal arts institution that values dedicated undergraduate teachers" or "salesperson with an innovative firm where self-motivation and discipline are encouraged"; (3) *educational background*—majors and minors in college, knowledge acquired, degrees received, other special training, and dates associated with each; (4) *geographic preferences and willingness to relocate;* (5) *awards, scholarships, and honors;* (6) *work experience*—including jobs held, responsibilities associated with and skills developed in each, and dates and places of employment; (7) *memberships in organizations and offices held*—could include service clubs, sororities, and athletics. In addition, some organizations will want to know something about salary expectations (although this information is more often discussed during the interview). Others will be concerned with grades, particularly in majors and minors, and may even request a transcript. Any subsidiary interests or talents—such as typing, operating computers, or public speaking skills—may be listed on the resume. A list of references may be included or furnished upon request. Each resume should be carefully planned and structured, checked for spelling and wordiness, and professionally printed on white, off-white, or light beige bond paper. Figures 7.3 and 7.4 present sample resumes. Your resume should create a first impression of you as an individual—with unique skills and contributions to offer. Thus, no two resumes should be exactly alike.

Figure 7.2
Sample cover letter.

February 15, 1994

208A Clark House—Read Center
Indiana University
Bloomington, IN 47406

Philip Johnson
College Recruitment Director
General Telephone of Indiana
1633 North Meridian Street
Indianapolis, IN 46208

Dear Mr. Johnson:

In a recent meeting with Tim Hill, Director of Public Relations for General Telephone here in Bloomington, he suggested I write you concerning your research for individuals interested in working in public relations.

As my enclosed resume indicates, I am about to graduate from Indiana University with a double major in public relations and organizational behavior. I am very much interested in pursuing a career in public relations, preferably with a large organization. My past work experiences have taken me into several organizations where I assisted in advertising efforts, worked with the layout and design of company brochures, wrote newspaper articles and made speeches. This past summer, I worked part-time for the Bloomington branch of your organization—particularly with designing public relations brochures. I found my experience with General Telephone to be rewarding. I was especially impressed with the opportunities you provide for geographic mobility and continuing education. I am eager to investigate the possibility of full-time public relations employment.

Would it be possible for us to discuss this further in an interview? I am available every afternoon (1:00 to 5:00), Monday through Friday. I may be reached at (812) 337–4697, or at the above address. I'd be delighted to travel to Indianapolis anytime of convenience to you. Thank you for your consideration.

Sincerely,

Emily C. Henson

Behavior during the Interview

After you have engaged in the kind of self-assessment and organizational research that we have suggested, you are in an excellent position to approach the employment interview. Not only have you considered such practical issues as whether or not you work well under pressure and where you prefer to live geographically, but you have examined the more philosophical issues involving your personal and professional goals, such as the meaning of success to you, the kinds of people you desire to associate with professionally, the things you value in life, and the kind and amount of recognition necessary for

Figure 7.3
Sample employment resume.

EMILY C. HENSON

CURRENT ADDRESS:
208A Clark House—Read Center
Indiana University
Bloomington, IN 47406

PERMANENT ADDRESS:
1706 Maple Avenue
Elkhart, IN 46207

PROFESSIONAL GOAL:
To obtain a public relations position in a corporate setting where creativity and self-motivation are stressed.

EDUCATION:
B.A. in Public Relations and Organization Behavior. Indiana University, Bloomington, May, 1994.

Diploma of Graduation from North High School granted June, 1990 in Elkhart, Indiana, with majors in English and speech, minors in history and art.

GEOGRAPHIC PREFERENCES:
Midwest or West; willing to relocate.

SUBJECTS STUDIED IN DEPTH:
Public relations, artistic layout and design, journalism, speech, organizational behavior and development, and advertising.

G.P.A. (on a 4.0 scale):
B.A. degree, overall: 3.2
    public relations major: 3.5
    organizational behavior major: 3.3

WORK EXPERIENCE:

Sept. 1993–Present
Editorial staff of *Indiana Daily Student;* researched and wrote over 50 news stories and 12 editorials; also assisted in preparation (layout and design) of Indiana University *Alumni Magazine.*

June 1993–August 1993
Worked as part-time assistant to the Director of Public Relations, Bloomington office of General Telephone; made speeches, designed brochures, and wrote news releases.

Sept. 1992–May 1993
Worked part-time to assist the Indiana University Director of Alumni Affairs in designing public relations brochures, making public speeches, and conducting alumni telethons.

June 1992–August 1992
Staff writer for the *Elkhart Tribune;* wrote 15–20 news stories, conducted interviews, and typed.

Sept. 1991–May 1992
Wrote occasional articles for the *Indiana Daily Student.*

AWARDS AND HONORS:
Dean's List three of four college years; "Outstanding Journalist" for *Indiana Daily Student,* 1993; One of America's Outstanding Young Women, 1992.

CLASS ACTIVITIES:
B.P.W. (1990 to present); Alpha Chi Omega, member (1990–1992) and vice president (1992–1993); Student Speaker's Bureau (1991–1994); Indiana University Student Foundation (1991–1994); tennis team (1992–1994).

REFERENCES:
Furnished upon request.

Figure 7.4
Sample employment resume.

Mary E. Kelly

409 S. Ramble Road
Cincinnati, OH 45201
(513) 794–6308

Objective

Human Resource Specialist. To use my graduate education, knowledge of training, recruitment, and performance appraisal to develop highly trained, motivated, and productive employees for a progressive organization.

Education

Indiana University Graduate School, Bloomington, M.A. Organizational Communication, 1993
- M.A. Thesis: Conflict Management and Performance Appraisal, GPA 3.9/4.0
- Awarded Indiana University Arts and Sciences Full Fee Scholarship

Indiana University, Bloomington, B.A. Telecommunications, 1990, GPA 3.4/4.0
- Kappa Alpha Theta Women's Fraternity: Panhellenic Representative and Rush Counselor

Boston University, London (England) Journalism Internship Program, August–December 1988

Summary of Qualifications

- Developed and taught courses for the Indiana University Department of Speech Communication and School of Business. Topics included EEO policies, management theory, interviewing, and group decision making.
- Developed and presented workshops on conflict management, briefing techniques, and diversity.
- Recruiting experience in both academic and business environments.

Skills

Training

Trainer, <u>Atlanta Executive Services Corps</u>, *Present*. <u>U.S. Defense Intelligence Agency</u> *July 1993* <u>Bloomington (IN) Department of Human Resources</u> *May 1992–May 1993.* Design, develop and facilitate training on diversity, briefing techniques, and conflict management.

Associate Instructor, <u>Indiana University</u>, Bloomington, *August 1991–June 1993* Designed and presented lectures, activities, and examinations to teach the fundamentals of business and professional communication. Received 1992 Arts & Science Excellence in Teaching Award. Selected to teach a course previously reserved for Ph.D. level instructors.

Entertainment Supervisor, <u>Kings Island Theme Park</u>, Cincinnati, OH *Summers 1985–1987* Trained and supervised crew of forty people, managed entertainment facilities.

Organizational

Account Executive, <u>WBWB FM Radio Station</u>, Bloomington, IN *May 1990–June 1991* Consulted with clients regarding advertising needs, budget, development of advertising campaign, and production of commercials. Managed over eighty accounts, recognized by corporate president for having tripled productivity of accounts within first six months.

Guest Relations Manager, <u>Kings Island Theme Park</u>, Cincinnati, OH *April 1988–August 1988* Addressed needs of park guests through problem solving and advising park management.

Recruiting

Masters Faculty Representative, <u>Indiana University</u>, Bloomington, IN *August 1991–May 1992* Interviewed candidates applying for faculty positions. Gathered information on candidates' qualifications and graduate students' impressions and reported findings to department faculty.

Recruiting Assistant, <u>Management Recruiters</u>, Cincinnati, OH *June–August 1991* Matched human resource needs of client organizations with suitable applicants.

Recruiter, <u>Indiana University Admissions Office</u>, Bloomington, IN *April 1989–May 1990* Traveled with admissions staff, made presentations to prospective I.U. students and parents.

Technical

Computer, proficient in Wordperfect, Microsoft Word, and Vax Mail System
Audio/Visual, experience in audio and video production.

References available upon request.

you to be satisfied. Indeed, each individual should approach the employment interview by giving considerable thought to current events, morality, and personal value orientations. It is not uncommon for an employer to be concerned about prospective employees' stands on these matters.

The Initial Impression

Just as it is important for the interviewer to establish rapport early in the interview, it is also critical for you as an interviewee to make a favorable *initial impression.* Most interviewers make their decisions during the first four or five minutes of the interview.[14] Being on time is essential. In our culture, punctuality is indicative of good manners and interest in the forthcoming interaction. You should secure the name of the interviewer and use it throughout the interview.

A critical part of the initial impression will be determined by your appearance. Stewart and Cash point out that "philosophically it might be wrong to judge a man by how he dresses, but we in fact do just that."[15] It is not possible or even desirable to describe in detail the ideal attire for a selection interview. Each interview should be approached with intelligence and common sense regarding the sort of image you wish to convey (casual versus formal), the sort of position for which you are interviewing (an assembly-line foreman versus a college professor), and the kind of organization represented by the interviewer (industrial firm, elementary school, or research and development branch of an organization). Regardless of the specific garb chosen, you should appear neat and clean. In general, if there is some doubt regarding the most appropriate attire, it is best to err on the conservative side.

Throughout the interview, you will communicate both verbally and nonverbally. Through the use of body, voice, and language, you will articulate ideas and, perhaps more subtly, express attitudes and reveal values. Many aspects of nonverbal communication that apply to any communication encounter were discussed in chapter 5. You will be evaluated by the manner in which you walk (slovenly, aggressively, aimlessly); shake hands (limply, warmly, vigorously); sit (slumped, rigidly, reasonably relaxed); express yourself facially (darting eyes, full open-eye contact, animated versus expressionless face); and move (animated versus inert, tense versus relaxed).[16]

The use of your voice is also important. Vocal quality, pitch, audibility, intelligibility, and expressiveness all count, and so does language usage—especially vocabulary and grammar. It is usually best, for example, to avoid slang, to use a "normal" vocabulary (devoid of attempts to impress the interviewer with your knowledge of "big" words), and to speak grammatically. It is also vital that you articulate your views persuasively.

Several studies have revealed that the applicant's communication effectiveness has a profound impact on how she or he is rated by the interviewer and on whether or not she or he receives a job offer.[17] Whenever possible, communicate positive information about yourself. In discussing your skills and abilities, try to relate them to the specific organization with which you are interviewing. Specify how and why you think you are well suited to this particular organization. By so doing, you demonstrate your knowledge of the organization and match the organization's needs with your talents. Whatever claims you make about your positive qualities, abilities, or skills, always substantiate them with support. It is not enough to say, " I'm really motivated." You need to support that assertion with examples of situations in which you demonstrated motivation or quote the testimony of others who concur with your self-perception.

Finally, you must recognize that *nervousness is natural*. What normal person can approach a situation, whose outcome might affect him or her for many years ahead, with an attitude of "who cares?" No one does, nor should anyone. Nervousness in selection interviews, like stage fright in public speaking, can best be controlled through adequate preparation and the recognition that the decision making is not unilateral but *shared*. Most interviewees discover that once they begin to concentrate on responding to questions and expressing their views articulately and honestly, much of their initial nervousness disappears. It is well to remember that *moderate* anxiety is usually a stimulus for improved performance. Some nervousness is not only natural, but may actually be an asset.

Qualities to Reveal during the Interview

As we saw in chapter 1, there are many qualities interviewers look for during an employment interview: oral communication skills, motivation, initiative, and so on. Your behavior during the interview must exhibit these characteristics; it is hardly persuasive to say to the interviewer, "Oh, by the way; I'm motivated, assertive, loyal, mature, enthusiastic, and a natural leader." Thus, during the interview, you should show several behavioral and attitudinal characteristics indicative of these desirable traits. The first behavior that is desirable during an interview is *directness*. Directness is revealed, in part, through appropriate eye contact, posture, and other mannerisms. An applicant who is withdrawn will often shrink back into her chair, will seldom gesture, and usually avoids eye contact with the interviewer. Equally important, however, is verbal directness. As an interviewee, you should never evade questions but respond to them thoroughly and directly. Avoid starting your statements with such phrases as, "Well, I could be wrong, but . . ." or "I guess I think this would work. . . ." Instead, phrase your ideas decisively and clearly.

Closely related to directness is *responsiveness*. The interviewer should not feel that he is "prying" information from you. After all, an important purpose of the interview is for the organizational representative to gain additional data from you. Thus, you should approach the interview with an expectation of actively participating. Active involvement requires good listening on your part. We have already discussed listening in detail in chapter 5, but here we might also point out that many an inadequate answer can be avoided if the interviewee listens actively and empathically.

Interviewers also expect interviewees to be *mentally alert*. This, of course, is not synonymous with brilliance but is related to one's comprehension of questions and articulateness in responding to them. Your mental alertness may also be judged by your willingness to substantiate your assertions with evidence. Alertness should be matched by general *emotional control*. Particularly when confronted with questioning techniques such as reactive or hypothetical probes, you should remain reasonably poised and

An unusually exhaustive hiring process is used by Toyota Motor Manufacturing U.S.A. in Georgetown, Kentucky:

Step 1: The Kentucky Department of Employment Services has applicants complete application forms and view a one-hour videotape describing Toyota's work environment and selection system.

Step 2: Applicants take the Situation Judgment Inventory, which tests their interpersonal skills and ability to work in a team environment. The test is administered and scored by the Kentucky Department of Employment Services.

Step 3: Applicants participate in four hours of group and individual problem-solving and discussion activities conducted at Toyota's assessment center. In addition, applicants for assembly-line jobs participate in a five-hour assembly simulation, with other candidates playing the role of manager.

Step 4: A one-hour group interview is conducted by Toyota with several candidates, allowing their group communication skills to be assessed.

Step 5: Applicants undergo two and one-half hours of physical and drug and alcohol tests at an area hospital.

Step 6: New hires are closely monitored and coached on the job for their first six months at work; those unable to perform acceptably are immediately discharged.

From Gary Dessler, "Value-Based Hiring Builds Commitment," *Personnel Journal* 72 (November 1993): 98–102.

emotionally in command. Interviewers can (and occasionally do) ask questions that confuse, startle, or even embarrass. When this happens, do not panic, but take a few seconds to think carefully before you respond. You should also make some assessment of the reason for the question (for example, to test creativity or to see how you respond to unanticipated conditions). In general, whenever a difficult or unclear question is posed, the best strategy is to ask for clarification or admit to some difficulty in responding.

Highly personal questions that have no bearing on the job should probably be deflected. In fact, as we pointed out earlier in this chapter, they are often illegal. Employers who ask an engaged woman how getting married will affect her job or how soon she plans to have children are engaging in illegal questioning. Responding to such questions is difficult. Some interviewers reason that "if you want the job badly enough, you'll answer the question." On the other hand, such questions often are asked by interviewers who simply do not know any better or want to test the applicant's assertiveness. A smiling response (such as, "Well, I really don't think that has a bearing on how well I would perform here. Let's talk about job-related things.") that redirects the interview back to work-related subjects probably would be most effective.

All of these attitudinal qualities relate directly or indirectly to *openness*. An interview is not the place to be coy or evasive. Whenever you attempt to distort or rationalize your behavior (for example, a poor grade or a long period of unemployment), you succeed only in confusing or alienating the interviewer (remember, she's heard these tales before). Honesty is not just the best policy, but the *only* policy to follow in selection interviews. Interviewees who can honestly assess themselves, who are not afraid to admit to weaknesses or mention strengths, who can say with poise and openness, "I don't understand how you're using the word *ethics*," and who sincerely attempt to be clear, direct, and straightforward will gain a positive evaluation from most interviewers.

In addition to behaviors and attitudes, there are several other qualities employers often consider important. Interviewees should anticipate having to provide or expound on information relating to their ability, desire to work, social-emotional maturity, and character.[18] *Ability* can be demonstrated in several ways and can have a variety of meanings to different organizations. Some organizations believe that the important thing is to hire bright people, and they will learn (via training and experience) to do the job well, regardless of their lack of specific education, training, and previously acquired skills and experiences related to the job. Needless to say, strive to communicate so as to reveal intelligence and adaptability. But as we have said throughout this chapter, before the interview, you need to reflect on your skills, experiences, and training related to the job. Only in this way can you understand and subsequently articulate how these experiences increase your capability for the position.

Another critical quality is your *motivation to work*. Achievements in past endeavors (such as high grades or promotions in other jobs) are often indicative of high motivation. Frequent job changes in the past may be viewed as indicative of motivational instability. You should anticipate having to explain such changes. Once again, careful preparation leading to the interview can be most beneficial in expressing motivation. Interviewees who are extremely well informed about the organization and can articulate precisely why they are seeking employment are usually perceived as being highly motivated to work productively in the organization.

Social/emotional maturity is also important and is largely related to your personal goals. Although few individuals seek employment solely for the contributions they can make to the organization, many mature persons desire to contribute substantially to their professions and to society. Organizations are also increasingly seeking individuals who are imaginative, self-reliant, and independent.

Certainly not the least important of the qualities to be demonstrated during the interview is your *character*. Ethical judgments are never easy to make. Sometimes information regarding personal integrity and responsibility can be gleaned from your credentials. For example, any existing history of financial responsibility or testimony provided in letters of recommendation may serve as evidence. For the most part, however, character will be judged on the basis of the personal behavior you exhibit during the interview—particularly in relationship to openness, honesty, and objectivity in self-assessment. If, for example, your record has some flaws—low grades, a firing incident—the wisest course is to admit it, take responsibility for it, and discuss what you learned from the incident and how you think you have grown.

At the conclusion of the interview, you should pose any questions you have not yet had an opportunity to ask. It is imperative that you know what to expect next procedurally. The interviewer should provide this information. In the event that he or she does not, you need to find out where you stand and when and how the next communication is to occur. Immediately following the interview, you might send a note to the interviewer, thanking the person for her time and reiterating the fact that you will be pleased to hear from the organization soon. It is also appropriate to offer to send any additional data the interviewer might desire. A sample thank-you letter follows in figure 7.5.

Conclusion

There is one overriding problem that, more than anything else, contributes to poor employment interviewing: the natural desire on the part of each participant to be wanted by the other. As a result, each participant tries to sell the organization or self to the other. Neither participant provides the other with complete, accurate information; and each participant concentrates too much upon making a good impression on the other.

To avoid this pitfall, both parties must take a problem-solving approach. As an applicant, you have a problem: finding a compatible, interesting, rewarding job. As an interviewer, you also have a problem: finding a qualified, productive, and—it is hoped—satisfied new employee. Really, these two problems are one and the same. Rather than trying to sell each other a product, the interviewer and the applicant should work toward the resolution of a common problem: determining whether the position's requirements and the applicant's qualities are compatible.

The problem-solving perspective is the key to success in employment interviewing, both as an applicant and as an interviewer. When seeking a job, you must learn enough about the organization to make an intelligent decision about spending part of your future there, but you must also give the interviewer enough information about yourself so that he or she can make an informed decision about your suitability for the position. After all, the interviewer knows the organization and the position far better than you. You, on the other hand, know yourself better than does the interviewer. Only by exchanging information can each of you educate the other to the extent that both of you can make the best possible decision. So be prepared, make a good impression, ask good questions, and follow up after the interview. Above all, be open and honest as you communicate with representatives of the organizations with whom you interview.

Appraisal Interviews

The director of the Medical Records Department at St. Luke's Hospital, Nancy Walser, had a reputation for being one of the toughest managers in the hospital. She disapproved of socializing among the Medical Records employees, constantly emphasized that they get as much work done as quickly as possible, and closely watched everyone's activities at work. Productivity in the department was extremely high, and very few errors were made by the employees. On the other hand, morale among employees was not particularly good, and conflicts between Medical Records personnel and the physicians and nurses working in the hospital were common.

Figure 7.5
Sample "thank-you" letter.

April 10, 1994

208A Clark House—Read Center
Indiana University
Bloomington, IN 47406

Philip Johnson
College Recruitment Director
General Telephone of Indiana
1633 North Meridian Street
Indianapolis, IN 46208

Dear Mr. Johnson:

Thanks again for taking the time to meet with me last Tuesday. I enjoyed very much the time I spent with you, and I left the interview even more convinced that I could make a positive contribution to General Telephone of Indiana.

During the interview, you indicated that you are looking for two things: practical experience and an ability to be flexible. In both areas, I feel I have something to offer. My work on the editorial staff of the *Indiana Daily Student,* with the public relations office of General Telephone in Bloomington, and in the Director of Alumni Affairs office at I.U., all have given me the firsthand experience that is so important to success in any organization. And in each of these positions, changing dead-lines, priorities, and events in the community taught me flexibility. No one could have survived in those positions without being able to adapt almost instantaneously!

You asked me to provide some references. May I suggest you contact the following:

Mr.Robert Jordan	Richard L. Enos, Editor	Mr. Timothy A. Hill
Faculty Advisor, *Indiana Daily Student*	*Terre Haute Tribune*	Director, Public Relations
Indiana University	12 Terre Haute Ave.	General Telephone of Indiana
Bloomington, IN 43703	Terre Haute, IN 42802	Bloomington, IN 43703
(203) 555–8713	(212) 555–8989	(203) 555–8713

Each of these individuals would be able to give you their perceptions of my work performance and my ability to adapt to changing priorities.

Again, I appreciate your having taken the time to meet with me. Please feel free to contact me if you need any additional information.

Sincerely,

Emily C. Henson

Emily C. Henson

Mary Skeen had worked in Medical Records for eight years, making her the second longest-term employee in the twenty-four-person department. She did not particularly like working for Nancy but needed the job and, in fact, took some pride in the quality of her work. Her annual appraisal interview was scheduled soon, and she expected to receive good ratings and a substantial raise.

The date for Mary's appraisal came and went. In fact, four weeks passed and she had heard nothing. One day, however, Nancy walked up to Mary's desk and said, "Mary, I'd like to see you for a minute." "Sure," Mary replied. Nancy handed her three sheets of paper. "Here are three copies of your performance review. I've already filled them out, so read them and sign them, and then give them back to me. I didn't give you much of a raise; your attitude hasn't been good lately, and you were late coming to work last week. Try to improve." Nancy walked off before Mary could reply.

This appraisal interview, such as it is, illustrates almost everything that commonly is done wrong in interviews of this type. The interview was late. No notification was given the employee. No review of job requirements occurred. No review of performance standards or measures happened. The "recency" effect prevailed. No strengths were noted and no plans for improvement made. Small wonder that Mary filed a grievance that same afternoon and that Nancy eventually was removed from the directorship of the department.

Few situations create more discomfort for both managers and employees than performance appraisals. McGregor undoubtedly was correct when he observed that "managers are uncomfortable when they are put in the position of 'playing God.' "[19] He probably could have added that employees are equally uncomfortable about having their bosses enact that role. Yet performance appraisals are a necessity if employee performance is to be evaluated and rewarded.

Purposes

While there is no substitute for good day-to-day communication between supervisor and employee, the formal yearly (or semiyearly) performance appraisal serves some specific functions.[20] Ideally, such an appraisal should

1. Tell the employee where she stands—how the supervisor judges that employee's performance to have been during the review period.
2. Give the employee guidance for doing a better job in the future by clarifying what is expected of him.
3. Plan developmental and growth opportunities for the employee and identify specific areas in which the employee needs to improve her knowledge and skills.
4. Give the employee an opportunity to express his feelings about performance-related matters.

Problems

Research has revealed a number of common failings in performance interviews. Lahiff found that appraisal interviews often tend to *dwell upon the individual's negative characteristics.* This is a highly destructive approach, as is indicated by Kay, Meyer, and French's discovery that the more weaknesses the manager mentions during the interview, the poorer the worker's performance becomes, and the lower he or she rates the organization's appraisal system.[21]

A second common fault is the *halo effect,* a term first used in 1920 to describe the tendency people have to see one positive trait in someone and then to attribute to that person a variety of other positive traits. Thus, we mentally place a halo around the head of that person. If an employee arrives early and leaves late every day, we probably will be impressed. However, if this causes us to overlook the poor quality and quantity of his work or his inability to get along with his peers, then we have fallen victims to the halo effect.

The *central tendency effect* is yet another common problem. We may tend to classify others as "average" and not do the hard work necessary for spotting gradations. If we assign the same average rating to everyone, then we do not have to think very much about the characteristics that distinguish their performance levels. Similarly, the *leniency effect* occurs when everyone is given an equally high rating. The *critical effect* takes place when no employee can measure up to the supervisor's standards, so that all of them are judged deficient.

The *recency effect* occurs when we allow more recent events to outweigh past history. A recent mistake by an employee may, psychologically, cause us to erase from the record the many previous occasions on which the employee did well. Nancy's comments in the beginning of this section that Mary's "attitude hasn't been good lately" and that she was late coming to work last week typifies the influence that many supervisors allow the recent past to have.

The question thus arises: How can we avoid all of these problems and use appraisal interviews in ways that maximize their effectiveness as analytic and motivational tools? Our own experience suggests that *effective appraisal interviewing is a result of two things: careful preparation and skillful procedures.* We will consider each of these in turn.

Preparation

You should do three things as you prepare for an appraisal session. First, you should *review the requirements of the employee's job.* Much evidence suggests that supervisors and subordinates have quite different perceptions of the employee's job and that supervisors rarely are able to provide accurate descriptions of their employees' written job duties as expressed in job descriptions.[22] It is vital that you review the tasks that the employee ought to have performed and that you decide in your own mind which of them

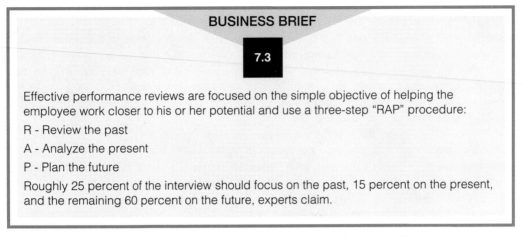

From "Making the Most of Employee Reviews," *Practical Supervision* 1 (September 1992): 2.

is more important than the others. If you have conducted past appraisals for this employee, you should also review those to remind yourself of any plans for performance improvement that the two of you developed in previous meetings.

Second, you should *obtain input from the employee concerning his level of performance.* Using a written questionnaire (perhaps similar to the preappraisal form in table 7.1), the employee should describe for you those objectives he felt he was to achieve, the behaviors he was to perform, the strengths and weaknesses of his performance, and his short- and long-range career objectives. Remember, superiors and subordinates typically have different perceptions. By obtaining this sort of information, you are able to review the employee's perceptions before your interview begins.

Third, you should *complete the performance review form,* if any, that your organization requires. These forms are important, for they provide a written record of the decisions you and your employee make about his or her performance.[23] As such, they may serve as the basis for future personnel decisions (such as promotions, transfers, or discharge), or they may protect you from action taken against you by an employee.

When completing the review form before the interview, you must make one final decision: Will the ratings you provide serve as the final appraisal of the employee, or will they simply be a worksheet that you will use to guide the interview, which you will revise when the interview is over? Strong arguments can be offered for each alternative. If your ratings stand, then you will not be persuaded by employees who are not good workers but who are good salespersons. More than once we have seen good workers suffer because they are not very skilled interviewees and poorer workers come out well because they are good at "slinging the bull." If your rating is to be final, then the principle of cooperative problem solving is violated. Thus, you may want to take a compromise approach: Use the rating forms to provide your final rating of the employee's performance (perhaps taking into account the self-perception information you have obtained in advance), and use the interview to communicate those ratings to the employee and then to cooperatively develop a plan for future improvements in his or her performance.

Table 7.1 Employees' Preappraisal Summary

Instructions: In the space provided below, answer the questions posed.

1. Since your last interview, how well do you think you have performed? Give specific examples, details, information, and so on that indicate why you . . .

2. Looking toward the future, in what ways do you think your performance can be improved, and how can your supervisor help you to achieve those improvements?

3. What long-term goals for personal development or achievement do you have? How can your supervisor help you achieve them?

4. What long-term objectives for personal and professional development do you have? How can your supervisor help you to achieve them?

5. What additional comments, if any, do you have concerning your performance during the past year, your future objectives, or your upcoming performance appraisal?

Performance evaluations can help people to reach their potential when they include such questions as:

What are five key projects or goals you have here, and how can I help to support them?

Does our company need you? What do you want to do here? What are you planning to do to reach your goals?

What will you do in the coming year to develop the three highest-potential people who work for you?

What are your personal plans for continuing education and development for the coming year?

From "Performance-Review Questions," *Communication Briefings* (February 1993): 6.

Procedures

While a number of approaches to the appraisal interview are available, one of the most reasonable systems is that suggested by Brett and Fredian.[24] They suggest a seven-step model for performance appraisal. The first step is to *get to the point of the interview.* The appraisal should begin with a statement of the purpose of the meeting and a brief overview of the structure that the interview will follow.

The supervisor next should *describe specifically the important elements of the employee's past performance.* She should talk about criteria that both of them understand (amount of work, quality of work) and should give both good and bad examples of the employee's performance. These specifics are important: The employee learns nothing if he is simply told that "you are doing a good job." The discussion should focus on work-related matters and should deal only with performance areas that are really important. Perhaps the best way to ensure these things is to state the specific job requirement and then provide specific indications of performance. For example:

> Pat, part of your job is to write monthly summary reports of employee relations activities in each production plant and to have those to all members of top management by the fifteenth of the next month. In five of your twelve reports, you were more than one week late in getting those reports out. I want to discuss this with you.

This statement indicates the job requirement, provides specific information, tells Pat what is important to the supervisor, and indicates that he will have a chance to discuss the matter before any final decisions are reached. This is far superior to simply saying, "Pat, your ER reports are often late."

Third, the supervisor should *provide employees with a chance to give their own observations.* As you invite them to describe their performance, you perform step four in the appraisal process: *listen.* Using the techniques reviewed in earlier chapters, actively

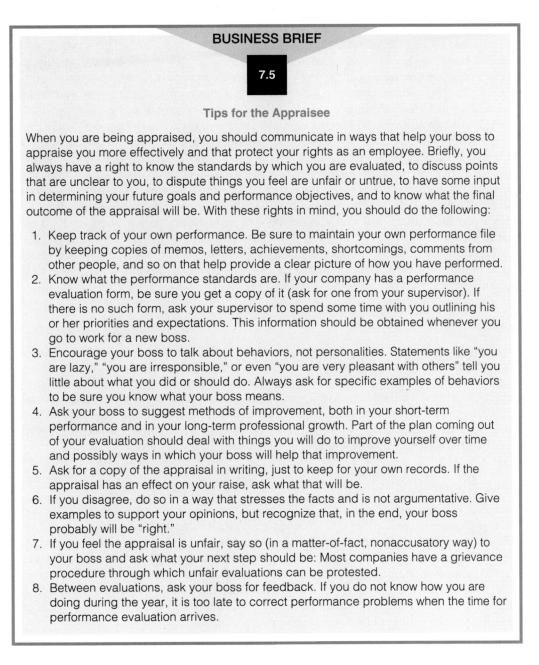

BUSINESS BRIEF

7.5

Tips for the Appraisee

When you are being appraised, you should communicate in ways that help your boss to appraise you more effectively and that protect your rights as an employee. Briefly, you always have a right to know the standards by which you are evaluated, to discuss points that are unclear to you, to dispute things you feel are unfair or untrue, to have some input in determining your future goals and performance objectives, and to know what the final outcome of the appraisal will be. With these rights in mind, you should do the following:

1. Keep track of your own performance. Be sure to maintain your own performance file by keeping copies of memos, letters, achievements, shortcomings, comments from other people, and so on that help provide a clear picture of how you have performed.
2. Know what the performance standards are. If your company has a performance evaluation form, be sure you get a copy of it (ask for one from your supervisor). If there is no such form, ask your supervisor to spend some time with you outlining his or her priorities and expectations. This information should be obtained whenever you go to work for a new boss.
3. Encourage your boss to talk about behaviors, not personalities. Statements like "you are lazy," "you are irresponsible," or even "you are very pleasant with others" tell you little about what you did or should do. Always ask for specific examples of behaviors to be sure you know what your boss means.
4. Ask your boss to suggest methods of improvement, both in your short-term performance and in your long-term professional growth. Part of the plan coming out of your evaluation should deal with things you will do to improve yourself over time and possibly ways in which your boss will help that improvement.
5. Ask for a copy of the appraisal in writing, just to keep for your own records. If the appraisal has an effect on your raise, ask what that will be.
6. If you disagree, do so in a way that stresses the facts and is not argumentative. Give examples to support your opinions, but recognize that, in the end, your boss probably will be "right."
7. If you feel the appraisal is unfair, say so (in a matter-of-fact, nonaccusatory way) to your boss and ask what your next step should be: Most companies have a grievance procedure through which unfair evaluations can be protested.
8. Between evaluations, ask your boss for feedback. If you do not know how you are doing during the year, it is too late to correct performance problems when the time for performance evaluation arrives.

and attentively listen to the employees, both encouraging them to talk and retaining the information for use in the last portions of the interview.

When we have analyzed past performance, the fifth step is to *lay out future plans and goals*. Here, we need to take the problem-solving approach to two things—improving performance weaknesses from the past and assessing new objectives or goals to be accomplished in the future. What does the employee feel he should do to achieve his goals, and how does he feel you should evaluate the quality of his performance in doing them? Naturally, you have your own ideas about his goals and objectives, so you will need to work together to arrive at an action plan for next year's performance. Finally, just as the employee commits to achieving certain things, so too must the supervisor commit to providing any assistance he might need. Part of the performance action plan, therefore, should include the assistance and resources that the supervisor is to provide.

The last two steps of the procedure make up the interview's closing we described in the preceding chapter. First, to make sure that both parties understand what decisions have been reached, *the employee should be asked to summarize the discussion.* Second, *supervisor and subordinate should agree on some follow-up procedure.* Rather than waiting until the next annual review, they should schedule meetings for progress reports and feedback, enabling both of them to adjust their behaviors as necessary. If performance problems arise, they can correct them quickly rather than waiting for the entire year to elapse.

Typically, all of these things are put in writing, signed by both parties, and placed in the employee's permanent file. Again, this sort of *record keeping is important* to the employee, the supervisor, and the entire organization.

Conclusion

As a management tool, nothing should be more useful than the performance appraisal interview. Done properly, such an interview serves to clarify the employees' job responsibilities and motivates them toward greater achievement.[25] By devoting time to appraisal interviews, supervisors save a great deal of time later on, for they will not need to monitor and correct the work efforts of employees continually. Employees should know what to do and why. Doing appraisal interviews effectively requires considerable time, but it is a worthwhile investment in employees' future performances.

Disciplinary Interviews

Disciplinary interviews are a necessity in every organization. Organizations must have rules, policies, and procedures. Employees may violate them for a wide variety of reasons. When a violation occurs, it becomes the responsibility of the supervisor or manager to determine why it occurred, to motivate the violator not to do it again, and to deter others from committing the same violation. All of this should be achieved via disciplinary interviews. In this section, we will consider the pitfalls surrounding disciplinary interviews and suggest procedures whereby such interviews can be used to improve employee performance while respecting employee rights.

Purposes

The disciplinary interview achieves a number of necessary things. First, *it corrects behaviors that violate the rules of the organization.* The key word in that phrase is *corrects.* The goal of discipline in an organization is not punishment; it is correction.

Disciplinary interviews also serve as a notice to other employees that rules are enforced and that violations of those rules are simply not ignored. When it becomes clear that violations of rules, policies, and procedures are confronted and corrected, employees will take greater care to conform to the rules.

Protection of employees is another purpose of disciplinary interviews. Many organizational rules relate directly to employee safety. Rules against horseplay, drinking on the job, using drugs, theft, sabotage, and failing to follow established work procedures are all designed to protect employees from other employees or even from themselves.

Disciplinary interviews should preserve justice and fairness. They should ensure that everyone is treated equally and that the rights of all employees are respected and preserved. This is perhaps the most important purpose of disciplinary actions.

Problems

A virtually limitless number of problems occur during disciplinary proceedings. For example, as Alpander notes, *supervisors generally are reluctant to criticize or discipline in the first place.*[26] Lacking the knowledge they need to discipline constructively and desiring popularity with their people, they simply avoid taking action against employees at all. The opposite problem is *overcriticism*—angrily bawling out the employee in front of others. In such situations, the employee usually is taken by surprise, is embarrassed in front of others, and is given no opportunity to respond or react.

Still *other problems stem from procedural matters*—failure to document disciplinary action so that appropriate records are retained and the supervisor is protected against charges of bias or discrimination, failure to take action promptly, failure to learn all the facts before taking action, failure to follow written policies concerning disciplinary proceedings, failure to discipline in privacy, failure to develop a positive plan of action. Many of these failures are similar to the problems encountered in appraisal interviews; indeed, there are many parallels between these two types of supervisory action.

Unfortunately, there is one important way in which disciplinary interviews and appraisal interviews differ. When appraisal interviews are done badly, they adversely affect the performance of the employee, but they do not typically lead to spectacular consequences. Not so with disciplinary proceedings. If an employee feels he has been wronged through disciplinary action, he may file a grievance. In unionized situations, this grievance may be accompanied by union demands for redress or management action against the offending supervisor. If such action is not forthcoming, strikes or work slowdowns could result. In nonunion settings, the employee may take her grievance to an outside arbitrator, who may rule against the organization. In cases of dismissal, for example, this may result in the employee being reinstated and given back pay. Either way, the supervisor is caught up in a swirl of controversy and often is sorry he or she took the action in the first place. This fear only makes other supervisors more hesitant to discipline their employees.

Briefly put, *disciplinary procedures can be dangerous to the supervisors who invoke them.* Nevertheless, discipline must be invoked on occasion, and if the supervisors

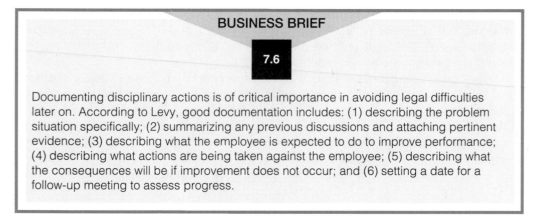

From Martin Levy, "Discipline for Professional Employees," *Personnel Journal* 69 (December 1990): 27–28.

know what they are doing, the disciplinary interview can be an effective way of correcting behavior and improving performance. Our purpose in the following sections is to suggest ways to minimize the risks of disciplining and to maximize the utility of those encounters.

Preparation

Like performance appraisals, disciplinary interviews depend heavily on thorough preparation for their success. Before calling an employee in for a disciplinary meeting, you should do a number of things.

First, identify and analyze the problem. Identify specifically what has been happening and determine why it has happened. Be sure a problem exists that calls for disciplinary action before you confront the employee.

Second, check the employee's work record. Determine whether she has been disciplined before and, if so, for what. Determine whether she has been a good, dependable worker in the past and whether the present situation represents a continuation of bad behaviors or a sudden change in behavior. While you must be consistent in the way you administer the organization's rules, you also must adapt your own behavior to the individual case.

Third, review the organization's disciplinary rules. In most organizations, work rules have been developed that specify the types of punishable infractions and perhaps the severity of the action to be taken in each case. Repeated lateness, for example, is typically handled by an oral warning, while theft and sabotage are handled by immediate suspension or dismissal. You need to know what the appropriate action is.

Finally, examine your own attitudes and motives. The relationship that exists between you and the employee has a significant impact on the disciplinary interview that is about to take place. You must be certain that your actions are based on objective facts and behaviors and not on your personal biases or feelings about the employee.

While formalized procedures for taking disciplinary action with hourly employees are relatively common, corrective action for salaried professionals tends to be done much more haphazardly. One company, HR Textron, Inc. in Valencia, California, has attempted to implement a four-step policy specifically designed for salaried employees. These steps include:

1. A formal, documented discussion between the employee and his or her supervisor, with the supervisor keeping the paperwork generated by this discussion.
2. Another formal, documented discussion, with the paperwork being placed in the employee's personnel file along with the write-up from the first step.
3. A third documented discussion that may involve a probationary period or some time off from work, along with a warning that continued behavioral problems will lead to termination.
4. Termination.

All supervisors and managers were trained to implement this procedure effectively, and legal charges associated with discipline of professional staff dropped dramatically.

From Martin Levy, "Discipline for Professional Employees," *Personnel Journal* 69 (December 1990): 27–28.

Procedures

The *first* step is to *notify the employee that you want to meet with him*. Obviously, you should not confront the employee in front of his peers and publicly embarrass the employee by yelling at him. The interview should be held privately and after any emotions or anger have cooled down, and it should be done as soon after the infraction as possible (again allowing time for the preparation described above).

When the employee arrives (and the door is closed), *get directly to the point*. Engaging in small talk to relax the employee would probably be counterproductive. She would only become more tense, waiting for the ax to fall. The way in which you state the point, however, is crucial. *Under no circumstances should you begin by condemning or accusing the employee*. The most certain way to make the employee defensive and to stop two-way communication is to begin with statements like:

"Karen, what are you trying to do to this department (or me)?"

"Ralph, I'm fed up with you always being late to work."

"You've goofed off for the last time, Maria. I'm writing you up."

Like performance reviews, disciplinary interviews should be treated as problem-solving sessions. You and the employee have a mutual problem, and the two of you

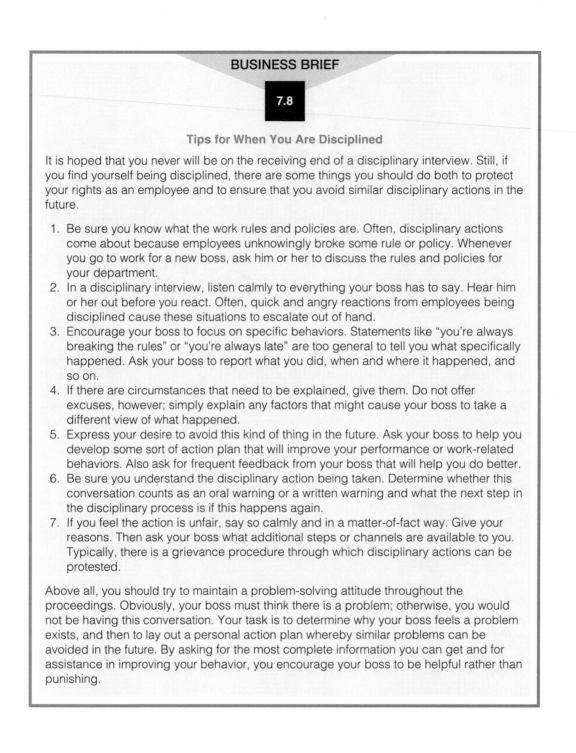

BUSINESS BRIEF

7.8

Tips for When You Are Disciplined

It is hoped that you never will be on the receiving end of a disciplinary interview. Still, if you find yourself being disciplined, there are some things you should do both to protect your rights as an employee and to ensure that you avoid similar disciplinary actions in the future.

1. Be sure you know what the work rules and policies are. Often, disciplinary actions come about because employees unknowingly broke some rule or policy. Whenever you go to work for a new boss, ask him or her to discuss the rules and policies for your department.
2. In a disciplinary interview, listen calmly to everything your boss has to say. Hear him or her out before you react. Often, quick and angry reactions from employees being disciplined cause these situations to escalate out of hand.
3. Encourage your boss to focus on specific behaviors. Statements like "you're always breaking the rules" or "you're always late" are too general to tell you what specifically happened. Ask your boss to report what you did, when and where it happened, and so on.
4. If there are circumstances that need to be explained, give them. Do not offer excuses, however; simply explain any factors that might cause your boss to take a different view of what happened.
5. Express your desire to avoid this kind of thing in the future. Ask your boss to help you develop some sort of action plan that will improve your performance or work-related behaviors. Also ask for frequent feedback from your boss that will help you do better.
6. Be sure you understand the disciplinary action being taken. Determine whether this conversation counts as an oral warning or a written warning and what the next step in the disciplinary process is if this happens again.
7. If you feel the action is unfair, say so calmly and in a matter-of-fact way. Give your reasons. Then ask your boss what additional steps or channels are available to you. Typically, there is a grievance procedure through which disciplinary actions can be protested.

Above all, you should try to maintain a problem-solving attitude throughout the proceedings. Obviously, your boss must think there is a problem; otherwise, you would not be having this conversation. Your task is to determine why your boss feels a problem exists, and then to lay out a personal action plan whereby similar problems can be avoided in the future. By asking for the most complete information you can get and for assistance in improving your behavior, you encourage your boss to be helpful rather than punishing.

need to arrive at a solution. *The best way to begin the interview is to define that problem by stating two things: (1) the appropriate rule or job requirement and (2) the information you have about the employee's behavior.* For example:

> Jim, you know that shop rules prohibit drinking on the job. When people drink, their own work suffers, and they become dangerous to everyone else. Now, I've been told by three different people that you've been seen drinking during break periods. I'm concerned about that, and that's why I asked you to come in. What can you tell me about this?

Through this statement, you have posed the problem, and you have asked the employee for input. You have not said, "What do you have to say for yourself?" which would create a trial-like atmosphere. Instead, you've simply indicated a desire for information from the employee.

Your next task is to listen. By letting the employee talk, and by asking questions when necessary, you should determine what, in the employee's view, actually took place. You should also obtain her explanation of why it happened, and you should ask her to explain the appropriate rules to you.

Having heard these things, you then face two tasks. First, *you must tell the employee what disciplinary action is to be taken* against him. This action may range from a written warning placed in his file, to a suspension from work, to outright termination. Then, *if termination is not the action,* you should *work with the employee to determine how he will improve in the future.* This step is much like the performance action plan developed during a performance appraisal. Through two-way, cooperative communication, the two of you decide what the employee is to do, how he is to achieve that, and what you might do to help. Then you set some sort of follow-up schedule whereby you meet again to determine what progress, if any, has occurred.

When the interview has been completed and a behavioral action plan has been agreed to, the proper documentation must also be completed. Most organizations have forms for this purpose, and the supervisor is required to indicate the actions taken, reasons for discipline, and plans for future improvement. The supervisor then signs the form, as does the employee, and the completed paperwork is sent to the supervisor's immediate superior or to the personnel department. All of this, as we indicated earlier, is important as a protection for the supervisor against future charges of discrimination or bias and as part of the ongoing record of the employee's performance. Since most organizations have disciplinary policies that say that subsequent offenses receive more severe punishment, this record will guide future disciplinary actions for this employee.

Conclusion

Several things are implied in the actions outlined in this section. First, the emphasis of the proceedings is upon the employee's *behavior,* not upon the employee. You are not evaluating her worth as a human being. Rather, you are working with the employee to develop new ways of behaving that conform to the requirements of the organization and the employee's job.

Second, you do not negotiate the disciplinary action. As a supervisor, you are the one to decide the appropriate action to be taken. This should not be a topic for discussion or debate during the interview. You must take care that the penalty is a reasonable one. It must fit the nature of the offense, but it also must be such that it allows you and the employee to continue working together after the discipline has taken place.

Finally, we must emphasize again the problem-solving nature of the disciplinary interview. You have a goal: to improve the behavior of one of your employees so that it conforms to the rules of the organization and ensures that the employee is making a positive contribution. Likewise, your employee probably has goals: to remain employed, to maintain the esteem of his coworkers, and perhaps to succeed and advance in the organization. By working together, the two of you strive to achieve these goals and overcome the problem of the employee's errant behavior. Above all, the emphasis of the disciplinary interview must be on the future.

Persuasive Interviews

While employment, appraisal, and disciplinary interviews are daily occurrences in all organizations, the most frequent type of interview is the persuasive interview. Such interviews occur in every possible setting: between members of different organizations, as when a tire manufacturer tries to sell a product to an automobile manufacturer; between members of the same organization but different work groups, as when an industrial engineer tries to convince the vice-president of manufacturing that an assembly process should be changed; between members of the same work group ("Hey, Bob, want to buy some of my daughter's Girl Scout Cookies?"). Much of the politicking that goes on in organizations occurs in persuasive interviews. Many of the formal presentations we will describe in later chapters are preceded by private interviews in which the groundwork for the presentation is laid.

Purposes

The goals of persuasive interviews usually involve some change in the person playing the role of interviewee: beliefs are changed, attitudes are changed or strengthened, or behaviors are changed. As an interviewer, you seek to cause the interviewee to think something he previously had not thought, to feel something he had not felt, or to do something he was not going to do. However, we do not include coercive interviews. Coercion occurs when someone is forced to do something against her will (as when the boss walks up and asks, "Do you want to contribute to the United Way this year, or shall I have your resume typed for you?"). *Persuasion occurs when people change beliefs, attitudes, or behaviors because they want to do so*—they have been convinced that such a change is desirable. According to Hatch, a "persuasive situation" exists when "you need to get somebody to do something that they wouldn't do if you just asked them to do it."[27]

The other important purpose of this kind of interview is the achievement of mutual goals. *Ideally, a persuasive interview ends in victory for everyone involved.* If you are successful, the other person thinks, feels, or does what you want. At the same time, though, that other person should feel that she has gained something from making the change. Stewart and Cash elaborate, explaining that our chances for success are significantly increased: (1) when our proposal appears to satisfy some need, desire, or motive held by the other person; (2) our proposal is consistent with the person's current beliefs or attitudes; (3) when our proposal seems practical; and (4) when the advantages of our proposal seem to outweigh any disadvantages or when no better alternative seems available.[28] Thus, there are a number of specific purposes that need to be achieved if our two main purposes—producing change and achieving mutual objectives—are to be accomplished. In this section, we will examine techniques for effective persuasive interviewing.

Preparation

As with all other types of interviews, the key to successful persuasive interviewing is careful preparation. Nierenberg, in his analysis of negotiating, argues that the first step is *establishing objectives*.[29] You need to decide specifically what you want the other person to think, feel, or do. The best way to do this, Baird suggests, is to *begin by answering six questions*.[30]

Who (do I want to influence)?

What (do I want him to do, think, or feel)?

How (do I want her to do it)?

When (do I want this to happen)?

Where (do I want this to happen)?

Why (do I want him to do it)?

Having answered each of those questions, you should then phrase a single declarative statement: "I want (who) to do (what) (how, when, where) because (why)." Consider some examples:

I want these customers to buy this 1988 Pontiac by making a 40 percent down payment today (and financing the rest with our credit department) because this car has been here so long and because I need the commission.

I want my boss to give me a pay increase by raising my salary 12 percent starting next month because I need the money, have done a good job and deserve a raise, have not had a raise in three years, and will leave the company if I don't get a raise soon.

I want the vice-president to support my proposal for a new research and development group by sending a memo to all appropriate executives tomorrow because I want to have a group reporting to me and because we need to have R&D people gathered together in a single group to promote better cooperation and productivity.

Each of these examples follows the pattern outlined above, but each has some unique characteristics that deserve mention. Each of them does a good job of specifying who and what, and indicating as much as necessary how, when, and where. However, the why portions are substantially different. In the first example, "because I need the commission," the why is honest, but it probably would not be very persuasive to the customers. In the second, several whys are given, some that might be persuasive to the boss, but others that might not. Finally, two reasons are given in the third example: one that the vice-president might support and one that could get the persuader in trouble (appearing to be power-hungry is considered negative in most organizations). When preparing this purpose statement, then, you should *list as many whys as possible and then note those that might be appealing to your interviewee and those that are irrelevant* (or perhaps damaging) to your case. Then, as a last step, determine which "why" statements will need proof before anyone will believe them. For example, the statement in the third objective concerning better cooperation and productivity would need some kind of support before the vice-president would be likely to believe it.

Having set your objective, your second step is to *analyze,* as much as possible, *your interviewee.* If you know who that person is ahead of time, you can do a complete, careful analysis. However, if you encounter total strangers (as when a retail salesperson works with anyone who comes into the store), then you must make some quick judgments (or ask some good questions) at the beginning of the interview.

Generally, there are five aspects of the interviewee that you should attempt to analyze. First, try to judge her *interests.* What things are important (and hence interesting) to this individual? You also need to ascertain her *beliefs* and *attitudes.* Beliefs are learned judgments about matters of fact, truth, or falsity. Such statements as "The world is round," "Wool wears better than polyester," or "BMW cars hold their value" are belief statements. Attitudes are the person's feelings, positive or negative, about those beliefs. Attitudes have an object (the thing we have some feeling about), direction (positive or negative), intensity (how much positive or negative), and commitment (how firm the attitude is in our minds); and, like beliefs, they are learned. To the greatest extent possible, we must determine what relevant beliefs this interviewee holds, and what effect their direction, intensity, and commitment levels are likely to have on our proposal.

Values and *needs* are the last two things to consider. Values are the interviewee's concept of what is good or bad, desirable or undesirable, moral, right, just, acceptable. These are similar to attitudes but are more deep-seated and usually serve as the basis for attitudes. Needs also are deep-seated and consist of the motives, drives, or internal forces that produce behaviors designed to satisfy, or at least reduce, them. Theorists have suggested a variety of motives or needs that people have, as we saw in earlier chapters.

Conducting this sort of analysis gives us some vital information. Above all, it enables us to choose "why" statements that are likely to be most effective with this particular individual. It also allows us to prepare for "why not" statements that the interviewee is likely to give us in response. In addition, it helps us to plan the sequence of the interview—to know what to talk about first (interests), what relationships to draw (between beliefs and attitudes), and ultimately, what specific proposal statement we should use to close the deal. For that reason, it is imperative that this sort of preparation be done.

Procedures: General Persuasion

A persuasive interview generally should consist of five basic steps.[31] *Getting attention* occurs when interviewer and interviewee first meet. Burstein claims that this moment is the "point when [the interviewer's] appearance, demeanor, and what he says will determine if he will have an opportunity to make an adequate presentation."[32] We have already seen (in chapter 5) the impact of appearance in communication. We will focus here on verbal strategies. According to Hatfield, there are two approaches we might take to opening the interview: the *service* approach ("May I help you?"), used when the interviewee seems not to be interested in a specific item; or the *merchandise* approach ("You don't see Cadillacs like this baby anymore, do you?"), in which the object being considered by the interviewee is mentioned.[33] The first is weak, may convey disinterest on the part of the interviewer, and usually elicits a "No, I'm just looking" answer. The second approach immediately focuses attention on the object, and gives impetus to further conversation. In a sales situation, the merchandise opening seems most desirable.

Other ways to get attention are to make a statement about some recent incident that pertains to the topic or to quote some respected member of the organization. A startling statement emphasizing a key point could serve the same purpose, as could a vivid example of some problem that you want to discuss.

Identifying some need that is important to the listener is the next step. A question like "Have you ever been irritated by . . . ?" or "Have you noticed that people here never . . . ?" is one method. By using questions or providing examples of your own, you must convince the other person that a problem exists that needs to be solved.

Once the person seems to agree that a need exists, the next step is to *offer a proposal* that can satisfy that need. You might say, "I believe that a good solution to this situation is to . . ." and then describe how your idea would resolve the problem you have identified.

Next, you must make the solution of the problem real to the other person by *causing him to visualize* what things will be like once the problem is solved. This visualization hopefully makes the person more willing to go along with your idea and more motivated to take the action you are about to recommend.

Finally, ask the other person to *take the action* you desire: to make some decision, communicate to someone, and so on. Suppose, for example, you want your boss to start a day-care center for children of the office staff. To convince her to take this action, you might go through the following interview sequence:

You: Excuse me, Ms. Taylor. Could I see you for a minute?

Boss: Sure. What's on your mind?

You: Well, I'm worried about absenteeism. I think a lot of people in this company aren't showing up as often as they should at work, and that people seem to be sneaking in late or out early. (Attention)

Boss: Really? I hadn't seen that. Who's doing it?

You: It's true. I've been watching for the last few months, and while I don't want to rat on anyone, it seems as though it's the young single parents who have the most problems. And I'm really concerned that it's affecting the morale and productivity of the department. (Need)

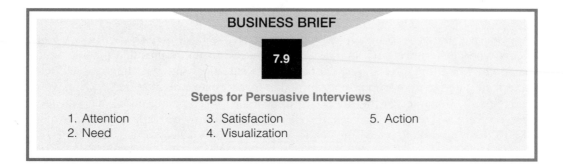

Boss: Well, I suppose it could be a problem.

You: I really believe it is. (Need)

Boss: So? Got any ideas?

You: Well, I've talked to a few people in the department, and the problem really seems to involve child care. They have trouble getting baby-sitters, or their kids are sick, or school is called off, and they have to stay home or sneak out in order to take care of things. The people whose kids are grown or who have no kids don't seem to have the same kinds of attendance problems. (Need)

Boss: What can we do?

You: Well, something a lot of companies are doing now is providing child care at work or near work so that parents don't have to worry about baby-sitters or sick kids. There have been several studies done that show attendance and productivity improve if a company starts a child-care center. (Satisfaction)

Boss: Is that so?

You: Here are some copies of the articles. Personally, I think it would be great. Imagine having a group of people who can concentrate fully on their jobs without worrying about child care. Plus, imagine how grateful the people would be to the company for providing this to them. I bet it would help cut turnover and improve our chances at recruiting new employees, too. (Visualization)

Boss: Hmmmmm. You could be right.

You: I'm sure of it. But I need your help.

Boss: What do you need?

You: I've discovered a funding agency that provides grants for new child-care programs in small to medium-size companies. I'd like to develop a proposal for us to go after one of these grants. Will you write a letter of support? (Action)

Boss: Sure, I'd be glad to. Sounds like an *excellent* idea.

By carefully analyzing your objectives and the nature of the interviewee, you can prepare a five-step persuasive interview that is likely to lead to the conclusion you desire.

The art of selling: adapting product features to customer.

While the procedures for a persuasive interview apply to any situation, there are special procedures that have proven effective specifically in a sales interview. Our experience has shown that the best approach uses four steps: introduction, need, presentation, and close. We call this the "INPC" method, and in the last chapter, we will discuss this model as it applies to a sales speech. Refer to chapter 14 for a detailed discussion of the sales presentation. The principles discussed there are readily adaptable to the sales interviewing context.

Summary

In this chapter, we examined four very important types of interviews: the employment interview, the appraisal interview, the disciplinary interview, and the persuasive interview. While the strategies and objectives of each differ significantly, all four of them have three important characteristics. If you keep these characteristics in mind when you interview, your chances for success will be greatly enhanced.

First, all four types require a good deal of preparation. You cannot interview off the top of your head and expect to be successful. In each case, you must examine yourself, the interviewee, the situation, and your objectives carefully, and then you must plan a strategy that takes each of those things into account.

Second, all four types involve open, honest sharing of information. In no case should you try to trick or deceive the interviewee. You may be able to achieve some short-term goal by doing so (such as hiring a new employee quickly, avoiding making the interviewee mad at you, or selling a shoddy product), but in the long term, the result will be negative.

Third, all four types require that you have the interviewee's best interests at heart. While you naturally must be concerned about yourself and your own goals, selfish interviewing leads to disaster. You must want to help the interviewee do the right thing, and your open sharing of information must be aimed toward facilitating that.

If you follow these principles, your success in selection, appraisal, disciplinary, and persuasive interviews will be greatly enhanced.

Questions for Discussion

1. Why is employment interviewing complicated and potentially problematic?
2. Describe the problem-solving approach to employment interviewing.
3. What requirements should you consider when you determine the qualifications for a certain job? What things must you not consider?
4. What is a BFOQ?
5. How would you initially screen out the clearly unqualified candidates, leaving only those who seem better suited for the job?
6. What are four major question areas on which you should focus your attention during an employment interview?
7. What are some techniques useful for implying a question?
8. What are some possible approaches to self-assessment in preparing for an employment interview?
9. What are some important attitudes and personal characteristics that an interviewee should possess? How, as an interviewee, might you show these things to an interviewer?
10. What are some common problems associated with appraisal interviews?
11. What objectives should an appraisal interview achieve?
12. What should be done to prepare for an appraisal interview?
13. How does the "shared problem-solving" concept apply to performance appraisal?

14. What are the goals of a disciplinary interview?
15. What are some common problems associated with disciplinary interviews?
16. What should be done to prepare for a disciplinary interview?
17. How does the "shared problem-solving" concept apply to discipline?
18. What is your understanding of the difference between persuasion and coercion?
19. How does one establish the objective for a persuasive interview?
20. What should be done when closing a persuasive interview?

Exercises

1. Select some specific job that interests you. Then, as precisely as you can, list all sources you would consult if you were a personnel manager seeking someone to fill that job. In addition, list all the qualifications you would look for as you sought potential candidates.
2. Imagine you are interviewing for a job and the interviewer asks you your age, race, religion, whether you have ever been arrested, and whether you intend to have children. What do you say? Why?
3. Create a resume and cover letter that you might use as an entree for an interview to obtain the job you had in mind in exercise 1.
4. List five questions you would ask in every employment interview you conducted as a personnel manager. Explain your choices.
5. Check with several local organizations to see what kinds of performance evaluations they use. What are the strengths of their systems? What are the weaknesses? How would you improve their systems?
6. Obtain a copy of a nearby organization's disciplinary policy or work rules. Using the skills described in this book, how would a supervisor in that organization deal with an employee who repeatedly was late to work? Be specific.
7. Visit two or three local stores and observe the persuasive interviewing techniques used by the salespeople. What sort of opening do they use? What pattern of questioning? What information about you do they try to obtain before making their sales presentations?
8. Select a current topic of interest and controversy, and choose an interviewee who feels differently than you do. Conduct a thorough analysis of that person; then plan an overall persuasive interviewing strategy: Indicate specifically what your closing question would be.
9. Review the Bates resume in table 7.2. Evaluate it, making suggestions (if any) for improvement.

Table 7.2 Sample Resume

LISA MARIE BATES

St. Olaf College **Northfield, MN 55057** **(507) 555–6529**	**R.R. 4, Box 418** **Pine City, MN 56398** **(218) 555–2732**

Statement of Purpose: I seek a full-time position with a public radio station where I can continue to develop my announcing and producing skills.

Education:

9/84–5/88   *Wadena Senior High School, Wadena, MN*
3.9 GPA. Valedictorian, graduated first in class.

9/88–5/92   *St. Olaf College, Northfield, MN*
3.6 GPA. Will graduate magna cum laude with B.A. degrees in Political Science and Speech-Theater. Department distinction in Speech-Theater.

Activities: Co-chair of St. Olaf Democrats, Chair and Founder of Speech Majors Social Organization, Worship Leader for St. Olaf Student Congregation, member of Political Science Student Association, member of Pi Sigma Alpha (national political science honor society), student representative to Speech-Theater department.

Work Experience:

12/85–9/88
Summer 90   *KWAD-AM/KKWS-FM Radio, Wadena, MN*
Duties: Announcing news, weather, sports, music. Operating board for all aspects of radio broadcast, including phone-link sports coverage. Writing and producing commercials, some news stories. Typing and formatting community events and funeral service announcements for on-air use.

9/88–Present   *WCAL-FM Radio, Northfield, MN*
Duties: Announcing regional news, weather, music. Operating board for all aspects of radio broadcast, including broadcasts of live music events. Editing, scripting, hosting, and producing full-length lectures for broadcast. Production experience with news features for use on morning music and information program and music concerts for broadcast. Experience compiling community announcements for on-air use, organizing and updating files for development department. On-air and volunteer participation in fund drives.

1/92–Present   *U.S. Arbitration & Mediation of Minnesota. Inc, Northfield, MN*
Internship duties: Compiling file information and statistics for quarterly report. Acting as assistant to executive director to conduct training and information sessions on mediation services. I am gathering material to produce a radio documentary on alternative dispute resolution.

References available upon request.

Small Group Communication

PART

3

Groups, like individuals, have shortcomings. Groups can bring out the worst as well as the best in man. Nietzsche went so far as to say that madness is the exception in individuals but the rule in groups.

—IRVING JANIS, GROUPTHINK

CHAPTER

8

Functions and Socioemotional Variables

s professionals or business persons, all of us will function in numerous small groups throughout our productive lives. We will put in hundreds of hours attending staff meetings, departmental meetings, subcommittee meetings, and unit gatherings. As we participate in groups, we will learn, form friendships, and contribute knowledge and skills vital to the task of solving the organization's problems. Participating in a group is not the same kind of experience as dealing individually with one other person or solving a problem alone. A group is both dynamic and complex. These qualities can inspire innovative decision making, or, by contrast, create the conditions for groupthink.

The frequency with which you will participate in groups is in itself reason enough to make the next three chapters important ones. We must also emphasize one other point: Your success in any organization will be influenced significantly by your performance in group settings. Every meeting represents an opportunity for you to impress your superiors, have your ideas adopted, assert positive influence over others, and demonstrate your capabilities for greater responsibility. On the other hand, we have seen careers stalled because of group participation. Employees who frequently arrive late or unprepared, fail to talk during meetings, behave disagreeably or discourteously or who otherwise perform poorly in the group setting rapidly develop a bad reputation among their peers and superiors—one that is virtually impossible to overcome. Finally, organizations are increasingly placing emphasis on participative problem solving at the lowest levels of the hierarchy, so the opportunities for you to perform well or poorly in a group are increasing. In some countries, such as the Scandinavian nations, workers are required by law to participate in industrial decision making. In American organizations, labor and management groups come together to attempt to keep companies open, to increase productivity, and to fight competition from foreign producers. For all of these reasons, then, developing skill in group participation is vital to you and your organization's short- and long-term well-being.

The Small Group Defined

Before going further, it is important to examine the concept of a small group. It is quite possible for several individuals to be together for some period of time and yet not really constitute a small group. Patients waiting in a dentist's office, students sitting in a classroom on the first day of the semester, or a dozen travelers snoozing in the TWA departure area waiting to catch a midnight flight are all examples of small groups of people, but not in the sense we are using the term here.

For small groups to exist, it is essential that group members perceive themselves as something other than a collection of independent individuals. Bales was among the first to point to the importance of group members developing a *psychological relationship,* a sense of a mutual awareness and interdependence.[1] The creation of this mutual psychological awareness rarely occurs all at once. Rather, it usually develops over some period of face-to-face interaction. Members' relationships are furthered by repeated encounters, normally accomplished through communicative exchanges.

When one of the authors left university teaching to accept a position as "Corporate Management Development Specialist" at Baxter Travenol Laboratories, a large manufacturer of health-care products, he found himself to be a member of several formal and informal organizational groups:

The Department of Training and Development in which he worked.

The "Management Effectiveness Training" instructor's group, consisting of all trainers who taught that course.

The Corporate Labor Relations Task Force, a group of people from many different departments who were sent on a moment's notice to any company facility experiencing labor relations problems.

The Corporate Personnel division, a very large collection of units and departments that met occasionally to receive news from the company executives.

The company softball team.

The Employee Opinion Survey Task Force, a small group of people selected to participate in the development of the organization's new employee opinion survey process.

A small, informal group of ex-college teachers who all had found their way into the company and who liked to talk over lunch about "the bad old days."

When he initially accepted his position, he knew about only one of these groups—the first.

Communication facilitates interaction and, by doing so, helps to define the psychological relationship that develops within the small group. Small group members also have some degree of shared interest. Often this interest is expressed as a *goal* upon which there is mutual agreement.[2] When small groups form to meet the personal needs of group members (such as the informal coffee break group), the goal may grow naturally from the group itself. Group members may meet to provide mutual support, listen to one another's complaints, or provide some diversion from routine work. Other small groups form in response to a formal organizational assignment. These groups are largely task-oriented and are often asked to make decisions or solve problems.

The number of people needed to constitute a small group has been a subject of controversy. Usually, the lower limit is set at three (with two being a dyad); but the upper limit is variable, with twenty considered a ceiling by some.[3] In general, the larger the group, the more complex the patterns of interaction and the more formalized the procedures necessary to handle the group's functioning efficiently. Studies of committees have revealed the most *common* group sizes to be five, seven, and nine.[4] For the most part, however, most researchers agree that face-to-face interaction, the existence of a psychological relationship, and some degree of

BUSINESS BRIEF

8.2

In an effort to improve quality and productivity, many companies are attempting to shift from classical organizational thinking (specialized jobs and narrowly defined tasks improve performance) toward a broader team-oriented approach (a more flexible, multiskilled work force performs best).

Even traditionally unionized companies, such as General Motors and National Steel, have improved morale, speed, and efficiency by loosening job classifications and developing a more flexible work force through intensive cross-training and job rotation. For example:

Motorola dissolved six pay categories at its Arlington Heights, Illinois, cellular phone factory. Now all workers are in the same category, and their pay increases are based on learning new skills while maintaining high work quality.

Lechmere, Inc., a twenty-seven store retail chain, bases pay raises on the number of jobs employees learn: cashiers are encouraged to also sell products, salespeople are taught to drive forklifts, and so on.

AT&T created nearly a dozen cross-functional teams to participate in developing a new cordless phone and through cross-training and employee involvement was able to cut development in half.

From D. Keith Denton, "Multi-Skilled Teams Replace Old Work Systems," *HR Magazine* 37 (September 1992): 48–56.

common interest (often involving a goal) are the salient characteristics of the small group rather than the specific number of group members.

Groups in organizations do not exist as isolated units. They are, instead embedded within the larger organizational system. Their members are part of, as Jablin has noted, "an interlocking network of organizational roles."[5] Moreover, each individual typically belongs to multiple groups and is often subjected to conflicting pressures. Finally, organizational groups operate within formal hierarchies and normally function with appointed leaders.[6] Even so, organizational groups can be distinguished according to type or purpose.

Small Group Types

You may recall that one of the findings of the Hawthorne studies was the significance of the informal work group as a source of employee motivation.[7] Indeed, we create small groups in organizations for various purposes, some of which relate only indirectly to organizational tasks. Many small groups form because of our personal needs for social interaction. These groups are *casual* or *cathartic*. Coffee break groups, lunch groups, and groups that form spontaneously are examples of casual groups. As we saw in chapters 1 and 5,

Informal groups are very important to workers at all organizational levels.

many progressive organizations encourage the formation of informal small groups to develop a more participative organizational culture. These organizations provide centrally located gathering places (such as break areas or conference rooms) and meeting "support equipment" (such as blackboards or easel pads) to encourage informal problem solving. Often, other groups form casually without management's awareness or approval. Disgruntled employees, for example, may gather together regularly to share their discontent and, occasionally, to mobilize against management. Communication in such casual or cathartic groups is unstructured and varied in content. In this small group context, the sharing of feelings, attitudes, and opinions usually is the goal, although resolution of some specific problem may also occupy the participants' attention.

On occasion, casual groups evolve into a more intimate kind of group experience. Close friendships may develop among colleagues in an organizational context, so that they begin spending a great deal of their nonworking time in each other's company. In this manner, casual groups grow into *primary* groups. Each of us experiences our first primary group in the family. Later, as children and adolescents, we feel the force of peer group influence. When we enter organizations, our work-related contacts often evolve into close friendships that may continue even after one or more of us have left that organization. Indeed, one of the greatest sources of job satisfaction is often the relationships we form with our peers. The relationships that make up our primary groups are very strong in the dimensions of attraction and involvement, and they are probably among the most important and influential relationships we experience.

In every organization, individuals need to be receptive to new information. The "knowledge explosion" is real to everyone, but nowhere is it more marked than in the organizational setting, where flexibility, innovation, and personal and technological change are everyday occurrences, necessary for institutional survival. Thus, many small groups function in organizations as *learning* or *training* groups. Most of us will be exposed to learning groups early in our organizational affiliation as part of orientation and training. But learning is a continuous process. Particularly in business and industry, yesterday's innovative technique is today's outmoded procedure. As a result, there is the constant need for reorienting, retraining, and helping individuals to adjust to the changing demands of the organizations in which they work. Management seminars may allow groups of administrators to learn new techniques of worker motivation, how to use a computer to store information, or how to conduct different kinds of interviews. Finally, learning takes place in most meetings held on a day-to-day basis.

Individuals in organizations make decisions every day. In highly centralized organizational structures, the "lonely man at the top" makes important decisions alone or perhaps with the assistance of only a few trusted advisors and friends. But in many modern organizations, decentralization has resulted in the spread of problem solving and decision making throughout the levels of the organizational hierarchy. Usually, such communication activities occur in small *decision-making* groups. These groups are task-oriented and goal-directed. They exist for the purpose of responding to some organizational need. While we may obtain personal satisfaction from our participation in decision-making groups, the primary objective of such groups is always the accomplishment of some task, usually making a high-quality decision.

Teams

We have already discussed the teamwork philosophy of organization theory, as well as the use of self-managing teams as a current application of human resources management. As small groups within organizations, teams generally consist of either project or work teams. *Project teams* have existed for many years in organizational settings. Typically consisting of employees representing an array of specialties (such as marketing, sales, and engineering), they coordinate the successful completion of a particular project, product, or service. Project teams have been part of the space program for many years and are common in electronic, computer, and other research-based industries. These teams typically work quickly to clarify goals, roles, and responsibilities. They often possess little history, are likely pressured by deadlines, and may have difficulty establishing mutually satisfying working relationships. Nevertheless, crossfunctional project teams are potentially valuable in that they keep individuals from different organizational divisions communicating with and educating each other, while reminding them of the importance of customer needs and satisfaction.

The other, and most innovative, kind of team is the *work team*. Wellins, Byham, and Wilson define the work team as "an intact group of employees who are responsible for a 'whole' work process or segment that delivers a product or service to an internal or external customer."[8] Work teams have become increasingly popular and are used in such diverse organizations as 3M, General Electric, AT&T, and Corning. Each of the companies that has won the Malcolm Baldrige National Quality Award (such as Millikin, Motorola, Westinghouse, and Xerox) fostered teamwork among employees as a crucial component of their improvement efforts.[9] Furthermore, through work teams, employee empowerment may be realized. However, there are no guarantees. Managers must first make a commitment to empowerment by demonstrating a willingness to give teams the actual authority to get the job done. This means providing access to resources, information, and technical assistance while allowing the team to make decisions about how to proceed, how to delegate responsibility, and so forth. Whether or not a team is effective, then, depends upon members' skills, knowledge, and initiative—as well as factors external to the group. When managers are truly committed to empowerment through teamwork and are willing to put aside constraints associated with the traditional hierarchy and to think in fresh, creative ways, work teams can serve as true vehicles of empowerment. In its "Statement of Aspirations," Levi Strauss & Company defines empowering leadership as that which "increases the authority and responsibility of those closest to our products and customers. By actively pushing responsibility, trust, and recognition into the organization, we can harness and release the capabilities of all our people."[10] Not surprisingly, work teams are an intrinsic component of the Levi Strauss culture.

Quality Circles

One of the most contemporary approaches to organizational problem solving and employee participation is the use of *quality circles*. These are small groups of people who meet voluntarily to define, analyze, and solve work-related problems.[11] Typically these people come from the same department or work group, or at least perform similar job functions, so that the problems they discuss are familiar to all of them, and each member can contribute to the development of solutions.

Many employees dread Monday mornings, the start of another work week. Not so for Al Reynolds and Amanda Dunston, employees at Northern Telecom's Morrisville, North Carolina, repair facility. "I now look forward to coming to work. I don't *have* to go to work, I *get* to go to work," claims Reynolds. Dunston adds, "I enjoy the challenge. Every day, I'm learning something new."

Both are part of a set of self-directed work teams recently formed by their company. As team members, they are involved in ordering materials, tracking and scheduling overtime work, calculating and monitoring productivity, reviewing budgets, and interviewing perspective team members. Soon, they also will be conducting peer performance reviews and taking corrective action when their peers do not perform adequately.

The key to successful implementation of self-directed teams at Northern Telecom was top-level management involvement. All members of supervision and management participated in intensive workshops designed to change how they think about worker-management relations and how they manage on a day-to-day basis. But not all managers were able to make the transition: company statistics indicate that about 25 percent of its first-line supervisors left after the team approach was adopted.

From Jana Schilder, "Work Teams Boost Productivity," *Personnel Journal* 71 (February 1992): 67–71.

At a general level, quality circles, meet to analyze and solve the organization's problems. More specifically, however, their functions are often detailed and diversified. Among the things quality circles do are:

improve the quality of services or products

reduce the number of work-related errors

promote cost reduction

develop better work methods

improve efficiency in the organization

improve relations between management and employees

promote participants' leadership skills

enhance employees' career and personal development

improve communication throughout the organization

Quality circles are increasingly common in the United States. Ninety percent of *Fortune* 500 companies reportedly use quality circles.[12] However, the concept initially developed in Japan following World War II and was aimed at reviving the Japanese economy. Throughout the 1950s and into the early 1960s, the Japanese conducted a nationwide drive to improve quality. Awards were given to individuals and corporations achieving unusual improvement in quality, and the Japanese government developed the "JIS" symbol to be put on only those products that had exceptionally high quality.

The quality circles (QC) concept spread to the United States in the early 1970s when a visiting team of quality circle leaders was invited by the American Society for Quality Control to present their programs to a conference at Stanford University. This conference sparked the interest of several representatives from the Lockheed Corporation, who studied the concept at length and ultimately installed a QC program at Lockheed. This program was enormously successful and was followed by other similarly successful quality circles programs in such corporations as J. C. Penney, Uniroyal, Firestone, Bendix, and Michigan Bell Telephone. Health-care institutions have also found quality circles to be valuable. At Norfolk (Virginia) General Hospital, for example, a food service quality circle found a way to cut overtime costs by $100,000 a year.[13] Because of the program's success, the manager of that department was promoted to the staff of Norfolk General's controlling corporation to implement participative management programs there.[14]

Although quality circles have been used with reported success in many organizations, group communication experts have pointed out that little is known about quality circle failures.[15] One writer reported that quality circles have a short life expectancy, with as many as 70 percent of them failing.[16] Case studies by Meyer and Scott suggest that quality circles may be no different from other committee meetings in some organizations in that supervisors may dominate them; the groups may lack a sense of clearly defined purpose, stray from problem solving, and get bogged down in never-ending problem analysis; and group members may be unequally committed to the group tasks.[17] Equally critical is the fact that for many organizational members, there are simply no tangible rewards associated with participating in quality circles, and supervisors themselves may send mixed messages, inviting criticism and open discussion during QC meetings, but rarely asking for suggestions or criticisms in other contexts.[18]

In spite of these potential problems, quality circles continue to thrive in many organizations when participation in them is voluntary. By helping build employee problem-solving and communications skills, management leadership and communications skills, and creating a formal structure for ongoing communication throughout the organization, the quality circles system has the potential for developing a more goal-oriented and team-centered management climate. With an effective QC program, many positive outcomes are possible. In some instances, as Stohl has written, "Workers will have information never before available, management will be talking to workers in ways they never did before, and workers' perceptions of the company will change."[19] Ultimately, this kind of climate works toward the long-term well-being of the organization.

Discussion in Public Settings

Most of the time, communication taking place in small groups in organizations occurs in *private* settings. When we participate in groups such as quality circles, we share

Types and Functions of Groups in Organizations

Type of Group	Setting	Function	Examples
1. Casual	Private	To satisfy the needs of group members for social interaction	Coffee break & lunch groups
2. Primary	Private	To provide the individual with a sense of social unity	Family & close friendship groups
3. Learning or Training	Private or Public	To disseminate & share information	Orientation & training groups & educational panels
4. Decision-making	Primarily private	To solve organizational problems or respond to other task-oriented needs	Committees, such as financial, public relations, production, & employee relations

information, persuade, and respond to the remarks of others without regard for any audience beyond the members of the group.

On occasion, however, we will be called upon as professionals to participate in a small group discussion for the benefit of an audience. These *public* discussions are important, for they provide the opportunity for organizational representatives to interact directly with a portion of the organization's relevant environment. Most public discussions are planned for the enlightenment of an audience. While some controversy may pervade the discussion, usually the discussion's main purpose is to provide information—possibly involving the expression of varied and perhaps relatively divergent points of view. Public discussions often bring together representatives from several different organizations, all of whom share some expertise on the discussion topic, but each of whom possesses a different perspective.

Public discussions can occur in several different formats or patterns of discussant interaction. A *panel discussion* is a type in which the participants interact directly and spontaneously with the guidance of a moderator. No participant has a planned speech. Instead, each speaks briefly, rather frequently, and within the realm of courtesy, whenever he or she desires. A more formal mode of public discussion is the *symposium,* in which discussants prepare brief speeches representing their viewpoints. Each group member speaks in turn without interruption or interaction. As the panel moderator, the symposium leader usually introduces the group members and provides a summary at the end of the discussion. During the actual discussion, however, there is no need for moderator intervention or guidance—except for providing transitions between speakers. In a sense, the symposium more closely approximates public speaking than group discussion since participants do not interact but function as relatively independent communicators. Both the panel discussion and the symposium may be followed by a *forum* period during which members of the audience are encouraged to ask questions and express opinions. The forum is generally guided by the moderator, and questions may be directed to individual members or to the group as a whole. Business Brief 8.5 summarizes the types and functions of groups in organizational settings.

Public discussions may include more than one format of discussant interaction. For example, all three elements were incorporated in a program on labor relations. Three attorneys and one consultant were participants in the program, which was attended by 150 personnel managers from companies throughout the United States. It began with a symposium: Each participant presented his ideas and positions in a speech lasting approximately thirty minutes. The panel moderator introduced each speaker and provided transitions between each presentation. When the speeches were concluded, a panel discussion (billed as a "free-for-all") ensued. Participants interacted with one another, discussing (and generally attacking) one another's ideas while trying to support their own. Finally, the program shifted to a forum. Audience members were encouraged to ask questions of the panel and to state their own opinions or ideas. The end result was a lively, varied, and entertaining program.

Public discussions in organizations take a similar variety of forms and are conducted for a variety of "publics." As the need for a consumer-oriented corporate culture grows, an increasing number of organizations are holding symposiums, panels, and forums for community groups, stockholders, customer groups, and others. One large manufacturer of hospital supplies, for example, has begun conducting seminars on "Managing Hospital Resources" across the country for hospital executives. During these seminars, attendees listen to short speeches by experts in many areas of management, watch as these experts discuss with one another, and then ask questions related to their own concerns. Similarly, many companies have started conducting such meetings for their own employees to increase the visibility of their executive group and promote interaction among employees and management. Our own observations indicate that public meetings, both inside and outside the organization, will become increasingly common.

The preceding discussion has not attempted to cover every type of small group that may exist in organizations in either private or public contexts. Rather, we have tried to demonstrate the wide variety of functions performed by small groups in organizations, with an emphasis on those forms of small group communication we believe to be most prevalent and significant.

Critical Socioemotional Variables

At the beginning of this chapter, we said that one of the characteristics of the small group is the existence of a psychological relationship among group members. The development of this relationship may be influenced by the nature of the task before the

Figure 8.1
A line discrimination task typical of Asch's research.

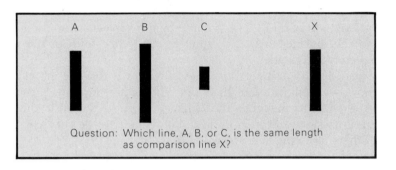

Question: Which line, A, B, or C, is the same length
as comparison line X?

group and the cognitive functionings of group members in relation to that task. But it is largely socioemotional factors that contribute to the development of interpersonal bonds within the group. Chief among these are pressure for uniformity, role structure, status and power, and cohesiveness.

Pressure for Uniformity

The phenomenon of social influence has long fascinated scholars in a variety of disciplines. In the field of organization theory, researchers of the Human Relations school were the first to recognize the potent influence of small informal work groups on the behavior of individuals. As early as 1911, however, Taylor noted the presence of group norms that appeared to affect industrial productivity.[20] Over the past half-century, the collective efforts of social science researchers have identified the small group as the foundation of social control.

One of the pioneering efforts in the field of intragroup relations was Sherif's research on the "autokinetic effect."[21] For all individuals, whether alone or in groups, a pinpoint of light projected through an opening in a wall into a completely darkened room has the appearance of moving. The perceived quantity and direction of its movement are completely different for each person. But Sherif found that when subjects in small groups publicly expressed their estimates of direction and degree of light movement, those judgments would eventually converge toward a common group standard. There was, of course, no correct estimate since the light only gave the appearance of motion. Thus, individuals, without the aid of any objective reality, were greatly influenced by the estimates of others.

Another classic social influence investigation was conducted by Asch, who performed a series of experiments involving simple line discrimination tasks.[22] In fact, the perceptual task of matching one of three comparison lines with a test line was so easy (as illustrated in figure 8.1), Asch discovered any individual with normal vision could make the correct match nearly 100 percent of the time. The investigator subsequently coached a group of confederates to make deliberately erroneous judgments on the same perceptual tasks. When a naive individual was placed among Asch's group of confederates and asked to listen to the judgments of others before stating his or her own estimates, the results were radically skewed in the direction of the majority. Approximately one-third of all estimates made by the subjects were identical with or in the direction of the distorted majority estimates. Only one-forth of the naive subjects remained completely independent.

What is especially provocative about these findings is that the individuals were not acquainted with one another before their brief encounter. Moreover, the confederates made *no overt attempts* to influence the behavior of the naive individual. Finally, the line discrimination tasks had no real intrinsic importance to the subjects, to their future relations with others, or to the fate of anyone in the room.

We have mentioned *norms* and *conformity behavior* several times in the preceding discussion. Schein defines a norm as "a set of assumptions or expectations held by the members of a group or organization concerning what kind of behavior is right or wrong, good or bad, appropriate or inappropriate, allowed or not allowed."[23] Individual group members who exhibit conformity behavior, then, act in a way they perceive to be consistent with group norms. Within small groups, norms are often *implicit:* that is, they are never actually articulated, but they are understood and accepted. *Explicit* norms, on the other hand, are more formal and are usually verbalized. Organizations often provide explicit norms in the form of rules, regulations, and other codes or conduct. These norms may include such varied items as personal appearance (hair length, cleanliness, appropriate attire), language usage, length of lunch and coffee breaks, and strategies and procedures to be used in committee meetings. Informal norms are even more potentially diverse, dealing, for example, with one's political views, the make of car one drives, or even the kind and quantity of dinner parties one gives. Whether or not we adhere to the norms of our group or organization depends upon a variety of factors. Chief among them is the degree to which we value our membership and identify strongly with the group or organization.[24]

While it is easy enough to recognize conformity behavior, it is much more difficult to tell whether the behavior being exhibited or the words being mouthed really reflect the person's genuine feelings. That is, individuals often comply publicly with the norms of the group but privately continue to hold a different set of beliefs. There is always the question of whether or not those who comply also accept the norm privately.

By interviewing his subjects after the experiment. Asch discovered that only a small percentage of the yielding subjects really believed the majority estimates were correct. In most cases, the group's judgment had been accepted publicly while private views remained the same.[25] In actual organizational settings, it is not uncommon for an employee to accept publicly the stated positions of others, especially if those others are in positions of power. This kind of compliance may be ingratiating, strategically aimed at increasing the worker's attractiveness in the eyes of his or her boss, or it may reveal the subordinate's fear of open discussion.

There are additional factors that allow us to predict the likelihood of an individual complying with group norms. *Situational* or *stimulus ambiguity* is the first. When individuals

BUSINESS BRIEF

8.6

The impact of group pressure is especially potent when the group's majority is composed of those in power. John Z. De Lorean's account of committee meetings inside General Motors dramatizes this point:

> Original ideas were often sacrificed in deference to what the boss wanted. Committee meetings no longer were forums for open discourse, but rather either soliloquies by the top man, or conversations between a few top men with the rest of the meeting looking on. In . . . meetings, often only three people . . . would have anything substantial to say, even though there were fourteen or fifteen executives present. The rest of the team would remain silent, speaking only when spoken to. When they did offer comment, in many cases it was just to paraphrase what had already been said by one of the top guys.

Clearly, this kind of pervasive conformity is detrimental to good decision making.

Source: J. Patrick Wright, *On a Clear Day You Can See General Motors* (New York: Avon Books, 1979), 47.

are placed in unfamiliar situations or are asked to perform tasks about which they know little or are generally uncertain, they are quite likely to look to the opinions of the group for the most appropriate action or attitude. *Unanimity* is also critical. That is, if an individual discovers that even one other group member has doubts about the majority's views, he or she is much less likely to "go with the flow." This is true, whether the two dissenters agree with each other or support varied points of view. The *personality characteristics* of the individual are another relevant variable. Those persons who are submissive, low in self-confidence, lack intelligence and originality, and need social approval are quite likely to conform to the norms of the groups to which they belong.[26] Moreover, those individuals who are involved in the discussion of issues not central to their value systems are low in ego-involvement and hence are likely to go with the prevailing view. Finally, those who are sensitive to others' expectations for them are more vulnerable to social influence attempts than those who are less sensitive to such social cues.[27]

Still other factors affecting conformity behavior relate to the *environment* in which the group functions. If a state of crisis or emergency exists or if the group is in a position of *having* to reach consensus, individual group members are likely to go along with the views of the group.[28] One of the most critical variables affecting social influence is *cohesiveness*. Highly cohesive groups demand, and usually obtain, high degrees of conformity behavior. We will define and discuss cohesiveness in a later section of this chapter.

Groups exert pressure for uniformity in a variety of ways. Schachter's early research revealed that one basic method is through *increases in the quantity of communication* directed toward the deviant member.[29] Subsequent research by Taylor found that the verbal behavior of majority group members was characterized by *reasonableness, dominance,* and *hostility*.[30] More recently, Thameling described the communication behavior of majority group members as being characterized by cooperativeness, opinionatedness, and emotionality.[31] Finally, Wenburg and Wilmot have identified five sequential steps taken by most groups as they attempt to influence opinion deviates. These are: (1) delaying action (doing little overtly and hoping the deviate will conform without pressure); (2) chatting among themselves (perhaps involving joking with the deviate); (3) ridiculing the deviate (overtly recognizing his or her behavior as different and unacceptable); (4) engaging in severe criticism (possibly including threats); and (5) rejecting the deviate (ignoring, isolating, and prohibiting future interaction with the group).[32]

The response of the deviate to pressure for uniformity is interesting and relatively unexplored. Bradley discovered the following trends as characteristic of deviant communication behavior in small group discussions: (1) decreased reasonableness from beginning to end (although relatively high reasonableness throughout); (2) increased emotionality from beginning to end; and (3) moderate dominance throughout (involving a short period of marked increases in assertive, aggressive behavior near the middle of the discussion).[33] Virtually nothing is known of the influence that might be exerted by the deviate under varying circumstances. However, one study demonstrated that an articulate, intelligent deviate might exert considerable influence on the views of the majority, particularly on topics about which the deviate knows much and the other group members know little.[34] But if those group members composing the majority are more informed, the deviate's influence may be lessened.[35] Table 8.1 summarizes critical issues related to social influence and conformity behavior.

Considered by themselves, pressure for uniformity and conformity behavior are neither good nor bad. They are simply facts of group and organizational life. Most decision-making groups have certain procedural norms whose purpose is to expedite the decision-making process. Adherence to these norms, like sticking to the agenda, refusing to interrupt others, and allowing everyone to speak, is usually a virtue. Yet pressure for uniformity and conformity behavior are hazardous. The best group decisions are made through the exploration of a variety of points of view. When minority positions are stifled and the quantity of potentially significant input reduced, there is little chance that the group will make a good decision.

Role Structure

The norms that develop in groups typically suggest (or require) appropriate modes of conduct for all group members. At the same time, however, groups need considerable role diversity among their membership to function effectively. Group members perform different, although often interdependent, functions as they work together on varied tasks. Conceptually, roles include behaviors and how those behaviors *function* within the group. For instance, a group member may use humor during a meeting. Her humor, however, may function in diverse ways—to relieve tension, to diminish someone else's ego (especially if the humor is sarcastic), to get the group off track by distracting members from the task at hand, or to build group cohesiveness. Clearly, some of these are

Table 8.1 A Summary Perspective of Pressure for Uniformity and Conformity Behavior

The Deviate is Likely to Conform When:	The Majority Responds to the Deviate by:	The Deviate Responds to the Majority by:
1. the situation is ambiguous or the task is difficult.	1. increasing the quantity of deviate-directed communication.	1. decreasing reasonableness.
2. the majority consists of three or more.	2. moving through these progressive steps:	2. increasing emotionality.
3. the majority is unanimous.	A. delaying action	3. displaying moderate dominance.
4. the deviate is submissive, low in self-confidence, unintelligent, very sensitive to others' expectations, low in ego-involvement, or needs social approval.	B. chatting among themselves	4. exerting counterinfluence.
	C. ridiculing the deviate	
	D. engaging in severe criticism	
	E. rejecting the deviate.	
5. the group must reach consensus, or there is a crisis or emergency.	3. communication behavior characterized by reasonableness, dominance, hostility, emotionality, opinionatedness, and cooperativeness.	
6. the group is highly cohesive.		

more functionally related to group goal accomplishment and maintenance than others. Similarly, asking a question can function as a simple request for information ("Do we have projected trends for next month yet?"); as a strategy for changing the subject; as a vehicle for introducing a new topic; or as a put-down or challenge ("What would *you* know about working in a factory?"). Thus, *roles are behaviors that perform some function in a specific group context*. The individual's enactment of a role will depend upon his interpretations of a given situation.

Various classification schemes have been developed to describe the roles or behavioral functions that group members enact. Typically, these roles fall into one of two main categories, group task roles and group building and maintenance roles.

Task roles involve the communication functions necessary for a group to accomplish its task, which often involves problem solving, decision making, information exchange, or conflict resolution. Based on the classic work of Benne and Sheats, these roles include:

1. *Initiator*—proposes new ideas, procedures, goals, and solutions; gets the group started.
2. *Information giver*—supplies evidence, opinions, and related personal experiences relevant to the task.
3. *Information seeker*—asks for information from other members, seeks clarification when necessary, and makes sure that relevant evidence is not overlooked.
4. *Opinion giver*—states her own beliefs, attitudes, and judgment; is willing to take a position, although not without sensitivity to others' views.
5. *Opinion seeker*—solicits the opinions and feelings of others and asks for clarification of positions. Ideally, those who give opinions will be equally willing to seek opinions.

6. *Elaborator*—clarifies and expands the ideas of others through examples, illustrations, and explanations. This role is valuable so long as elaborations are task-relevant.
7. *Integrator*—clarifies the relationship between various facts, opinions, and suggestions and integrates the ideas of other members.
8. *Orienter*—keeps the group directed toward its goal, summarizes what has taken place, and clarifies the positions of the group.
9. *Evaluator*—expresses judgments about the relative worth of information or ideas; proposes or applies criteria for weighing the quality of information or alternative courses of action.
10. *Procedural specialist*—organizes the group's work; suggests an agenda, outline, or problem-solving sequence.
11. *Consensus tester*—asks if the group has reached a decision acceptable to all; suggests, when appropriate, that agreement may have been reached.

Although early discussions of group task roles treated them as a unidimensional construct, the contemporary view suggests that they represent two task dimensions: those roles focusing on the substance or content of the issue being discussed (such as giving information) and another set of roles that deals with procedural matters (such as orienting and organizing the group). These two dimensions may function in tandem, if, for example, someone initiates the discussion (a procedural act) by tossing out an idea (a substantive move). Nevertheless, the distinction may be important since research on ad hoc groups suggests that group task behaviors that provide procedural guidance may be perceived as especially valuable. In one study, for instance, those who were viewed as having provided significant procedural guidance were most likely to emerge as group leaders.[36] The extent to which procedural acts are valued may also depend upon the characteristics of group members. Individuals have been shown to vary significantly in their need for procedural order in group communication settings.[37]

The second major category of group roles is *group building and maintenance roles*. These roles build and sustain the group's interpersonal relationships. Discussants playing these roles help the group to feel positive about the task and to interact more harmoniously. By reducing the competition between individual group members and their ideas, these behaviors nurture an enhanced sense of cooperation.[38] These roles include:

1. *Supporter*—praises and agrees with others, providing a warm, supportive interpersonal climate.
2. *Harmonizer*—attempts to mediate differences, introduce compromises, and reconcile differences.
3. *Tension reliever*—encourages a relaxed atmosphere by reducing formality and interjecting appropriate humor.
4. *Gatekeeper*—exerts some control over communication channels, encouraging reticent discussants, discouraging those who tend to monopolize the discussion, and seeking diversity of opinion.
5. *Norm creator*—suggests rules of behavior for group members and challenges unproductive ways of behaving; gives a negative response when someone violates an important group norm.

6. *Solidarity builder*—expresses positive feelings toward other group members; reinforces sense of group unity and cohesiveness.
7. *Dramatist*—evokes fantasies about persons and places other than the present group and time; may test a tentative value or norm through hypothetical example or story; dreams, shows creativity, and articulates vision.

Although these roles are presented as largely desirable and constructive, they must be evaluated as they are enacted in a specific group context. For instance, establishing and maintaining norms is quite valuable so long as the norms are sound. If the group is committed to encouraging dissent, for instance, and someone attempts to stifle a minority view, reminding the group of its norm (tolerance for diversity) would clearly have a positive function. However, helping the group maintain an attitude of intolerance would, by maintaining that norm, be counterproductive. Moreover, stereotypically, roles in the building and maintenance category are associated with pleasant, harmonious social interaction. However, enacting some of them could readily produce tension and conflict—such as discouraging those who are dominating the discussion or challenging someone who is behaving unproductively. This suggests that if groups are to maintain themselves over time, they will of necessity go through moments of conflict and norm-testing.

As noted earlier, most group members will perform diverse roles, and often the roles can be grouped together to form broader role clusters (see figure 8.2). Thus, those who function largely as opinion leaders, for instance, likely give their opinions rather frequently—but they also seek the views of others, evaluate everyone's views, support ideas they like, and occasionally offer procedural guidance. Similarly, the supportive role cluster might involve everything from supporting others to relieving tension to showing solidarity—while also offering information and opinions as task behaviors.

Finally, not all roles function constructively in groups. To be avoided are those roles that tend to further self-interests over group interests and goals. The *self-centered roles* include:

1. *Blocker*—constantly objects to others' ideas and suggestions, insists that nothing will work, is totally negative; may also repeatedly bring up the same topic or issue after the group has considered and rejected it.
2. *Aggressor*—insults and criticizes others, shows jealousy and ill will.
3. *Storyteller*—tells irrelevant, often time-consuming stories, enjoys discussing personal experiences.
4. *Recognition seeker*—interjects comments that call attention to his or her achievements and successes.
5. *Dominator*—tries to monopolize group interaction.
6. *Confessor*—attempts to use the group as a therapeutic session, asks the group to listen to his or her personal problems.
7. *Special-interest pleader*—represents the interests of a different group and pleads on its behalf.
8. *Noncontributor*—is reticent and uncommunicative; refuses to cope with conflict or take a stand; fails to respond to others' comments.[39]

Figure 8.2
Group role clusters.

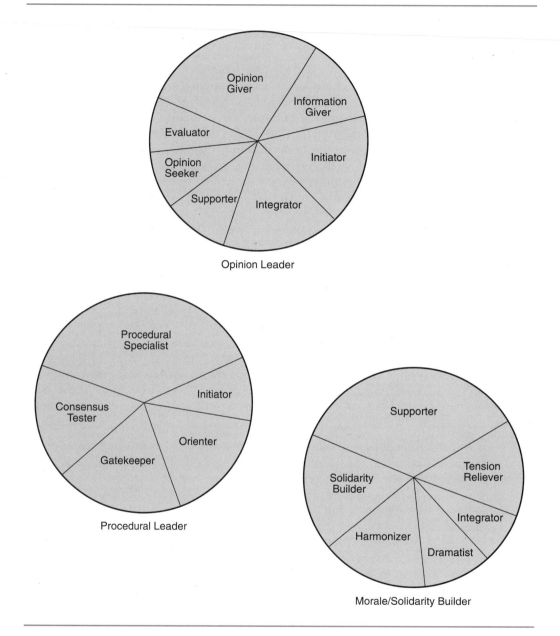

Opinion Leader

Procedural Leader

Morale/Solidarity Builder

Types of Roles in Small Groups

Task Roles	Relationship Roles	Self-Centered Roles
Initiator	Supporter	Blocker
Information giver	Harmonizer	Aggressor
Information seeker	Tension reliever	Storyteller
Opinion giver	Gatekeeper	Recognition seeker
Opinion seeker	Norm creator	Dominator
Elaborator	Solidarity builder	Confessor
Integrator	Dramatist	Special-interest pleader
Orienter		Noncontributor
Evaluator		
Procedural specialist		
Consensus tester		

In general, when positive roles are enacted and shared in groups (with negative roles minimized), positive group outcomes, such as enhanced morale and sound decision making, are more likely. Moreover, from a functional view, those who perform the positive task and building and maintenance roles are actually serving as group leaders (see chapter 10) insofar as their behaviors assist the group in accomplishing its goals.

While much of the research on groups roles has been conducted in laboratory settings, enacting roles in actual organizations is more complex. When individuals participate in committee, team, or quality circle meetings, they do so with the potential constraints and complexities associated with whatever formal organizational role they play. Someone may be a department chair, a clerical worker, a factory supervisor, or the company's latest recruit. The clerical worker who is part of a quality management team might consider it appropriate only to ask questions, support the views of others, and so forth. The department chair might assume that she is expected to come armed with ideas and information. Moreover, if the group functions with a formally appointed leader, that individual is likely to assume that he or she is supposed to provide the group with an agenda and background information and exert some semblance of control over group interaction. Thus, in organizational groups, individuals bring with them *role perceptions* (notions of what their role should consist of) and *role expectations* (their understanding of what others expect of them). Weighing and balancing those, individuals choose how to enact their roles, a process to be negotiated and renegotiated over time.

Status and Power

So long as the concept of hierarchy prevails in organizations, issues of status and power will remain potent variables affecting small group and organizational behavior. Most of the time persons who occupy positions of high status in the organizational hierarchy also possess considerable power. Thus, the two concepts are practically associated but conceptually quite distinct. Specifically, *status* is the value, importance, or prestige associated with a given role or position. *Power,* on the other hand, focuses on the opportunity to influence or control others. Throughout organizations of all kinds, individuals occupy positions that are highly valued by others (that is, high status positions); yet, in fact, they have little opportunity to influence the behavior of others (that is, they possess little power). The vice-presidency of the United States is a classic example of a position of considerable importance and prestige that carries minimal power.

Just as the concepts of power and status differ, the type of power varies from situation to situation. French and Raven distinguish six types of social power, or power base, and designate them as (1) reward, (2) coercive, (3) referent, (4) legitimate, (5) expert, and (6) information.[40] *Reward power* refers to one's ability to elicit a desired response from another due to one's ability to provide the other with positive reinforcement. A realtor may show houses to prospective clients each evening, working long after traditional hours are over in hopes of gaining a large sales commission when a house is finally sold. Besides hoping for this monetary reward, however, she may also toil for fear that her employer will fire her if she doesn't make a significant sale soon. The latter thinking represents an example of *coercive power,* or, in this case, the ability of her employer to elicit a desired response (hard work leading to sales) by means of potential punishment (firing).

The third type of social power is *referent,* and it functions most potently when a person strongly identifies with another, holding him or her in high esteem and respecting the individual's judgment on appropriate behavioral standards. Small, informal work groups within organizations are often potent sources of referent power. Individual workers within them may increase or decrease their productivity, not in accordance with the formal reward and punishment system of the organization, but simply because other members of their small informal work group are doing it (and, in this manner, indicating it to be the appropriate way to behave.)

The next power base discussed by French and Raven, *legitimate power,* focuses on recognized authority. Individuals responding to this type of power do so, not because they anticipate a specific reward or fear some punishment, but simply because they believe that the person requesting the response is fully authorized to make the request. People holding organizational status higher than our own are often accorded this sort of power. The manager of some other department, for example, probably does not have direct power to discipline or fire us; yet when he makes a request that we provide his staff with some information, we probably will comply simply because we believe he has the right to make such a request. Similarly, when a security guard for the company asks us to sign in or out when we come to work early or leave late, we probably will comply, even though we might have status higher than his or hers; again, we accord the guard the right to make that request of us.

Figure 8.3
The bases of power.

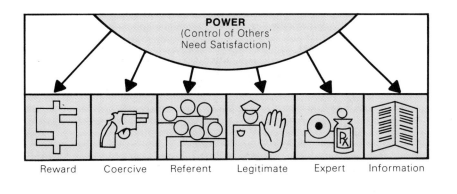

When we follow the directions or take the advice of another because of that person's recognized competence, we are behaving in response to *expert power*. An intelligent supervisor or manager, in fact, makes much use of this sort of power, not by exerting it but by being influenced by it. The most effective executives surround themselves with expert advisors, frequently ask those people for advice, and use the advice when making decisions. They recognize that their advisors know more about marketing, engineering, sales, the law, and so on, and they allow the advisors to exert expert power by acting on their advice. Of course, by increasing your own expertise in a specific topic or area, you increase your own ability to exert expert power over others.

Finally, *information power* refers to the power to control the availability and accuracy of necessary information. If we can control the flow of information someone receives, we can control his or her behavior to some degree (again, consider the powerful secretaries who significantly influence organizational functioning by determining what information their bosses receive). Similarly, we all want to do the correct thing; thus, we are influenced by information we perceive to be accurate. People who can supply such information are likely to be influential for us. Figure 8.3 depicts these bases of power.

In comparing the effects of different types of power, it is important to remember that these categories are not mutually exclusive. The same persons can have, and often do have, several sources of power, particularly in organizational settings. The vice-president of a corporation has the power both to hire and to fire and may be, in addition, a recognized expert in a specific field, such as marketing or economics. Finally, even if an executive is only a figurehead with no particular power to reward or punish or is even incompetent in terms of professional expertise, still he or she is a vice-president, and a great many individuals respond to the position rather than the person. Thus, in real life settings, we are subjected to several types and combinations of power.

Individuals in organizations often belong to small groups composed of members with varying power and status. In these groups, persons do not communicate as equals, a fact that is often an obstacle to effective interaction and decision making.[41] Several studies have shown that those possessing high status are treated with more deference by fellow group members than are those of low status. High-status members are also less likely to be held personally responsible for behaving in ways normally viewed as inappropriate by others.[42] Communication directed to those possessing high status is also distorted in certain important ways.

A number of experimental studies have investigated the nature of upward-directed communication distortions. One early investigation, for example, explored role relations among psychiatrists, clinical psychologists, and psychiatric social workers.[43] The researchers found that communication directed toward the highly influential psychiatrists was extremely supportive and cautious. In a similar study, Cohen discovered that high-power figures received significantly greater numbers of communications and longer verbalizations than their lower-power counterparts.[44] Moreover, he found that when a low-power individual perceived the possibility for upward mobility, his or her verbal behavior became more task-oriented, friendlier, and more supportive of the high-power individual.[45] For the most part, upward communication is associated with approval-seeking behavior, but on occasion, it may be characterized by aggression and even hostility.[46] Perhaps, as Cartwright and Zander have noted, it is the simultaneous desire for power and fear of it that have led to such seemingly ambivalent reactions.[47] Moreover, it may well be that our reactions to individuals who can reward us differ significantly from our responses to those who rely primarily on punishment as a means of controlling our behavior.

In every organization, there are many persons who possess considerable status and power. Not all of them use their positions and influence in the same manner, however. A powerful organizational executive can stifle opinions contrary to his or her own and encourage superficial analysis of problems and explorations of solutions. But the same person can wisely recognize the difficulties that attach to speaking with one's superiors, reward accurate, honest expressions of opinion, and elicit the articulation of divergent points of view.

In the film *Effective Decisions,* Peter Drucker tells the story of Alfred P. Sloan, who for years was the brilliant chief executive of General Motors. On this particular occasion, the executive board of GM was considering a proposal that sounded innovative, interesting, and financially sound. Not one member of the board raised an objection. Sloan asked each one, "Do you see anything wrong with this proposal?" Each one responded negatively. Sloan wisely commented, "Well, I don't see anything wrong with it either. For that reason, I move that we postpone its consideration for one month to give ourselves some time to think." Drucker reports that the proposal was soundly defeated one month later. A poor proposal was appropriately rejected in this instance because a wise manager believed that those in power had the obligation to ensure that dissenting views were voiced, and he insisted on hearing conflicting views before he would act.[48]

All group members must be concerned with the effectiveness of the group's problem-solving ability. By virtue of their power or status, some group members are in strategic positions for greatly influencing the quality of the groups's decision-making process. The judicious use of authority to encourage the free expression of ideas and to reward initiative and innovative thinking can go far in eliminating the doubts and skepticism of less powerful group members.

From Bob Smith, "Employee Committee or Labor Union," *Management Review* 83 (April 1993): 54–57.

Cohesiveness

A final significant socioemotional variable affecting group interaction is *cohesiveness*. As a small group characteristic, cohesivesness is related to solidarity, the group's "stick-togetherness," and its ability to maintain itself over time and through crisis.[49] Not surprisingly, cohesiveness and conformity are related in that the highly cohesive group usually clings to its norms, attitudes, and values. Individuals who are members of such groups feel a strong sense of belonging, prefer membership in those groups to that in most others, and have close friends who also belong.

As a socioemotional variable, cohesiveness often facilitates group functioning. The sense of "we-ness" in cohesive groups often transcends individual differences and motives.[50] High cohesiveness and high group member morale are often closely associated. Early studies of decision-making conferences reported significant positive correlations between cohesiveness and members' satisfaction, both with the group experience and with the total meeting.[51] In addition, cohesive group members like each other. They rate each other highly with respect to attractiveness, motivation, and performance.[52] In general, these group members communicate more frequently with one another than do members of noncohesive groups, and they tend to be friendlier.[53]

While it is clear that the atmosphere in highly cohesive groups is usually pleasant and moral runs high, we often erroneously assume that these groups will necessarily make superior decisions or be highly productive. Of particular interest from an organizational viewpoint is the relationship between cohesiveness and productivity. Research has demonstrated that cohesiveness neither increases nor decreases group productivity.[54] Rather, it serves to heighten the susceptibility of group members to mutual influence. If a highly cohesive group establishes a standard of low productivity, persons belonging to that group are quite likely to conform to the norm and produce little.

Moreover, cohesiveness can have an even darker side. Consider psychologist Irving Janis's account of events occurring a few days before disaster struck the small mining town of Pitcher, Oklahoma, in 1950. Janis reports that the local mining engineer had warned the town's citizens to leave immediately because the land the town sat on had been accidentally undermined and was in danger of caving in at any moment. But the day after the warning was issued, at a meeting of leading citizens belonging to the Lions Club, the members joked about the warning and "laughed uproariously when someone arrived wearing a parachute."[55] In their complacent and cohesive way, these club members seemed to be saying that disasters of this sort just couldn't happen to fine folks like them in a nice little town like theirs. Within a few days, this reasoning cost some of these men and their families their lives.

Although the Pitcher, Oklahoma, incident occurred over four decades ago, it is far from an isolated event. Groups and organizations in many communities regularly make poor decisions—in part because their cohesiveness leads them into a mind-set that discourages dissent and the rational examination of alternative courses of action. We know, for instance, that pressure for uniformity is great in groups characterized by high cohesiveness.[56] This pressure serves to reduce the range and quality of information and opinions presented and diminishes the advantages of having groups rather than individuals make decisions. We have already discussed some of the problems associated with pressure for uniformity. In cohesive groups, group pressure can also be accompanied by choice shifts in which the group gradually shifts toward the position initially taken by the majority or by its most vocal members. Since these shifts depend more on intragroup pressures than on the quality of argument and information available, the group may end up making extreme decisions—ones that mindlessly continue existing policies or are inordinately risky.[57] Moreover, since cohesiveness generates high levels of member commitment to group decisions and high levels of motivation to implement them, group members may do all they can to implement a poor or foolish decision or to ignore or distort information that suggests that their decision or proposed course or action might be unwise.[58]

One of the most extensive investigations of the potentially negative impact of cohesiveness on a group's ability to make intelligent decisions was conducted by Irving Janis. Janis examined the decision-making processes leading to several historic military and political fiascoes, including the decision to cross the 38th parallel in Korea, and the decision to invade the Bay of Pigs, the choice to escalate the war in Vietnam, and the decisions surrounding the Watergate cover-up. To explain how poor decisions were made in each of these instances, Janis introduces the concept of groupthink, which he defines as "a model of thinking that people engage in when they are deeply involved in a cohesive in-group, when the members' striving for unanimity overrides their motivation to realistically appraise alternative courses of action. . . ."[59]

Janis goes on to identify eight negative qualities that commonly lead to groupthink:

1. An *illusion of invulnerability,* creating excessive optimism and encouraging excessive risk taking.
2. *Collective rationalization* to discount warnings that might lead members to reconsider their assumptions.
3. An unquestioned *belief in the group's inherent morality,* causing members to ignore the ethical consequences of their decisions.
4. *Stereotyped views of opposition leaders* as either too evil to warrant genuine attempts to negotiate or too weak or stupid to be a viable threat.
5. *Direct pressure exerted on any member who expresses dissenting views,* making clear that such dissent is unacceptable.
6. *Self-censorship* by group members, attempting to minimize the importance of any doubts they might have.
7. A *shared illusion of unanimity* concerning opinions conforming to the majority view.
8. The *emergence of self-appointed "mindguards"*—members who protect the group from conflicting information that might shatter their shared complacency.[60]

Janis does not argue that all highly cohesive groups fall prey to groupthink. Rather, he points out that strategies do exist for counteracting it. Janis believes that the cohesive group's leader is a critical individual, one capable of insisting on the open-minded pursuit of available options. Specifically, he suggests that the group's leader should (1) assign to everyone the role of critical evaluator, (2) avoid stating personal views, particularly at the outset, (3) bring in outsiders representing diverse interests to talk with and listen to the group, (4) play and ask specific others to take turns playing the devil's advocate, (5) let the group deliberate without the leader from time to time, and (6) after a tentative decision has been made, hold a "second chance" meeting where each member is required to express as strongly as possible any residual doubts.[61] When leaders insist on and groups accept these kinds of norms, cohesive groups should function extremely effectively. Certainly, these guidelines are consistent with Courtright's study of groupthink in which he found that the "absence of disagreement" is perhaps the most powerful aspect of the groupthink syndrome.[62]

Group cohesiveness generally contributes to the development of the group's socioemotional climate, and it has great potential for enhancing the group's performance. Members of highly cohesive groups need to recognize, however, that cohesiveness does not automatically facilitate positive group outcomes. Such groups should carefully scrutinize the norms they develop, as well as the way in which they elicit conformity to those norms. In this manner, highly cohesive groups stand a better chance of meeting their task responsibilities in a socioemotional climate that is pleasing to all.

Summary

As members of organizations, we spend considerable time interacting in small groups. Some small groups, such as casual or primary groups, are informal and exist primarily to satisfy personal needs. Others are more formally structured and focus on the accomplishment of specific tasks, often involving decision making and problem solving. Group discussions occur in both private and public settings and involve all levels of the organizational hierarchy. Many socioemotional variables affect the functioning of small groups, including social influence, role structure, status, power, and cohesiveness. These variables play powerful roles in determining the climate in which decision-making groups carry out their responsibilities. Highly cohesive groups often develop groupthink tendencies that hinder effective decision making. But perceptive leaders can do much to encourage these groups to give fair consideration to conflicting opinion.

Questions for Discussion

1. How would you distinguish a collection of individuals from an interacting small group?
2. Name and define several types of small groups commonly encountered in organizational settings. What are some examples of each? Be sure to comment on teams and quality circles.
3. Compare and contrast a panel discussion with a symposium.
4. Discuss your understanding of norms. What are some examples of established norms in specific organizations of your experience?
5. What are some of the personal, group, and situational variables contributing to conformity behavior? How do groups exert pressure for uniformity? How do deviates respond to social influence?
6. What types of roles do individuals play in small groups? What, in your view, is the relative significance of each?
7. Compare and contrast status and power, both their definitions and their effects on human communication behavior.
8. Discuss the five bases of power. Provide examples of each based on your own experience. What combinations of power are most common in your views? Most effective? Least effective?
9. What are some of the positive and negative factors associated with highly cohesive groups? How is groupthink related to cohesiveness?

Exercises

1. Think of an organization to which you now belong or to which you belonged for some length of time in the past. Make a list of several norms (both implicit and explicit) operating within this organization. Then think of a time when some

member (possibly you) deviated from one of those norms? How did the group treat the deviate? What was the deviate's response?

2. Break into groups of five to seven members and discuss a controversial question of the group's choice. After twenty minutes, terminate the discussion and analyze the role behavior of each group discussant. Some, for example, serve as information givers or seekers, others as clarifiers, others as facilitators, and still others as blockers. Which roles seemed most useful to your particular group? Why?

3. Suzanne Martin has been hired recently as a sales representative of a prestigious women's clothing store in New York. The job is extremely important to Suzanne, as she hopes to rise to the position of assistant buyer and ultimately to buyer for the store. In this particular organizational setting, there is great potential for advancement, and Suzanne is thrilled with her new job. There is, however, one problem. Every Friday at the close of the workday, all seven of the sales personnel in Suzanne's division visit a nearby cocktail lounge and chat informally for some time. The chatting invariably involves organizational gossip, rumor transmission, and speculation. Suzanne finds the custom distasteful but has been warned that those who fail to "be sociable" often have trouble working with the rest of the group throughout the workweek. Others who have developed such interpersonal problems were unable to move upward in the organization.

   a. What norm(s) is operating in this situation?
   b. Is it implicit or explicit?
   c. What are the advantages of conforming?
   d. What are the disadvantages?
   e. What would you advise Suzanne to do in this situation? Why?

4. Consider the following brief description:

   Michael Carr is a lower-level manager in Organization ABC. He is young, assertive, extremely bright, and particularly innovative in his approach to problem solving. Among his subordinates, he is known as "the brain."

   Richard Walls is vice-president in charge of sales in the same organization. In terms of the organization's chart, he is two levels above Carr. Walls is an autocrat who rewards liberally and punishes only occasionally. When he does punish, he often does so by firing.

   Peter Arden is president of Organization ABC. Near retirement, he has an impressive record with the company, but lately, he has grown relatively out of touch with the cutting edge of the organization.

   a. Discuss the relative status of each of these individuals.
   b. What kind of power base is each operating from?
   c. If the three gave conflicting orders, which one would most workers obey? Which would you obey? Why?

The Process of
Decision Making

ommittee work abounds in organizations. Yet anyone who has spent more than a few minutes in a committee meeting knows that being in a small group can be a frustrating experience. Groups often get off the track, bicker among themselves, and consume seemingly endless hours. Managers who decide to share problem-solving and decision-making responsibilities with their employees need to begin by considering both the assets and the liabilities associated with group work.

First, from a negative perspective, groups take time. Because an individual decision maker doesn't have to deal with diversified perspectives or interruptions, he or she is usually able to reach a solution unimpeded. In organizations, time and money are interdependent. When an executive who makes fifty dollars an hour takes four hours to consider a problem and make a decision, that decision costs the company two hundred dollars. If five such executives meet to make a decision about the same problem, even if they take only the same amount of time, that decision costs the organization one thousand dollars!

Besides the time-cost factor, many people lack training in group discussion skills. As a result, group meetings are often poorly organized, and members come unprepared, expecting others to carry the major burden. Some group members are overly talkative and dominate the discussion, while others remain mute. Finally, some leaders do not really allow groups to make decisions. Instead, they use the meeting as an arena to sell their own ideas. Other leaders allow the group to discuss an issue for a limited time period and then require a vote rather than letting a genuine consensus develop from the group's deliberations. Still others listen (or pretend to listen) to the group and then go off and quietly make the decision alone.

Given these potential liabilities, the obvious question is: Why bother with groups? Researchers who have pursued this question have found some rather encouraging results. There is some evidence to suggest that groups who reach decisions through a process of cooperative deliberations do, in fact, generate more ideas and produce better quality decisions than do individuals who work on problems alone.[1] Certain discussion techniques, such as brainstorming, nominal grouping, and the use of idea-generating agendas, can also stimulate creativity.[2] Among group members, there is much knowledge and information, typically more than would be in the possession of any one member trying to solve the problem alone. Certainly, there is a greater diversity of perspectives, and this diversity can serve to discourage the thinking ruts that often characterize the problem-solving attempts of individuals.[3]

Equally important, people who help make decisions understand how and why they were made. Participating in decision making increases group members' commitment to decisions and generally improves their morale.[4] We may give our time to committee work grudgingly on occasion, but in the long run, most of us feel more useful, more productive, and more valued as professionals when we have a chance to share in making significant decisions. Most of the so-called liabilities we discussed are not inherent to small-group deliberations. They tend to occur, rather, when group members are ignorant of group processes and are poorly informed regarding sound decision-making procedures.

Group decision making offers significant advantages to organizations. It is important to remember, however, that skill in decision making may be even more important to individual group members. As management becomes more participative, employees are becoming more involved in making decisions that affect them and the organization directly. Well-made decisions improve the employee's own working life and the success of the organization; poorly made decisions adversely affect both. And, as we have seen, people skilled in group decision making are much more likely to rise both in the esteem of their peers and superiors and in the organizational hierarchy.

Of course, there is nothing magic about making decisions in groups. Some groups work quite effectively and consistently make pretty good decisions, while others flounder. Researchers have attempted for some years to compare effective and ineffective groups, trying to distinguish their behaviors and communicative activities. Based on their research, Hirokawa and Scheerhorn point to five factors that can potentially lead a group to a low-quality decision: the improper assessment of a choice-making situation, the establishment of inappropriate goals and objectives, the improper assessment of positive and negative qualities associated with various alternatives, the establishment of a flawed information base, and faulty reasoning based on the group's information base.[5] Attempting to further distinguish effective from ineffective groups, Hirokawa and Pace argue that the quality of a group's decision depends on four things:

1. *The way in which group members attempt to evaluate the validity of opinions and assumptions advanced by fellow discussants.* Evaluations tend to be more rigorous in effective groups.
2. *The careful, rigorous manner in which groups try to evaluate alternatives, measuring them against established criteria.*
3. *The kind of premises on which decisions are made.* Effective groups are more likely to use high-quality facts and inferences, whereas ineffective groups rely more on questionable facts and assumptions.
4. *The sort of influence exerted by prominent group members.* In highly effective groups, leaders are more supportive and facilitating and less inhibiting. They ask appropriate questions, challenge invalid assumptions, clarify information, and keep the group from going off on irrelevant tangents.[6]

As you approach working in a small group, you should be aware that decision making is a *process* rather than a procedure. As with other processes, the operative elements are interdependent and delicately balanced. A personality clash among members not only disrupts interpersonal relations but also affects the problem-solving ability of the group. In addition, as you interact with other group members throughout the discussion, there will be constant fluctuations within you, between and among you and others, and in the group as a whole. It is impossible, therefore, to point to a given procedure that should be followed in all decision-making groups. Rather, it is critical that you be sensitive to the situations that might develop moment to moment and have within the realm of your knowledge and experience some potentially useful approaches or strategies to deal with such contingencies.

Working in Groups: A Balance Sheet

Pros	Cons
Groups stimulate thought.	Groups take time.
Groups share information.	Group work is costly.
Groups build commitment.	Meetings can be inefficient.
Groups promote self-esteem.	Groups can be undemocratic.
Groups make better decisions.	Group pressures can mislead.

Preparing for Participation

In organizational settings, you will find yourself working in decision-making groups for three basic reasons. First, you will *acquire* some group memberships simply by joining the organization. You will participate in department or unit meetings, for example, and you will attend companywide meetings, employee training sessions, and other meetings directly related to your responsibilities. Second, you will be *assigned* other group memberships. Your boss may ask you to work with some task force comprising people from several departments, or your turn to be your department's representative on a fundraising committee may come up. Finally, you will be *appointed* to groups whose membership you seek. Quality circles, for example, consist only of employees who volunteer to participate. If you are one of the volunteers chosen, you have been appointed to membership. Many of the most prestigious groups in an organization have appointed members, and your performance in other decision-making group settings will determine whether you win the appointment you seek.

However you obtain group membership, your initial responsibility to that group will be to prepare carefully. Often, your assignment or appointment to group membership is based on expertise you happen to have; however, even in those situations, you will gather and organize information that you can contribute to the group's functioning. As we have already suggested, failure to prepare adequately for a group meeting is one of the most common causes of poor performance.

Taking a Personal Inventory

The first step to discussion preparation is to take an inventory of the ideas, information, and other relevant data already in your possession. As we noted earlier, most decision makers in organizations would not belong to the group exploring a particular problem unless they were believed to possess some useful information, perspectives, or insights.

In the classroom setting, discussion groups are usually free to select the subjects they wish to consider, with only reasonable restrictions. Thus, choosing a topic for group exploration is probably based on some shared interest in subjects, such as the parking problem on campus, how the community should dispose of PCBs, the most recent tax law, or academic dishonesty. In actual organizations, topics or tasks are more likely to be assigned.

Initially, then, group members should take stock of their existing attitudes, opinions, and knowledge. In fact, it is often useful for some members of the group to meet prior to the actual meeting to assess the nature and quality of the members' collective knowledge. The deficiencies that are found in this store of existing data provide the guidelines for subsequent research. If you know how you feel about a problem but recognize that these feelings are based largely on some specific personal experiences, then perhaps the most productive strategy for you is to read widely regarding the issue or problem, attempting to be as open-minded as possible.

Collecting Information

Few of us know everything we need to contribute our best efforts to the group's task responsibilities. Thus, most of us must engage in some collection of information. It is true that group decisions can be superior to the judgments of individuals, particularly with tasks requiring the pooling of data,[7] but this is never the case when the discussion involves the pooling of ignorance. Whenever groups are able to make high quality decisions, it is usually because each group member is prepared for discussion.

You can collect information from many sources, including your own personal observation and experience, interviews and surveys, and reading. We all base a great many of our attitudes on *personal experiences*. In solving organizational problems, these experiences are especially vital sources of information. Generally, personal observation is best when it is substantiated by other types of evidence. The assembly-line foreman who has had twenty years' experience handling blue-collar workers may believe that his style of supervision works best for achieving maximum worker productivity. That opinion is made more credible if he can provide evidence to show that workers under his supervision have actually increased their output (both qualitatively and quantitatively), and perhaps that his style of leadership compares favorably with that of other supervisors who deal with similar personnel performing similar tasks.

On some occasions, you may wish to conduct *field research* as you gather information. Field research often involves *interviews* or *surveys*. Organizations frequently conduct surveys to discover how the public is responding to a particular marketing strategy. The major advantage of the survey is the breadth of response it provides. If you decide to conduct your own survey, you should recognize that, to be valid, the survey must be conducted on a sample representative of the population to which the responses are being generalized. Most of you are not expert pollsters or statisticians. Even so, the appropriate strategy to follow for reasonable safety in conducting surveys is to select respondents at random and to gather relatively large samples. It is also wise to draw several samples independently from the same population to check the validity of your results. Under these conditions, if you obtain consistent results across all samples, you can reasonably assume that the data accurately reflect the population of interest.

The construction of valid survey questions is a task that should be undertaken with particular care. This matter is also of special concern for anyone who elects to collect data by means of interviews. In either case, one of the more common problems encountered by inexperienced researchers is the tendency to ask leading or loaded questions. These are questions that, intentionally or unintentionally, reveal your opinions or feelings. Often, they elicit a response that reinforces the questioner's prejudices rather than measures the actual attitudes of the respondents. To be avoided, then, are such leading questions as: "Why do you think this company has adopted such an inequitable approach to dealing with male and female employees?" "Doesn't it seem to you that the president's economic program has failed?" or "Why would anyone want to work for a government-funded institution these days, anyway?" While the survey taps the views of a large number of individuals, through the interview it is possible to acquire greater depth of information. Whenever you want to know the reasons behind specific positions (rather than have a general profile of the views of the overall population) or wish to explore the ideas of experts in a given area, you will probably find the interview a useful research tool.

Of course, great care must be taken in interpreting responses. If the person being interviewed uses an ambiguous word in response, you should ask him or her for a definition or elaboration rather than guess at an appropriate interpretation after the fact. And it is usually a wise strategy to interview individuals representing a variety of points of view or perspectives. For example, because of declining enrollments, many elementary and secondary schools have been closed in recent years. In an attempt to make judicious decisions regarding which particular schools are to close in a given community, school boards have conducted polls and interviewed citizens. The typical procedure has been to tap the views of parents, students, administrators, government leaders, and concerned citizens. By interviewing a selected number from each of these categories, these decision-making boards can probe for evidence supporting each person's ideas and explore the feelings underlying his or her attitudes.

A final source of information you may wish to examine before participating in a discussion is written materials. For each of you as students of group decision making, this often includes a thorough exploration of resources that reside in the library. Certainly, the holdings catalogue is one source of information, allowing you to explore authors, titles, and general subject areas. However, other research sources abound. There are a number of standard sources for locating reference works, such as *Basic Reference Sources, Guide to Reference Books,* and *The Guide to the Use of Libraries.* Because the sources of specific bibliographies are seemingly endless, researchers should become familiar with such indexes as the *Bibliographic Index: A Cumulative Bibliography of Bibliographies and of Bibliographical Catalogues, Calendars, Abstracts, Digests, Indexes. The Reader's Guide to Periodical Literature* is a familiar index whose citations are largely from popular magazines. Other guides to articles published in professional journals include *Applied Science and Technology Index, Psychological Abstracts, The Education Index,* the *International Index: Guide to Periodical Literature in the Social Sciences and Humanities,* and *Business Periodicals Index.*

Libraries contain a wealth of information that is often essential in preparing for a group meeting.

If you wish to acquire information on a news event, you should begin by exploring *The New York Times Index.* On occasion, you will need materials that pertain to official government records. *The Catalogue of the Public Documents of Congress and of All Departments of the Government of the United States* is the major comprehensive index of government documents from 1893 to the present. A helpful source of information for recently published books is *Books in Print.* A less complete reference is the *Book Review Digest,* but its advantage is that it contains summaries of works cited so that you can glean some notion of the book's relevance to your particular needs. Finally, many research projects are never actually published. Much of this material is indexed in *Dissertation Abstracts.* In general, every student of group decision making who desires to contribute substantially to the group's effort should familiarize himself or herself with the available library resources, including computerized bibliographies and abstracts.

In the organizational world, surprisingly little use is made of the library resources we have just listed. Instead, decision makers tend to rely heavily on other sources that, in our view, may not be as reliable. The first, of course, is other people in the organization. Prior to a meeting dealing with a problem in work methods, for example, a supervisor in accounting probably would meet with someone from the industrial engineering department to obtain any knowledge he or she might have of the problem at hand. For information about their own area of expertise, most professionals maintain memberships in professional associations, attend conventions of those associations at which current issues and ideas are discussed, and subscribe to the journals those associations publish. Most read the *Wall Street Journal* for business-related information, and like everyone else, they rely on television and newspapers for information about current events. In larger organizations, they also may have access to a company library in which various periodicals and books are housed, and they may be able to use one of the computer-based information retrieval systems (such as Internet, ERIC, or the Lockheed system) now gaining prominence. However, our observations suggest that most people in organizations simply do not take maximum advantage of the information sources available to them, nor do they conduct in-depth investigations in areas outside their own job responsibilities.

Analyzing Collected Data

Obviously, the collection of relevant information is important. Equally critical, however, are its interpretation and evaluation. In other words, the mere accumulation of abundant evidence is not adequate preparation for participation in a decision-making discussion. Rather, it is important that you analyze the data you have collected. Four general criteria for processing your information are helpful: (1) accuracy, (2) recency, (3) completeness, and (4) reliability of the source.[8] Not all of these criteria need be applied to every piece of information, but in most cases, using one or more of them will allow you to make judicious evaluations of the basic quality of your evidence.

The *accuracy* of information is related to its truth and verifiability. An individual should be able to do research in several independent sources and discover essentially the same information. For example, doctors should be able to agree on the *major* causes of heart disease. Statistics describing the number of teenage pregnancies or the cost of a college education should be relatively consistent in different sources. When serious inconsistencies occur, you should question the accuracy of your sources.

You should also strive to obtain the most recent information possible. The significance of *recency* as a criterion for evaluating information depends on the subject being discussed. Most decision making in organizations *must* be based on the most recent data available. Economic trends, consumer demands, and productivity figures are a few examples of kinds of data that change rapidly. They are also the sorts of data upon which organizations base some of their more critical decisions.

It is seldom possible for any group member to obtain all existing information of relevance to the group's decision. But while *completeness* is never possible, it is best for you to strive toward obtaining the most complete information you can in the time available. Completeness and accuracy are closely related. If you explore a great quantity of evidence representing a wide variety of sources, you are in a better position to determine its accuracy than the person who is familiar with only a narrow range of information.

Finally, it is imperative that, as a group discussant, you assess *the reliability of your sources*. Decision makers in organizations often rely on personal observations or recently published reports and surveys conducted by the industry or institution itself. On many occasions, however, individuals find themselves participating in discussions of topics about which they know little or, at least, need to learn a great deal more. Under these conditions, group members must make some judgment about the reliability of their sources. If the source has a well-established reputation for trustworthiness and competence, you can feel reasonably confident about its reliability.

Meetings are notorious time wasters in most organizations. To conduct meetings more effectively, G. Laborde Associates, a communication consulting firm in Mountain View, California, recommends use of the "Pegasus" procedure:

P—present desired outcomes for meetings—make the goal of the meeting crystal clear;

E—explain evidence so that anyone can hear, see, or feel proof that the meeting accomplished its goals (that is, what should people experience if the meeting is successful?);

G—gain agreement from each person concerning the goal of the meeting;

A—activate sensory acuity—be perceptive to others' nonverbal cues;

S—summarize each decision after all decisions have been reached;

U—use a relevancy challenge—ensure that all points brought up during the meeting fit the meeting's objective; and

S—summarize the next step and report back on it—make sure any required follow-up is clear.

From Gary M. Stern, "Here's a Way to Stop Wasting Time at Meetings," *Communication Briefings* (April 1991): 8a–8b.

Of course, from time to time, even the most reputable of sources will be in error. No one is perfect, and ultimately one or more established authorities may be proven mistaken. There exist, for example, several different theories of the origin of the earth. Ranging from the most scientific to the most theological, each theory is expounded (with considerable supporting evidence) by a number of recognized geologists. The greatest safeguard against siding with the "wrong" expert is to engage in the most complete research possible so that you are aware of controversies and divergent points of view. Again, notice the interrelatedness of these criteria. Using one of them often assists you in making valid judgments about the others.

A final critical factor concerning preparation is that you approach the decision-making discussion with an attitude of *open-mindedness*. There is a strong tendency for group members to reach definite conclusions about the best solution to the group's problem before the discussion. They then enter the discussion as advocates of a given position. This prohibits the group from exploring the problem together, for it creates a situation in which a number of adversaries attempt to convince each other of the superiority of their points of view. Obviously, such a confrontation is more like a debate than a decision-making discussion.

To discourage this confrontational sort of situation from developing, it is important to recognize that the *group* has been asked to reach a decision. While each person's contributions are both solicited and appreciated, no one individual should attempt to dominate the group's effort. Controversial questions, by definition, invite several different interpretations, analyses, and potential solutions. Differences of opinion exist on these issues, even among experts. Through the open-minded consideration of each group member's ideas, feelings, and points of view, a maximum number of perspectives can be revealed and explored. Only under these circumstances can any small group hope to reach a judicious decision, one that demonstrates the value of decision making by groups.

Discussion Questions: Types, Characteristics, and Examples

Earlier in this chapter, we pointed out that group decision making should be viewed as a *process* rather than a *procedure*. Thus, although several patterns of organization are often used to structure the communication activities of decision-making groups, these patterns should be approached with flexibility and open-mindedness. One important determinant of an appropriate organizational strategy is the kind of question the group is addressing.

Questions of Fact

Four types of questions are appropriate for decision-making discussions: questions of *fact, conjecture, value,* and *policy. Questions of fact* concern matters of truth or falsity. They can be answered affirmatively or negatively without consulting the beliefs or attitudes of group members. This is not to imply that attitudes and motives do not affect the manner in which you and others deal with the question or perceive evidence pertinent to its discussion. The correct answer to the question of fact is a matter of actual events, particular properties, or specific states of affair, not simply *perceived* truth. Here are some examples of questions of fact relevant to decision making in organizations: "Is this organization meeting the antipollution standards established by the federal government?" "Is this hospital meeting the health-care standards recently established by the AMA?" and "Is this company equipped with facilities to accommodate the needs of handicapped employees?"

Too often, the assumption is made that the group that reaches a consensus on a question of fact has automatically discovered the truth. Unfortunately, this is not necessarily the case. The only way to increase the probability that your group will agree on the correct response to a question of fact is to direct your collective efforts toward conscientiously gathering and skillfully analyzing pertinent data. It is also critical that your members explore and agree on the meaning of particular terms. In the question about handicapped employees, you need to reach a common notion of such terms as *equipped, facilities,* and *handicapped.* The group defining *handicapped* primarily in relation to employees confined to wheelchairs might reach quite different conclusions from a group that conceives of it as involving blindness, deafness, and perhaps certain learning disabilities.

Questions of Conjecture

Similar to the question of fact is the *question of conjecture*. Instead of dealing with the present, it focuses on the future. Organizations must live with (and perhaps learn from) mistakes made in the past. The only events they can influence, however, are those that lie ahead. In fact, organizations are constantly involved with analyzing the future, trying to anticipate future needs and demands of the population they serve. Since questions of conjecture focus on events as yet unseen, in discussing them, your group must base its conclusions on probabilities. Even so, you should avoid the temptation to rely excessively on guessing. It is often possible to base an intelligent prediction of the future on a substantial knowledge of the past.

In this manner, it is possible to gain some sensitivity to the variables contributing to certain kinds of effects. In essence, the discussion of a question of conjecture demands the same knowledge and intelligent analysis as the question of fact. Examples of questions of conjecture include: "Will the demand for Product X increase in the coming months?" "Will the demand for mathematics teachers increase in the years ahead?" and "Will the number of fathers seeking joint custody of their children increase during the next decade?"

Questions of Value

Not unlike questions of fact or conjecture, the *question of value* can usually be answered affirmatively or negatively. But value questions deal neither with truth nor probability. Rather the beliefs, attitudes, values, and motives of the members of your group are sought in discussing value questions. In general, values refer to modes of conduct or desired states of existence. Once a value has been internalized, it becomes a standard for guiding behavior, for developing and maintaining attitudes, and for judging your own and others' actions.[9] Values are formed in various ways, and, once established, they tend to endure. Because values cannot be "proven," questions of value should never be treated like questions of fact. When your group discusses value questions, you must recognize that it is simply *approving* the conclusions reached, not demonstrating them irrevocably. Examples of questions of value are "Are our investments in companies in South Africa justified?" "Is teaching the most important mission of this university?" "Is training our employees in communication skills worth the cost?" and "Is hiring and retaining employees with AIDS a justifiable practice?" Value-related issues underlie many contemporary problems confronting organizations.

Questions of Policy

The kind of question most frequently discussed in organizational settings is the *question of policy*. In discussing this, your group will be involved in determining the most appropriate course of action to be taken or encouraged. In a sense, the question of policy is not really a distinct kind of question because underlying almost every question of policy are one or more questions of fact, conjecture, and value. As your group makes judgments about the most suitable course of action to be taken in a specific situation, it will be continually confronted with factual and conjectural questions, as well as issues related to the opinions, attitudes, and motives of individuals within the group.

You need to anticipate the complexity associated with the discussion of policy questions, develop a sensitivity for recognizing the specific issue being discussed, and handle each issue appropriately. Examples of questions of policy include: "Which presidential candidate should this newspaper support?" "What should be the stand of this church regarding the acceptance of homosexuals as members?" and "Should this organization appropriate additional funds to support research and development?"

Notice the diversity of subsidiary questions that might logically arise within these discussions. The policy question relating to homosexuality might include the discussion of factual questions, such as "What is the present stand of the church regarding homosexuals?" and "What is the attitude of church leaders regarding this question?" Conjectural issues might also be raised, including, "What will be the reaction of the average church member if this church grants membership to homosexuals?" Finally, questions of value include "Is homosexuality immoral?" and "What are our personal reactions to this issue?"

Characteristics of Appropriate Discussion Questions

Regardless of the specific kind of question discussed, your group should make every effort to phrase the question appropriately. Gouran has pointed out that the three most important criteria for determining the quality of any discussion question are *simplicity, objectivity, and controversiality*.[10] Simplicity is related to clarity and demands avoiding unnecessary ambiguity or complication. Complicated questions are often pretentious and confusing. Questions should also be phrased objectively. While total objectivity is never possible, your group should make every attempt to remove highly subjective language and phrasing from the discussion question. Objective questions are free of loaded language and implied premises.

Consider, for example, the question, "What should be done in this community to stop the spread of drug abuse?" The subjectivity in this question resides in its assumption that drugs are being abused in the community and that abuse is *spreading*. Further, it is assumed that the correct solution must involve halting such drug usage. A more objective way of phrasing the question would be, "To what extent are drugs used in this community?" This kind of phrasing does not preclude the discussion of drug abuse, but it does begin with the assumption that abuse exists.

Finally, discussion questions should be characterized by controversiality. This is not to imply that all discussions should be full of argument and emotional confrontations. There should be, however, at least *two* points of view for which support can be gathered. The discussion of a question lacking in controversiality is really not a discussion but a simple meeting to confirm previously existing and agreed upon beliefs. It is useless for a manager to call a meeting of several subordinates to discuss the merits of a newly implemented wage incentive plan if she already knows that all members of the group share the same opinion of the plan. She would do better to acknowledge the individual opinions of group members and not waste the group's time in discussing an issue about which a decision has already been reached on an individual basis.

Patterns of Organization for Decision-Making Groups

Many organizational approaches are available to your group as you plan a discussion. Before we explore some of these approaches, it may be useful to review some of the research findings related to effective patterns of group problem solving and decision making.

Research Relating to Problem-Solving Patterns

The manner in which a group discusses a problem is definitely related to the group's success. Early research by Bales and Strodtbeck identified three clearly discernible stages of analysis in successful problem-solving groups: *orientation, evaluation,* and *control.*[11] During the orientation phase, group members spend a good deal of time coordinating decision-relevant information, that is, exchanging information, orienting, repeating, and confirming. In the second stage, evaluative behavior is predominant. Group members exchange opinions, ideas, and feelings in an attempt to reconcile their differences over judgments of fact and the appropriateness of proposed courses of action. In the final (control) stage, individuals exchange suggestions, consider alternative courses of action, and generally express considerable agreement and disagreement in arriving at a commonly accepted solution.

Another fairly linear model of task group development was proposed by Tuckman and Jensen.[12] Their group stages include *forming, storming, norming, performing,* and *adjourning.* Formative behavior involves establishing new relationships and seeking some sense of group spirit. In the next stage, group members begin to react to the demands of the situation. They may question the group's charge and the authority of others in the group, articulating some assertions of differences and independence. The norming stage sees the group agreeing on rules of behavior, criteria for decision making, and ways of doing things. Only during the fourth phase does the group really examine the task or problem since it has focused on relationship development during earlier phases. Finally, as group members' time together draws to a close, they strive for closure on both task and relationship issues, moving toward adjournment. This model emphasizes relationship development and, thus, is most appropriately applied to newly formed groups. It provides less specific information about ongoing groups' decision-making processes.

Process Models of Decision Making

As early as the 1960s, some small group researchers challenged the linear view of group decision making. Scheidel and Crowell, for instance, began with the assumption that if group decision making were essentially linear, it would be characterized by statements that initiate, extend, modify, and synthesize discussion topics. When they observed actual groups, however, they found that these statement types accounted for only about 22 percent of a group's total interaction. Instead, Scheidel and Crowell observed a *reach-test* cycle in which one participant would reach forward with a new idea that was then tested by elaboration, acceptance, or rejection by the other group members. Then a different member would reach out with another idea, and the process would repeat itself. Far from a linear progression toward a decision, these groups followed a *spiraling* model in which members bounced ideas back and forth as they moved toward consensus.[13] Subsequent research by Gouran and Baird[14] and Baird[15] examined the width of the spiral as it progresses. Both studies noted a tendency for disagreement to be followed relatively closely by changes in topic—suggesting that the tension conflict creates may account for changes in the spiral's direction. The width of the spiral was found to be associated with the type of group (social groups changed topics more quickly when conflicts surfaced than did task groups) and group motivations (cooperative groups changed topics more readily than competitive groups when disagreements arose).

Fisher conducted yet another significant study of the interaction process leading to group consensus on decision-making tasks. He found that groups moved through four interrelated phases as they approached consensus. During the first, the *orientation* phase, discussants offered their ideas with some measure of tentativeness and ambiguity; much clarification of opinions and general agreement behavior also occurred. The second phase, *conflict,* was characterized by considerable disputation, with opinions being expressed more assertively. In general, comments were as likely to be unfavorable as favorable, and such communication behavior was persuasive, even argumentative, in nature. Phase three, the *emergence* phase, involved a decline in argument and conflict as group members moved toward a decision that occurred during the final phase, *reinforcement.* This is a time of confirmation and substantiation. Discussants seek a fuller understanding of the group's decision. Much of their communication involves interpretation and support, with little dissent. Fisher also reported that groups do not progress steadily toward a final decision.[16] Instead, they seem to move in jumps by making amendments to different aspects of the proposal being considered.

Several recent studies by Poole suggest that groups develop according to a "multiple sequence model."[17] That is, the groups he studied tried to implement logical, orderly problem-solving sequences, but frequently other factors, such as lack of information, task difficulty, and conflict, interfered. Moreover, periods of idea development and exploration were often broken by periods of integrating activity, such as joke-telling, sharing personal stories, and mutual compliment passing.[18] More recently, Poole and Roth found that groups go through periods of disorganization that are unpredictable and fail to follow a linear model.[19] Taken as a whole, Poole's research suggests that group development may not be as orderly as earlier models proposed.

Distinguishing Effective from Ineffective Groups

Even though groups approach their problem-solving ventures with considerable diversity, researchers have continued to seek factors that might distinguish effective from ineffective groups. In her longitudinal field study of eight project teams, Gersick reported that each team developed its own approaches during its early meetings and tended to stick with those until it reached a midpoint in the time available for completing the project.[20] At this midpoint, each group experienced a transition, "a powerful opportunity to alter

To improve communication throughout the Hyland Therapeutics Division of Baxter Healthcare Corporation, senior management unanimously decided to convene an employee advisory committee (EAC). The group consisted of three supervisors, four working leaders, two nonsupervisory production employees, an executive secretary, and a facilitator for the human resources function, all of whom volunteered to participate.

Initially, the group was asked by management to develop a recommendation for revising the work schedule from a five-day to a seven-day work week—an action needed quickly because of increased demand for company products. They were told not to deal with people problems, wages, benefits, or other topics not directly related to changing the work schedule.

Early meetings were devoted to getting acquainted and to discussing each member's expectations for the group. Then the group moved to a listing of the criteria that had to be met for a work-scheduling option to be considered. Alternative schedules then were proposed and evaluated in terms of those criteria. When they agreed on a final solution, EAC members took it back to their departments for review and modification by their peers. Ultimately, the group proposed developing two different shifts, one covering weekends and the other working only Monday through Friday.

The proposal was approved unanimously by the management group. In the view of the group members, they succeeded because they followed the seven-step process of "multi-attributed decision making" (MAD): (1) determine essential requirements each option must meet; (2) prioritize those requirements and assign weights of importance to each; (3) mathematically normalize each requirement so each option can be compared against the standard; (4) rate each option on each requirement; (5) for each option, multiply each normalized requirement by the corresponding requirement weights; (6) add up the ratings; and (7) select and recommend the option with the highest combined score. This systematic approach to decision making was, the group members felt, the single most important factor contributing to their success.

From Lanny Blake, "Group Decision Making at Baxter," *Personnel Journal* 70 (January 1991): 76–82.

the course of its life midstream."[21] Depending on whether or not the transition functioned constructively, the teams' final products or outcomes varied in quality. Successful groups used the transition as a time to examine and possibly change their basic operating assumptions. Unsuccessful groups tended to ignore the opportunity for self-examination and plowed ahead using the same, often self-defeating patterns. More recently, Gersick has further advanced a *punctuated equilibrium model* of group process in which she offers three concepts as the key to understanding group development. First is "deep structure," or the set of assumptions or performance strategies a group uses to approach its problem. Next is the equilibrium period, in which groups work within their established patterns without questioning their basic approach to the task. Third is the revolutionary period, or the transition time, in which groups examine

Figure 9.1
Phases in group problem solving.

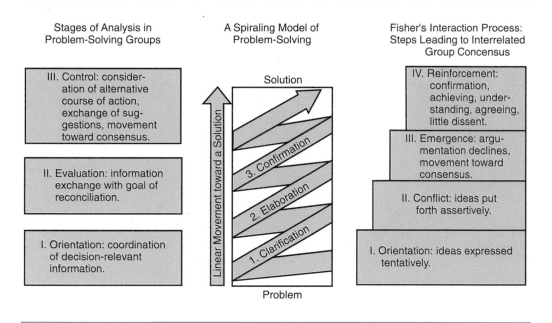

their operating framework and have the chance to reformulate what they are doing as a basis for moving forward (the strategy taken by effective groups).[22]

Task group effectiveness was also studied in a laboratory investigation by Hirokawa. He attempted to distinguish successful from unsuccessful problem-solving groups on the basis of the phases that characterized their discussions. The results, though based on a small sample, indicated that no single uniform sequence of phases is necessarily associated with effective or ineffective problem solving. The study found, rather, that both "successful" and "unsuccessful" groups took their own unique paths to solving their problems, often depending on the conditions present at critical points in the problem-solving process. However, one potentially important difference did emerge. "Successful" groups tended to begin their discussion by attempting to analyze the problem before trying to search for a viable solution, while "unsuccessful" groups tended to begin the discussion by immediately trying to search for a viable solution.[23] Other studies have suggested that real work teams rarely proceed in an orderly, predictable fashion.[24] Figure 9.1 summarizes three different perspectives on group problem solving.

Although the research on group decision models is mixed, the ambiguities may reflect a rather restrictive focus on procedures, stages, phases, or process interventions rather than a broader examination of these in the context of other potentially salient group characteristics. Some have argued that decision outcomes are mediated by vigilant information processing, wherein group members approach their work conscientiously and carefully.[25] As Gouran put it, "although [decision-making procedures] can be very useful in keeping a decision-making discussion focused on the requirements of the question, you fall prey to the belief that the sequence itself rather than the qualities of mind it represents is what determines a group's effectiveness."[26] Endorsing this view, Hirokawa and Rost recently advanced *vigilant interaction theory,* based on the belief that effective groups are more attentive to the group process than are ineffective groups. They argue that effective groups are vigilant in their assessment of the nature of the task, their choice of criteria for evaluating alternatives, and their approach to weighing both positive and negative qualities associated with different decision options.[27] Thus, the spirit with which the problem is tackled significantly influences the quality of the group's work.

Some writers are skeptical of any approaches to problem solving or decision making that are based on the premise of rationality.[28] For instance, in Cohen, March, and Olson's *garbage can model,* decision making is seen as a garbage pail in which people, problems, alternatives, and solutions slush around until there is sufficient contact among these elements for a decision to emerge. According to these theorists, groups will attempt to make their decisions seem rational retroactively through retrospective sense-making, but the decisions are really due to chance. They argue that the effectiveness of a decision should be judged according to group members' abilities to implement it and make it work rather than on the intrinsic effectiveness of the decision itself.[29]

While acknowledging that decision making is scarcely a completely rational process, most scholars subscribe to the view that groups could benefit from discovering and adopting procedures that minimize the widely acknowledged disadvantages or process losses frequently associated with group interaction, such as looking at solutions before understanding the problem. For instance, Poole and Roth analyzed the sequences of activities in forty-seven decisions made by twenty-nine groups. They found that over half of the forty-seven decisions began with some form of solution focus. Fourteen of the groups never engaged in problem definition or other activities and spent the entire time focusing on solutions.[30] Similarly, Nutt reviewed seventy-six cases of organizational decision making and reported that in 84 percent of them, a solution-centered process was used.[31] An initial focus on solutions may cause a truncated search and cursory consideration of alternatives. Even more serious, real problems may go unidentified in favor of problems that fit existing solutions. When this happens, the group actually formulates and attempts to solve the wrong problem.

The studies described here clearly do not prescribe the "best" pattern for decision-making groups to follow. Instead, they describe the kinds of interaction processes that do occur as groups engage in problem solving. Even so, some scholars have examined the relationship between different organizational strategies and decision-making outcomes. One early study demonstrated that groups who develop an orderly attack on the problem before them, considering only one issue at a time, have a greater probability of reaching consensus than groups who do not proceed in such an orderly manner. Subsequent studies have supported the value of methods of problem solving that are thorough and systematic.[32]

While problem solving can be effective when it is systematic, group members may engage in behaviors that disrupt their problem-solving efforts. One potential problem is impatience: One or more members may become too eager to get to a solution (or possible solutions) and cause the group to neglect careful evaluation or orientation. Another is conflict avoidance. In their eagerness to maintain nice relations, members may avoid or smooth over conflict, again to the detriment of the group's critical thinking. Still another problem concerns the reconfirmation groups find necessary. Sometimes members become frustrated and say something like, "Hey we've talked about that ten times already; why don't we get on it?" In fact, restatement, elaboration, and clarification are important elements of the group spiral, and members must be willing to tolerate (and the group leader willing to support) reconsideration of issues discussed earlier.

Now that we have discussed some of the research on decision-making strategies, it might be helpful to examine some useful problem-solving patterns from which any decision-making group might choose. One of the greatest problems group members must overcome is the tendency to make judgments about the quality or feasibility of one another's ideas too early in the discussion. As a result, some researchers have proposed problem-solving strategies that encourage the generation of a maximum number of ideas without premature interpretation or analysis. Brilhart and Jochem found that a *creative problem-solving pattern* (involving the generation of possible solutions prior to the statement of criteria for their judgment) produced more high-quality solutions than the more traditional pattern of first establishing criteria and then considering appropriate solutions.[33] Other scholars have found support for the value of *brainstorming,* where ideas are proposed and listed without any type of judgment or criticism. Research has shown that this procedure can produce fresher, better quality ideas than more ordinary problem-solving procedures.[34] A final approach, the *nominal group procedure,* gives each group member an opportunity to brainstorm privately (that is, on paper). An appointed clerk or "grouper" then collects the lists of ideas and compiles a master list. Ultimately, group members vote on the items they consider most important.[35] Some research comparing brainstorming groups with nominal groups has found that the nominal group procedure is more effective than brainstorming for groups composed of highly apprehensive individuals; nominal grouping also appeared better than brainstorming in terms of idea generation.[36] Group members also can brainstorm, organize, and evaluate their ideas using computer-based group support systems, which we discuss later in this chapter.[37]

The Reflective-Thinking Sequence

First articulated by John Dewey in 1910, the reflective-thinking sequence for problem solving was for many years the only organizational pattern taught in group discussion classes. While many problems arise if one attempts to employ this pattern without regard to the type of question being considered, it is, nevertheless, a common problem-solving pattern, and it is often quite useful when discussing questions of *policy.* The reflective-thinking sequence consists of the following:

1. How shall we define and limit the problem?
2. What are the causes and extent of the problem?
3. What are the criteria by which solutions should be judged?
4. What are the alternative solutions and the strengths and weaknesses of each?
5. What solutions can we agree upon?
6. How can we put the solution into effect?[38]

There are, of course, variations of this sequence. Sometimes the established criteria are not formally stated before the discussion of alternative solutions. In some instances, the groups will not have the power, or perhaps the desire, to actually put a solution or policy into effect. In this case, the last question in the sequence is omitted from consideration.

The Creative Problem-Solving Sequence

Brilhart's research with the creative problem-solving pattern has demonstrated that it is a pattern preferred by groups discussing policy problems of personal relevance to them. It can lead to the generation of more alternative solutions and better quality solutions than patterns based on the reflective-thinking method.[39] The following is an adaptation of Brilhart's creative problem-solving sequence:

1. What is the nature of the problem facing us?
2. What might be done to solve the problem? All group members' ideas are listed *without* evaluation.
3. By what specific criteria shall we judge among our possible solutions? During this phase, the group considers its standards and values, particularly in terms of the extent to which the established criteria are relative or absolute.
4. What are the relative merits of our possible solutions? This process is one of elimination and synthesis, evaluation and judgment.
5. How will we put our decision into effect? Here, the group considers procedural matters involving who, what, when, and how.

The creative problem-solving sequence is similar to Dewey's system, but it differs in its emphasis on suspension of judgment and its encouragement of the generation of unlimited alternative solutions. It can be used with the discussion of any question appropriate for the reflective-thinking format.[40]

Nominal Group Procedure

We have already discussed some of the potential hazards associated with interacting groups. One problem-solving strategy circumvents these hazards by creating a process by which a group works on a problem but does *not* interact. Since the group does not actually have a discussion, the group is labeled *nominal,* that is, in name only.[41] Following are the steps to be used in the nominal group procedure:

1. A group convener ("grouper") poses the problem to be considered (for example, "What can we do to cut production costs?").
2. Each group member writes down his or her ideas on the problem. No discussion is permitted. Brainstorming is encouraged.
3. The grouper may ask group members to divide their lists in some manner. (Given the question above, they might make a list of things they could do personally and a list of things the organization could do.) This step is optional.

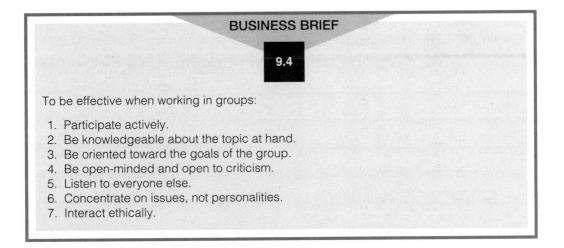

4. Individuals read their lists in round-robin fashion. That is, each person reads his or her first item, then on to the second item, until all lists are exhausted. All items are recorded in clear view of everyone as they are read.
5. The group votes and identifies the highest priority items.
6. Without any discussion, the group is disbanded.

The nominal group procedure is advantageous in that (1) brainstorming is encouraged, (2) no one can be discouraged by the evaluative remarks of others, and (3) equality of participation is a likely outcome. One disadvantage of any noninteracting group, however, is that since the brainstorming is private, group members cannot be stimulated by hearing the ideas of others.[42]

Question-Agenda Model

Earlier, we discussed the kinds of questions appropriate for decision-making groups. We suggested that different kinds of questions should be approached from different perspectives for a maximally productive discussion to occur. Gouran has outlined several different agenda that he believes to be conducive to structured and yet reasonably spontaneous interaction among discussants.[43] The agenda selected depends upon the kind of question being discussed. Gouran's agenda follows:

Agenda for Discussions on Questions of Fact and Conjecture

1. What evidence do we have to support an affirmative position?
2. What weaknesses, if any, exist in this body of evidence?
3. What evidence do we have to support a negative position?
4. What weaknesses, if any, exist in this body of evidence?
5. Have we accumulated enough information to reach a decision?
6. In the light of the evidence examined, what position on the question appears to be most defensible?

Agenda for Discussions on Questions of Value

1. What are our individual positions on the question?
2. On what bases have we arrived at these positions?
3. Which of these bases for our respective positions are sound, and which are questionable?
4. Are there positions other than those represented in the group that we should explore?
5. Which of the bases for additional positions are sound, and which are unsound?
6. Has our evaluation led to any changes in position?
7. Is there one position we can all endorse?

Agenda for Discussions on Questions of Policy

1. What problems, if any, exist under the status quo?
2. What are the alternatives among policies that we could endorse?
3. What are the relative strengths and weaknesses of each of the alternatives?
4. On the basis of our analysis, which policy shall we endorse?

These suggested agenda are proposed only as tentative models, as potentially fruitful structures for the discussion of each kind of question. The advantage of using a different agenda for each type of question is that it is virtually impossible to neglect the nature of the question under consideration. Using these agenda, for example, your group is more likely to treat value questions as ones involving attitudes and motives and factual questions as ones necessitating the collection of considerable evidence before the discussion.

Using Technology to Facilitate Groups: Group Support Systems

Group support systems (GSS), interactive, computer-based systems, are rapidly being adopted and used by more corporations. GSS meeting rooms (see figure 9.2) incorporate the use of a local-area network, individual personal computer (PC) workstations, and GSS software to support such traditional meeting activities as idea generation, idea consolidation, the evaluation of alternatives, and decision making.

Originally, GSS were designed with several specific features intended to enhance the group interaction process.[44] First, GSS enable *parallel communication*. Because group participants brainstorm, consolidate ideas, and vote using their networked PCs, GSS allow each participant to contribute simultaneously; therefore, no group member need wait for another group member to finish "speaking." Second, GSS support *group memory* by recording all typed comments electronically, allowing participants to withdraw from the group process to think or type comments and then rejoin the group discussion. Third, these systems enable participants to contribute to the group *anonymously,* thus reducing the pressure to conform and diminishing both communication and evaluation apprehension.[45] Since ideas typed into the computer do not reveal the identity of the contributor, participants can evaluate their merits on the basis of their content rather

Like many companies, the Reynolds and Reynolds Company in Moraine, Ohio, was looking for ways to improve productivity without increasing costs. Company management decided to structure an employee-run problem-solving team that funneled ideas to management, to provide cross-training to most employees, and to put in place a series of small employee-suggested changes that could result in large gains in efficiency.

An initial investigation of barriers to effective performance revealed conflict between the repair and distribution functions of the plant. Since each function blamed the other for any problems, a five-person task force comprised of people from both areas and one from internal engineering was formed and named ACT—the Accomplishing Communications Team.

The ACT members funneled employee ideas to management over the next several months, including proposed revisions in the weekly work schedules (which would be drawn up by employees themselves), a plan for cross-training repair technicians, and an improved method for labeling repaired parts. All of these measures, and many others, were implemented, with significant cost savings to the company.

Ultimately, the approach increased productivity by nearly 40 percent, reduced the time parts wait for repairs from two weeks to twenty-four hours, and eliminated the need to recheck returned parts.

From Raju Narisetti, "Bottom-up Approach Pushes Plant's Performance to the Top," *Chicago Tribune,* 29 November 1992, sec. 7, p. 13.

than their contributor. Finally, GSS can be used to *deliver a decision-making heuristic (or structure) and channel group behavior* to maintain the group's focus on the task.[46] Ventana Corporation, maker of GroupSystems™, argues that these features help meeting participants contribute more fully, keep meetings on track, complete projects more rapidly, and stay focused and develop consensus.

Although there are clearly potential advantages associated with the use of technology like group support systems, group process losses are also possible. These advantages and disadvantages must be thoughtfully weighed.[47] For instance, typing comments into GSS PCs takes more time than speaking, thus, potentially reducing the amount of information available to the group. On the other hand, the group benefits in that reading is faster than listening. Using a keyboard in the GSS session reduces both verbal and nonverbal cues and yields slower feedback. This reduction in media richness, however, can be offset by more careful and better worded communication. Because GSS anonymity separates the identity of the participants from their comments and votes, they are depersonalized—and thus, presumably better able to express their true opinions. At the same time, however, this condition may also promote "deindividuation," that is, a loss of self- and group-awareness, which itself is associated with both positive and negative communication effects. For instance, deindividuation can increase socializing and decrease negative reactions to criticism. However, reducing inhibitions may cause "flaming," in which feelings (especially negative sentiments) are expressed quickly and without reflection. Moreover, keyboarding may actually inhibit socializing, resulting in reduced group cohesiveness and satisfaction. Finally, the PC screen typically displays only twenty-four lines of text at one time. While this limitation may encourage "information chunking," or the combining of data, and reduce information overload, it may also cause participants to lose a global view of the task, resulting in the incomplete use of information.[48]

One important GSS feature, group memory, allows participants to pause and think during the group keyboarding activity without missing information being submitted by other group members. The GSS capacity to record information can also reduce memory and attention losses, attention blocking, and the incomplete use of information.[49] However, voiced comments and important nonverbal cues may go unnoticed and are, in any event, not documented.

Anonymity is widely heralded as a GSS feature that can reduce status consciousness, pressures to conform, and evaluation apprehension. However, it may also increase free riding because it is more difficult to determine who is not doing his or her fair share.[50] Anonymity may encourage group members to challenge others, allowing the group to catch more errors and realize more objective evaluations of group ideas. But at the same time, anonymity also makes it difficult to attribute value to ideas since participants are unable to match ideas to contributor expertise.[51]

The final notable GSS capability, parallel communication, reduces interruptions and increases air time—providing equality in both access and voice. No one need wait for someone else to stop talking. However, this feature can also generate information overload and increase redundancies since, at times, no one is electronically listening to what others are electronically saying.

Some GSS researchers contend that the rationality of decision making can be improved if people are provided with step-by-step procedures, or heuristics, that substitute for or supplement their own (often deficient) approaches to problem solving.[52] This contention has received some empirical support, since several studies have shown that the use of supplemental heuristics has led to improvements in problem definition, generation of alternative solutions, and even the quality of decisions themselves.[53]

After reviewing empirical GSS research, Dennis and Gallupe conclude that the research "paints a cloudy picture"[54] regarding the overall impact of this kind of group technology on group processes and outcomes. They point out that field research shows that using GSS appears to improve meeting outcomes, such as performance, efficiency, and satisfaction. In laboratory research, however, the results are mixed. Some laboratory studies show influence to be more equally distributed among group members using GSS, while others report no effect from GSS use. Moreover, on occasion, GSS use has been found to decrease consensus or has shown mixed results.

Nunamaker, Dennis, Valacich, Vogel, and George suggest that the discrepancy in laboratory and field research findings may be largely a function of group attributes.[55]

They note that most field groups use GSS to address complex tasks. In these instances, the reduction in group process losses afforded by using GSS appears to have a substantive and meaningful impact on group outcomes. Most field studies also involve groups of a larger size than those used in laboratory experiments. Reducing process losses probably has a greater proportional impact on larger groups than on smaller ones. Moreover, laboratory groups tend to share a common pool of information, whereas field group members tend to exhibit a greater disparity of information and viewpoints when assembling for a meeting. Thus, the improved information exchange through the use of GSS may be more critical and valuable for real groups meeting in organizational contexts.

We should also note that there are nontechnology elements of the GSS meeting environment that may affect the nature of the group-member interaction process. Because GSS meetings do not take place in anyone's office, no participant is disadvantaged by having to travel to someone else's office for the meeting, perhaps finding him or herself on something less than neutral turf. GSS facilities suggest by their very design and layout a concern for equality and a commitment to task. For instance, a number of meeting rooms are organized (as depicted in figure 9.2) so that participants are seated at equal distances around a U-shaped table. All can see a large screen that is prominently situated at the front of the room. At times, a meeting facilitator may stand in front of the group to provide instructions or assist the group process. What is important, however, is that this kind of meeting environment promotes equitable interactions.

In traditional meeting rooms, those with higher rank or status are often advantaged while those with lower rank, confidence, or skill are disadvantaged. For instance, a group member with higher status, often the group's leader, typically elects to sit at the head of the table, giving him or her greater visual access to others (while being the focus of everyone's attention), as well as the potential for greater influence. Studies have shown that those seated in key positions will, in fact, talk more than others and will also be perceived as more influential. At the other extreme, those with high communication apprehension will invariably choose the most obscure seats, allowing them to withdraw from communication more easily and to avoid being the focus of attention. Interestingly, the GSS meeting environment neither promotes the would-be star nor provides hideouts for the apprehensive.

The adoption and use of GSS and other such "groupware" products are increasing rapidly. Many organizations have chosen to downsize, and they want to make the time spent by managers and professional staff in meetings (30 to 70 percent of their time) as productive as possible. Corporations now employ GSS to support a wide range of purposes (such as team building, strategic planning, quality control, joint applications design, and project management) and productivity gains as high as 90 percent have been reported by firms using this technology.[56]

Daniel Petre cautions that too many companies are buying groupware such as GSS as if it were just another word processor or spreadsheet. This carries a high risk, he warns, because groupware's potential is so great and its scope of impact so broad. Petre contends that successful implementation depends less on technological logistics and more on organizational culture—especially in terms of the willingness of employees to share information.[57]

Figure 9.2
A GSS meeting environment.

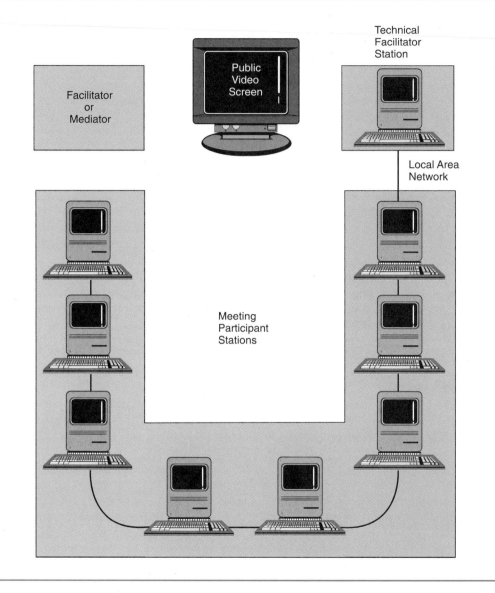

An innovative use of group dynamics was attempted by Lutheran Brotherhood, a Minneapolis-based financial services company. When it learned that the laptop computers used by members of the sales force had become outdated and virtually useless, management decided that new laptop technology—and new sales force computer skills—was desperately needed.

Rather than employing traditional training methods, Lutheran Brotherhood decided to use direct sales force participation in developing a training program and to require interdepartmental involvement by employees throughout the company. A twenty-one member task force was formed and spent six months researching available laptops before making a final selection. It then initiated an organizationwide communication effort to announce the new system and upcoming training—including news articles in company publications and a music video featuring Lutheran Brotherhood executives in ponytails and spiked hair.

The task force received training in use of the new technology and in turn trained a 110-member deployment team consisting of employees from all functional areas of the organization. Training sessions then were conducted by the task force and deployment team members, each of whom had walkie-talkies with which to contact technical experts when difficult questions arose during the sessions. In just five weeks, almost all of the fifteen hundred salespeople learned how to use the new technology.

From Victoria Obenshain, "Peer Training Yields Speedy Results," *Personnel Journal* 71 (April 1992): 107–110.

Groupware essentially facilitates collaborative communication, but it can't be used effectively so long as people view possessing information as a personal competitive advantage within an organization. If the corporate culture emphasizes and reinforces individual effort and ability and does not promote cooperation and information sharing, the underlying premise, or spirit, of the groupware technology is undermined.

Organizations wanting to emphasize collaboration should introduce groupware in such a way that it benefits them immediately without drastically altering the way they operate.[58] Ronni Marshak, vice-president of the Patricia Seybold Computing Group in Boston, suggests that companies "tell employees honestly what groupware will or will not do for them, and let them know that it may be difficult to use in the beginning. Then be sure to offer some sort of incentive to those who use groupware . . . and don't forget training. Without training, groupware is a guaranteed mess."[59]

Regardless of the kind of question being discussed or the organizational or technological approach chosen by your group, there are certain kinds of behaviors that group members should display throughout the discussion. We will now focus on these behaviors and suggest appropriate guidelines.

When common goals are negotiated and trust runs high, group work can lead to increased cohesiveness and enhanced morale.

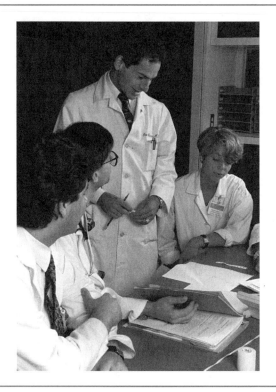

Behavioral Guidelines for Discussion Participants

A discussion is only as good as its participants. Informed, participative members bring about an effective discussion. Uninformed, uninvolved, or unskilled interactants virtually guarantee the group's failure. To help you develop your own group decision-making skills and to provide you with standards for evaluating the behaviors of other group members, this section will lay out some behaviors we have found effective in promoting both your own success as a group member and the overall success of the group.

To begin with, *every group member must take an active part in the discussion and activities of the group*. If you sit back silently during group meetings, you contribute nothing to the group or to your own credibility in the group or the organization. On the other hand, if you participate actively and make positive contributions to the group, you will help the group achieve its goals, improve your own standing within that group, and build an organizationwide reputation as someone who is valuable to have in group situations. Such a reputation will do much to enhance your long-term success.

Every group member needs to be as knowledgeable as possible regarding the subject of discussion. It is probably inevitable that some members of your group will be better informed on certain aspects of the discussion subject than you. But it is still vital that you explore all facets of the question as thoroughly as possible, given the constraints of time. You should assume that you might be the only one to find any relevant evidence regarding specific subpoints of the question. Having abundant information will also allow you to anticipate possible misunderstandings of your ideas and to be prepared to explain them in alternative ways, possibly providing different perspectives and examples.

We previously noted the importance of approaching the discussion with a desire to be a part of the *group's* decision-making effort. You should not make irrevocable judgments in advance. Rather, *each person should be group-oriented* throughout. The point of participation in the discussion is not to satisfy your need for social approval or to gain acceptance for a personal prejudice or point of view. Each person shares some responsibility for the success or failure of the entire group. Whenever anyone allows personal ambitions to replace commitment to the objectives of the group, he or she is functioning in a manner detrimental to the group's success.

Closely related to a group-oriented attitude is one of open-mindedness. *Group members should enter the discussion as open-minded as possible and strive to maintain an attitude of open-mindedness throughout the decision-making process.* There are several ways in which this attitude can manifest itself. For example, you might encourage the expression of all points of view. Discussants who are interested in seeing the group make the best decision possible recognize that the suppression of any point of view, however deviant, is potentially damaging to the quality of the group's effort. Furthermore, individual stands should be tentative. Any person can carefully examine an issue before a discussion and yet, during the course of the discussion, reach the conclusion that some previously obtained information is wrong or a conclusion reached is in error. Unfortunately, we are all susceptible to the problem of feeling embarrassed about having to back down from a point of view we have publicly espoused. Nevertheless, such embarrassment must be weighed against the negative outcomes for the group as a whole. If, after weighing the evidence and analysis brought forth during the discussion, you discover your position is no longer defensible, you have the responsibility to concede and allow the discussion to continue.

Throughout every phase of the discussion, *all discussants should carefully listen.* Attentiveness to the ideas of other group members is, of course, common courtesy. But careful listening has important implications for the effective functioning of your group as well. If you listen carefully, you are less apt to introduce irrelevant or redundant ideas and information. You are also better able to legitimately challenge the opinions of others whenever those ideas seem to lack supporting evidence. It is not uncommon to hear sweeping generalizations during discussions such as: "This organization is totally stifled by bureaucracy!"; "The public is completely ignorant of what we are trying to do!"; "Professors in this university are only interested in their research, not their students!"; or "The head of this department is a real dictator." All of these statements sound brash, and it is impossible to discern their truth or falsity on the basis of the generalizations alone. A discussant who is listening carefully will be quick to probe for evidence underlying these kinds of statements. Unsupported and unchallenged statements pose a threat to the validity of the group's conclusions.

Closely related to challenging unsupported assertions is the important function of asking for clarification of ideas, evidence, or opinions that are unclear to the listener. Most of us are only too skilled at pretending to understand things we do not, in part because we fear revealing our ignorance and, occasionally, because we are too lazy or uninterested to seek further understanding. The responsible, intelligent discussant will recognize when someone uses an unfamiliar or ambiguous word or expresses an idea in an obscure fashion, will realize that the other group members also probably don't understand, and will see that the statement is clarified before the group continues.

Every group member should strive to concentrate on substantive concerns. Every decision-making group has a task before it; the individuals composing the group, however, are human beings who possess personalities that occasionally conflict. Severe personality clashes can destroy the socioemotional climate of the group and render the accomplishment of the group's task an impossibility. While it is good that group members feel reasonably uninhibited about expressing their ideas and feelings openly, still it is unwarranted to assume that the decision-making group provides a suitable context for the resolution of interpersonal hostilities. As a mature group member, you should realize that it is impossible to be equally attracted to every other member. It stands to reason that some of your fellow discussants will seem insensitive, uninformed or unintelligent, domineering, or rude from time to time. Even so, the important consideration from the viewpoint of the group's welfare is to assist all members, regardless of personality peculiarities or irritations, to contribute their best effort toward the group's task. Table 9.1 provides one example of an evaluation form that can be used in reacting to any group member's contribution.

Finally, *every group member should strive to interact ethically.* This means showing concern for others' ideas, respect for their feelings, and willingness to give them time to reflect on new information. The ethical discussant is less interested in winning an argument than in achieving a consensus based on mutual understanding and respect. He or she does not use the group as an arena for promoting special interests or ruthlessly advancing his or her own status at the expense of others. The ethical discussant is as eager to learn and listen as he is to offer opinions and sage advice. He insists on accuracy in information and is willing to take extra time and put up with extra meetings for the sake of a better, more fully informed, decision. Ethics involves developing a sense of responsibility for the good of the group as a whole, while not losing a feeling for the relationship between the group and the rest of the organization. The ethical discussant is mature enough to realize that other groups have different priorities and that no matter how hard this group works or how excellently it performs, others work hard as well and have legitimate needs to be fulfilled. Thus, the ethical discussant is a good thinker, a good listener, a hard worker, and a responsible member of the organizational community.

Table 9.1 Discussion Participation Evaluation

For _____

Instructions: Circle the number that best reflects your evaluation of the discussant's participation on each
scale: 1 = Superior;   2 = Good;   3 = Average;   4 = Somewhat lacking;   5 = Poor.

1 2 3 4 5	1. Was prepared and informed.
1 2 3 4 5	2. Contributions were reasonably brief and clear.
1 2 3 4 5	3. Comments were relevant and well timed.
1 2 3 4 5	4. Spoke distinctly and audibly to all.
1 2 3 4 5	5. Contributions made readily and voluntarily.
1 2 3 4 5	6. Frequency of participation: If "Poor," indicate too low ( ) or too high ( ).
1 2 3 4 5	7. Nonverbal responses were clear and constant.
1 2 3 4 5	8. Listened to understand and follow the discussion.
1 2 3 4 5	9. Appeared open-minded.
1 2 3 4 5	10. Cooperative and constructive.
1 2 3 4 5	11. Helped keep discussion organized, following agenda.
1 2 3 4 5	12. Contributed to evaluation of information and ideas.
1 2 3 4 5	13. Respectful and tactful with others.
1 2 3 4 5	14. Encouraged others to participate.
1 2 3 4 5	15. Assisted in leadership functions.

Comments:

Evaluator _____

Summary

There is nothing magic about making decisions and solving problems in groups. Although "participatory management" has been a buzzword for several years, getting employees involved in committee meetings and task groups is a challenging affair—one with hazards as well as positive outcomes. A small group can function effectively only under conditions where its members know something about group process and are interested in and willing to try to work together to share information and make good decisions. When individual group members are ignorant of group dynamics or are using the group as an arena for airing their prejudices or demonstrating their management potential, the group as a whole is likely to suffer.

This book has stressed the positive side of small group communication, providing information, principles, and guidelines needed for effective group participation. As with other communication skills, we assume that any organizational member can *learn* to interact effectively in a small group setting. But effective group membership does require knowledge, the right kinds of attitudes, and a willingness to work at it. Every group is different. One group may be confronted with a particulary difficult task. Another may have few members who really care about the group's assignment. Another may have a poor leader. Still others may contain at least two people who try to dominate the group, perhaps in a contest for leadership. Each of these groups will present special challenges for group members who are primarily interested in facilitating the group's decision-making process. By following the principles advanced in this book, it is hoped, you will be well equipped to deal with difficult committee assignments and to help other group members move toward satisfying and productive outcomes.

Questions for Discussion

1. In what sense is group decision making a process rather than a procedure?
2. What are some ways (methods) of preparing for participation in a group discussion? Which seem to you to be most useful? Why?
3. What are several important factors to consider in the processing of any information? Provide examples to demonstrate their relevance.
4. What is meant by "having a group orientation"?
5. Identify each of the following discussion questions in terms of *fact, conjecture, value,* or *policy*. Then evaluate the merit of each as a potential discussion question in terms of *simplicity, objectivity,* and *controversiality*.
    a. What should be the policy of the United States concerning gun control?
    b. What is the value of a post-high school education?

c. Is there a positive correlation between violence on television and the crime rate?

d. Is cohabitation usually culturally degrading or stimulating?

e. Is teenage alcoholism a serious problem in our society today?

f. What should be our attitude toward women's rights?

6. Compare and contrast the reflective-thinking sequence, the creative problem-solving sequence, the nominal group procedure, and the question-agenda model. What are the strengths and weaknesses of each? Can you think of other potential approaches? Elaborate.

7. What are some of the advantages and disadvantages of group support systems?

8. Discuss some of the behavioral characteristics of effective discussion participants. Refer to examples from your own experiences.

Exercises

1. Take any two of the following topics and phrase them into all four types of discussion questions (fact, conjecture, value, and policy). Check each question carefully to make sure it meets the criteria of simplicity, objectivity, and controversiality.

a. euthanasia
b. pass/fail grading system
c. ethics in advertising
d. noise pollution
e. pornography
f. labor unions
g. profit motive
h. interracial marriage
i. charismatic movement in religion
j. the government's approach to dealing with the homeless

2. Break into groups of five to seven members each. Choose a topic of mutual interest and some controversiality and phrase it into a question for a decision-making discussion. After appropriate time for individual preparation, meet again as a group and discuss the question, attempting to reach consensus.

3. Following the above discussion, critically consider the quality of the group's decision-making efforts in terms of the problem-solving pattern used, the quality and quantity of the contributions of individual group members, and the socioemotional variables operating within the group, especially group pressure for uniformity, role relations, status and power variables, and cohesiveness.

4. Stan Ralston is a new medical technologist in Marquette's Memorial Hospital, a three-hundred-bed private hospital and the only one near the town of Bloomingdale, where Stan and his family reside. Within the hospital, there are many close-knit groups. The laboratory where Stan works has five medical technologists, six

laboratory technicians, and several part-time employees. The chief medical technologist holds a weekly staff meeting where announcements are made and problems discussed. As a newcomer, Stan quickly learns that the laboratory staff is one of the more cohesive and homogeneous groups in the hospital. At the next weekly meeting, the lab staff is scheduled to discuss the acquisition of some new laboratory equipment, particularly a new blood-gas machine. Stan's previous experience with a variety of these machines leads him to favor a particular brand and model. He knows from informal conversations, however, that the rest of the staff favors a completely different machine, one with which Stan is familiar and to which he is opposed.

   a. Considering the laboratory is a small group, how should Stan approach participation in it?

   b. How is the cohesiveness of the group a relevant factor?

   c. Should Stan speak primarily from his personal experience, or should he attempt to engage in additional research?

   d. Should he enter the discussion as an advocate or as a group-minded discussant?

   e. To what extent will social influence function here? How is Stan likely to respond?

Conducting Group Meetings

One of the most common complaints we hear from supervisors, managers, and executives is that "there are too many meetings." Indeed, the higher one goes in an organization's hierarchy, the more time one is going to spend conducting or participating in meetings. It seems likely that the use of meetings in organizations is going to increase rather than decrease in the future. In his book *Megatrends: Ten New Directions Transforming Our Lives,* John Naisbitt claims that "people whose lives are affected by a decision must be part of the process arriving at that decision." He goes on to argue that "whether or not we agree with the notion or abide by it, participatory democracy has seeped into the core of our value system. Its greatest impact will be in government and corporations."[1] Already this trend is clear in the business setting. In response to a survey of management practices conducted nationwide, only 15.3 percent of all top executives and 12.3 percent of all managers said they make major decisions without consulting all their direct subordinates in meetings; all the rest used participative decision making to some extent.[2]

With this increasing emphasis on participative decision making has come an increased need for two other things: skills among employees and supervisors in participating in meetings and skills among supervisors, managers, and executives in conducting meetings. James O'Toole of the Center for Future Research at the University of Southern California claims that "what America will require is workers who are humane individuals, with analytical and entrepreneurial skills, who know how to work in groups, and who know how to solve problems."[3]

In keeping with this growing need, the previous two chapters discussed the factors of group participation. In this chapter, we will consider techniques for leading group meetings. Specifically, we will discuss the times at which meetings should and should not be called; how to prepare for meetings; how to announce meetings; general approaches to leading meetings; specific formats by which certain types of meetings can be run; things to do as a follow-up to a meeting; and strategies for dealing with problem participants in groups. All of this should help you develop your skills in conducting group interactions in the organizational setting.

Before turning to the practical aspects of conducting or leading meetings, however, we want to consider leadership more theoretically. Historically, there have been several different approaches to the study of leadership, each providing contrasting insights into this complex process. In the next section, we will explain four of these approaches.

Approaches to the Study of Leadership

The Trait Approach

Probably the earliest view of leadership was based on the notion that "leaders are born, not made." This approach suggested that there were certain qualities, such as physical energy or friendliness, that were *essential* for effective leadership, regardless of the nature of the group being led, the task assigned the group, or other situational factors. The essential leadership qualities or traits would simply be transferred appropriately from situation to situation. Thus, it was believed possible to separate leaders from followers.

Approaches to the Study of Leadership

Approach	Assumptions	Communication Emphasis
Trait	Leaders are born, not made.	Effective communication traits
Stylistic	Leaders' effectiveness is based on what they do, not what they are.	Autocratic versus democratic versus laissez-faire styles
Situational	Leader effectiveness is based on how styles fit group contexts.	Positional power, nature of task and social relationships
Functional	Leadership is behaviors, not people.	Communication behaviors that influence group members

Unfortunately, the inherent leadership traits discovered in empirical investigations varied greatly from study to study. One scholar reported that only 5 percent of the identified leadership traits consistently appeared in four or more investigations.[4] Perhaps the most encouraging collection of information on the trait approach was compiled by Stogdill.[5] In an exhaustive review of leadership research published since 1945, Stogdill was able to identify a relatively stable number of leadership traits. Among the most frequently occurring factors were social and interpersonal skills, technical skills, intellectual skills, leadership effectiveness qualities, group task supportiveness, and task motivation. A final set of factors Stogdill identified focused on the personality characteristics of leaders, which included willingness to share responsibility, emotional balance and control, ethical conduct, personal integrity, communication ability, energy, enthusiasm, experience, courage, maturity, and independence.

These factors provide an elementary sketch of characteristics associated with leadership. It is important to remember, however, that a leadership trait that is an asset in one situation may function as a liability in other situations. Furthermore, the kinds of skills the leader needs to exhibit may vary as the group or organization develops. That is, leadership traits necessary for emerging as a leader may differ substantially from those required for maintaining one's position of leadership.[6]

More recent attempts to contribute to our understanding of the differences between leaders and nonleaders have focused on the characteristics of the individual's *communication behavior* rather than on his or her personality. One researcher identified five negative traits that consistently prevented an individual from emerging as the group leader: being uninformed, not participating, demonstrating extreme rigidity, exhibiting authoritarian behavior, and engaging in offensive verbalization.[7] On a more positive note, another investigator discovered that appointed leaders who were able to maintain their leadership status throughout a meeting were more agreeable and less opinionated then their unsuccessful counterparts.[8]

It is unlikely that any investigation will ever reveal an unvarying set of leadership traits completely free of environmental, task, and socioemotional conditions within and surrounding the group or organization. Even so, it is important to identify the communication characteristics associated with leadership emergence and maintenance, high-quality interaction, and positive group outcomes. These are the kinds of qualities that can be developed. Managers within organizations can learn communication skills to facilitate important management responsibilities, such as problem solving and conflict resolution.

The Stylistic Approach

Another approach to the study of leadership has focused on what leaders *do* rather than the kinds of people they are. This stylistic approach was given impetus by the now classic investigation of White and Lippitt, who studied leadership in three different social climates: authoritarian, democratic, and laissez-faire.[9] White and Lippitt concluded that the democratic style was superior to the others in several respects, including the level of group cohesiveness developed, the amount of independent behavior exhibited by the subjects, the quality of the product created by the group, and overall member satisfaction with the group experience.

Many other studies have reinforced the value of the democratic style of leadership. One investigator found that groups with more permissive leaders developed higher levels of cohesiveness than groups with less permissive leaders.[10] A classic study by Coch and French pointed to employee participation as a significant variable in reducing resistance to altered working conditions in a large industrial organization.[11] Finally, in a summary of the Massachusetts Institute of Technology studies of human behavior, Galbraith reported great support for participative decision making as a means of increasing productivity and morale.[12]

Yet not all studies have supported the complete superiority of democratic leadership. Shaw reported that groups working under autocratic leadership took less time, committed fewer errors, and produced more than groups working under the direction of democratic leaders. These autocratically led groups, however, evidenced greater aggression and hostility and lower morale.[13] Moreover, a number of studies conducted in actual organizations have demonstrated that the best managerial style depends on a number of situational variables, among them the nature of the workers and the kind of work being carried out.[14]

In part, it is difficult to compare the results of stylistic studies of leadership because of the wide variance in how investigators define the different leadership styles. "Participation" may range from total involvement in significant decision making to the mere opportunity to approve an already sanctioned policy. Furthermore, as Gouran has noted, "the democratic and participatory styles at their best are frequently studied in relation to more autocratic styles at their worst."[15] It is possible to lead a group in a relatively autocratic, directive fashion and still be fair, considerate, and responsive to the needs of group members.

Given the wide variety of organizations, types of human beings, and other situational concerns, it is unlikely that one style of leadership will ever be found consistently superior in all significant respects. Situational factors will greatly influence the success of any given style of leadership.

The Situational Approach

If no one style of leadership can be declared to be universally superior, then the context in which leadership is exercised can be explored. Perhaps the best known exponent of the situational school is Frederick Fiedler. His research efforts spanned some fifteen years and focused on such diverse groups as athletic teams, business management groups, bomber crews, surveying teams, and policymaking committees.[16] Fiedler concluded that the style of leadership most effective in any given situation depends on three factors: the *power* of the leader's *position*, the *nature* and *structure* of the *task* being performed, and the *social relationships* between the leader and other group members. The ideal situation is one in which the leader has high position power and a clearly structured task and is able to maintain good social relations with other group members. Under such circumstances, it is the authoritarian leader who seems to be most effective. Interestingly enough, the authoritarian is also more effective when conditions are extremely unfavorable: that is, when the task is not clearly structured, when the leader has little position power, or when group members must work with a leader whom they dislike. The democratic style is most successful when the group is functioning under only moderately favorable conditions. In practice, most organizational settings in which leaders find themselves are moderately positive. Thus, Fiedler's research tends to suggest that in many situations, democratic leadership is the preferred management strategy.

In addition to the contextual factors enumerated by Fiedler, others appear to influence the effectiveness of a given style of leadership. The *self-confidence* of group members will influence the style of leadership they are willing to accept. For example, discussants who are confident that they are knowledgeable on the topic under discussion and are capable of contributing substantively to the group's decision-making effort are not likely to be supportive of an authoritarian leader. On the other hand, group members who have little confidence in their abilities to function constructively are more likely to appreciate authoritarian leadership. They may, in fact, feel lost and inadequate with a leader who strongly encourages them to participate in the discussion and share in making decisions.

Still another important situational variable is the leader's actual or perceived *competence*. Leaders who are highly intelligent and possess abundant knowledge on the discussion subject are quite likely to be accepted by the group—regardless of their particular leadership style. This is especially true when there are vast discrepancies between the information levels or perceived competence of the leader and the other group members.

Finally, and of particular relevance to organizational decision making, we know that groups will tend to accept a style of leadership that has allowed them to function successfully in the past. Groups that make high quality decisions and produce excellent products are much more likely to continue under the same leader's guidance than groups that experience continual or significant failure.

What is important, then, is flexibility in our attitudes toward preferred leadership styles. Some situations demand a relatively directive style of leadership, especially those situations in which nonleaders in the group lack confidence, knowledge, or even the desire to take the responsibility for shared decision making. In such instances, autocratic leadership is probably appropriate. In other situations, however, providing too much direction might stifle creativity, extinguish enthusiasm, and result in impaired decision making. Thus, it is the "fit" between the leader and the situation that is important.

The Functional Approach

All the perspectives discussed so far have focused on the behavior and characteristics of those individuals who are acknowledged or appointed leaders. The functional approach conceives of leadership differently. The behavior of *any* group member that promotes the achievement of group goals is viewed as leadership. Leadership functions are usually performed by more than one group member, and it is conceivable that all individuals in the group might contribute to the achievement of the group's objectives. In this latter instance, all group members function as leaders, although the extent of their goal-directed influence would undoubtedly vary both qualitatively and quantitatively.

Research has not identified all potentially relevant leadership behavior. Moreover, among those variables believed to be positively associated with the exertion of influence within a group, no one has actually identified those functions uniquely related to leadership. It is possible that a group member could perform several different tasks or socioemotional roles (for example, requesting information and relieving tension) and still fail to lead the group toward the accomplishment of its task. Perhaps leadership should be viewed as a characteristic that each member will likely exhibit *in some form;* however, only some members will function as leaders to any significant extent. Then the issue becomes determining what constitutes a significant amount of a given function.

The important thing to remember about the functional approach to leadership is that *each person* is capable of leadership regardless of whether or not he or she is ever formally appointed "leader." All too often, group members perceive the need for elaboration or clarification. They sense that someone needs encouragement. Or they possess abundant and necessary information for the critical analysis of the problem before the group. Yet they fail to assert themselves and perform the needed function simply because they believe that the appointed leader ought to be the one to do it.

When to Call Meetings

Many of the complaints or "bad press" that meetings receive are due to their inappropriate usage. Too many meetings are held when no meeting really is needed. Conversely, too many decisions are made without a meeting when, in fact, a meeting should have occurred. As a first step in knowing when and when not to have a meeting, Auger suggests you keep in mind the following principles:[17]

First, you *should* call a meeting when you need to:

1. Reach a group judgment as the basis for a decision.
2. Discover, analyze, or solve a problem.
3. Gain acceptance from the group for an idea, program, or decision.
4. Achieve a training objective.
5. Reconcile conflicting views.
6. Provide essential information for work guidance or for the relief of insecurities or tensions.
7. Insure equal understanding of company policy, methods, or decisions.
8. Obtain immediate reactions to a problem that requires a speedy response.

On the other hand, you *should not* call a meeting when:

1. Other communications, such as telephone, telegram, letter, E-mail, or memo, will produce the desired result.
2. There is not sufficient time for adequate preparation by participants or the meeting leader.
3. One or more key participants cannot attend.
4. The meeting is not likely to produce satisfactory results because of personality conflicts or conflicts with overall management strategy.
5. Expected results do not warrant spending the money it will cost to hold the meeting.

When deciding whether to call a meeting, always remember the old saying that "time is money." Meetings consume a lot of both, and you must be sure the investment is worthwhile before convening any meeting.

Preparing to Conduct Meetings

Much of the effort that goes into making a meeting successful occurs before the meeting happens. Only through careful planning can you be sure that the meeting will be as successful as possible. Yet research conducted by Frank suggests that preparation often is lacking: When asked "How frequently are group meetings well planned?", 40.6 percent of the respondents in his survey of 416 organizations responded "almost never" or "sometimes."[18]

To insure thorough preparation, you should ask yourself several questions, such as

1. Have I clearly defined the purpose or purposes of the meeting?
2. What are the outcomes that should emerge from this meeting? (Information? Plans to gather information? Possible courses of action? A solution to a problem? A policy statement?)
3. Who should participate? As a rule, invite to the meeting people who are expected to carry out a decision to be reached at the meeting, people who possess unique information that they can contribute to the meeting, people whose approval may be

needed, people who have official responsibility for the matter under discussion, and people who have a personal contribution to make from a strategic standpoint (that is, whose support you want or whose opposition you want to avoid politically).

4. How should people be notified of the meeting? We will talk further about methods of announcing meetings in the next section.
5. How much time will the meeting probably take?
6. What information, if any, do members need before the meeting?
7. What follow-up, if any, will be needed after the meeting?
8. What agenda will the meeting follow?
9. What is the best time and place for the meeting?
10. What physical arrangements need to be made for the meeting?

Answering these questions will probably provide adequate preparation for a meeting.

The *facility* in which the meeting is to be held should be given careful consideration as part of the planning process. The physical location of a meeting and equipment used during that meeting have a powerful impact on the meeting's success. As a result, you must plan carefully the physical facilities to be used during the session. Generally, you should consider five basic elements: *task, comfort, acoustics, visibility,* and *interference.*

Task is a consideration of the work to be done in the meeting and of the equipment necessary to do that work. If a presentation is to be given, for example, an overhead transparency projector or a slide or film projector and a screen may be needed. If participants' comments are to be solicited and discussed, a "flip pad" or easel pad of large sheets of paper will be needed. A blackboard also may be needed. Occasionally, videotaping equipment, such as cameras, playback units, and monitors, is used. The leader should insure that all such equipment is at the meeting site, that spare bulbs for projectors are on hand, that electrical outlets have been located and the necessary extension cords procured, and that there are markers or chalk for use on the flip pad or blackboard.

Comfort involves several aspects of the environment. Temperature and ventilation are important. You need to determine how to control the room's temperature and ventilation, should the room become too cold, hot, or stuffy during the meeting. In all instances, speed of change is the primary concern. Any room can have its temperature or ventilation changed; the issue during a meeting is whether the change can be achieved quickly enough.

Another aspect of comfort is the chairs: Are they padded enough or flexible enough to provide comfort for a long meeting? Are they too comfortable (creating the possibility of people dozing off during the meeting)? Are they moveable so that people can face each other if necessary? Will desks or tables be needed? Any equipment that participants may need, such as writing tablets, pencils, or erasers, should also be set out at each person's seating place before the meeting begins.

Acoustics, or the ability of people to hear one another, is also an important consideration. You should be sure that sound carries well even when the room is full of people (sound always carries better in an empty room) and that the room is not overly large so that people will sit too far from one another. If necessary, obtain microphones and loudspeakers so everyone can be heard.

Visibility is also important. People should be able to see anyone who is talking, whether that person is the meeting leader or another group member. If charts, graphs, slides, movies, or other visuals are to be used, everyone must be able to see these as well. All of this should be taken into consideration when arranging the room. Consider the impact of any seating arrangement on group interaction. As we have indicated in earlier chapters, people are more likely to talk with people seated next to them or across the table from them and far less likely to talk with people seated some distance away. Be sure that everyone has equal access to everyone else if group discussion is to be an important part of the meeting (sitting around a circular table might be helpful in this regard) or that committee members who need to work together are seated next to one another.

Interference is one final concern. Interruptions should be prevented and background noise eliminated if at all possible. You need to investigate what things, if any, will be happening in adjoining rooms during your meeting. You also need to select a meeting location that is away from the normal work area, unless the meeting is to be very brief and informal. A "do not disturb" notice on the door may be helpful, and participants should be told ahead of time to have messages taken for them during the meeting so interruptions will not occur.

Announcing Meetings

Too often meetings fail because they are poorly announced. The wrong people show up, participants arrive unprepared, or members have to leave before the end of the meeting because no one knew how long the meeting would take. To avoid such problems, you should send a written announcement at least one week in advance to everyone involved in the meeting. Do not rely on telephone calls, face-to-face interactions, or even E-mail (since some don't check their mail regularly).

The written announcement of the meeting should say:

Why the meeting is being held. Members should know what the purpose of the meeting is and what their role is to be. This gives them a chance to prepare for the meeting if necessary, and it lets them know what matters will not be part of the meeting's contents.

When the meeting starts and ends. Most announcements indicate the starting time; too few say how long the meeting is expected to last. To avoid people leaving early due to other commitments, state in the announcement how long the meeting is expected to go or when it will adjourn.

Where the meeting is to be held. If attendees are likely to be unfamiliar with the location, a map or some description of how to find it should be included.

Who is going to attend. The complete list of attendees should be provided for everyone to see. The list need not give everyone by name ("the entire training force" would be sufficient), but each attendee should know who else is coming.

What is going to be considered in the meeting. An agenda or outline of the meeting's proceedings should be included. If attendees are allowed to suggest items for inclusion in the agenda, this fact also should be stated, and attendees should be told to whom their items should be sent and by what date those items should be received.

Sample Meeting Announcement

To: All Training Department Members
From: H. K. Thompson, Director of Training & Development
Re: Upcoming Department Meeting
Date: November 10, 1994

On Friday, November 21, we will have a meeting of the Training Department, to be held in Training Room C in the Training Center, Building C. It will begin at 12 noon and be over by 1:30 p.m.

Mr. Don Johnson, Vice-President of Personnel, will be present to talk about his objectives for the training function next year, and Mr. Gary Howard, Director of Employee Relations, will attend to discuss the role of Corporate Training support for in-plant locations.

The purposes of the meeting are (1) to discuss plans for the department and to choose specific programs to offer next year, (2) to review participant responses to this year's programs, and (3) to discuss any matters of concern to you. *Please bring all of your participant rating sheets to the meeting; you will be asked to present the average ratings received for each of your programs to the rest of the group.*

Our agenda is as follows:

1. Plans for next year
   a. Objectives of the Vice-President—Mr. Johnson.
   b. The Role of Corporate Training for In-Plant Location—Mr. Howard.
   c. Specific programs we should offer at Corporate facility (group suggestions).
   d. Specific programs we should offer at individual plant sites (group suggestions).
2. Program evaluations
3. Training staff's matters of concern

Business Brief 10.2 presents a sample announcement letter. While the contents of such a letter will change from one meeting and group to the next, the basic types of information contained in this announcement should be included in every meeting notification.

Approaches to Conducting Meetings

An important element of group leadership is the extent to which the leader shares power with the group members. Some leaders, for example, take total control of the meeting and decision making, simply telling everyone else what is going to happen, who is going to do what to whom, and so on. Other leaders are just the opposite: they allow a great deal of participation by the group members, both in interacting and in making decisions.

Regarding the concept of shared or conserved power, we can identify four basic approaches to conducting meetings:

Autocratic (highly directive) leadership occurs when the leader does virtually all the talking and decides everything (or virtually everything) the group will do. Meetings led by such leaders consist primarily of announcements the leader makes to the attendees, followed by any questions the attendees have for the leader. In other words, communication is almost exclusively downward and decision making is virtually nonexistent.

Consultative leadership encourages input from group members, although the leader still makes the final decisions. In effect, the leader "consults" with the members, asking for their thoughts and ideas concerning problems, decisions, actions, and so on. They participate in the interaction, and they have some influence over the leader's thinking. However, they have power only to the extent that they can persuade the leader to adopt their suggestions or proposals.

Democratic leadership adheres to the principle of "one person, one vote." The leader simply facilitates the meeting; he or she has no more power than does anyone else. The group members interact, make decisions, and solve problems.

Laissez-faire leadership occurs when the leader has virtually no role in the meeting. If, for example, a supervisor asks an employee to conduct the meeting while the supervisor sits at the back of the room or if the boss announces in advance that he or she will not attend a particular meeting so that a less inhibited discussion might occur, he or she is practicing laissez-faire leadership. If this leadership style is to be effective, it ought to be occasional and strategic. Since the laissez-faire leader gives away power, the group takes on both control and responsibility for its actions.

No one approach is always best. Each situation must be examined to determine which style of leadership will be most effective. Several factors should be considered when selecting a style (and corresponding meeting agenda). First, *group expectations* are important. What sort of leadership does the group expect you to provide? *Group purposes* should also be taken into account. What is the group trying to achieve? Learning, socializing, or team building require minimum leader control, while communicating specific information to the group is much more directive. *Group methods* are another consideration. Some group processes, such as brainstorming or rating problem priorities, require strict procedural control, while others, such as discussing a problem's underlying causes, can be done with virtually no leadership. *Time* is also a consideration. Participation takes time, while announcements can be given quickly. If a decision must be made at once, autocratic leadership may be required.

In choosing a leadership style, group *members' skills and maturity* should also be considered. Experienced, mature group members require less guidance and control than do new, inexperienced members. Moreover, the more people participate, the better they become at participation. Thus, gradually giving more and more participation to group members is one way of increasing the skills and maturity of the group. The *leader's own skill and confidence* are also factors to be considered. In general, directive leadership is easier to exert than consultative or democratic leadership. The latter two require skill in listening, handling conflict, controlling group interaction, and so on. Thus, as leaders become more skilled, they tend to become more participative over time.

Finally, the kind of leadership style most appropriate in a given situation will depend, in part, upon the *need for group support* and the *group's interest and involvement* in the issues under discussion. Some decisions need the active endorsement of the group. In addition, participation in decision making increases the commitment of those making the decision. Simply being told what to do or how to do it minimizes commitment and motivation. And, of course, the more controversial, involving, and interesting the issue being discussed, the more the members of the group will want, and should be encouraged, to participate.

Types of Group Meetings

Having identified general leadership styles, we can now examine types of meetings through which those styles are implemented. Once again, we will examine the autocratic, consultative, democratic, and laissez-faire styles, describing some meeting formats that fit each style.

Autocratic Meetings

Generally, autocratic meetings are not really meetings but rather presentations by the group leader to the group. As we already have seen, some situations demand this sort of meeting. Time may be of the essence, the group may not know enough about the topic to participate, the group may have no control over the topic so that participation would be meaningless, and so on. Whatever the case, the leader chooses to use the one-to-group setting to communicate information to the participants.

The autocratic meeting is really an exercise in public presentation. Therefore, the principles described in chapters 12, 13, and 14 will be of help in conducting this type of meeting. At this point, however, we can offer an agenda and some principles to follow when conducting the autocratic meeting:

I. Introduction
   A. Call the group to order.
   B. Announce the purpose of the meeting.
   C. If appropriate, explain why the meeting is being handled this way and why the group is not participating in making the decision or formulating plans.
   D. Preview the meeting agenda. List the order in which the topics will be covered, when breaks (if any) will be taken, when questions should be asked (any time; at the end of each announcement; at the end of the meeting), and when the meeting will probably end. The agenda might be written on a blackboard or flip pad at the front of the room to help keep participants oriented to the topic.
II. Presentation
   A. Announce the first topic; where appropriate, give the background of the topic, current actions or decisions, and future implications for this group.
   B. Announce the second topic; handle in the same way.
   C. Announce the third; continue through announcements.

D. As much as possible, use visual aids: handouts, charts, graphs, overhead transparencies, and the like. Accompanying visual stimuli help participants both to understand and remember the announcements.

III. Conclusion
  A. Ask for and answer any questions.
  B. State again any future implications the announcements have for the group.
  C. Tell the group what follow-up will occur. ("I'll send each of you a memo saying in writing what I've announced today. If you have any questions or concerns later, give me a call.")
  D. Dismiss the meeting.

The keys to successful autocratic meetings are clarity, completeness, and comprehension. The information you provide must be as clear as possible to the members (watch their feedback carefully for signs of puzzlement or confusion, and let them ask questions). It must be complete, particularly if the members are to have a role in implementing the decision or if it will affect them. Finally, they must comprehend the reasoning behind the decision or the implications of the information.

Consultative Meetings

In consultative meetings, the leader maintains decision-making authority but asks the group to suggest alternatives, ideas, causes, and so on. At the beginning of the meeting, it is important to make this situation clear to the participants. The leader should state the problem, decision, or situation she is facing, tell the group that their ideas or suggestions are desired, but make it clear that the leader ultimately will have responsibility for the decision. Thus, while the leader promises to listen, she does not promise to do everything (or anything) the group suggests.

As an agenda for the meeting, the leader might choose to use one of those outlined in chapter 9: the reflective-thinking sequence, the creative problem-solving sequence, the nominal group procedure, or a questions-agenda model. Regardless of the agenda he suggests, however, the leader will have to solicit participation from the group. Several strategies may be useful here.

First, the leader might use an *overhead question*—one asked of the group as a whole. Such a question might be "What do you think of this?" or "What ideas do you have concerning solutions to this problem?" The problem with overhead questions, however, is that they may go over everyone's head; no one has responsibility for answering the question, so often no one answers. The silence that follows an overhead question is often deafening. If the overhead question does not produce participation or discussion, a more specific approach might prove useful.

One way to encourage participation is to use the *directed question*. That is, call on someone for an answer. While this guarantees that someone will say something to you, there are some principles you should observe when asking direct questions. First, be sure the member has an answer. If you ask someone a question about which she has neither an opinion nor information, the member (and you) will be embarrassed and discussion will be even more difficult to initiate. So make an effort to call on someone you

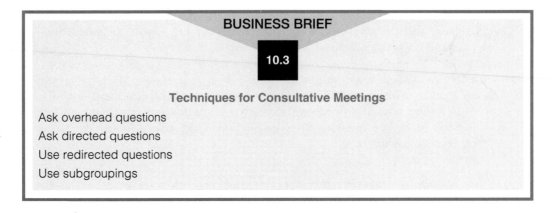

know to have information, whose nonverbal cues indicate he has an opinion (for example, a member who shakes his head negatively when you introduce the topic), or with whom you have spoken prior to the meeting to let her know she will be called upon at the beginning of the meeting.

Directed questions should also be sufficiently open, requiring more than a yes or no response. Asking "Bill, do you agree with that?" and having Bill grunt "uh-huh" hardly produces stimulating interaction. Ask "What are some things you think we should do, Bill?" or "Bill, how do you feel about this issue?" Directed questions also should be passed around the group. There is a temptation to call again and again on the same member, either because he is such a good answer-giver or because you are personally acquainted with that member and feel comfortable calling on him. You must make a deliberate effort to call on different members at different times.

Finally, encourage participation by asking *redirected questions*. That is, when a group member asks you a question, redirect the question back to the group, rather than immediately providing a response. For example, you might make it an overhead question: "What do all of you think of that?" You might direct it to another member: "Diane, how would you answer Bill's question?" Or you might redirect it back to the original questioner: "Well, I have some ideas of my own, but maybe you have something you could suggest." Again, your purpose is to stimulate interaction among the members; conducting a question-and-answer session with individual members does not achieve active group discussion.

In larger groups (more than ten people), another participation-producing device is to *subdivide the group into smaller groups,* give them a topic to discuss, and have them report back a few minutes later. For example, you might divide your group of ten into two groups of five members each and instruct them: "Now I want each of your groups to come up with the longest list possible of things we might do to improve the courtesy we show patients in the hospital. After about ten minutes, I'll stop you and have you report your answers for everyone." The small group setting and specific assignment of topics are very effective in getting people to talk with one another, and this interaction will continue when the larger group is reformed later on.

At the end of a consultative meeting, one of two things should occur. First, if you have the ability and inclination to make decisions on the spot, you should do so. Tell the group which of their recommendations you will accept and which you reject (along with reasons why you choose not to do those things) or which suggestions you will pass along to upper management and which seem not to be feasible (again offering explanations why). While some members may be disappointed that their ideas are not used, they nevertheless feel that some action will be taken based on their input, and this feeling is far more satisfying than being told "I'll get back to you with my decision" (particularly if the leader never gets back to them).

In some situations, however, you may not have the ability or desire to make an on-the-spot commitment. Then you must use the "I'll get back to you" statement, but you also should tell them when and how you'll get back to them: "I'll send you all a memo next week telling you what I have decided" or "We'll meet again next Tuesday at this same time so I can present my decisions to you and answer any questions." Do not, under any circumstances, leave the group hanging without any feedback or follow-up.

Democratic Meetings

In democratic meetings, decision-making power and group interaction are shared among all members. The principle of "one person, one vote" is followed, and the leader has no more power in making the decision than does any other group member. However, the leader does control the methods used by the group, setting the agenda they will follow, controlling interaction among them, and even deciding how decisions will be made.

In democratic groups, decisions can be made in several ways:

Consensus. Consensus is probably the ideal method of decision making. The group simply discusses the topic until everyone agrees. In Japan and among some religious sects (such as the Quakers), decision making by consensus is rigidly followed; nothing is decided until everyone agrees. Such decision making is desirable in that everyone supports the decision arrived at by the group, but it is also disadvantageous if there are time limits. As an extreme example, the Quakers debated the issue of slavery during the nineteenth century for nearly fifty years; they finally concluded their debates (without reaching consensus) long after the Civil War was over. If your group cannot reach consensus within a reasonable time period, you should move to some other technique for making a decision.

Group ratings or rankings. There are mathematical techniques for arriving at compromise solutions. If, for example, two alternatives remain and the group cannot choose between them, hand everyone a sheet of paper and ask them to rate each alternative on a scale from 0 to 10 (with 0 meaning it is a totally unacceptable solution, 5 meaning the solution is largely neutral, and 10 meaning it is the perfect solution to the problem). Then collect the ratings, calculate the average rating for each alternative (that is, add up the ratings given the first alternative and then divide by the number of members; then do the same for the second alternative, and select the alternative that comes out with the highest rating). If several alternatives remain, you might ask the group members individually to rank order them (a ranking of 1 for their favorite, 2 for their second favorite, and so on). Collect the rankings, calculate the average ranking for each alternative, and select the one with the lowest number (remember, the lower the number, the more preferred the alternative is). Either ratings or rankings can help the group make a decision without there being any "winners" or "losers"; everyone's ratings or rankings had an impact on the decision.

Process of elimination. Sometimes no alternative emerges as clearly the best. The strategy then might be to eliminate the worst. One technique for achieving this is called the "murder board." An alternative is written on a large sheet of paper or blackboard at the front of the room, and the group then tries to "kill" the idea by listing everything that could possibly be wrong with it. When they have run out of ideas, the next alternative is put up and subjected to the same treatment. The alternative that receives the fewest objections or has the fewest serious problems is chosen. Sometimes, however, all the alternatives are "killed"; then the group must generate new solutions to the problem or new decisions they can make.

Majority vote. In small groups, the majority vote method generally should be avoided. Whenever there is a vote, someone loses. This minority may be embarrassed, resentful, angry, frustrated, and so on, and they are not likely to support the group's decision. Granted, there are times (such as when parliamentary procedure is used) when majority votes are called for, but in most meetings, some other method of decision making should be employed whenever possible.

Many of the principles we have seen in this chapter and in the preceding two apply to the conduct of a democratic meeting. However, one democratic method of conducting a large-group meeting requires special knowledge on the part of the leader. We will consider that method in the section on parliamentary procedure.

Laissez-Faire Meetings

In a sense, any meeting can be a *laissez-faire* meeting; the leader has only to appoint a substitute leader, sit in back, and let things happen as they may, or for strategic reasons (like discouraging groupthink) not attend the meeting at all. In one type of laissez-faire meeting, facilitation by a leader is required, but decision making and interaction are almost entirely within the control of the group. This type is the *team-building* meeting.

While different authors suggest different team-building strategies, they generally agree on the goals team building should achieve.[19] First, it should cause the group members to agree on their common goals and objectives. Second, it should sort out the roles each member will play in working toward the goals and objectives. Third, it should cause the group to decide on the procedures they will follow when working together. Fourth, it should help them arrive at mutually satisfactory relationships with one another. All four of these might be achieved in a single meeting lasting as long as three or four days, or they might be accomplished one at a time through a series of meetings.

Littlejohn describes one common approach to team building that requires two one-day sessions.[20] The first day is devoted to a discussion of members' perceptions of the organization and of the team members themselves. They exchange opinions and ideas about the organization as a place in which to work, and they exchange knowledge about themselves. The second day focuses on planning and goal setting. Members deal with such issues as mission (Why do we as a team exist?), situation (Where are we now?), and strategies (How are we going to reach our goals?). Procedures such as these ultimately achieve the goals of team building.

Several specific techniques can be used to encourage interaction and achieve team-building objectives. For instance, you might have participants individually (or in small groups) develop a list of habits or practices they think the team should develop, modify, or improve. You might have them address the question "Why do we exist as a functioning team?" Have them report their answers. Then, from the composite list produced by all groups, have the groups meet again and rank the answers according to their importance. Another interesting question members might discuss in small groups is "What would we be like if we were the 'ideal' team?" Have each group report its answers and write them on a blackboard or flip pad. Then have the groups meet again and, taking each characteristic one at a time, answer the question "Is this us?" That is, does the overall team have that characteristic? Again, have the groups report their answers. Finally, for those characteristics where the consensus of the group is no, ask everyone "Is this characteristic important?" If the consensus is yes, an area needing change has been identified.

The next step is to move the group toward analyzing and solving the problem. To begin, you might put the members into small groups and then assign each group one or more of the characteristics needing change. For each characteristic, have the group answer the question, "Why are we not like this now?" Have them report their answers. In doing so, they will have identified the causes for the problems confronting the team. Then, assign each small group one or more of the characteristics identified as needing change. Ask the groups to develop the longest possible list of ways the group might achieve each characteristic. Practicality should not be a concern; wild and crazy ideas should be encouraged. Have the groups report their lists of possible solutions. For each possible solution reported by a small group, ask the entire group "Will you do this?" If the general feeling seems affirmative, ask "How?" Record the answers as the team's action plan.

Finally, to improve relationships among group members, give each individual member enough sheets of paper so that he or she can write a message to every other individual member. Then instruct the participants to write their own name and the name of the participant to whom they are writing at the top of each page. Finally, ask them to provide information related to three statements:

"If you were to do more of the following, it would help me to do my job better."

"If you were to do less of or stop doing the following, it would help me to do my job better."

"If you would continue to do the following, it would help me to do my job better."

When everyone has finished writing, have them exchange messages so that everyone has one message from every other member. Then have them write their own personal action plan, listing their commitments for the following statements:

"I will keep doing the following."

"I will do less of or stop doing the following."

"I will continue doing the following."

These statements of personal commitment should be taped to the walls of the meeting room for everyone to see, and members should be allowed to walk around the room and read everyone else's sheet. Copies of the sheets also are kept after the meeting to serve as reminders of the pledges each member made.

In a sense, the team-building meeting is not really a laissez-faire meeting in the stereotypic sense, because the leader actively participates by asking questions, recording answers, and assigning tasks to individuals or small groups. However, all decisions are made by the group with no input from the leader or facilitator, so that all authority is delegated by the leader to them. Indeed, some executives hire consultants specializing in team building to come to the organization and conduct these meetings. In those situations, the executive exerts true laissez-faire leadership.

Following Up Meetings

Whenever a meeting has been concluded, regardless of the style used to conduct that meeting, some follow-up must occur. At least three things need to be done. First, the group should be asked to examine their own proceedings and evaluate how effective the meeting was. Such evaluation can be done at the end of the meeting (by asking the participants to take a moment to express their thoughts in writing or to discuss briefly how well they thought the meeting went) or some time after the meeting (by distributing questionnaires about the meeting to the members and asking them to return the completed questionnaires to the leader). As a brief, informal approach to evaluating a meeting, we have found it useful to ask the participants to write their answers to three questions:

What part(s) of the meeting did you like most?

What part(s) of the meeting did you like least?

How might future meetings of this type be improved?

More complicated, but thorough, is the "Meeting Effectiveness Questionnaire" shown in table 10.1. By having members complete the questionnaire, the leader can get quantitative feedback on each element of the group's proceedings. Regardless of the form and timing of feedback, groups should almost always be asked to evaluate the quality of the meeting in which they participated.

When someone dominates the groups' talking time, other group members may withdraw or pretend to listen.

Second, the actions of the meeting should be reported to those who need to be advised. The report need not necessarily be a long set of notes or minutes but should contain enough information that those who could not attend or who will be affected by the results will know what was done and what was planned. In our view, such reports serve as useful reminders to the group participants and as notice of the group's achievements to other groups and individuals throughout the organization. Thus, we recommend that after every important meeting, a report be distributed both to the attendees and to anyone else who might have even a passing interest in the group's actions.

Third, the leader must check to be sure that commitments made during the meeting are carried out. Are people doing what they said they would do? Are they staying on schedule? Have they encountered new or unanticipated problems? Are there things the leader is committed to do for the group (such as get back to them with an answer)? In effect, the leader must monitor herself and the progress of the members as they do the things agreed to. Such monitoring might be achieved by speaking with members individually, asking for written progress reports, making occasional telephone calls to members, or calling another meeting.

Clearly, the work done by a group does not stop when the meeting concludes. Often, in fact, the meeting is only the beginning of the real effort. Effective, thorough follow-up is vital to the continuation of the things the group meeting began.

Table 10.1 Meeting Effectiveness Questionnaire

Circle the number that best describes how you feel about each statement below.

Key: 1 = Strongly Disagree   3 = Neutral   5 = Strongly Agree
       2 = Disagree   4 = Agree

1. I clearly understood the purpose of the meeting.	1	2	3	4	5
2. The persons most directly involved with the purpose of the meeting were present.	1	2	3	4	5
3. All members had the opportunity to participate by expressing their views and opinions.	1	2	3	4	5
4. I had sufficient time and information to prepare for the meeting.	1	2	3	4	5
5. The leader of the meeting kept things on track and minimized time wasted on side issues.	1	2	3	4	5
6. I understand what the results of the meeting mean for me.	1	2	3	4	5
7. I support the results of the meeting.	1	2	3	4	5
8. The leader of the meeting was open to all ideas presented.	1	2	3	4	5
9. I understood what was expected of me at the meeting.	1	2	3	4	5
10. Ideas were presented clearly and were easily understood by everyone present.	1	2	3	4	5
11. The participants seemed to want to work for the good of the group.	1	2	3	4	5

Handling Problem Participants

As group leader, you frequently will encounter group members whose behavior is not helpful to the group. And as group leader, it will become your responsibility to deal with these people. On occasion, group pressure or some assertive group member will bring the problem participant back into line, but as a rule, the group will look to you, literally and figuratively, to take some action.

While it is impossible to anticipate every bizarre behavior that can occur in a group, we have compiled some common problem behaviors and some techniques whereby a leader can address them. Problem behaviors fall into two types: *members who talk*

Table 10.1 continued

Circle the number that best describes how you feel about each statement below.

Key: 1 = Strongly Disagree   3 = Neutral   5 = Strongly Agree
        2 = Disagree   4 = Agree

12. At the conclusion of the   1   2   3   4   5
    meeting, it was obvious to me
    that everyone knew what was
    expected of him or her.

13. The proper amount of time   1   2   3   4   5
    was allocated to this meeting.

14. The agenda/topics of the   1   2   3   4   5
    meeting were clear and easy
    to follow.

15. The meeting facilities were   1   2   3   4   5
    comfortable and appropriate.

16. Participation was spread   1   2   3   4   5
    evenly among the members;
    everyone talked about the
    same amount.

17. Conflicts between group   1   2   3   4   5
    members were resolved
    quickly and to everyone's
    satisfaction.

18. Decisions were made in ways   1   2   3   4   5
    that were fair to all group
    members.

19. Members dealt courteously   1   2   3   4   5
    with one another.

20. Each participant and all visual   1   2   3   4   5
    aids used during the meeting
    were easily visible to
    everyone.

In the future, we might improve similar meetings by:

---

too much and prevent others from participating and *members who don't talk or participate* enough. Specific problem types in each category are listed next, along with some strategies you might use to deal with them.

Members Who Talk Too Much

Show-offs know a great deal about the topic and are eager to prove it. They dominate the interaction out of a desire to exhibit their in-depth knowledge, and in so doing, they prevent everyone else from talking. To deal with a show-off, you might politely interrupt with a summarizing statement and ask someone else a direct question or interrupt with an observation: "Ken, you've made some interesting points, but I want everyone to have a chance. Let's hear what Tanya thinks about this." In addition, you could assign the member some specific project, such as gathering information or developing recommendations, and then have him present these to the group for their discussion. Finally, you could put the member in charge of a subcommittee of the group, and again have the entire group discuss their recommendations.

Quick and helpful members know all the right answers, but in providing them, they keep other members from participating. Unlike the show-off, their motive is not to exhibit skill and win approval but simply to help the group. You might manage such members by tactfully interrupting them and asking direct questions of other members, by talking about the interaction ("Juan, I really appreciate your ideas. Now let's see what someone else might contribute.") or by assigning the member a communication role, such as "idea evaluator." Before a meeting or during a break, for example, you might approach the member and say, "You really know a lot about this. Would you mind helping me evaluate the ideas that the other members contribute? We'll get their ideas, and then you indicate which seems best." Generally, the member will appreciate having such a clear and important function.

Ramblers babble incessantly during meetings, and invariably take the group away from the topic and on to something else. Other group members are quick to recognize and react to this sort of person: As soon as she begins to speak, they look at each other or cast their eyes heavenward out of frustration. The leader must step in. For example, when the rambler stops for a breath, thank her, rephrase one of her statements to make it relevant to the topic, and move back to that topic with a question to the group. Alternatively, you might interrupt and ask a direct question of someone else or talk about the interaction: "Thanks for your comments, Jean. Would anyone else like to comment now?" Finally, you could refer to the agenda or, if the topic is written on the blackboard or easel pad, point to the board or pad and ask the member which topic she is discussing. This method is potentially embarrassing to the member, however, and could cause anger or resentment.

Arguers constantly disagree with others, try to make trouble, and seem generally hostile. Such behavior disrupts the group, and it may be motivated by any number of things: frustration at not being the leader, dislike for the other group members, general crankiness, and so on. To prevent this behavior from upsetting and frustrating the other members, the leader must deal with it relatively quickly. You could seat the disruptive member next to you, making it easier for you to control him and to break in when arguments begin. You also might talk with the member privately and describe the behaviors you have observed. Ask the member to tell you what problems or concerns he has. Third, you could assign specific responsibilities to this member, just as you would the show-off. The feeling of being special may bring a hostile member back into the group, but it also may give him even greater opportunity to disrupt the group if that is his aim. Finally, if all else fails, you might privately ask the member to leave the group.

Side conversationalists insist on conducting private meetings of their own. Usually, a group will have two such problem members, who will be seen whispering or muttering to each other during the meeting. Such behavior is disruptive to other members and distracts these two participants from the group proceedings. To deal with this situation, you could direct a question to one of the conversationalists: "Kim, what do you think of that?" Kim either will have to answer, which automatically brings her back into the discussion, or she will have no idea what you are talking about, and her embarrassment will keep her involved in the discussion, at least for a while. In addition, you could talk privately to the conversationalists and express your concern about their behavior. Finally, if the same two people continually converse during meetings, assign seats for the next meeting with these two members at opposite sides of the group.

Complainers blame the group's problems on things not under the control of the group: management, company policy, the economy, and so on. They would rather gripe about the evils of these things than deal with the problem the group faces. In addition, they adopt a "what's the use" attitude that may cause apathy among other group members. To manage a complainer, you might address her directly and point out that some things cannot be changed by the group. Rather, the goal of the group is to operate as best it can under the present system. Alternatively, you might ask the member for a solution to her problem: "Well, Carol, what do you think we should do about the economy?" When she answers, "We can't do anything about it," ask, "Then should we just give up and go home?" She and other members will say no, enabling you to say, "Then what should we do?" In so doing, you will bring the group back to the topic and illustrate the futility of the member's complaints. Finally, you could interrupt the complaints and reorient the group to the topic under discussion.

Selfish members have a problem of their own that they want to discuss. They continually bring the group back to that problem, thus moving the group away from the topic at hand. To handle a selfish member, you could have the group discuss the member's problem. Get their opinions and recommendations; than return to the original topic. In addition, you might talk about the behavior and suggest that the member's problem be considered when the group has completed its current task: "John, you keep raising this problem. How about if we hold off on it for a while and talk about it when we have finished what we're doing?" Then deal with the member's problem when the group finishes the topic at hand. Finally, you could talk privately with the member about his problem and see if a solution can be developed outside the group.

Poor speakers lack communication skills: they speak too softly, do not speak clearly, express ideas poorly, and so on. The ideas may be good, but no one can tell because the member is inaudible or incomprehensible. To assist this sort of group member, repeat her ideas in your own words: "In other words, you're suggesting that. . . ." In addition, you may need to repeat the member's comments for everyone to hear, ask the member to repeat her comments while she stands, faces the group and speaks loudly. However, do not use this strategy if it is likely to embarrass the member.

Squabblers are two or more members who simply dislike one another and argue frequently as a result. You must be careful to distinguish between personality conflicts, which are disruptive to the group, and topic-based conflicts, which are based on real disagreements over the topic. When two members argue over several different conflicts and give off nonverbal cues indicating real dislike for each other, the leader needs to step in. For example, interrupt their argument with a direct question to one of them. This forces that member to talk to you, enabling you then to get other members involved in the interaction. Or you could summarize the comments each has made and then move on to another topic. Third, you might seat the two so that it is difficult for them to see one another (such as on the same side but at opposite ends of a long conference table). This makes it more difficult for them to argue. Finally, if other strategies fail, you might meet privately with the two of them, describe how their behaviors are affecting the group, and involve them in solving their own conflict.

There are other types of members who talk too much. However, the basic strategies described above can be applied to any member who prevents others from talking. The key is to determine the motives underlying the member's behaviors and then take action appropriate to those motives.

Members Who Do Not Talk

Uninterested members simply do not care about the group or its topic. As a result, they sit silently, perhaps looking out the window or doing something of their own (like writing notes or reading a book). To deal with this situation, you might direct a question to the member; ask for experiences as they relate to the topic. Be careful, however, to ask something the member can answer; otherwise, you add embarrassment to the apathy he is already feeling. In addition, you could assign the member specific responsibility. Have him collect information, list possible solutions, and so on. Be careful of giving that person some task vital to the group, however; the member might not come through on the task he is assigned. Other approaches are to meet privately with the member to discuss what the problem might be, form groups only on a voluntary basis (allowing uninterested members to leave), or seat the member in the middle of the group so that all interaction occurs around him (apathetic members usually try to sit at the back or on the fringes of the group where they go largely unnoticed). Finally, you could play the devil's advocate: ask the member for his opinion, and when it is given, disagree. By starting an argument with the member, you draw him into the group, and you may stir his interest.

Listeners are interested in the topic but prefer to listen rather than speak. They do nothing disruptive and may even provide helpful nonverbal reinforcement (head nods, attentive posture) to those who talk. But they do not contribute any ideas. To build a listener's participation, you might ask her to give an opinion whenever the member shows either agreement or disagreement nonverbally: "Susan, you seem to agree with Nancy's point. Why do you feel that way?" This sort of question is useful because you know Susan has an answer (she has been showing agreement nonverbally) and because your question draws her into the discussion. You also could direct questions to the member or, if you know something about the member, try to bring the topic around to an area in which the member has some experience. Then ask the member to recount those experiences. Assigning the member some specific duty, such as collecting information, also might be effective. Or finally, you could simply accept her preference to listen.

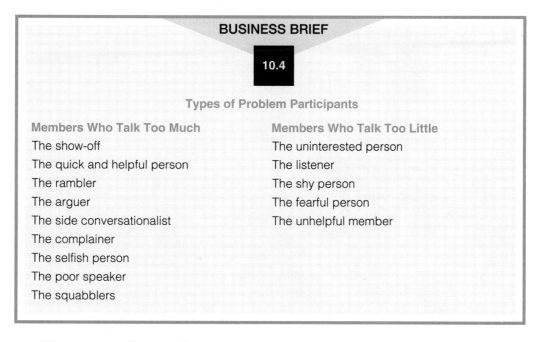

BUSINESS BRIEF

10.4

Types of Problem Participants

Members Who Talk Too Much	Members Who Talk Too Little
The show-off	The uninterested person
The quick and helpful person	The listener
The rambler	The shy person
The arguer	The fearful person
The side conversationalist	The unhelpful member
The complainer	
The selfish person	
The poor speaker	
The squabblers	

Shy group members simply are not very assertive. Nonverbal cues help you to identify them: they occasionally seem about to speak, but then some other member begins talking and they remain quiet. Directing a question to the member (be sure it is a question he can answer) can be helpful, or you might frequently ask the member for his agreement. By turning to him for approval, you increase the member's standing in the eyes of the other group members, making them more likely to involve the member as well. In addition, when the member seems to want to talk, call on him, even if it means cutting off a more assertive member who has just begun to speak. Finally, you could assign the member some specific responsibility.

Fearful members suffer stage fright in group situations. They are afraid of ridicule or failure or seeming stupid in the group's eyes. Rather than risk rejection or disapproval, they simply sit quietly. To gain a fearful member's participation, you could ask her a question that you know she can answer and then praise the answer given. In addition, you might turn frequently to the member for agreement or approval, thus building her status in the eyes of other members. During meetings, you should try to protect the member from ridicule or attack; take her side and help provide a defense any time another member launches an attack. Finally, you might seat the member next to you in an effort to build an association between the two of you. Your status in the group will reflect well on her.

Unhelpful members simply choose not to help others. They may have expertise on the topic but see no point in assisting the other members. An experienced employee, for example, might say, "It took me twenty years to learn my job; now you go learn yours like I did." To handle an unhelpful member, draw bits of information and experience from him with direct questions and compliment contributions each time.

In addition, you might assign the member some specific responsibility or appoint him chairperson of some group subcommittee, asking for a report of the committee's progress at each large group meeting.

Again, there are many other reasons why members choose not to participate. However, by controlling the overtalkative members and drawing out the nonparticipants, you can equalize members' contributions to the group interaction.

Handling Large Group Meetings: Parliamentary Procedure

Generally speaking, the larger the group, the more difficult it is for the group leader to control the meeting. In very large group meetings, such as stockholders' meetings or meetings of legislative bodies, the leader frequently chooses to use a very structured format to ensure orderly communication. Perhaps the most commonly used large group format is *parliamentary procedure.*

The rules of parliamentary procedure were not developed by any single person or group of people. Rather, they evolved over hundreds of years through the experiences of thousands of self-governing assemblies. They have become somewhat complicated over time, but their basic principles have rarely changed. If you understand the principles, the rules make more sense and are easier to apply. These principles include:

The majority rules. Obviously, this is a democratic approach to group communication. Rarely can total agreement be reached on any issue. To have some basis for action in cases where disagreement occurs, the principle is followed that the preferences of the majority are carried out.

The rights of the minority are protected. The majority cannot be granted unlimited power. Every member of the assembly has individual rights, regardless of whether he or she happens to agree with the majority. These rights include the right to a secret ballot, the right to nominate for office, and the protection of the constitution and bylaws of the organization. As leader you must insure that these rights are protected and that no one is steamrollered by the majority.

Business must be accomplished. Meetings are held to bring about some action. The group welcomes free presentation of all the facts and opinions on any problem under discussion, but that discussion cannot consume an entire meeting, nor should it get in the way of getting things done.

Feelings must be respected. We must be careful not to lose sight of individual feelings as we conduct the group's business and control its interaction. Just as courtesy is important in all our social relationships, so too must it be maintained in large group meetings.

Obviously, these four principles will contradict one another at times; for example, the rights of a minority may interfere with the rapid accomplishment of the group's business or with the rule of the majority. As group leader or chairperson, you must do all you can to maintain a balance among these principles. The rules of parliamentary law have been developed to help you achieve such a balance.

The order of business used by a large group will vary somewhat. However, a typical group agenda includes the following elements:

1. *Call to order.* After determining that a quorum (the minimum number needed to transact business, usually a simple majority of the total membership) is present, the chairperson gets the attention of the group (often by rapping a gavel on the podium) and says, "The meeting will please come to order."

2. *Opening ceremonies.* Many groups open their meetings with a prayer, pledge of allegiance, song, and so on. If such a ceremony is used by this group, the chairperson next would say, "Let us open our meeting by. . . ."

3. *Roll call.* If a roll call is desired to determine who is in attendance, the chairperson would say, "The secretary will please call the roll." Occasionally, she might add, "Members will answer to their names by . . . ," stating the way in which members should respond to their names.

4. *Reading of the minutes.* The chairperson next says, "The secretary will read the minutes of the last meeting." When the minutes have been read, he or she then asks, "Are there any corrections or additions to the minutes?" If none is offered, the chairperson states, "The minutes stand approved as read." If corrections are offered (and agreed to by the chairperson and the assembly), the secretary is instructed to make the necessary changes. Then the chairperson states, "The minutes stand approved as corrected."

5. *Reports.* After the reading of the minutes, the chairperson typically calls on the chairpersons of standing and special committees to make reports to the group. For example, the chairperson might ask the chairperson of the membership committee to read that committee's report. If there are no objections, the report is accepted by the group (not endorsed but *filed* for future reference). If any proposed action grows from a committee report, it is introduced later under "new business." Normally, standing (or permanent) committees report first, followed by special (or temporary) committees.

6. *Unfinished business.* The chairperson says, "We now will consider any unfinished business." Anything left over or postponed from the previous meeting may be discussed and voted on at this time.

7. *New business.* The chairperson says, "We will now consider any new business." As a rule, this portion of the meeting consumes most of the time spent by the group.

8. *Program.* Occasionally, the group has some program (such as a speaker, film, or presentation) planned as part of the meeting. When no more new business is forthcoming, the chairperson asks, "Is there any further new business to come before this meeting? If not, will the chairperson of the program committee (or other member in charge of the program) please take charge of the program planned for this meeting." The chairperson and secretary may then sit in the audience for the program.

9. *Miscellaneous, announcements, and so on.* Before adjourning, the chairperson may ask if there are any announcements to be made, notes to be read, or other routine matters not requiring group action. Some groups do this earlier in the meeting, following the reading of the minutes.

10. *Adjournment.* One of two procedures may be used to adjourn a meeting. If the meeting always adjourns at a fixed time and that time arrives, the chairperson may say, "The meeting is adjourned." If not, the chairperson may ask, "Is there a motion to adjourn?" In the latter case, some member of the group says, "I move we adjourn." This motion must be seconded by another group member, and it cannot be discussed. The motion is put to a vote, and the result announced: "The motion is adopted; the meeting is adjourned." In the highly unlikely event that the motion to adjourn is defeated, the chairperson would announce the vote and call for any additional new business on the assumption that the majority had something else they want to do before closing the meeting.

In large group settings where parliamentary procedure is used, the purpose of the meeting generally is to decide on various courses of action. Possible courses of action are suggested by the group members, who do so in the form of motions for discussion by the group. One such motion, as we already have seen, is the motion to adjourn—a suggestion that the meeting be terminated and everyone leave. Almost all decisions made by the group are handled in a similar fashion: A member suggests a course of action (that is, she states a motion), the group considers it, and ultimately a decision to adopt or reject that motion is made. The real "work" involved in leading a large group meeting is handling the members' motions and ensuing discussion while preserving the four principles we stated earlier.

Several steps are followed in handling motions offered by members. First, *the member obtains the floor.* The member rises, calling out, "Mr. (or Madam) Chairperson." In smaller or more informal groups, the member might remain seated and address the chair. The member should not rise without addressing the chair if he wants to obtain the floor. The chairperson then *recognizes the member* by saying the member's name, nodding in the member's direction, or in some other way referring to the member. The member should not speak until receiving recognition from the chair. Only then does the member have the right to address the assembly.

The *member states the motion* by saying, "I move that we . . . ," thus suggesting the action she wants the group to take. The motion should be as complete as possible so that no unnecessary amendments need be made but it should not be overly long and complicated. Long motions should be submitted in writing.

For a motion to be considered, it usually must be supported by at least one other group member. Thus, the next step is that the *motion is seconded.* The person giving the second need not rise; he only needs to call out "second" or "I second the motion." If no one seconds the motion, the chairperson may ask, "Is the motion seconded?" If still no one seconds the motion, the chairperson states, "The motion is lost for lack of a second." If a second is given, the *chairperson then states the motion* to the group by saying, "It has been moved and seconded that we. . . ." Then the *chair calls for discussion:* "Is there any discussion on the motion?"

The next step in the process is that *members discuss the motion.* Several points should be kept in mind here. Each member who wants to speak must first obtain the floor (be recognized by the chairperson), just as if a new motion were being offered. Discussion must be confined to the motion at hand, and the one who offered the motion usually is given first opportunity to discuss it. Usually, people are recognized as they stand and address the chair; however, if someone rises and interrupts the previous speaker, she is ruled out of order and not given the floor. If many people desire to speak, the chair tries to "alternate the floor," first recognizing someone in favor of the motion and then recognizing someone against it, giving each position a turn to speak. Any member who has already spoken once is not recognized until all members wanting to express themselves for the first time have done so. Finally, the chair does not offer her or his opinions on the motion; his or her job is simply to keep order.

Ultimately, *the chair determines that the discussion is finished.* When members stop rising to request recognition, the chairperson asks, "Is there any further discussion?" If some is offered, the chair repeats the question later. When no further discussion is offered, she or he proceeds to the next step, *restating the motion.* He or she might say, "If there is no further discussion, we are ready to vote. The question is on the motion to. . . ."

Next, *the members vote on the motion.* This can occur in several ways. Frequently, the group uses a voice vote, where the chairperson says, "As many as are in favor of the motion say aye; those opposed no." If the number of ayes (pronounced "I") clearly is larger than the number of nos, or vice versa, the decision is announced. The group also can vote by raising hands or by standing to show support for or opposition to the motion. If the motion requires a two-thirds majority, standing or hand-raising votes should be taken to enable the chairperson to count the votes. Members can request this type of vote by calling, "division," or by saying, "I call for a division of the house." Then the chairperson must request that a standing vote be taken. Finally, a group can vote by secret ballot or by general consent. In the latter case, the chairperson says, "If there is no objection, we will . . ." (stating the action that the motion requires). The chairperson then pauses to allow members to object. If no one does, the motion is considered to be passed by unanimous approval; if an objection is offered, a vote is taken by voice, show of hands, standing, or ballot.

The chairperson has a right to vote whenever her or his vote will change the outcome. However, the chairperson may not want to reveal her or his opinions and thus may choose not to vote except in the case of a secret ballot. However, if the chairperson's vote will either create or break a tie, he or she may want to vote openly. A tie vote defeats a motion (majority rule means that half of those voting plus one must support the motion). By creating a tie with her or his vote, the chairperson would defeat a motion; by breaking a tie, the chairperson would carry the motion.

When the vote is taken, the *chairperson announces the result of the vote*. If there is no doubt of the result, the chairperson says, "The ayes have it; the motion is carried." or "The nos have it; the motion is defeated." Then the *chairperson indicates the effect of this vote*. He or she says, "We will therefore . . ." (stating the action that the motion requires the group to take). Finally, the *chairperson moves to the next piece of business*. If a main motion was voted on, the chairperson asks, "Is there any further business to come before us?" If the group was voting on an amendment to a main motion, the chairperson says, "The question is now on the main motion, which has been amended to read . . ." (repeating the main motion as amended).

There are different types of motions that group members can offer, and these must be handled in different ways. So far, we have primarily discussed main motions, motions that bring a subject before the group for consideration and action. However, other types of special motions require unusual handling. To be effective, the chairperson must be able to answer several questions in his or her own mind whenever a motion is offered and to then take appropriate action. These questions include:

What type of motion is it?

What motions may it displace in receiving the attention of the group, and which motions may displace it?

Does it require a second?

May it be discussed?

What vote does it require: majority or two-thirds?

To help you understand the types of motions you or other group members might make, we will consider some special motions that commonly occur. The first group are all considered *main motions*.

1. *The motion to take a matter "off the table."* When some motion has been tabled or "placed on the table," discussion of that motion has been suspended temporarily. A member can bring the matter to the attention of the group again by moving that the original motion be taken off the table and considered by the

group. This motion cannot be offered immediately after the group has voted to table the initial motion; some other business must transpire before this motion to take a matter off the table can be considered.

2. *The motion to reconsider action previously taken.* This motion can be offered only by someone who voted in favor of the original motion, and its effect is to place the original motion before the group again as though a vote never had been taken. It is important to note, however, that a motion to reconsider is appropriate only for matters the group can undo; things that now cannot be changed should not be reconsidered. This motion is also appropriate only during the same meeting in which the original motion was passed or during the next meeting the group holds.

3. *The motion to repeal or rescind an action previously taken.* This motion is similar to the preceding but is used in later meetings when the motion to reconsider is no longer appropriate. It can be offered by any member, and its effect is to reverse the action previously taken (again assuming that what was done now can be undone).

A second group of motions are *subsidiary motions,* which are applied to main motions to get them in proper shape so the group can take action on them. They include:

1. *The motion to amend.* When the group does not like the wording of the main motion, they may change that wording by amending the motion. The group may add words, remove words, or substitute words; however, they can do only one of these things at a time (that is, they cannot simultaneously add some words, remove others, and substitute for still others). The maker of the main motion does not need to approve these changes; the majority vote of the group determines whether the main motion is amended. To amend a motion, a member rises, addresses the chair, and says, "I move we amend the motion by adding (removing, substituting) the words. . . after the words . . . so that the motion will read. . . ." This motion requires a second before it can be considered. The group may also want to amend the amendment, and this is moved in the same way. The process cannot be carried any further, however (that is, you cannot amend an amendment to an amendment). The voting order is (1) amendment to the amendment, (2) amendment, and (3) motion.

2. *The motion to refer to a committee.* The group may want to have some committee handle a matter rather than devoting time to the matter in this meeting. Thus, a member might rise, address the chair, and say, "I move we refer this motion to. . . ." or "I move that a . . . committee be created to handle this matter." The latter motion should state what the composition of the new committee is to be, how it should be appointed, what power it should have, when it will report, and what its name should be.

3. *The motion to postpone to a particular time.* A member might rise, gain recognition, and say, "I move that we postpone consideration of this matter until our next meeting" or "I move that we postpone consideration of this matter for ten minutes." A specific time must be stated, and it may not be beyond the next regular meeting of the group.

4. *The motion to put an end to discussion and vote at once.* If this motion is made and passed by two-thirds of the group, it immediately stops discussion and brings about an immediate vote on the matter before the group. To make such a motion, a member rises, is recognized, and says, "I move that we put an end to discussion on this matter." An alternative way of stating this motion is "I move the previous question."

5. *The motion to lay a matter on the table.* Like the motion to postpone consideration, this motion delays consideration of the matter at hand; however, it does not state any time limit. The person offering the motion simply says, "I move that this matter be laid on the table." If the motion is seconded and supported by a majority vote, discussion of the matter stops until the matter is taken off the table at some future time. If not seconded or supported by a majority vote, the motion to table is defeated, and discussion on the original matter continues.

Incidental motions make up the third motion group. They are offered during the course of a meeting when an unusual situation arises that needs immediate action by the group. These may be offered at virtually any time, and they must be decided upon before discussion returns to the matter at hand. Some common incidental motions are:

1. *A point of order.* When anyone makes a mistake in parliamentary law, any member may rise without being recognized and say, "Mr. (or Madam) Chairman, I rise to a point of order." The chairperson then will say, "State your point of order." The member then explains the error that was made. Usually, the chair will rule on the matter by stating, "Your point of order is well taken" (then making the necessary changes) or "Your point of order is not well taken" (with no changes being made). On rare occasion, the group may be asked to vote for or against the point of order, and their decision determines whether the point is upheld.

2. *An appeal from the decision of the chair.* Whenever the chairperson makes a decision that a member believes is wrong (including a decision on a point of order), the member may rise and say, "I appeal from the decision of the chair." If this motion is seconded, the member has a right to explain her position, the chair may defend himself or herself, and other members may speak on the matter. A vote is then taken, and the decision of the majority is followed no matter what the chairperson may think. A tie vote serves to uphold the chairperson's decision since it is assumed the chairperson would vote for himself or herself.

3. *A motion to suspend the rules.* This is done so that some procedure or motion normally out of order can be used or discussed. Rules may be suspended only for a specific purpose and for the limited time necessary to accomplish the proposed action. Many rules cannot be suspended, such as basic rules governing a quorum, voting requirements, or voting methods. For the most part, only procedural rules are suspended. The motion to suspend the rules requires a two-thirds majority for adoption.

4. *A motion to object to the consideration of some matter.* This allows the group to avoid the discussion of an issue because it is viewed as embarrassing, unnecessarily contentious, frivolous, or inopportune. This motion also requires a two-thirds majority for adoption. The only time the motion to object is in order is immediately after the objectionable motion has been stated by the presiding officer. If discussion of the motion has begun, it is too late to object to its consideration. The person who objects may be any member of the organization, including the chairperson, and this person is free to state or withhold his reasons for the objection.

5. *A parliamentary inquiry.* This motion's purpose is simply to seek advice from the chairperson. This advice usually focuses on issues such as the appropriate

parliamentary procedure to follow in making a particular motion. Whenever a group member is uncertain about how to refer some matter to a committee, how to word a motion properly, or how to nominate a candidate for office, she might conduct a parliamentary inquiry. Like other special motions designed to maintain the rules, the parliamentary inquiry may interrupt a speaker, although the chairperson may choose to hold her or his reply until the person who has the floor has concluded.

The final group of motions, *privileged motions,* are of such importance that they can be made at almost any time. They include:

1. *The motion to adjourn.* This motion is for closing the meeting or sometimes, strategically, for terminating the discussion of a particular question. This motion may not interrupt a speaker, but it is in order at any time. As we pointed out earlier, it is neither amendable nor debatable, and it must be put to an immediate vote.
2. *The motion to recess the group.* Unlike the motion to adjourn, the motion to recess the group is intended to temporarily disband the meeting. Recesses are occasionally needed to obtain additional information, to discuss voting procedures, to rest, or to count votes. The motion to recess may interrupt any business other than the process of voting. It may not interrupt a speaker.
3. *The question of privilege.* This motion requires that the presiding officer deal with some situation affecting the welfare of the organization's members, such as fire, offensive remarks, or poor acoustics. The question of privilege is unusual in that it needs no second, and it can interrupt both business and speaker. The presiding officer may decide the matter or may submit it to a vote of the group.

This list is not intended to be exhaustive but to highlight major motions that are often used in formal business meetings.

As we said earlier, the chairperson must know not only the types of motions, but their precedence—that is, what motions may displace other motions. One motion may replace another already before the house if the new motion has sufficient power or *precedence* to do so. It is important that you know which motions have which levels of precedence. If one motion is under consideration and another is made, you must decide whether the new motion is appropriate for consideration (so that it should be considered before attention is returned to the original motion) or whether consideration of the new motion should be denied until discussion of the original motion is completed.

To help you keep track of precedence, the chart in table 10.2 lists types of motions in order of precedence. It also indicates whether each motion requires a second from another group member, whether discussion of the motion is allowed, whether the motion can be amended, and what level of voting support (simple majority or two-thirds) is needed.

Again, parliamentary procedure is complicated, and our purpose here is simply to acquaint you with basic decisions you will have to make when conducting large group meetings under these rules. For a more detailed and complete understanding of parliamentary procedure, you should consult one of the many excellent books devoted to that topic.[21]

Table 10.2 Order of Precedence of Motions

Types of Motions (Listed in Order of Precedence from Highest to Lowest; A Second Motion Cannot Be Considered Unless It Has Higher Precedence Than the Motion Already before the Group)	Requires Second?	May Be Discussed?	May Be Amended?	Vote Needed
Privileged:				
To fix the time of the next meeting	Yes	No	Yes	Majority
To adjourn	Yes	No	No	Majority
To recess	Yes	No	Yes	Majority
Question of privilege	No	No	No	Chair[d]
Incidental:				
An appeal from the decision of the chair	Yes	Yes[a]	No	Majority
A point of order	No	No	No	Chair[d]
To suspend the rules	Yes	No	No	2/3
To object to consideration	No	No	No	2/3
Parliamentary inquiry	No	No	No	Chair[d]
Subsidiary:				
To lay on the table	Yes	No	No	Majority
To put an end to discussion (to call the previous question)	Yes	No	No	2/3
To limit debate	Yes	No	Yes	2/3
To postpone to a certain time	Yes	Yes	Yes	Majority
To refer to a committee	Yes	Yes	Yes	Majority
To amend a motion	Yes	Yes[a]	Yes	Majority
To postpone indefinitely	Yes	Yes	No	Majority
Main:				
An ordinary main motion	Yes	Yes	Yes	Majority
To take a matter off the table	Yes	No	No	Majority
To reconsider action previously taken	Yes[b]	Yes[a]	No	Majority
To repeal or rescind action previously taken	Yes[b]	Yes	Yes	Majority[c]

[a]May be discussed, unless it applies to an undebatable question.

[b]Opens the main motion to discussion as well.

[c]If prior notice is given that such a motion is forthcoming, a majority is needed; if no such notice is given, two-thirds vote is needed.

[d]Requires only chairperson's decision; a majority vote is needed if appealed from chair.

Summary

At one time or another, most of us find ourselves in the role of committee chairperson. We may not be managers or administrators in the formal sense, but we are *leaders* in that we plan and organize meetings, call and arrange for meeting rooms, and conduct the meeting when the other members arrive. Sometimes we chair on a one-shot basis, especially if we are working with an ad hoc group—or, more likely, we chair an ongoing committee, which may continue for months, or even years. Our ability to manage these meetings effectively will influence many important outcomes, such as our own professional well-being. Moreover, when we lead groups to sound decisions, we make a really important contribution to the organization as a whole.

Most of our opportunities to lead groups occur in the context of small committee meetings, but on certain occasions, we are elected to leadership positions that require us to conduct business meetings involving much larger groups of people. These sorts of meetings necessitate the use of parliamentary procedure. Although the rules of parliamentary procedure may seem complicated at first, most can be learned with relative ease as one uses them over time. The rules of parliamentary procedure are all based on important principles, like the right of all members to have their views aired. That's why, for instance, limiting or restricting discussion requires the support of two-thirds of the organization's members. Other important motions grow from such principles as turn-taking, the right of the majority to prevail, and the right of the minority to be protected. Most chairpersons have the support of a parliamentarian, so that parliamentary questions can be resolved as expediently and judiciously as possible. Even so, the more the chairperson knows about parliamentary procedure, the more smoothly each business meeting will proceed.

Whether we are leading small, informal groups or large business meetings, we will function more effectively if we think carefully about the meaning of leadership, prepare carefully, follow a plan or agenda, and understand something about the principles of group dynamics discussed earlier in this book. Through the way we communicate, by asking appropriate sorts of questions, by making timely procedural and organizational suggestions, and by listening carefully to the ideas of other group members, we have an excellent chance of being able to conduct really effective meetings.

Questions for Discussion

1. Why have meetings gained such a bad reputation in most modern organizations?
2. Why is it important to an organization to have effective meetings?
3. When should you avoid calling a meeting?
4. How do the facilities in which a meeting is held affect the success of that meeting?

5. In what types of situations are autocratic meetings most desirable? Consultative meetings? Democratic meetings? Laissez-faire meetings?
6. Why should majority vote be avoided as a decision-making device?
7. Why are team-building meetings important in an organization?
8. As a leader, how can you judge whether a group member's actions are harmful to the group as a whole?
9. In your view, is leadership more a matter of traits, style, or situation? Why?
10. How do you react to the functional approach to leadership? In organizational settings, can leadership, realistically, be shared?

Exercises

1. Write an announcement for a meeting (create your own purpose, list of attendees, and so on).
2. Conduct a mock meeting using the principles of parliamentary procedure.
3. Conduct a mock meeting using one of the autocratic, democratic, consultative, or laissez-faire approaches outlined. Then have members complete the "Meeting Effectiveness Questionnaire." Have members report and explain their answers for each item on the questionnaire.
4. Conduct a mock meeting, and at the beginning of the meeting, assign some of the problem-member roles to some group participants. Do not announce which member has which role. Assign a leader to conduct the meeting. At the meeting's end, discuss how effectively the leader handled each problem participant.

CHAPTER
11

Managing Conflict

S omeone once observed that "life is just one damned thing after another." In most organizations, those "damned things" are conflicts of various sorts, for all too often corporate life seems to be one conflict after another. Indeed, organizational conflict seems to be inevitable. Throughout this text, we have stressed the interdependence of organizational members and the continuing need for them to behave cooperatively. Yet this interdependence, this continuing necessity for interaction among people, makes conflict unavoidable. As Bernard points out, stress and conflict will occur in organizations because they are "inherent in the conception of free will in a changing environment."[1]

As we shall soon see, conflict is not in and of itself bad. Indeed, in many situations, some conflict is necessary for the organization to function at maximum efficiency. If some conflicts remain unsolved or if they are managed poorly, the organization as a whole will suffer. In this chapter, we turn our attention to yet another aspect of communication among groups of people: identifying, analyzing, and managing conflict. Communication to manage conflict comprises a complex set of strategies involving both informative and persuasive elements. In an effort to understand these strategies, we will consider the role of conflict in organizations, noting attitudes toward conflict and the settings, causes, and consequences of organizational disputes. Then we will examine several methods by which each type of organizational conflict may be managed. In so doing, we hope to develop communication strategies by which organizational conflict may be managed for the benefit of the organization as a whole.

The Role of Conflict in Organizations

Attitudes toward Conflict

As we saw in chapter 1, a great number of changes have occurred in the thinking of organizational and management theorists during the past century. None of these changes has been as dramatic as the change in theorists' attitudes toward organizational conflict. Classical organizational theorists, such as Taylor[2] and Fayol,[3] said rather little about organizational conflict, probably because they assumed that managers were basically rational, unlike workers. Because of their rationality, they could clearly see the objectives of their organization and plan logically. When disputes broke out among irrational workers, the function of the manager was to act as a sort of fire fighter, stamping out the conflict so that the workers could return to the rational task of doing work and making money. In effect, then, conflict had no role in organizations in the view of Classical management and organizational theorists.

In the Human Relations approach to organizations, conflict played a more prominent role. Theorists of the Human Relations school[4] felt that the key to organizational functioning was the maintenance of satisfactory social relationships. Since conflict was indicative of a breakdown in human relationships, they felt the success of the organization rested upon management's ability to prevent conflicts from ever occurring. Human Relations managers thus spent considerable time and energy making sure that everyone was happy and no one was arguing. Workers in Human Relations organizations spent an equal amount of time and energy hiding conflicts from their managers lest they be reprimanded for engaging in such antisocial behaviors. As a consequence, conflicts were "swept under the rug," not managed, so that while they disappeared temporarily, they often reappeared some time later, bigger and more difficult to handle than before. By stressing conflict avoidance, Human Relations managers and theorists did not succeed in truly avoiding conflict. Rather, they created frustrations and conflicts that were far greater than the original problem.

More recent views of organizational conflict happily have been somewhat more realistic. Evan typifies these views in his characterization of recent attitudes about conflict.

1. Conflicts always occur because of disagreement about expectations or organizational goals.
2. Conflicts can be good or bad for both the organization and the individual.
3. Conflicts can be validly minimized for crisis (armies) or routine (manufacturers) organizations but may not be best minimized for knowledge and technology (research and development) organizations.[5]

Thus, theorists and practitioners in organizational development all have arrived at the realization that conflict in organizations not only is inevitable but may be beneficial.

In fact, some organizational leaders take the view that creating conflict can be a useful strategy for achieving organizational change. As a manager, one is constantly battling inertia. If no tensions are felt, the status quo is likely to continue. That's why some leaders create conflict: to demonstrate, for example, how organizational values are not reflected in employee behavior, how advertising is false or misleading, or how supervisors have different standards for their employees than they have for themselves. The tension generated by conflict typically leads to some attempts to reduce or eliminate the tension level—and that means that the conflict must be confronted. With effective leadership, it will be confronted and managed in an appropriate way. To manage conflict effectively, one must know something about the settings, causes, and consequences of conflict. We turn now to these matters.

Settings of Conflict

Berelson and Steiner define social conflict as "the pursuit of incompatible, or at least seemingly incompatible, goals, such that gains to one side come about at the expense of the other."[6] Herbert provides another view of conflict, defining it as occurring "whenever the attainment of a goal is hindered."[7] While these definitions disagree in some minor respects, both imply that *conflict involves the simultaneous presence of two or more incompatible elements*. In this section, we will examine some of the settings in which such conflicting elements often are found.

Intrapersonal Conflict

Two conflict forms, frustration and goal conflict, occur commonly within individuals in organizations. *Frustration* is the simpler of the two, occurring when one's ability to attain a goal is hampered by the imposition of some barrier. For example, we may have a strong desire to perform in a superior fashion, yet because of some limitation (limited

Conflict Settings

Intrapersonal conflict	Conflict within the person, such as frustration or goal conflict
Interpersonal conflict	Conflict between people, such as individual versus individual or individual versus group
Intergroup conflict	Conflict between two or more groups
Interorganizational conflict	Conflict between entire organizations

ability, inadequate education, or a supervisor who does not like us), our performance evaluations consistently are "average." We then might try somehow to improve matters, perhaps by working harder, taking evening courses at a local college, or trying to obtain a transfer to another department. If these measures fail, frustration results and less productive behaviors are likely to follow.

More complex than frustration is a second sort of intrapersonal conflict, *goal conflict,* where the attainment of one goal excludes the possibility of attaining another. Three principal types of goal conflict can be identified.

1. *Approach-approach conflict*—in which the individual is caught between trying to decide on one or another of two attractive goals that are mutually exclusive. The college graduate with two attractive job offers has to deal with this kind of conflict.
2. *Approach-avoidance conflict*—in which the individual has both positive and negative feelings about trying to attain a goal because the goal possesses both attractive and unattractive characteristics. The individual faces this kind of conflict when she is offered a promotion and a pay hike but must transfer from San Francisco to Antarctica to take the new job.
3. *Avoidance-avoidance conflict*—in which the individual must choose between two mutually exclusive goals, both of which are unattractive. Here, alas, the job hunter must pick between selling used cars and selling encyclopedias, neither of which seems like a good idea.

Interpersonal Conflict

Conflict between organizational members also takes two forms: *individual versus individual* and *individual versus group.* Examples of the first are infinite: two managers competing for the same promotion, two women vying for a tennis championship, two students vying for the top grade in the class. In each instance, the competitors are striving for possession of some resource available to only one of them. Although the competition may even be enjoyable to the participants, uncontrolled conflict of this sort is often destructive to the organization.

On occasion, conflict also occurs *between an individual and a group*. As we pointed out previously, some groups demand absolute conformity by their members, so that a "rugged individualist" who happens to join that group might find himself in conflict with other members. Or an individual who is particularly eager to promote her own interests may do so by breaking group norms. Work groups, for example, typically have informal but rigidly enforced production limits such that anyone outproducing the rest of the group is labeled a "rate buster" and pressured to conform.

Interpersonal conflicts produce stress within the organization and must be managed correctly if they are to become beneficial rather than detrimental to the organization.

Intergroup Conflict

As we already know, much of our life in organizations is spent in groups: work groups, decision-making groups, social groups. Often these groups come into conflict with one another. Two particular types of intergroup conflict deserve mention. *Functional conflicts* occur when business functions are divided up into departments that often have entirely different perspectives of organizational processes. Manufacturing divisions tend to have short time perspectives and seek to maximize their own goals of long production runs and standardized products to meet unit cost goals. Marketing divisions tend to have long time perspectives, to evaluate products and services from the perspective of the consumer, and to endeavor to customize and provide many options to suit each customer individually. Conflicts between these groups are common, and managers must seek means for their resolution.

Line and staff conflicts represent a second type of intergroup conflict, as staff groups are responsible for measuring, monitoring, analyzing, and projecting the work and results of the organization, while line groups are concerned only with the actual execution of the work. Line may see staff as being impractical, overeducated, inexperienced, or abstract; while staff may view line as dull, narrow, inflexible, or unimaginative. Perceptual incongruities such as these are virtually guaranteed to produce conflict between line and staff groups.

Interorganizational Conflict

While individuals and groups within organizations often are embroiled in conflicts, the organizations themselves usually are involved in disputes as well. For example, consider some of the organizations with which an automobile manufacturer comes into contact. General Motors buys automotive parts from Borg-Warner. Although these two corporations are acting cooperatively to build automobiles, they are also in conflict: Borg-Warner wants to get the highest possible prices from General Motors for the parts it supplies, while General Motors wants to pay the lowest possible prices. Similarly, advertising agencies handling the General Motors account want to charge the highest possible prices, while General Motors wants to keep its advertising budget as low as possible. Executive recruiting firms are eager to charge high fees for finding new executives to staff General Motors, while GM wants to keep recruiting costs low. The United Auto Workers want as many union members as possible to be employed by General Motors (since those people must pay dues to the UAW), and they are eager to have their members well paid by General Motors. General Motors wants to keep its

When the Boss Is Wrong

A particulary ticklish conflict situation arises when you feel your boss is wrong. Submission to authority is expected in most organizations, but thinking employees will ask, "Don't I have a responsibility to speak up if I see something wrong?" Of course, you do. But the key issue is authority: how can you provide your boss with information he or she needs about his or her decision without usurping the boss's decison-making authority?

When you need to disagree with your boss, try to offer alternatives rather than direct opposition. For example:

If your boss asks you to do something you feel should not be your responsibility, don't say,"But that isn't in my job description." Instead, you might offer to take the work to some other more appropriate person ("Maria does this kind of thing a lot. Do you mind if I ask her to do this?"), or ask your boss what activities you should give up to perform this new task ("I'd be happy to do this, but I need your help in deciding what things I should leave until later.").

If your boss has an idea you feel won't work, don't say, "That won't work; I have a better idea." Rather, ask the boss, "Help me to understand why we are going to do it this way." After hearing the reasons, you might add, "If that's what you want, I'll do it; but could I suggest a way that might be faster (cheaper, more efficient, and so on)?"

If your boss gives you a directive that contradicts some other boss' instructions (particularly instructions given you by your boss' boss), you are caught in the middle. But don't say, "That goes against this other boss' directives." Instead, let your boss know of the other instructions you have been given and suggest that the three of you meet to identify what the priorities are.

If your boss asks you to do something you feel is not right, don't say, "I won't do that; it's unethical." Try to prevent this situation from ever arising by discussing ethical issues with your boss well in advance: what things does the company stand for, and what do you personally believe in? If, nevertheless, you are asked to do something you feel is unethical, explain the conflict between the request and your ethical standards and ask the boss not to ask you to do that.

Presented by Don Michael McDonald, "How to Tell Your Boss He's Wrong," *Management Solutions* 43 (December 1988): 3–9; Fernando Bartolome, "When You Think the Boss is Wrong," *Personal Journal* 69 (August 1990): 66–73.

labor costs down. The federal government imposes regulations concerning safety and pollution that are supposed to reflect the public interest. General Motors tries to keep manufacturing costs minimal. The automobile-buying public wants quality cars at low prices, while General Motors wants to make a profit. In all of these instances, partial conflict (but also a partial sharing of goals) exists between each group. Yet only by overcoming these conflicts can each group have its needs met to some degree.

Causes of Conflict

Implicit in our discussion of the settings of conflict have been several conflict causes. Although conflict can arise for many different reasons, we will next discuss some common contributors to organizational conflict.

1. *Competition for rewards.* Every organization offers a limited number or amount of rewards to its members. Individuals compete for promotions, raises, and status symbols; departments compete for budget allocations; organizations compete for a larger share of the market. These situations are called "win-lose" or "zero-sum" conditions. What one competitor wins, another loses, so that if the amount won and the amount lost are summed, they add to zero.

2. *Interlevel incompatibilities.* The organization is composed of many levels of hierarchy. Some research suggests that as we move from one level of the hierarchy to the next, our perceptions of the corporation tend to change. For instance, Likert discovered that top staff, foremen, and line workers all felt that they understood other people's problems but were themselves misunderstood, and in fact discovered that none of them shared congruent perceptions of what the other's problems were.[8]

3. *Functional conflicts.* As we already have seen, conflicts occasionally arise when organizational subgroups have overlapping functions. In fact, any situation involving functional overlap may produce conflict. If the individuals, groups, or organizations involved have different values, perceptions, or ideas concerning how the job should be done, disagreements will spring up that must be resolved if the work is to be completed.

4. *Differences in values and goals.* Production and sales units often conflict in this way since sales is more geared toward rapid production for high volume and speedy delivery, while production prefers a slower pace that emphasizes quality. When speed as a value and quality as a value clash (as they often do when the sales division puts in a rush order or when production slows down), conflict is likely to result. Whenever groups or individuals within organizations possess different values, the resulting conflicts can be quite difficult to resolve.

5. *Deficiencies in the organization's information system.* An important message may not be received, a supervisor's instructions may be misinterpreted, or decision makers may arrive at different conclusions because they used different data bases. Conflicts based on missing or incomplete information tend to be straightforward in that clarifying previous messages or obtaining additional information generally resolves the disputes. Since value systems are not being challenged, these conflicts tend to be easily addressed by dealing directly with the information deficiency.

6. *Specialists versus generalists.* As jobs have become increasingly complex and science has made technology more intricate, the need for specialists to perform those jobs and use those technological innovations has become more and more pressing. Yet management functions typically require generalists to perform them. Most organizations are constructed so that a large number of specialists must be governed by a small number of generalists, which creates a host of potential

conflicts. The generalist manager often knows less about the job than does the specialist worker, so that the worker may find it frustrating or nonproductive to communicate with his boss. The worker may "short circuit" the organization's formal lines of communication, often to the dismay of the supervisor. Or there may be conflicting loyalties. Among professionals, loyalty to a discipline often conflicts with loyalty to the organization, as when a researcher feels himself a chemist first and a member of the organization second.

7. *Role conflict.* Occasionally, the job behaviors (termed one's organizational "role") expected of an individual provide a source of conflict. Generally, these sorts of conflicts fall into three categories. First, *intrarole conflict* occurs when an individual occupying a single role is subjected to stress. Organizational foremen often are subjected to contradictory expectations, as when management expects them to represent management interests during negotiations, while labor expects them to act as representatives of labor.

   Interrole conflict, on the other hand, occurs when someone is expected to simultaneously perform two different roles. Killian reports an instance of this sort of role conflict in his study of the disastrous Texas City fire.[9] When oil refineries caught fire and the blaze threatened the entire town, police were confronted with competing role demands: to play their "police" role by trying to protect the town's populace or to undertake their "father" role by looking after their families. In every case except one (a policeman whose family was out of town), the policemen chose the role that was more important to them and tended to their families. They experienced role conflict and resolved it by selecting the role they judged most important.

   Finally, *interpersonal role conflict* occurs when two or more individuals seek the same role position, as when two young executives compete for the same promotion or when roles overlap so that two or more people are called on to do the same things in different ways at the same time. Parents disciplining a child in different ways are an example of this second role-conflict type.

8. *Status conflict.* An important element of any organization is status, or the ranking of roles in the organization according to importance. Organizational members usually seek increases in status, which are achieved through promotions and accompanied by an increased number of status symbols: a bigger office, perhaps with a window; a larger desk; a personal parking space; or a key to the executive washroom. However, an item symbolizing status may be not only a source of motivation but a source of conflict. In past years, new members of an organization have entered at the bottom of the hierarchy and "worked their way up the ladder." With the advent of new technologies and an increased emphasis upon expertise and specialization, highly qualified and trained young specialists now are superseding older organizational members, much to the latter's dismay. Working for someone who is younger and has less seniority has produced a great deal of status conflict among older subordinates in modern organizations.

9. *Personal differences and incompatibilities.* Individuals may simply not like one another, thus contributing to organizational conflict. Differences in background,

education, socialization, age, and expectations can produce different needs, perceptions, and goals. As noted above, if those differences stem from different attitudes and values, the resulting conflicts can be severe. In communicative exchanges involving individuals who are personally incompatible, discussions can become highly emotional and take on moral overtones.

10. *Environmental stress.* From a systems perspective, such stress is a major source of conflict. Other conflict sources can only become more salient in a stressful environment. Over the past few years, for instance, many large organizations have been downsizing, resulting in many people losing their jobs. When workers feel their jobs are threatened, and especially if there is much uncertainty about the rules by which the organization is operating, they will likely respond with frustration, hostility, and increased competitiveness.

Styles of Conflict Management

Researchers have discussed different conflict management styles since the mid-1960s. Among the first were Blake and Mouton, whose five-category conflict management grid was soon replicated and refined by others.[10] Blake and Mouton conceptualized conflict style as a characteristic mode or a habitual way that a person handles a dispute. Style can also be viewed as an orientation toward conflict or conflict tactics and strategies

Figure 11.1
Conflict management styles.

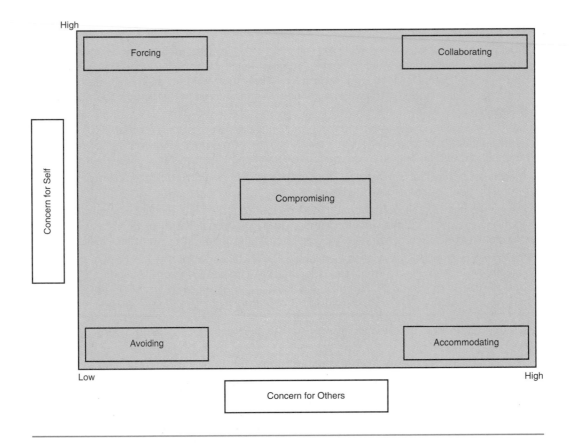

(either planned or enacted).[11] The styles studied generally emanate from a five-category scheme based on concern for self (or task) and concern for others. The five conflict styles (while variously labeled) are depicted in figure 11.1.

The first conflict style is *avoiding*. Although aware of conflict at a cognitive level, the person using this style may withdraw by removing herself (psychologically or physically) from the conflict situation, refraining from arguing, or simply failing to confront. If the conflict is over serious or complex issues, avoidance behaviors may contribute to frustration, deny others' feelings, and generally aggravate the problem. Moreover, at a practical level, in organizational settings where interdependent tasks are commonly addressed, long-term avoidance is probably not an achievable strategy.

At the other extreme of managing conflict is *forcing*. Those who employ this style rely on coercion rather than on persuasion or collaboration. They use assertiveness, verbal dominance, and perseverance. When all else fails, they resort to their position power or formal authority, ordering others to comply simply because they are in charge.

Less direct, manipulative forms of forcing are also possible, however. For instance, a manager with a forcing style might manipulate the composition of a committee so that the solution he prefers emerges through a "democratic" process. Although forcing may be effective in some situations (where, for instance, quick action is required), when repeatedly used as a conflict style, it tends to breed hostility and resentment.

The third conflict style is *accommodating,* an approach that glosses over differences, plays down disagreements, and generally trivializes conflict. In the ultimate sense, those who accommodate simply give in, setting aside their own concerns and surrendering to those of others. Those who smooth over conflicts basically accommodate others, often with the goal of maintaining pleasant interpersonal relationships. Occasionally, accommodating is used strategically when someone sets aside her concerns on a particular issue, with the hope that the next time there is conflict, the other person will "owe her one." Whether or not this strategy is effective depends upon whether the terms of the accommodation are understood, as well as the standards governing the other party's actions. Accommodating is most appropriately used when the person who chooses to accommodate truly perceives the issue as trivial.

As an even-handed approach to conflict, the *compromising* style carries considerable appeal. Compromising involves searching for an intermediate position, splitting the difference, and meeting the opponent halfway. Thus, for both parties, partial satisfaction is achieved. Unlike the first three approaches, compromising appears fair and requires considerable effort and interaction (presumably involving both persuading and listening). The difficulty with compromising as a typical conflict style is that it is, above all, expedient. When used consistently, it sends the message that the individual is more interested in resolving the conflict than in actually finding an excellent solution to the problem. Moreover, no one is ever fully satisfied. While there are no real losers, neither are there any real winners. The feeling of accomplishment that can grow from working through a problem to consensus is never realized through compromise.

Finally, the preferred conflict style in many organizational contexts is *collaborating* or *problem solving.* This style calls upon the disputants to face the conflict openly and directly and to seek, by working together, an integrative solution. Collaboration grows from a trust-building process. It encourages everyone to express themselves assertively while reinforcing the value of listening to others and approaching the problem constructively. Consistent with notions of supportive communication behaviors and attitudes discussed in chapter 2, the collaborative approach demands a focus on the problem and its thoughtful analysis rather than on placing blame. It works best in organizational environments that foster openness, directness, and equality. With collaboration, the integrative approach to problem solving (as defined earlier) must prevail wherein the "pie" is expanded by avoiding fixed, inflexible, incompatible positions. For complex, important issues, the collaborative approach is preferable, both in the quality of the outcome achieved and the feelings of empowerment that grow from people having successfully exercised their problem-solving skills in addressing a significant issue.

While the collaborative approach is consistently hailed as effective in managing conflict, it is not always the most appropriate conflict management style for every situation. For instance, collaboration is not appropriate when the conflict is trivial and quick decisions are required. Avoidance may be quite effective for handling less important and highly volatile issues, and forcing may be appropriate for crisis situations or for moving forward with unpopular courses of action.[12] Problem solving or collaboration generally works well in situations where parties are interdependent, where supporting and implementing the solution is required, and where the conflict stems from ambiguity or inadequate shared information.

The limited or inadequate use of the collaborative style in managing conflicts has resulted in considerable speculation. Some argue that problem solving is not taught by our society as a way of life. Instead, the emphasis is upon obeying authority figures, such as teachers and parents. When children mature and eventually become authority figures, they may expect to be obeyed or to dominate others. This power-oriented view inhibits the individual's ability to choose problem solving or collaboration as a natural conflict management style.[13] Moreover, in comparison with any other style, collaboration requires a greater degree of time, energy, and commitment.[14] Thus, the combined problems—lack of skill in constructive confrontation and an unwillingness or inability to expend the necessary time, energy, or commitment—serve to diminish the extent to which collaboration is used in conflict situations.

Whatever the conflict style or strategy chosen, its effective implementation will depend on the disputants' ability to adapt to the situation, their fairness and objectivity in approaching the conflict, and the way in which they communicate.[15] There are many different ways of forcing, for instance—ranging from soft, persistent argument to unpleasant, loudly projected references to one's power and authority. Others will react differently, depending on the specific verbal and nonverbal communicative behaviors that make up the overall conflict style. Moreover, timing is important. Executives report that early intervention is critically related to effective conflict management—the longer the delay, the more likely the conflict will escalate, perhaps out of control.[16]

Structural Intervention in Managing Conflict: Third-Party Methods

When the conflicting parties are unwilling or unable to arrive at a resolution to their situation, they may resort to calling in a neutral third party for assistance. In this way, they extend or elaborate on the negotiation process. The third party could be a supervisor (in conflicts between employees), an upper-level manager (in conflicts between two departments), the chief executive officer (in conflicts between divisions), a government-appointed mediator (in labor-management disputes), or a judge in a courtroom (in conflicts between organizations). In these situations, the third party could play one of two roles: the *arbitrator,* who, after hearing both sides of the issue, makes a decision that both parties must live by, or the *mediator,* who tries to facilitate communication between the parties so that they can work through their problems and arrive at a decision of their own. Although both processes rely on communication to manage information and exert social influence, mediation is a type of facilitation that hinges almost exclusively on communication for its success.[17]

The mediator's task requires sensitivity. Assisting with the logical, decision-making part of the conflict is only a small part of the mediator's role. Because conflicts have usually escalated before the mediator becomes involved, she or he often finds that the parties are no longer particularly logical. Thus, the mediator will have to deal with a number of nonrational postures shaped by hurt feelings, a preoccupation with settling old scores, defensiveness, and distorted perceptions. Mediators, however, also have an advantage in this task. Because they are not as emotionally involved as are the disputants, they are usually much better able to maintain a proper perspective.

Mediators use varied tactics, including directive, nondirective, procedural, and reflexive techniques.[18] *Directive tactics* allow the mediator to exert substantive control over the negotiation by recommending proposals, giving opinions about positions, assessing the costs associated with demands, and occasionally including compliance.[19] In general, directive tactics are more effective in the latter stages of mediation than in early meetings.[20] *Nondirective tactics* capitalize on the mediator's role in securing information for the disputants and in clarifying misunderstandings. Thus, the mediator may act as a conduit by passing information between the parties or as a clarifier by paraphrasing messages and narrowing topics for discussion.[21] As *procedural tactics,* the mediator may organize separate or joint sessions, establish protocol for the sessions, regulate the agenda, and establish deadlines. Finally, mediators may use *reflexive tactics* by influencing the affective tone of the mediation—developing rapport with participants, using humor, and speaking the language of both sides. Effective mediators use a combination of these tactics, although they report that reflexive tactics are more effective than directive and nondirective ones in facilitating joint collaboration.[22] Clearly, communication is central to the mediation process. As Kolb points out, mediators are like the directors of a drama, who set the scene, manage impressions, orchestrate the script, and maintain dramatic inquiry throughout the process.[23]

Fortunately, most groups and organizations are able to manage their own conflict through negotiation and bargaining rather than having to call in third parties. Effective outcomes are more likely to be realized when individuals voluntarily solve their own disputes than when leaders or other third parties are asked to intervene. Thus, developing an understanding of productive collaborative approaches to managing conflict is crucial.

Collaborative Conflict Management

Where it is possible and desirable to approach conflict from a problem-solving perspective, several integrative negotiation strategies have been shown to foster collaboration.[24] First, and perhaps most important, is *establishing superordinate goals*. The parties involved in the conflict should begin by focusing on what they share in common. As individuals become aware of the salience of their shared goals—for example, greater productivity, a safer work environment, lower costs, a fairer evaluation system, or improved working relationships—they tend to become sensitized to the merits of resolving their differences so that these mutual goals will not be jeopardized. When consensus on common goals is achieved, the disputants can begin to examine their specific differences. Once established, superordinate goals must be referred to throughout the deliberations. Some researchers have cautioned, however, that superordinate goals are more likely to reduce perceived rather than underlying conflict.[25] Whether or not superordinate goals are helpful depends on the groups developing a culture for mutual understanding and constructive interaction patterns.[26]

Another important collaborative behavior involves *separating the people from the problem*. Having defined the mutual benefits to be gained by successfully resolving the conflict, attention must be directed to the real issue at hand—solving a problem. Negotiations are more likely to result in mutual satisfaction if the parties depersonalize the discussions. The participants might benefit from viewing each other as advocates for differing points of view rather than rivals. They may need to suppress their desire for personal revenge or one-upmanship. From a communicative perspective, a person would refer to "an unreasonable argument" rather than calling her counterpart "an unreasonable person." In general, it is crucial to avoid loaded language, such as labeling others' ideas as stupid, crazy, naive, fascist, or ill-conceived.

In the preceding chapter, we discussed the importance of groups identifying and using criteria for determining the quality of alternative solutions to a problem.

BUSINESS BRIEF

11.5

Problem-Solving Negotiations

Participants in the Harvard Negotiation Project suggest an alternative to positional bargaining that they call "principled negotiation" or "negotiation on the merits." This problem-solving approach can be summarized in four points:

People: Separate the people from the problem. The participants should see themselves as working side-by-side, attacking the problem rather than each other.

Interests: Focus on interests, not positions. Rather than focusing on people's stated positions, the object of a negotiation should be to satisfy their underlying interests.

Options: Generate a variety of possibilities before deciding what to do. Searching for one "right" solution inhibits creativity and narrows vision. A designated time should be set aside to develop a range of possible solutions that advance shared interests and creatively reconcile differing interests.

Criteria: Insist that the result be based on some objective standard. Developing a set of criteria whereby possible solutions might be judged (such as market value, expert opinion, custom or law) ultimately will help to arrive at a fair solution.

From Roger Fisher and William Ury, "Getting to Yes," *Management Review* 48 (1982): 16–21.

In situations involving conflict, *articulating and using objective criteria* is equally crucial. No matter how many goals are shared, some interests are bound to be incompatible. Rather than seizing on these as opportunities for testing wills, determining what is fair is far more productive. This requires that both parties agree on how fairness should be judged. As objective criteria are discussed and agreed upon, individuals begin to shift their thinking from "getting what I want" to "deciding what makes most sense"—fostering an attitude of reasonableness and open-mindedness.

Also related to the open-minded pursuit of solutions is *focusing on interests, not positions*. In bargaining and negotiation settings, positions are thought of as bottom-line demands the negotiator makes. By contrast, interests constitute the substructure of the evidence and reasoning underlying the demands. Establishing agreement on interests is easier because they tend to be broader and multifaceted. Achieving agreement, however, even on interests, involves a fair measure of creativity in redefining and broadening the problem to make it more tractable. For instance, once a problem has been defined, there are a variety of ways to enlarge, alter, or replace it. If a problem such as sagging productivity has been defined in a specific way (for example, worker laziness), other contributing causes exist and can be articulated. Thus, one way to proceed is by generating at least two alternative hypotheses for every problem discussed. The strategy is to broaden the problem definition by thinking in plural rather than singular terms.

In recent years, Chrysler Corporation and the United Auto Workers (UAW) have worked cooperatively to develop a more effective, less acrimonious approach to contract negotiations. A key element of that effort has been the development of "modern operating agreements" (or MOAs) for some Chrysler plants.

The MOA concept evolved in 1986–1987 as a joint effort between Chrysler management and the UAW to improve quality and productivity on the assembly line. The objective of the MOAs was to create a more democratic work environment, and they eliminated superficial labor-management distinctions and inefficient practices; reduced job classifications, supervisory personnel, and union representatives; and established self-directed work teams and a pay system that rewards workers for their job-related knowledge.

Each MOA has a team that participates in daily audits, assists in developing work assignments, corrects minor and reports major tooling and maintenance problems, provides input regarding production standards, assists in planning work methods, monitors and controls performance, coordinates overtime work, arranges vacation schedules, and performs various other tasks.

Generally, MOA plants have reported reduced operating costs, lower turnover, fewer grievances, and lower absenteeism. All of this has been a direct result of the realization that the company and the union share common interests and that working together rather than as adversaries more effectively serves those interests.

The questions should be phrased, "What are the problems?" "What are the meanings of this?" "What are the results?" Another possibility is to reverse the problem's definition by contradicting the currently accepted definition to expand the number of perspectives considered. For instance, a problem might be that morale is too high instead of too low or that a work environment is characterized by too little rather than too much structure. Opposites and backward looks often enhance creativity. When a variety of interests and problem definitions are examined, individuals are better able to understand each other's points of view and place their own views in perspective. The integrative question is "Help me understand why you are advocating that position?"

Another negotiation strategy requiring creativity is *inventing options for mutual gains*. Here, however, the creativity is focused on generating unusual solutions. While some negotiations may necessarily be distributive, negotiators should never begin by adopting a win-lose posture. By focusing both parties' attention on brainstorming alternative, mutually agreeable solutions, the negotiation dynamics naturally shift from competitive to collaborative. Moreover, the more options and combinations there are to explore, the greater the probability of reaching an integrative solution. Both goodwill and creativity are required as the parties ask, "What can we do that we haven't tried before?"

Several small group techniques discussed in the preceding chapter might prove useful, both in defining interests and problems and in generating solutions. Brainstorming (where ideas are tossed out without evaluation) is one potential technique. In addition, the nominal group procedure might be used, in which each participant brainstorms on paper, then the ideas are collected, shared, and discussed. Finally, group support systems allow for computer-assisted brainstorming, encouraging creativity and preserving anonymity. Whatever approach to brainstorming is employed, those who participate in the process are basically asking, "Now that we better understand each other's underlying concerns and objectives, let's brainstorm ways of satisfying both our needs."

Finally, the parties' approach to the notion of "success" is critical. By maintaining a realistic, optimistic attitude, *success can be defined in terms of gains, not losses.* The employee who seeks a 12 percent raise and receives an 8 percent raise can choose to view that outcome as either an accomplishment (that is, a gain over the present situation) or as a disappointment (in that expectations were not realized). Whichever interpretation, the objective outcome is the same, but the employee's satisfaction is likely to vary significantly. Individual reactions to an outcome are greatly influenced by the standards used to judge it. Thus, the agreed-upon criteria are especially salient and should be called upon to judge the value of the proposed solution or outcome. The question to be asked is, "Does this outcome constitute a meaningful improvement over current conditions?"

Using Technology as a Tool to Manage Conflict

In other chapters, we have shown how technology might be used to facilitate communication, team building, leadership, and organizational change. Here, we examine how technology can be used to manage conflict, and, in particular, we identify factors that may influence its impact on *groups* experiencing conflict.

All groups experience conflict at one time or another. In decision-making ventures aimed at building consensus, for example, actions taken or decisions made will clearly not meet with everyone's complete approval. Consensus is difficult to reach since most of us find it difficult on occasion to compromise our views. To help us make progress, we may choose to adopt external ground rules or guidelines to structure our group interactions, with the goal of approaching our tasks more positively and productively. For instance, Hall and Watson's guidelines might be used to help minimize conflict.[27] These guidelines instruct group members to:

1. Avoid arguing for your own evaluation. Approach the task on the basis of logic.
2. Avoid changing your mind only to avoid conflict. Support only solutions with which you are somewhat able to agree.
3. Treat differences of opinion as indicative of an incomplete sharing of relevant information.
4. View differences of opinion as both natural and helpful rather than as a hindrance in decision making.

Kare Anderson offers a three-step procedure that she terms "triangle talk" as a means of handling conflict more effectively. In her view, the tendencies most people have to either fight back or withdraw from conflicts can best be overcome by:

1. Knowing exactly what you want. By asking yourself "What do I want in this situation," you can gain greater control and focus.
2. Finding out what the other person wants and making him or her feel heard. Knowing the other person's objectives provides a basis for negotiations.
3. Proposing action in a way the other person can accept. This helps create the top of the triangle—the common ground between the two sides.

These three steps are best achieved by asking questions, Anderson contends. Vague, general questions should be used initially (such as "What do you think about this situation?"), but more specific questions should be used as negotiations continue ("Exactly what would make this proposal work better for you?").

From Kare Anderson, *Getting What You Want: How to Reach Agreement and Resolve Conflict Every Time* (New York: Penguin Books, 1993).

During group meetings, conflicts may surface as ideas are generated, explored, consolidated, and evaluated—in other words, throughout the decision-making process. In an idea generation activity, for example, the brainstorming process can create polarization effects since each individual learns, perhaps for the first time, how other group members view the issue being discussed. In some cases, a particular group member may assume, before the meeting, that others support the same job candidate, course of action, or policy that he does. As views are expressed during a meeting, however, he may learn that he is wrong. When brainstorming is used to generate ideas, McGrath recommends that groups adopt techniques designed to:

1. Make sure that the creativity of each individual is not stifled by social influence processes that often operate in groups. Fear of social embarrassment, conformity pressures, and status systems that inhibit participation by low status members should be actively discouraged.
2. Take maximum advantage of whatever creativity-enhancing forces may operate in groups. Social support, reinforcement for contributing, and cross-stimulation of group members should be promoted.[28]

We have already seen that technology provides unique opportunities for channeling and supporting group work. Computer systems, particularly group and negotiation support systems, can act as intervention mechanisms to specifically address issues related to group conflict management.

Technology plays an increasingly prominent role in collaborative problem-solving ventures.

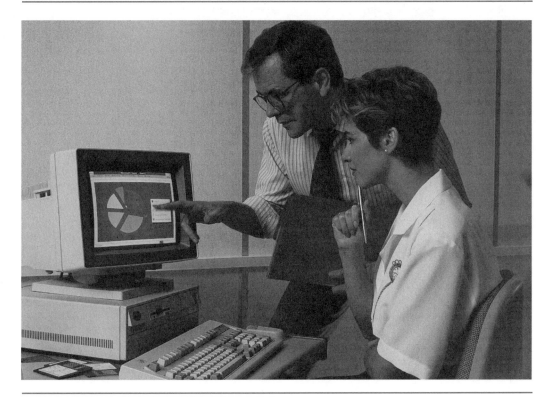

According to Argyris, *intervention* involves entering into a system of relationships, coming between or among persons, groups, or objects for the purpose of helping them.[29] The interventionist is someone or something that enters an ongoing system or set of relationships primarily to achieve three tasks:

1. to help generate valid and useful information,
2. to create conditions in which individuals can make informed and free choices, and
3. to help clients develop an internal commitment to their choice.

With regard to conflict management, group process interventions should consist of activities that help to promote:

a cooperative climate,

a focus on problems, not emotional issues,

an orderly and organized process,

consideration of a wide range of alternative solutions, and

avoidance of artificial conflict-reducing techniques, such as relying on the leader for making the final decision.[30]

Group support systems employ software and hardware to promote and enforce these conditions. GSS act as a group process intervention by:

1. imposing process-related structure on the meeting,
2. providing an electronic meeting channel that can improve communication among group members, and
3. delivering a structured heuristic to analyze the problem or task.

As we noted in chapter 9, GSS allow anonymous input and parallel and simultaneous processing, encouraging group member participation since views can be aired without inhibition or constraints. GSS also facilitate the imposition of decision-making heuristics and meeting agendas. These can help keep groups on track while allowing them to systematically work through conflict. And the ability of GSS to provide an electronic record of the meeting can help group members share a common understanding of what has transpired in their meetings.

Researchers Poole, Holmes, and DeSanctis conducted one of the first and the most extensive studies designed to test the impact of GSS on group conflict management.[31] In their study, they compared groups using GSS to groups using only paper and pencils and groups using no support at all. Discovering mixed results, the researchers concluded that GSS does not necessarily directly determine conflict interaction or outcomes. Rather, they argue, it is the *way* groups use the technology that mediates its impact. They found, for instance, that some GSS groups used the structure better than others.

Despite their mixed findings, Poole, Holmes, and DeSanctis remain confident that GSS can provide a number of benefits for conflict management. Because of the anonymity feature, GSS can, they argue, distance people from ideas, thereby depersonalizing and sometimes defusing difficult conflict situations. GSS make conflict management procedures salient to group members, bringing order to group meetings. In addition, procedures such as voting can surface hidden conflicts.

The impact of GSS on conflict management likely depends on the nature of the GSS and how the group applies it. Poole, Holmes, and DeSanctis note that the GSS used in their study had no specialized conflict management capabilities. Moreover, a facilitator was not used in these GSS sessions. In all likelihood, a facilitator might have been able to help more groups adapt GSS in a manner conducive to productive conflict management. Users of any technology are influenced by expectations. How GSS is explained to users and the level of training they are provided will surely influence how they will use the technology in conflict situations.

Another technology available for groups to use in resolving conflicts is *negotiation support systems*—decision support technologies that specifically focus on providing computerized assistance for situations in which group members strongly disagree on factual or value judgments.[32] Negotiation support systems are interactive, computer-based tools that are specifically intended to support negotiating parties in reaching an agreement.[33] These systems focus on enhancing the prospect of consensus with the intent of making compromise possible.

Negotiation support systems may include decision support software with modeling capabilities, such as decision trees, risk analysis, forecasting methods, and multiattribute functions, as well as software supporting structured group methods, such as electronic brainstorming, nominal grouping, and delphi techniques. Some of these systems even include artificial intelligence to help groups define and solve problems. Many commercial software products are available (including GSS) that encompass some or all of these features.

Ironically, computer systems themselves have been a source of conflict in employee-management relations. Savage points out that many labor unions were once vociferous in their crusade against office automation.[34] They felt, with some justification, that technology threatened a loss of jobs for their members. However, many unions have come full circle and now offer training in computer use to enhance their members' development and advancement opportunities. Instead of simply using technology training to retrain members whose skills are being passed by, Savage notes, many unions have embraced technology to further their goals and to keep members abreast of computer skills. For example, the Air Line Pilots Association, whose pilots are already computer-literate, has established services for members to access information about new technologies and to facilitate communication and negotiations with their employers.

Summary

Conflict is a controversial subject. Even among those who herald its virtues, ambivalence persists. In organizations, however, the reality of interdependence, competition for scarce resources, and the necessity of coping with change while working together on all sorts of tasks create conditions where conflict is inevitable. The types and sources of conflict are numerous, perplexing, and often tenacious. Even so, individuals at all organizational levels can learn under the appropriate circumstances to approach conflict cooperatively and collaboratively. On occasion, technology may function as a source of conflict, but it also offers new and ever-changing tools for groups to use in managing conflicts. With conflict comes the opportunity for growth and change, for innovation and empowerment, for problem solving and consensus building. Those who learn to confront their differences openly and honestly, to communicate about their differences with sensitivity and integrity, can contribute to a constructive and satisfying organizational climate.

Questions for Discussion

1. What are some ways in which conflict can be good for an organization and some ways that it can be bad?
2. In what settings can conflict occur?
3. What are approach-approach, approach-avoidance, and avoidance-avoidance conflict?
4. Explain the idea that "every organization is in partial conflict with every other social agent it deals with."

5. How can conflict become institutionalized?
6. Describe three types of role conflict.
7. When does increased communication fail to reduce conflict?
8. How effective is avoidance in resolving conflict? Why?
9. Compare and contrast the five styles of conflict management.
10. Describe some of the key steps in collaborative conflict management.
11. How can technology be used as a tool in managing conflict?

Exercises

1. Relate the systems concept of organizations and the concepts of conflict resolution discussed in this chapter. From a systems perspective, what sorts of conflict should be expected most often, and what methods of conflict reduction should be most effective?
2. Think of an organization to which you now belong or to which you belonged in the past. List one instance of each conflict setting that occurred in that organization and how it was (or should have been) resolved.
3. Tim Hill is a mediator who has been asked to work with the Major League Baseball Player's Association and the Major League Owner's Association to help them resolve their long-standing feud over players' salaries and right not to be traded without the player's consent. What advice would you give Tim before the meetings begin?
4. Think of a time in your life when you experienced some conflict, preferably in a job-related situation. In a brief essay, describe the nature and extent of your conflict, the contexts in which it occurred, and the methods you and others used to manage the conflict. To what extent did you resolve the conflict? What other methods would you have tried if you had it to do over again?
5. Choose an organization and arrange for an interview with someone in a management position. As you interview this individual, address some of these issues:
   a. In what ways has this organization experienced conflict?
   b. What role, if any, has the union played in conflicts that have occurred?
   c. What kinds of groups or departments within the organization experience the most conflict? Why?
   d. What approaches to resolving conflicts have been tried? To what extent have they been successful?
   e. Is conflict beneficial in any way? If so, how? If not, why not?
   f. What are some different techniques of conflict resolution that might yet be tried?

Public Communication

PART
4

Public speaking, which is the best way to motivate a large group, is entirely different from private conversation. A speaker may be well informed, but if he hasn't thought out exactly what he wants to say today, to this audience, he has no business taking up other people's valuable time.

—LEE IACOCCA, IACOCCA: AN AUTOBIOGRAPHY

CHAPTER
12

Preparing for and Supporting the Public Speech

peaking in public is an increasingly common organizational communication activity. While administrators, board directors, and other executives have always made speeches, today professional men and women of varied occupations are called upon to speak with increasing regularity.[1] Consider these examples: (1) A lawyer talks to an organization of concerned parents about the legality of textbook censorship; (2) An obstetrician informs a group of expectant mothers about alternative methods of childbirth; (3) An accountant speaks to a local Rotary Club, giving them some tips on how to file their income tax returns; (4) An educator addresses a group of fellow teachers in an effort to get them to unionize; and (5) A social worker speaks to a group of junior high school students about the use of illegal drugs. Clearly, regardless of your occupation—whether you are an educator, a social worker, a realtor, or a salesperson—you are likely to be asked to make some speeches throughout your professional life.

Many believe that the most critical skills any prospective organizational employee can possess may be the ability to speak effectively and write clearly. Economist Peter Drucker exemplifies this view when he notes that colleges teach the one thing that is most valuable for the future employee to know: the ability to organize and express ideas in writing and speaking.[2] Unfortunately, many bright young men and women graduate from college every year without having mastered these vital skills. In fact, it is often only when they are confronted with the realities of their first jobs that they recognize how frequently they must write reports and letters and inform and persuade varied audiences in public speaking situations.

Among the decisions each public speaker must make are how to choose a good speech subject, how to analyze the audience's interests and values, how to find and assess information, how to organize information coherently, and how to deliver the speech effectively. The first task, however, is choosing an appropriate topic.

Selecting the Speech Topic

Whenever you are asked to make a speech, you are faced with one of two basic situations: (1) the topic is suggested, or (2) you are told to speak about anything of your choice (occasionally, within some rather broad perimeters). Often a topic is suggested that is related to your job. Automotive executives are asked to speak about the impact of the nation's economic woes on their industry; journalists are invited to discuss media coverage of controversial trials; and teachers are asked to talk about pedagogical innovations.

The other kind of public speaking invitation you may receive is to "talk about anything you like." You may be asked to speak because someone in the audience knows you are a good speaker, or perhaps the audience wants a prominent citizen (you) to speak to them so that they can receive positive publicity and attract a sizable crowd. On still other occasions, you will be given a general subject area within which you are free to select a specific topic. You may be told to talk about the economy, law, religion, or politics. Because such broad subjects can be pursued in countless ways, the major job of choosing a topic remains your responsibility in these situations. For many speakers, having to choose the subject presents a problem, since though the possible topics seem endless, no *one* is quite appropriate. In fact, many speakers spend an inordinate amount of time on topic selection and are left with inadequate time for researching, organizing, and practicing. Yet topic selection can be approached rather systematically if potential topics are examined in relationship to four major perspectives: (1) *personal,* (2) *audience,* (3) *situational,* and (4) *organizational.*

Personal Perspective

Certainly the richest source of speech ideas resides within you as an individual. Begin, then, with some assessment of your *personal knowledge, experiences, attitudes,* and *beliefs.* Speeches vary in purpose; yet each is essentially a *personal statement* from you as a speaker to others who choose or are asked to listen. You may want to select a topic about which you already know a good deal but would like to learn more. Sometimes with this approach, it is necessary to engage in thorough library research. On other occasions, you need only organize your thinking into some effective, appealing strategy. More often, some of both procedures is required. Your personal interest in a subject may evolve from intellectual enthusiasm and curiosity as well as from firsthand experiences. Not every speaker has traveled extensively, worked for twenty years in a hospital, or written speeches for a prominent political candidate. What is important, however, is that you have certain kinds of *secondary experiences.* You have read books, seen movies, and listened to lectures and speeches. You have access to great quantities of information concerning current events from such sources as newspapers and news magazines. Moreover, because of your interests, values, and beliefs, you have acquired information and ideas on some subjects of persistent controversy—such as suicide, religion, the role of government, marriage, and drug use and abuse. With controversial topics such as these, you have the challenging task of focusing them specifically to avoid an overly general, superficial analysis. Since most audience members are probably familiar with the basic aspects of these issues, it is particularly crucial that you approach these subjects with freshness and creativity.

Sometimes conducting a self-inventory of your interests and experiences can be helpful. Business Brief 12.1 presents some factors to consider as you go through a thorough, thoughtful self-assessment.

The Perspective of the Audience

The second major perspective from which any potential topic should be considered is the *audience.* It is usually wise to select a subject about which the audience has some information but would enjoy learning more. Normally, speech requests are accompanied by some reference to time limits; that is, no speaker is free to talk for three or four hours. In fact, most public speeches are delivered in twenty to thirty minutes. If you elect to pursue a substantive topic, it is imperative that the audience have some initial information so that your remarks are understood.

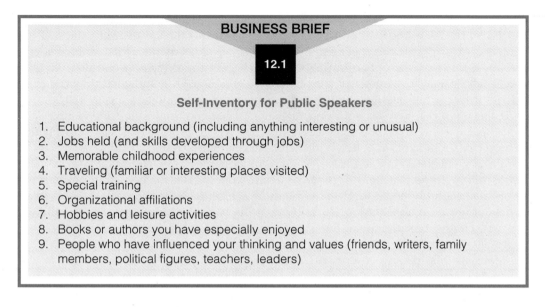

Let us say, for example, that a representative of General Motors chooses to speak on some of GM's automotive innovations in response to the fuel shortage to an audience composed of business and professional women. Although the speaker may assume that his all-female audience is not extremely knowledgeable about automotive technology, he can be reasonably sure that they are well aware of the nation's overall economic condition, of the basic dimensions of the energy shortage, and of some general responses of automobile designers and manufacturers to fuel consumption problems. As a result, the speaker can spend most of his time discussing specific features of particular models (probably with the assistance of visual aids) and plans for future innovations. Notice that this topic is a good, manageable choice for this audience because of the assumed level of audience knowledge and predicted interest in the subject.

Every speech topic, then, should be selected with an equal concern for speaker and audience needs, values, and interests. Both you and your listeners must be "turned on" if the communication exchange is to be meaningful and reciprocal. Too often we view public speaking as singularly source-oriented—that is, a chance for one person to hold another group captive while the former "speaks his or her mind." Yet, communication can be personally and socially significant only if *reciprocal exchange* occurs.

In choosing a subject, there are a number of *audience-related dimensions* to be considered. At the most basic level, contemplate potential subjects with regard to the *demographic characteristics* of the audience, including age, gender, socioeconomic status, and educational level. This kind of information helps you select a topic, and it also provides clues to *how* to handle a given topic tastefully and persuasively. The subject "Death and Dying" is a topic relevant to everyone. Yet the manner in which you approach its discussion would vary considerably if you were addressing a group of teenagers rather than a group of elderly citizens.

Also, seek information about the *social, economic, political,* and *religious beliefs* of the audience. Such knowledge may provide insights into the needs and values of the audience. With persuasive speaking, in particular, an assessment of such values is crucial. As soon as you accept an invitation to speak, it is appropriate to question the individual who contacted you about his or her perceptions of the audience's interests and values. If the group has regularly scheduled meetings, you might want to visit one of their meetings before your speaking engagement, spend some time interacting with them, and observe their reactions to another speaker. It is important to avoid making stereotypic assumptions about an audience based on minimal information.

Finally, in selecting a topic, you might consider the *audience's immediate background.* Some people, for example, share concerns and have common interests in problems simply because of the context or setting in which they find themselves. Speakers are commonly asked to address groups such as prison inmates, military officers, clergy, or college students. As a student enrolled in a basic business and professional communication course, you will often address your classmates. Your audience in this instance represents a diversity of religions, political views, intelligence, and socioeconomic levels. But because they share the bond of attending college, they have common interests. So such topics as grade inflation, the job market, the university's grading system, graduation requirements, faculty evaluation, and university ratings would all be potentially relevant.

The Situational Perspective

Closely related to this last dimension of audience analysis is the third major perspective from which you might consider speech subjects, the *occasion.* Every year organizations celebrate anniversaries, schools go into virtual hysterics over sports victories, and towns have parades and festivals in honor of their own. If you are asked to speak for such an occasion, it is vital that you be sensitive to its meaning in the lives of your audience. Once in a while a speaker is unaware of the occasion being marked until he or she arrives to make the speech. If this should ever happen to you, seriously consider the impact of the occasion on your audience and the degree to which you might alter your handling of the subject to meet the demands of the situation.

Time is a critical factor. As we stated earlier, most public speeches last from twenty to thirty minutes. It is not unusual, however, for a speaker to be restricted to fifteen minutes or, at the other extreme, allotted a full hour. The focus of your topic would vary greatly in each of these instances. There are occasions when it is appropriate to provide a kind of broad overview of a topic or problem (if, for example, the audience is poorly informed). More commonly, a narrower subject with a greater depth of handling is preferable.

The Organizational Perspective

The final perspective from which you might consider topic selection is that of the *organization* you are representing. When you are called upon to make a public speech, it is often because of your affiliation with a specific organization. Consider the young

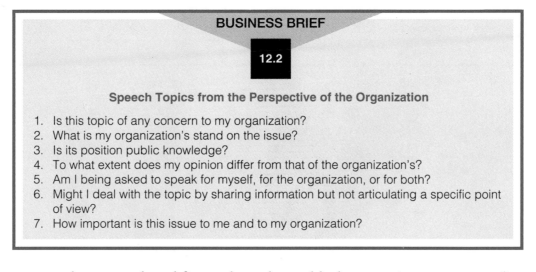

BUSINESS BRIEF

12.2

Speech Topics from the Perspective of the Organization

1. Is this topic of any concern to my organization?
2. What is my organization's stand on the issue?
3. Is its position public knowledge?
4. To what extent does my opinion differ from that of the organization's?
5. Am I being asked to speak for myself, for the organization, or for both?
6. Might I deal with the topic by sharing information but not articulating a specific point of view?
7. How important is this issue to me and to my organization?

woman who was a talented first-grade teacher and had a reputation as an outstanding speaker. Whenever she was asked to speak, she usually selected a topic related to her professional organizational membership, such as stimulating creativity in the very young child, the advantages and disadvantages of teaching children to read before formal schooling, or dealing with hyperactivity in children.

Of course, once the topic is actually selected, the notion of organizational representation may have some added impact. If the chosen subject is controversial—perhaps one about which the organization has taken a formal public stand—consider the degree to which your personal view coincides with the organization's and the possible advantages and disadvantages of any dissension.

In the teaching example just mentioned, suppose that the school's formal policy is to discourage parents from teaching their children to read before school. Assume further that the speaker's position is that children should be stimulated as much as possible before going to school, including learning to read if they express interest and ability in this area. Clearly the position of the school and the personal views of the teacher do not coincide on this issue. The speaker must then make a choice. Should she discard this subject due to the incompatibility of views? Should she make it a point to speak her mind, in part, perhaps, to test the open-mindedness of the school's administrators? Might she speak on the topic but handle it in such a way that she presents a good deal of information and a variety of viewpoints in a descriptive manner without actually identifying her own? These are questions of practical and ethical significance. Clearly, you need to consider the organization you are representing as you go about the task of selecting a speech topic. This does not mean that you are simply an outlet through which your organization communicates its views to the public. But the organization does create some constraints and a framework in which you must operate. As you begin to think about possible speech topics, you might consider the questions raised in Business Brief 12.2. In addition, figure 12.1 depicts the four subject selection perspectives we have discussed.

Figure 12.1
Perspectives for topic selection.

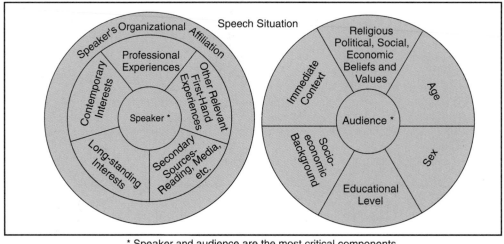

* Speaker and audience are the most critical components.

Just as the nature of the topic chosen should reflect a consideration of the individual, the audience, the situation, and the organization, the way in which the topic is *narrowed* and *focused* should also reveal a sensitivity to these factors. The general topic of pollution, for example, might focus on the issue of noise pollution for a group of teenagers, on the practical concerns of "how pollution affects our daily lives at the university" for a classroom audience, and how the automotive industry is attempting to cope with air pollution for an audience of business people. Once the topic has been selected with these considerations in mind, you are ready to think about the basic goal or purpose of your speech.

Choosing the Purpose

In many instances, the speech purpose is virtually assigned or, at best, tactfully implied. Not long ago we were asked to make a speech as part of the opening session for a weekend-long leadership retreat. The contact person suggested to us at once, "Now these kids [college juniors and seniors] really want something *interesting*. I mean, they've been studying and listening to lectures all week; they've got finals coming up in two or three weeks. So . . . use a little humor, make them laugh! I mean, I know you're both professors, but frankly the *last* thing we want is a *lecture*."

Aside from our amazement that he had bothered to seek out such dull, lifeless "professor types" to reduce this audience to giggling hysteria, we were perplexed by what he asked us to achieve. Specifically, he wanted us to introduce the audience to all of leadership theory, cite supporting research for each theory, give them practical guidelines for their own leadership behavior, and uplift them in such a way that they would feel moved to go forth with great pride in their positions and faith in themselves. Thus, we were to interest and entertain, inform and instruct, persuade and inspire—be combination comedians, master teachers, and evangelists! Although this example represents a rather dramatic and unusual set of public speaking demands, its atypicality is a matter of degree rather than of kind. In fact, most successful speeches *do* interest, inform, and persuade in varying proportions. Yet as you choose your topic and begin the task of narrowing and focusing, you should do so with some *basic purpose* in mind.

To Interest

Some public speeches do little more than entertain. Often the speaker has no serious intention of being either informative or persuasive. Comedians and after-dinner speakers often speak to entertain. Sometimes the speech is built around a kind of theme, frequently involving recounting a series of personal experiences, each with a humorous point. Comedian Bill Cosby does a great deal of this kind of speaking, focusing on such themes as going to the dentist, paying one's bills, and having a baby.

Most of us seldom speak publicly for the single purpose of entertainment. Even so, the general notion of entertainment in the sense of listening to something for intrinsic enjoyment or interest does have a critical place in effective public speaking. All too often we overlook the importance of *interest*. We assume that if a speech is packed full of good, factual information, and well-reasoned appeals, it is sure to be a success. We overlook the fact that information, statistics, ideas, and visual aids all must be related to the interests and needs of the audience. Without attention, listeners cannot learn; neither can they be moved, uplifted, inspired, or incited to action. Thus, every speech must interest.

It is not always easy to determine what subjects audiences will find interesting. But most audiences will respond with interest to information they perceive to be

1. *Relevant.* An audience of single parents struggling with child discipline problems, financial woes, and loneliness would be interested in hearing a family therapist discuss strategies for dealing with these problems. For an audience of happily married couples whose children are grown, however, this subject would not be particularly relevant.
2. *Useful.* A group of graduating college seniors is motivated to learn about the job market in a way that a group of retiring executives is not. For the seniors, the subject is useful.
3. *Startling, unusual, or new.* Novelty sustains attention. The speaker who presents new insights into Japanese productivity, opportunities for installing computers in homes, or innovations in genetic engineering is more likely to interest the audience than one who presents a standard treatment of drug abuse, the dangers of smoking, or abortion.
4. *Worth knowing or repeating.* Not everyone would agree on what is worth knowing. However, speeches dealing with such topics as religion, the economy, or education are likely to be perceived as substantive and worthy of invested time.

5. *Amusing or entertaining.* Some speakers' primary goal is to make the audience laugh and enjoy themselves. While this goal may sound frivolous, it is one of the most difficult to accomplish. Speeches to entertain must be carefully adapted to the particular interests and knowledge of the audience.

To Inform

For most public speakers, however, interest is only the beginning. Much public discourse is primarily *informative.* Its purpose is to teach, to impart information. On occasion, you will actually present the audience with new information; at other times, you may take familiar data and present some different perspective or interpretation.

Whenever you choose to give an informative speech, your major purpose is to *gain audience understanding.* Informative speeches should meet several criteria: (1) accuracy—the result of careful observation, study, and research; (2) completeness—the inclusion of information essential to a proper understanding of the subject; (3) unity—adherence to a central theme and clarity of thought progression; and (4) meaningfulness—related to the audience's needs, interests, and levels of understanding.[3]

Often in organizational settings informative speaking takes the form of oral technical reports, a subject we will return to in chapter 14. For example: (1) A floor supervisor explains to assembly-line workers the reason for a new job rotation schedule; (2) An attorney enlightens a group of citizens about the laws governing child abuse cases; (3) An electrical engineer explains to a school board the plans for wiring a new school complex; and (4) A salesperson presents figures to her department depicting the successful marketing of a new fluoride mouthwash. Informative speeches usually require the use of visual aids to increase clarity and enhance understanding. Because achieving audience understanding is so important, informative speeches should be followed by a question-and-answer period.

Finally, it is important to remember that not all informative speeches are purely informative. Many speakers transmit information to build a common ground of understanding before urging the audience to support a given point of view or to act in a specified way. In this manner, then, information dissemination creates a foundation for persuasion.

To Persuade

Persuasion is the final goal or purpose of public speaking. Some would argue that all communication is inherently persuasive, for even the speaker who provides factual information about specific subjects, such as how legislation is passed, how to take excellent pictures, or what the federal regulations are regarding advertising, does so with some persuasive intent of getting the audience to understand and *accept* the speaker's presentation of the facts. However, speeches that are explicitly persuasive fall into three basic categories: those whose purpose is to *stimulate, to change belief,* or *to incite to action.*

Often you will be asked to address an audience whose interests, values, feelings, and beliefs are virtually identical with your own. In this case, your strategy may be to reinforce already existing beliefs. Thus, the *speech to stimulate* does not attempt to effect change except in the sense of changing the degree of listener commitment, that is, intensifying and enhancing an already existing belief or attitude. Speeches that stimulate are quite common in political and religious settings.

Most of the time as a public speaker you will not find yourself in the position of addressing large groups of totally supportive listeners. Instead, you usually face a mixed group—some members supportive, some negative, and many undecided. On occasion, you may encounter a totally hostile audience, but these instances are also relatively rare. In any event, your strategy with many audiences is to *persuade them to believe* in your advocated proposition, solution, or interpretation. For a great many listeners, this will involve some significant change in or realignment of previously held beliefs. Changing people's beliefs is difficult, particularly those beliefs that are rooted in deep clusters of attitudes and values and have developed in response to personal experiences and observations.

It is not uncommon for listeners to respond positively to a speech, demonstrating appreciation for its language and delivery, and yet remain unmoved by its appeals. This is especially true when the speaker is advocating a *behavioral commitment* on the part of the audience. Many persuasive speeches go beyond the realm of idea acceptance and attempt to move the audience to *action*. The political candidate wants more than an affirmation of belief; he wants committed listeners who will support him at the polls. The minister desires more than believing church members; her hope is for active, involved, behaviorally committed Christians. As public speakers, we are often in positions of soliciting votes and money, of requesting commitments of time and talent, of asking people to give, to share, to show their involvement in their beliefs in some measurable way. These tasks are immensely challenging. It is quite possible to succeed in changing listeners' beliefs and still not actually move them to action.

The practical impact of this can perhaps best be illustrated by a personal example. Early in our research careers (and long before AIDS was an issue) we conducted a study in which we assembled a group of people who all had indicated rather strong negative attitudes toward the idea of giving blood to the Red Cross. We subsequently exposed them to a persuasive speech in which a young hemophiliac made a poignant plea for personal blood donations. Immediately following the speech, we administered another attitude questionnaire similar to the first. Interestingly enough, impressive reversals in attitude seemed to occur. In fact, over 70 percent of those previously opposed to giving blood now indicated not only that they favored it, but that they would donate blood if provided the opportunity! Yet when these same individuals were confronted with official Red Cross sign-up cards (as soon as the attitude questionnaires were collected), informed that the Bloodmobile would be in town during the following month, and told that transportation would be provided to and from the Bloodmobile, nearly 80 percent of those with "altered" attitudes declined to commit themselves to the *action* of donating blood. Moving listeners to believe is difficult; inspiring them to act is even more demanding. In chapter 14, we will examine persuasive strategies for changing audience attitudes and moving them to action.

Specific Purposes

Once you have some basic notion of your speech's general purpose, you are ready to consider your specific purpose. It is not adequate to say that you want to persuade the audience regarding sound investment practices. Rather, be specific about the kind of response you are seeking; have a precise goal. With that goal in mind, choose evidence, draw conclusions, organize your arguments, and select a fitting delivery style.

The specific purpose of your speech should be phrased in terms of the audience response you are seeking. It is a good practice to write out a precise purpose statement specifying what you intend to accomplish. Some examples follow:

My purpose is to persuade the audience to invest their savings in money market CDs.

My goal is to help the audience recall and recognize the seven warning signs of cancer.

I want to persuade the audience to reexamine their views on child custody.

I want to convince the audience to attend the next school board meeting and vote against closing any elementary schools.

Writing a specific purpose statement encourages you to think concretely about what you are trying to achieve. With an established goal, you are more likely to make sound judgments about how to develop your speech. Moreover, after you have delivered your speech, a goal can help you determine your success.

In formulating your purpose statement, check it against these guidelines:

1. *What is the basic purpose of the speech?* To interest, inform, stimulate, change beliefs, or move to action? How do you hope to be interesting? What kind of audience understanding do you hope to gain? For what kind of persuasion are you aiming?
2. *What is the specific audience response you are seeking?* As examples: "I want the audience to enjoy my discussion of Japanese tradition"; "I want my audience to understand the differences in Japanese and American values that cause workers in the two societies to view their jobs differently"; or "I want to convince the audience to sign up for a weekend seminar on Japanese management."
3. *Is your purpose realistic?* Can it be managed within the time limits? Is it a reasonable topic, given your knowledge of the audience's needs, interests, values, and demographic characteristics?
4. *Is your purpose clear?* If your purpose is vague, both you and your audience may experience a good deal of confusion. If you say, for example, "I want my audience to understand about Japanese management," that is about the same as saying that you are going to talk about Japanese management. In contrast, the statements in number 2 are clear about the kind of audience response sought.

Figure 12.2 summarizes general speech purposes and criteria for assessing specific purposes.

Figure 12.2
Public speaking purposes.

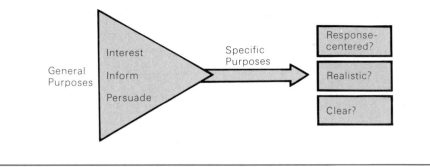

Supporting the Speech with Evidence

Once you have agreed to make a speech, and have chosen your subject and purpose, you can begin to consider what you want to say. Regardless of your speech's specific purpose, you will be articulating several ideas, contentions, and propositions throughout your speech. Suppose you were speaking to a congregation of the United Methodist Church. You might assert, "What we need is a ministry that reaches out to singles within this church." On the basis of that assertion alone, the audience could not determine whether your argument was strong or weak. To convince the congregation that your contention is sound, you need to support it with evidence. Evidence is *the body of fact and opinion pertaining to a subject.*

In most of your speeches, you should use varied kinds of evidence. Some kinds of speeches, such as technical reports, rely heavily on statistical evidence, often presented with the assistance of visual aids. But informative reporting may also be enhanced by the use of examples, comparisons, and the opinions of experts. Therefore, it is best to assume that for most public speeches you will need to use several different kinds of evidence. Figure 12.3 illustrates the different types of evidence that may be used to support contentions.

Facts as Evidence

Much of the evidence you collect will be factual; that is, it will involve the relatively objective description of something without interpretation or judgment. It is important to recognize that facts are not absolute truths. We make assertions about what we view as reality. If our view of reality is accurate and verifiable, then it is factual. In collecting factual information, it is important to seek reliable sources and to look through different sources to make sure you are finding consistent factual information. You ought to be able to look in more than one place and find a consistent account of how many people voted for Bill Clinton in the 1992 presidential election, what the unemployment rate was

Figure 12.3
Illustrates the different types of evidence that may be used to support contentions.

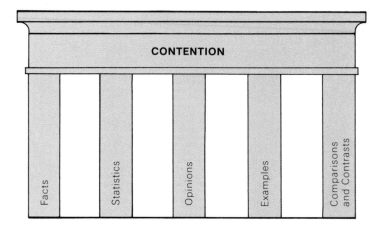

for the first six months of 1994, and what the major causes are of early blindness. Whenever you discover inconsistencies, carefully examine your sources for bias or possibly conclude that there are simply different approaches to explaining a particular phenomenon. In the latter case, avoid presenting such information as factual.

Facts are needed in most speeches and are a potentially compelling form of evidence. Compare the following assertions, the first presented without facts and the second with facts.

> Most people in this organization are happy with their jobs and are always trying to find ways to better themselves. **(Without facts.)**

> Last year, our employee survey revealed that over 80 percent of our employees are extremely satisfied with their jobs. Among the areas of greatest satisfaction were working relations with peers, treatment by the boss, and wages and other tangible incentives. What's more, this is a company on the move with people who are interested in growing. Over half of our employees are presently enrolled in some college or university, updating their education with our financial support. And, perhaps most impressive, five of our upper-level managers received excellent job offers from competing companies last year and decided to stay with us! **(With facts.)**

Because of its factual development, the latter is more concrete and convincing.

Factual evidence was also used effectively by Bob Rackleff, who, as a consulting writer, spoke before the Friends of Lloyd Environment Defense Fund Conference in Chicago late in 1991. Rackleff was trying to persuade his audience of the frequency with which oil pipelines have leaked in recent years, mostly without the public even being aware of the problem. He shared these facts:

> In March, 1991, a pipeline spill of 1.7 million gallons of crude oil flowed into a frozen marsh and the Prairie River near Grand Rapids, Minnesota.

Speakers often use visual aids as one form of evidence.

In April, 1991, a Marathon Oil pipeline near Carlsbad, New Mexico, leaked 1.5 million gallons of crude oil before workers spotted the leak.

In January, 1990, a New Jersey pipeline leaked 576,000 gallons of home heating oil into the Arthur Kill Waterway. New York City filed criminal charges that Exxon had submitted false reports that its pipeline safety equipment was working.

At about the same time, 210,000 gallons of kerosene spilled from a pipeline into the Rappahannock River, shutting down Fredericksburg, Virginia's water supply.

In July, 1989, a pipeline in North Dakota spilled 1.3 million gallons of crude oil.

These are some of the worst of the petroleum spills and leaks in recent years—from any source—but they go largely unnoticed by the American public and most environmentalists.

That's because our idea of oil pollution comes from televised images of oil slicks, oil-soaked beaches and wildlife from spills by damaged tanker ships—not underground leaks from our nation's 225,000 miles of pipelines.[4]

By citing a string of concrete factual instances of pipeline disasters, the speaker dramatizes the significance of the problem.

Statistics as Evidence

One type of fact often used in public speaking is statistical. Many people are intimidated by the thought of using statistics, yet statistics simply provide a numerical method of handling large numbers of instances. When statistics are used appropriately, they provide the most precise information about factual matters available to any public speaker.

Notice how John Jacob, president and CEO of the National Urban League, used statistics effectively to portray the economic plight of African-Americans:

> The economic picture is ugly. The nation is in a recession these days, and when America is in recession, black America is in a depression.
>
> We start from a weaker base and are far more vulnerable to downturns. Here are some of the *State of Black America 1992's* findings about the black economy:
>
> The median net worth for blacks is less than 10 percent of the median net worth for whites in America.
>
> Blacks own about 424,000 businesses out of a total of 17.5 million businesses in America.
>
> Total income per black person in America in 1990 was about nine thousand dollars, versus well over fifteen thousand dollars for whites.
>
> Median black family income was only 58 percent of that for whites—$21,423 versus $36,915.
>
> About 25 percent of black families earn under ten thousand dollars a year, compared to about 7 percent of white families. Put another way, African-American families are three-and-a-half-times as likely as whites to be making less than ten thousand dollars a year.[5]

Statistics fall into two general categories: descriptive and inferential. A descriptive statistic states a population fact; for example, 30 percent of all Americans smoke cigarettes. Frequently, however, it is inconvenient or impossible to obtain descriptive data. In this instance, you can turn to inferential statistics. The collection of inferential statistics involves gathering a sample and, on the basis of that sample, reaching a conclusion about the population of interest. When Louis Harris samples a few thousand Americans and predicts the election day behavior of all the American people, he is using inferential statistics. For past elections, he and other professional pollsters have done this with impressive accuracy.

The important fact to remember about *inferential statistics is that each has a confidence interval or margin of error*. Since inferential statistics are always probabilistic in nature, you can never be certain that you have accurately described the population in question. For example, if you were to report on the basis of a survey of one thousand assembly-line workers that 50 percent of all such workers are dissatisfied with their health insurance plans, it would be important to recognize that this particular percentage is only one of a number of different figures that might represent the workers in question. In this instance, you might report that the sample statistic is significant at the .05 level of confidence. This simply means that there is a 95 percent chance that the true percentage falls within a range of 47 to 53 percent; thus, there is only a 5 percent chance that the actual percentage of dissatisfied workers is less than 47 percent or greater than 53 percent.

Figure 12.4
Tests for statistical evidence.

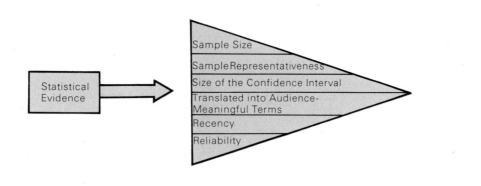

Another important statistical issue is *sample size and representativeness*. In general, as the size of the sample approaches the size of the population, the more confidence you can have in the accuracy of the statistic. Thus, if you want to know how workers in an organization of three thousand employees are responding to a new incentive plan, you are more likely to reach valid conclusions if you sample the views of three hundred than if you sample only thirty. Moreover, your sample should tap the views of all kinds of workers, male and female, experienced and inexperienced, supervisors and underlings. If you examine the views of only managerial personnel, you may well obtain a distorted view of employees' attitudes.

When using statistics, a few practical concerns should be kept in mind. Speeches should never be padded with statistics. Statistics should be used only when they are needed and when they represent the most precise way of demonstrating a point. They should *never* be used simply because they sound impressive. Moreover, every attempt should be made to make the statistics as clear and personally meaningful to the particular audience as possible. To say that a bond issue will cost the city $89 million sounds overwhelming, but the same figure presented as approximately five dollars per taxpayer clearly makes the proposal appear manageable. Finally, you should seek statistics that are as *recent* as possible. Nothing is more useless than an outdated statistic. Figure 12.4 summarizes tests for statistical evidence.

Opinions as Evidence

While evidence of fact is rooted in the notion of objectivity and suspended judgment, *evidence of opinion* is the application of interpretation and judgment to the known facts. There are three different types of opinion evidence you might use: *personal opinion, lay opinion,* and *expert testimony.*

It is probably safe to say that all speakers support their presentations with personal views from time to time. Your success in using *personal opinions* for support will largely depend on your credibility with the audience in question. If you are perceived as highly intelligent, accomplished in your area of endeavor, sincere and trustworthy in your motives, and objective in your views, you might rely extensively on personal testimony. This is especially true if you are speaking about a problem with which you have had years of experience. In his speech to the Iowa Poultry Association, for instance, John W. Megown, vice-president for public affairs and governmental regulations, at Vigortone Products Company, offers his personal views and stresses his years of professional experience.

> Early in 1977, shortly after Dr. Donald Kennedy took over as commissioner of the Food and Drug Administration, we started hearing some strange stories coming out of Washington, D.C.
>
> The gist of the stories was that some bureaucrats were speculating about a theory that consumers of meat from animals fed antibiotics might possibly develop resistance to antibiotics and that maybe they should be banned.
>
> Over a quarter of a century ago, I first became involved with antibiotics. Back in 1953 and 1954, I carried out one of the early research projects with antibiotics in swine feeds.
>
> For the next fourteen years, I was a professional animal nutritionist and had the opportunity to observe first-hand the use of low-level antibiotics in all types of livestock and poultry feeds.
>
> Because of my long-time experience with antibiotics, this theory about possible antibiotic resistance is very hard for me to swallow.[6]

Regardless of high credibility, seldom will any public speaker rely on his or her own views without additional reference to other support, such as statistics or examples.

Another kind of opinion evidence is *lay opinion*. Suppose you wanted to argue that most employees in your department were dissatisfied with the food being served in the company cafeteria. To support this argument you might cite the results of a poll you have taken that indicate 85 percent of all employees in your department found the food to be "extremely poor." In this case, lay opinion is good evidence because the matter being judged does not require the testimony of an expert; nor would your personal views suffice. Thus, lay opinion is useful when you want to describe the habits, attitudes, and behaviors of ordinary people. Normally, you would collect information about lay opinion by conducting a survey or by interviewing.

The final kind of opinion evidence is *expert testimony*. Most of us are not such renowned experts in our own fields that we could not profit from quoting others of greater renown who happen to support our views. In some instances, you might be able to combine different kinds of opinion evidence. To continue the example above, you might point out, "I have been very discouraged by the quality of food in our cafeteria [personal opinion]. My poll revealed that 85 percent of the employees in my department rate the food as very poor [lay opinion]. And even the company dietician, Lois Peterson, revealed to me in an interview last week that she was not pleased with the quality of many of the products purchased by our firm for use in food preparation. In particular, she objected to the quality of meats, fruit, and vegetables [expert opinion]." This is an especially good example of expert testimony because the company dietician is known to the audience and, more important, is in a position of being able to offer some insights into the reasons for the poor food quality. Moreover, we might even view her as a "hostile witness" in that we would expect her to feel defensive about the food issue, since she shares considerable responsibility for its quality. That makes her testimony even more persuasive.

Whenever you decide to use expert testimony to support your views, you need to observe a few guidelines. First, you must be concerned with the issue of *actual expertise*. That is, the person must be a recognized authority in the area in which he or she is being quoted.

You should also be concerned with the *expert's objectivity*. It is entirely possible for an expert to be competent in a given area and yet be a poor source of testimony because of some known bias in his or her views. It is far better, for example, to know the views of lay persons concerning the quality of a particular brand of television set than to quote the opinion of the president of the company that manufactures them. While the president may well be an expert in electronics and quite knowledgeable about television sets in general, his views in this instance are probably influenced by self-interest. Thus, he lacks trustworthiness and objectivity in his credibility as a source.

Once you have collected some highly credible expert testimony to support your presentation, the task still remains of *identifying the expert for the audience*. It is critical that the quoted expert be known and acceptable to the listeners; if he or she is not, then it is up to you to provide the necessary information. Assume that you are addressing a topic related to medicine; an appropriate identifying phrase might be stated as follows: "Dr. William Johnson, chief of neurosurgery at Johns Hopkins University Medical Center, has pointed out that. . . ." This kind of identification is specific, precise, concise, and adequately informative.

Examples as Evidence

One of the most difficult problems public speakers face is trying to make general principles or abstract notions interesting and meaningful to the audience. One of the best ways of doing this is through examples. Examples provide concrete frames of reference and by doing so interject life and meaning into the point you are making.

Examples can be either actual or hypothetical. They can be elaborate or brief. *Actual examples* point to real events or people. In the example that follows, Mario Cuomo, governor of New York, uses a moving extended example in his keynote address to the 1984 Democratic National Convention:

> It's a story I didn't read in a book, or learn in a classroom. I saw it, and lived it. Like many of you.
>
> I watched a small man with thick calluses on both hands work 15 and 16 hours a day. I saw him once literally bleed from the bottoms of his feet, a man who came here uneducated, alone, unable to speak the language, who taught me all I needed to know about faith and hard work by the simple eloquence of his example. I learned about our kind of democracy from my father. I learned about our obligation to each other from him

In certain speaking situations, real objects may be the most vivid kind of example.

and my mother. They asked only for a chance to work and to make the world better for their children and to be protected in those moments when they would not be able to protect themselves. This nation and its government did that for them.

And that they were able to build a family and live in dignity and see one of their children go from behind their little grocery store on the other side of the tracks in south Jamaica where he was born, to occupy the highest seat in the greatest state of the greatest nation in the only world we know, is an ineffably beautiful tribute to the democratic process.[7]

In a classroom speech, a student recently shared this example, one which her student audience found extremely thought-provoking:

One of my friends is a girl named Amy. Amy went to Florida this year over spring break. One day on the beach she met the most incredible guy named John. The rest of her vacation was filled with excitement and romance. Amy thought she had met the man of her dreams. She and John talked about seeing each other in the future—as much as possible. When John pushed a sealed envelope into her hand, kissing her as she boarded the plane, Amy was pleased. Assuming it was a love note, she eagerly opened it on the plane.

As her plane gathered speed on the runway, these were the words she read: "I'm so sorry Amy. You see, I have AIDS. I will always love you. Signed John." Amy never heard from "John" again. The name and address he had given her were false.

The other kind of example you might want to use is hypothetical. *Hypothetical examples* are ones that might reasonably or plausibly take place, but in using them you are not referring to an actual event or person. Although hypothetical examples are concocted, they should not be unrealistic or distorted. In the following example, William J. McCarville, director of environmental affairs for the Monsanto Company, used hypothetical examples effectively when he addressed the American Institute of Chemical Engineers:

> Let's suppose that instead of being a chemical engineer, you drive a truck for a soft drink manufacturer. Suppose you turn a corner too quickly and your truck turns over. Then suppose that because of the impact, the cases fall out of your truck, the bottles break and there's sugary, carbonated cola running all over the street.
>
> What you would have is a hazardous waste, according to definitions proposed under the Resource Conservation and Recovery Act.
>
> Now, you've lost your job with the soft drink company, so you go out and get another job driving another truck. This time, you're hauling tankers of sulfuric acid for a chemical company. As it happens, one day you skid around the same corner, turn the truck over and spill the contents all over the street.
>
> By this time, I know you're ahead of me. According to the proposed regulations, both liquids would be classified as hazardous waste. Both would require disposal under the same stringent methods.
>
> The result may be that we find ourselves filling up our Class I landfills with soft drinks. And at the same time the neighbors are out marching trying to get all the landfills shut down anyway.[8]

Because examples are so easy to identify with, they can be a powerful way of supporting your ideas. Even so, they must be used with care. Most of the time when we use examples we are arguing that the example represents the general principle we are discussing. Thus, one test of a good example is its *typicality*. If you are talking about the reading habits of children, you might, during your research, run across an example of a nine-year-old who regularly reads *Penthouse,* "trashy" comic books, and other questionable materials. Of course, you would not use this example to illustrate the point that children's reading habits were impoverished these days, unless you had reasons to believe that this child was typical.[9]

Comparisons and Contrasts as Evidence

One of the primary ways we learn is through *comparison*. We compare the known with the unknown, the more familiar with the less familiar. Whenever we encounter a new problem, we compare it with similar problems we have experienced in the past. New jobs, friends, and concepts are compared with old ones. Thus, a good way to help an audience understand what you are talking about is to compare your idea with something with which they are quite familiar or experienced. You might compare the job of managing a company with the job of managing a family. You might discuss the architectural design you had in mind for a new municipal complex by comparing it to one in a neighboring town with which you know the audience is familiar. Or you might compare a new book with one you know they have read. By using these comparisons, you hope to enlighten, to make the unknown more familiar, perhaps to make your audience less afraid of something you are advocating, more comfortable and at ease. What is important to remember in using comparisons as evidence is that they are only useful or enlightening when they are justified—that is, when the events, people, or phenomena you are comparing are similar enough to warrant the comparison.

In his speech to the Conference Board in New York, A. Thomas Young, president and CEO of the Martin Marietta Corporation, used the following comparison in discussing ethics and breaking the law:

> Whether in Washington, New York or Peoria, most people seldom set out with the deliberate intent of breaking the law. They are drawn into it, almost as a boa constrictor defeats its prey.
>
> Most of us probably think a boa crushes its target in the powerful folds of its body. Actually, this snake places two or three coils of its body around its prey. Each time the victim exhales its breath, the boa simply takes up the slack. After three or four breaths, there is no more slack. The prey quickly suffocates.
>
> This deadly phenomenon of a victim becoming the unwitting accomplice of its own destruction is not confined to the world of reptiles. It exists in the human behavior that characterizes all walks of life anywhere on the globe. The boa we have to face—and sometimes fail to face—is following our ethical values: each lapse is another coil of the snake.[10]

On occasion, you may want to inform an audience about a concept or principle by showing them its opposite. By using *contrast* rather than comparison, you are highlighting differences. This can be a compelling form of evidence when your goal is to stress the value of your advocated approach or plan in comparison to the approaches of others. For example, when Edward M. Kennedy addressed the 1980 Democratic convention, he devoted a large portion of his speech to contrasting the Democratic and Republican parties. After defining the Democratic party as that of the common man and woman—the party of farmers, mechanics, and laborers—he went on to paint a strikingly contrasting view of the Republicans:

> The 1980 Republican convention was awash with crocodile tears for our economic distress but it is by their long record and not their recent words that you shall know them.
>
> The same Republicans who are talking about the crisis of unemployment have nominated a man who once said—and I quote: "Unemployment insurance is a prepaid vacation plan for freeloaders." And that nominee is no friend of labor.
>
> The same Republicans who are talking about the problems of the inner cities have nominated a man who said—and I quote: "I have included in my morning and evening prayers everyday the prayer that the federal government not bail out New York." And that nominee is no friend of this city and of our great urban centers. . . .

The same Republicans who are talking about preserving the environment have nominated a man who last year made the preposterous statement—and I quote: "Eighty percent of air pollution comes from plants and trees." And that nominee is no friend of the environment.

And the same Republicans who are invoking Franklin Roosevelt have nominated a man who said in 1976—and these are his exact words: "Fascism was really the basis of the New Deal." And that nominee, whose name is Ronald Reagan, has no right to quote Franklin Delano Roosevelt.

The great advantage which our opponents offer is a voyage into the past. Progress is our heritage, not theirs.[11]

Similarly, Janet Martin, vice-president of Administrative Bank, CIBC, offered these comments regarding women in organizational leadership positions when she spoke to the Business and Professional Women's Club of North Toronto, Canada. She makes her case by using both expert testimony and contrast:

Might the glass ceiling exist because the personal trade-offs and sacrifices women must make are greater than their male counterparts? John Kenneth Galbraith once [said]:

In the modern world, women's liberation consists of submerging a personality to a corporation rather than a husband.

Harsh as Galbraith's view may be, he does have a point. Reports published in the *Wall Street Journal* a few years ago revealed that while 94 percent of male executives were married, only 41 percent of their female counterparts were. Ninety-five percent of male executives had children, compared to 39 percent for women. A very small percentage of men were divorced or never married. For women executives, the number was 45 percent.[12]

Regardless of the kind of supporting materials you select as evidence, you must be concerned about quality. Here, it might be appropriate to return briefly to chapter 9, where we discussed several tests that can be applied to any piece of evidence to assess its adequacy. Moreover, evidence standing alone means very little unless we are able to examine it critically and, based on it, reach reasonable conclusions.

Drawing Sound Conclusions

Whenever you stand before an audience and propose a particular solution as the best response to a problem or suggest some innovation, your proposal is based on some conclusion you have reached on the basis of supporting materials you have discovered. The cognitive process by which you do this is *reasoning,* the process of drawing conclusions from evidence.

Inductive Reasoning

The first basic reasoning process is *induction*. Induction is a method of drawing generalizations from some set of observations; thus, it moves from the particular to the general. We all engage in inductive reasoning. Unfortunately, some of us fail to reason with care and sensitivity to the hazards peculiar to the process.

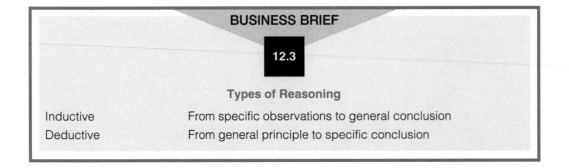

Inductive Fallacies

Probably the most common fallacy associated with inductive reasoning is the *hasty generalization*. Too many persons have experiences with an extremely limited and unrepresentative number of individuals or instances. Yet they jump hastily to general conclusions about the characteristics of the group or population as a whole. A few years ago, a noted minister in a small town in southern Indiana was convicted of theft (specifically, personally pocketing donations from the congregation for a new church). The affair received a great deal of state and national news coverage. Many persons concluded on the basis of this *one* instance that all ministers are dishonest hypocrites who squander the people's hard-earned contributions in the name of Christianity. Clearly, a single and undoubtedly unrepresentative instance is hardly adequate for reaching such a generalization.

Another common inductive fallacy is *faulty analogy*. In making an analogy, you compare two events, persons, ideas, and so forth on the basis of their similarity. You may encounter a problem, however, if the two things being compared are not similar enough to justify the comparison. A college administrator once stated, "The notion of restoring student direction and control of intercollegiate athletics is silly. You might just as well talk about giving horse racing back to the horses." The inference that students and horses are equally inept at directing their own "athletic" activities is absurd. There might be a number of reasons why students should not be given this sort of control. On the basis of this analogy, however, it is impossible to discern what those reasons are.

A third inductive fallacy is *faulty causal reasoning*. This fallacy confuses a chronological relationship with a causal relationship. The simple fact that one event usually follows another in time does not necessarily mean that the first caused the second. There are often other less obvious factors that contributed to the second event. An undergraduate history student once made a study of European war for a final term paper. He noticed that during the years immediately preceding the outbreak of recent wars, there occurred an increase of armaments among the aggressive nations. On the basis of this observation, he concluded as the thesis of his paper, "Increased armaments are one of the major causes of European wars." It is probably far more likely that increased armaments were the reaction to other causative factors, such as political upheaval or international tensions. Thus, increased armaments could reasonably be viewed as an *effect* rather than a cause.

A final consideration regarding inductive reasoning is not actually a part of the reasoning process but has to do with *perceptual biases*. No two persons' perceptions are exactly alike. Because of differences in ability, experiences, and expectations, our worlds are highly personalized. The inconsistency in witnesses' accounts of accidents is a familiar example of such perceptual discrepancies. Specifically, most individuals engage in both *selective perception* and *selective retention*, seeing and recalling only certain parts of something perceived, while distorting, filtering, or omitting the remainder. Often such selectivity is unintentional, occurring well below the level of consciousness. Selective perception and retention create difficulties with inductive reasoning in that the quality of the conclusions reached can be no better than the perceived and remembered data on which they are based.

Deductive Reasoning

The other major reasoning process is *deduction*. When you reach a conclusion deductively, you begin with a generally accepted idea or premise and apply it to a specific instance. Unlike induction, deduction moves from the general to the particular. An individual may believe that all research scientists are highly intelligent. Whenever he or she meets a particular person who is identified as such a scientist, our deductive thinker will probably conclude that this person, too, is quite bright. Of course, the quality of any deductively reached conclusion always depends on the validity of the generalization on which it is based.

As with inductive reasoning, deductive reasoning leads us to conclusions that are probable rather than absolutely true. Generalizations from which we reason are seldom based on all possible cases; therefore, there is always room for some error. In addition, it is quite possible to go through a reasoning process that is apparently logical and still reach an erroneous conclusion. We know, for example, that people who drink excessively throughout much of their lives usually die at an earlier age than others, partly because of the great likelihood of liver damage. If we know one such individual, we are likely to predict a shortened life span for him or her. Most of the time we will be correct, but sometimes our deduced conclusion will be wrong. Consider the example of the ninety-two-year-old man whose picture appeared in the news recently. He attributed his longevity to "women, cigars, and whiskey!" Moreover, he noted that his indulgence in each had been "excessive" for as many as seventy-five years!

Deductive Fallacies

Fallacies associated with deductive reasoning usually result when you draw conclusions from questionable assumptions or premises. It is critical, then, that you continually evaluate the quality of the premises from which you are reasoning. One common fallacy associated with deductive reasoning is *circular reasoning*. Not long ago, one of our students informed us that a mutual acquaintance had abandoned high school teaching to go into professional theater. The remainder of our conversation went something like this: Friend: "She's really a gifted actress, you know." Us: "Oh, you've seen her act?" Friend: "No, but she is currently acting on Broadway!" The circularity in this reasoning results from accepting a questionable assumption: namely, that anyone who acts on Broadway is gifted in acting. If one were to accept this peculiar premise, then the conclusion could be viewed as logical. The difficulty here is not rooted in the deductive thought process but in an erroneous assumption affecting that process.

Another common deductive fallacy is *guilty by association*. Here, the quality of an idea or the worth of a person or program is determined solely on the basis of other ideas, persons, or programs with which it is associated. An idea may be demeaned or rejected simply because it is attributed to a particular source. Abundant research on source credibility has demonstrated that speeches, poems, or pieces of art are consistently judged of high quality when attributed to persons held in high esteem by the judges and of poor quality when attributed to low-credibility individuals.[13] In all of these studies, the actual quality does not vary, only the source to which the product is attributed. Real-life examples of the guilt-by-association fallacy abound. During the 1960 presidential campaign, for example, John F. Kennedy attempted to associate Richard M. Nixon with Republican candidates of the previous half-century or more by saying: "I stand tonight where Woodrow Wilson stood, and Franklin Roosevelt stood, and Harry Truman stood. Dick Nixon stands where McKinley stood and Taft—listen to those candidates—Harding, Coolidge, Landon, Dewey. . . . Where *do* they get those candidates?" Kennedy made no attempt to establish the common ideas, programs, and principles of Nixon and the other candidates. He simply associated their names with his. The assumption operating here is that there are no substantial differences among any of a party's presidential candidates, even over a considerable historical span. Certainly this premise is open to argument.

A third fallacy associated with deduction is the *confusion of definitions with facts*. Some individuals rather arbitrarily define or label a group of people in a particular way, apply that definition to a specific person, and assume that they have given a factual description of that person. The important consideration, of course, is whether or not the label or definition has any basis in reality. There are those who define all men as "male chauvinist pigs," serious students as "nerds," college administrators as "pencil-pushing bureaucrats," and women as "broads." The implications of each of these labels are many and derogatory. If, for example, all women are indeed "broads," it follows that any individual woman should fit into this rather neat, if repugnant, category. This definition has no factual or empirical foundation; thus, the intelligent thinker will reject it.

The final fallacy of deduction is often referred to as the *bandwagon effect*. No one is completely free from the influence of others, especially the influence of those who are significant in their lives. When you are asked to make some judgment about a matter of physical reality, such as determining whether or not a stove is hot, it is relatively easy to decide without knowing the views of others. For matters involving social reality, however, it is often comforting to know that others support our views. Children learn how to employ this fallacy early in life when they beg their parents to be allowed to play outside after dark, go swimming for the afternoon, or wear blue jeans to church, on the grounds that all their friends are allowed to do it. The assumption is that these children's parents simply couldn't be all wrong! Bandwagon appeals continue to haunt us as we are asked to drink, smoke, eat, and enjoy because others are doing it. There may be some valid reasons why we should jump in the lake, but jumping in simply because others have done so is not a particularly valid one.

Summary

Early in their careers, many people believe that they will never have to make a speech. They do not see initially why a doctor or accountant or police officer would need to acquire public speaking skills. After several years on the job, they have a different view. They have found themselves being asked to present their ideas or areas of expertise to others, often in a public situation. They have learned that it is not enough to be a competent professional. One must also be able to communicate effectively with others—to present ideas for change persuasively, to brief new employees, and to convince others to act.

In this chapter, we have introduced you to some of the fundamentals of public speaking, such as selecting an appropriate topic, choosing a purpose, framing it in terms of the audience response you are seeking, and finding evidence to support the assertions you plan to make. We have also discussed logical ways of reasoning, so that your arguments will be sound and persuasive. Many speakers fail—not because they are stupid, not because they lack presentational skills or experience on the job—but because they have not taken the time to fit their subject to the particular speech situation, or they have not spoken with a clear sense of purpose, so that the audience *understands* what they are expected to do, believe, or think. If audience members leave a speech scratching their heads and asking, "What does she want me to do about it?" the speaker has not been clear about her purpose, and that creates problems for everyone.

Speakers who know what they are talking about, who have gathered sound and sufficient evidence, and who have reached logical conclusions in advancing their arguments are well on the road to effective public communication. The next steps, then, involve choosing an appropriate organizational pattern and delivering the speech effectively. In the next chapter, we will address these issues.

Questions for Discussion

1. To what extent should a public communicator consider his or her responsibilities as an organizational representative when speaking to an audience beyond the organization's boundary?

2. Which situation do you generally find most difficult as a public speaker: one in which you are asked to speak but may choose your own topic or one in which you are asked to speak and are assigned a topic? Be specific in discussing your rationale.

3. We mentioned four perspectives to be considered in selecting a topic for a public speech: personal, audience, situational, and organizational. Which of these (or combinations of these) do you feel are generally most important? Why? What kinds of contextual factors might influence your decision?

4. What are some of the basic purposes or goals of public speaking? Which, in your view, are most common or significant? Provide at least one example of a topic that would work well with each basic purpose you name. Phrase a specific purpose statement for each topic.

5. What are some of the hazards in using statistics as evidence? How can they be avoided?

6. Compare and contrast personal, expert, and lay opinion. What are some important considerations in the use of each?

7. How important are examples in developing persuasive arguments? Be specific.

8. Compare and contrast inductive and deductive reasoning, defining and giving an example of each.

9. Name at least two fallacies commonly associated with inductive reasoning. Do the same with deductive reasoning.

10. How does perception relate to reasoning? Be specific.

Exercises

1. You have just been chosen to represent your college or university as a public speaker. Your audience is to be the powerful finance committee in the state legislature. They tell you to speak on any topic related to your interests or to higher education. You have approximately twenty minutes to speak. Your speaking is part of a statewide program designed to allow government officials and their constituents to better understand each other, while interacting and exchanging ideas.
   a. What topic would you choose? Why?
   b. To what extent would you consider yourself a representative of the university and to what extent are you speaking just for yourself? How would your view of your role affect your communication behavior?
   c. What are some of the values, demographic characteristics, and other salient factors with this audience?
   d. Given the audience, topic, and situation, what would be your goal? Be specific and elaborate.

2. Michael Williams is an upper-level supervisor in a research and development laboratory. For several months, the company has had much internal bickering over the proposed purchase of a highly sophisticated, multimillion dollar computer. Williams is a brilliant man and committed to innovation—but not without a tinge of conservatism. For weeks, he has spoken out against the purchase of the computer in committee meetings within the laboratory organization. His opinions were considered with care but ultimately rejected, with a narrow majority supporting the costly expenditure. Until recently, no one has discussed the matter publicly. Now, however, news of the decision has reached the press, precipitating considerable public curiosity. As an outgrowth of this interest, Williams has been asked to address the local Lions' Club (of which he is a lifelong member) regarding the lab's decision to purchase the new computer.
   a. Should Williams agree to speak on this topic? Why or why not?
   b. If so, how should he approach it in terms of his personal views versus the position of the organization?
   c. What strategy might he use?
   d. What should be his specific purpose?
   e. How might his dual allegiance to both audience and the lab affect his presentation?

3. You are the head of the public relations division of a large industrial organization. One of your responsibilities is establishing a training program for those members of the organization who are often asked to meet the public as speakers. You have enough money allotted for this task to allow you considerable flexibility and creativity.
   a. What kind of training would you provide as the basis for this program? (That is, what topics would you cover, what services would you provide, and so forth?)
   b. What kinds of people would you hire to assist you?
   c. Would you require all managers within the organization to participate in this program or would you wait for individuals to ask for help?
   d. How long and under what conditions would the program be conducted? Why?
4. Is there anything wrong with any of the following? Why or why not?
   a. Quoting the president of General Motors regarding the superiority of the Oldsmobile.
   b. Using only statistical evidence to support a point of view.
   c. Relying exclusively on your own opinion to support a proposal.
   d. Comparing a managerial approach at a small private business with that at IBM.
5. Provide one example of each of the following reasoning fallacies:
   a. guilt by association
   b. bandwagon effect
   c. faulty causal reasoning
   d. false analogy
   e. hasty generalization
   f. selective perception

Your examples may be either real or hypothetical. You may choose them from any communication context, that is, advertisements, social exchanges, formal speeches, or others.

CHAPTER 13

Organizing and Delivering the Public Speech

any speakers carefully select and focus their topics, judiciously choose a specific purpose, seek out good supporting materials, and still never really experience success in their speaking endeavors. Part of their failure may be attributed to bad luck, but more commonly, a good measure of it is related to some significant problem with the way they have organized their ideas or delivered their speeches. In this chapter, we will examine speech organization, delivery, and style with the objective of helping you better accomplish your purpose as an effective public communicator.

Organizing the Speech

Rhetorical theorists have long observed that speeches must be well structured if they are to be effective. Among the earliest to comment on the importance of organization was the Greek philosopher Plato, who wrote, "Every discourse ought to be a living creature, having a body of its own and a head and feet; there should be a middle, beginning, and end, adapted to one another and to the whole."[1] In keeping with Plato's metaphor, we will next examine the three basic parts of speeches: the *introduction,* the *body,* and the *conclusion.*

The Introduction

If you have ever had the experience of rising to confront a room filled with chattering high school students, excited, noisy convention folks, or even a group of contented and disinterested Kiwanians following a luncheon, you are well aware of the first problem encountered by every public speaker: *gaining the attention and interest of the audience.* Every speech introduction should do this, although the manner in which it is done will vary greatly. Sometimes with serious topics about which there is great common interest, you may assume that the topic itself has captured the audience's attention. As a result, the best approach is to move directly into its discussion. This was the approach Jimmy Carter used in his speech to the nation on October 1, 1979. He began his remarks concerning U.S. response to Soviet military force in Cuba by moving directly to the subject:

> Tonight I want to talk with you about the subject that is my highest concern, as it has been for every President. That subject is peace and the security of the United States.[2]

It is more common, however, for public speakers to address audiences with mixed interest levels; thus, it is important to make an early attempt to gain their attention. In a moment, we will consider specific devices for doing this.

The other major function of the introduction is *orienting the audience to the speech's subject.* Although a speaker can choose to do many different things during this time of orientation (such as providing background or defining difficult or ambiguous terms), the speech's orientation phase should include four basic components: stating the speech's purpose, adapting the topic to the audience, establishing credibility, and providing a preview. Taken together, the attention-getter and the orientation prepare the audience for listening to the speech, while engaging their interest.

For the first part of the orientation phase, you should *state the purpose of your speech*. This does not mean that you literally reiterate the formal purpose statement that you developed in preparing the speech. Instead, you articulate your purpose more subtly. For instance, rather than saying, "My purpose is to persuade the audience to start using E-mail more regularly to improve their on-the-job efficiency," you might say, "Using E-mail on the job is an excellent way to improve your efficiency and productivity." Similarly, instead of stating, "My purpose is to convince my audience that donated blood is not being safely screened," you might argue, "Unfortunately, the methods used to screen donated blood are simply not safe." By using a more subtle form in articulating your objective, your purpose should be clear. But at the same time, you will follow principles of good oral style by speaking directly to the audience—and avoiding referring to your listeners in the third person as "the audience."

In the previous chapter, we stressed the importance of choosing a topic of mutual interest to both you and your audience. Even so, during your introduction, it is critical to *adapt your topic to the audience* by telling them why they should care. You, after all, have been preparing your speech for some time and are well aware of its importance to you. The audience, however, may not focus on the topic until they begin to listen to your speech. So, those early moments are a crucial time to explain to them why the subject of your speech is relevant to them and their concerns. For instance, in the sample outline in Business Brief 13.2, Indiana University sophomore Jennifer Bradley adapts to her audience in her speech about health care in America by saying: "Each of us will some day have some sort of health problem. One of us may just get a cold every now and then, while another may break a bone, and a third may have to have major surgery. Each of us will, at some point in life, have to cope with the reality of paying expensive medical bills. So clearly, we all need to be concerned about what kind of insurance coverage we have to pay these expenses." Her point, quite simply, is that everyone will have to cope with health care issues. It is only a matter of time. In a practical sense, adapting to the audience causes the speaker to address the question, "What's in it for us?"

The third part of orienting the audience involves *establishing your credibility*. In a sense, credibility is an ongoing issue throughout any speech, but for every speaker, the introduction represents an especially critical time to establish her or his credentials. For established professionals, this may be a less daunting task. We expect doctors to know about medicine, attorneys to know about the law, and accountants to be able to answer questions about taxes. For student speakers, however, the issue of establishing credibility is somewhat more challenging. In the student speech, for instance, Bradley initially establishes her credibility by referring to her numerous experiences with her grandfather's multiple major and costly surgeries. (Later in the speech, she further enhances her credibility by showing her extensive research on the subject of health care). As a speaker, you might establish your credibility by referring to a personal experience (for example, studying in Paris or learning CPR and saving someone's life), referring to the experiences of those close to you or about whom you care deeply (such as speaking of a friend who was injured by a drunken driver or addressing your ongoing concern for the poverty-stricken children of America), or by demonstrating your extensive knowledge or education in a particular field or with a special subject (for example, your ten years of experience as a jazz musician or your knowledge of the author Kurt Vonnegut from having read all of his books). By addressing the issue of your credibility, you are answering the audience's question: "Why should we listen to or believe you?"

Finally, before you launch into the body of your speech, you should complete your orientation phase by *enumerating a preview*. The preview introduces your major points and gives your audience a clear idea of what to expect from the remainder of your speech. In previewing, you are also signaling what it is that you feel is most important, those things you want the audience to remember and to reflect on long after you have finished speaking. If, after enumerating your preview, you follow through with your plan, you will have further enhanced your credibility by demonstrating your careful organization and preparation.

Common Attention-Getting Devices

Effective introductions vary with the specific demands of the speech situation. Even so, experienced speakers have found a number of introductory devices helpful in gaining the attention of the audience. These include: (1) establishing common ground with the audience, (2) paying the audience a deserved compliment, (3) asking a rhetorical question, (4) using humor, (5) using a narrative or illustration that leads into the subject, and (6) using an appropriate combination of these techniques. This list is not intended to be exhaustive; it merely suggests approaches that have been used successfully in the past.

Sometimes as a speaker you are separated from your audience in some significant way. You may hold a position of high status or influence or have vastly different experiences or knowledge. When this is the case, you may feel it necessary to establish an early bond with the audience through the introduction. Notice how Neal W. O'Connor, chairman of the board of N. W. Ayer ABH International, *establishes common ground* with his audience, the Syracuse Press Club:

> Thanks for the warmth of your welcome, a welcome back to Syracuse. One does feel old when he comes back to a place where he's been young. . . .
>
> I owe a lot to Syracuse. My father and mother both graduated from the University. Two of my father's brothers made their careers in this city. One was even president of this very hotel. I met a certain Nancy Turner, class of 1950, here. She is now Mrs. O'Connor. One of our oldest and most valued clients, the Carrier Corporation, has made this its headquarters city. I have many good friends here whom I see all too seldom. . . . I have a great respect for Syracuse, for the city and its people.[3]

We talked earlier about the potential significance of the speech occasion. Often the introduction is the most appropriate place to make direct reference to either the occasion or the efforts of the audience if praise or recognition is deserved. Eric Rubenstein, president of the Single Room Operators Association, paid the audience an honest compliment when he spoke to a group representing Job Resources, Inc. in Chicago:

> I am delighted to be here. Let me compliment your fine organization, Job Resources, on having counseled and job-trained more than 7,000 individuals, and having also obtained permanent employment for over 2,000 men and women since 1979. Clearly, much of your success is due to the hard work and dedication of your founder and Executive Director, Ms. Michal Rooney.

Job Resources' track record is especially impressive because you only assist disabled individuals, economically-disadvantaged people, and displaced workers. Your non-profit agency truly helps needy people train for and obtain jobs, and this is appreciated.[4]

The third attention-getting device is the *rhetorical question*. Unlike ordinary questions, rhetorical ones do not seek an outward verbal or behavioral response; rather, they are meant to stimulate thought and perhaps pique curiosity. In the following speech introduction, John D. Garwood, dean of instruction at Fort Hays State University, describes a hypothetical situation involving value judgments and then poses a thought-provoking rhetorical question:

O'Hare Airport in Chicago was about one hour away from being fogged in for the night. One plane would be leaving for New York in thirty minutes. Five seats were left; six people bought tickets. No other planes would leave that night.

John Jones, laborer, had won a trip to Europe and the boat left that evening.

Mark Johnson, serviceman, back from two years overseas, is returning to his wife and baby in New York.

Marie Wilson is hurrying to the bedside of her father, a heart attack victim, who is dying.

Thomas Roberts is scheduled to attend a father-son banquet in New York with his son, who has been having some problems.

Sam Brown, rock star, is on stage at Madison Square Garden that evening before 15,000 fans.

Barbara Wright, retired schoolteacher, is being honored that evening at a class reunion.

Which of the six would you leave behind?[5]

The fourth introductory device is *humor*. Several words of caution are necessary here. Humor should be used only as an introductory device when it is appropriate and tasteful. Some speakers seem to believe that every speech should begin with a joke—all too often of the standard, canned variety. Some humor can be planned in advance, but often the best kind of humor grows naturally from the speech situation and includes some references to persons present or preceding events. Moreover, some individuals are more skilled with humor than others. As a public speaker, you must honestly assess yourself with regard to this issue. There is probably no worse way to begin a speech than by telling a joke that flops. When tastefully employed, however, humor that is relevant to the topic and occasion can serve as an extremely effective attention-getting device. In the following introduction, George H. Dixon, president of First Bank System, begins his speech to the International Trade Seminar with a humorous anecdote:

It is a genuine pleasure to be here in Duluth again today and to have this opportunity to share with you some thoughts on trade with the People's Republic of China. This being a speech, we might as well begin with a brief anecdote about another speech, which can give us an early insight into the nature of the Chinese people.

It is a story about a young American who at a banquet found himself seated next to the eminent Wellington Koo, a Chinese diplomat. Completely at a loss as to what to say to a Chinese, this young man ventured, "Likee soupee?" Mr. Koo smiled and nodded. Later when called upon to speak, Wellington Koo delivered an eloquent talk in exquisite English, sat down while the applause was still resounding, turned to the young man and said, "Likee speechee?"[6]

Another attention-getting device is a *narrative* or *illustration* leading into the topic. Sometimes these devices focus on a personal experience; on other occasions, they simply recount an example or event read or remembered. They may be true to life or hypothetical, literary, or historical—so long as they gain attention in a meaningful manner. We might note here that good introductions often employ more than one attention-getting device. In the following example, the speaker begins by going directly to the topic and follows that with a brief, interesting narrative. Herbert Richey, chairman of the board of the Chamber of Commerce, begins his speech to the Ohio Chamber of Commerce in this way:

> I'd like to talk about modern economics today. I'm sure many of us are already familiar with that. But for those who are not, I can illustrate the theory with a story: Jed is a part-time farm worker with a flair for applied economics. One day he "borrowed" a country ham from the farmer who employs him . . . without bothering to tell the farmer. He went downtown and sold the ham to the grocer for $27. Then he used $20 of that money to buy $80 worth of food stamps. With the food stamps, he bought $48 worth of groceries. He used the remaining $32 worth of food stamps to buy back the ham. Then he returned the ham to the farmer's smokehouse. So the grocer made a profit, the farmer got his ham back, and Jed has $48 worth of groceries plus $7 in cash. If you see no flaw in that process, then you are already familiar with modern economics. On the other hand, if you suspect that someone, somewhere, has been "taken" for $80, then the rest of this speech is dedicated to you.[7]

A final way to introduce a speech in an interesting and creative way is to use several different attention-getting devices in some appropriate combination. Gary Trudeau, cartoonist and satirist and husband of Jane Pauley, formerly of the *Today* show, delivered some clever introductory remarks when he spoke at Wake Forest University's commencement on May 19, 1986. In his introduction, Trudeau shared some intriguing statistics, used humor (and satire), and referred directly to the occasion:

> Ladies and gentlemen of Wake Forest: My wife, who works in television, told me recently that a typical interview on her show used to run ten minutes. It now runs only five minutes, which is still triple the length of the average television news story. The average pop recording these days lasts around three minutes, or, about the time it takes to read a story in *People* magazine. The stories in *USA Today* take so little time to read that they're known in the business as "News McNuggets."
>
> Now, the average comic strip only takes about 10 seconds to digest, but if you read every strip published in the *Washington Post,* as the President of the United States claims to, it takes roughly eight minutes a day, which means, a quick computation reveals, that the Leader of the Free World has spent a total of 11 days, 3 hours and 40 minutes of his presidency reading the comics. This fact, along with nuclear meltdown, are easily two of the most frightening thoughts of our time.
>
> There's one exception to this relentless compression of time in modern life. That's right—the graduation speech. When it comes to graduation speeches, it is generally conceded that time—a generous dollop of time—is of the essence.

This is because the chief function of the graduation speaker has always been to prevent graduating seniors from being released into the real world before they've been properly sedated.

Like all anesthetics, graduation speeches take time to kick in, so I'm going to ask you to bear with me for about a quarter of an hour. It will go faster if you think of it as the equivalent of four videos.[8]

The length of the introduction varies with the needs of the speech situation. Some formal speech occasions demand extensive introductory reference to the events at hand, as well as to significant persons present. Some audiences are already basically attentive; others need considerable coaxing. In general, introductions should not be too extensive, particularly in the classroom context. The introduction does, however, create an important initial impression and should be constructed with care and creativity.

The Body

The part of the speech where you present your major ideas is the body. Most of your speaking time (80 to 90 percent) will be spent here. Within the body of your speech will appear the bulk of your information. It is here that you will develop your line of thinking and reveal your informative or persuasive strategy.

Common Patterns of Organization

One commonly used pattern of arrangement is *chronological order*. You begin with a given time and then move forward, or backward, depending on the nature of the subject. Chronological order may be useful with a variety of topics, so long as you are dealing with a subject involving chronological relationships. Thus, the life of Albert Schweitzer, the development of the labor movement in the United States, the evolution of the moral majority movement in religion, or changing views of management theory are all appropriate subjects for time arrangement.

A second common pattern is *spatial arrangement*. You employ space as your ordering principle. You could discuss any of the topics mentioned in the preceding paragraph spatially rather than chronologically simply by talking of them in terms of locations. For example, you might discuss Schweitzer's contributions in several specific geographical locations without regard to the order in which those contributions occurred. Or you might talk of the inception of the moral majority movement in the South and its spread to the Midwest, the West, and the East. These examples illustrate an important notion: *most topics can be approached from a variety of ordering perspectives*. Your task is to make a judicious decision in choosing the most appropriate one for the particular situation in which you are speaking.

Another pattern is *topical*. When you arrange your ideas topically, you often deal with types, forms, qualities, or aspects of the speech subject. You might discuss higher education by looking at vocational and technical institutes, community or junior colleges, four-year colleges, and universities. Similarly, you might speak about dogs according to breed; people according to religious beliefs or socioeconomic status; or

BUSINESS BRIEF

13.1

Patterns of Organization

Chronological	In order of time
Spatial	In order of location
Topical	In order of types, forms, qualities, or aspects of speech subject
Cause-effect	In order of causes to effects
Problem-solution	In order of problem to possible and/or best solutions

the writings of Shakespeare in terms of type, including sonnets, histories, comedies, and tragedies. It is often possible to look at the same subject from several topical perspectives. You might discuss Shakespeare as we just suggested; but you might also rank Shakespeare's work qualitatively and speak about the lesser, the average, and the best of Shakespeare. Moreover, you might discuss the major social issues brought forth in his works or interesting male or female characters. Some topics clearly lend themselves well to varied topical arrangements.

Whenever you choose to make an analytical speech, you may wish to consider using a *cause-and-effect* arrangement. This pattern can move from effect to cause or from cause to effect. Sometimes it can be incorporated as part of an overall problem-solution pattern; for usually within the structure of such a speech, you will analyze the problem (effect) in terms of contributing causes. It is important to remember that a chronological relationship does not necessarily equal a causal relationship. One event following another may represent chance as easily as cause. Furthermore, whenever you look at a given effect to seek its causes, you must continually guard against oversimplification. The quest for the single cause is usually hopeless. The cause-and-effect pattern of organization should be used with care.

Finally, the *problem-solution pattern* is one of the most frequently used by public speakers. In instances where the audience is well aware of the nature and causes of the problem, you might only briefly describe it and spend the remainder of the time exploring viable solutions. It is also acceptable for you to discuss a problem and consider a number of alternative solutions without actually selecting one as the best. When, as a result of your preparatory research, a preferred solution naturally emerges, you would do well to support it; but you should also consider leaving the selection of a preferable alternative up to the audience.

Given the wide variety of organizational patterns from which you can choose, a few general principles should be kept in mind. First, select your organizational pattern carefully. *The way you present your ideas and information should be strategic,* designed to enhance the chance that you will elicit the audience response you are seeking. If you are talking to an audience about a technical area in which they have little background and experience, you have to devote a good portion of your speech to educating them—giving them information they need so that they can understand what you want them to do. Second, *give some thought to symmetry and balance.* Normally, you would develop each of your main points so that each idea is given equal emphasis. But, if you decide that one idea is clearly more controversial, complex, or important than the others, you may consciously decide to devote more time to that idea. Again, what is important is that the decision be strategic. Finally, *be aware of primacy and recency effects.* Although researchers have not been able to agree on whether arguments are more memorable and persuasive if they are placed first (primacy) or last (recency), they do agree that those two positions are the most powerful—and that information or arguments embedded in the middle of a message are less likely to have the same impact.

The Transition

A final vital aspect of organization is the *transition,* the bridge connecting one idea with another. Good transitions are critical to the coherence and continuity of the speech. Each major idea needs to be rounded off and related to that which follows. Too many speakers believe that they can move magically from one main point to another. Thus, they concentrate on remembering the main concepts in the speech while paying little attention to the problem of moving smoothly from point to point. Many basically well-structured speeches have been seriously hindered by poor transitions.

Sometimes transitions can be relatively brief. For example, "Now that we've considered the basic dimensions of the problem, let's attempt to analyze its causes." On other occasions, an entire paragraph may be needed to maintain the flow of thought or demonstrate the nature of the relationships involved.

Speakers can sometimes employ rhetorical questions as transition devices. Some examples are: "But what do we really mean by the word democratic?" "How do you think a well-educated person would approach this kind of complex problem?" "What, then, are the ways we can best prepare our children for responsible adulthood?"

If a preview is used at the beginning of the speech, it may be necessary only to say subsequently, "first, second, and third" in moving from point to point. No speaker should rely exclusively on this manner of transition.

Internal summaries can also be useful as transitions. With the internal summary, you usually review the points already covered, and you may even preview the ideas or approaches to follow; for example, "Now that we've looked at some of the major dimensions of our economic plight, let's move on to consider some ways of improving the situation."

Unfortunately, transitions are often ignored by speakers. Without the skillful use of transitions, speeches seem incoherent. One of the best ways of ensuring that audiences *perceive* the unity and interrelatedness of your ideas is to make these relationships clear through good transitions. In sum, transitions can create bonds by revealing the speech's main ideas as integral parts of a coherent whole.

The Conclusion

We've all heard speakers who pause slightly near the end of their speech and then mumble, "Well, I guess that's all I have to say. I sure appreciate your attention. [Further pause.] Thank you." Some might call this a conclusion, but we would contend that the speaker did not conclude; he or she simply stopped. The specific purpose of a conclusion will vary from speech to speech, but the general purpose is to *bring the speech to a strategic close—thus creating a final impact.* We turn now to a consideration of some specific concluding devices.

One common method of concluding persuasive speeches is with a *challenge.* You may challenge the audience to act, to believe, to meet the need, to demonstrate concern, or even to live a different kind of life. At the 1992 Democratic convention in New York City, presidential candidate Bill Clinton concluded his acceptance speech with this compelling challenge:

> Somewhere at this very moment, another child is born in America. Let it be our cause to give that child a happy home, a healthy family, a hopeful future. Let it be our cause to see that child reach the fullest of her God-given abilities. Let it be our cause that she grow up strong and secure, braced by her challenges, but never, never struggling alone; with family and friends and a faith that in America, no one is left out; no one is left behind.
>
> Let it be our cause that when she is able, she gives something back to her children, her community and her country. And let it be our cause to give her a country that's coming together and moving ahead, a country of boundless hopes and endless dreams, a country that once again lifts up its people and inspires the world.
>
> Let that be our cause and our commitment and our new Covenant.
>
> I end tonight where it all began for me: I still believe in a place called Hope.[9]

A second concluding device useful with informative as well as persuasive discourse is the *summary.* In summarizing, you may repeat the main points in a straightforward, almost literal fashion; or you may choose to restate the major ideas in different, and often more concise, phraseology. Summaries are often used in conjunction with another concluding device. A student used the following summary, followed by a rhetorical question, to conclude his speech on LAMP, a new interdisciplinary curriculum at Indiana University:

> In short, the Liberal Arts and Management Program is an excellent alternative to a traditional college degree. Indiana is one of only a few schools offering this interdisciplinary degree (so, it's a unique opportunity). It combines a broad education in the liberal arts and sciences with a substantial cluster of business courses (giving you the best of both worlds). And, you have a lot of contact with your professors because LAMP is small, with several courses team-taught by faculty from the liberal arts and business. At a time when business leaders are calling for more liberally educated employees, why not look into LAMP?

Yet another concluding device is the *quotation.* Quoted material can take the form of expert testimony, poems, songs, or striking, memorable slogans. Quotations should be pertinent and meaningful; they *must* be brief. In a speech from which we quoted earlier, President Carter concluded with a striking quotation:

> The struggle for peace—the long, hard struggle to bring weapons of mass destruction under the control of human reason and human law—is the central drama of our age.

At another time of challenge in our nation's history, President Abraham Lincoln told the American people: "We shall nobly save, or meanly lose, the last best hope of earth."

We acted wisely then, and preserved the union. Let us act wisely now, and preserve the world.[10]

A good way to demonstrate the effects of an advocated plan is to conclude by *visualizing the future*. This device allows you to picture concretely the projected results of your ideas in an appealing way. One of the most famous examples of an entire speech that visualizes the future is Martin Luther King, Jr.'s speech, "I Have a Dream." In his conclusion, he further imagines the future in this way:

> And when this happens, and when we allow freedom to ring, when we let it ring from every village and hamlet, from every state and city, we will be able to speed up that day when all of God's children—black men and white men, Jews and Gentiles, Catholics and Protestants—will be able to join hands and to sing in the words of the old Negro spiritual, "Free at last, free at last; thank God Almighty, we are free at last."[11]

More recently, New York Governor Mario Cuomo, in his speech to the 1992 Democratic convention nominating Bill Clinton for the presidency of the United States, concluded by vividly portraying the future under Democratic leadership:

> A year ago, we had a great parade in New York City to celebrate the return of our armed forces from the Persian Gulf. I'm sure you had one, too. But as joyous as those parades were, I'd like to march with you in a different kind of celebration—one, regrettably, we cannot hold yet.
>
> I'd like to march with you through cities and rural villages where all the people have safe streets, affordable housing and health care when they need it.
>
> I want to clap my hands and throw my fists in the air, cheering neighborhoods where children can be children, where they can grow up and have the chance to go to college and one day own their own home.
>
> I want to sing—proud songs, happy songs—arm in arm with workers who have a real stake in their company's success, who once again have the assurance that a lifetime of hard work will make life better for their children than it's been for them.
>
> I want to be part of a victory parade that sends up fireworks, celebrating the triumph of our technology centers and factories, outproducing and outselling our overseas competitors.
>
> I want to march—with you—knowing that we are selecting justices to the Supreme Court who are qualified to be there, and who understand the basic American right to make our own individual moral and religious judgments.
>
> I want to look around and feel the warmth, the pride, the profound gratitude of knowing we are making America surer, stronger—sweeter. Some day I want to march to Washington, not to beg for what we need, but to shout our thanks because we made the greatest nation in the world freer than it's ever been, provided new opportunities to new generations of seekers, justified our gifts by showing the world how much better we can be!
>
> So step aside, Mr. Bush, You've had your parade.[12]

A final concluding device involves *referring to materials used in the introduction*. This is most readily accomplished when you earlier introduced your speech with some attention-getting illustration or narrative. Because this device unites the conclusion and the introduction, it has great potential for giving the speech a sense of unity. Consider the following example in which Janice Carlat, a freshman at the University of Kansas, speaks to her classmates on the subject of Pablo Picasso's art and its meaning. During the introduction, she quotes Picasso as saying, "Reality is more than the thing itself. I always look for its super-reality. A green parrot is also a green salad." Carlat subsequently refers to this introduction in the conclusion that follows:

> In contrast with other artists, Picasso, unlike the cool, constricted, specialized artist of today, is haunted by a need to search and find. He is probably one of the last humanists in the problematic history of art. His works will always be a study to the individual, and, as long as there continue to be problems in our world, Picasso will continue to communicate—to communicate in his world of abstraction where faces are not faces but conglomerations of eyes and ears, where baby buggies are not baby buggies but piles of nuts and screws, and where green parrots are not green parrots but green salads.[13]

Conclusions, like introductions, should be tailored to the needs of the specific speech situation. As a general rule, they should be brief. Probably the most irritating thing a speaker can do is to say, "In conclusion . . . ," and then drone on and on. Once again, conclusions are used to create a final impact, to remind, to reinforce, and to round out the strategy.

Outlining the Speech

Although we have chosen to discuss outlining at this point in the chapter, the outline is, in fact, something that develops as you prepare the speech. Most speakers construct a rough outline quite early, representing their initial thinking and ideas they would like to explore. Later, as they read widely and begin to choose some strategy of organization, the outline will grow, change, and be refined. The outline, then, evolves as your ideas emerge. Sometimes it is rearranged; often it is expanded to include more detail or support. The outline from which you ultimately deliver your speech will reflect your total speech preparation process. This final outline serves several useful purposes.

First, the outline allows you to examine your speech's structure to see if you are satisfied with the way you have organized your ideas. You can see whether or not you have consistently followed the pattern of organization you set out to pursue. Have you, for example, examined all aspects of the problem before moving on to the solution—or have you jumped back and forth? By examining your outline, you can see if you have given each main point the emphasis you had intended. You can also note if you have developed your arguments properly, that is, with adequate supporting material. Finally, by constructing an outline, you encourage yourself to go over your speech. This helps to fix the main points in your mind and will later assist your memory during the actual delivery of the speech.

The sample outline in Business Brief 13.2 illustrates the kind of outline you will develop. Some speakers prefer to write out their introductions and conclusions, especially if they are concerned about beginning and ending in a specific, carefully planned way.

SAMPLE OUTLINE

Health Care: A Basic Right of Every American

By Jennifer E. Bradley

Specific Purpose: I want my audience to agree that America is experiencing a severe health care crisis and that *everyone* has a right to quality health care.

Introduction

I. **Attention-Getting Device:** I'd like to tell you the story of a woman without health insurance. This story was reported by Steven Miles in the November 11, 1992, issue of the *Journal of the American Medical Association (JAMA).* The woman had been assaulted by a man she knew and he had broken her arm. After this, she had taken an overdose of an anticonvulsant on impulse, and a friend took her to the emergency room. There, her overdose, which was considered an emergency, was treated, and her arm was temporarily splinted. She was admitted to the hospital and stabilized within two days. A surgeon said that the woman's arm needed to be operated on in order to set the fracture, but he refused to perform the surgery because the woman had no insurance, and he didn't think that Medicaid, which she was eligible for, would cover the whole cost. This surgeon was legally able to refuse this necessary treatment, and in the United States of America, no less, where equality is supposed to prevail (Testimony-Miles, 1992).

II. **Orientation Phase:** This story illustrates the health care crisis that is going on in America right now.

Adaptation: Each of us will some day have some sort of health problem. One of us may just get a cold every now and then, while another may break a bone, and a third may have to have major surgery. The same is true of our parents, grandparents, and children. Each of us will, at some point in life, have to cope with the reality of paying expensive medical bills. So clearly, we all need to be concerned about what kind of insurance coverage we have to pay these expenses.

Credibility: My grandfather has had eleven major surgeries in the past twelve years, including open heart surgery, prostate surgery, and back surgery. The huge fees for the surgeries themselves are only made worse by the operating room and hospital fees, plus any post-surgical therapy. If it's amazing that his body has survived all this cutting, then it's even more amazing that his wallet has survived it. Luckily, he has the best health insurance policy money can buy, as everyone should have. There's just one catch. He has the money to buy it, while many who need even more medical care don't.

Enumerated Preview: I'd like to talk to you today about the health care crisis we are currently experiencing in America. Then I'd like to discuss why we should care about fixing this problem and why all deserve quality health care.

Transition: First, let's look at the severity of the health care crisis.

Body

III. America is in the middle of a huge health care crisis.

   A. Health care costs are out of control.

      1. According to the November 1992 issue of *Scientific American,* we were spending 4% of our GNP (gross national product) on health care in 1940. In 1990, the figure jumped to 12.2% (Statistic-Fein, 1992). That's more than a 300% increase in only 50 years.

      2. And the December 14, 1992, *New York Times* reported that the Congressional Budget Office predicts that we will be spending 18% of our GNP on health care by the year 2000 (Statistic-Reinhardt, 1992).

      3. *Scientific American* reports that we are currently spending more of our GDP (gross domestic product) on health care than any of the 23 other nations in the Organization of Economic Cooperation and Development (Statistic-Fein, 1992).

      4. The March 8, 1993, issue of *Time* reports that in 1991, 100 Tylenol with Codeine 3 tablets cost $19.38 wholesale here in the U.S., whereas the same amount cost only $3.32 in Canada (Statistic-Greenwald, 1993). That is, we paid nearly six times as much for the same medicine here, just because we don't control costs. And the situation is the same with numerous other drugs.

      5. So, as you can see, our huge health care costs are not only taking money away from other important programs, but are also hurting us in terms of international competition, since our companies have proportionately less money to invest.

Internal Transition: But dollars and cents are only one part of this huge problem.

   B. In addition, many Americans who badly need health care just aren't getting it.

      1. The December 4, 1990, *Washington Post* reports that 37 million Americans have no health insurance whatsoever, and that an additional 50 million more have only partial coverage that wouldn't pay for a serious illness (Statistic-Matthiessen, 1990).

      2. Sadly, as the December 14, 1992, *New York Times* tells us, one third of these uninsured Americans are children (Statistic-Reinhardt, 1992).

      3. The November 1992 copy of *Scientific American* points to three other groups who, being uninsured or underinsured, are particularly at risk in the health care crisis (Testimony-Fein, 1992).

         a. First, there are the unemployed, the homeless, and those who work part-time.

         b. Second, there are those whose employers don't provide coverage or provide only inadequate coverage.

         c. And finally, there are those with preexisting conditions, including high-risk individuals such as those who are HIV positive or who have histories of medical conditions in their families, and the elderly, who represent a growing proportion of the population.

         d. Clearly, these are many of the people who most need medical care.

Transition: Health care costs are so high (and increasing) that only the richest can afford good health insurance policies. In addition, many of those who most need care (the unemployed, underprivileged, and poor) are unable to get it. Clearly, this shows not only that America is in a severe health care crisis, but also, as Uwe E. Reinhardt so aptly put it in the December 14, 1992, *New York Times,* it illustrates the " 'God-bless-me-and-to-hell-with-you' ethic of the 1980's" (Testimony-Reinhardt, 1992). This kind of attitude has only served to exacerbate the health care crisis and must be changed. Let me tell you why we need to start caring more about a national health care program and why each and every person has a fundamental right to quality medical care.

IV. Two basic principles shape the argument that all deserve health care: those of human dignity and caring for the least well-off. Much of the following is based on an article in the November 4, 1992, issue of *JAMA,* written by Charles Dougherty.
   A. The first ethical principle is that of human dignity.
      1. As caring individuals, most of us believe that human beings have a certain intrinsic value, commonly referred to as human dignity or worth. This value is, as Dougherty puts it, "beyond any relative estimation, beyond the contingencies of supply and demand" (Testimony-Dougherty, 1992). We cannot put a price tag on the worth of a human—humans are priceless.
      2. The implication of this is that we respect people because of their intrinsic value.
      3. This respect, in turn, creates two duties in terms of health.
         a. We must not only avoid destroying the health of others,
         b. but must also make an effort to protect and maintain health.
         c. According to Dougherty, "Failure to act on this duty, by allowing lives to be shortened or diminished in quality because of lack of access to basic health care, expresses a callous disregard for the dignity of human life" (Testimony-Dougherty, 1992).

Internal Transition: While this argument is reason enough to support universal health care, another ethical issue must also be considered.

   B. The second moral value central to the health care debate is that we should take care of those who are least able to care for themselves.
      1. This is why people donate clothes to the Salvation Army, work at the Community Kitchen, and give food to food banks. People daily support and act on this basic moral principle by donating time, goods, and money to various charitable organizations.
      2. Since all people have human dignity, even the least well-off deserve respect, which includes the opportunity to live a "life fit for a human being" (Testimony-Dougherty, 1992).
      3. In keeping with this idea, we all have a social responsibility to help those who are least able to help themselves.
      4. As Dougherty points out, "this is the very point of health care: that the well should assist the sick and dying" (Testimony-Dougherty, 1992).

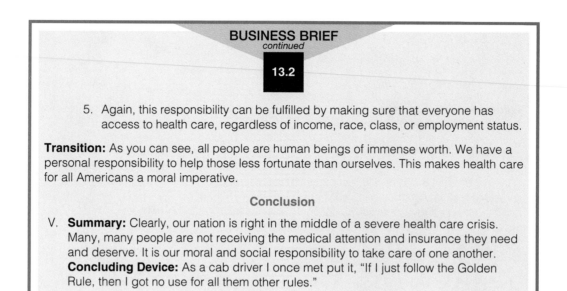

BUSINESS BRIEF
continued

13.2

5. Again, this responsibility can be fulfilled by making sure that everyone has access to health care, regardless of income, race, class, or employment status.

Transition: As you can see, all people are human beings of immense worth. We have a personal responsibility to help those less fortunate than ourselves. This makes health care for all Americans a moral imperative.

Conclusion

V. **Summary:** Clearly, our nation is right in the middle of a severe health care crisis. Many, many people are not receiving the medical attention and insurance they need and deserve. It is our moral and social responsibility to take care of one another.
Concluding Device: As a cab driver I once met put it, "If I just follow the Golden Rule, then I got no use for all them other rules."

Others write out each transition to ensure a clear movement from one main point to another. Most speakers write out certain kinds of supporting details, such as statistics and quotations taken from experts, where precision is vital.

Although some variations are appropriate in the outlining format, some rules apply to all outlines. First, *each point in the outline should contain only one piece of information or idea*. For example:

I.   Refined sugar should be minimized in the diet to decrease obesity and reduce one's susceptibility to high blood pressure.

Because more than one point is made here, this part of the outline should be altered as follows:

I.   Refined sugar should be minimized in the diet.
     A. Minimizing sugar intake decreases obesity.
     B. Minimizing sugar intake reduces one's susceptibility to high blood pressure.

Here the main idea is presented with a Roman numeral. The subpoints are subordinated with capital letters.

Second, *the outline should accurately reflect relationships between ideas*. The most general ideas should be listed with Roman numerals, the next most general with capital letters, the next with Arabic numbers, and so on. Consider this *poor* example:

I.   Too much refined sugar leads to hyperactivity in children.
     A. Sugar should be minimized in the diet.
     B. Most breakfast cereals consumed by children are over 75 percent sugar.
     C. Consuming too much refined sugar as children encourages adult obesity.
     D. Refined sugar can be replaced by other natural sweeteners in most recipes.

The most general idea here is that sugar should be minimized in the diet. Yet that point is made subordinate to the one claiming that sugar leads to hyperactivity. In fact, none of the subpoints is related directly to I. Here is a better way to approach this outline:

I. Refined sugar should be minimized in the diet.
   A. Diets containing much refined sugar produce several negative effects.
      1. Children often develop hyperactivity.
      2. Adults often develop high blood pressure.
      3. All age groups tend to become obese.
   B. Minimizing refined sugar does not mean that sweets cannot be consumed.
      1. Many foods are naturally sweet.
      2. Honey may be substituted in many recipes.
      3. Brown sugar may be used for most baking.

In this outline segment, one general idea is introduced with a Roman numeral. That main idea is developed by two slightly less general subpoints appearing under *A* and *B*. These, in turn, are elaborated through more specific subpoints appearing in *1, 2,* and *3*.

The example we just presented illustrates another important outlining rule: *Each subpoint should be logically related to the main point under which it falls.* In the poor example, that rule was consistently violated. That is, what one can do with recipes or adult obesity has little to do with hyperactivity in children. In the second outline, however, each subpoint is logically related to the main idea of the need to minimize refined sugar in the diet.

You should also *use a consistent system of symbols and indention.* All main points should be listed with Roman numerals; all major subpoints should have capital letters; all supporting statements following major subpoints should have Arabic numbers. You should follow the system we have illustrated in this section. In addition, when an entry runs longer than one line, indent the second line the same amount as the first line. For example:

I. Finding ways to cook enticing meals without using refined sugar can be challenging.
   A. One way of approaching this challenge is to purchase one of the several new "sugar-free" cookbooks that have appeared in recent months.

By using this sort of consistent indention and symbol system, you visually establish the logical relationship among your ideas.

Most of the time you should *avoid having single subpoints.* Usually, subpoints indicate subdivisions of the main points under which they fall. Thus, for every *A* you should have a *B;* for every *1* there should be a *2;* for every *a* you need a *b,* and so forth.

Finally, *be consistent in the kind of phraseology used.* Some speakers prefer *full sentence outlines,* such as the one dealing with sugar above. Others prefer a topical or key word outlining approach. Outlines should not jump back and forth between phrases and sentences. An example of a *key word outline* follows:

I. Reasons for regular exercise
   A. Weight control
   B. Muscle tone

      C. Cardiovascular health

      D. Attitude improvement

      E. Sleep enhancement

  II. Ways to get regular exercise

      A. Joining a YMCA

      B. Finding a partner

      C. Beginning or ending the day with exercise

For the actual delivery of your speech, a key word outline may be most beneficial. In fact, some experts believe that the best way to achieve really effective delivery is by using a key word outline.[14] If you practice with this kind of outline, and go on to deliver your speech with it as well, you may find that your presentational style will be more direct and spontaneous.

Although outlining rules are often violated, they are not difficult to master. A well-constructed outline is of great help during the delivery of a speech. Equally important, it stands as a tangible symbol of the time, effort, and thought you have put into your speech.

Presentation of the Public Speech

However well organized you are, the actual delivery of the speech is of paramount importance. Many an intelligent, well-intentioned, and well-prepared speaker has failed to move his or her listeners simply because of an inability to present the speech directly, spontaneously, and emphatically. To deliver any speech effectively requires that the speaker approach the situation with some measure of confidence; yet stage fright remains a nearly universal phenomenon.

Developing Confidence

The term *stage fright* originated in the theater, but most people do not have to participate in a dramatic production to experience this unfortunate malady. Quaking limbs, quivering voices, and dry mouths are only a few of the dreaded symptoms. It is a paradox of human nature that most of us desire attention; but when we receive attention in the form of an audience, we respond with some measure of fear. Essentially, it is a fear of personal failure, for we expose a good deal of ourselves through our public expression of attitudes and ideas.

Even so, many speakers lack confidence because they hold a number of erroneous notions about stage fright. Among these fallacious assumptions are (1) the speaker is virtually alone in experiencing anxiety in public speaking; (2) only beginners experience stage fright; (3) everyone in the audience can tell exactly how frightened a speaker is; and (4) stage fright is always debilitating for the speaker. Let us consider each in turn.

Anxiety in public speaking is not an uncommon occurrence. In fact, only rarely do public speakers experience no anxiety before or during the actual delivery of their speeches. One study demonstrated that 77 percent of all experienced speakers admitted to some stage fright on each speaking occasion.[15] Of course, "experienced" speakers are not necessarily synonymous with "great" speakers. Yet, historically, some of the most eloquent orators of all time were besieged by stage fright, including Cicero, Abraham Lincoln, and Winston Churchill. Clearly then, anxiety is not infrequent; nor is it experienced by only the small and insignificant.

Although exceptions exist, normally stage fright decreases as individuals gain experience as public speakers.[16] It is not uncommon for students in basic public speaking courses to experience fairly intense anxiety during their first speech performance. As public speaking becomes a part of their normal classroom activities, however, they meet future assignments with greater confidence.

Speakers frequently overrate the accuracy with which listeners can judge the extent of their nervousness. Even if there are no physical reactions to anxiety, we often assume that the audience can see through our smiles and calm appearance to the turmoil and uncertainty lurking beneath. Once again, studies do not support this assumption. *Listeners,* including college speech teachers, *are notoriously poor judges of the amount of anxiety speakers experience.*[17] The typical tendency is to underrate stage fright, attributing greater confidence to the speaker than he or she claims to feel. In fact, it is not uncommon for speakers to believe they "acted nervous" while audience members will comment on the degree to which the speakers seemed completely in control and self-assured!

Earlier in this section we referred to stage fright as an "unfortunate malady." While this represents a commonly held view, in truth, anxiety is a hindrance to your performance only if it is severe or uncontrolled. A number of psychological studies have demonstrated that *moderate anxiety can be an asset in performance,* whether you are taking an examination or giving a speech.[18] You should welcome some anxiety as a possible stimulus for a better presentation. Whenever you become anxious before giving a speech, your flow of adrenalin is increased. Unfortunately, this increased source of energy often manifests itself in shaking hands and other signs of nervousness. Yet that same energy can be channeled into positive behaviors that may enhance the effectiveness of your presentation. Moderate tension can provide a creative edge, a more dynamic style of delivery, a more animated presentation. When viewed from this perspective, stage fright becomes a tool for creating a more involving presentation.

Finally, there is perhaps no better way to control anxiety than to *know that you are well prepared* for the speech event. When you have carefully analyzed your audience, engaged in thorough research, strategically structured the organizational pattern of the speech, practiced the delivery of the speech, and are committed to the ideas therein, you are in an excellent position to control your anxiety. Without such diligent preparation, however, anxieties are not only present but quite likely well founded.

Types of Delivery

There are three major styles of delivering a speech: *impromptu, extemporaneous,* and *manuscript.* We will discuss each one briefly.

Impromptu

Impromptu speeches are essentially off-the-cuff; they are delivered without preparation, other than perhaps a few minutes to organize your thoughts. As you function in professional and social groups and organizations, you are often called upon to articulate a point of view, make a brief report, or explain a procedure. More often than not, requests for these speeches arise directly within the meeting when someone needs information. While impromptu speaking is a common occurrence in daily organizational life, you should *never* elect to give an impromptu speech whenever you are asked in advance to make a speech. By definition, impromptu speaking excludes the opportunity for research, audience analysis, arranging some strategic plan, and practicing delivery. As a result, you have minimal control over most crucial speech variables.

Extemporaneous Speaking

A second type of delivery is extemporaneous. Many individuals confuse impromptu and extemporaneous speaking, believing that one does little to prepare for an extemporaneous address. On the contrary, extemporaneous delivery requires a great deal of preparation. The extemporaneous speech is carefully prepared, thoroughly outlined, practiced but not memorized, and delivered from notes.[19] When speaking extemporaneously, you commit key ideas to memory, but precise words, specific phrases, and particular examples vary during practice sessions as well as during the actual presentation of the speech. The outline used in extemporaneous speaking should meet your needs and follow the guidelines we established earlier in this chapter.

Outlines can be placed either on full sheets of paper or on four-by-six-inch note cards, depending upon a number of variables in the particular speech situation. If you plan a great deal of bodily movement, including perhaps the use of a chalkboard, it is probably best to use note cards rather than carrying sheets of paper around the room. On the other hand, papers are entirely appropriate if they are placed on the podium and left there; in fact, they allow you to visualize a greater portion of the speech in one glance. The greatest difficulty with the use of notes is preventing them from becoming a crutch, reducing eye contact and directness. When properly employed, however, the notes used for extemporaneous speaking have the potential for allowing maximum flexibility, directness, and spontaneity. This is especially likely if you use a key word outline. Your notes serve as a reminder of strategies planned and ideas developed; but you should feel able to deviate from them whenever the situation demands it. As an extemporaneous speaker, you can make structural alterations, clarify or elaborate with additional examples or illustrations, and omit unnecessary passages because you are creating the speech as you deliver it.

This is not to imply that extemporaneous speakers can do no wrong. There are times when they will flounder for precise words (and sometimes will never find them); they may ramble or use too many examples, especially of a personal nature. With appropriate criticism and guidance, however, these problems usually decrease with experience. Perhaps the greatest advantage of extemporaneous delivery is that it requires total involvement on the part of the speaker.

Speaking from a Manuscript

The final delivery mode is manuscript. You write the speech out word for word and read the manuscript to the audience. The use of the manuscript is not infrequent among business and professional speakers. Furthermore, manuscripts are often *required* whenever the speaking occasion is an especially important one. If an organizational representative is speaking on a controversial issue and the press is likely to be present, the manuscript provides a record of what the speaker actually said so that there will be minimal distortions in reporting. Within the political world, manuscript speaking is widespread. Nearly all major presidential addresses are delivered with the assistance of a manuscript. If poorly handled, however, the manuscript can become a most deadly form of delivery.

Common problems associated with manuscript speaking are limited eye contact, poor oral style, difficulties associated with reading, and inflexibility. Unless speakers practice frequently before delivering the manuscript, they are apt to become bogged down in the manuscript itself during the presentation. We have all seen speakers who are glued to their manuscript, looking up only sporadically or failing to look up at all. Without eye contact, a sense of directness and involvement cannot be effectively communicated. Actually, if manuscript speaking is to be successful, it should sound very much like a good extemporaneous speech. Its words, phrases, and sentences should have a conversational quality. All too often we write manuscript speeches as we would write essays—with long, complicated sentences and complete impersonality (for example, "one might think" rather than the more direct "you might think").

When properly used, the manuscript speech provides the opportunity for maximum speaker control. Time limitations are important and often overlooked by public speakers. By using a manuscript, you can plan precisely with regard to time, again leaving some room for "during delivery" alterations. The potential for excellence in language usage is also great with the use of the manuscript. Descriptive passages can be created with attention to color, precision, simplicity, and figurative elements. Precise verbs can be chosen and incorporated throughout the speech. The manuscript speech can become a work of art so long as you are constantly aware of the need for keeping a conversational quality. Finally, because the manuscript is ordinarily rehearsed with approximate similarity to the speech as actually presented, you should find it possible to practice the delivery with relative precision. This, in turn, makes it possible to face the speaking occasion with an increased sense of confidence.

Before we leave the specific subject of manuscript speaking, it may be appropriate here to consider a form of speaking often associated with the professional conventions of organizations. Many professional persons are asked to read scholarly or research papers at conventions several times throughout their lives. These papers are not speeches but essays, critical or methodological studies, and other forms of scientific and artistic endeavors. Audiences are usually persons quite familiar with the content and jargon of the field. Our personal experience with such "speaking" occasions reveals that, while the presented ideas are often excellent, the oral deliveries are usually less than satisfactory.

When faced with the necessity of presenting a paper in this kind of situation, it is usually best to have copies of the paper available for all audience members so they can seek out any details of interest or inquiry. It is most effective, then, to talk about the paper extemporaneously, highlighting major ideas and adjusting the style and length of the presentation to the needs of the audience and situation. Sometimes it is possible to read certain important passages off the paper, including, for example, the introduction and conclusion; seldom is it effective to read the entire paper word for word. The only exception to this is when the paper is fashioned in good oral style—that is, when it is not written as it would subsequently appear in a scholarly journal. Even then, the paper should be altered, as any manuscript speech should, whenever the situation demands it.

Characteristics of Effective Delivery

In discussing the three major styles of delivery, we have alluded to the qualities of effective delivery. In general, effective delivery in public speaking is characterized by *spontaneity, directness, flexibility,* and *involvement.*

Spontaneity is particularly important in the use of gestures and bodily movement. Neither should be planned in advance; they should emerge naturally from the speech, the enlarged conversation. Both gestures and bodily movement should reinforce the spoken words so that movement does not involve aimless wandering around the room. As a general rule, you ought to gesture whenever you feel like it, making some attempt to adjust the size of the gesture to the size of the room (the small classroom versus the five thousand-seat auditorium).

Directness is another critical quality of effective delivery. Probably the best way to communicate directly with others is to look directly into their eyes while articulating your ideas. We recognize this fact at an interpersonal level, but the importance of eye contact often escapes us when we communicate as public speakers. Whenever possible, you should strive to establish eye contact with everyone in the audience as often as possible. When speaking in a large lecture hall, it is also important to look at least in the direction of everyone in the audience.

Directness can also be communicated through the language and supporting evidence used. Speaking in the second person, translating statistics into figures of direct relevance to the audience, and using examples and illustrations of great personal interest to the listeners are some approaches to stylistic directness.

Finally, directness may be demonstrated through appropriate vocal qualities. You should speak so as to be heard—but not so that you blast listeners from the room. Some speakers talk with an overly projected, artificial vocal quality, leaving the impression of a dramatic production rather than a speaking occasion. On the other hand, no one cares to listen to a monotone. Ideas are best communicated directly to audiences by speakers who employ vocal variety and expressiveness.

Flexibility is a third quality of effective delivery. To be a flexible speaker, you must be alert to information, responses, and other stimuli that might indicate a need for change in your planned strategy and choice of words. Speakers who insist on delivering the speech precisely as they have practiced it often fail to meet important needs of audience members. They are not responsive to boredom, confusion, or hostility. Thus, they say what they want to say, but the listeners cannot, will not, or do not receive the message. Once again, the most effective public speakers are usually those who are especially responsive to audience feedback.

The final important delivery characteristic is *involvement.* It is imperative that you appear concerned about your communicated message. Involvement is a total delivery

concept, including eye contact, movement, word choice, and facial expression. We believe that you are committed to your ideas when you reinforce your words with appropriate nonverbal and inflectional emphasis. The speaker who says, "I couldn't believe in this more" in a deadpan manner without communicating an image of total commitment might as well say, "I couldn't care less about this"; certainly the latter is more likely the meaning the audience will perceive.

Responding to Unexpected Events

In every public speaking situation, we can never completely predict audience responses nor be completely certain of the kinds of questions audience members are likely to pose after the speech. That kind of uncertainty is part of the speech environment and should be anticipated and even welcomed. But from time to time, every speaker faces other sorts of unexpected events that may be more unsettling.

Consider some of the following examples. One woman scheduled to speak at a convention became flustered before the presentation and left all of her notes in her hotel room, several blocks from the convention center. She had planned to use extemporaneous delivery with considerable reliance on her notes. Yet only a few minutes before she was scheduled to speak, she realized her notes were missing. On a different occasion, one of the authors was planning to speak from a manuscript but arrived at the restaurant meeting room only to discover that there was no podium.

Obviously, the list of unexpected events could continue indefinitely, and that is precisely the point. Because of the endless array, you must approach each speaking situation recognizing that unforeseen events may occur. For the most part, they are the exception rather than the rule; most listeners are polite and receptive, most rooms do have podiums, and notes seldom get shuffled or lost. When unfortunate unexpected events do occur, the best approach is one of calmness, common sense, and good humor. In most instances, audience members and others who planned the program are more than happy to help you overcome a difficult situation. We have seen listeners' seats moved, podiums created out of boxes, and outside noise sources removed to accommodate the needs of the speaker. After all, the mere fact that you have been invited to address a group of listeners indicates some regard, interest, and respect for you as a person.

Responding to Questions

Every public speaker should be prepared to answer audience questions, usually following the presentation. There are situations in which the speaker encourages listeners to interrupt him or her during the speech whenever they have a question, when something is unclear, or when they simply wish to relate a personal view. The typical procedure, however, is for the speaker to present her or his ideas without interruption and entertain questions during a forum period following the speech.

No speaker should underestimate the importance of responding meaningfully to listeners' questions. In a sense, the *questioning* or *forum period* is simply an extension of the more formally structured presentation, for the skill with which questions are answered will be a major determinant of listeners' overall response to the speech. The forum period represents yet another opportunity to reinforce important ideas, build credibility, provide additional interesting information, and even deal with aspects of the topic untouched by the speech itself.

In handling the forum period procedurally, it is important that each listener hear and understand the question being answered. Sometimes it is helpful to have the questioning audience member rise and state his or her question; or if the room is especially large, you may simply repeat the question before answering it. If several persons have questions, deal with as many as time permits.

No one questioner should be allowed to dominate the forum period, nor should you pursue irrelevant questions for long. If an irrelevant issue is raised or a question so technical that you suspect only a few listeners are interested in hearing the response, you might ask the person who raised the inquiry to talk with you following the forum period. You should never attempt to fake your way through a difficult question. It is best to admit that you do not have that kind of experience or perhaps never uncovered that kind of data during your research. While continual responses of "I don't know" damage your credibility, a single admission of ignorance tends to humanize you and give you a positive mark for openness. And just as you should know how long you are expected to speak, it is equally important to learn how much time is available for answering questions. Time limits vary greatly, but whatever they are, they should be respected.

Language: Striving for Good Oral Style

When we speak of good *oral* style, we are really stressing the fact that speaking and writing are not the same. Even though both deal with words, sentences, and language in general, there are several important differences. Speakers who read from a written text often sound stuffy or overly formal. In listening to them, we may feel that their remarks really do not speak to us directly. This is especially the case if they are reading from a written report. Actually, most of the differences between oral and written style are more a matter of degree than of kind. While most people couldn't list the differences, they could easily identify a speech that violated good oral "rules."

Differences Between Oral and Written Style

Generally speaking, in contrast to written prose style, good oral style uses:
1. *More personal pronouns* (we, ours, I, mine, you, yours)
2. *More simple sentences* (Although good speakers use variety in sentence structure, they rely mostly on the simple "subject-verb-predicate" sentence structure.)
3. *Shorter sentences* (This is related to number 2 and will be elaborated shortly.)
4. *Many more rhetorical questions* (We have already discussed these as potentially good attention-getting devices to be used in the introduction. Used throughout the speech, they tend to sustain the audience's attention by challenging them to think.)
5. *More repetition of words, phrases, and sentences* (Readers can go back and reread something they have missed or focus on a phrase that strikes their fancy. Listeners cannot do this. Thus, good speakers often intentionally repeat key ideas, colorful phrases, or slogans that they want the audience to remember and ponder after the speech is over.)
6. *More monosyllabic than polysyllabic words* (As we said above, good speeches must be instantly intelligible. Listeners do not carry dictionaries in their hip pockets. It is vital, therefore, to use familiar, relatively simple words with most audiences.)
7. *More contractions* (Good public speaking should have a conversational quality. In daily conversation, we use many contractions—"I've," "you can't," "he won't," rather than "I have," "you cannot," or "he will not." Speakers sound more natural when they use contractions.)
8. *More figurative language* (By using metaphor, simile, alliteration, repetition, and other figures of speech, the public speaker makes her words more pleasing to the ear and stimulates the audience's imagination. Figures of speech also make abstract ideas concrete, add color and life to the speech, and reinforce key ideas.)[20]

Choosing Words

Certainly a primary goal of any public speaker is to be clear. One way of achieving clarity is to choose your words with great care. *Concrete words,* for example, are usually preferable to abstract words. Concrete words point to real events or objects that the audience can associate with objective experience. As your words become more and more concrete, the pictures you paint in the minds of your audience tend to become clearer and clearer. Concrete words appeal to the senses. They point to something the listeners can hear, touch, see, taste, or feel: lemon, motorcycle, boots, tea, roses, picnic table, the howl of a wolf, the smell of freshly perked coffee. Whenever you must deal with a relatively abstract concept in your speaking, you can make it clearer and more concrete by providing specific illustrations and examples.

Besides being concrete, your words should also be *simple*. Simplicity is related to clarity. When you use simple words, you avoid being vague, pretentious, or verbose. But simplicity is not the same as simpleness. In fact, many great speakers of the past, including Winston Churchill and Franklin Delano Roosevelt, have been masters of simplicity. Although simple words are usually familiar ones as well, there are some phrases that have become clichéd by overuse. Among the *clichés that should be avoided are*

it goes without saying	in the final analysis
after all is said and done	tired but happy
easier said than done	all in all
last but not least	drastic action
method in his madness	reigns supreme
more than meets the eye	worked like a horse
ignorance is bliss	clear as a crystal
few and far between	

These are only a few examples of expressions that were probably amusing and interesting at one time but are now stale from overuse.

Besides striving for concreteness and simplicity in word choice, you should also seek *precision*. Although we often speak of synonyms, rarely do we find any two words that have *exactly* the same meaning. If you looked up the following five words, you would soon discover that while each has to do with being poor, they still represent subtly different shades of meaning: *destitute, impoverished, bankrupt, impecunious,* and *needy*. Precise words are accurate. Rather than using the verb *walked*, for instance, you might describe the *way* a person walked by using such verbs as *staggered, ambled, strutted, sauntered, waddled,* or *raced*. By selecting the best word in these cases, you also eliminate unnecessary modifiers, such as, "walked *slowly*" or "walked *drunkenly*." Thus, precise language is usually compact.

Constructing Sentences

As you choose your words carefully and begin to place them into sentences, some additional guiding principles are useful. First, *construct your sentences so that the subject and the verb are close together*. This increases the intelligibility of the sentence. It is also a practical characteristic of daily conversation; therefore, it sounds more natural. Consider the following sentence in which subject and verb have been separated: "This plan, which has been tested in other companies like our own and has resulted in enormous profits, is worthy of your support." To place the subject and the verb together and thus increase the sentence's intelligibility, you might create two separate sentences, as follows: "This plan is worthy of your support. It has been tested in companies like our own and has resulted in enormous profits."

Another important guideline is to *keep your sentences relatively short,* with some variety in sentence length and type. Short sentences are easier for audiences to follow and comprehend. Supposedly, a "standard" sentence is made up of seventeen words.[21] Even so, some variety is essential. Longer sentences can be clear if properly constructed. In writing sentences, you should avoid needless repetition, unnecessary modifiers, and circumlocutions, such as "*The reason why* I think this plan will work is *because.* . . ." One of the best ways to delete unnecessary words is to *use the active voice* whenever possible. Compare the following:

"Much dissatisfaction with this new rotation schedule has been expressed by line workers." (passive voice)

"Line workers have expressed much dissatisfaction with this new rotation schedule." (active voice)

Sometimes the passive voice is unclear because it is wordy, but often it is intrinsically unclear. For example, "This product was chosen because it met governmental standards and . . ." What this sentence does not tell us is who did the choosing. Depending upon the issue being discussed, that might be very important information.

Also related to the issue of sentence length is the use of modifiers. Specifically, *use only necessary modifiers.* There are two kinds of modifiers in the English language, those that comment and those that define. Commenting modifiers include *very, most,* and *definitely.* These modifiers tell us nothing new; instead, they try to boost the meaning of the word they modify. Yet if your words are selected carefully, with a concern for precision, they should be able to stand alone without the assistance of modifiers that simply try to make their meaning more emphatic. Of course, some modifiers are essential; they tell us something we need to know. Depending upon whether a plan is described as "innovative," "costly," "sensible," or "outdated," we will and should respond differently. Defining modifiers provide information that the noun standing alone cannot convey.

Sometimes we add other kinds of unnecessary words to our sentences. Often we load up on prepositions, conjunctions, adverbs, and relative pronouns that add nothing to the sentence but empty words. To be concise, you need to *eliminate* these *low information content (LIC) words* from your speaking (as well as from your writing). Business Brief 13.5 lists LIC words and phrases, specifying those that should be eliminated completely and noting how the remaining ones should be modified.

Yet another way of enhancing the intelligibility of your remarks is to *use straight-forward sentences.* Sometimes we begin our sentences with an accumulation of clauses. We might say, for example, "When you try to think of a less expensive way, when you

BUSINESS BRIEF

13.5

Examples of Low Information Content (LIC) Words and Phrases

The LIC words and phrases in this partial list are followed by an expression in parentheses (to illustrate a better way to write the phrase) or by an (X), which means that it should be dropped entirely.

actually (X)

a majority of (most)

a number of (many; several)

as a means of (for; to)

as a result (so)

as necessary (X)

at the rate of (at)

at the same time as (while)

bring to a conclusion (conclude)

by means of (by)

by use of (by)

communicate with (talk to; telephone; write to)

connected together (connected)

contact (talk to; telephone; write to)

due to the fact that (because)

during the time that (while)

end result (result)

exhibit a tendency (tend)

for a period of (for)

for the purpose of (for; to)

for this reason (because)

in an area where (where)

in an effort to (to)

in close proximity to (close to; near)

in connection with (about)

in fact (X)

in order to (to)

in such a manner as to (to)

in terms of (in; for)

in the course of (during)

in the direction of (toward)

in the event that (if)

in the form of (as)

in the neighborhood of; in the vicinity of (about; approximately; near)

involves the use of (employs; uses)

involves the necessity of (demands; requires)

is designed to be (is)

it can be seen that (thus; so)

it is considered desirable (I/we want to)

it will be necessary to (I, you, or we must)

of considerable magnitude (large)

on account of (because)

prior to (before)

subsequent to (after)

with the aid of (with)

Note: Many of these phrases start and end with little connecting words such as *as, at, by, for, in, is, it, of, to,* and *with.* This can help you to identify LIC words and phrases in your writing.

consider the issue of practicality, and when you look for a plan that is really forward-looking, I am convinced that the plan I've outlined here tonight is the one to pursue." Because of the way this sentence is constructed, audience members may never make it to the persuasive point at the end. A more straightforward way to say it is: "I am convinced that the plan I've outlined here tonight is the one to pursue. It is practical, inexpensive, and forward-looking."

Similarly, you can keep your sentences straightforward by refusing to invert them. Inverted sentence structures may look sophisticated on the page, but they are hard for listeners to follow. Here is an example: "That we have a severe morale problem, reduced productivity, and high levels of absenteeism were the findings of our recent organizational analysis." This sentence is not the kind you would utter naturally; it is contrived. Here is the same sentence, but with normal word order: "The findings of our recent organizational analysis were that we have a severe morale problem, reduced productivity, and high levels of absenteeism."

Delivery: Using Visual Aids

In each speaking situation, the need for communicating information clearly, concretely, and concisely is great. One way of doing this is through the use of visual aids. By using visual aids, you reinforce your ideas by letting your audience see them as well as hear about them. You may choose from numerous visual vehicles.

Probably the simplest and most basic is the *chalkboard*. This allows you to put diagrams and sketches on the board as an explanation unfolds. If you are counting on using a chalkboard, however, you had better check in advance to make sure the room has one. The chalkboard is a convenient and potentially effective means of depicting important data. Moving to and from the chalkboard allows you to be active in communicating your ideas. It may serve to spark your own interest, as well as the audience's. Moreover, physical activity may help you to manage any speech anxiety you are experiencing. Of course, the chalkboard has its limitations. Because it is so familiar to most audiences, it tends to be less interesting than other forms of visual aids. But if your handwriting is legible, if you are working on a clean board, and if you can practice so that you do not lose contact with the audience while you write, then the chalkboard may be a sensible choice of visual support. You can also enhance the rather ordinary appearance of most chalkboards by using several different colors of chalk. If possible, prepare the board in advance and cover it with a screen, to be lifted at the appropriate moment.

Other visual aids can be prepared in advance and brought with you to the speaking event. For example, if you want to use color or a sophisticated design, you may elect *posterboard drawings* as a presentational aid. These can be prepared in advance and can be as professional and impressive as budget and talent will allow. Since posterboards can be somewhat clumsy to handle, especially if two or more are used during the presentation, you may want to use a *flipchart*. With this method, you place the drawings on a rather large tablet and display them on a convenient frame that facilitates movement from one drawing to the next. It is also possible to use *flannel boards* to create a picture during the presentation by adding relevant elements as you discuss them, rather than unveiling the entire visual at once. This visual aid encourages listeners to follow you progressively as you discuss an idea or sequence of events point by point. Finally, if you need to demonstrate a progression of information, you may choose to use the *cutaway*, a visual aid that begins with a basic outline or simple picture and adds parts to it so that it progresses into a complex drawing. A speaker explaining the value of specific features of a particular automobile design might find a cutaway useful to depict, first, the basic car body. The speaker might then add each part one by one so that, eventually, the automobile is completed. Cutaways are rather difficult to construct. If you want to use one, you may have to consult the design department of your organization for assistance.

On occasion, you may decide to prepare copies of a *handout* to aid the audience's comprehension. These are especially useful when you are referring to extensive lists of figures, such as budgetary statements in the context of a technical report. You can also use handouts to outline essential information to which the audience can refer during subsequent decision-making sessions. By using handouts, you reduce the need for audience notetaking. Thus, listeners can devote greater attention to your ideas. The handout serves as an outline for you, potentially assisting you in your organization and delivery. While many teachers have discovered the virtues of the handout, in general, duplicated materials tend to be underused by speakers. When using handouts, you should pass them out at the moment you plan to discuss them (not in advance) and make sure that copies are available for everyone.

A final kind of frequently used visual aid is the *model*. Models may be either *single-dimensional* or *three-dimensional*, depending on the subject of the presentation. In chapter 1, we presented a single-dimensional model depicting the role that communication plays in organizational life. These models are typically rather simple and straightforward. Three-dimensional models, on the other hand, are miniatures of the real, often larger, object. Suppose an architect has been asked to make a presentation in which he is to discuss his concept of a new museum. He may elect to construct a three-dimensional model of the proposed building so that the audience will have a precise picture of the structure he envisions. One major advantage of these models is the clarity and precision with which they allow you to demonstrate your ideas.

Depicting Statistics

In most speaking situations, you will find yourself using statistics as support from time to time. Visual aids can often help you to present statistical information clearly and concisely. One common method is to use *summary tables*. These tables allow you to analyze raw data and present the data's major conclusions in such a way that important relationships are clarified. Table 13.1 provides an illustration of a summary table. In this example, assume that the speaker is describing a problem that has developed in the financial stability of one branch of the organization's clothing stores. In the

Table 13.1 A Comparison of the Fashion Corner with the Fashion Nook in Terms of the Average Number of Different Garments Sold Daily

	Average Number Sold Daily	
Garment Types	Fashion Corner	Fashion Nook
Dresses	11	24
Coats	2	7
Blouses	8	16
Slacks	12	22
Pantsuits	3	13

summary table, she is comparing the average number of garments sold per day in the problem store (Fashion Corner) with the average number sold daily in a successful branch in a similar town (Fashion Nook).

Statistical summary tables may contain only one main idea, or they may be more complicated and introduce several summaries. Even with relatively sophisticated audiences, however, you should not attempt to crowd too much information onto one summary table. Fairly complicated summary tables should be presented on handouts, or the data should be separated so that it is depicted on several different tables.

Another common method for presenting statistical summaries is by a *graph*. A graph is a representation of numbers by geometric figures drawn to scale.[22] Speakers often use graphs to make statistical information more vivid and to depict relationships. Two of the more familiar and useful kinds of graphs are line and bar graphs. *Line graphs* are especially useful for depicting comparative relationships through time. Many business and professional presentations focus on information relating to time-based trends—for example, comparing gross or net profits, production, or wages. As a result, the line graph is one of the more useful tools of the presentational speaker. Figure 13.1 presents an example of a line graph depicting gross income.

It is possible to place more than one curve on a single graph, but it may be at the expense of clarity. Moreover, you should recognize that a trend can be distorted simply by compressing or elongating the space allotted to time periods, while keeping the other dimension of the graph constant. The ethical speaker will not knowingly distort a trend simply to dramatize a particular point.

The other kind of commonly used graph is the *bar graph*. These graphs usually depict quantity. Thus, a simple bar graph literally uses bars to indicate amounts and is well suited to presenting comparative statistics. Figure 13.2 depicts comparisons of worker productivity, focusing on five known time periods and one projected one.

Bar graphs are particularly useful as visual aids in that they can be made large enough for the audience to see and easily understand the point being made. As with the line graph, it is possible to depict a number of different statistical comparisons simultaneously on the same bar graph, often through the use of different colors or shadings. Once again, however, when a graph is shown from the front of the room, simplicity should be sought to avoid confusion.

Figure 13.1
Line graph of gross income.

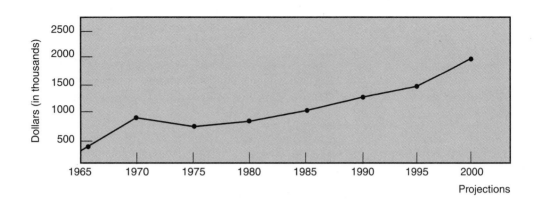

Figure 13.2
Bar graph of worker productivity.

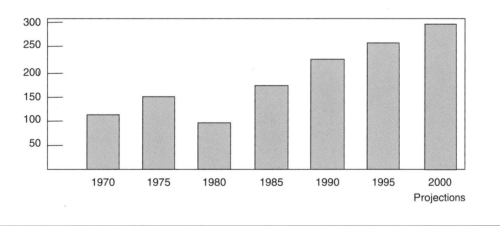

Other Visual Devices

There are many other types of visual aids from which to choose. *Maps,* for example, can be used in a great variety of ways. They are particularly useful if you are dealing with geographical locations. Locations are often important when you are addressing issues such as sales progress in different territories, when the company is considering opening branch offices, and when specific populations are concentrated. As visual aids, maps should be prepared with care to add color and clarity to the presentation.

When McDonnell Douglas was forced to lay off many of its employees, it made extensive use of video as a communication tool. In a tape sent to 100,000 employees, John F. McDonnell, chairman of the company, used a series of charts and graphs to describe the company's financial difficulties and explain the reasons behind his decision to lay off 17,000 workers.

The video, along with a series of "town hall" meetings between McDonnell and employees, were part of a strategy to regain the support and confidence of employees who had become progressively less productive and made an increasing number of on-the-job mistakes over the previous several years. Brief statements by selected employees also were included in the video in an effort to express concerns other employees might have as well.

These efforts drew positive reactions. Some felt it was an effective way of sending warnings to less productive employees, and one employee remarked that the video could signal a new approach to management-employee relations throughout the company.

From Stephen Franklin, "New Candor in the Air at McDonnell Douglas," *Chicago Tribune,* 10 September, 1990, Sec. 4, p. 1.

You can also use actual *objects* as visual aids. Assume that a speaker is proposing the adoption of a new line of toys aimed at fostering creativity and teaching certain critical concepts, such as numbers and spatial relationships. Assume further that samples of these toys exist. What better way to persuade the audience of the uniqueness and value of the toys than by displaying and demonstrating them?

Overhead projectors are useful for displaying detailed or complex information on a large screen. However, certain principles should be observed when using an overhead projector. The transparencies should be as simple and readable as possible. When displaying transparencies, avoid "keystoning," or the wide-at-top, narrow-at-bottom effect that occurs when the light is projected upward at too steep an angle. Attempt to have the lens sufficiently high to project the light head-on, and if the screen is hanging from the ceiling, secure the bottom to the wall behind it to create an appropriate angle. In addition, stand next to the screen, not the machine, when speaking (thereby presenting a unified image to the audience), and be sure you do not stand between audience members and the projected image. When using a pointer, do not hold it over the platform of the machine (thereby magnifying by a thousand times any shakiness of the hands you are experiencing); instead, point directly to the screen.

When changing transparencies, try to accomplish the switch quickly and smoothly so that the audience is not blinded by a bath of hot, white light between every slide. Try to avoid "lightheads," or askewed positioning of the overheads, by placing each squarely on the machine.

Slide projectors are particularly useful in showing pictures or delivering presentations that must be repeated in the future. For maximum effectiveness, slide presentations should be planned in advance to maintain a relatively steady pace. As each new slide is shown, allow a moment of silence so the audience has an opportunity to grasp its contents, then describe and discuss what they are viewing. In addition, avoid turning your back to the audience and talking to the screen; glance at the screen to determine what slide is showing, and then speak directly to the audience as you provide added information.

Finally, with increasingly sophisticated technology, *electronic presentation systems* are becoming widely available. These include an array of electronic aids that can be used to enhance oral presentations. For instance, some presentational rooms are now equipped with a multipurpose, large projection screen. The speaker uses one centralized system to shift among color slides, overhead transparencies, videotapes, and computer graphics—all of which are projected onto the large screen. Even in more traditional rooms, software can still be used to generate computer graphics. Some are predicting a revolution in this area.[23] For instance, cumulative graphics (for example, ones that start with an empty pie and add pieces) and dynamic (moving) graphics are already available. Standard graphics packages offer about sixteen colors from which to select, but one package offers nearly a thousand colors.[24]

Some Practical Considerations

Regardless of the type of visual aid you choose to clarify the presentation, here are some general guidelines you should follow:

1. *Use visual aids only when they are justified.* Some speakers try to jazz up their presentations by using visual aids. But unnecessary visual aids can annoy or distract an audience as easily as persuade them. Visual aids should be used to clarify, to make more concrete, or to demonstrate something that is difficult to describe without them. They should reinforce main points to help the audience understand and remember them.
2. *Don't hesitate to use essential visual aids.* You cannot tell an audience what a proposed budget is "like." To be clear and complete, you must present it in detail visually, usually by providing a handout. Similarly, it would be foolish to describe a building plan, a surgical procedure, or an automobile design without the aid of visuals.
3. *Your visual aids should be large enough so that each member of the audience can see and decipher them with ease.* A visual aid that cannot be seen is actually a hindrance and would best be omitted entirely.
4. *Your visual aids should be clear and, if appropriate, colorful.* Your writing or printing should be neat and clear. In general, a black-and-white chart is not nearly so striking as one that includes red, purple, or blue. Whatever color scheme you choose, your visual aid should enhance clarity and be pleasing to the eye.
5. *Your visual aids should be simple.* The inclusion of many complicated details will serve only to distract the audience and obscure the point being made. In general, it is best to illustrate only the essentials, with one concept featured with each diagram.

6. *Consider the needs of each audience member in presenting your visuals.* It is quite possible for the visual aid to be large enough, but due to nervousness or insensitivity on the part of the speaker, many listeners are never given the opportunity to see it. Visual aids should be placed high enough so that those in the front of the room do not obstruct the view of those in the back. On other occasions, it may be necessary to turn the aid and display it at varied angles so that all persons in the room can see it with ease.

7. *Do not inadvertently obscure the view of your visual aid by standing in front of it.* Often a part of the graph or chart is hidden from some of the audience, but those individuals cannot be rationalized out of existence—particularly since they could be critical group leaders! There is often a tendency, when writing on the chalkboard, to hide a great deal of the writing with one's body while, at the same time, talking to the board rather than to the audience.

8. *Point to the part of the visual aid you are discussing.* In this way, you can help the audience follow your remarks. You can point by using your finger or, with large visual aids, a pointer.

9. *Visual aids should be displayed only when they are being discussed in the presentation.* When you are finished with them, remove them from view. When visual aids are randomly displayed at the beginning of the presentation or left in view after they have functioned as aids, you are inviting the audience to continue to look at the visual and ignore your message.

10. *Practice with your visual aid before the presentation.* Make sure you are comfortable with the equipment. More important, be sure you can move smoothly from your notes at the podium to the visual aid and back again without losing either your composure or your sense of directness with the audience.

Visual aids are potentially useful supportive devices for the presentation of speeches. Not every speaker should use them, but most presentations would benefit from their skillful use. The careful preparation of visual materials is simply one way for the speaker to demonstrate a concern for clarity, precision, and concreteness. When properly prepared, visual aids should, as the name suggests, *aid* audience comprehension. Furthermore, they indicate that you believe you are engaging in a significant form of organizational communication.

Summary

There are many reasons why public speakers fail to communicate effectively. Chief among them is the speaker being perceived by the audience as disorganized. Poor organization leaves the audience feeling confused and frustrated. What were the speaker's *main* ideas? How did the arguments progress throughout the speech? How were the main points related? Did the speech hang together so that it seemed like a coherent whole? What information or arguments should be remembered? If the answers to these questions are unclear, the speaker probably had some difficulty organizing his or her thoughts—or difficulty communicating them to the audience in a way that let them see the speech's underlying logic and coherence.

Organizing your speech into a form well suited to the audience's needs and your specific purpose is a step crucial to your success as a public speaker. Your task is to choose a pattern of organization that makes sense in terms of your overall speaking strategy. One useful tool for accomplishing this is the outline. By outlining, you can begin to put your ideas down on paper and examine the way your speech is developing. Later, you can use the outline to assist you in delivering your speech extemporaneously.

For most public speaking contexts, the extemporaneous style of delivery is best. Extemporaneous delivery allows you to be direct with your audience, as well as flexible and spontaneous. In general, these qualities will serve you well as you speak within your organization or as a representative of your organization addressing the general public. Through extemporaneous delivery, you are also more likely to use conversational language, so that your sentences are less stilted and your word choice is simple and appropriate. One hazard associated with extemporaneous delivery, however, is that your word choice may be less than perfect, and occasionally your sentences may ramble. As you speak more and more frequently and as you work to improve over time (using the criteria outlined in this chapter), your oral style will surely improve.

Finally, using carefully prepared visual aids is an excellent way to enhance your speech. With visual aids, you can highlight your main ideas, depict statistics, picture things that otherwise have to be imagined, and show the audience that you did, in fact, prepare very well for your presentation. Almost any speech can benefit from the use of at least one visual aid. As with other aspects of your speech, visual aids will be more effective if they are prepared well in advance (using the criteria discussed in this chapter) and if you practice using them *before* you deliver your speech. Visual aids are a virtual requirement in certain types of speech situations, such as those involving sales or proposal presentations. In our last chapter, we turn our attention to some of these special kinds of public speaking contexts.

Questions for Discussion

1. What are some of the elements of an effective speech introduction? Be specific. What are some methods of gaining the audience's attention? Cite examples whenever possible.
2. What are some speech topics that would be well suited to each of the following patterns of organization?
   a. chronological order
   b. spatial order
   c. topical order
   d. cause-and-effect order
   e. problem-solution order
3. Discuss the basic characteristics of good speech conclusions. What are some specific devices that might be used to conclude speeches? Examples?

4. Describe the components of a good speech outline. In what ways do you see outlines as important?
5. Refute or defend the following: "Stage fright is a nearly universal phenomenon." Cite evidence to support your position. What are some strategies for developing confidence as a public speaker?
6. Compare and contrast impromptu and extemporaneous speaking. What are the conditions under which each is appropriately used?
7. If given the choice, would you elect to speak extemporaneously or from a manuscript? Why? How would you prepare for the mode of delivery you have chosen?
8. What are some problems you might anticipate with regard to answering questions after a speech? How might you cope with each? Again, be specific.
9. List some of the differences between oral and written style. What happens when a public speaker violates the "rules" of good oral style?
10. What are some of the characteristics of good word choice and sound sentence structure? Cite examples of each quality you name.
11. List several guidelines for the effective use of visual aids.

Exercises

1. Choose one of the following topics. Assume that you have been assigned to speak on this chosen topic to your classroom audience. Compose a good introduction and conclusion. Select a basic purpose for your speech. Then choose a tentative strategy of organization for the body and outline it briefly. Discuss the reasoning behind your choices.
   a. grade inflation
   b. the job market
   c. reverse discrimination
   d. the institution of marriage
   e. accomplishments of the present federal administration
   f. United Way
   g. ethics in advertising
   h. heart disease
   i. sugar in the diet
   j. postretirement years
   k. exercise
2. Take a topic of your choice and deliver it to the classroom audience using extemporaneous delivery. Try to capitalize on the qualities of effective delivery that are particularly well suited to the extemporaneous mode of delivery. If possible, ask your instructor to make a videotape of your speaking so that you can later watch yourself and gain from self-analysis. At the very least, ask the audience to focus specifically on your delivery and how it might be improved.
3. Choose another speech topic and develop it into a manuscript speech. Be sure to guard against composing it like an essay rather than a speech, and practice it several times so that you can overcome some of the problems associated with manuscript speaking. Then follow the same procedure in delivering the speech outlined above. Which mode of delivery do you prefer, or does it depend on the context, topic, and so forth?

4. After each of the speeches, allow the audience to ask you questions. In answering them, make every effort to follow the guidelines established in the chapter. After the question-and-answer period, ask the class to evaluate that part of your speaking as well. To what extent, for example, did your responding to questions contribute to your clarity, credibility, and responsiveness?

5. Go to the library and look up *Vital Speeches of the Day*. Select any speech delivered during the past two years. Make a copy of it. Then determine to what extent the speaker used good oral style. Mark specific instances where either word choice or sentence structure is especially good or bad. Then write a brief speech analysis in which you discuss the extent to which the speaker developed her or his speech using good oral style. Be sure to define the criteria you use to assess oral style.

Special Speaking Applications

R ecently, a group of professionals from a prominent manufacturing company in the East approached a professor of communication, asking her to teach them how to make good oral presentations. The group was quite diverse, composed of, among others, a twenty-one-year-old college intern working in sales as part of his field experience for a degree in marketing, a thirty-year-old woman who had just moved into a supervisory position, and a fifty-year-old upper-level manager who had been with the company for more than twenty-five years. Besides their differences in age and status within the firm, their speaking needs also varied. The young man wanted to know how to make better persuasive presentations to customers, the woman was interested in learning how to present concise, informative reports to her newly acquired staff, and the senior manager needed to learn how to make high-quality public presentations to promote the company at conferences around the world. In spite of the differences in their speaking needs, they all had two things in common. Not a single person in the group (nine in all) had ever studied public speaking, nor had they anticipated doing any public speaking when they started their careers.

We begin the chapter with this illustration because these individuals are typical of the general business and professional population. Most people assume they will not be making oral presentations, and when they *are* asked to (because it is expected of successful professionals), they feel poorly equipped to do so. In chapter 12, we pointed out that most managers and a great many professionals of all sorts need to develop public speaking skills. Yet we recognize that not everyone will be asked to make general speeches to some large public outside the organization. Much public speaking occurs regularly inside the organization, some of it requiring special skills and understanding. In this final chapter, we turn our focus to two kinds of public speaking with which many of you will be involved in the future: the oral report (sometimes called the informative or technical report) and the persuasive speech, which includes proposal and sales presentations.

Informative Oral Reports

In every organization, there is a compelling need to share information. If individual employees fail to inform one another of their actions, ideas, and experience, the likely result is wasted time, poor decisions, and uncoordinated efforts. Much information sharing occurs informally and grows out of the context of private meetings and small groups, but there are also many times when important information needs to be shared with a significant number of employees. At those times, managers may tap individuals to prepare and present their information more formally in the form of oral reports. This section will focus on oral reporting as a special instance of public speaking and will offer some practical suggestions for developing and delivering effective oral reports.

Defining the Oral Report

Suppose you are asked to attend a state meeting in place of your supervisor. Upon your return, she asks you to come into her office and brief her on what happened at the conference. Or suppose that your company is preparing to introduce some new computer software into the market. Your boss asks you to examine the major competitors and prepare a thorough report of your findings, which you will deliver to all personnel in your organization who are involved with marketing and selling the new product. Or imagine yourself as a research chemist employed by a large drug manufacturing firm. You have discovered some possible dangers associated with a new drug your company is planning to market. At the weekly staff meeting with your fellow chemists, you are asked to present a progress report on your research.

As you begin to think about the kind of jobs you hope to hold in the future, you can probably think of many different situations where you may be called upon to give an oral report. The preceding examples point to the diversity of oral reports, highlighting the different sizes and types of audiences you may be asked to address. Every oral report involves a face-to-face presentation of information, except in a few unusual cases where you participate in a teleconference or are asked to brief someone by telephone.

Most oral reports are made in response to an inquiry. Your supervisor wants you to share information, or some group within the organization indicates that they need information. The oral report, then, grows from that expressed request or need. Typically, you are asked to make a report because someone assumes that you know something of particular interest to others. Because of your experience, expertise, or both, you are asked to share what you know or have experienced. Regardless of the specific nature of the oral report, its general purpose is to *facilitate understanding and retention*.[1] As Wilcox has put it, "Our success . . . in informing will be measured by the degree to which our listeners are able to comprehend and recall accurately and meaningfully what we are talking about."[2]

Developing the Oral Report

From the time you are asked to give an oral report, everything you do should be geared toward the general purposes of helping your listeners understand the information and retain it. In many cases, the information you share will have a direct impact on how well others perform their jobs. In other instances, they may need it simply to better understand the organization in which they work and how their unit or department relates to others. Given this perspective, the following guidelines may be helpful:

Know Your Audience and Their Expectations

Most oral reports are given within the organization rather than to some external constituency. That suggests that you are more likely than not to be acquainted with your listeners or at least able to acquire information about them with relative ease. Gaining this information is a crucial step, since listener needs and expectations vary significantly even within the same organization. Let's say, for example, that you have developed an innovative training program for new members of your department. Your supervisor is impressed with your work and asks you to present a brief description of this program to the company's executive board. In this case, you are dealing with executives who take a very broad view of the organization and are generally interested in any program within the company that promotes morale and productivity. This audience does not want to hear the details of how you developed your program. They are not interested in how to set up one of their own. What they want is a highlighting overview.

On a different occasion, you might be asked to discuss your training program with another department interested in the possibility of establishing a similar one of their own. In this case, you need to deal with the specifics of goals, planning, and implementation. These listeners *need* to know how to do it when you are finished. Given the diversity of these two audiences, their needs and expectations, you would approach your topic so differently that the two resulting reports would represent entirely different presentations. This kind of audience adaptation is crucial.

Be Prepared to Adapt to the Listeners' Norms

Many groups within organizations listen regularly to oral presentations, possibly as part of their regular staff meetings. Because these individuals have frequent meetings, work together, and may even socialize together, they tend to develop strong preferences or norms regarding communicative interaction. Some of these groups can be very difficult audiences. Some, for instance, are very informal. Their meetings begin with considerable joking and horseplay, and they continue to tease one another throughout their meeting session. Should you be asked to present a technical report to such a group, you may feel that the nature of your information and the climate in which you are speaking are simply incompatible. Rarely is that the case. With this kind of group, you might want to consider arriving early so that you can participate in the informal banter, to establish goodwill and common ground with them. Then, in your introductory remarks you might make some reference to how much you have enjoyed their company and good cheer before turning your attention to the serious subject at hand.

On other occasions, you may have to make more sweeping kinds of adjustments. A prominent engine manufacturing company in the Midwest, for instance, prides itself on having much interaction between departments. This involves inviting individuals from other departments to make oral presentations with some regularity. Often the presenters are newer members of the organization, since one of the company's objectives is to assist their employees in acquiring public speaking skills. In this case, then, the oral reporter often faces a group of employees with a good deal more experience than himself or herself. Equally important, the company has developed a style of interacting so that listeners frequently interrupt the presenter in the middle of his or her presentation, questioning and probing for further information—or occasionally challenging the information presented.

This example highlights the importance of understanding the norms and customs of one's listeners *before* presenting an oral report. Armed with this information, you can plan intelligently. As with any public speech, different options exist. In this case, the speaker might choose to break his report into short segments, stopping after each to ask if there are any questions. Or he might choose to create a more integrated kind of report, but practice it aloud several times with a friend who agrees in advance to interrupt him with questions, thus letting him practice retaining his stream of thought when being interrupted. Finally, he might consider stating politely to the listeners that he will be delighted to respond to questions at the *end* of the presentation and ask them to hold their questions and comments until then. The last technique is risky. It places the speaker in the position of attempting to gain control over the flow of the interaction, asks the audience to adjust to his expectations, and is particularly tricky, given the status difference described above.

What is important to recall is that every group has norms; one must find out what those norms are and then select from among sensible and available strategies the one most likely to result in a positive listener response.

Know the Material

Every public speaker is expected to be knowledgeable. The individual who presents an oral report, however, is expected to be particularly expert. In addition, the oral report is often given to fellow experts within the organization: the marketing strategist is talking to others who are engaged in marketing, the teacher is speaking to other educators, the computer analyst is addressing others who program computers. In short, these are not general audiences. They may need or request a report because they want information. But they are typically operating from a base of experience and knowledge related to the topic that is different from that of most general audiences.

As you prepare to give an oral report, then, it is imperative that you be well versed. Much of your knowledge may grow from your direct experience. When it does not, however, you will need to supplement it with reading, research, and other data collection methods we discussed in chapter 9. Figures must be recent; facts must be accurate and verifiable. Equally crucial is establishing your expertise if it has not already been established. You can make tactful references to your experiences as a teacher, a student, a trainer, a developer, or a fundraiser that will make your presentation more interesting and your comments more credible.

In examining the information you plan to use for your oral report, be sure to consider what the audience already knows. If you are to be truly informative, you must take the audience into partially uncharted waters and give them something new that they can think about or use. Some organizational members are automatically skeptical of anyone who stands up and makes an oral presentation. They may believe that they know as much as you. They may prefer to read about the information rather than having to listen to a presentation. And they may have had some negative experiences with oral presenters in the past. Moreover, in many cases these listeners are listening to your presentation because they were *required* to attend; that is, their supervisor thought you knew something that might be valuable to them. Thus, they may perceive themselves as captive. Perhaps the best way to overcome these kinds of objections is to show the audience that you possess substantive information worth their listening time. You must also organize and present your information so that it is as understandable and interesting as possible.

Carefully Organize Your Materials in Light of Your Specific Purpose

The person who asks you to present an oral report will typically assign your general purpose. You may be asked to report on the status of a fundraising project with which you are associated, to discuss the way quality circles might be used in your organization, to summarize survey information you have acquired about some market-relevant segment of the population, or to outline plans for a building's renovation. Beyond this general purpose, you must think in terms of the specific audience response you desire. You want them to gain an understanding of your ideas and information. But beyond that, what do they need to be able to do with it? Is your report to serve as background so that they can begin to explore and discuss an issue? Is your report supposed to give them enough information by itself so that they can intelligently choose some course of action? Do they need this information to function smoothly, or is the information enriching and interesting but not essential to their professional and personal welfare? As you seek answers to these kinds of questions, you will discover a clearer sense of how to proceed.

As we pointed out in the last chapter, the pattern of organization should reflect your goal or purpose. If, for instance, you want to teach a group of new employees how to write grant proposals, you might choose chronological order, and discuss progressive steps in planning, researching, phoning, writing, and revising over time. If you were reporting on a proposed new building, you would be more likely to use spatial order, moving from the first floor up to the top floor. Finally, many informative oral reporters choose to use a straightforward topical approach involving the choice and development of subject-relevant categories. One popular topical approach, for example, is Who? What? When? Where? Why? How? Not all of these questions will be relevant with every topic, but the general approach is good because it encourages you to look at the subject comprehensively and provides an organizational mechanism for linking the main points together. Suppose you were going to present a report on how to give a speech. You might use the following topical approach:

1. Why is public speaking important?
2. Who is asked to make speeches?
3. What is an effective speech?
4. What are its basic components?
5. How does one learn?
6. Where might one go to learn?

Since the oral informative report is usually given in a situation where time constraints are great, the report must be organized with a maximum concern for conciseness. Refer to the characteristics of effective organization for proposal presentations presented later in this chapter; they apply to oral reports as well.

Deliver Your Report Extemporaneously

A few delivery characteristics are particularly important for oral reports. First, deliver your report from an outline, using extemporaneous delivery. Since so much of the material you present in this kind of context is technical, often either factual or statistical, you need the directness, good eye contact, and conversationality that using an outline allows. Although your information may be dry, in the sense of factual, your presentational manner can demonstrate to the audience that you still find it useful and interesting. Take particular pains with your pacing. Listeners have difficulty absorbing great quantities of

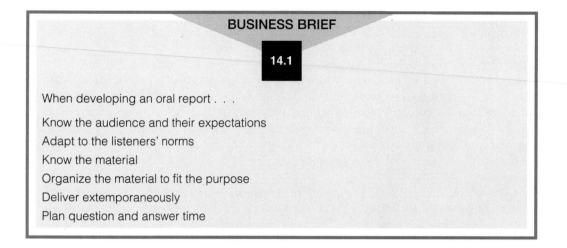

factual, technical information unless they have the time to do so. Slowing down to emphasize crucial information can be helpful. Finally, reinforce your oral comments with appropriate audiovisual aids. These can be useful both during and after your presentation. You may, for instance, use an overhead projector, display charts, and show graphs during your report. Afterwards, you may provide a handout summarizing your remarks, providing additional information, or listing sources of specific kinds of information.

Plan a Definite Time for Questions and Answers

Many public speaking situations do not allow for interaction between speaker and audience. As a special form of informative speaking, however, the oral report must include time for audience questions. Listeners who are presented with information and ideas that are new to them need the opportunity to clarify misunderstandings and to ask for some missed point to be repeated. Good teachers know how important it is to give students time to probe, ponder, and occasionally challenge them through questions and comments. The same is true when you make an oral report. New information is often misunderstood. Or it may raise more questions than it answers. If listeners are to go away feeling satisfied and informed, they, too, must have a chance to talk.

Probably the best context in which to present an oral report is one in which you are presenting information that the listeners will soon be using. Under those conditions, they see its significance and their supervisor has a chance to test what they have retained and can apply. In most reporting situations, however, the information is not used immediately. In those cases, it is particularly useful to provide handouts or follow-up information sheets to reinforce previous learning and increase the chances of retention.

Persuasive Speaking: Basic Principles

Without the ability to communicate persuasively, most organizations could not survive, and most professionals would find their ability to solve problems and achieve upward mobility severely hampered. Managers must communicate persuasively whenever they

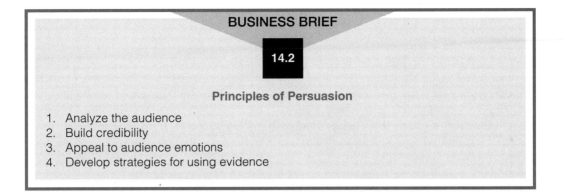

talk to the public about the excellence of their firm or product. Every supervisor toils daily to convince his or her employees that their jobs are important and that they should continue to strive for excellence. Any worker who has a bright idea is immediately confronted with the problem of selling it to others. And all employees involved with sales and promotion are regularly required to approach customers or potential clients and persuade them to make a purchase or investment. As with informative oral reporting, persuasive speaking is a common communication activity in contemporary organizations. Similarly, it is a form of communication that can occur during a private conference, in a small decision-making group, or in front of audiences of varied sizes. We will deal here with persuasion in an audience context, with the understanding that persuasive principles can readily be adapted to other organizational situations. In addition, chapter 7 presents specific issues and techniques important to conducting persuasive or sales interviews.

In our earlier discussion of speech purposes in chapter 12, we suggested that accomplishing a persuasive purpose can be one of the most complex and difficult. The persuasive speaker typically sets out to convince an audience to work harder, consider a product innovation, vote for some new policy or procedure, or invest their time or money in some endeavor. Listeners can absorb information without feeling threatened, but they often squirm when asked to think creatively, to spend money, to cast a vote, or to invest their valuable time in some specific way. To be a successful persuasive speaker, then, you must begin by thoroughly acquainting yourself with the audience and their needs and values.

Analyze the Audience

Every audience can be described according to their basic demographic characteristics, as we pointed out in chapter 12. Some are mostly male; others are basically youthful, mostly well educated, or rather well-to-do. Thus, you might want to consider the basic listener characteristics of age, gender, socioeconomic status and educational level, and religious and political beliefs. If you wanted, for instance, to convince a group of supervisors in your organization that sexual harassment was a problem, you would need to consider both your gender and your listeners' gender before formulating a persuasive plan. If you were a woman addressing a group of male supervisors on this subject, your approach would have to be designed to minimize defensiveness. Listeners' characteristics are a reality with which you must work as a persuasive speaker. Having made a preliminary assessment of those characteristics, you are then ready to ask some questions about what is likely to motivate your audience. Motives are variable energy sources. Coming from within, they tend to guide the options we choose to pursue.[3] The options we select depend on many factors, including our background experiences, the state of our present needs, and our general philosophies of life and human behavior. Some human motivation theorists, including Maslow, contend that individuals are motivated by unfulfilled needs, some of which are more basic to existence than others. One might conclude from this view, then, that audience members must be comfortable with their physiological needs before one can appeal to their higher needs for love, security, and belonging.[4] Anyone who has been forced to attend a lecture before lunch without the benefit of breakfast is well aware of the learning distraction created by hunger pains! While it is difficult to help people learn when their basic needs are unsatisfied or poorly understood, it is virtually impossible to stimulate their thinking, change their beliefs, or move them to act under such circumstances.

Although there are many sources of human motivation, for many audience members habits serve as motives. They will prefer now and in the future what they have felt comfortable with in the past. But individuals vary greatly in the rigidity of their response patterns. At one extreme are the persons who are comfortable only with the status quo. They are cautious, conservative, and low in risk-taking in nearly all circumstances. These individuals are invariably opposed to any idea that involves risk. They may not think the present system perfect, but they take considerable consolation in the knowledge that they are accustomed to it. *Creative, innovative,* and *new* are words that automatically elicit negative responses from these persons. At the opposite end of the habit continuum are those individuals who are consistently flexible, open-minded, and ever responsive to change. In extreme cases, a listener may actually be attracted to an idea or purchase a product simply because it carries the label "new" or "improved."

Habits are only one perspective from which to consider human motivation. Every individual has needs that must be satisfied for the person to live and function happily and productively in society. When personal needs go unfulfilled, they create voids, distress, weakness, and other kinds of physical and psychological discomfort. Earlier we referred to the human motivation research of Maslow that identified a hierarchy of human needs. Beginning at the bottom of the needs hierarchy, they are (1) physiological (health and well-being); (2) safety (personal security, fear of the unknown); (3) love and belonging (the social need of knowing that one is regarded warmly and belongs comfortably to groups that are significant to him or her); (4) esteem (moves beyond being accepted to being respected and held in high regard); and (5) self-actualization (striving for ultimate personal fulfillment).[5] Figure 14.1 illustrates this point.

Some audience members will listen to a persuasive speech with the aim of endorsing the best solution or making the best decision for the welfare of the organization. But while organizational representatives, executives, and managers are "organization men and women" in one sense, they are at the same time human beings with personal needs and motives. Thus, it is critical to consider the diversity of needs. An audience member

Figure 14.1
Factors influencing human motivation.

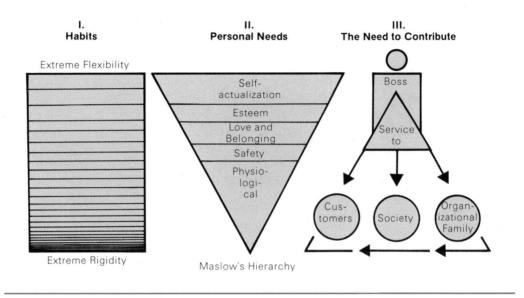

I. Habits — Extreme Flexibility — Extreme Rigidity

II. Personal Needs — Self-actualization, Esteem, Love and Belonging, Safety, Physio-logi-cal — Maslow's Hierarchy

III. The Need to Contribute — Boss — Service to — Customers, Society, Organizational Family

who is insecure about his own capabilities, is uncertain of his acceptance within his department, and believes that he is held in low esteem presents a different type of persuasive problem than a listener who is completely confident, affectionately regarded by all, and respected as a talented, innovative leader.

Not all writers believe that the needs identified by Maslow are the most telling. McClelland argues, for instance, that all needs are socially acquired. He identifies three major sets of needs: (1) *the need for achievement*—being driven to succeed, extremely hardworking, and desiring feedback; (2) *the need for power*—having (in the negative sense) the need to dominate, force, or coerce others or (in the positive sense) the ability to make subordinates feel inspired to excel; and (3) *the need for affiliation*—having the desire to be with others, to belong, and to interact socially.[6] The audience member with strong achievement needs may be listening to your speech from the perspective of "What's in it for me?" She may wonder if the change you are proposing would give her an opportunity to use her abilities and to excel. That kind of person's motivation is very different from the one who is more affiliative and, hence, concerned with how the proposed change might affect the organization's social environment or the well-being of the immediate group as a whole. As you construct your persuasive strategy, you need to consider the motivational bent of each audience member so that you can make your presentation as *personally compelling* as possible.

The final set of important motivating factors is externally directed. Many professional people have genuine concern for the welfare of the organization as a whole. Ideas they perceive as enhancing the position of the organization will receive their hearty support. Secure in their personal and professional positions within the organization, they are committed to advancing the goals of the institution, usually including maximizing profit and rendering some public service. Drucker deals with this last notion in his book, *The Effective Executive,* in which he points to "commitment to contribution" as a characteristic of many successful high-level managers.[7] In this instance, the person is motivated by a desire to contribute substantively to society. Such sentiments often involve a widening of the listener's perspective to include not only his or her own specialty or department, but the processes, purposes, and goals of the entire organizational family.

This, then, is yet another dimension of human motivation that you need to consider as a persuasive speaker. A proposal for organizational change that aims to increase the quality of a specific company product, ensure a safer environment for its public, or create, in general, a better, more harmonious society would have great intrinsic appeal to a group of employees who are motivated by external, other-oriented concerns. Figure 14.1 summarizes some major factors influencing human motivation.

Often the key to gaining support for an idea or plan resides not in a rational justification of the idea or solution, but in one's ability to comprehend the forces within the audience that predispose them to believe and behave in predictable ways. Such knowledge makes it possible to create a persuasive strategy that will relate the virtues of the plan to the motives already present within the listeners.

Build Credibility

Think of the last time someone tried to sell you something and failed. Why didn't you buy? Perhaps you simply didn't have the money, but beyond that, the would-be persuader may have "turned you off" in some way. Maybe he seemed deceptive and you worried that the product wasn't as great as he claimed. Or perhaps you asked him some questions he couldn't answer, and so you grew to doubt whether he knew what he was talking about. Possibly his personal style was offensive. Maybe he came on too strong, or at the other extreme, seemed to be more interested in going to lunch than in making the sale. In short, he may have done something that caused you to view him as lacking credibility. He might have been selling a marvelous product, perhaps the exact kind of self-cleaning microwave oven you have always wanted. But because you were unimpressed with him as a person and a communicator, you decided to keep on looking.

What is true for the salesman in this case is true for any public speaker with a persuasive purpose. Aristotle pointed out thousands of years ago that the speaker's *ethos* or credibility is her or his most powerful source of influence. Even the most carefully constructed and soundly supported speech will fail if the speaker is viewed as low in credibility. Most researchers agree that several factors combine to influence listener perceptions of speaker credibility.[8] In general, if audiences perceive speakers to be *competent, trustworthy, objective,* and *enthusiastic,* they will view them as highly credible. Of course, these dimensions are interrelated. Listeners have little regard for the sincere speaker who is not terribly well versed. Nor will they tolerate the bright but deceptive. Objectivity is important in that listeners, while recognizing that a persuasive speaker has taken a stand, still want to believe that he or she has given fair consideration to more than one point of view. Listeners also prefer to feel that the speaker would still be willing to hear opposing views. Finally, most listeners find it easier to be convinced by a persuasive speaker who is genuinely enthusiastic and dynamic than by one who is either too pushy or too bland.

What can you do to enhance your credibility as a public speaker? First, you must recognize that even before you begin to speak, your listeners will likely have some impression of your credibility. If, for example, you are known within your organization as an expert on nutrition and you are speaking on the need for a balanced diet, the audience's perception of your credibility should be quite positive. Even if the audience knows nothing about you, however, they will begin to assess your credibility as soon as they see you. Your *appearance* counts. The way you dress is important, as is the way you walk, sit, smile, and shake hands. Looking professional, suiting your attire to the occasion, and appearing neatly groomed are also essential.

If you are in a rather formal public speaking situation, your listeners will also gain some impression of your credibility from the remarks of the person who introduces you. If you know you are to be introduced, you might send your introducer pertinent information several days beforehand—information geared, in part, toward enhancing your credibility. Avoid sending a long, detailed resume. Introducers often have trouble picking out the really crucial information.

You can also do things *during* your speech to alter your perceived credibility. Building credibility is a process that unfolds as you share your thoughts with the audience. Here are some techniques you might try:

1. *Establish common ground* with the audience. In general, audiences enjoy listening to speakers with whom they believe they have something in common. If you once worked in a department like theirs, say so. Whenever you can demonstrate values, concerns, or aspirations that you and your audience hold in common, you help your credibility.

2. *Build trust.* Normally, trust building is a process that evolves only over time. Even so, you can often establish yourself as a trustworthy source of information on a particular subject by techniques such as self-disclosure (admitting that you were terribly out of shape before joining the company's fitness program) or by establishing your individuality (speaking as an executive who once viewed most administrators as incompetent).

3. If appropriate, *reinforce your status.* If your introducer does the job well, you may not have to do this. If not, however, *tasteful* references to your experience, education, or position are entirely appropriate. Mention your experience with supervision, student government, sales, and so forth as you address each of these subjects. Obvious name-dropping or repeated references to a prestigious award or position must be avoided.

4. *Support your views with evidence.* We have already discussed the importance of using evidence. In general, the better your evidence, the more the audience will perceive you as credible. In the next section, we will discuss specific ways to use evidence that are designed to enhance your persuasiveness.

5. *Strive for good delivery.* We have already discussed principles of effective delivery in detail. Here let us simply note that persuasive speakers who can deliver their speeches fluently and with apparent confidence, who can sound sincere and committed to their ideas, will go a long way toward establishing themselves as trustworthy, competent, and enthusiastic communicators.

6. If appropriate, *use visual aids.* Visual aids are not necessary for every speech. If they make sense and if you want to take the time to prepare them, however, they can add color and interest to your presentation. Using handouts or overhead transparencies highlighting your main points may lead the audience to perceive you as well organized. And the presence of any carefully constructed visual aid suggests that you went to some pains to prepare for the presentation. That implies you took the task seriously.

There is no standard way of building one's credibility. Each topic, audience, and speech situation presents its own set of obstacles to be overcome. No speaker is equally credible on every topic he or she addresses. In some instances, your credibility may be almost automatic. In others, you may want to consider using all of the credibility-building devices listed. In most speaking situations, even highly credible speakers nurture their image by establishing common ground, using evidence, and striving for excellent delivery. To be an effective persuasive speaker, your credibility can never be too high.

Appeal to Audience Emotions

As a persuasive speaker, you often want to get your audience excited about some cause, move them to action, or help them to become less complacent. You will have difficulty achieving those goals on the basis of logical appeals alone. You may decide then to use some emotional appeals designed to make your listeners feel sad, happy, angry, guilty, sympathetic, compassionate, or proud. To get people to act, to move them to change some policy, you often have to move their hearts as well as their heads.

If your persuasive goal is to move your listeners to action, be sure to use emotional appeals in conjunction with sound evidence and reasoning. You should always build your persuasive speech on a firm, rational foundation of facts and logic. Discerning listeners will not be moved by your emotional appeals unless you can prove your case. Once you have presented convincing arguments, you can use emotional appeals to kindle your audience's feelings, engage their beliefs, and incite them to action.

One of the most common ways of appealing to listeners' emotions is through the use of an *emotionally moving story or illustration*. Discussing basic facts about pay inequity, crowded student housing, or alcoholism among workers is not enough. You need to use specific examples. In this way, the emotional appeal grows from the content of the speech itself. Sometimes *your language can* also *evoke emotional responses*. You might describe a competitor, for instance as "unfair, dishonest, and power-hungry." Or you might describe the philosophy of your own company as "fair-minded, worker-oriented, and loyal to the American tradition of progress." You must be careful if you choose to move your audience in this way, however. Sometimes this technique is simply too obvious. This is especially true if the moving phrases are not developed or supported later in the speech. Thus, stirring words, phrases, and slogans must be used tastefully and with restraint. Finally, perhaps *the most powerful source of emotional appeal is your sincerity, commitment, and conviction as. a persuasive speaker*. You cannot move an audience simply by using the right words and plugging in colorful examples. Audiences are amazingly good at detecting insincerity or apathy. If you are feeling the emotions you wish to arouse in your audience, then everything you say and the way you say it will reinforce your commitment and hopefully convey a compelling message.

Develop Persuasive Strategies for Using Evidence

We suggested earlier that persuasive speakers are more likely to be successful if they support their views with evidence. In this section, we want to elaborate on the relationship between persuasiveness, the organization of evidence, and credibility.

One factor you might want to consider in gathering evidence is whether or not the audience has already heard it. Using evidence with which the audience is familiar does little to enhance your persuasive impact. If the audience already knows that "professors at this university are paid about two thousand dollars a year less than those at other Big Ten institutions," they have probably either accepted this evidence as true or rejected it as false. In either case, you have persuaded no one. In short, *evidence with which the audience is not familiar is more persuasive than evidence to which they have already been exposed*.[9]

Next, you need to assess your own credibility in the eyes of the audience. If you are not well known to your audience, if they are hostile to your position, or if they in any way question your authority or motives, you should plan to use abundant evidence. That is, only those speakers with the highest credibility can make unsubstantiated assertions and still be persuasive.[10] Equally important, no one has high credibility with all audiences. The president of the United States is usually highly credible when speaking to members of his own party, but not so when he is addressing members of the opposing party or even audiences of mixed political predispositions. Similarly, when you present a proposal, your credibility may be extremely high with those who know you well or those who would profit from your advocated plan. However, for those audience members who perceive themselves to be in competition with you, the ones who have never worked with you or even heard of you, or those who are hostile toward anyone who advocates change, your credibility may be more questionable. Since most of us are rarely in speaking situations where our credibility is uniformly high with all audience members, *the safest strategy is to use evidence to enhance our persuasiveness*.[11]

Using evidence also plays an important part in long-term attitude change.[12] That is, whenever you are in a position of arguing for some principle of enduring value, something that you want the audience to think about over an extended period of time, or something about which they do not have to act immediately, you will be more persuasive if you present them with supporting evidence. Moreover, if you know that the audience will be exposed to opposing arguments after listening to you, *you can make them more resistant to counterinfluence by using evidence*. If your arguments are well supported with evidence, you have a better chance of being persuasive as you compete with other speakers in the long run.

Another issue you need to consider is whether or not you should acknowledge opposing points of view. That is, should you simply present arguments to support your ideas, or should you devote some time to discussing opposing arguments? Most plans, however well conceived, have both advantages and disadvantages. A brilliant idea is expensive. Creating a new division may cause some established departments to be trimmed. Most innovations are accompanied by some risk. Obviously, it is more pleasurable and easier to discuss the strengths of your ideas than to address potential risks or weaknesses. Even so, in most situations, *you will be more persuasive if you set forth your own arguments and acknowledge opposing points of view*.[13] The only exception to this generalization is when you are speaking to an audience who already agrees with you. But when you talk with those who are opposed or ambivalent, those who are bright and well educated, or those who have already heard opposing arguments, you should present both sides. Since most audiences fall into at least one of these categories, the latter is the preferred route.

So far, we have discussed persuasive strategies aimed at inducing audiences to accept some change. Sometimes, however, you will be in a position of trying to prevent change—that is, you want to reinforce the audience's present convictions and make them more resistant to change. Suppose that your child attends a fine old elementary school located only two blocks from your home. You really like this arrangement and genuinely believe in the neighborhood school concept, a concept to which your local school board has also been consistently committed over the years. Now, however, you learn that in order to save over $200,000, the superintendent is going to present the school board with a proposal for closing three elementary schools (one of them yours) and busing the children to other schools around the community. You decide to attend the next school board meeting and voice your objections. Since the public is always allowed to speak first at these meetings, you know that it is only after you speak that the board will hear the superintendent's proposal for closing the schools. What kind of persuasive strategy should you use to "immunize" the board against the superintendent's proposal?[14]

Two basic strategies exist. First, you might try using what is called "supportive message pretreatment." That is, you can introduce evidence that provides additional support for the neighborhood school concept (for example, citing studies demonstrating the superiority of a child's education under these circumstances). Or you can use "refutational pretreatments," where you attack the idea of busing children out of the neighborhood (for example, by making comparisons with schools where this procedure has led to overcrowding, decreased achievement test scores, and increases in transportation costs). If time is very limited, you should use the refutational strategy over the supportive one. But if you have enough time, *the best approach is to combine the two strategies so that you both support your position and refute the arguments of others*. Once again, the two-sided message is superior; but in the context of immunization discussed here, the emphasis should be on refutation rather than support.[15]

Once you have decided to present both supporting and opposing arguments, the next concern is how best to arrange them. *Should you begin by attacking the opposition or by presenting arguments supporting your own point of view? Usually, the latter course of action is preferable.* Receivers who first listen to a speaker's case often move in the direction of the speaker's views. When this happens, they are more likely to listen to his or her reasons for being against the opposition. If, however, the speaker begins by pointing to flaws in the opposing arguments (and especially if those arguments have any audience appeal), audience members may react defensively, moving even closer to the opposition and becoming more resistant to the speaker's own position when they finally hear it.[16]

Whenever you have to argue against an audience's beliefs, the best approach is to begin by establishing some substantive common ground. Talk about some things both you and the audience hold dear. In the school closings example, you might begin by talking about your mutual commitment to the welfare of the children of the community and the quality of education within the school corporation. Then you can begin to develop your arguments. Not only is establishing common ground an attention-getting device, but an early affirmation of commonly held values tends to increase the audience's assessment of your credibility as a speaker and makes them more open to hearing your claims.[17]

Persuasion: Proposal Presentations

Assume for a moment that you have worked in an organization for several years. Throughout your professional experience you have been interviewed and conducted interviews; you have developed various kinds and qualities of interpersonal relationships; and you have learned to listen to the views of others as well as to communicate effectively yourself. Together, your task competence and interpersonal skills have led you into important group experiences within the organization; you presently belong to several influential committees. But now you find yourself in a slightly different position: you have been asked to present one of your creative marketing concepts to the board of directors, and you must develop a proposal for the board's consideration.

In a sense, you now are a kind of public communicator in that you face a group of receivers and individually defend a point of view. But the small interacting group is not a typical audience; and you are not facing the general public, but a group of employees with considerable status and decision-making power. Your success in this kind of situation depends as much on your understanding of the dynamics of the small group as it does on the quality of the proposal you put forth.

Defining the Proposal Presentation

Proposal presentations are developed by some member of the organization, often at a superior's request, and delivered to a small group of decision makers. Sometimes presentations are made to small groups of peers, but more often they are delivered to superiors. On occasion, the speaker is not personally acquainted with most members of the group to whom he or she is making the presentation. The presenter knows them, perhaps, only by reputation and other information received by way of the organizational grapevine. At other times, an expert in, for example, computer technology, is asked to present a proposal to a small group of high-level executives with whom she consults nearly every day. Proposal presentations require careful preparation and practice. They are, after all, being presented to small groups of important decision makers, organizational representatives with great demands on their time and energies. As Howell and Bormann point out: "Presentations are the most carefully prepared, structured, developed, tested, and rehearsed speech messages given by a member of an industry, a unit of government, or a profession."[18]

Preparing for the Presentation

Presentational speaking clearly involves the communication of much information; yet it cannot be said that presentations are primarily informative. Those who present proposals usually explain, for example, the meaning of consumer trends and report on matters such as end-of-the-year financial statements. Explaining and reporting are often crucial speaker functions in this context, but the presentational speaker acts largely as a *persuader* in that he or she supports a specific proposal in the presence of decision makers who have the power to accept or reject it.

To be persuasive, these presentations must be proposal-oriented and audience-centered. Presentational speakers are almost invariably proponents of change, agents of innovation. Successful presentational speaking begins with a proposal worth presenting; but it is equally critical that the speaker engage in painstaking preparation, focusing on an analysis of the audience as members of the organizational structure, as individuals, and especially as decision makers within a small group.

Know the Organization

As you approach the creation of a presentation, you should recognize that the organization offers a highly structured environment for communication interaction. To varying degrees, all of the formal and informal channels and constraints discussed in the second chapter will be operant. For example, we have already noted that organizational employees are usually called upon to give presentations at the request of a superior. Thus, the proposal is generated as a result of the organization's formal demand. By the same token, the proposal is often presented to a group of powerful decision makers; thus, the presentational speaking event represents an instance of upward communication. Those to whom you communicate in this context possess both power and status; they are successful executives who can hire and fire and, most significant in this case, accept or reject you and your proposal. Thus, as a presentational speaker, it is important for you to guard against the tendency to distort information, a common upward communication problem.

Another important aspect of the organizational context is the increasing trend toward specialization. Concomitant with the knowledge explosion came the organizational tendency to seek individuals with increasing depths of expertise. Such depth, however, is often accompanied by considerable narrowness of focus. As a result, the expert who is called upon to make a presentation to a small group of decision makers faces the task of relating her or his expert knowledge to the understanding and needs of the group members. While the problem of audience adaptation is not unique to presentational speakers, the often critical nature of the proposal being presented and the complexities associated with upward communication heighten the importance of it being skillfully accomplished.

Know the Immediate Audience

It is only on rare occasions that public speakers know their audiences personally. In this sense, you have an advantage in a presentational speaking situation. First, you are usually addressing a *small* group, and that makes the individual analysis of audience members a manageable task. Often, particularly in smaller organizations, you will know all of the decision makers on a daily working basis. Even if you lack firsthand knowledge, belonging to the organization is an asset; for this allows you access to the information needed to analyze your audience judiciously.

Let us assume that you are a marketing analyst who has been called upon to present a proposal focusing on a new strategy for advertising one of the company's major products. Let us assume further that your audience is composed of two organizational vice-presidents, the head of the company's marketing operation, the organization's comptroller, and the research director in charge of quality control. Since you are a marketing analyst, you know the head of the company's marketing operation both personally and professionally. (In fact, he was the one who asked you to create and present the proposal.) This first group member is an innovator; he is concerned with creativity and originality and will engage in moderate risk-taking to ensure that the organization remains a leader in its marketing innovations. In contrast, the company's comptroller is cautious, conservative, and continually committed to operating within the realm of modest realism. You do not know her personally, but her reputation for conservatism is widely acknowledged. The third group member, the quality control expert, should present little problem as an audience member since he is a close friend of yours and generally supports innovations so long as they do not threaten the quality of the company's products. Finally, there remain the two vice-presidents. The first is an older man, clearly recognized as a figurehead within the hierarchy. He is within one year of retirement, and his presence on certain key committees is more a tribute to his loyalty in the past than an index of his actual influence. The last member of the decision-making team is a relatively young, aggressive vice-president who has achieved her present position by her relentless commitment to innovation and change. She is known for her brilliance, assertiveness, and her notion that the organization must continually be on the cutting edge in all significant areas of management, quality, and production. This final member holds a high position of power within the organization, and she is informally influential as well.

Now that you are armed with specific knowledge of each member of your audience, you are ready to prepare your proposal. In this instance, you might well elect to pursue a theme of innovation, stressing the potential of your new advertising scheme for moving the organization forward in sales while projecting an image of creativity and innovation. Such a strategy should engage the enthusiastic support of the group's two most powerful and prestigious members, the young vice-president and the marketing head. In all probability, the quality control member will support the proposal since his interests are in no way threatened. The figurehead vice-president can be counted on to vote with the prevailing point of view. Finally, even the objections of the comptroller can be reduced with your assurance that the new strategy, while initially expensive, will pay for itself rather quickly and soon will effect substantive increases in product sales. Our point is that specific knowledge of the prejudices, interests, and values of each member of the small group audience is a critical preliminary consideration for presentational speaking.

Understand the Dynamics of the Group

Occasionally, as a presentational speaker, you will address an ad hoc group meeting on a one-time basis for the purpose of listening to a specific presentation; thus, the group has no history and no anticipated future. Most of the time, however, you will talk to some group that meets regularly and has established patterns of interaction.

Small group audiences are different from the audiences faced by most public speakers. They have a dynamic quality, possessing psychological bonds, goals, and relatively predictable patterns of interaction.

A general understanding of group dynamics allows you to focus on a more specific, in-depth knowledge of the particular group in question. It is important to discover which members of the group function as leaders. The person ignorant of leadership research might assume that the appointed leader is the person to whom she should focus the majority of her appeals. But as a student of group dynamics, you know that appointed leaders may or may not lead the group in a significant sense and that the important information to obtain relates to which group members consistently influence the group. Your appeals should be aimed at the most influential individuals.

Equally important is an understanding of how power and status are distributed within the group. Most decision-making groups consist of persons having rather high status within the organization. One might be tempted to assume automatically that a vice-president would have more power than a floor supervisor. Yet, you will recall from our comments on group dynamics that we must identify the functionally powerful figures within the group, since high status and power are not invariably associated. Once you have engaged in audience analysis of the sort outlined in the preceding paragraphs, you are ready to plan a fruitful strategy of organization. As we pointed out in the last chapter, it is not enough to know the material.

Organize the Proposal

Whenever you rise to make a speech, it is important that your remarks be clearly organized. The elements of the proposal should be arranged in such a way that they reveal some purposive design. Although different proposals will use different persuasive strategies, several general principles of arrangement take on particular significance because of the organizational context in which the proposals are presented. In this sense, then, all proposals should be arranged in accordance with the principles of *unity, coherence, emphasis, completeness,* and *conciseness.*

The principles of unity and coherence are closely related and often confused, yet both are critical elements of any well organized presentation. We usually say that *a speech is unified when we can discover a central theme to which each element of the message logically relates.* In the context of a proposal presentation, the central purpose is to get the decision-making group to accept and support a given course of action. In a unified presentation, every major subdivision relates to and supports that basic action-oriented theme. This unity is strengthened by the coherence of the arguments as well. *Coherence* here means that *the parts of the message are interrelated.* They are not held together simply because they relate to the basic proposal; they go together because they are logically interrelated.

Another basic quality of a well-arranged presentation is emphasis. It is not possible for audiences, even highly skilled decision makers, to digest and remember everything a speaker says. Thus, it is critical that presentations be *constructed so that the most important ideas and data are stressed.* There are many strategies for emphasizing information.

Proposals may be presented quite informally to small groups of decision makers.

Audiences tend to pay more attention to those arguments they hear first and last. One strategy, then, is to place the strongest arguments early and late in the speech, with less essential ideas in the middle. You can employ a certain amount of repetition as a means of emphasis, although *never* at the expense of conciseness. It is also possible to use internal summaries, transitions, and conclusions for reiterating key ideas. Finally, using visual aids is an effective method of stressing critical data.

The fourth characteristic of a well organized presentation is completeness. *Complete presentations are comprehensive—they deal with all the important topics relating to the central theme.* Speakers with restricted information, a biased perspective, or inadequate research are poorly equipped to deal with their proposals competently and completely. The notion of completeness does not imply that you say everything there is to say about a given topic. Rather, it suggests that you present the proposal as completely as possible given the constraints of time and the needs, understanding, and interests of the audience.

Perhaps the notion of completeness can best be grasped in relation to the final important organizational characteristic, *conciseness.* Organizational decision makers need complete information on which to base their decisions. Because of the demands on their time, it is crucial that a complete picture be created in the most concise manner possible. Many beginning speakers repeat themselves unnecessarily. In an effort to ensure completeness, they sacrifice *economy of word and thought*. Effective presentations are filled with pertinent information and compelling arguments, but they are never wastefully wordy or unduly repetitious.

Patterns of Arrangement for Presentational Speaking

As we pointed out in the last chapter, every effective public presentation should have an introduction, a body, and a conclusion. But there are some special patterns of organization that work particularly well with proposal presentations: *the scientific problem-solving pattern, state-the-case-and-prove-it,* and *the psychological-progressive pattern*.[19] We will consider each in turn.

The first pattern, *scientific problem solving,* is the same as the reflective-thinking approach to problem solving discussed in chapter 9. As such, it is based on Dewey's notion of how the trained mind inductively attacks a problem, usually in the context of the laboratory. This pattern of organization is most often effective in discussing a relatively complicated problem—especially if the audience is largely ignorant of the facts or if audience hostility is anticipated. Through the scientific approach to problem solving, you lead the audience through a systematic series of steps involving an introductory definition of the problem, an exploration of the problem (including an examination of causes and effects), an enumeration and evaluation of representative solutions, and finally the objective selection of the best solution.

There are numerous advantages to this arrangement. When handled properly, it creates an image of you as an open-minded, objective communicator. You encourage the audience to examine the problem along with you and to consider a variety of possible solutions—not just the particular one you are advocating. With such an approach, members of the audience can be made to feel that they have participated in selecting the best alternative. It is difficult to maintain hostility in the face of such a disarming approach to problem solving.

When the audience is poorly informed, this inductive development of the topic provides a natural framework for the communication of essential information. As a speaker, you do not assume that the audience is already familiar with the problem, its causes, and potential remedies. Rather, you assume that you possess important descriptive information, which, when shared with the audience, will allow you to objectively and logically discover the best alternative—together. In this sense, then, the scientific pattern of problem solving creates a feeling of audience participation and has potential for bringing speaker and listeners closer together.

The second pattern of organization often useful for presentational speaking is *state-the-case-and-prove-it*. This is a relatively simple arrangement entailing the straightforward development of a central thesis with supporting arguments. Normally, each supporting element begins with a contention or topic sentence, followed immediately by substantiating material. Typically, the pattern consists of an introduction followed by the thesis statement, each supporting contention with appropriate elaboration and support, and a concluding summary that repeats the proposition.

Patterns for Proposal Presentations

Scientific Problem-Solving	State-the-Case-and-Prove-It	Psychological-Progressive
Define problem	Introduction	Arouse
Explore problem	Thesis	Dissatisfy
Causes	Contention 1	Gratify
Effects	Evidence	Picture
Possible solutions	Contention 2	Move
Best solution	Evidence	
	Summary	

Whereas the scientific problem-solving pattern is an inductive approach to organization, state-the-case-and-prove-it is deductive. You begin with a general conclusion and, through the use of specific arguments, attempt to show that it is justified. The speech, then, is one of proof and reinforcement.

This second pattern of arrangement is useful in situations considerably different from those that call for the scientific problem-solving approach. Specifically, state-the-case-and-prove-it is appropriate for organizing the discussion of familiar, much argued topics of controversy. When the audience is familiar with a particular problem and has perhaps heard it discussed many times before, there is no need for the speaker to explore it gradually and comprehensively. In fact, to ignore audience members' experience and knowledge will only bore, frustrate, and possibly insult them. The appropriate strategy, then, is to state one's position and clearly and systematically support it.

During the introduction of a state-the-case-and-prove-it presentation, you usually acknowledge the fact that the audience is familiar with the problem. Then you explain your reason for reopening a discussion of the issue. It may be that new information has been accumulated or that recent events have modified a previously satisfactory or stable situation. Thus, the controversy needs to be considered from this new perspective. This kind of introduction should leave the audience eager to learn the effects of the new information or situation relating to the old problem.

Throughout the presentation, you must clearly state the relevance of each supporting element to the general thesis you are advocating. Often this can be accomplished through the skillful use of transitions that make clear the supporting nature of each contention. In the summary, highlight the significance and valence of your arguments, encouraging the audience to reflect on the quality of the proof presented.

The final pattern of arrangement for proposals is the *psychological-progressive pattern*. This approach, based on Monroe's Motivated Sequence, can be useful in a wide variety of speaking situations.[20] *It involves five steps:* (1) *arouse,* (2) *dissatisfy,* (3) *gratify,* (4) *picture,* and (5) *move.* Using this pattern, first concern yourself with capturing the audience's attention. The next task is to demonstrate the nature of the problem, depicting the difficulties, tensions, or tragedy of a specific situation of immediate concern. Then link your recommendation or proposal with the problem so that the audience can understand and accept the proposal as a probable solution to the problem. It is not enough, however, that the audience *understand* the advantages of your solution, for the *accepting* audience is usually one that has been moved both rationally and emotionally. Thus, you should focus on helping the small group audience to *see* the manner in which your proposal will remedy the situation. Finally, you culminate the persuasive attempt through appeals and challenges that reflect an understanding of the audience's needs and values and will move them to accept the proposal with enthusiasm and commitment.

Speakers using the psychological-progressive pattern often comment on the ease with which it can be remembered and subsequently used. Another virtue of this pattern is that you can readily omit the early steps if the audience is already familiar with the problem or has an extremely high initial level of interest. In such a situation, it is possible to move almost immediately to the advantages of your proposal and spend a great deal of time elaborating and picturing its merits. In general, this pattern encourages more of an emphasis on a specific solution than the others.

Persuasion: Sales Presentations

The key to success for any organization is sales: unless someone can sell the organization's services or products to someone else, that organization simply will not survive. Unlike proposal presentations, sales presentations occur between an organization and its environment (such as an individual customer or another organization) rather than within the organization. The speaker acts as a representative for himself or herself, his or her organization, and that organization's products or services.

Like the proposal presentation, the sales presentation typically is given before a small group (although, as mentioned in chapter 7, sales interviews in a one-on-one situation are also common). Groups to which sales presentations are made may take many forms, depending on the product or service being sold and the organization of which the group is a part. As consultants, for example, the authors have found themselves trying to sell their consulting services to groups of top-level university administrators; members of the personnel department of a major airline; a nursing task force consisting of staff nurses and first-level nursing supervisors; a vice-president of engineering and his immediate staff; the vice-president of human resources, director of training, director of labor relations, and training manager of a major insurance company; and the entire middle management group (approximately ten people) of a small manufacturing firm. In situations like these, success depends on several things: knowledge of your own product or service, an understanding of the organization to which you are selling, and a sensitivity to the characteristics, needs, and biases of the group to which you are speaking directly.

Preparing for the Sales Presentation

As in any speaking situation, the most important work occurs before the actual presentation takes place. Careful preparation significantly enhances your chances for success; poor preparation virtually guarantees failure.

When preparing your sales presentation, you need to do several things. First, gain information about your audience and the speaking situation. Second, use that information to outline your presentation. And finally, prepare supporting materials (such as visual aids or handouts) to use during the presentation.

Gaining Information

Typically, you will not be acquainted with the group to whom you are selling. However, you will probably have some contact with at least one member of that group, if only to schedule your presentation. During that initial contact, try to learn as much of the following information as you can:

1. *Who will make the decision concerning purchase of the service or product?*
2. *Who will be attending the meeting?* Learn how many people are coming (so you know what to expect and how many copies of handout materials you need to bring) and what positions these people hold.
3. *If the decision maker is not scheduled to be part of that meeting, why not?* Typically, meetings that do not include the decision maker are not very productive for the sales presenter.
4. *How long is the meeting to last?* Obviously, you will need to tailor your presentation to fit the time limitations.
5. *Why is this organization considering purchasing this service or product?* In other words, what are the needs? Some needs analysis questions (see chapter 7 on sales interviewing) can be extremely helpful, enabling you to show specifically how your service or product will help this organization.
6. *What criteria will be used to make the decision?* This information occasionally is not known by the person making the arrangements with you, but if you can get it, you will know what things to emphasize in your remarks.
7. *What physical arrangements or equipment are or can be available?* Be sure to ask for any room arrangement you prefer and for any equipment (such as an overhead projector or videotape player) you need.

By obtaining this sort of information and then using it to shape your presentation, you will be able to provide a much more efficient, effective view of your service or product.

Outlining the Presentation

In the preceding section, we considered several organizational patterns for proposal presentations. Any of these patterns might be appropriate for a sales presentation as well. However, there is another pattern we find equally effective and that parallels the procedures followed during a sales interview: the INPC model, outlined in Business Brief 14.6.

The INPC Sales Presentation

Introduction

    Establish identity and credibility
    Establish purpose
    Establish climate

Need

    Ask questions of the group, or
    Describe organization's needs, or
    Describe typical needs

Presentation

    Provide overview of product or service
    Show or describe features
    Tie features to needs to show benefits

Close

    Summarize benefits
    Summarize reasons to choose your product or service
    Ask for questions

Following this model, the *Introduction* phase should do several things. First, it should identify who you are and what organization you represent. In a brief statement, give your name and title in your organization, your organization's name, how long your organization has been in this business (if appropriate), your organization's specialties or notable achievements, and some customers who use your products or services. This information helps the group to feel that they are dealing with an experienced, reputable organization and sales representative.

Next, briefly state the purpose of your presentation: to ask some questions of the group (if you have a need and desire to do so), to describe your product or service, and then answer any questions they might have.

Finally, establish the climate for the presentation. Experience shows that informal, extemporaneous presentations are more effective in sales situations. To create such a climate, you might make a statement like "I intend to be fairly informal in my remarks, so please feel free to ask questions whenever you like. And I'll ask you any questions that I have as well." This statement encourages two-way communication between you and the group, and it provides a more relaxed atmosphere for everyone.

The *Need* portion of the presentation is important as well. Obviously, some need must exist; otherwise it is unlikely that you would have been asked to make this presentation in the first place. To establish the need, you might simply address a question to the group as a whole, such as "Why are you considering this service or product now?" The group spokesperson or leader probably would provide an answer, looking to other group members for support. However, since this approach might make you seem unprepared, it probably would be better simply to describe the organization's needs as you see them, based on your preparatory conversations. Finally, you could describe typical needs you have found in other similar organizations. By watching audience reactions to the typical needs you describe, you probably will be able to determine which needs are present here.

Presentation of your product or service occurs once the needs have been established. Typically, this presentation will consist of three steps: provide an overview of what the product is and how it works or of how the service is performed (taking the group through a step-by-step sequence); describe particularly important features of your product or service as they respond to the group's needs; and explain the benefits of your product or service to the group or their organization.

The *Close* in a sales presentation is not as straightforward as in a sales interview. Typically, the group will need to meet after you have left to make their decision. Indeed, they may also have met with other sales representatives or have such meetings scheduled in the near future, so that they need to consider the competitors' services or products as well. In short, it is highly unlikely that the group will be able or willing to make a decision while you are there. Therefore, to ask for such a decision (as you would during an interview) would be inappropriate and potentially embarrassing.

Instead, the Close of a sales presentation should do two things. First, it should summarize the benefits you illustrated when you tied the features of your product or service to the organization or group's needs. Again, it is these benefits that should cause the group to select your product or service, and you must make sure they are understood and remembered. Second, you might summarize why the group should choose you and your organization. Refer to the information you provided during the Introduction about your organization's experience and reputation. Many products and services are very similar; the unique qualifications of your organization may be the determining factor that gets you the sale.

Finally, ask for *questions*. If the group has asked questions during your presentation, there may be few or none at this point. Our experience, however, has been that many questions are asked and that this is one of the most important elements of the sales presentation. The questions you are asked reveal those things that the group found most important (or most difficult to understand) and thus those things that you need to stress again. The questions may also reveal the individual biases or preferences of the members, allowing you to direct your remarks even more specifically to their concerns. By handling questions effectively, you not only maintain the positive impression you have created up to this point but advance your cause significantly. When preparing for the presentation, try to anticipate questions the group might ask and have answers ready.

Preparing Supporting Materials

The Presentation phase of the presentation often benefits significantly from the use of visual aids. As chapter 13 indicates, aids such as chalkboards, flipcharts, overhead transparencies, models, and maps add clarity and interest to the presentation. As a rule, *every sales presentation should be accompanied by some form of visual aid.* In preparing for the presentation, develop aids that are professional in appearance, neat, communicative and add to the credibility of your organization and product or service.

Delivering the Sales Presentation

We have already noted some elements of delivering the sales presentation:

It should be delivered extemporaneously.

It should be somewhat informal in tone.

It should involve the use of visual aids.

It should allow for questions and answers.

In addition, we should note that the characteristics of effective delivery presented in chapter 13 apply here as well. An effective sales presentation is characterized by a delivery that is spontaneous, direct, flexible, and involving.

Particularly important in a sales presentation are the elements of spontaneity and flexibility. As you present your Introduction, Need, Presentation, and Close, you must be sensitive to feedback (verbal and nonverbal) from the audience and adjust to that feedback appropriately. Sometimes the feedback and adjustment are obvious: someone interrupts your presentation to ask a question, and you adjust by giving an answer. More often, however, feedback and adjustment are subtle, requiring extreme sensitivity and flexibility on the part of the speaker. In this section, we will consider briefly how to read reactions, interpret them, and adjust to them.

Reading Reactions

While knowledge of your product is important, perhaps even more important is knowledge of people. You need to understand the people to whom you talk. You need to know how to read their feelings and reactions accurately and what to do about the things you perceive. With this ability, you are almost certain to be successful. Without it, success will be very difficult to achieve.

At the outset, you must remember one important fact: words often tell very little about how a person feels. We express most of our feelings with our eyes, gestures, and voice. Research suggests that only about 7 percent of what we feel is expressed through our words. Another 38 percent (roughly) is expressed through the tone of voice we use—rate of speech, voice inflection, pitch, volume, and so on. Finally, our face, eyes, and gestures account for about 55 percent of the feeling we convey.

To read people accurately, then, you must become skillful at noticing quick changes in the eyes and face. These changes may be incredibly fast, lasting only a half to a quarter of a second. But if you are observant, you can perceive changes as specific as enlargement of someone's pupils (often a sign of interest), as well as general changes in body posture.

While you speak, the group is constantly sending messages about their feelings and reactions. Most informative are the eyes: if someone likes you or is interested in your presentation, her or his eyes will seem to brighten as the muscles around the eyes tense.

On the other hand, if the person wishes you would go away, the muscles around the eyes may be relaxed, with the face drooping slightly. More than any other factor, the eyes reveal what the mind is thinking.

There are two important dangers in trying to read body language. First, you cannot assume that specific actions have particular meanings. Folded arms may mean rejection, but they also may mean that the individual is cold or is just comfortable in that position. Second, you should not try to keep track of so many actions that you lose your concentration. But if you are able to focus on some general body language groupings, then you might be able to use nonverbal cues to your advantage.

There are five basic groups of nonverbal cues that indicate how a person is feeling:

Group 1: Approval

Nonverbal cues may indicate positive acceptance of you and your claims. Signs of approval include leaning forward toward you, maintaining eye contact, changes in vocal inflection (an animated voice), frequent gestures, a pleasant, smiling expression, frequent head nods, raised eyebrows, willing responses to your questions, and vocal indications of agreement ("Uh-huh," "Yeah," and so on). Sometimes a customer will express approval verbally as well, using approval statements such as "That sounds good" or "I really like that." Such verbal and nonverbal expressions should indicate to you that the customer likes what you are saying and accepts the feature, benefit, or proof you have offered.

Group 2: Confusion

While describing features or benefits, you may perceive signs of puzzlement. These signs are important: many people will choose not to ask questions, either because they do not wish to appear uninformed or stupid or because they do not want to prolong the meeting. It is important that you be sensitive to these signs and respond to them appropriately. Nonverbal signs of confusion or lack of understanding include a slight scowl or frown, narrowing of the eyes, tilting the head to one side, raising the eyebrows, or pursing the lips. Verbally, a confused person might ask to have a point repeated, give a response that is "off the wall," ask for an explanation, or give vocal cues such as "Huh?" or "What?" It is important to pick up such signs. Understanding must be achieved if the group is to be convinced to buy what you are selling.

Group 3: Skepticism

Sometimes listeners find it difficult to believe what you are saying. After all, they may have been subjected to dozens of sales calls from representatives and have heard the same claims repeated by each. It is only natural for them to be a little suspicious of the things you (and all the other reps) say. Common nonverbal signs of skepticism include raising one eyebrow, tilting the head backward or tilting the head forward and peering out from under the eyebrows, shifting from an open posture to one that is more closed (perhaps by folding the arms or crossing legs), frowning or scowling, narrowing the eyes, looking away from you, or shaking the head. Some verbal signs of skepticism include "Do you really expect me to believe that. . . ?" or "Well, I rather doubt that. . . ." Each of these statements suggests that your points are not being accepted and that you will need to take some action to convince the group.

Group 4: Indifference

When customers see sales representatives frequently, it becomes easy for them to adopt an attitude of indifference. They have sat through countless presentations, each of which makes the same claims and uses the same buzz words. They have become jaded, adopting an unspoken attitude of "All right, so tell me how *your* product or service is better than all the others." The more experienced they are, the more likely they will adopt such an indifferent attitude. Several nonverbal cues convey indifference, including "hanging" facial muscles, a slumped or overly relaxed posture, an expressionless face, a posture that leans away from you, a tapping or wiggling foot, heavy sighs, frequent changes of posture (squirming), drumming the fingers or tapping with some object, and providing very little response to your questions. In addition, the group may simply agree with everything you say, giving no direct expression of indifference but at the same time giving you nothing to go on. To get a sale, you have to motivate them before they will have any interest in the features and benefits you describe.

Group 5: Objection

Several nonverbal cues, when shown in combination, often indicate objections to you and your product or service: folded arms, crossed legs, clenched fists or tense hands, posture turned away from you (with shoulders at an angle), frowns, tight lips or facial grimace, avoidance of eye contact, flat voice with very little variance in volume or pitch, and very short answers to your questions. Verbal objections generally show clear disagreement with your arguments or focus on perceived disadvantages of your product.

Certainly, there may be other groups of nonverbal and verbal cues that indicate specific reactions or feelings. For our purposes, however, the groups listed above are most relevant, and it is these you should look for and try to read when making a presentation.

Handling Reactions

As you describe features, advantages, benefits, and evidence, watch and listen for client responses. Those responses in turn dictate what you should do next. Again, we will consider the five types of reactions described above, this time noting some appropriate strategies for handling them.

Handling Approval

When you see signs of approval, what do you do? First, consider closing. If the meeting has gone on for some time, with the group agreeing with or showing interest in the features and benefits you described, you may ask for questions at this point. However, if it is still very early in the meeting, you may decide closing is premature. Instead, you might reinforce the approval. Sales usually are the result of a series of agreements. If the group seems to be approving, try to get them to make an open commitment that they agree with a benefit you have described. For example, you might ask the entire group, "You seem to feel that the cases in this book are particularly good. Is that right?" Such reinforcement makes these small battles you have won more memorable and influential when you try to win the entire war later on. Finally, move on to another point. Once agreement has been obtained or interest shown, it is tempting to continue to "beat the point to death." After all, agreement and interest are pleasant for you, and you are likely to do what you can to get them to continue. However, when agreement has been obtained, note the point of agreement in your mind and then move on to the next point.

Handling Confusion

When you perceive confusion, first review what you just said but in a different way. Say something like, "Let me go over that again, because it's important." Give the group another chance to follow your thinking. If that seems ineffective, blame yourself and ask for a reaction. Noting continued puzzlement, you might say, "I'm really not explaining this very well. Is this making any sense at all?" Alternatively, you might note that others often find this point confusing and again ask for a reaction. For example: "It seems like a lot of people have trouble understanding this. Am I explaining it all right?" Finally, you might simply respond to the reaction. If someone is reluctant to indicate confusion or lack of understanding, your question may prompt the person to admit confusion and tell you what specifically is unclear. However, if the person's reluctance to indicate confusion stems from a desire to get the conversation over with, he or she may insist that everything is perfectly clear, even though he or she is genuinely confused. Therefore, you might review the point one more time, still watching for nonverbal signs of confusion, and then move on to your next point. If you are not convinced that the person understands, look for an opportunity later in the meeting to return to the source of confusion and review it one last time.

Handling Skepticism

When you perceive skepticism, you first might ask about the behaviors you have observed: "You seem skeptical about this. Do you have some reservations about what I'm saying?" This question invites the group members to state openly any concerns they might have—concerns that otherwise might go unspoken and unanswered. Then respond appropriately to stated reservations and invite the group to raise any other reservations in their minds. Finally, to handle persistent skepticism, you must offer some sort of proof for what you have claimed. In other words, you must give some evidence to support the validity of your features or benefits. Continue to provide proof until the group accepts the validity of your point or it becomes clear that someone is expressing a personal objection rather than skepticism about a particular feature. When such an objection emerges, handle it as you would any other objection.

Handling Indifference

When you see indifference, stop selling and ask questions designed to uncover needs. The specific question you ask to identify needs is determined by the reason for the group's indifference. If the group sees no need for your product, ask questions for background information. For example:

"Tell me about your work."

"What things need to be improved?"

If the organization has a self-developed procedure, ask about the procedure to see if there might be any problems. For example:

"What have you liked best about that procedure?"

"What things would you improve if you could?"

"What problems have you had?"

"Tell me more about how your system works."

If the client is satisfied with a competitor, ask about the competing product or service to identify possible problems. For example:

"What do you like most about. . . ?"

"What things might be improved. . . ?"

"What problems have you had. . . ?"

"What complaints have employees offered?"

Often, customers do not want to express their lack of interest. They know you will try to give answers, and rather than taking the time to hear your answers, they decide to suffer through the presentation in silence, ask for a brochure, and let you leave. You cannot afford this type of treatment; you have invested time to put yourself in front of this group, and a meaningful conversation is important. By forcing them to talk to you, you are more likely to uncover some needs that can be met or some problems that can be answered, and in so doing increase the chances of getting a sale.

Handling Objections

During your presentation, people are likely to raise complaints, objections, questions, and other roadblocks to a potential sale. Much of your effectiveness throughout the sales call will be determined by how well you deal with the objections that come up. While each client and each situation is different, there are some common reasons why objections are raised and, in some cases, why a particular client seems to be more resistant than others.

Some clients raise objections because they simply want more information or because they don't know what they want or need. Rather than resisting your sales effort, they are expressing an objection to receive assurance on some doubtful point or because they have not properly understood your presentation. For example, they might object because not enough benefits are yet apparent. Indeed, this is the reason for most objections, and once a client sees enough benefits, there is no longer a reason to object.

On the other hand, some clients raise objections based on hidden motives: to show you that they are intelligent, clever, and not an easy sale; because they are tired of seeing the parade of sales representatives knocking at their door; as a stalling tactic to avoid making a decision at this time; because they already have made up their minds but do not want to say no to your face; or because they are resistant to change.

There are many other reasons, of course, why clients raise objections to your claims. Most objections reflect legitimate concern or curiosity about the content and features of your product or service. And each objection gives you an opportunity to exercise your skills as a sales representative.

There are four basic strategies for dealing with objections a client raises. First, you could *meet the objection directly*. This sort of approach handles the objection in an assertive manner, supported by specific evidence. It requires that you be well organized and thoroughly familiar with the features of your product or service. It can be an extremely effective way of dealing with objections as they arise.

Second, you could *sidestep the objection*. If an objection does not seem to be a major concern in the client's mind, you can simply avoid it. But be careful; while sidestepping an objection avoids wasting time discussing trivial matters, you must judge carefully whether the objection is trivial or not. If you sidestep an objection that really is important to the client, you may lose the sale.

Minimizing the objection is a third approach, which strives to reduce the impact of objections. You can implement this approach verbally (through the things you say in response) and nonverbally (through your physical reactions). To minimize an objection verbally, you first might remind the client of benefits he or she already has accepted—benefits that might outweigh the objection that has been raised. In reviewing those benefits, first begin with some introductory phrase, such as

"Let's look again at your overall needs."

"Remember some of the things we have talked about."

"Look at the big picture for a second."

Then summarize the benefits already agreed to. However, if there are no benefits to review or if the list does not seem to outweigh the objection, then you need to question to uncover needs. In other words, you start the Need and Presentation steps over again in an effort to build a case for your product. Eventually, you hope to compile a list of agreed-to benefits that will outweigh this objection.

Nonverbal reactions can be used to minimize objections, although they must be used carefully. Raising your eyebrows in surprise, for example, indicates your amazement that such an objection would even be raised. Similarly, frowning or shaking your head indicates that, in your opinion, a minor point has been raised. A heavy sigh, shrugging your shoulders, turning your head away are other signals that you do not view this matter to be important. The client then may simply drop the objection, realizing that it is not a major issue, and you can proceed to more important matters. However, the client also may press the point, which lets you know that the objection is not minor in her or his mind, necessitating a discussion of why the objection can be overcome or is of secondary importance.

The biggest danger in using nonverbal cues to minimize objections is that you may anger the client. The issue may indeed be very important in the client's mind, and your sigh or shrug may offend the client. For that reason, minimizing objections nonverbally should be used very carefully.

Giving in to an objection is appropriate when you just cannot win the point. For example:

You: I really think this book would meet your needs.

Client: Well, that may be. But I have already decided to adopt another text.

You: Which one?

Client: The one I just wrote.

Or:

You: This new edition is far more attractive visually than the second edition was.

Client: Actually, I don't think so. All the illustrations are blue, and there is scientific evidence that blue is more difficult for the eye to distinguish. I absolutely refuse to use a book with all blue illustrations.

When there is no way of overcoming an objection or the objection shows a legitimate preference for a competitor, you may have to give in. But there still may be other ways to get a sale. For example, you might suggest the client use one of your other products or services, admit this one problem but try to counter with other more important advantages, or simply move to other needs the client has. Giving in on an objection does not mean giving up.

By watching for, interpreting, and responding to feedback from the client group, you add significantly to the effectiveness of your sales presentation.

Summary

This concluding chapter has introduced you to some of the specific kinds of "public" speaking contexts you are likely to encounter as you move into jobs requiring professional training and perhaps involving some managerial responsibility. We place quotation marks around the word *"public"* because many of these special sorts of speeches are presented to relatively small groups and in that sense are quite different from the stereotype of the public speech delivered to a large audience. In spite of audience size, many of these special public speaking situations involving sales, proposal presentations, and oral reports are delivered to listeners who are very important people—board members, upper-level managers, potential customers—in short, people who can make the difference in your professional opportunities and the success of your organization.

Although we have suggested specific concerns and techniques that may be useful in particular public communication contexts, we also want to emphasize that *the underlying principles of effective public speaking are quite similar across situations*. That is, in every speech situation, you must prepare carefully, know your material or product, carefully analyze the audience, clearly and strategically organize your remarks, and present your ideas or information using effective (usually extemporaneous) delivery. And *each* time you prepare to give a speech, you must not lose sight of the transactional nature of communication. When you deliver public speeches, you still exchange roles of sender and receiver. You hope to influence others' ideas and decisions, but as you watch and hear others react to your thinking and arguments, you, too, are often influenced. That is, in public speaking, as in other communication contexts, you participate in a dynamic process in which all participants share control.

Questions for Discussion

1. If you were asked to make a fairly technical oral report, what are some guidelines you would keep in mind?
2. What are some of the most important things to remember when making a persuasive speech?
3. Discuss some of the basic elements influencing human motivation. How significant do you consider each of these elements?
4. What are some of the ways in which organizations demonstrate their "commitment to contribution"? Cite specific examples.
5. In what ways might a small group audience differ from a traditional speech audience? How does the difference affect your preparation as a speaker?
6. Define and explain the following: unity, coherence, emphasis, completeness, and conciseness. In what sense are these important qualities of organization?
7. Under what circumstances (topic, audience, personal point of view) would you elect to use the following patterns of arrangement? Why?
   a. scientific problem solving
   b. state-the-case-and-prove-it
   c. psychological-progressive pattern
8. How can you use evidence most persuasively? Be specific.
9. What advice would you give to someone who has to prepare and present a sales speech?

Exercises

1. Choose any small group to which you have belonged for at least a year. Imagine that you have been asked to present a proposal to this group for its consideration and possible acceptance. Analyze the group, both the interacting whole and the individual members. Be specific in terms of their habit patterns, needs, and typical interpersonal relationships. In view of your analysis, how might you motivate them to accept your proposal?

2. Choose a social or organizational issue for which you would like to propose some change. Consider your classmates as your audience. With this audience, topic, and your ideas in mind, describe your persuasive strategy. What kind of evidence would you use and why?

3. James Goodman is a computer analyst in an automobile manufacturing organization. His boss has asked him to present a proposal advocating the purchase of a new, expensive, and fairly controversial computer for the organization. The group to which Goodman is to make the presentation is composed of (1) the vice-president for research and development (young, innovative, flexible, liberal); (2) the director of finance (middle-aged, rigid, conservative, for the status quo); (3) the supportive boss who made the request; (4) the director of data analysis (young, brilliant, cautious, conservative); and (5) the president (near retirement, moderate on most issues, listens mostly to the advice of the vice-presidents in the organization).

   a. Given the expense of the computer, the controversiality concerning its worth, and the nature of the audience, what strategy should Goodman adopt?
   b. What assumptions might he make about the dynamics of this particular small group?
   c. What pattern of arrangement would be most appropriate? Why?
   d. What are some lines of argument that might be especially effective?
   e. How should he deal with the persuasive presentation of his evidence?

Appendix
Careers in Communication

We often have been asked "What can I do with a background in speech communication?" Unlike many other areas of study, speech communication does not have a clear career path. As a result, people of that educational background often do not know what sorts of positions they should seek or what other kinds of training they should acquire. To assist your own career planning, we include this supplement on career opportunities that emphasize communication.

At the outset, we should emphasize that a background in speech communication provides you with two things: a set of communication skills that enables you to perform more effectively in virtually any position and a body of knowledge about communication that you can transmit to others. In our view, careers in "communication" are ones that place primary emphasis on your communication skills or that involve teaching others the skills you possess.

Listed below are some general career areas in which people with speech communication backgrounds frequently find employment and some specific position or job titles those people are likely to hold. We also have described the responsibilities those positions typically entail and the educational background you would need to obtain such a position and function effectively in it.

Human Resources Management

The personnel function in an organization goes under various labels: *personnel, employee relations, labor relations, human resources,* and the now widely used *human resources management.* Many communication-related positions exist within this function.

1. *Personnel interviewer.* As the name implies, this entry-level position in personnel involves reviewing employment application forms and letters, and often resumes as well, and conducting initial screening interviews with applicants. Typically, this person does not make the final hiring decision; rather, he or she simply passes along to the department that has the position opening a list of candidates who, after the initial interview, seem qualified. The department then conducts second interviews and selects a candidate.

Effective performance in this position requires interviewing skills, of course. In addition, you should acquire some knowledge of current equal employment opportunity and affirmative action laws in particular and of personnel management programs in general. Coursework in personnel management and general business is often an important addition to studies in speech communication. Since many organizations are now using various forms of preemployment tests, some work in psychological tests and measurement and in statistical analysis would prepare you for the most sophisticated of employment functions and for the future of personnel interviewing.

2. *Personnel recruiter.* Large companies (and many small ones) have their own recruitment staffs to seek out qualified candidates for upper-level positions in the organization. In addition, personnel recruitment firms (called headhunters) hire people who act as consultants to other organizations, helping those organizations find qualified candidates for executive and management slots. Like the personnel interviewer, the recruiter conducts initial screening interviews with potential candidates. However, while the interviewer typically talks to people who have responded to advertisements in newspapers or who have simply walked in, the recruiter must actively find and solicit potential candidates. Thus, most recruiters spend a great deal of time on the telephone and almost as much time traveling about the country meeting with potential applicants.

The recruiter needs the same general educational background as the personnel interviewer. However, she or he also needs much more assertiveness, persuasiveness, and determination than does the interviewer. Therefore, skill in effective sales techniques is a desirable addition to the skills outlined above.

3. *Employee relations representative.* Many organizations have an employee relations or labor relations staff whose function is to deal with employee concerns and complaints and to do everything possible to encourage positive employee morale. These people meet privately with employees who come to see them, they may conduct group meetings with employees to learn their concerns and complaints, they may help in the resolution of employee grievances, and they may assist in writing and publishing all or part of the employee newsletter.

Skills in interviewing, conducting meetings, resolving conflict, and written communication are obviously important for success in this career category. In addition, knowledge of personnel administration systems, such as compensation and benefits, union-management contracts, and labor law, is a virtual necessity. Thus, coursework in business law, labor relations, personnel management, and organizational and industrial psychology all are important in preparing for this sort of position.

4. *Training coordinator.* Many human resource management departments have a training arm. Such training falls into two categories: management or supervisory training and development, and basic job skills or technical training. People with communication backgrounds typically conduct training seminars for managers and supervisors; skilled senior employees who are effective communicators are more likely to conduct the technical training courses. Among the supervisory and management seminars taught in most organizations are the following: styles of

management, oral communication skills, effective business writing, performance appraisal, effective discipline, employment interviewing, setting performance standards, delegating work, decision making, problem solving, and conducting effective meetings.

Keys to effective performance as a management or supervisor trainer are public speaking and teaching skills and a knowledge of management and supervision techniques. Coursework in business management may provide some background in the latter. However, current books sold in "trade" (as opposed to "text") books sections that deal with supervision and management methods are more likely to provide the type of information that should be included in these sorts of seminars.

Public Relations or Marketing

As organizations of all types try to become "close to the customer," the role of the public relations or marketing specialist takes on greater importance. Again, these people must have skills in human communication to perform effectively.

1. *Speech writer.* More and more executives in large- and medium-sized corporations are hiring people to write speeches for them. Of course, politicians long have had staffs of writers to assist them in preparing their major addresses. Traditionally, speech writers have had backgrounds in journalism, public affairs, or marketing; now, however, people with speech communication backgrounds are becoming more prevalent. The role of the speech writer is to analyze the situation in which a speech is to be given, meet at length with the speaker to gather his or her ideas on the topic, conduct research on the topic, prepare a first draft of the speech, and then meet repeatedly with the speaker to arrive at a final draft. In effect, everything is done that normally would be done in preparing a speech, except that the final speech is delivered by someone else.

   Of primary importance in this career category are skills in speech preparation and written communication. Some knowledge of the type of business in which you function is also vital (such as a knowledge of business administration in industry, of public policy and current affairs in government, and so on). Finally, a knowledge of sales and marketing strategies is helpful in planning overall communication campaigns; typically, the speech writer is involved in these activities as well as in the preparation of individual addresses.

2. *Organizational spokesperson.* On occasion, very large organizations will have spokespersons whose function is to deal with the media, investor groups, and other elements of the organization's environment. Such people may conduct press conferences, stockholder meetings, community programs, and so on, and they may be interviewed by members of the press when the organization's position on a particular issue is sought.

   Again, skill as a communicator is vital here. Platform skills are particularly important, as are skills in handling questions from hostile questioners and in dealing with the mass media. A general understanding of business administration and print and broadcast journalism is also useful, and coursework in those areas would be an important supplement to communication training.

3. *Customer or patient relations representative.* Many organizations have always placed heavy emphasis on good relations with their customers. Others only recently have recognized the importance of good customer relations. For example, changes in Medicare and Medicaid reimbursement procedures have forced hospitals to become concerned about maintaining good patient relations. As a result of all this, new career opportunities are being created in customer and patient relations. Typically, this person interacts with customers of the organization. He or she will receive complaints, investigate them, and provide the complainer with some response. As this field becomes more sophisticated, customer or patient relations representatives also will interview customer groups, conduct telephone surveys, distribute and analyze customer questionnaires, and generally conduct market research that used to be the exclusive responsibility of marketing analysts. Again, skill in face-to-face communication is vital for this sort of position.

Skills in interviewing, conducting meetings, and interpersonal conflict resolution are important, as are skills in active listening. In addition, coursework in survey research and statistical analysis will become increasingly vital, as will some background in psychology. Obviously, you must understand the industry in which you work (retailing, manufacturing, health care, government, and so on) to know how customer complaints should be handled; coursework there also is useful.

4. *Fundraiser or director of development.* Many organizations rely heavily on voluntary contributions of money for their existence. Social service agencies, hospitals, educational institutions, political organizations, religious organizations, and other nonprofit agencies have a staff of people whose function is to develop sources of income from the outside. Typical job titles are director of development, development officer, or occasionally, fundraiser or community relations director. This person's responsibility is to meet with community leaders and groups to present the organization's functions and contributions in the best possible light, and to convince these people to make large donations.

Platform skills are at the heart of this sort of position, as are skills in interviewing and salesmanship. Some understanding of finance and economics is also helpful, as is a knowledge of the industry in which you work. Above all, determination, assertiveness, persuasiveness, and a genuine belief in the value of what you are doing enable you to communicate effectively with those you encounter.

5. *Communication specialist.* Traditionally, organizations have used their public relations arm to communicate both to outside groups and to internal "publics"— employees, management, and so on. While there is a move now toward specialization, many organizations still hire people with speech communication backgrounds to communicate both internally and externally. These people traditionally have dealt primarily with written communications: newsletters, magazines, annual reports, special announcements, and so on. As a result, journalism majors most often were hired into these positions. However, as the communication function has become more sophisticated in most organizations, there has developed an increased appreciation for the broader skills and knowledge possessed by speech communication experts.

Oral communication skills remain important: interviewing skills assist in the collection of information, just as public speaking and meeting leadership skills help in disseminating information. A broad knowledge of human communication behavior and of marketing strategies is also helpful. Written communication skills are, of course, vital.

Sales, Advertising, and Marketing

By definition, sales involves communication. Thus, it is not uncommon to see people skilled in communication do extremely well in all aspects of sales. However, some areas in which speech communication graduates have recently begun to find success fall somewhat outside the traditional sales positions.

1. *Investment account executive.* Investment companies such as Merrill Lynch, Shearson/Lehman/American Express, Prudential-Bache, and others hire people to solicit new accounts and manage old ones. Typically called account executives, these people convince new customers to invest through their brokerage, and then provide advice on investments the client should make. While people with backgrounds in accounting, economics, or finance traditionally have been hired into these positions, most organizations now are realizing that communication skills are most important and that knowledge in investments can be taught. Their strategy has thus changed; they now hire good communicators and train them in investments.

    Obviously, skills in interviewing and sales are vital for success in this career. Coursework in accounting, finance, economics, and business administration would also be extremely helpful. A few brokerage houses do not offer training for their new account executives, and so some background in finance would be necessary to obtain a position; most of the larger firms, however, will provide their own training.

2. *Market research specialist or opinion research specialist.* Most organizations are concerned with gathering information from their customer groups to determine how their products or services are perceived, what new products or services should be initiated, what old ones should be deemphasized, how well the organization's advertising is being received, and so on. In large organizations, the marketing department will have people skilled in collecting and analyzing such data. Smaller organizations often turn to outside consulting organizations for such assistance. Market or opinion researchers are skilled in conducting individual interviews and focus group discussions with customers, in designing and administering survey questionnaires, in analyzing the accumulated data, and in presenting the findings to the management.

    Traditionally, people with marketing backgrounds have been hired into such positions, and some coursework in market research and consumer behavior is useful. However, people with backgrounds in speech communication and some expertise in survey research and statistical analysis are welcomed into such positions, because they have an understanding of human behavior and communication processes often not possessed by marketing specialists. Coursework in psychology and mass media is also useful in developing expertise in this area.

3. *Sales representative.* Typically, when one thinks of a sales representative, one thinks of door-to-door encyclopedia salespersons, used car dealers, or insurance salespersons. While all of these certainly are career paths into which someone with good communication skills could go, other less obvious sales positions with more long-term career potential are available. Most companies sell products or services to other companies, and they always are looking for (and willing to pay premium salaries to) people who will be effective in those sales encounters. Moreover, the path to executive positions is usually direct for good sales representatives; positions as regional sales director, national sales manager, and so on can be acquired quickly, and movement into even higher positions is common for people with sales backgrounds.

The most important skill in this sort of position is, of course, skill in conducting sales interviews. Personal qualities such as assertiveness, determination, and persuasiveness also are important, as is an understanding of the industry in which you will work. Most companies provide product-oriented training to their sales representatives, so product expertise is not necessary initially. Coursework in psychology, marketing, accounting, business administration, and statistics also is helpful in developing an appropriate background.

Consulting

A consultant is anyone who can provide an information service to an individual or organization, a service that they cannot or choose not to do themselves. Accounting firms, for example, act as consultants. They do the books for small companies that do not have their own accountants, and they audit the books of large companies to provide an objective check on the accounting functions there. Similarly, consultants in communication provide a variety of services to organizations and individuals who need assistance in those areas, or they provide an outsider's view of how well the organization is doing things on their own.

There is a virtually limitless range of communication-related areas in which consulting assistance can be provided. Any skill you can offer to an organization (or teach to members of that organization) represents a consulting opportunity. To give some understanding of the range of consulting done by people with speech communication backgrounds, we will simply list some of the services of which we are aware.

1. *Communication skills training.* These consultants offer group seminars and individual instruction to people at all levels of an organization in such skills as public presentations, dealing with the mass media, effective writing, interviewing techniques, conducting meetings, and so on. Some consulting firms are entirely devoted to providing such services; the Executive Technique, Inc., a division of the J. Walter Thompson advertising agency, teaches public speaking skills to groups of executives. Most supervisors, managers, and executives need improvement in their communication skills (and are aware that they need such improvement), and people with speech communication backgrounds do well as consultants in this area.

2. *Public relations consultants.* Some consulting firms assist organizations in communicating with the public. Hill and Knowlton, Inc., of Chicago, for example, helps companies plan and implement their entire long-term public relations campaign. Speech communication experts often are hired by such consulting firms to serve as consultant/employees, and a few individuals have their own consultancies in the public relations area.

3. *Labor relations consultants.* Speech communication experts who can help organizations measure the attitudes of their employees and improve their overall communication efforts also are in demand as consultants. Some labor relations consulting firms (such as Modern Management, Inc., of Bannockburn, Illinois) hire people with speech communication backgrounds to perform such services for client organizations, while several individuals also market their services to companies of all types.

4. *Compensation and benefits consultants.* Communication about compensation and benefit programs is just as important in an organization as the actual quality of those programs. As a result, many compensation consulting firms (such as Hewitt Associates in Bannockburn, Illinois, or Hay Associates, with offices all over the country) will hire communication specialists to work with their compensation and benefit experts in planning communication campaigns to be implemented after changes in compensation and benefit plans have been made.

5. *Productivity improvement consultants.* Traditionally, industrial engineers have been considered the source of productivity improvement consulting expertise. With the new emphasis on employee participation in achieving better productivity, however, consultants who can teach problem-solving skills to groups of employees, group leadership skills to supervisors and managers, and listening and communication skills to executive groups have come into demand. Many such consultants offer assistance to companies in installing quality circles, while others have their own participation-based programs for sale.

6. *Guest or customer relations consultants.* People who can teach employees, supervisors, and managers basic interpersonal skills to improve guest, customer, or patient relations now are in increasing demand. Generally, these people teach very basic communication techniques, such as active listening, nonverbal communication, and effective interviewing to large groups of employees, showing them how to use these techniques in their day-to-day relations with the organization's customer groups.

7. *Career planning consultants.* These people work with organizations and individuals in a variety of ways. Outplacement consultants help people who have been fired or laid off find new employment; often, such consultants are hired by the company doing the firing as a gesture of goodwill toward the displaced workers. Other consultants help organizations conduct career "assessment centers," in which lower level employees and supervisors have their communication and management skills assessed to determine their potential for upward advancement. Still others help individuals develop their interviewing and job-seeking skills to assist their search for new employment.

Certainly, there are other areas in which people with speech communication backgrounds can provide consulting assistance. Any area in which you can identify skills of your own, needs of organizations, and a willingness of those organizations to purchase your skills is an area in which you will be successful as a consultant. But one final note is in order: while the career positions described in the previous sections are entry-level positions requiring little or no experience and a B.A. or B.S. degree, consulting typically requires advanced degrees and/or extensive experience. After all, before an organization will pay eight hundred or fifteen hundred dollars per day for consultant assistance, it wants some proof that the assistance it will receive is worth its investment.

Finally, we will repeat advice offered in chapter 7: To market your skills effectively, you must first take an inventory of those skills. Corporate interviewers and recruiters probably will not understand the names of the courses you have taken. To help them assess you, you must tell them specifically the things you are able to do, or the things you can teach their employees to do. Only when you translate your educational and work background into specific skills will you be able to take advantage of the speech communication background you have developed and the advantages it offers.

Notes

CHAPTER 1

1. John C. Hafer and C. C. Hoth, "Selection Characteristics: Your Priorities and How Students Perceive Them," *Personnel Administrator* (March 1983): 25–28.
2. W. O. Underwood. "A Hospital Director's Administrative Profile," *Hospital Administration 9* (1963): 37–39.
3. M. J. Cetron, W. Rocha, and R. Luchins, "Into the 21st Century: Long-term Trends Affecting the United States," *The Futurist* (1988): 29–40.
4. Everett Rogers and Rehka Agarwala-Rogers, *Communication in Organizations* (New York: Free Press, 1976), p. 6.
5. Peter Drucker, *The Practice of Management* (New York: Harper & Row, 1959), p. 92.
6. Herbert A. Simon, *Administrative Behavior,* 2d ed. (New York: Macmillan, 1958), p. xvi.
7. Linda L. Putnam, "The Interpretive Perspective," in *Communication and Organization: An Interpretive Approach,* eds. L. L. Putnam and M. E. Pacanowsky (Beverly Hills: Sage, 1983), p. 45.
8. Alex Bavelas and Dermot Barrett, "An Experimental Approach to Organizational Communication," *Personnel* 27 (1951): 368.
9. Thomas J. Peters and Robert H. Waterman, Jr., *In Search of Excellence* (New York: Harper & Row, 1982), p. 124.
10. Raymond G. Smith, *Speech Communication: Theory and Models* (New York: Harper & Row, 1970), p. 14.
11. John Wenburg and William Wilmot, *The Personal Communication Process* (New York: John Wiley & Sons, 1973), p. 6.
12. S. Axley, "Managerial and Organizational Communication in Terms of the Conduit Metaphor," *Academy of Management Review* 9 (1984): 428–37.
13. Frederick Taylor, *Scientific Management* (New York: Harper & Row, 1911).
14. Henri Fayol, *General and Industrial Management* (London: Sir Isaac Pitman and Sons, 1949); Luther Gulick and L. Urwick, *Papers on the Science of Administration* (New York: Institute of Public Administration, 1937); Max Weber, *The Theory of Social and Economic Organization* (New York: Oxford University Press, 1947).
15. Weber, *The Theory of Social and Economic Organization,* pp. 329–36.
16. Fritz J. Roethlisberger and William J. Dickson, *Management and the Worker* (Cambridge: Harvard University Press, 1939).
17. Douglas McGregor, *Professional Manager* (New York: McGraw-Hill, 1967); Rensis Likert, *The Human Organization* (New York: McGraw-Hill, 1967); Robert Blake and Jane Mouton, *The Managerial Grid* (Houston: Gulf Publishing, 1964); Raymond Miles, "Keeping Informed— Human Relations or Human Resources?" *Harvard Business Review* 43 (1965): 148–63.

18. Rogers and Agarwala-Rogers, *Communication in Organizations,* pp. 3–36.
19. Kenneth Boulding, "General Systems Theory—the Skeleton of a Science," *Management Science* (April 1956): 323–35; Herbert A. Simon, *Models of Man* (New York: John Wiley & Sons, 1956); William G. Scott, *Organization Theory* (Homewood, Ill.: Richard D. Irwin, 1967); Paul R. Lawrence and Jay W. Lorsch, *Organization and Environment: Managing Differentiation and Integration* (Boston: Harvard University Graduate School of Business and Administration, Division of Research, 1967).
20. Daniel Katz and Robert L. Kahn, *The Social Psychology of Organizations* (New York: John Wiley & Sons, 1966), pp. 16–17.
21. Robert B. Duncan, "Characteristics of Organizational Environments and Perceived Environmental Uncertainty," *Administrative Science Quarterly* 17 (1972): 313–27.
22. Bro Uttal, "The Corporate Culture Vultures," *Fortune,* 17 October 1983, p. 66.
23. Michael E. Pacanowsky and Nick O'Donnell-Trujillo, "Organizational Communication as Cultural Performance," *Communication Monographs* 50 (1983): 146; Nick Trujillo, "Organizational Communication as Cultural Performance: Some Managerial Considerations," *Southern Speech Communication Journal* 50 (1985): 201–24.
24. Peters and Waterman, *In Search of Excellence,* p. 248.
25. Terrence E. Deal and Allen A. Kennedy, *Corporate Cultures* (Reading, Mass.: Addison-Wesley, 1982).
26. Also see *Administrative Science Quarterly: Special Issue on Organizational Cultures* 28 (1983): 331–502.
27. *Behavioral Sciences Newsletter,* 25 June 1984. See also George F. Truell, *Building and Managing Productive Workers* (Buffalo, N.Y.: PAT Publications, 1984).
28. William G. Ouchi, *Theory Z: How American Business Can Meet the Japanese Challenge* (Reading, Mass.: Addison-Wesley, 1981), p. 207.
29. Edward E. Lawler, *High-Involvement Management: Participative Strategies for Improving Organizational Performance* (San Francisco: Jossey-Bass, 1986), p. 3.
30. Brian Dumaine, "Who Needs a Boss?" *Fortune,* 7 May 1990, pp. 52–60.
31. *Ibid.,* p. 54.
32. Craig Eric Schneier, Amy Brown, and Seymour Burchman, "Unlocking Employee Potential: Managing Performance," *Management Solutions* 33 (January 1988): 17.
33. William J. Weisz, "Employee Involvement: How It Works at Motorola," *Personnel Journal* 62 (February 1985): 29.
34. Lawler, *High-Involvement Management,* p. 1.
35. See Patricia Hayes Andrews, *Speech Communication S223: Business and Professional Communication* (Bloomington, Ind.: School of Continuing Studies, 1990), pp. 33–34.

CHAPTER 2

1. Paul Hersey and Kenneth H. Blanchard, *Management of Organizational Behavior* (Englewood Cliffs, N.J.: Prentice-Hall, 1972), p. 67.
2. Henry Mintzberg, *The Nature of Managerial Work* (New York: Harper & Row, 1973); and Nick Trujillo, " 'Performing' Mintzberg's Roles," in *Communication and Organizations,* eds. L. L. Putnam and M. E. Pacanowsky (Beverly Hills: Sage, 1983), pp. 73–97.
3. Douglas McGregor, *Human Side of Enterprise* (New York: McGraw-Hill, 1960).
4. *Ibid.*
5. Abraham Maslow, *Motivation and Personality* (New York: Harper & Row, 1954).
6. John J. Morse and Jay W. Lorsch, "Beyond Theory Y," *Harvard Business Review* 48 (1970): 146–55.
7. Douglas McGregor, *Professional Manager* (New York: McGraw-Hill, 1967).
8. Rensis Likert, *New Patterns of Management* (New York: McGraw-Hill, 1961); Rensis Likert, *The Human Organization* (New York: McGraw-Hill, 1967).
9. Likert, *New Patterns of Management.*
10. Bureau of Labor-Management Relations and Cooperative Programs. *Labor-Management Cooperation: 1989 State-of-the-Art Symposium* (Washington, D.C.: U.S. Department of Labor, 1989).

11. Dorwin Cartwright and Alvin Zander, eds., *Group Dynamics: Research and Theory,* 3d ed. (Evanston, Ill.: Row, Peterson, 1968).
12. Robert Blake and Jane Mouton. *The Managerial Grid* (Houston: Gulf Publishing, 1964).
13. Paul Hersey, Kenneth H. Blanchard, and R. K. Hambleton, *Contracting for Leadership Style: A Process and Instrumentation for Building Effective Work Relationships* (Columbus: Ohio State University Center for Leadership Studies, 1977).
14. *Ibid.,* p. 4.
15. *Ibid.*
16. Paul Hersey and Kenneth H. Blanchard, "Life Cycle Theory of Leadership," *Training and Development Journal* 23 (1969): 26–34; Paul Hersey and Kenneth H. Blanchard, *Management of Organizational Behavior: Utilizing Human Resources,* 3d ed. (Englewood Cliffs, N.J.: Prentice-Hall, 1977).
17. Frederick Herzberg, *Work and the Nature of Man* (Cleveland: World Publishing, 1966); Herzberg, "One More Time: How Do You Motivate Employees?" *Harvard Business Review* 46 (1968): 53–62.
18. Victor Vroom. "Organizational Choice: A Study of Pre- and Postdecision Processes," *Organizational Behavior and Human Performance* 1 (1966): 212–25.
19. Richard Tanner Johnson and William G. Ouchi, "Made in America (Under Japanese Management)," *Harvard Business Review* 52 (September–October 1974): 61–69; William G. Ouchi, *Theory Z: How American Business Can Meet the Japanese Challenge* (New York: Addison-Wesley, 1981).
20. Richard Tanner Pascale, "Zen and the Art of Management," *Harvard Business Review* (March–April 1978): 153–62.
21. Johnson and Ouchi, "Made in America," pp. 65–66.
22. Stephen P. Robbins, "The Theory Z Organization from a Power-Control Perspective," *California Management Review* 25 (1983): 67–75; B. Bruce Briggs, "The Dangerous Folly Called Theory Z," *Fortune,* 7 May 1982, pp. 41–53.
23. Lea P. Stewart, William B. Gudykunsz, Stella Ting-Tomey, and Tsnkasa Nishida, "The Effects of Decision-Making Style on Openess and Satisfaction within Japanese Organizations," *Communication Monographs* 53 (1986): 236–51.
24. Randy Hirokawa and Akira Miyahara, "A Comparison of Influence Strategies Utilized by Managers in American and Japanese Organizations," *Communication Quarterly* 34 (1986): 250–65.
25. Brian Dumaine, "Who Needs a Boss?" *Fortune,* 7 May 1990, 52–60.
26. Henry P. Sims, Jr., and James W. Dean, Jr., "Beyond Quality Circles: Self-Managing Teams," *Personnel* 62 (January 1985): 26.
27. Robert Tannenbaum, *Leadership and Organizations: A Behavioral Science Approach* (New York: McGraw-Hill, 1961), p. 11.
28. Warren Bennis and B. Namus, *Leaders: Strategies for Taking Charge* (New York: Harper & Row, 1985).
29. Jay A. Conger, "Leadership: The Art of Empowering Others," *Academy of Management Executive* 3 (1989): 17–24.
30. Michael E. Pacanowsky, "Communication in the Empowering Organization," in *Communication Yearbook 11,* ed. J. Anderson (Beverly Hills: Sage, 1987), pp. 356–79.
31. K. Thomas and B. Velthouse, "Cognitive Elements of Empowerment: An 'Interpretive Model' of Intrinsic Task Motivation," *Academy of Management Review* 19 (1990): 666–81.
32. *Ibid.*
33. See Gary M. Shulman, J. Douglas, and S. L. Schultz, "The Job Empowerment Instrument (JEI): A Replication" (Unpublished manuscript, Miami University, 1993).
34. Kent Hodgson, "Adapting Ethical Decisions to a Global Marketplace," *Management Review* 81 (May 16, 1992): 53–57.
35. Charlene Marmer Solomon, "Transplanting Corporate Cultures Globally," *Personnel Journal* 72 (October 1993): pp. 78–88.
36. Mary A. DeVries, quoted in "Words and Phrases to Avoid," *Communication Briefings* (April 1993): 7.

37. Marcy Huber, quoted in "Dealing with Different Cultures," *Communication Briefings* (June 1993): 5.
38. "The Quality Imperative: Questing for the Best," *Business Week,* 16 December 1991.
39. "TQM/CQI: The CEO Experience," *Hospitals,* 5 June 1992, pp. 24–32.
40. Michael S. Leibman, "Getting Results from TQM," *HR Magazine* 37 (September 1992): 34–38.
41. Dale E. Basye, " 'Quality' Touches off Born-Again Fervor," *San Francisco Chronicle,* 11 January 1993, p. E3; Tamara J. Erickson, "Beyond TQM: Creating the High Performance Business," *Management Review* 81 (June 1992): 58–61.
42. Ken Myers and Ron Ashkenas, "Results-Driven Quality . . . Now!" *Management Review* 82 (March 1993): 40–44.
43. Shari Caudron, "Keys to Starting a TQM Program," *Personnel Journal* 72 (February 1993): 29.
44. "The Horizontal Corporation: It's about Managing Across, Not Up and Down," *Business Week,* 20 December 1993, pp. 76–81.
45. *Ibid.*
46. Vicki Clark, "Employees Drive Diversity Efforts at GE Silicones," *Personnel Journal* 72 (May 1993): 148–53.
47. Shari Caudron, "Training Can Damage Diversity Efforts," *Personnel Journal* 72 (April 1993): 51–55.
48. *Ibid.*
49. Kathleen Murray, "Companies Rethink One-Shot Diversity Training as New Problems Are Created," *Chicago Tribune,* 13 September 1993, Sec. 4, p. 6.
50. R. Roosevelt Thomas, Jr., *Beyond Race and Gender* (New York: American Management Association, 1991).
51. Jim Kennedy and Anna Everest, "Put Diversity in Context," *Personnel Journal* 70 (September 1991): 50–54.
52. Thomas J. Peters and Robert H. Waterman, Jr., *In Search of Excellence* (New York: Harper & Row, 1982), p. 261.
53. Rodman L. Drake, "Leadership: It's a Rare Blend of Traits," *Management Review* 74 (August 1985): 25.
54. Lawrence R. Wheeless, Virginia Emon Wheeless, and Richard D. Howard, "The Relationships of Communication with Supervisor and Decision-Participation to Employer Job Satisfaction," *Communication Quarterly* 32 (1984): 230.
55. Robert Levering, *A Great Place to Work* (New York: Random House, 1988).
56. Jack Gibb, "Defensive Communication," *Journal of Communication* 11 (1961): 141–48.

CHAPTER 3

1. Peter Drucker, *Management: Tasks, Responsibilities, Practices* (New York: Harper & Row, 1974), p. 481.
2. Charles Goetzinger and Milton Valentine, "Problems in Executive Interpersonal Communication," *Personnel Administration* 27 (1964): 24–29.
3. Karl B. Clark, "Oral Business Communication Needs as a Basis for Improving College Courses," (Ph.D. Diss., University of Michigan, 1968).
4. Allan Cox, *The Cox Report on the American Corporation* (New York: Delacorte Press, 1982).
5. William V. Haney, *Communication and Organizational Behavior: Text and Cases,* 3d ed. (Homewood, Ill.: Richard D. Irwin, 1973), pp. 278–88.
6. Edgar H. Schein, "Organizational Socialization and the Profession of Management," *Industrial Management Review* 9 (1968): 1–6.
7. Patricia Hayes Bradley, "Socialization in Groups and Organizations: Toward a Concept of Creative Conformity," in *Intercom: Readings in Organizational Communication,* ed. S. Ferguson and S. Devereaux-Ferguson (Rochelle Park, N.J.: Hayden, 1980), pp. 388–402.
8. Terrence E. Deal and Allen A. Kennedy, *Corporate Cultures* (Reading, Mass.: Addison-Wesley, 1982).
9. William P. Anthony, *Participative Management* (Reading, Mass.: Addison-Wesley, 1978).

10. David W. Ewing, "Practical Incentives for Helping Employees Make Themselves Heard," *Management Review* 72 (January 1983): 14–18.
11. Thomas W. Hourihan, "Help Employees to Understand Their Benefits," *Personnel Administrator* 28 (April 1983): 92–98.
12. John Garnett, "Team Briefings' Improving Communications in U.K. Firms," *AMA Forum* 72 (June 1983): 29–30.
13. Mike Hopkins-Doerr, "Getting More Out of MBWA," *Supervisory Management* (February 1989): 17–20.
14. S. L. Yenney, "In Defense of the Grievance Procedure in a Nonunion Setting," *Employee Relations Law Journal* 2 (Spring 1977): 437.
15. Phillip K. Tompkins, "Organizational Communication: A State of the Art Review," in *Conference on Organizational Communication,* ed. G. Richetto (Monograph NASA, G. C. Marshall Space Flight Center, Huntsville, Alabama, 1967).
16. William H. Read, "Upward Communication in Industrial Hierarchies," *Human Relations* 15 (1962): 3–15.
17. Janet Fulk and Sirish Mani, "Distortion of Communication in Hierarchical Relationships," *Communication Yearbook* 9 (Beverly Hills: Sage, 1986), pp. 483–510.
18. Alan Zaremba, "Communication: The Upward Network," *Personnel Journal* 68 (March 1989): 34–39.
19. Frederic M. Jablin, "Superior-Subordinate Communication: The State of the Art," *Psychological Bulletin* 86 (1979): 1201–22.
20. Henri Fayol, *General and Industrial Management* (London: Sir Isaac Pitman and Sons, 1949).
21. "The Horizontal Corporation," *Business Week,* 10 December 1993, pp. 76–81.
22. Rosabeth Moss Kanter, *The Change Masters: Innovation for Productivity in the American Corporation* (New York: Simon & Schuster, 1983), p. 30.
23. Valorie A. McClelland and Richard E. Wilmot, "Communication: Improve Lateral Communication," *Personnel Journal* 69 (August 1990): 32–38.
24. Frank Corrado, *Getting the Word Out* (Homewood, Ill.: Business One Irwin, 1993).
25. Anthony Downs, *Inside Bureaucracy* (Boston: Little, Brown, 1967).
26. Tompkins, "Organizational Communication."
27. K. H. Roberts and C. A. O'Reilly, "Organizations as Communication Structures: An Empirical Approach," *Human Communication Research* 4 (1978): 283–93.
28. Deal and Kennedy, *Corporate Cultures.*
29. Thomas J. Peters and Robert H. Waterman, Jr., *In Search of Excellence* (New York: Harper & Row, 1982), pp. 121–22.
30. Walter Kiechel III, "Beat the Clock," *Fortune,* 25 June 1984, p. 148.
31. Keith Davis, "The Care and Cultivation of the Corporate Grapevine," in *Readings in Interpersonal and Organizational Communication,* 3d ed., ed. R. C. Huseman et al. (Boston: Holbrook Press, 1973), pp. 131–36.
32. Gordon Allport and Leo Postman, *The Psychology of Rumor* (New York: Henry Holt, 1947).
33. Davis, "Corporate Grapevine," pp. 131–36.
34. J. K. Sheperd, "The Spread of Rumors," *Indianapolis Star Magazine,* 21 November 1979, p. 4.
35. Davis, "Corporate Grapevine," p. 132.
36. James L. Exposito and Ralph L. Rosnow, "Corporate Rumors: How They Start and How to Stop Them," *Management Review* 72 (April 1983): 44–47.
37. Beverly Davenport Sypher and Theodore E. Zorn, Jr., "Communication Related Abilities and Upward Mobility: A Longitudinal Investigation," *Human Communication Research* 12 (1986): 420–31.

CHAPTER 4

1. Bowen H. McCoy, "Applying the Art of Action-Oriented Decision Making to the Knotty Issues of Everyday Business Life," *Management Review* (July 1983): 20–21.
2. Robert C. Solomon and Kristine Hanson, *It's Good Business* (New York: Harper & Row, 1985), p. 5.

3. LaRue Tone Hosmer, *The Ethics of Management* (Homewood, Ill.: Richard D. Irwin, 1987), p. 106.

4. John F. McMillan, "Ethics and Advertising," in *Speaking of Advertising,* ed. J. S. Wright and S. S. Warner (New York: McGraw-Hill, 1963), pp. 453–58.

5. Wroe Alderson, "The American Economy and Christian Ethics," in *Advertising's Role in Society,* eds. J. S. Wright and J. E. Mertes (St. Paul: West, 1974), pp. 163–75.

6. Lawrence J. Flynn, "The Aristotelian Basis for the Ethics of Speaking," *Speech Teacher* 6 (1957): 179–87.

7. Kenneth Burke, *The Rhetoric of Motives* (Cleveland: World, 1962); Kenneth Burke, *Language as Symbolic Action* (Berkeley: University of California Press, 1966).

8. Kate Ludeman, *The Worth Ethic* (New York: E. P. Dutton, 1989), p. xv.

9. Milton Rokeach, *Beliefs, Attitudes and Values* (San Francisco: Jossey-Bass, 1968), p. 124.

10. Franklyn Haiman, "Democratic Ethics and the Hidden Persuaders," *Quarterly Journal of Speech* 44 (1958): 385–92.

11. Karl Wallace, "An Ethical Basis of Communication," *Speech Teacher* 4 (1955): 1–9.

12. "Looking to Its Roots," *Time,* 25 May 1987, p. 27.

13. See Richard L. Johannesen, "The Emerging Concept of Communication as Dialogue," *Quarterly Journal of Speech* 57 (1971): 373–82; Paul W. Keller and Charles T. Brown, "An Interpersonal Ethic for Communication," *Journal of Communication* 18 (1968): 73–81; David W. Johnson, *Reaching Out: Interpersonal Effectiveness and Self-Actualization* (Englewood Cliffs, N.J.: Prentice-Hall, 1972); John Stewart, "Foundations of Dialogic Communication," *Quarterly Journal of Speech* 64 (1978): 183–201; Richard L. Johannesen, "Perspectives on Ethics in Persuasion," in *Persuasion: Reception and Responsibility,* ed. Charles U. Larson (Belmont, Calif.: Wadsworth, 1973).

14. Johannesen, "The Emerging Concept," pp. 373–82.

15. Edward Rogge, "Evaluating the Ethics of a Speaker in a Democracy," *Quarterly Journal of Speech* 45 (1959): 419–25.

16. F. G. Bailey, *Humbuggery and Manipulation: The Art of Leadership* (Ithaca, N.Y.: Cornell University Press, 1988), p. ix.

17. Eric L. Trist, "Urban North America: The Challenge of the Next Thirty Years," in *Organizational Frontiers and Human Values,* ed. W. H. Schmidt (Belmont, Calif.: Wadsworth, 1970), p. 82.

18. Thomas. J. Peters and Robert H. Waterman, Jr., *In Search of Excellence* (New York: Harper & Row, 1982).

19. Warren H. Schmidt and Barry Z. Posner, "Managerial Values in Perspective," *AMA Survey Report,* 1983.

20. "What's Wrong?" *Time,* 25 May 1987, p. 15.

21. "Having It All, Then Throwing It All Away," *Time,* 25 May 1987, pp. 22–23.

22. "Keating's Group 'Looted' Lincoln S&L, Judge Says," *Chicago Tribune,* 24 August 1990, Sec. 3, p. 3.

23. "Looking to Its Roots," p. 26.

24. "Looking to Its Roots," p. 29.

25. "Looking to Its Roots," pp. 29–41.

26. James L. Hayes, *Memos for Management: Leadership* (New York: American Management Association, 1983), p. 103.

27. Thomas J. Peters, *Thriving on Chaos* (New York: Knopf, 1987), p. 519.

28. Schmidt and Posner, "Managerial Values in Perspective," p. 11.

29. Theodore Levitt, "The Morality (?) of Advertising," *Harvard Business Review* 50 (1972): 84–92.

30. Raymond A. Bauer and Stephen A. Greyser, *Advertising in America: The Consumer View* (Boston: Harvard University School of Business and Adminstration, Division of Research, 1968).

31. Eli P. Cox, "Deflating the Puffer," *Business Topics* 21 (1973): 29–38.

32. Otis A. Pease, "Advertising Ethics," in *Advertising's Role in Society,* eds. J. S. Wright and J. E. Mertes (St. Paul: West, 1974), pp. 271–77.

33. Pradeep K. Korgaonkar, George Smith, and Marlene Jones, "Correlates of Successful Advertising Campaigns," *Journal of Advertising Research* 24 (1984): 47–53.
34. Pease, "Advertising Ethics."
35. Charles H. Sandage and Vernon Fryburger, *Advertising Theory and Practice,* 6th ed. (Homewood, Ill.: Richard D. Irwin, 1963), p. 84.
36. Colston E. Warne, "The Influence of Ethical and Social Responsibilities on Advertising and Selling Practices," in *Speaking of Advertising,* eds. J. S. Wright and D. S. Warner (New York: McGraw-Hill, 1963), pp. 381–92.
37. E. J. Kottman, "Truth and the Image of Advertising," *Journal of Advertising* 33 (1969): 64–75.
38. Levitt, "The Morality (?) of Advertising," p. 85.
39. John K. Galbraith, *The New Industrial State* (Boston: Houghton Mifflin, 1967).
40. "Documentation of Advertising Claims," *Trade Regulation Reporter* 1 (June 1971): para. 7996.
41. Debra L. Scammon and Richard J. Semenik, The FTC's 'Reasonable Basis' for Substantiation of Advertising: Expanded Standards and Implications," *Journal of Advertising* 12 (1983): 3–11.
42. Jeffery Mills, "Anacin Told How to Spell Relief," *Washington Post,* 25 September 1981.
43. Stephen M. Shortell, Ellen M. Morrison, and Bernard Friedman, *Strategic Choices for America's Hospitals* (San Francisco: Jossey-Bass, 1990).
44. "Hospice Firm Pays Nurses to Recruit Patients," *Chicago Tribune,* 26 August 1990, Sec. 2, p. 1.
45. "Health Care in the 1990s: Forecasts by Top Analysts," *Hospitals* (20 July 1989): 34–40.
46. Solomon and Hanson, *It's Good Business,* p. 184.
47. "On Sneaker Battlefield, PUSH Is Just One More Foe for Nike," *Chicago Tribune,* 26 August 1990, Sec. 7, p. 1.
48. See Charles J. Stewart and William B. Cash, *Interviewing Principles and Practices,* 3d ed. (Dubuque, Iowa: Wm. C. Brown, 1982), pp. 163–67.
49. Such discrimination is forbidden by Title VII of the Civil Rights Act of 1964. Since 1972, the Equal Employment Opportunity Commission has had the power to take organizations to court. See Ruth G. Schaeffer, *Nondiscrimination in Employment, 1973–1975—A Broadening and Deepening National Effect* (New York: Conference Board, 1975).
50. "Age Discrimination Actions Flooding Courts, New BNA Special Report Funds," *Labor Relations Week* 3 (1989): 1109.
51. Lin Farley, *Sexual Shakedown: The Sexual Harassment of Women on the Job* (New York: McGraw-Hill, 1978).
52. *Federal Register,* Vol. 45, no. 219, 10 November 1980.
53. Gary N. Powell, "Sexual Harassment: Confronting the Issue of Definition," *Business Horizons* 26 (1983): 24–28.
54. Donald J. Peterson and Douglass Massengill, "Sexual Harassment—A Growing Problem in the Workplace," *Personnel Administrator* (October 1982): 79.
55. "With Problem More Visible, Firms Crack Down on Sexual Harrassment," *Wall Street Journal,* 8 August 1986, p. 12.
56. Peterson and Massengill, "Sexual Harassment," p. 85.
57. *Ibid.*
58. Carolyn C. Dolecheck and Maynard M. Dolecheck, "Sexual Harassment: A Problem for Small Businesses," *American Journal of Small Business* 7 (1983): 45–50.
59. James C. Renick, "Sexual Harassment at Work: Why It Happens, What to Do About It," *Personnel Journal* (August 1980).
60. Dolecheck and Dolecheck. "Sexual Harassment."
61. Peterson and Massengill, "Sexual Harassment."
62. *Ibid.*
63. Eric Rolfe Greenberg, "Workplace Testing: Results of a New AMA Survey," *Personnel* 65 (April 1988): 36–44.
64. "Phone Monitoring a Fairness, Privacy Call," *Chicago Tribune,* 27 August 1990, Sec. 4, p. 1.
65. "Phone Monitoring."
66. "Bosses Peek at E-Mail," *USA Today,* 24 May 1993, Sec. B, p. 1.
67. Solomon and Hanson, *It's Good Business,* p. 188.

68. Carol Kleiman, "20 Million Industrial Jobs Hinge on 'Fetal Protection' Court Case," *Chicago Tribune,* 27 August 1990, Sec. 4, p. 2.

69. Kleiman, "20 Million Industrial Jobs."

70. "Nuclear Safety Law Not Pre-Empted by Employee's Wrongful Discharge Suit," *Labor Relations Week* 3 (1989): 529.

71. Solomon and Hanson, *It's Good Business,* p. 167.

72. Richard Lacayo, "Nowhere to Hide," *Time,* 11 November 1991, pp. 34–40.

73. Jerome H. Want, "Corporate Mission: The Intangible Contributor to Performance," *Management Review* 75 (August 1986): 46–50.

74. Alan Weiss, "The Value System," *Personnel Administrator* 34 (July 1989): 40–41.

75. Michael Davis, "Working with Your Company's Code of Ethics," *Management Solutions* 33 (June 1988): 5–10.

76. Robert Hershey, "Corporate Mottos: What They Are, What They Do," *Personnel* 64 (February 1987): 52–56.

77. Anthony J. Rutigliano, "Steelcase: Nice Guys Finish First," *Management Review* 74 (November 1985): 46–51.

78. Maynard M. Dolecheck, "Doing Justice to Ethics," *Supervisory Management* 10 (July 1989): 35–39.

79. Sally Blank, "Hershey: A Company Driven by Values," *Management Review* 75 (November 1986): 31–35.

80. Bureau of Labor-Management Relations and Cooperation, *The Changing Role of First-Line Supervisors and Middle Managers* (Washington, D.C.: U.S. Department of Labor, 1988), p. 8.

CHAPTER 5

1. John Naisbitt, *Megatrends: Ten New Directions Transforming Our Lives* (New York: Warner Books, 1982), p. 45.

2. Timothy Leary, *Interpersonal Diagnosis of Personality* (New York: Ronald, 1957).

3. William C. Schutz, *FIRO: A Three-Dimensional Theory of Interpersonal Behavior* (New York: Holt, Rinehart & Winston, 1958); William C. Schutz, *The Interpersonal Underworld* (Palo Alto, Calif.: Science and Behavior Books, 1966).

4. Robert F. Bales, *Personality and Interpersonal Behavior* (New York: Holt, Rinehart & Winston, 1971).

5. See Ronald B. Adler and Neil Towne, *Looking Out/Looking In,* 4th ed. (New York: Holt, Rinehart & Winston, 1984), p. 299.

6. Ellen Berscheid and Elaine H. Walster, *Interpersonal Attraction* (Reading, Mass.: Addison-Wesley, 1969).

7. John Daly, "Homophily-Heterophily and the Prediction of Supervisor Satisfaction" (Paper presented at the annual meeting of the International Communication Association, Portland, Oregon, April 1976).

8. Thomas M. Rand and Kenneth N. Wexley, "Demonstration of the Effect: 'Similar to Me,' in Simulated Employment Interviews," *Psychological Reports* 36 (1975): 535–44.

9. David Landy and Elliott Aronson, "Liking for an Evaluator as a Function of His Discernment," *Journal of Personality and Social Psychology* 9 (1968): 133–41.

10. John R. P. French and Bernard Raven, "The Bases of Social Power," in *Group Dynamics,* eds. D. Cartwright and A. Zander (New York: Harper & Row, 1960), pp. 259–68.

11. Irwin Altman and Dalmas Taylor, *Social Penetration: The Development of Interpersonal Relationships* (New York: Holt, Rinehart & Winston, 1973).

12. See, for example, Michael L. Hecht, "Satisfying Communication and Relationship Labels: Intimacy and Length of Relationship as Perceptual Frames of Naturalistic Conversation," *Western Journal of Speech Communication* 48 (1984): 201–16; Donald J. Cagala, Grant T. Savage, Claire C. Brunner, and Anne B. Conrad, "An Elaboration of the Meaning of Interaction Involvement," *Communication Monographs* 49 (1982): 229–48.

13. Albert Mehrabian, *Public Places and Private Spaces* (New York: Basic Books, 1976).

14. W. Barnett Pearce, "The Coordinated Management of Meaning: A Rules Based Theory of Interpersonal Communication," in *Explorations in Interpersonal Communication,* ed. Gerald R. Miller (Beverly Hills: Sage, 1976), pp. 17–35.
15. Marsha Houston Stanback and W. Barnett Pearce, "Talking to 'The Man': Some Communication Strategies Used by Members of 'Subordinate' Social Groups," *Quarterly Journal of Speech* 67 (1981): 21–30.
16. Charles M. Rossiter and W. Barnett Pearce, *Communicating Personally* (New York: Bobbs-Merrill, 1975).
17. Albert Mehrabian, *Silent Messages* (Belmont, Calif.: Wadsworth, 1971).
18. Robert A. Bell, Sheryl W. Tremblay, and Nancy L. Bverkel-Rothfuss, "Interpersonal Attraction as a Communication Accomplishment: Development of a Measure of Affinity-Seeking Competence," *Western Journal of Speech Communication* 51 (1987): 1–18.
19. William Haney, *Communication and Organizational Behavior* (Homewood, Ill.: Richard D. Irwin, 1967), p. 56.
20. Mark L. Knapp, *Nonverbal Communication in Human Interaction,* 2d ed. (New York: Holt, Rinehart & Winston, 1978), pp. 94–95.
21. Theodore R. Sarbin, Ronald Taft, and Daniel E. Bailey, *Clinical Inference and Cognitive Theory* (New York: Holt, Rinehart & Winston, 1960).
22. Eugene Jacobson, W. W. Charters, and Seymour Liberman, "The Use of the Role Concept in the Study of Complex Organizations," *Journal of Social Issues* 7 (1951): 947–99; John E. Haas, *Role Conception and Group Consensus* (Columbus: Bureau of Business Research, Ohio State University, 1964); Bond L. Bible and James D. McComas, "Role Consensus and Teacher Effectiveness," *Social Forces* 42 (1963): 225–32.
23. Henry W. Riecken and George C. Homans, "Psychological Aspects of Social Structure," in *Handbook of Social Psychology,* ed. G. Lindzey (Cambridge, Mass.: Addison-Wesley, 1954), pp. 786–832; A. Paul Hare, *Handbook of Small Group Research* (New York: Free Press, 1962).
24. Gary T. Hunt and Louis P. Cusella, "A Field Study of Listening Needs in Organizations," *Communication Education* 32 (1983): 368–78.
25. Donald T. Campbell, "Systematic Effort on the Part of Human Links in Communication Systems," *Information and Control* (1958): 334–69.
26. Erving Goffman, *Interaction Ritual* (New York: Doubleday, 1967).
27. " 'Listening' Errors Prove Costly for Firms," *San Jose Mercury News,* 14 March 1984, p. 1F.
28. Andrew D. Wolvin and Carolyn Gwynn Coakley, *Listening,* 2d ed. (Dubuque, Iowa: Wm. C. Brown, 1985).
29. William P. Sullivan, "Have You Got What It Takes to Get to the Top?" *Management Review* 72 (April 1983): 7–11.
30. Charles Ogden and I. A. Richards, *The Meaning of Meaning* (New York: Harcourt Brace Jovanovich, 1923).
31. David W. Ewing, "Practical Incentives for Helping Employees Make Themselves Heard," *Management Review* 72 (January 1983): 14–18.
32. Edward J. Hegarty, *How to Talk Your Way to the Top* (West Nyack, N.Y.: Parker, 1973).
33. G. Michael Barton, "Communication: Manage Words Effectively," *Personnel Journal* 69 (January 1990): 34.
34. Ray Birdwhistell, "Background to Kinesics," *ETC* 13 (1955): 10–18.
35. Michael Maas, "In Offices of the Future . . . The Productivity Value of Environment," *Management Review* 72 (March 1983): 16–20.
36. Fred I. Steele, *Physical Settings and Organizational Development* (Reading, Mass.: Addison-Wesley, 1973).
37. Pat Gerlach, "Offices Get Down to the Business of Looking Good," *Chicago Sunday Herald,* 26 August 1984, Sec. 2, p. 1.
38. Mehrabian, *Public Places and Private Spaces.*
39. Michael Korda, *Power! How to Get It, How to Use It* (New York: Random House, 1975).
40. Edward W. Miles and Dale G. Leathers, "The Impact of Aesthetic and Professionally Related Objects on Credibility in the Office Setting," *Southern Speech Communication Journal* 49 (1984): 361–79.

41. David Joiner, "Office Territory," *New Society* 7 (1971): 660–63.
42. D. W. Stacks and J. K. Burgoon, "The Persuasive Effects of Violating Spacial Distance Expectations in Small Groups" (Paper presented at the Southern Speech Communication Association, Biloxi, Miss., 1979).
43. Peter A. Andersen, "Nonverbal Communication in the Small Group," in *Small Group Communication: A Reader,* 5th ed., eds. R. Cathcart and L. Samovar (Dubuque, Iowa: Wm. C. Brown, 1988), pp. 333–50.
44. Albert Mehrabian, "Inference of Attitude from the Posture, Orientation, and Distance of a Communicator," *Journal of Consulting and Clinical Psychology* 32 (1968): 308.
45. Thomas J. Peters and Robert H. Waterman, Jr., *In Search of Excellence* (New York: Harper & Row, 1982), p. 220.
46. M. Lefkowitz, Robert Blake, and Jane Mouton, "Status Factors in Pedestrian Violation of Traffic Signals," *Journal of Abnormal and Social Psychology* 51 (1955): 704–6.
47. John T. Malloy, *Dress for Success* (New York: Warner Books, 1978).
48. Andersen, "Nonverbal Communication in the Small Group," pp. 334–35.
49. Mehrabian, "Inference of Attitude from the Posture, Orientation and Distance of a Communicator."
50. Albert Mehrabian and M. Williams, "Nonverbal Concomitants of Perceived and Intended Persuasiveness," *Journal of Personality and Social Psychology* 13 (1969): 37–58.
51. J. O'Connor, "The Relationship of Kinesic and Verbal Communication to Leadership Perception in Small Group Discussions" (Ph.D. diss., Indiana University, 1971); John E. Baird, Jr., "Some Nonverbal Elements of Leadership Emergence," *Southern Speech Communication Journal* 42 (1977): 352–61.
52. Andersen, "Nonverbal Communication in the Small Group," p. 337.
53. A. E. Scheflen, *Body Language and the Social Order* (Englewood Cliffs, N.J.: Prentice-Hall, 1972).
54. Howard M. Rosenfeld, "Instrumental Affiliative Functions of Facial and Gestural Expressions," *Journal of Personality and Social Psychology* 4 (1966): 65–72; Mehrabian and Williams, "Nonverbal Concomitants of Perceived and Intended Persuasiveness."
55. Paul Ekman and W. V. Friesen, *Unmasking the Face* (Englewood Cliffs, N.J.: Prentice-Hall, 1975).
56. R. Exline and C. Eldridge, "Effects of Two Patterns of a Speaker's Visual Behavior upon the Perception of the Authenticity of His Verbal Message" (Paper presented to the Eastern Psychological Association, Boston, 1967).
57. Mehrabian, "The Significance of Posture and Position."
58. Joseph A. DeVito, *The Interpersonal Communication Book,* 4th ed. (New York: Harper & Row, 1986), p. 208.
59. Ashley Montagu, *Touching: The Human Significance of the Skin* (New York: Columbia University Press, 1971).
60. Kenneth Blanchard and Spencer Johnson, *The One Minute Manager* (New York: Morrow, 1982).
61. Nancy Henley, *Body Politics: Power, Sex, and Nonverbal Communication* (Englewood Cliffs, N.J.: Prentice-Hall, 1977).
62. Sidney M. Jourard, *Disclosing Man to Himself* (New York: Van Nostrand Reinhold, 1968).
63. *Ibid.*
64. DeVito, *The Interpersonal Communication Book,* pp. 211–13.
65. David W. Addington, "The Relationship of Selected Vocal Characteristics to Personality Perception," *Speech Monographs* 35 (1968): 492–503.
66. M. H. L. Hecker, "Speaker Recognition: An Interpretive Survey of the Literature," *ASHA Monographs,* no. 16 (Washington, D.C.: American Speech and Hearing Association, 1971).
67. Howard Giles and Richard Y. Bourhis, "Voice and Racial Categorization in Britain," *Communication Monographs,* 43 (1976): 108–14; Norman J. Lass, Karen R. Hughes, Melanie D. Bowyer, Lucille T. Waters, and Victoria T. Broune, "Speaker Sex Identification from Voiced, Whispered and Filtered Isolated Vowels," *Journal of the Acoustical Society of America* 59 (1976): 675–78.

68. Joel R. Davitz, *The Communication of Emotional Meaning* (New York: McGraw-Hill, 1964); Mark Snyder, "Self-Monitoring of Expressive Behavior," *Journal of Personality and Social Psychology* 30 (1974): 526–37.
69. Andersen, "Nonverbal Communication in the Small Group," p. 340.
70. John E. Baird, Jr. and Gretchen K. Wieting, "Nonverbal Communication Can Be a Motivational Tool," *Personnel Journal* 58 (1979): 607–10.
71. Hegarty, *How to Talk Your Way to the Top.*
72. French and Raven, "*The Bases of Social Power.*"
73. Arlene Yerys, "How to Get What You Want through Influential Communication," *Management Review* 71 (June 1982): 12–18.
74. Natasha Josefowitz, "Getting through to the Unreachable Person," *Management Review* 71 (March 1983): 48–50.
75. Frank Stagnaro, "The Benefits of Leveling with Employees: ROLM's Experience," *Management Review* 71 (July 1982): 16–20.
76. Rossiter and Pearce, *Communicating Personally.*
77. Samuel Culbert, *Interpersonal Process of Self-Disclosure: It Takes Two to See One* (Washington, D.C.: NTL Institute for Applied Behavioral Science, 1967).
78. Joseph Luft, *Group Processes: An Introduction to Group Dynamics* (Palo Alto, Calif.: National Press Books, 1970).
79. Rafael Steinberg, *Man and the Organization* (New York: Time-Life Books, 1975).
80. Rossiter and Pearce, *Communicating Personally.*

CHAPTER 6

1. Iain Carson, "What Are the Causes of Executive Stress?" *International Management* (January 1972): 14–19.
2. Andrew J. J. Brennan, "Worksite Health Promotion Can Be Cost-Effective," *Personnel Administrator* 28 (April 1983): 39–42.
3. James M. Lahiff, "Interviewing for Results," in *Readings in Interpersonal and Organizational Communication,* eds. R. C. Huseman, C. M. Logue, and D. L. Freshley, 3d ed. (Boston: Holbrook Press, 1973), pp. 395–414.
4. John R. Hinrichs, "Employees Going and Coming: The Exit Interview," *Personnel* (January-February 1971): 27–32.
5. Charles J. Stewart and William B. Cash, *Interviewing: Principles and Practices,* 3d ed. (Dubuque, Iowa: Wm. C. Brown, 1982), p. 7.
6. Robert E. Carlson, "Improvements in the Selection Interview," *Personnel Journal* 6 (1971): 268–75.
7. Robert Widgery and C. Stackpole, "Desk Position, Interviewee Anxiety and Interviewer Credibility: An Example of Cognitive Balance in a Dyad," *Journal of Counseling Psychology* 19 (1972): 173–77.
8. Gary Richetto and J. P. Zima, *Fundamentals of Interviewing* (Chicago: Science Research Associates, 1976).
9. Stewart and Cash, *Interviewing: Principles and Practices,* p. 14.
10. *Ibid.,* p. 15.
11. Richetto and Zima, *Fundamentals of Interviewing,* p. 23.
12. Craig D. Tengler and Frederic M. Jablin, "Effects of Question Type, Orientation, and Sequencing in the Employment Screening Interview," *Communication Monographs* 50 (1983): 245–63.
13. *Ibid.,* pp. 262–63.
14. Marvin Gottlieb, *Interview* (New York: Longman, 1986), pp. 47–49.
15. Carl Rogers and Richard E. Farson, "Active Listening," in *Organizational Communication,* eds. S. D. Ferguson and S. Ferguson, 2d ed. (New Brunswick, N.J.: Transaction, Inc., 1988), pp. 319–34.
16. Lahiff, "Interviewing for Results," p. 335.

CHAPTER 7

1. Joseph A. Raelin, "First-Job Effects on Career Development," *Personnel Administrator* 28 (August 1983): 71–92.

2. Diane Arthur, "Preparing for the Interview," *Personnel* 63 (May 1986): 37.

3. For an analysis of the sorts of illegal questions commonly asked in employment interviews, see Fredric M. Jablin, "Use of Discriminatory Questions in Screening Interviews," *Personnel Administrator* 27 (March 1982): 41–44.

4. American Psychological Association, *Principles for the Validation and Use of Personnel Selection Procedures,* 1975; Equal Employment Opportunity Commission, *Uniform Guidelines on Employee Selection, Federal Registrar,* 25 August 1978; also see Micheale Snyder Battles and Suzanne Bitzer, *The Manager's Guide to Equal Employment Opportunity* (New York: Executive Enterprises, 1977), and Jerome Siegel, *Personnel Testing under EEO* (New York: American Management Association, 1980).

5. Eric Rolfe Greenberg, "Workplace Testing: Who's Testing Whom?" *Personnel* 66 (May 1989): 39–45.

6. Eric Rolfe Greenberg, "Workplace Testing: Results of a New AMA Survey," *Personnel* 65 (April 1988): 36–44.

7. Arthur A. Witkin, "Commonly Overlooked Dimensions of Employee Selection," *Personnel Journal* 59 (1980): 573–88.

8. For additional suggestions, see D. Trevor Michaels, Seven Questions That Will Improve Your Managerial Hiring Decisions, *Personnel Journal* 59 (1980): 199–225.

9. H. L. Sheppard and H. Belitsky, *The Job Hunt: Job-Seeking Behavior of Unemployed Workers in a Local Economy* (Baltimore: Johns Hopkins University Press, 1971).

10. Richard N. Bolles, *What Color Is Your Parachute? A Practical Manual for Job-Hunters and Career-Changers* (Berkeley, Calif.: Ten Speed Press, 1980).

11. Lois J. Einhorn, Patricia H. Bradley, and John E. Baird, Jr., *Effective Employment Interviewing* (Glenview, Ill.: Scott, Foresman, 1982).

12. Howard M. Sherer, "Effective Entry-Level Organizational Communication as Assessed through a Survey of Personnel Recruiters" (Ph.D. diss., Indiana University, 1984).

13. Harold D. Janes, "The Cover Letter and Resume," *Personnel Journal* 48 (1969): 732–33.

14. Mary Bakeman, Peter Weaver, and Jo Ash, *Job Seeking Skills Reference Manual,* 3d ed. (Minneapolis: Rehabilitation Center, 1971), p. 57.

15. Charles J. Stewart and William B. Cash, *Interviewing: Principles and Practices,* 3d ed. (Dubuque, Iowa: Wm. C. Brown, 1982), pp. 163–204.

16. Rosalia Sears, "Nonverbal Communication in the Employment Interview: A Review of the Literature," *Indiana Speech Jounral* 18 (1986): 20–32.

17. Steven M. Ralston, "The Relative Influence of Interviewee Communication Behavior, Job Application and Job Description upon Simulated Personnel Selection Decisions" (Ph.D. diss., Indiana University, 1986).

18. William D. Brooks, *Speech Communication* (Dubuque, Iowa: Wm. C. Brown, 1971).

19. Douglas McGregor, "An Uneasy Look at Performance Appraisal," *Harvard Business Review* 58 (1957): 66–71.

20. Randall Brett and Alan J. Fredian, "Performance Appraisal: The System Is Not the Solution," *Personnel Administrator* 26 (1981): 61–68.

21. James M. Lahiff, "Interviewing for Results," in *Readings in Interpersonal and Organizational Communication,* eds., R. C. Huseman, C. M. Logue, and D. L. Freshley, 2d ed. (Boston: Holbrook Press, 1973); Emanuel Kay, Herbert H. Meyer, and John R. P. French, "The Effect of Threat in a Performance Appraisal Interview," *Journal of Applied Psychology* 49 (1965): 311–17.

22. Cal W. Downs, G. Paul Smeyak, and Ernest Martin, *Professional Interviewing* (New York: Harper & Row, 1980).

23. J. Key, "Many Employee Evaluation Systems Are Rating Bad Scores," *Chicago Tribune,* 25 January 1982, Sec. 8, p. 3.

24. Brett and Fredian, "Performance Appraisal."
25. For a more detailed consideration of employee performance appraisal, see Elaine F. Gruenfeld, *Performance Appraisal: Promise and Peril* (Ithaca, N.Y.: Cornell University Press, 1981); Charles A. Dailey and Ann M. Madsen, *How to Evaluate People in Business* (New York: McGraw-Hill, 1980); and Donald H. Brush and Lyle F. Scheonfeldt, "Performance Appraisal for the '80s," *Personnel Administrator* 27 (December 1982): 76–83.
26. Guvenc G. Alpander, "Training First-Line Supervisors to Criticize Constructively," *Personnel Journal* 59 (1980): 216–21.
27. Richard A. Hatch, *Communicating in Business* (Chicago: Science Research Associates, 1977), p. 178.
28. Stewart and Cash, *Interviewing: Principles and Practices,* pp. 230–36.
29. Gerald I. Nierenberg, *Fundamentals of Negotiating* (New York: Hawthorn Books, 1973).
30. Jonn E. Baird, Jr., *Speaking for Results* (New York: Harper & Row, 1981), pp. 22–24.
31. See Alan H. Monroe, *Principles and Types of Speech* (Chicago: Scott, Foresman, 1935), pp. vii–x; also Douglas Ehninger, Bruce Gronbeck, and Alan H. Monroe, *Principles of Speech Communication,* 9th brief ed. (Glenview, Ill.: Scott, Foresman, 1984).
32. M. Burstein, *Selling and Salesmanship* (Dobbs Ferry, N.Y.: Oceana Publications, 1969), p. 7.
33. J. Hatfield, "Communication in Retail Salesmanship: A Balanced Approach," in *Readings in Interpersonal and Organizational Communication,* eds. R. C. Huseman, C. M. Logue, and D. L. Freshley, 2d ed. (Boston: Holbrook Press, 1973), pp. 395–407.

CHAPTER 8

1. Robert F. Bales, *Interaction Process Analysis: A Method for the Study of Small Groups* (Cambridge, Mass.: Addison-Wesley, 1950).
2. William Scott, *Organization Theory* (Homewood, Ill.: Richard D. Irwin, 1967).
3. Michael S. Olmstead, "Orientation and Role in the Small Group," *American Sociological Review* 19 (1959): 741–51.
4. Clovis R. Shepherd, *Small Groups* (Scrantan, Pa.: Chandler, 1964).
5. Frederic M. Jablin, "Groups within Organizations: Current Issues and Directions for Future Research" (Unpublished ms., University of Texas at Austin, 1980).
6. Also see R. Greenwood and K. Legge, "Policy-Making Groups," in *Groups at Work,* eds. R. Payne and C. L. Cooper (New York: John Wiley & Sons, 1981), pp. 9–40.
7. Fritz J. Roethlisberger and William J. Dickson, *Management and the Worker* (Cambridge: Harvard University Press, 1939).
8. R. Wellins, W. Byham, and J. Wilson, *Empowered Teams* (San Francisco: Jossey-Bass, 1991), p. 3.
9. David A. Whetton and Kim S. Cameron, *Developing Management Skills,* 2d ed. (New York: HarperCollins, 1991).
10. See Gay Lumsden and Don Lumsden, *Communicating in Groups and Teams: Sharing Leadership* (Belmont, Calif.: Wadsworth, 1993).
11. *Quality Circles Participants' Manual* (Prospect Heights, Ill.: Waveland Press, 1982), pp. 5–16.
12. E. E. Lawler and S. A. Mohrman, "Quality Circles after the Fad," *Harvard Business Review* 85 (1985): 65–71.
13. Donald E. L. Johnson, "Managers with Participative Skills Will Thrive in Cost-Conscious Market," *Modern Healthcare* 14 (March 1984): 48–53.
14. *Quality Circles Participants' Manual,* pp. 8–13.
15. Tom D. Daniels and Barry K. Spiker, *Perspectives on Organizational Communication* (Dubuque, Iowa: Wm. C. Brown, 1987), pp. 202–3.
16. J. Leonard, "Can Your Organization Support Quality Circles?" *Training and Development Journal* 37 (1983): 67–72.
17. G. W. Meyer and R. G. Stott, "Quality Circles: Panacea or Pandora's Box?" *Organizational Dynamics* 13 (1985): 34–50.
18. *Ibid.*

19. Cynthia Stohl, "Quality Circles and Changing Patterns of Communication," *Communication Yearbook* 9 (Beverly Hills: Sage, 1986), pp. 483–510.
20. Frederick Taylor, *Scientific Management* (New York: Harper & Row, 1911).
21. Muzafer Sherif, *The Psychology of Social Norms* (New York: Harper & Row, 1936).
22. Solomon E. Asch, "Studies of Independence and Conformity: A Minority of One against a Unanimous Majority," *Psychological Monographs* 70 (1956).
23. Edgar Schein, *Process Consultation* (Reading, Mass.: Addison-Wesley, 1969), p. 59.
24. George Cheney, "On the Various and Changing Meanings of Organizational Membership: A Field Study of Organizational Identification," *Communication Monographs* 50 (1983): 342–62.
25. Asch, "Studies of Independence and Conformity."
26. Robert Blake and Jane Mouton, "Conformity, Resistance, and Conversion," in *Conformity and Deviation,* eds. I. A. Berg and B. M. Bass (New York: Harper and Brothers, 1961), pp. 1–37.
27. For a comparison of these two approaches to conformity, see Patricia Hayes Andrews, "Ego-Involvement, Self-Monitoring, and Conformity in Small Groups: Communicative Analysis," *Central States Speech Journal* 36 (1985): 51–60.
28. Lawrence B. Rosenfeld, *Human Interaction in the Small Group* (Columbus, Ohio: Charles E. Merrill, 1973).
29. Stanley Schachter and Kurt Back, "An Experimental Study of Cohesiveness and Productivity," *Human Relations* 4 (1951): 229–38.
30. K. Phillip Taylor, "An Investigation of Majority Verbal Behavior toward Opinions of Deviant Members in Group Discussions of Policy" (Ph.D. diss., Indiana University, 1969).
31. Carl L. Thameling, "Majority Responses to Opinion Deviates: A Communication Analysis" (Ph.D. diss., Indiana University, 1990).
32. John R. Wenburg and William Wilmot, *The Personal Communication Process* (New York: John Wiley & Sons, 1973).
33. Patricia Hayes Bradley, "An Experimental Study of Deviate Responses to Pressure for Uniformity in Group Discussions of Policy," *Small Group Behavior* 9 (1978): 149–60.
34. Patricia Hayes Bradley, Alan M. Harris, and C. Mac Hamon, "Dissent in Small Groups," *Journal of Communication* 26 (1976): 155–59.
35. Thameling, "Majority Responses," pp. 80–83.
36. Judith M. Bunyi and Patricia Hayes Andrews, "Gender and Leadership Emergence: An Experimental Study," *Southern Speech Communication Journal* 50 (1985): 246–60.
37. Dennis S. Gouran and Randy Y. Hirokawa, "Counteractive Functions of Communication in Effective Group Decision-Making," in *Communication and Group Decision-Making,* eds. R. Y. Hirokawa and M. S. Poole (Beverly Hills: Sage, 1986), pp. 81–90.
38. *Ibid.*
39. Kenneth D. Benne and Paul Sheats, "Functional Roles of Group Members," *Journal of Social Issues* 4 (1948): 41–49.
40. John R. P. French, Jr., and Bernard Raven, "The Bases of Social Power," in *Studies in Social Power,* ed. D. Cartwright (Ann Arbor, Mich.: Institute for Social Research, 1959), pp. 65–84.
41. Gouran and Hirokawa, "Counteractive Functions," pp. 88–89.
42. See, for example, Dennis S. Gouran and Patricia Hayes Andrews, "Determinants of Positive Responses to Socially Prescribed Behavior," *Small Group Behavior* 15 (1984): 525–42.
43. Alvin Zander, Dorwin Cartwright, and Stanley Schachter, "Power and the Relations among Professions," in *Studies in Social Power,* ed. D. Cartwright (Ann Arbor, Mich.: Institute for Social Research, 1959), pp. 15–34.
44. Arthur Cohen, "Upward Communication in Experimentally Created Hierarchies," *Human Relations* 11 (1958): 41–53.
45. Harold H. Kelley, "The Warm-Cold Variable in First Impressions of Persons," *Journal of Personality* 18 (1950): 431–39.
46. Jacob I. Hurwitz and Alvin Zander, "Some Effects of Power in the Relations among Group Members," in *Group Dynamics,* eds. D. Cartwright and A. Zander (New York: Harper & Row, 1960), pp. 483–92.

47. Dorwin Cartwright and Alvin Zander, *Group Dynamics* (New York: Harper & Row, 1968).
48. Peter Drucker, *Effective Decisions, Effective Executive Series,* 1968.
49. Shepherd, *Small Groups.*
50. William Foster Owen, "Metaphor Analysis of Cohesiveness in Small Discussion Groups," *Small Group Behavior* 16 (1985): 415–24.
51. D. G. Marquis and Kurt Back, "A Social Psychological Study of the Decision-Making Conferences," in *Groups, Leadership, and Men,* ed. H. Guetzkow (Pittsburgh: Carnegie Press, 1951), pp. 55–67.
52. Leonard Berkowitz, "Group Norms among Bomber Crews," *Sociometry* 19 (1956): 141–53.
53. Kelley, "The Warm-Cold Variable," pp. 431–39; Kurt Back, "Influence through Social Communication," *Journal of Abnormal and Social Psychology* 46 (1951): 9–23; Martin Grossack, "Some Effects of Cooperation and Competition upon Small Group Behavior," *Journal of Abnormal and Social Psychology* 49 (1954): 341–48; John R. P. French, Jr., "The Disruption and Cohesion of Groups," *Journal of Abnormal and Social Psychology* 36 (1941): 361–77.
54. Schachter et al., "An Experimental Study of Cohesiveness and Productivity," pp. 229–38; Leonard Berkowitz, "Group Standards, Cohesiveness, and Productivity," *Human Relations* 7 (1954): 509–19.
55. Irving L. Janis, *Groupthink,* 2d ed. (Boston: Houghton Mifflin, 1982), p. 3.
56. Back, "Influence through Social Communication"; Leonard Berkowitz, "Liking for the Group and the Perceived Merit of the Group's Behavior," *Journal of Abnormal and Social Psychology* 54 (1957): 353–57.
57. David Siebold and Renee Meyers, "Communication and Influence in Group Decision-Making," in *Communication and Group Decision-Making,* eds. R. Y. Hirokawa and M. S. Poole (Beverly Hills: Sage, 1986), pp. 96–115.
58. Irving Janis, *Decision Making: A Psychological Analysis of Conflict, Choice, and Commitment* (New York: Free Press, 1977).
59. Janis, *Groupthink,* p. 9.
60. *Ibid.,* pp. 197–98.
61. Richard C. Huseman and Russell W. Driver, "Groupthink: Implications for Small Group Decision Making in Business," in *Readings in Organizational Behavior: Dimensions of Management Actions,* eds. R. C. Huseman and A. B. Carroll (Boston: Allyn & Bacon, 1979), pp. 100–110.
62. John A. Courtwright, "A Laboratory Investigation of Groupthink," *Communication Monographs* 45 (1978): 229–46.

CHAPTER 9

1. Keith Davis, *Human Behavior at Work* (New York: McGraw-Hill, 1972).
2. Irvin Summers and Major David E. White, "Creativity Techniques: Toward Improvement of the Decision Process," in *Intercom: Readings in Organizational Communication,* eds. S. Ferguson and S. Devereaux Ferguson (Rochelle Park, N.J.: Hayden Book, 1980), pp. 338–48.
3. Norman R. F. Maier, "Assets and Liabilities in Group Problem-Solving: The Need for an Integrative Function," *Psychological Review* 74 (1967): 239–49.
4. *Ibid.*
5. Randy Y. Hirokawa and Dirk R. Scheerhorn, "Communication in Faulty Group Decision-Making," in *Communication and Group Decision-Making,* eds. R. Y. Hirokawa and M. S. Poole (Beverly Hills: Sage, 1986), pp. 63–80.
6. Randy Y. Hirokawa and R. Pace, "A Descriptive Investigation of the Possible Communication-Based Reasons for Effective and Ineffective Group Decision Making," *Communication Monographs* 50 (1983): 363–79.
7. Douglas Bunker and Gene Dalton, "The Comparative Effectiveness of Groups and Individuals in Problem Solving," in *Managing Group and Intergroup Relations,* eds. J. Lorsch and P. Lawrence (Homewood, Ill.: Richard D. Irwin, 1972), pp. 204–11.

8. Dennis S. Gouran, *Discussion: The Process of Group Decision-Making* (New York: Harper & Row, 1974).

9. Milton Rokeach, *Beliefs, Attitudes, and Values* (New York: Jossey-Bass, 1968).

10. Gouran, *Discussion,* pp. 66–80.

11. Robert F. Bales and Fred L. Strodtbeck, "Phases in Group Problem-Solving," *Journal of Abnormal and Social Psychology* 46 (1951): 485–95.

12. B. W. Tuckman and M. A. C. Jensen, "Stages of Small-Group Development," *Group and Organizational Studies* 2 (1977): 419–27.

13. Thomas M. Schiedel and Laura Crowell, "Idea Development in Small Groups," *Quarterly Journal of Speech* 50 (1964): 140–45.

14. Dennis S. Gouran and John E. Baird, Jr., "An Analysis of Distributional and Sequential Structure in Problem-Solving and Informal Group Discussions," *Speech Monographs* 39 (1972): 16–22.

15. John E. Baird, Jr., "A Comparison of Distributional and Sequential Structure in Cooperative and Competitive Group Discussions," *Speech Monographs* 41 (1974): 226–32.

16. B. Aubrey Fisher, "Decision Emergence: Phases in Group Decision-Making," *Speech Monographs* 37 (1970): 53–66; B. Aubrey Fisher, "The Process of Decision Modification in Small Discussion Groups," *Journal of Communication* 20 (1970): 51–64; B. Aubrey Fisher, "Content and Relationship Dimensions of Communication in Decision-Making Groups," *Communication Quarterly* 27 (1979): 3–11.

17. Marshall Scott Poole, "Decision Development in Small Groups I: A Comparison of Two Models," *Communication Monographs* 48 (1981): 1–24.

18. Marshall Scott Poole, "Decision Development in Small Groups II: A Study of Multiple Sequences in Decision Making," *Communication Monographs* 50 (1983): 206–32.

19. Marshall Scott Poole and J. Roth, "Decision Development in Small Groups IV: A Typology of Group Decision Paths," *Human Communication Research* 15 (1988): 323–56.

20. Connie Gersick, "Time and Transition in Work Teams: Toward a New Model of Group Development," *Academy of Management Journal* 31 (1988): 9–41.

21. *Ibid.,* p. 32.

22. Connie Gersick, "Revolutionary Change Theories: A Multiple-Level Explanation of the Punctuated Equilibrium Paradigm," *Academy of Management Review* 16 (1991): 10–36.

23. Randy Y. Hirokawa, "Group Communication and Problem-Solving Effectiveness: An Investigation of Group Phases," *Human Communication Research* 9 (1983): 291–305.

24. Gersick, "Time and Transition in Work Teams."

25. Irving L. Janis and L. Mann, *Decision Making: A Psychological Analysis of Conflict, Choice, and Commitment* (New York: Free Press, 1977).

26. Dennis S. Gouran, *Making Decisions in Groups: Choices and Consequences* (Prospect Heights, Ill.: Waveland Press, 1982).

27. Randy Y. Hirokawa and K. Rost, "Effective Group Decision-Making in Organizations," *Management Communication Quarterly* 5 (1992): 267–288.

28. Charles Conrad, *Strategic Organizational Communication: An Integrated Perspective,* 2d ed. (Orlando, Fla.: Harcourt Brace Jovanovich, 1990).

29. M. D. Cohen, J. G. March, and J. P. Olson, "A Garbage Can Model of Organizational Choice," *Administrative Science Quarterly* 17 (1972): 1–25.

30. Marshall Scott Poole and J. Roth, "Decision Development in Small Groups V: Test of a Contingency Model," *Human Communication Research* 15 (1988): 549–89; also Poole and Roth, "Decision Development in Small Groups IV."

31. P. C. Nutt, "Types of Organizational Decision Processes," *Administrative Science Quarterly* 29 (1984): 414–50.

32. Harold Guetzow and John Gyr, "An Analysis of Conflict in Decision-Making Groups," *Human Relations* 7 (1954): 367–82; Norman R. F. Maier and Richard A. Maier, "An Experimental Test of the Effects of Developmental versus 'Free' Discussion on the Quality of Group Decisions," *Journal of Applied Psychology* 41 (1957): 320–23.

33. John K. Brilhart and Lurene M. Jochem, "Effects of Different Patterns of Outcomes of Problem-Solving Discussion," *Journal of Applied Psychology* 48 (1964): 175–79.

34. Marvin D. Dunnette, John Campbell, and Kay Jaastad, "The Effect of Group Participation on Brainstorming Effectiveness for Two Industrial Samples," *Journal of Applied Psychology* 47 (1963): 30–37; Thomas J. Bouchard, "Whatever Happened to Brainstorming?" *Industry Week,* 2 August 1971, pp. 26–27.

35. Thad B. Green and Paul H. Pietri, "Using Nominal Grouping to Improve Upward Communication," *MSU Business Topics* (Autumn 1974): 37–43; Donald C. Mosley and Thad B. Green, "Nominal Grouping as an Organization Development Intervention Technique," *Training and Development Journal* (March 1974): 30–37.

36. Frederic M. Jablin, David R. Siebold, and Rich L. Sorenson, "Potential Inhibiting Effects of Group Participation on Brainstorming Performance," *Central States Speech Journal* 28 (1977): 113–21; Jablin, "Cultivating Imagination: Factors That Enhance and Inhibit Creativity in Brainstorming Groups," *Human Communication Research* 7 (1981): 245–58.

37. B. Gallupe, G. DeSanctis, and G. Dickson, "The Impact of Computer-Based Support on the Process and Outcomes of Group Decision Making," *MIS Quarterly* 12 (1988): 277–298; Rob Anson, "Effects of Computer Support and Facilitator Support on Group Process and Outcomes: An Experimental Assessment" (Ph.D. diss., Indiana University, 1990).

38. John Dewey, *How We Think* (Boston: Heath, 1910).

39. Brilhart and Jochem, "Effects on Different Patterns."

40. Dewey, *How We Think.*

41. Green and Pietri, "Using Nominal Grouping."

42. Summers and White, "Creative Techniques," pp. 342–43; also see Brant Burelson, "Decision-Making Procedures and Decision Quality," *Human Communication Research* 10 (1984): 557–74.

43. Gouran, *Discussion,* pp. 76–77.

44. A. Dennis and R. B. Gallupe, "A History of Group Support Systems Empirical Research: Lessons Learned and Future Directions," in *Group Support Systems: New Perspectives,* eds. L. M. Jessup and J. S. Valacich (New York: Macmillan, 1993), pp. 78–96.

45. Suzanne Herrick-Walker, "The Effect of Group Decision Support Systems on Decision-Making Groups Containing High Communication Apprehensives: Satisfaction, Participation, and Productivity" (Unpublished master's thesis, Indiana University, 1991).

46. G. DeSanctis, M. D'Onofrio, V. Sambamurthy, and M. S. Poole, "Comprehensiveness and Restrictiveness in Group Decision Heuristics: Effects of Computer Support on Consensus Decision Making," *ICIS Proceedings* (1989).

47. J. Nunamaker, A. Dennis, J. Valacich, D. Vogel, and J. George, "Group Support Systems Research: Experience from the Lab and Field," in *Group Support Systems: New Perspectives,* eds. L. M. Jessup and J. S. Valacich (New York: Macmillan, 1993), pp. 78–96.

48. *Ibid.*

49. J. Nunamaker, A. R. Dennis, J. S. Valacich, D. R. Vogel, and J. F. George, *Electronic Meeting Systems to Support Group Work: Theory and Practice at Arizona* (Arizona Working Paper, University of Arizona, Tucson, 1990).

50. *Ibid.,* pp. 78–96.

51. *Ibid.*

52. P. Keen and S. Morton, *Decision Support Systems: An Organizational Perspective* (Reading, Mass.: Addison-Wesley, 1978).

53. Gallupe, DeSanctis, and Dickson, "The Impact of Computer-Based Support," pp. 277–98.

54. Dennis and Gallupe, "A History of Group Support Systems Empirical Research," p. 73.

55. Nunamaker et al., *Electronic Meeting Systems,* pp. 78–96.

56. D. Kirkpatrick, "Here Comes the Payoff from PCs," *Fortune,* 23 March 1992, pp. 93–100.

57. N. Wreden, "Regrouping for Groupware," *Beyond Computing* 2 (1993): 52–55.

58. *Ibid.*

59. *Ibid.,* p. 55.

CHAPTER 10

1. John Naisbitt, *Megatrends: Ten New Directions Transforming Our Lives* (New York: Warner Books, 1982), p. 159.
2. Allan Cox, *The Cox Report on the American Corporation* (New York: Delacorte, 1982), p. 136.
3. Perry Pascarella, *The New Achievers: Creating a Modern Work Ethic* (New York: Free Press, 1984), p. 106.
4. Charles Bird, *Social Psychology* (New York: Appleton-Century, 1940).
5. Ralph Stogdill, *Handbook of Leadership* (New York: Free Press, 1974).
6. Dennis S. Gouran, "Conceptual and Methodological Approaches to the Study of Leadership," *Central States Speech Journal* 21 (1970): 217–23.
7. John G. Geier, "A Trait Approach to the Study of Leadership in Small Groups," *Journal of Communication* 17 (1967): 316–23.
8. Hugh C. Russell, "An Investigation of Leadership Maintenance Behavior," (Ph.D. diss., Indiana University, 1970).
9. Ralph White and Ronald Lippitt, *Autocracy and Democracy* (New York: Harper & Row, 1960).
10. Leonard Berkowitz, "Sharing Leadership in Small Decision-Making Groups," *Journal of Abnormal and Social Psychology* 48 (1953): 231–38.
11. Lester Coch and John R. P. French, Jr., "Overcoming Resistance to Change," *Human Relations* 11 (1948): 512–32.
12. John R. Galbraith, "Influencing the Decision to Produce," *Industrial Management Review* 9 (1967): 97–107.
13. Marvin Shaw, "A Comparison of Two Types of Leadership in Various Communication Nets," *Journal of Abnormal and Social Psychology* 50 (1955): 127–34.
14. Paul R. Lawrence and Jay W. Lorsch, *Organization and Environment* (Boston: Harvard Business School, Division of Research, 1967); Joan Woodward, *Industrial Organization: Theory and Practice* (New York: Oxford University Press, 1965).
15. Gouran, "Conceptual and Methodological Approaches to the Study of Leadership," p. 219.
16. Frederick E. Fiedler, *A Theory of Leadership Effectiveness* (New York: McGraw-Hill, 1967); "The Leadership Game: Matching the Man to the Situation, in *Readings in Organizational Behavior: Dimensions of Management Actions,* ed. Richard C. Huseman and Archie B. Carroll (Boston: Allyn & Bacon, 1979), pp. 305–13.
17. B. Y. Auger, "Staff Meetings: Energy Waste or Catalyst for High Performance," *Data Management* 20 (May 1980): 39–41.
18. Allan D. Frank, "Trends in Communication: Who Talks to Whom?" *Personnel* 62 (December 1985): 41–47.
19. For example, see William G. Dyer, *Team Building: Issues and Alternatives* (Reading, Mass.: Addison-Wesley, 1977), and William I. Gordon and Roger J. Howe, *Team Dynamics in Developing Organizations* (Dubuque, Iowa: Kendall/Hunt, 1977).
20. Robert F. Littlejohn, "Team Management: A How-to Approach to Improved Productivity, Higher Morale, and Longer Lasting Job Satisfaction," *Management Review* 71 (January 1982): 23–28.
21. For example, see General Henry M. Robert, *Robert's Rules of Order Newly Revised,* (Glenview, Ill.: Scott, Foresman, 1970); Alice Sturgis, *Sturgis Standard Code of Parliamentary Procedure,* 2d ed. (New York: McGraw-Hill, 1966); John E. Baird, *A Guide to Conducting Meetings* (New York: Abingdon Press, 1965).

CHAPTER 11

1. Chester Bernard, *The Functions of the Executive* (Cambridge: Harvard University Press, 1950), p. 14.
2. Frederick Taylor, *Scientific Management* (New York: Harper & Row, 1911).
3. Henri Fayol, *General and Industrial Administration* (London: Pitman, 1949).

4. Fritz J. Roethlisberger and William J. Dickson, *Management and the Worker* (Cambridge: Harvard University Press, 1939).
5. William Evan, "Conflict and Performance in R&D Organizations," *Industrial Management Review* 7 (1965): 35–46.
6. Bernard Berelson and Gary A. Steiner, *Human Behavior: An Inventory of Scientific Findings* (New York: Harcourt Brace Jovanovich, 1964), p. 588.
7. Theodore Herbert, *Dimensions of Organizational Behavior* (New York: Macmillan, 1976), p. 347.
8. Rensis Likert, *New Patterns of Management* (New York: McGraw-Hill, 1961).
9. Lewis M. Killian, "The Significance of Multiple-Group Membership in Disaster," *American Journal of Sociology* 57 (1952): 309–14.
10. Robert R. Blake and Jane S. Mouton, *The Managerial Grid* (Houston, Gulf Publishing, 1964).
11. J. P. Folger and M. S. Poole, *Working through Conflict* (Glenview, Ill.: Scott Foresman, 1984).
12. A. Rahim and T. V. Bonoma, "Managing Organizational Conflict: A Model for Diagnosis and Intervention," *Psychological Reports* 44 (1979): 1323–44.
13. R. J. Mayer, *Conflict Management: The Courage to Confront* (Columbus, Ohio: Batelle Press, 1990).
14. Blake and Mouton, *The Managerial Grid.*
15. E. Phillips and R. Cheston, "Conflict Resolution: What Works?" *California Management Review* 21 (1979): 76–83.
16. *Ibid.*
17. A. Douglas, *Industrial Peacemaking* (New York: Columbia University Press, 1962).
18. P. J. D. Carnevale and R. Pegnetter, "The Selection of Mediation Tactics in Public Sector Disputes: A Contingency Analysis," *Journal of Social Issues* 41 (1985): 65–81.
19. D. M. Kolb, *The Mediators* (Cambridge: MIT Press, 1983).
20. J. M. Hilltrop, "Mediator Behavior and the Settlement of Collective Bargaining Disputes in Britain," *Journal of Social Issues* 41 (1985): 83–99.
21. J. A. Wall, "Mediation: An Analysis, Review, and Proposed Research," *Journal of Conflict Resolution* 25 (1981): 157–81.
22. Carnevale and Pegnetter, "The Selection of Mediation Tactics."
23. Kolb, *The Mediators.*
24. G. Northcraft and M. Neale, *Organizational Behavior* (Chicago: Dryden Press, 1990).
25. *Ibid.*
26. David A. Whetton and Kim S. Cameron, *Developing Management Skills,* 2d ed. (New York: HarperCollins, 1991).
27. J. Hall and W. H. Watson, "The Effects of a Normative Intervention on Group Decision-Making Performance," *Human Relations* 23 (1970): 299–317.
28. J. E. McGrath, *Groups: Interaction and Performance* (Englewood Cliffs, N.J.: Prentice-Hall, 1984).
29. Chris Argyris, *Intervention Theory and Method* (Reading, Mass.: Addison-Wesley, 1970).
30. Folger and Poole, *Working through Conflict.*
31. M. S. Poole, M. Holmes, and G. DeSanctis, "Conflict Management in a Computer-Supported Meeting Environment," *Management Science* 8 (1991): 926–53.
32. D. L. Olson and J. F. Cortney, *Decision Support Models and Expert Systems* (New York: Macmillan, 1992).
33. M. T. Jelassi and A. Foroughi, "Negotiation Support Systems: An Overview of Design Issues and Existing Software," *Decision Support Systems* 5 (1989): 167–81.
34. J. A. Savage, "Unions Cutting Bargain with High-Technology 'Devil' " *Computerworld 24* (July 23, 1990): 1, 115.

CHAPTER 12

1. K. E. Kendall, "Do Real People Ever Give Speeches?" *Central States Speech Journal* 25 (1974): 233.
2. Peter Drucker, "How to Be an Employer," *Fortune,* 5 May 1952, p. 126.

3. Cal Downs, David Berg, and Wil Linkugel, *The Organizational Communicator* (New York: Harper & Row, 1977).

4. Bob Rackleff, "The Hidden Dangers of Oil Pipelines: Try Toxic Pollution," *Vital Speeches of the Day* 58 (1992): 253.

5. John E. Jacob, "The State of Black America: Excellence, Perseverance, and Preparation," *Vital Speeches of the Day* 58 (1992): 533.

6. John W. Megown, "Topsy-Turvy Times for Agriculture," *Vital Speeches of the Day* 46 (1979–80): 17.

7. Mario Cuomo, "Keynote Address," *Vital Speeches of the Day* 50 (1984): 649.

8. William J. McCarville, "Waste Not—Want Not," *Vital Speeches of the Day* 46 (1979–80): 28.

9. There are rare occasions when an unusual example may be extremely pertinent. For example, knowing that a particular federally approved drug can be lethal for three out of every one thousand people is important information.

10. A. Thomas Young, "Ethics in Business," *Vital Speeches of the Day* 58 (1992): 726–27.

11. Edward M. Kennedy, "Principles of the Democratic Party: Common Hopes for the Future," *Vital Speeches of the Day* 46 (1979–80): 714–15.

12. Janet Martin, "Room at the Top," *Vital Speeches of the Day* 58 (1992): 348.

13. James C. McCroskey, *An Introduction to Rhetorical Communication,* 3d ed. (Englewood Cliffs, N.J.: Prentice-Hall, 1978), pp. 67–85.

CHAPTER 13

1. Irwin Edmond, *The Works of Plato* (New York: Simon & Schuster, 1928), p. 309.

2. Jimmy Carter, "U.S. Response to Soviet Military Force in Cuba," *Vital Speeches of the Day* 46 (1979–80): 2.

3. Neal W. O'Connor, "The Freedom to Communicate: An Advertising Man Re-reads the First Amendment," *Vital Speeches of the Day* 42 (1976): 179.

4. Eric Rubenstein, "Homelessness and Values: A Stopping Point or a Way of Life?," *Vital Speeches of the Day* 58 (1992): 401.

5. John D. Garwood, "Back to the Basics: A Commitment to Excellence," *Vital Speeches of the Day* 46 (1979–80): 42.

6. George H. Dixon, "Trade with China: Opportunity or Illusion?" *Vital Speeches of the Day* 46 (1979–80): 83.

7. Herbert S. Richey, "The Real Cause of Inflation: Government Services," *Vital Speeches of the Day* 46 (1979): 386.

8. Gary Trudeau, "The Impertinent Question," *Vital Speeches of the Day* 52 (1985–86): 619.

9. Bill Clinton, "Acceptance Address," *Vital Speeches of the Day* 58 (1992): 645.

10. Carter, "U.S. Response to Soviet Military Force in Cuba," p. 4.

11. Martin Luther King, Jr., "I Have a Dream," in *Contemporary American Speeches,* 3d ed., eds. W. A. Linkugel, R. Allen, and R. L. Johannesen (Belmont, Calif.: Wadsworth, 1972), p. 293.

12. Mario M. Cuomo, "Nominating Address," *Vital Speeches of the Day* 58 (1992): 650–51.

13. Janice Carlat, "A Green Parrot," in *Contemporary American Speeches,* 3d ed., ed. W. A. Linkugel et al. (Belmont, Calif.: Wadsworth, 1972), p. 63.

14. Michael Osborn and Suzanne Osborn, *Public Speaking* (Boston: Houghton Mifflin, 1988).

15. E. D. Wrenchley, "A Study of Stage Fright in a Selected Group of Experienced Speakers" (M.A. thesis, University of Denver, 1948).

16. William Hamilton, "A Review of Experimental Studies of Stage Fright," *Pennsylvania Speech Annual* 17 (1960): 44–45.

17. Theodore Clevenger, Jr., "A Synthesis of Experimental Research in Stage Fright," *Quarterly Journal of Speech* 45 (1959): 135–59.

18. John P. DeCecco and W. R. Crawford, *The Psychology of Learning and Instruction: Educational Psychology* (Englewood Cliffs, N.J.: Prentice-Hall, 1974).

19. Cal Downs, David Berg, and Wil Linkugel, *The Organizational Communicator* (New York: Harper & Row, 1977), p. 223.

20. Jane Blankenship, *A Sense of Style* (Belmont, Calif.: Dickenson, 1968), pp. 112–24.
21. Rudolph Flesch, *The Art of Plain Talk* (New York: Harper & Brothers, 1946), p. 38.
22. Helen M. Walker and J. Lev, *Elementary Statistical Methods* (New York: Holt, Rinehart & Winston, 1958).
23. Richard C. Huseman and Edward W. Miles, "Organizational Communication in the Information Age: Implications of Computer-Based Systems," *Journal of Management* 14 (1988): 191–92.
24. Edward W. Miles, et al., "Assessing the Utility of Computer-Generated Graphics in Problem-Solving" (Paper presented at the meeting of the Academy of Management, New Orleans, 1987).

CHAPTER 14

1. Vincent DiSalvo, *Business and Professional Communication* (Columbus, Ohio: Charles E. Merrill, 1977), pp. 131–55.
2. Roger P. Wilcox, *Oral Reporting in Business and Industry* (Englewood Cliffs, N.J.: Prentice-Hall, 1967), p. 22.
3. William S. Howell and Ernest G. Bormann, *Presentational Speaking for Business and the Professions* (New York: Harper & Row, 1971), p. 92.
4. See Abraham Maslow, *Motivation and Personality* (New York: Harper & Row, 1954); W. Clay Hamner and Dennis W. Organ, *Organizational Behavior: An Applied Psychological Approach* (Dallas: Business Publications, 1978), pp. 137–41.
5. Maslow, *Motivation and Personality*.
6. David McClelland, *The Achieving Society* (New York: Van Nostrand Reinhold, 1961); Hamner and Organ, *Organizational Behavior*, pp. 183–86.
7. Peter F. Drucker, *The Effective Executive* (New York: Harper & Row, 1967).
8. Jack L. Whitehead, "Factors of Source Credibility," *Quarterly Journal of Speech* 54 (1968): 59–63.
9. James C. McCroskey, *An Introduction to Rhetorical Communication,* 3d ed. (Englewood Cliffs, N.J.: Prentice-Hall, 1978), pp. 59–66.
10. See James C. McCroskey, "A Summary of Experimental Research on the Effects of Evidence in Persuasive Communication," *Quarterly Journal of Speech* 55 (1969): 169–76; Joseph A. Luchok and James C. McCroskey, "The Effect of Quality of Evidence on Attitude Change and Source Credibility," *Southern Speech Communication Journal* 43 (1977): 383–94.
11. Michael Burgoon and Judee K. Burgoon, "Message Strategies in Influence Attempts," in *Communication and Behavior,* eds. G. J. Hanneman and W. J. McEwen (Reading, Mass.: Addison-Wesley, 1975), pp. 149–65.
12. *Ibid.,* p. 153.
13. McCroskey, *An Introduction to Rhetorical Communication,* pp. 142–43.
14. William J. McGuire, "Inducing Resistance to Persuasion: Some Contemporary Approaches," in *Advances in Experimental Social Psychology,* ed. L. Berkowitz (New York: Academic Press, 1964), pp. 191–229.
15. *Ibid.*
16. Burgoon and Burgoon, "Message Strategies in Influence Attempts," p. 157.
17. *Ibid.,* p. 158.
18. Howell and Bormann, *Presentational Speaking for Business and the Professions,* p. 11.
19. *Ibid.*
20. Douglas Ehninger, Bruce Gronbeck, and Alan H. Monroe, *Principles of Speech Communication,* 9th brief ed. (Glenview, Ill.: Scott, Foresman, 1984), pp. 247–62.

Photo Credits

Author Index

Subject Index

skills, 3–5, 32–34
small group, 229
upward, 71–75
Communication functions, 65–67
Communication skills training, 459
Communication specialist, 457
Comparisons, as evidence, 369–71
Compensation consultant, 460
Competence, 97, 428
Competition, 12, 333
Conclusion of speech, 380, 388–90
Confidence, 396–98
Conflict
causes of, 333–35
defined, 328–29
management, 327–48
settings, 329–32
Conformity, 241–44
Conjecture, questions of, 268, 277
Conscientious objection, right to,
108–9
Consensus, 42
Consultative meetings, 301, 303–5
Consulting, 459–60
Contradicting, 140–41
Contrasts, as evidence, 369–71
Controversiality, 269
Corporate Cultures, 21
Corporate Mission Statements,
111–15
Corporate mottos, 112, 114
Counseling interviews, 165
Cover letter, 197–99
Creative problem-solving pattern,
276
Credibility, 381, 428–30
Cultural school, of organization,
20–24
Customer relations representative,
457

Data, analyzing, 265–67
Decision making groups, 235
Decision making models, 271–75
Deductive fallacies, 374–75
Deductive reasoning, 373–74
Delivery, effective, 401–2
Delivery, types of, 398–401
Democratic meetings, 301, 305–6
Dialogic ethics, 92
Diamond sequence, 176–77
Dichotomous listening, 134
Directive, 170–71

Directness, 203, 401
Disciplinary interviews, 163,
214–20
Discrimination, 103
Discussion questions, 267–69
Dissent, 58
Dissertation Abstracts, 264
Distortion, 70, 74
Diversity, managing, 54–56
Dominance, 122, 153–54
Downward communication, 68–71
Dress for Success, 147
Drug testing, 195
*Dun and Bradstreet's Middle
Market Directory,* 197
*Dun and Bradstreet's Million
Dollar Directory,* 197
Dun's Review, 197
Dyadic communication, 119–228
Dyadic settings, 64

Economic analysis, 89
Education Index, The, 263
EEOC, 192–95
Effective Decisions, 252
Effective Executive, The, 428
Elaborating, 141
Electronic media, 70, 73–74, 79
Emotional maturity, 205
Emotions, audience, 430–31
Empathy, 136–37
Employee relations representative,
455
Employment interviews, 163,
187–206
Empowerment, 45–48
Enthusiasm, 428
Environment, 141–45
Ethics, 59–60, 182–83, 286
Ethos, 428–30
Evaluation, 67
Evidence
persuasive strategies for using,
431–33
and speeches, 361–71
Examples, as evidence, 367–69
Exit interviews, 165
Expert testimony, 366–67
Extemporaneous speaking, 399,
423–24

Fact
confused with definition,
374–75

as evidence, 361–63
questions of, 267, 277
Fallacy
deductive, 374–75
inductive, 372–73
Feedback, 20, 67
Filtering, 70
Fitch's Corporation Reports, 197
Flexibility, 401
Following up meetings, 308–9
Fortune 500, 237
*Fortune's Plant and Product
Directory,* 197
Forum period, 240
Frustration, 329–30
Functional approach, to
leadership, 296
Functional conflicts, 333
Functional/transferable skills,
196–97
Fundraiser, 457
Funnel, 176
Furniture arrangement, 143

Generalization, hasty, 372
General semantics, 138
General systems theory, 17
Globalization, 48–50
Grapevine, 80–83
Graphs, 410
Grievance interviews, 164–65
Groups, effective, 271–75
Group Support System, 278–83,
346–47
Group task roles, 245–46
Groupthink, 254–55
Guest relations consultant, 460
Guide to Reference Books, 263
*Guide to the Use of Libraries,
The,* 263
Guilt by association, 374

Handout, 409
Harassment, sexual, 103–5
Hawthorne studies, 14–15
HEAR, 136–37
Helpfulness, 136–37
Hersey and Blanchard
management theory, 38–40
Herzberg management theory,
40–41
Horizontal communication, 75–78
Hourglass sequence, 177–78
Humanist ethics, 91–92

Human relationships, nature of, 121–24
Human relations school, of organization, 14–15
Human resources management, 15–16, 34–41, 43–44, 454–56
Human resources school, of organization, 15–17
Humor, 383–84
Hygiene factors, 40–41
Hypothetical examples, 369

Illustration, 384
Impression, initial, 202–3
Impromptu, 398–99
Inductive fallacies, 372–73
Inductive reasoning, 371
Informal communication, 80–83
Information collecting, 262–65
Information exchange, 65
Information interviews, 166–67
Informative oral reports, 419–24
INPC Model, 442–44
In Search of Excellence, 80
Integrity, 97
Interactions, 124
Interdependence, 95
Intergroup conflict, 331
International Index: Guide of Periodical Literature in the Social Sciences and Humanities, 263
Interorganizational conflict, 331–32
Interpersonal conflict, 330–31
Interpersonal similarity, 122
Intervention, 345
Interviews, 163–67
    appraisal, 164, 206–14
    conducting, 167–83
    counseling, 165
    defined, 162
    disciplinary, 163
    employment, 163
    exit, 165
    grievance, 164–65
    information, 166–67, 262–63
    persuasive, 167, 220–25
Intrapersonal conflict, 329–30
Introduction, of speech, 380–85
Inventory, personal, 196–97
Inverted funnel, 176–77

Investment account executive, 458
Involvement, 123, 155–59, 401

Japanese approach to management, 42–43
Job maturity, 38–40
Job requirements, 188
Job skills testing, 195
Johari Window, 156–59
Journal of Advertising Research, 98
Joyful living, 95–96

Kinesics, 148–49

Labor relations consultant, 460
Laissez-faire meetings, 301, 306–8
Language
    improving use of, 139–40
    and oral style, 404–8
Lay opinion, 365–66
Leadership, 31–45
    life cycle theory of, 38–40
    study of, 292–96
Learning groups, 235
Legal ethics, 89–90
Letters, 197–99, 206–7
LIC. See Low information content
Life cycle theory of leadership, 38–40
Likert management theory, 35–37
Listening, 58, 178–81
Low information content (LIC), 406–8

McGregor management theory, 34–35
MacRae's Blue Book—Corporate Index, 197
Maintenance/building roles in groups, 246–47
Management
    guidelines for, 56–60
    human resources, 15–17, 34–41, 43–44
    Japanese approach to, 42–43
    scientific, 12
Management skill clusters, 31–34
Manuscript, 399–401
Maps, 411
Marketing, 458–59
Market research specialist, 458
Maturity, social-emotional, 205

Mediation, of conflict, 339–40
Mediator, 339
Meetings, 291–326
Megatrends: Ten New Directions Transforming Our Lives, 121, 469
Memos for Management: Leadership, 97
Mental alertness, 203–4
Model, 499
Motions, 318–24
Motivation, 205
Motivators, 40–41

Narrative, 384
Negative support systems, 346–47
Network, 23
New York Times Index, 263
Nominal group procedure, 275, 276–77
Nondirective, 170–71
Nonverbal symbols, 129, 140–52
Norms, 242

Objectivity, 269, 428
Objects, 412
One Minute Manager, 150
Opening the interview, 169–70
Openness, 205
Open questions, 171–72
Opinion, as evidence, 365–67
Oral reports, informative, 419–24
Oral style, 404–8
Order of business, 317–18
Organization, common patterns of, 385–87
Organizational communication, 8–10
Organizational perspective, 354–56
Organizations
    communication in, 3–5, 9–10
    conflict in, 327–48
    contemporary views, 15–27
    defined, 6
    historical perspective, 10–15
    as open system, 17–18
Outlining, of speech, 390–96
Overhead projector, 412
Overload, information, 70

Panel discussion, 238–41
Parliamentary procedure, 316–24